"With the publication of this book, the Wel
take a giant leap forward. Chatterjee and W
impressive experiences building Web Services, painstakingly provide their readers with concise, but thorough understandings of the most important issues and their solutions. They unabashedly recommend best practices in application architectures, put key technologies together and show their readers how to step-by-step build world-class, enterprise Web Services and ebusiness applications. It's about time we had a book like this!"

—David Bunnell, former CEO & Editor of Upside Magazine, and founder of PC Magazine, PC World, Macworld, Publish, NewMedia, and BioWorld

"Developing Enterprise Web Services is the first of the next generation of Web services books, picking up where the introductory volumes leave off. Jim and Sandeep review the essential foundation (SOAP, WSDL, and UDDI) and then describe how to design and build real applications on top of it. This book includes essential information and examples about extended Web services specifications in the areas of security, transactions, and reliability, and others, and is invaluable as a resource for developers and managers who want to look past the standard stock quote service."

—Eric Newcomer, CTO Iona

Hewlett-Packard® Professional Books

HP-UX

Fernandez	Configuring CDE
Madell	Disk and File Management Tasks on HP-UX
Olker	Optimizing NFS Performance
Poniatowski	HP-UX 11i Virtual Partitions
Poniatowski	HP-UX 11i System Administration Handbook and Toolkit, Second Edition
Poniatowski	The HP-UX 11.x System Administration Handbook and Toolkit
Poniatowski	HP-UX 11.x System Administration "How To" Book
Poniatowski	HP-UX 10.x System Administration "How To" Book
Poniatowski	HP-UX System Administration Handbook and Toolkit
Poniatowski	Learning the HP-UX Operating System
Rehman	HP Certified: HP-UX System Administration
Sauers/Weygant	HP-UX Tuning and Performance
Weygant	Clusters for High Availability, Second Edition
Wong	HP-UX 11i Security

UNIX, Linux, Windows, and MPE I/X

Mosberger/Eranian	IA-64 Linux Kernel
Poniatowski	UNIX User's Handbook, Second Edition
Stone/Symons	UNIX Fault Management

Computer Architecture

Evans/Trimper	Itanium Architecture for Programmers
Kane	PA-RISC 2.0 Architecture
Markstein	IA-64 and Elementary Functions

Networking/Communications

Blommers	Architecting Enterprise Solutions with UNIX Networking
Blommers	OpenView Network Node Manager
Blommers	Practical Planning for Network Growth
Brans	Mobilize Your Enterprise
Cook	Building Enterprise Information Architecture
Lucke	Designing and Implementing Computer Workgroups
Lund	Integrating UNIX and PC Network Operating Systems

Security

Bruce	Security in Distributed Computing
Mao	Modern Cryptography: Theory and Practice
Pearson et al.	Trusted Computing Platforms
Pipkin	Halting the Hacker, Second Edition
Pipkin	Information Security

Web/Internet Concepts and Programming

Amor	E-business (R)evolution, Second Edition
Apte/Mehta	UDDI
Chatterjee/Webber	Developing Enterprise Web Services: An Architect's Guide
Kumar	J2EE Security for Servlets, EJBs, and Web Services
Mowbrey/Werry	Online Communities
Tapadiya	.NET Programming

Other Programming

Blinn	Portable Shell Programming
Caruso	Power Programming in HP OpenView
Chaudhri	Object Databases in Practice
Chew	The Java/C++ Cross Reference Handbook
Grady	Practical Software Metrics for Project Management and Process Improvement
Grady	Software Metrics
Grady	Successful Software Process Improvement
Lewis	The Art and Science of Smalltalk
Lichtenbelt	Introduction to Volume Rendering
Mellquist	SNMP++
Mikkelsen	Practical Software Configuration Management
Norton	Thread Time
Tapadiya	COM+ Programming
Yuan	Windows 2000 GDI Programming

Storage

Thornburgh	Fibre Channel for Mass Storage
Thornburgh/Schoenborn	Storage Area Networks
Todman	Designing Data Warehouses

IT/IS

Missbach/Hoffman	SAP Hardware Solutions

Image Processing

Crane	A Simplified Approach to Image Processing
Gann	Desktop Scanners

Developing Enterprise Web Services

An Architect's Guide

Sandeep Chatterjee, Ph.D.

James Webber, Ph.D.

www.hp.com/hpbooks

PEARSON EDUCATION
PRENTICE HALL PROFESSIONAL TECHNICAL REFERENCE
UPPER SADDLE RIVER, NJ 07458
WWW.PHPTR.COM

Library of Congress Cataloging-in-Publication Data

A CIP catalog record for this book can be obtained from the Library of Congress.

Editorial/production supervision: *Mary Sudul*
Cover design director: *Jerry Votta*
Cover design: *DesignSource*
Manufacturing manager: *Maura Zaldivar*
Acquisitions editor: *Jill Harry*
Editorial assistant: *Brenda Mulligan*
Marketing manager: *Dan DePasquale*
Publisher, HP Books: *Mark Stouse*
Manager and Associate Publisher, HP Books: *Victoria Brandow*

Published by Prentice Hall PTR
Pearson Education, Inc.
Upper Saddle River, New Jersey 07458

Prentice Hall books are widely used by corporations and government agencies for training, marketing, and resale.
The publisher offers discounts on this book when ordered in bulk quantities. For more information, contact Corporate Sales Department, Phone: 800-382-3419; FAX: 201-236-7141;
E-mail: corpsales@prenhall.com
Or write: Prentice Hall PTR, Corporate Sales Dept., One Lake Street, Upper Saddle River, NJ 07458.

Printed in the United States of America
1st Printing

ISBN 0-13-140160-2

Pearson Education LTD.
Pearson Education Australia PTY, Limited
Pearson Education Singapore, Ptc. Ltd.
Pearson Education North Asia Ltd.
Pearson Education Canada, Ltd.
Pearson Educación de Mexico, S.A. de C.V.
Pearson Education — Japan
Pearson Education Malaysia, Pte. Ltd.

Contents

Part 2 Advanced Web Services Technologies and Standards 143

Chapter 5 Conversations 145

Chapter 6 Workflow 175

Chapter 7
Transactions 249

Chapter 8
Security 305

FOREWORD

The singing workmen shape and set and join
Their frail new mansion's stuccoed cove and quoin
With no apparent sense that years abrade...
—Thomas Hardy, Rome: Building a New Street in the Ancient Quarter, 1887

OK, Rome wasn't built in a day, but once they got the sucker up and running, it was magnificent and, hey, it's still there and functioning quite nicely. Having first heard about Web services toward the end of the last century, I would have thought by now they would be ubiquitous. At this point in time, I should be able to replace My Yahoo with a personalized Web services portal uniquely suited to my quixotic needs and desires. Years ago, I started planning this portal when I heard Bill Gates waxing poetically about Hurricane—a.k.a. "My Services"—which was Microsoft's vision of creating a suite of personalized Web services for early adopters like me. Unfortunately, Microsoft abandoned this effort when critics complained it was really an insidious plot to own people's personal information.

Mostly by pure dumb luck, I've been at the forefront of technology for most of my life. As a young man just out of college, I was working in Albuquerque, New Mexico, at a small company called MITS which, with a little help from a then 19-year old Bill Gates and his buddy Paul Allen, started the personal computing revolution. Taking advantage of this happy situation, I leveraged my background in media to launch a magazine called *Personal Computing*. These experiences led me to found a number of other magazines including *PC Magazine*, *PC World*, *Macworld*, *Publish*, *NewMedia*, and *BioWorld*. Most recently I was CEO and Editor of *Upside Media, Inc*.

Throughout the years, I have been fortunate to have had a first-hand involvement in the evolution of many revolutionary new innovations, including the first personal computer (Altair), the first portal computer (Osborne), the first spreadsheet (VisiCalc), the Macintosh Computer, Multi-Media, the Internet, and even Biotechnology.

To say that I have seen my share of "paradigm shifts" is an understatement. Technology innovation has been all around me. Who would have thought that a couple of guys in a small company in Albuquerque would start what would later become the PC revolution? Shouldn't it have come out of IBM or Xerox or some other big technology company? That's exactly the rub. Innovative ideas don't always come from the big companies, sometimes they spring out from the big guys and at other times they spring out from the little guys.

Based on all the above, I am completely convinced that Web services will level the playing field between the little guy and the big guy as no technology has ever done before. Thanks to this new revolution, the mom-and-pop company down the street can market their innovative software and services to the neighborhood, to the global masses, as well as to the largest companies in the world. But, we're not only talking about the new and interesting. Even the most mundane and boring is supported. The procurement system of the mom-and-pop company can seamlessly interface with the billing system of a global multinational company and here's where things get really interesting. The systems of the multinational can also interface with the systems of the mom-and-pop company. The most innovative new systems to the most boring, existing tasks are all available on an anybody-to-anybody basis. This will ultimately happen but like many great technologies, it will require a lot of work and patience before the dream is truly realized.

As Sandeep Chatterjee and James Webber so eloquently and clearly explain in this book, real world Web services and Web services-based applications can't simply be put together in a haphazard manner by merely reading through one of the Web services technology specifications. You need to be familiar with these standards and they are extremely important, but they only represent the basic building blocks. To "architect" and construct world-class enterprise services, developers need a much deeper knowledge of a number of different standards and tools plus their "inter-relationships" and best practices for use.

Web services are small segments of larger applications and as such, quality-of-service issues loom large if they are to be truly useful and scalable. When building them, you have to factor in such considerations as: *Availability* (how often is the service available for consumption); Accessibility (can it serve a client's request now); *Performance* (how long does it take to respond); *Compliance* (is it really "standard"); *Security* (is it safe to interact with this service); *Energy* (suitable for mobile apps); and *Reliability* (how often does it fail). Like building Rome, building Web services gets complicated fast.

So how do you architect an application to be reliable if some of the Web services you are depending on become unavailable? Can an application be written to seamlessly scale to support new Web services from an expanding group of strategic partners? What about transactional guarantees or atomic coordination between multiple, independent services? And can you accomplish your design goal and still provide adequate safeguards for corporate and individual information and intellectual property?

I imagine that the software world would have given up in disgust by now, moved on to some new paradigm, except for two factors. The first is that all the major software companies are committed to Web services to the tune of several billion dollars, and the second is that Web services are, gosh darn-it, actually revolutionary. They are so revolutionary they represent a whole new amazing way of doing business, which will transform the software industry *forever* and change the very nature of the corporate IT department, thrusting it into the heart of strategic thinking.

Web services build on and extend the Web application model by allowing any client application to access and use its capabilities. By implementing capabilities that are available to other applications (or even other Web services) via industry standard network and application interfaces and protocols, Web services represent reusable software building blocks that are URL addressable. We're talking here about a concept called "anybody-to-anybody" communications—quoting from this book, "a person who implements a Web service can be almost one hundred percent certain that anybody else can communicate with and use the service."

Chatterjee and Webber aren't so concerned, however, about Web services for the masses. They tackle a much more difficult topic, which is Web services for enterprises. These are services that have to be totally reliable, absolutely secure and extremely functional. Referring back to the "building Rome" analogy, these guys aren't really talking about building foot paths or neighborhood streets, rather they are more interested in the avenues, aqueducts, and other major arteries that seamlessly and safely interconnect the Porticus of Gaius to the Forum of Caesar—the House of the Vestal Virgins to the Temple of Saturn, and back again. They are talking about the communication and transportation systems that made Rome the most magnificent functioning city of the Ancient World.

In today's global marketplace, world class enterprises need to interconnect with their customers and partners internationally using legacy systems that are mostly incompatible with each other, and they need to do this relatively fast and as inexpensive as possible. Web services provide the solution but not without overcoming some fairly difficult obstacles.

In the Web services world, nothing is as simple as it may seem. Take transactions, for example. Transactions are the bedrock on which B2B interactions rise or fall, they are a fundamental abstraction or requirement for what we sometimes refer to as "fault-tolerant computing." In a lucid and detailed style, the authors point out that the choices for transactions are scarce and, in fact, the OASIS Business Transaction Protocol (or simply BTP) is the "only Web services transaction protocol with implementation we can use today." They explain BTP and how to implement it, but just in case you get in over your head, they also suggest that unless you have specialist knowledge in this area, you should give "serious consideration" to buying or outsourcing it.

As with transactions, this book goes into great detail to describe the Web services technologies and standards that can be used in the real world today. These address the most challenging enterprise requirements including conversations, workflow, security, the challenges inherent in the development of mobile systems, how to build user-facing portals by aggregating back-end Web services, and how to manage an ever growing number and type of Web services within the enterprise. But more than this, the authors tell you in a concluding section filled with source code and a step-by-step guide how to put this together. You'll learn how to actually develop a

Web service application and deploy it onto the Tomcat application server and the Axis SOAP server (both freely available).

The ambitious goal of *Developing Enterprise Web Services: An Architect's Guide* is to give readers a "thorough understanding" of the steps necessary to build and deploy Web services and client applications that meet enterprise requirements. This is a lofty goal indeed, and you'll want to spend some serious time going through all the clear and concise content that the authors have spent well over a year developing. I found it really amazing.

Fortunately, with the publication of this book, the Web services vision is about to take a giant leap forward. We are building our "Rome" and the end is finally in sight. Chatterjee and Webber, drawing on their own impressive experiences building Web services, painstakingly provide their readers with concise, yet thorough understanding of the most important issues and their solutions. They unabashedly recommend best practices in application architectures, put key technologies together and show their readers step-by-step how to build world-class, enterprise Web services-based e-business applications. And darn it, it's about time we had a book like this!

David Bunnell
Berkeley, California
September 2003

ACKNOWLEDGMENTS

The authors would like to thank the many people who have helped and contributed to this book. First, we would like to thank Bob Bickel for supporting and sanctioning our writing of this book. We would also like to thank the following people who reviewed early drafts of the manuscript and provided insightful feedback: Tony Wasserman, Lionel Lavallee, Sriram Somanchi, Ravi Trivedi, Mark Little, Stuart Wheater, Andy Taylor, Savas Parastatidis, Lindsay Marshall, Scott Williams, Satish Thatte, and Farhat Kaleem.

We would also like to thank the people at Pearson Education and, in particular, our executive editor, Jill Harry, who supported, encouraged, and guided us throughout the process. And, of course, our most profound thanks go to our families for their constant love and encouragement. Jim would especially like to thank Katherine Neasham for her continued support.

To all of these and many others too numerous to mention, we give our heartfelt thanks and appreciation.

CHAPTER 1

Introduction

Web services technologies are fundamentally changing the software industry, making the role of enterprise IT organizations more strategic, and recasting the software vendor-consumer relationship. Web services are also being hailed by CEOs, CIOs, and CTOs as the next-generation vehicle for driving topline growth and controlling bottom lines. But, simply jumping on the Web services bandwagon won't lead to corporate success. Web services are simply a platform; how companies implement a solution using this new technology determines their success and ultimately their return on investment (ROI). In this book, we take a no-nonsense, strategic view of developing enterprise Web services and applications: looking at where the technologies are, where they are going and how companies need to architect their own Web services solutions to not get left behind.

Web services platforms provide the functionality to build and interact with distributed applications by sending eXtensible Markup Language (XML) messages. Additional technology layers are constantly emerging, others are being refined, and still others are being discarded. The platform is essentially a moving target.

To stay on the leading edge, companies are building and deploying their applications while work on the underlying platform continues. And, as with any industry standard initiatives which require building consensus, the Web services platform will remain a work in progress for some time.

How can you build any meaningful application, let alone mission-critical enterprise applications, on such a platform? If you are a developer or an architect charged with building Web services or applications that consume Web services, you have to know where the platform is today, and where it is going. Otherwise, the endless pit of application rewrite and maintenance overhead will far outweigh any benefits that can be garnered from this promising new technology.

Real world, enterprise Web services and applications cannot be developed by simply reading through the Simple Object Access Protocol (SOAP) or the Web Services Description Language (WSDL) specifications. Developers must understand a number of different standards and technologies, and more importantly, their inter-relationships as well as best practices for their use.

Consider an e-business application that requires interaction between multiple partner Web services. Understanding SOAP and WSDL gives developers the ability to write Web services and consume them within their application. But, how must the application be architected to be reliable in case some Web services become unavailable? How can an application be written to seamlessly scale and support new Web services from a growing list of strategic partner companies? What are the best practices for developing mobile Web service applications, and how can individual Web services be created to support quality-of-service (QoS)? How can transactional guarantees or atomic coordination between multiple, independent Web services be supported by applications? And, how can all of this be done securely so that corporate and individual information and intellectual property are safeguarded?

In this book, we focus on how to develop Web services and applications within real world enterprise environments. We describe not only the vanilla Web services platform consisting of SOAP, WSDL, and UDDI (Universal Description, Discovery and Integration), but also build on this to include the other technologies, standards, and emerging standards that provide support for transactions, security and authentication, mobile and wireless, quality-of-service, conversations, workflow, interactive applications and portals, as well as systems management.

We discuss the opportunities represented by Web services and, more importantly, describe best practices and architectural patterns for building enterprise systems that position you and your organization to most fully leverage those opportunities. We do not summarize any one Web services standard, but instead provide a sufficiently thorough discussion of all of the critical technologies and standards, as well as their inter-relationships, that are necessary for building enterprise Web services and applications. Our focus is on developing enterprise Web services and applications based on industry standard Web services technologies, not on summarizing standards.

Let's get started by reviewing what Web services are and why they are important.

What Are Web Services?

Web services represent a new architectural paradigm for applications. Web services implement capabilities that are available to other applications (or even other Web services) via industry standard network and application interfaces and protocols. An application can use the capabilities of a Web service by simply invoking it across a network without having to integrate it. As such, Web services represent reusable software building blocks that are URL addressable. The architectural differences between monolithic, integrated applications and Web services-based applications are depicted in Figure 1-1.

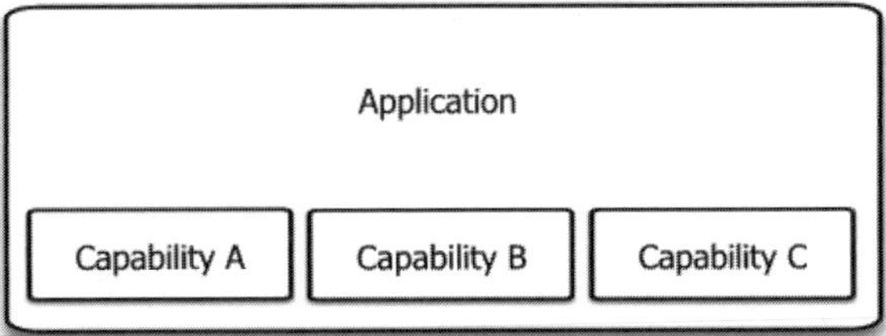

(a) Monolithic application with integrated capabilities A,B, and C.

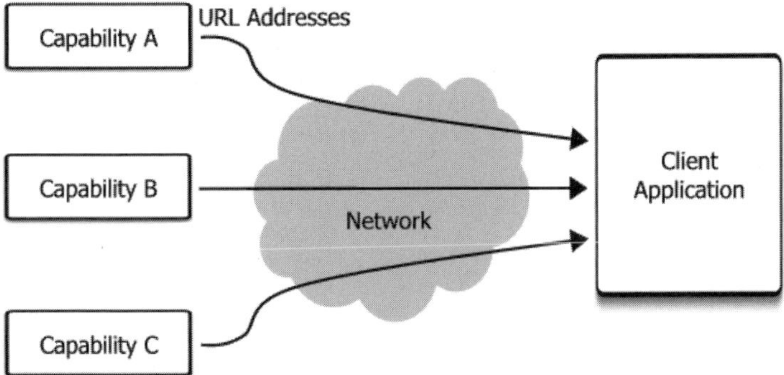

(b) Client application invoking remote Web services for capabilities A, B, and C.

Figure 1-1 The architectural differences between (a) a monolithic application with integrated capabilities, and (b) a distributed application using Web services-based capabilities.

The capabilities provided by a Web service can fall into a variety of categories, including:

- Functions, such as a routine for calculating the integral square root of a number.
- Data, such as fetching the quantity of a particular widget a vendor has on hand.
- Business processes, such as accepting an order for a widget, shipping the desired quantity of widgets and sending an invoice.

Some of these capabilities are difficult or impractical to integrate within third-party applications. When these capabilities are exposed as Web services, they can be loosely coupled together, thereby achieving the benefits of integration without incurring the difficulties thereof.

Web services expose their capabilities to client applications, not their implementations. This allows Web services to be implemented in any language and on any platform and still be compatible with all client applications.

Each building block (Web service) is self-contained. It describes its own capabilities, publishes its own programmatic interface and implements its own functionality that is available as a hosted service. The business logic of the Web service runs on a remote machine that is accessible by other applications through a network. The client application simply invokes the functionality of a Web service by sending it messages, receives return messages from the Web service and then uses the results within the application. Since there is no need to integrate the Web service within the client application into a single monolithic block, development and testing times, maintenance costs, and overall errors are thereby reduced.

Assume you want to build a simple calculator application that determines the appreciation in stock price for any company given its corporate name and the date the stock was originally purchased. The application must do the following:

- Determine the stock ticker symbol for the company based on the company name.
- Determine the latest price of the stock based on the ticker symbol.
- Determine the historical price of the stock for the given date based on the ticker symbol.
- Calculate the difference between the two stock prices and present it to the user.

This seemingly trivial application is in fact enormously complex. Right from the get go there are problems. We have to build a database with the names of all the companies in the country and their associated stock ticker symbol. More importantly, we must maintain this database as companies are newly listed, become delisted, change their names or their ticker symbol, or merge. To access the real-time price of a stock, we must have a relationship with a financial or brokerage firm. The legal complexities and hassles in architecting such a relationship is bad enough, not to mention the IT infrastructure that must also be put into place.

Unless you work for a brokerage firm or are in the business of maintaining stock information, the time and costs necessary to build the infrastructure necessary to support the stock appreciation calculator are enormous and, in most cases, prohibitively so. Until a brokerage firm itself decided to provide such a calculator, customers would have to make do without it.

Web services simplify and in many ways eliminate the need to build for yourself the support infrastructure—both legal and technical. The calculator can be developed by simply passing messages between the calculator application and the appropriate set of Web services. Figure 1-2 graphically depicts the flow of messages, and the fundamental architecture of a Web services-based stock price appreciation calculator.

Messages are sent between the calculator application and the following three Web services:

- `StockTickerNameToSymbolConverter`, which accepts a company's name and provides the ticker tape symbol.
- `RealTimeStockQuoteLookup`, which provides the latest price of a stock based on its ticker tape symbol.

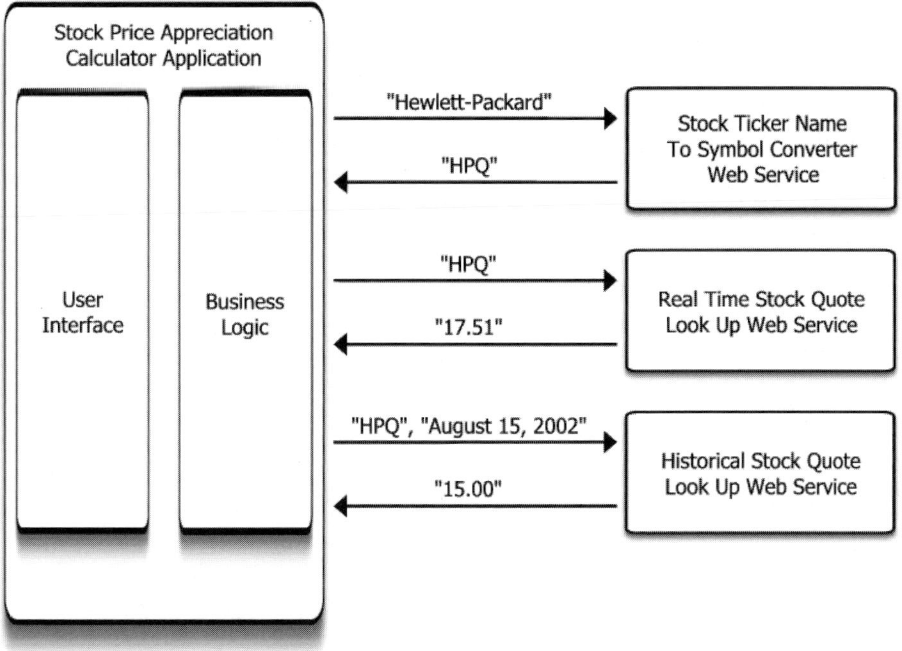

Figure 1-2 Sending and receiving Web service messages to build a stock price appreciation calculator.

- `HistoricalStockQuoteLookup`, which provides the historical price of a stock based on its ticker tape symbol and the desired date.

Since each of these three Web services is provided, hosted, and managed by another company, the developer of the calculator application has only to focus on his key insight or contribution alone. Complex, domain-specific issues such as the fact that Hewlett-Packard's ticker tape symbol was HWP and only recently became HPQ are (or should be) handled by the Web services directly. Using these three Web services, the application can easily determine the stock price appreciation for Hewlett-Packard from August 15, 2002, to be $17.51 - $15.00 = $2.51. Based on the data from the Web services, the calculator application can provide further analysis, such as the percentage appreciation, and present all of the information in an easy-to-understand, graphical manner.

Assuming the required capabilities exist and are available as Web services, developers can focus on their unique value-added piece and utilize third-party Web services for the remainder of the functionality. The benefits of using Web services are clear:

- Dramatically cut application development costs by focusing on your own value-added contribution and using third-party Web services for everything else.

- Integrate both data and business processes with market constituents and business partners that have desired domain expertise or capabilities.
- Reduce or eliminate many errors born out of complex and large monolithic applications.
- Simplify application maintenance and customization by segmenting an application into the client application and each of its consumed Web services.
- Significantly reduce time-to-market.

As we take this idea further, and more and more companies expose some of their internal capabilities as Web services, the real value of Web services lies in the *composition* of a set of Web services. Consider the following two companies. One is a traffic service company that monitors automobile traffic on major roads and highways and predicts expected travel times. The second is a taxi reservation service company that allows customers to reserve taxis for pickup at a specified location and time. Each of these companies and their products are compelling in and of themselves. However, if these companies exposed their capabilities as Web services, these services can be *composed* together into a single, more compelling and useful service—either by one of these two companies themselves or by a third company.

As an example, consider taking a taxi to the airport before catching a flight for a meeting. By leveraging the capabilities of both companies through their respective Web services, a traveler can reserve a taxi and rest assured that if an accident or other traffic conditions cause an unexpected increase in her travel time, the taxi reservation can be held and an alert sent to the traveler advising her of the updated taxi schedule as well as the traffic situation that caused the change. By simply and intelligently combining the individual services of the two companies, we are able to create a more compelling and useful service for travelers. The composition of Web services from different enterprises is depicted in Figure 1-3. The technologies that form the foundations of Web services are SOAP, WSDL, and UDDI.

SOAP

Simple Object Access Protocol (SOAP) is an XML-based mechanism for exchanging information between applications within a distributed environment. This information exchange mechanism can be used to send messages between applications and, more specifically, can be used to implement remote procedure calls (RPCs). RPCs allow one application to invoke and use a procedure (or capability) of another, possibly remote, application.

SOAP does not specify any application implementation or programming model. Instead, it provides a mechanism for expressing application semantics that can be understood by applications no matter how they are implemented. Accordingly, SOAP is application language- and platform-independent. SOAP is typically used in conjunction with HTTP, which supports easy traversal of firewalls and is sufficiently lightweight to be used within mobile and wireless environments.

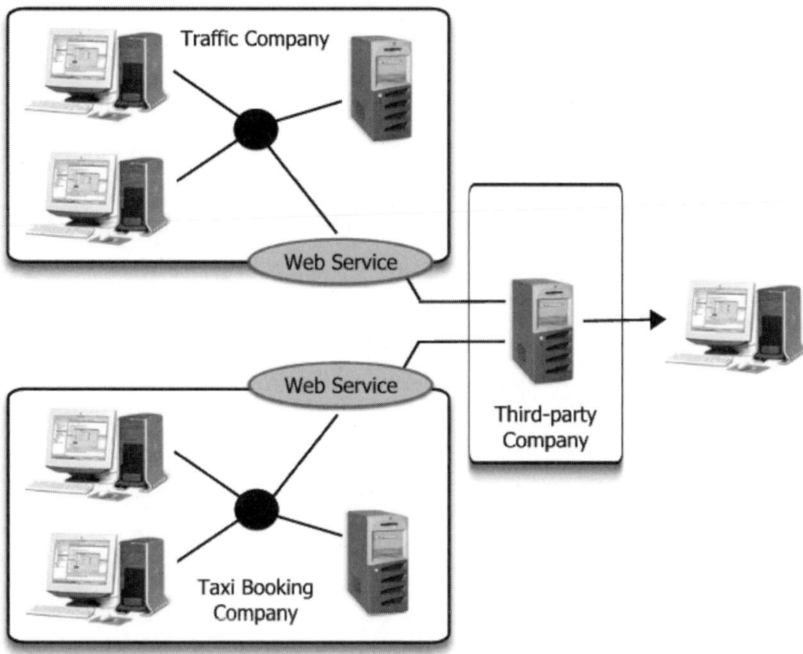

Figure 1-3 Composing together services exposed by multiple corporations to create a separate service offering.

WSDL

Web Services Description Language (WSDL) is an XML-based language for describing Web services. Through a WSDL description, a client application can determine the location of the remote Web service, the functions it implements, as well as how to access and use each function. After parsing a WSDL description, a client application can appropriately format a SOAP request and dispatch it to the location of the Web service.

WSDL descriptions go hand-in-hand with the development of a new Web service and are created by the producer of the service. WSDL files (or pointers thereto) are typically stored in registries that can be searched by potential users to locate Web service implementations of desired capabilities.

UDDI

Universal Description, Discovery, and Integration (UDDI) is a specification for a registry of information for Web services. UDDI defines a means to publish and, more importantly, discover (or search for) information about Web services, including WSDL files.

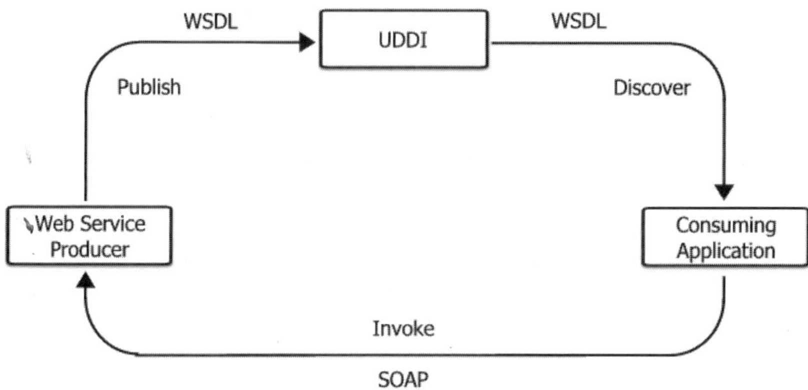

Figure 1-4 The relationships between SOAP, WSDL, and UDDI.

After browsing through an UDDI registry for information about available Web services, the WSDL for the selected service can be parsed, and an appropriate SOAP message can be sent to the service. Figure 1-4 graphically illustrates the relationships between SOAP, WSDL, and UDDI.

Now that we have a glimpse into what Web services are and how they can be used to build interesting applications and systems, we next discuss why this new technology is important.

Why Web Services Are Important

Web services represent a new paradigm in application architecture and development. The importance of Web services is not that they are new, but that this new technology addresses the needs of application development. To understand this new paradigm, let us first look at the application paradigm that preceded Web services—Web applications.

The Evolution of Web Applications

Web applications are applications that are available via the World Wide Web (Web) and allow any user anywhere in the world access to its capabilities. This is in contrast to older client-server applications in which only dedicated clients could access the applications residing on the server. Web applications grew the user base from just a few hundred client machines accessing a client-server application, to millions of users across the Web accessing a Web application.

The Web opened up the floodgates to Web applications by allowing users to simply specify a URL within a Web browser. Web applications also increased the difficulty of developing applications because a Web application client (a PC browser) has no knowledge of the application's communication requirements or underlying systems. Industry standard technologies such as HTTP and HTML were used to bridge this gap between Web application clients and the Web applications themselves. Application servers and other middleware emerged to reduce the complexities of building Web apps while still allowing pervasive access to each Web application.

Web services build on and extend the Web application model. Web applications allow any Web browser to access its functionality, with the application user interface presented through the browser. Web services take this a step further and allow any client application to access and use its capabilities.

A Web application allows universal user access to its capabilities by supporting industry standard interfaces to its user interface. They do not allow extending or adding to their capabilities through programmatic access. To leverage the functionality of a Web application and build on it, complex and often unreliable techniques, such as screen scraping, must be used. Web services address this issue by allowing programmatic access to the Web services' capabilities using industry standard interfaces and protocols. The evolution of Web applications to Web services is shown in Figure 1-5.

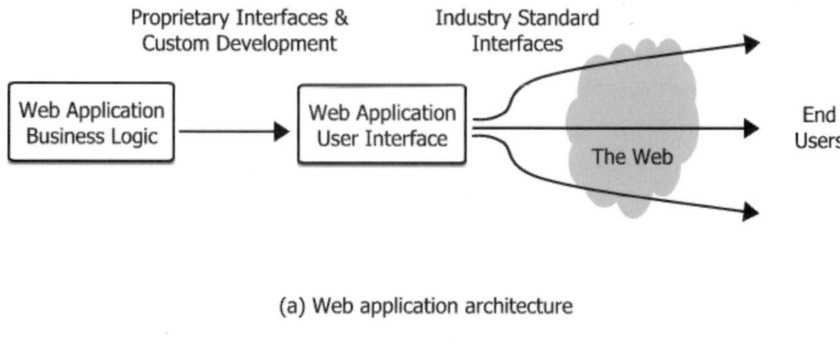

(a) Web application architecture

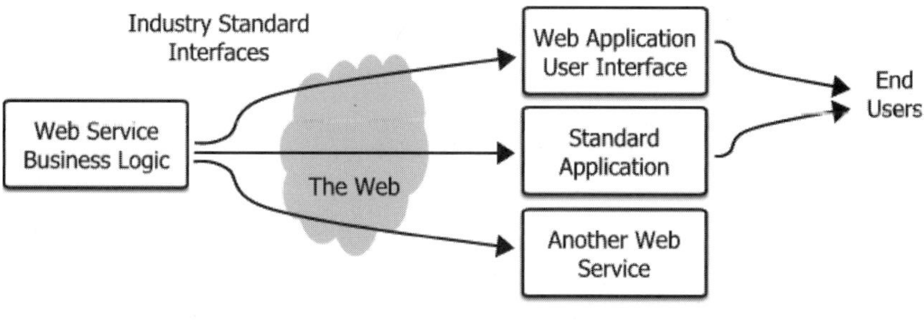

(b) Web services architecture

Figure 1-5 Evolution of Web applications to Web services and key architectural differences.

Web services advocate a services-oriented architecture for applications in which a software component provides its functionality as a service that can be leveraged by other software components. Such a service model abstracts away many complex issues that arise from software component integration, including platform compatibility, testing, and maintenance.

Since Web service clients do not have information necessary to communicate with a Web service, a set of standards is necessary to allow any-to-any communications. Web service standards build on previous standards for communications and data representation, such as HTTP and HTML.

The key enabler for Web services is XML. Although HTML and XML are similar in that both are human-readable markup languages, HTML is for presentation markup while XML is for semantic markup. This critical attribute of XML supports expressing application and functional semantics in a platform-independent manner that enables any-to-any information exchange.

Some argue that Web services are nothing new; they are simply the latest incarnation of distributed computing. In some sense that may be true, but what is it about Web services that is driving the incredible buzz? Why are entrepreneurs, CEOs of established companies, and industry analysts excited about this technology? In the next section, we see that Web services are not just another distributed computing platform.

Not Just Another Distributed Computing Platform

Web services are indeed a technology for distributed computing and there is one critical distinction between Web services and distributed computing technologies that have come before. A person who implements a Web service can be almost one hundred percent certain that anybody else can communicate with and use the service. The breakthrough of Web services is precisely the anybody-to-anybody communications that it enables. The confidence level Web services engender in its developers is similar to that of HTML Web pages. The developer of an HTML page is certain that anybody with a browser can view the Web page.

Web services grew out of a need for a distributed computing application environment that was not as difficult to deploy to as the Common Object Request Broker Architecture (CORBA) or Microsoft's Distributed Component Object Model (DCOM), and also offered greater interoperability. Both CORBA and DCOM aimed to provide a distributed computing environment across heterogeneous environments. Unfortunately, neither supported environments or technologies that were sufficiently far-reaching to enable heterogeneous communications at the anybody-to-anybody scale.

In a sense, Web services sacrifice the richness of capabilities that are provided by previous distributed computing environments, which are necessary to a small group of all applications, for a much simpler and more ubiquitous solution that is applicable for the vast majority of applications. This is not to say that Web services place restrictions on their use. Additional capabilities can be layered on top of the Web services platform to address varying needs.

Applications that are exposed as Web services have a large base of other applications (that are also exposed as Web services) with which to communicate. Since they are based on simple and open industry standards (or de facto standards), Web services make significant inroads toward ubiquitous interoperability. Interoperability here is on the scale of the Web or the Internet, not just a group or organization.

Based on industry standards and supporting anybody-to-anybody interoperability, Web services are poised to be the platform that delivers on the needs of e-businesses. All companies interact with other companies in the course of conducting their businesses. Manufacturing companies interact with component suppliers, distributors interact with manufacturing companies, retailers interact with distributors, and so on. Initially, these interactions were manual, conducted by mail, phone, and fax.

Web applications allowed companies to interact with one another by exposing some of their capabilities and business processes to others on the Web. But, most of the time, this still required a human being interacting with the Web application on the other side. Web services remove the need for constant human intervention while companies interact by enabling programmatic conversations between applications.

By removing this barrier to e-business interactions, Web services enable new business relationships as well as more fluid relationships that can be configured and reconfigured on-the-fly. Although Web services offer numerous benefits, they also present many challenges and risks within traditional enterprise environments. We discuss Web services and how they fit within enterprises next.

Web Services and Enterprises

On the surface, Web services appear to be a risky proposition for enterprises. Why will IT organizations that have demanded full control over all aspects of enterprise applications adopt a distributed and shared software architecture that moves administrative control over various parts of applications outside of the enterprise firewall? The runtime characteristics of Web services-based applications will have critical dependencies on remotely hosted and remotely managed external businesses. This is a severe departure from the centrally controlled as well as the guaranteed predictability and reliability that have become the hallmarks of enterprise software and the IT organizations that manage them.

The reasons for this break are clear. Web services enable the flow of data and business processes between business partners—between enterprises as well as between multiple organizations or groups within an enterprise—to a degree that have not been possible before. Businesses that could not previously communicate and applications that could not previously interoperate can now do so.

Web services enable companies to drive topline growth by integrating together different services and introduce new revenue-generating services. At the same time, Web services simplify integration, reducing time-to-market and costs, as well as support operational efficiencies that streamline the bottom line.

The potential benefits of Web services are enormous. The risks are equally great, if not greater. Enterprise IT organizations will find themselves in the middle, responsible for reconciling the benefits with the risks of adopting Web services within the enterprise.

IT organizations, in an effort to gain a controlling foothold over risky and potentially harmful Web services traffic, will insist on controlling which Web services applications interact with one another. A misbehaving Web service will simply be cut off from interacting with any enterprise applications; such cut offs may even be preemptive if there is a history of problems or a perception of a threat.

To accomplish this, IT will take on a more strategic role within organizations and align itself more closely with individual business units. Critical decisions by business units, such as the partners from which to source components, will have to be cleared by IT if those partners' Web services will interact with the applications or Web services of the company.

This will have major ramifications for enterprise application architectures. Enterprise applications will support dynamic and swappable Web services—hardwired Web service invocations will no longer suffice. Moreover, IT will use management environments to deploy enterprise-wide policies for Web services that will monitor and strictly enforce the Web services that applications can use.

There is no doubt that the uptake of Web services within the enterprise will require changes. Many of these changes will be to established procedures and existing policies that have been supported by years of experience and billions of dollars. Nonetheless, the potential benefits—both financial and strategic—to adopting Web services are sufficiently large to justify such changes.

Moving Forward

As organizations transition from researching Web services technologies and building internal prototypes to early-adopter deployments, and then eventually to mainstream adoption of Web services, the key differentiator and requirement is that these applications and systems are appropriate for "real world" deployment and usage. Some of the early prototypes built using Web services were in many ways toys. All of the Web services and client applications run on a single machine, hosted by the same application server, in a fully controlled environment. Many of these services and applications that once worked as prototype systems will no doubt break—some immediately, while others may take more time to break (which is much worse).

The next few years will see Web services and applications become hardened and ready for "real world" deployment. The real world is indeed a cold and hard place. Web services run remotely, sometimes go down and become unavailable, evolve into multiple versions, as well as encounter variances in network bandwidth and quality. Moreover, politics and competitive issues between organizations will result in unexpected outages and behaviors along critical dependencies within applications.

Already we see many standards bodies that have been convened to address these and other issues. Some of the technologies that are being developed to address these needs will eventually be automatic, transparent to developers as existing infrastructure and tools, such as middleware and IDEs, and incorporate the technologies. Nonetheless, architects and developers will need to have a keen understanding of these issues and technologies to develop enterprise-class Web services and applications.

In this book, we look at the Web services platform—where it is now and where it is going—with an eye toward developing robust enterprise Web services and applications. In the first of the three sections of this book, we begin by describing the core technologies that make up the Web services platform. These are XML, SOAP, WSDL, and UDDI. This platform provides a distributed computing environment based on standard interfaces and protocols, but it does not implement all of the capabilities necessary for implementing enterprise systems.

In the second part of this book, we look at some of the standards and emerging technologies that, once layered on top of the vanilla Web services platform, address some of the critical requirements of enterprise systems. These technologies include support for transactions, security and authentication, conversations, workflow, quality of service, mobile and wireless, services and systems management, as well as interactive applications and Web portals.

In the third part of the book, with both the vanilla Web services platform as well as some of the critical advanced technologies and standards under our belt, we take an in-depth look and provide step-by-step instructions for building an enterprise application using Web services. Addressing one of the biggest pain points in business processes today, we develop an enterprise procurement application that ties together the inventory and ordering Web services of multiple suppliers and facilitates the procurement process. We first develop the entire application using only the vanilla Web services platform (as described in the first part of the book). After identifying the shortcomings of this implementation based only on the vanilla platform, we add to and expand on the application using the advanced standards and technologies described in the second part of the book.

We conclude this book by summarizing and highlighting some of the key points to remember when developing enterprise Web services and applications.

Summary

Web services represent enormous opportunities and challenges. How organizations negotiate these hurdles will determine the benefits they incur. In this book, we describe the Web services platform—where it is and where it is going—so that developers building applications are cognizant of the fluid nature of the platform and can address enterprise system requirements within the context of a changing platform.

Architect's Note

- Web services are remotely hosted and managed applications whose capabilities can be accessed programmatically by client applications via an addressable URL.
- The core Web services platform, consisting of SOAP, WSDL, and UDDI, provides the means for building distributed applications based on industry standard technologies, interfaces, and protocols.
- The core Web services platform does not provide all of the necessary capabilities on which to build enterprise systems. Additional technologies are being developed and are being standardized that can be layered on top of the core platform and provide support for security and authentication, transactions, mobile and wireless access, quality-of-service, workflows, conversations, systems and service management, as well as interactive applications and Web portals.
- Web services are important and different from other distributed computing environments because they are based on industry standards that are nearly ubiquitous. This allows unprecedented interoperability between applications as well as companies and supports anybody-to-anybody applications.
- The adoption of Web services within enterprises will require fundamental changes to IT organizations that are responsible for deploying and maintaining enterprise systems. In an effort to maintain control over enterprise systems within a Web services environment, IT will take on a more strategic role that is aligned with individual business units and become part of the business decision process.

PART 1

Basic Web Services Standards, Technologies, and Concepts

In this first section of the book, we briefly review the industry standards, technologies and concepts that underlie Web services. These critical technologies support the development of Web services as well as applications that use (or consume) Web services. But, be forewarned that these foundational technologies do not provide everything necessary to build Web services and applications that meet enterprise requirements. We cover these advanced technologies in Section Two of this book.

In this section, we describe the following technologies that together make up the basic Web services platform:

Chapter 2: XML Fundamentals. In this first of three chapters in Part One, we start with a discussion of the fundamentals of the eXtensible Markup Language (XML), the basic technology on which Web services are based. From network protocols up the stack to back-end databases, XML in all its forms has had a commoditizing effect on enterprise computing systems and being both platform and language independent is a natural choice for the level of interoperability required of Web services.

Chapter 3: SOAP and WSDL. Here we describe in detail the two technologies that make up the foundations of Web services: SOAP and WSDL. SOAP (Simple Object Access Protocol) is an XML-based mechanism for exchanging information between applications within a distributed environment. This information exchange mechanism can be used to send messages between applications and, more specifically, can be used to implement remote procedure calls (RPCs). WSDL (Web Services Description Language) is an XML-based language for describing Web services. Through a WSDL description, a client application can determine the location of the remote Web service, the functions it implements, as well as how to access and use each function.

Chapter 4: UDDI. In this chapter, we describe UDDI (Universal Description, Discovery, and Integration), which is a specification for a registry of information for Web services. UDDI defines a means to publish and, more importantly, discover (or search for) information, including WSDL files, about Web services. We also describe the UBR (UDDI Business Registry), which is a global implementation of the UDDI specification.

After reading Section One, you will have a strong understanding of the technologies, standards and concepts underlying Web services. Refer to Section Three for a detailed, step-by-step guide and lots of sample source code to actually develop Web services and client applications.

CHAPTER 2

XML Fundamentals

The suite of technologies grouped under the XML umbrella provides the fundamental building blocks of the Web services architecture. From network protocols through back end databases, XML has had an advantageous effect on enterprise computing systems. Being platform and language independent is a natural choice for building interoperable systems via Web services. Given the importance of XML in enterprise computing, and specifically in Web services, this chapter recaps the fundamentals of XML before embarking on a discussion of more advanced topics such as namespaces and XML Schema.

XML: The Lingua Franca of Web Services

XML is a standard for data mark-up backed by the World Wide Web Consortium, which has been branded "the universal format for structured documents and data on the Web."[1] The entire XML suite of standards, models, and processing technologies have been under development since 1998 with the initial XML specification, and has since been augmented by several additional supporting standards and notes that have brought XML to its current rich state. In fact, though XML is undeniably a richly specified technology, it has retained its simplicity and the entire XML platform can be profiled as follows:[2]

1. From the W3C Web Site at http://www.w3c.org/XML/
2. These (fewer than 10) points are based on the W3C's "XML in 10 Points" available from http://www.w3c.org/XML/1999/XML-in-10-points

- *XML is for Structuring Data*
  Structured data includes things like spreadsheets, address books, configuration parameters, financial transactions, and technical drawings. XML is a set of rules for designing text formats that support the developer in creating structured data. Though it vaguely resembles source code, XML is not a programming language, but it does make it easy for a computer to generate data, read data, and ensure that the data structure is unambiguous. XML avoids common pitfalls in language design. It is extensible, platform-independent, supports internationalization and localization, and is fully Unicode-compliant.
- *XML Resembles HTML*
  Like HTML, XML makes use of tags (words surrounded by angle brackets, "<" and ">") and attributes (of the form *name="value"*). While HTML specifies what each tag and attribute means and often how the text between them will render in a browser, XML uses the tags only to delimit pieces of data and leaves the interpretation of the data completely to the application that reads it.
- *XML is Human Readable, but Humans Shouldn't Read It*
  Programs that produce structured data often store that data on disk, using either a binary or text format. An advantage of a textual format is that it allows people, if necessary, to look at the data without the program that produced it, using tools like text editors. XML files are text files that people shouldn't have to read, but may read as and when the need arises. Care must be taken when manually editing XML since its rules are strict. A forgotten tag or an attribute without quotes makes an XML document unusable. The official XML specification forbids applications from trying to second-guess the creator of a broken XML file; if the file is broken, an application has to stop and report an error.
- *XML is Verbose*
  Since XML is a textual format and uses tags to delimit the data, XML files are nearly always larger than comparable binary formats. That was a conscious decision by the designers of XML. The advantages of a text format are evident, and the disadvantages can usually be compensated at a different level by compression applications. In addition, the transfer of XML across networks can be hastened by communication protocols such as those used in modems protocols and HTTP/1.1, which can compress data on-the-fly, saving bandwidth almost as effectively as a binary format.
- *XML is a Suite of Technologies*
  XML 1.0 is the specification that defines what "tags" and "attributes" are. Beyond that specification, the XML family is a growing set of modules that offer useful services to accomplish important and frequently demanded tasks.
- *XML is Modular*
  XML allows you to define a new document format by combining and reusing other formats. Since two formats developed independently may have elements or attributes

with the same name, care must be taken when combining those formats. To eliminate name confusion when combining formats, XML provides a namespace mechanism that is supported in all XML-based technologies.

- *XML is License-Free, Platform-Independent, and Well-Supported*
  By choosing XML as the basis for Web services, we gain access to a large and growing community of tools and techniques on which to develop value. Basing Web services on XML is similar to basing a database strategy on SQL—you still have to build your own database, programs, and procedures that manipulate it, but there are many tools and commodity components available to help. Furthermore, since XML is license-free, Web services can be built without incurring royalty payments.

While a full discussion of the subject of XML is beyond the scope of this book, before delving deeply into developing Web services it is imperative that at least the basics of XML and XML processing are understood. Although some of the XML detail inherent in developing Web services can be abstracted by toolkits, the increasing popularity of XML at the application level means that any learning at this point will, in addition to accelerating the rate of understanding Web services technology, be generally valuable in day-to-day development. That said, it's time to get acquainted with some fundamental XML concepts.

XML Documents

The purpose of an XML document is to capture structured data, just like an object in an object-oriented programming language. Documents are structured into a number of *elements*, delimited by *tags* which may or may not be nested within other elements.

Anyone familiar with the syntax of HTML will immediately be comfortable with the look and feel of XML, although anyone thinking about coding XML like HTML must be wary—XML is extremely strict in its syntax, where the interpretation of HTML (particularly by browsers) is quite permissive. As we progress through the examples, it is worth remembering the fundamental document syntax:

1. All tags must have corresponding end tags unless they are devoid of subelements, in which case they can be represented as
   `<element-name … attributes … />`.
2. No element can overlap any other element, although nesting within elements is allowed.
3. A document can only have a single root element (which excludes the XML declaration `<?xml … ?>`).
4. Attributes of an element must have unique names within the scope of a single tag.
5. Only element names and attribute name-value pairs may be placed within a tag declaration.

The best way to understand XML is by example, and the XML document shown in Figure 2-1 is typical of the structure of most XML documents, though it is somewhat shorter than most we'll be seeing in the Web services world.

```
<?xml version="1.0" encoding="utf-8"?>
<dvd>
  <title>The Phantom Menace</title>
  <year>2001</year>
</dvd>
```

Figure 2-1 A simple XML document.

Figure 2-1 shows a simple XML document that contains data about a DVD. The document (as all XML documents should) begins with the XML Declaration, delimited by `<?` and `?>`. This declaration provides information for any programs that are going to process the document. In this case it informs any processors that the XML document is encoded according to version 1.0 (at the moment 1.0 is the first and only XML version and the 1.1 effort is underway) and the underlying textual encoding is UTF-8 as opposed to ASCII.

The remainder of the document is where the actual structured data is held. In this case we have a `root` element delimited by the `dvd` tag, which contains two subelements delimited by the `title` and `year` tags. Those subelements contain textual data that we assume relates to the name of the film on the disk and the year of its release (though this is a convention and we could name elements badly, just as we can poorly name variables when programming).

We can take this document one stage further and make it a little more useful for those programs who might want to derive richer information from it. The document shown in Figure 2-2 embellishes that from Figure 2-1 adding in the DVD regional information as an attribute to the root element `region="2"`. We have also added a comment to aid human readability that is delimited by `<!--` and `-->`.

```
<?xml version="1.0" encoding="utf-8"?>
<!-- This is the European release of the DVD -->
<dvd region="2">
  <title>The Phantom Menace</title>
  <year>2001</year>
</dvd>
```

Figure 2-2 A simple XML document with attributes and comments.

The addition of the attribute in Figure 2-2 would, for instance, be of great help to a DVD cataloging system that could use the region attribute to classify disks by their target geographical region.

XML Namespaces

Namespaces in object-oriented programming languages allow developers to name classes unambiguously. Given that different organizations (should) use different namespaces for the software components, even in the cases where two third-party software components contain a class with exactly the same name, the fact that those classes are in different namespaces means that they are easily distinguished from one another.

Unambiguous naming is a requirement that also permeates the XML world. For example, it may be the case that several versions of a document with a root element `dvd` may exist, but the structure of each is different. The way we distinguish the document that we want from a number of available `dvd` documents is by its XML namespace.

Unlike popular programming languages where specific scope resolution operators are used to build namespaces (e.g., `MyPackage.MyClass` in Java and `MyNamespace::MyClass` in C++) the convention in XML is to use a URI (Universal Resource Identifier) as the namespace identifier.

> In fact, XML namespaces use URIs by convention only. Strictly speaking, an XML namespace is just a string. The value in using URIs is that they ensure uniqueness that strings cannot.

The URI is the union of the familiar URL and the not-so-familiar URN (Uniform Resource Name) schemes as shown in Figure 2-3 and Figure 2-4.

```
ftp://src.doc.ic.ac.uk
gopher://gopher.dna.affrc.go.jp
http://www.arjuna.com
mailto:some.one@somewhere.com
news:uk.jobs.offered
telnet://foo.bar.com/
```

Figure 2-3 Some familiar URI schemes.

The general scheme for the construction of a URI is `<scheme>:<scheme-specific-part>`. An absolute URI contains the name of the scheme in use followed by a colon (e.g., `news:`), which is followed by a string which is interpreted according to the semantics of that scheme (i.e., `uk.jobs.offered` identifies a particular Usenet newsgroup).

While the URI scheme doesn't mandate the meaning of the `<scheme-specific-part>`, many individual schemes share the same form which most Web users will have experienced with URLs (Uniform Resource Locator) where the syntax consists of a sequence of four parts: `<scheme>://<authority><path>?<query>` (for example, `http://search.sun.com/`

search/suncom/?qt=java). Depending on the scheme in use, not all of these parts are necessary but given those rules any valid URI can be constructed.

> Another good convention to adopt for namespaces is that the URI chosen should have some meaning. For instance, if a document has a namespace which is a HTTP URL, then dereferencing that URL should retrieve the schema which constrains that document.

A URN is intended to be a persistent, location-independent, resource identifier. In typical situations a URN is used where a name is intended to be persistent. The caveat is that once a URN has been affiliated with a particular entity (protocol message, Web service, and so on), it must not be reused to reference another resource. The URNs in Figure 2-4 are typical of the kinds of identifiers we find in Web services applications (taken from OASIS BTP, see Chapter 7):

```
urn:oasis:names:tc:BTP:1.0:core
urn:oasis:names:tc:BTP:1.0:qualifiers
```

Figure 2-4 An example of the URN scheme.

XML namespaces affiliate the elements and attributes of an XML document with namespaces identified by URIs. This process is called qualification and the names of the elements and attributes given a namespace scope are called qualified names, or simply QNames.

Now that we understand we can qualify our documents with a namespace, we can extend the example in Figure 2-2 to include namespace affiliation. Given that it is likely there will be other DVD cataloging systems and those systems will also use elements with names like dvd (which will likely have a different structure and content from our own version), the addition of a namespace into our XML document confers the advantage that it cannot be mixed up with any other similar-looking dvd documents from outside of our namespace. Our newly namespaced document is shown in Figure 2-5.

```
<?xml version="1.0" encoding="utf-8"?>
<!-- This is the European release of the DVD -->
<d:dvd xmlns:d="http://dvd.example.com" region="2">
<d:title>The Phantom Menace</d:title>
<d:year>2001</d:year>
</d:dvd>
```

Figure 2-5 A simple namespaced XML document with attributes and comments.

We have introduced into Figure 2-5 an association between a *prefix* and a *URI* (in this case we've used a URL), using the xmlns attribute from the XML Namespace specification. We then used that prefix throughout the document to associate our elements with that namespace. Any XML processing infrastructure that reads our document does not see the elements as simply their element names but de-references the URI to arrive at the form `{URI}:<local name>` (e.g., `{http://dvd.example.com}:dvd}`) which is unambiguous, unlike the element name alone (i.e., just `dvd`). It is important to remember that the syntax `{prefix}:<local name>` is not understood by XML processing programs, it is a convention used when describing qualified elements.

> Although any element can contain a namespace declaration, the style convention in XML is to declare all namespaces that a document uses in its root element. Although this can make the opening tag of the root element quite large, it does improve overall document readability since we do not then pepper the document with namespace declarations.

Explicit and Default Namespaces

XML permits two distinct kinds of namespace declarations. The first of these as we have seen is the *explicit* form, whereby a prefix is given a namespace association (e.g., `xmlns:d="http://dvd.example.com"`), and then elements and attributes which belong to that namespace are explicitly adorned with the chosen prefix. The second of these is the default namespace declared as `xmlns=<uri>` that provides a default namespace affiliation which applies to any elements without a prefix.

> The default namespace can be used to improve the readability of an XML document. In documents where a particular explicit namespace is predominantly used (like the WSDL or SOAP documents in Chapter 3), declaring a default namespace alleviates the need to pepper the document with the same prefix all over. Using this strategy, only those elements outside of the default namespace will need to be prefixed, which can make documents significantly easier to understand.

We present a modified version of the XML from Figure 2 5 in Figure 2-6, where the default namespace declaration implicitly scopes all following elements within the `http://dvd.example.com namespace`, like this:

```
<?xml version="1.0" encoding="utf-8"?>
<!-- This is the European release of the DVD -->
<dvd xmlns="http://dvd.example.com" region="2">
<title>The Phantom Menace</title>
<year>2001</year>
</dvd>
```

Figure 2-6 Using default namespaces.

Adding a namespace affiliation to an XML document is analogous to placing a Java class into a specific package. Where the Java equivalent of in Figure 2-2 (which has no namespace affiliation) might have been referenced by a declaration such as `DVD myDVD`, the equivalent type of reference for the document in Figure 2-5 or Figure 2-6 would be `com.example.dvd.DVD myDVD`, which when reduced to Java terms is clearly unambiguous since only the owner of the `dvd.example.com` domain should be using that namespace (and by inference should be the only party using that namespace to name XML documents).

Inheriting Namespaces

Once a default or explicit namespace has been declared, it is "in scope" for all child elements of the element where it was declared. The default namespace is therefore propagated to all child elements implicitly unless they have their own explicit namespace.

> This arrangement is common in WSDL files (Chapter 3) where the WSDL namespace is the default namespace for an interface, but where the binding elements use their own explicit namespace.

The rule of thumb for choosing a default or explicit namespace is that if you can't see at a glance yourself which namespace an element belongs to, then no one else will be able to and, therefore, explicit namespaces should be used. If, however, it is obvious which namespace an element belongs to and there are lots of such elements in the same namespace, then readability may be improved with the addition of a default namespace.

And Not Inheriting Namespaces

Of course, a child may not necessarily want to inherit the default namespace of its parent and may wish to set it to something else or remove the default namespace entirely. This is not a problem with explicit namespaces because the child element can just be prefixed with a different explicit namespace than its parent, as shown in Figure 2-7, where the genre element has a different namespace affiliation than the rest of the document (which uses the default namespace).

```
<?xml version="1.0" encoding="utf-8"?>
<!-- This is the European release of the DVD -->
<dvd xmlns="http://dvd.example.com" region="2">
    <title>The Phantom Menace</title>
    <year>2001</year>
    <g:genre xmlns:g="http://film-genre.example.com">
        sci-fi
    </g:genre>
</dvd>
```

Figure 2-7 Mixing explicit and default namespaces within a document.

It is important to realize that any children of the `genre` element in Figure 2-7 that use the default namespace will be using the default namespace of the `dvd` element since the genre element only declares an explicit namespace for its scope. Similarly, with default namespaces, any element is at liberty to define a namespace for itself and any of its children irrespective of the namespace affiliations of any of its parent elements. This is shown below in Figure 2-8:

```
<?xml version="1.0" encoding="utf-8"?>
<!-- This is the European release of the DVD -->
<dvd xmlns="http://dvd.example.com" region="2">
    <title>The Phantom Menace</title>
    <year>2001</year>
    <genre xmlns ="http://film-genre.example.com">
        sci-fi
    </genre>
</dvd>
```

Figure 2-8 Mixing default namespaces within a document.

The `genre` element from Figure 2-8 declares that the default namespace for itself and its children (if any) are, by default, in the namespace `http://film-genre.example.com`. This differs from the example shown in Figure 2-7 since in the absence of any explicit namespace, children of the genre element belong to the `http://film-genre.example.com` and not to the `http://dvd.example.com` namespace as the outer elements do.

Of course it may be the case that an element does not require a default namespace and that the parent default namespace is inappropriate. In such cases, we can remove any default namespace completely, by setting it to the empty string `xmlns=""`.

> For default namespaces, remember that the scoping rules are based on the familiar concept of "most local" where the declaration nearest to the use has the highest precedence.

Attributes and Namespaces

So far all of our attention has been focused on the interplay between namespaces and elements. However, it is equally valid for attributes to be qualified with namespaces through the same prefix syntax. When namespace-qualifying attributes have a default namespace, different rules apply compared to elements. Attributes are not affiliated with any default namespace, so if an attribute is to be namespace qualified, then it must be done so explicitly since any attribute without a prefix will not be considered namespace qualified—even if declared in the scope of a valid default namespace.

> The convention in XML is to associate elements with namespaces, but to leave attributes unqualified since they reside within elements with qualified names.

At this point we now understand both basic XML document structure and some more advanced features like namespaces. These both set the scene for higher-level XML-based technologies (including Web services) which we shall continue by looking at XML Schema.

XML Schema

With the exception of the basic XML syntax, XML Schema is without a doubt the single most important technology in the XML family. In the Web services world, XML Schema is *the* key technology for enabling interoperation.

XML Schema is a W3C recommendation[3] that provides a type system for XML-based computing systems. XML Schema is an XML-based language that provides a platform-independent system for describing types and interrelations between those types. Another aspect of XML Schema is to provide structuring for XML documents.

> Document Type Definitions (or DTDs) were the precursor to XML Schema, and are a text- (not XML-) based format designed to convey information about the structure of a document. Unlike XML Schema, DTDs do not concern themselves with type systems, but simply constrain documents based on their structure. Furthermore, since the DTD language is not XML-based, many of the XML-friendly tools that we use are incapable of processing DTDs. Because of these reasons, and the fact that no recent Web services protocols have used DTDs, we can consider DTDs as a deprecated technology in the Web services arena. Instead, XML Schema has become the dominant metadata language for Web services (and indeed for most other application areas by this time).

In fact, the analogy between XML technologies and object-orientation is clear if we compare XML documents to objects and XML Schema types to classes. XML documents that conform to a schema are known as instance documents, in the same way that objects of a particular class are known as instances. Thus we can conceptually match XML Schema schemas with classes and XML documents with objects, as shown in Figure 2-9.

3. See http://www.w3.org/XML/Schema#dev for links to the XML Schema specifications.

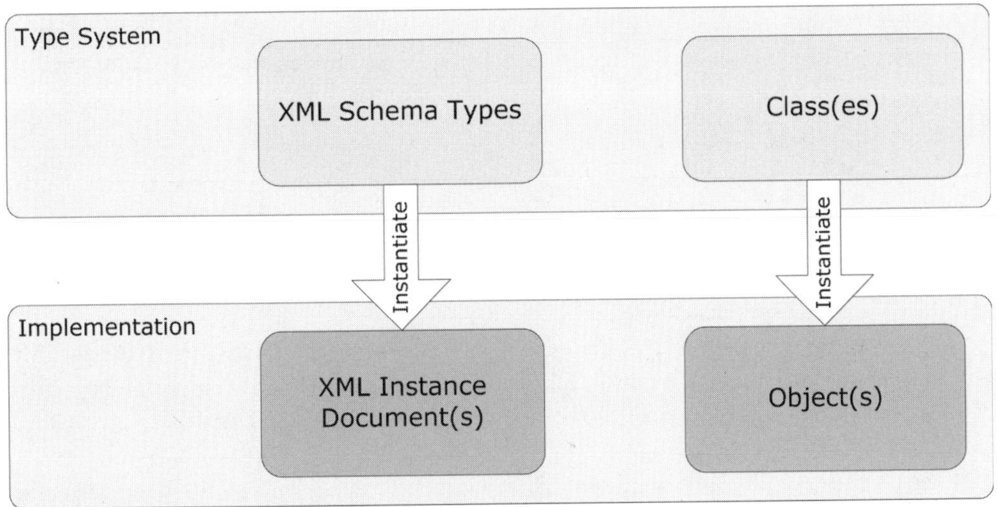

Figure 2-9 Comparing XML to object-oriented model.

The conceptual relationship between an object model and XML Schema is straightforward to comprehend. Where object-based systems classes and their interrelationships provide the blueprint for the creation and manipulation of objects, in the XML arena it is the type model expressed in XML Schema schemas that constrain documents that confirm to those schemas.

Like object-oriented programming languages, XML Schema provides a number of built-in types and allows these to be extended in a variety of ways to build abstractions appropriate for particular problem domains. Each XML Schema type is represented as the set of (textual) values that instances of that type can take. For instance the `boolean` type is allowed to take values of only `true` and `false`, while the `short` type is allowed to take any value from `-32768` to `32767` inclusively. In fact, XML Schema provides 44 different built-in types specified in the http://www.w3.org/2001/XMLSchema namespace. Additionally, XML Schema allows users to develop their own types, extending and manipulating types to create content models is the very heart of XML Schema.

XML Schema and Namespaces

As we have seen, the built-in types from XML Schema are qualified with the namespace http://www.w3.org/2001/XMLSchema. We must not use this namespace when we develop our own types, in the same way that we would not develop types under the `java.lang` package in Java or `System` namespace in .Net. However, like adding package or namespace affiliations in object-oriented programming, affiliating a type with a namespace in XML Schema is straightforward. Adding a `targetNamespace` declaration to an XML Schema to affiliate it with a namespace is analogous to adding a `package` declaration to a Java class, as shown in Figure 2-10.

XML Schema

```
<schema xmlns="http://www.w3.org/2001/XMLSchema"
targetNamespace="http://example.org"
xmlns:tns="http://example.org">

  <!-- Schema body here -->

</schema>
```

Java

```
package org.example;

class ...
```

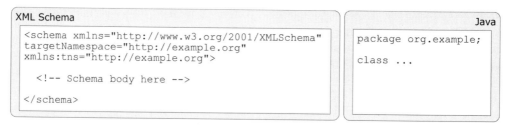

Figure 2-10 Adding namespace affiliation to an XML schema.

The skeletal schema shown in Figure 2-10 outlines the basic principle on which all XML Schema operate: the schema element delimits the namespace (like the keyword `package` delimits the package scope for a single Java source file) and the `targetNamespace` gives the namespace a name (like the period-separated string that follows the `package` keyword).

Don't be confused by the number of namespaces that exist in Figure 2-10. There are in fact only two of them and they play three distinct roles. The default namespace is the XML Schema namespace because the elements that we use in this document, such as the root element `<schema>`, are from the XML Schema namespace. The `targetNamespace` namespace is used to declare the namespace which the types that will be declared in this schema will be affiliated with. Finally, the explicit namespace `tns` (an abbreviation of Target NameSpace) will be used to allow types and elements within this schema to reference one another and, hence, it shares the same URI as the `targetNamespace` element.

A First Schema

Now that we understand the basics of XML Schema construction, we can write a simple schema with which we can constrain a document. This simple schema example does not explore any of the type-system features of XML Schema, but instead concentrates on constraining a simple document as a first step. Drawing on our experience with DVD documents earlier in this chapter we will create a schema that can validate a given DVD document. Let's recap the document that we want to constrain in Figure 2-11:

```
<?xml version="1.0" encoding="utf-8"?>
<dvd xmlns="http://dvd.example.com" region="2">
<title>The Phantom Menace</title>
<year>2001</year>
</dvd>
```

Figure 2-11 An XML document containing DVD information.

If we analyze the document in Figure 2-11, we see that it contains an element called dvd, which itself contains two elements, title and year, which are all qualified with the namespace http://dvd.example.com. From this, we immediately know that the targetNamespace is http://dvd.example.com. We also know that the schema requires two nested elements and a globally scoped element, and so we can construct the schema, as shown in Figure 2-12:

```
<?xml version="1.0" encoding="UTF-8"?>
<schema xmlns="http://www.w3.org/2001/XMLSchema"
  targetNamespace="http://dvd.example.com"
  elementFormDefault="qualified"
  attributeFormDefault="unqualified" >
  <element name="dvd">
    <complexType>
      <sequence>
        <element name="title" type="string"/>
        <element name="year" type="positiveInteger"/>
      </sequence>
      <attribute name="region" type="positiveInteger"/>
    </complexType>
  </element>
</schema>
```

Figure 2-12 A first DVD schema.

Since the elements in the document in Figure 2-11 have a namespace that matches the targetNamespace of the schema in Figure 2-12, we can assume that the document is a valid instance of the schema.

The schema dictates that the instance document must have an opening element with the name dvd from the line <element name="dvd"> at the opening line of the schema body.

> The conventional style for XML Schema documents is to declare the opening element with elementFormDefault= "qualified" and attributeFormDefault="unqualified" to ensure that elements in instance documents should be namespace qualified by default, while any attributes should lack any namespace qualification.

The schema then goes on to declare that there should be a sequence of two nested elements within that first dvd element, called title and year, respectively. Specifying this is done with four elements. The first of these is the complexType element which indicates that the parent dvd element consists of other elements nested within it. Inside the complexType element we see a sequence element. A sequence element places the constraint on any conformant document that elements nested within must follow the same sequence as the schema.

In this case, since the elements nested within the sequence are the `title` element followed by the `year` element, conformant documents must also specify `title` before `year`. The `title` element must contain information in string form because its type attribute is set to the `string` type from the XML Schema namespace. Similarly, the year element specifies that its information must be encoded as an XML Schema `positiveInteger` type.

The final aspect of this schema is to describe that the outer-most `dvd` element requires an attribute to hold region information. This constraint is applied with the `<attribute>` element which mandates an attribute called `region` whose value must be of type `positiveInteger`.

While we can now begin to create simple schemas to constrain simple documents, scaling this approach to large schemas and large documents is usually impractical and undesirable. Instead we need to look beyond the document—which after all is only the serialized, readable form of XML—to the real power of XML Schema: its type system.

Implementing XML Schema Types

The real beauty of XML Schema is that once a document has been validated against a schema, it becomes more than just a set of elements and tags—it becomes a set of types and instances. The elements contained within a document are processed and the type and instance information from them is exposed to the consuming software agent. After validation, the information contained in an XML Document is called a post schema-validation Infoset, or usually an Infoset. Infosets make it possible to reflect over the logical contents of a document, just like in some object-oriented programming languages, and so the power of XML Schema as a platform-independent type system is revealed. To demonstrate, let's start to build some types and see how the (logical) type system works with the (physical) document.

Creating Simple Types via Restriction

XML Schema provides a total of 44 simple types with which to build content models. However, unlike simple types in most programming languages, in XML Schema these types can be used as base types for the creation of specialized subtypes. There is a key difference though when we define a subtype of a simple type in XML Schema, in that we do not change the structure of the type (as we would do when we inherit from a base class in Java), but instead change the subset of values that the subtype can handle. For instance we might specify a subtype of the simple type `string` that can only be used to hold a value that represents a postcode. Similarly we might restrict the date type to valid dates within a particular century.

We create a subtype of a simple type in XML Schema using the `restriction` element. Within this element, we specify the name of the simple type whose set of permissible values we will be restricting (known as the base type) and how exactly the restriction will be applied. Restrictions are then specified by constraining *facets* of the base simple type, where the set of available facets in XML Schema is shown in Figure 2-13.[4]

4. Information from Part 2 of the XML Schema Specification at http://www.w3.org/TR/xmlschema-2/

Facet Element	Description
`length`	Specifies the number of characters in a string-based type, the number of octets in a binary-based type, or the number of items in a list-based type.
`minLength`	For string datatypes, minLength is measured in units of characters. For hexBinary and base64Binary and datatypes, minLength is measured in octets of binary data. For list-based datatypes, minLength is measured in number of list items.
`maxLength`	For string datatypes, maxLength is measured in units of characters. For hexBinary and base64Binary datatypes, maxLength is measured in octets of binary data. For list-based datatypes, maxLength is measured in number of list items.
`pattern`	Constrains the value to any value matching a specified regular expression.
`enumeration`	Specifies a fixed value that the type must match.
`whiteSpace`	Sets rules for the normalization of white space in types.
`maxInclusive`	Constrains a type's value space to values with a specific inclusive upper bound.
`maxExclusive`	Constrains a type's value space to values with a specific exclusive upper bound.
`minInclusive`	Constrains a type's value space to values with a specific inclusive lower bound.
`minExclusive`	Constrains a type's value space to values with a specific exclusive lower bound.
`fractionDigits`	For decimal types, specifies the maximum number of decimal digits to the right of the decimal point.
`totalDigits`	For number types, specifies the maximum number of digits.

Figure 2-13 XML schema facets.

Each of the facets shown in Figure 2-13 allows us to constrain simple types in a different way. For example, to create a simple type that can be used to validate a British postal code, we would constrain a string type using the `pattern` facet with a (complicated) regular expression as shown in Figure 2-14.

```
<simpleType name="PostcodeType">
  <restriction base="string">
    <xs:pattern value="(GIR 0AA)|((([A-Z][0-9][0-9]?)|(([A-
Z][A-HJ-Y][0-9][0-9]?)|(([A-Z][0-9][A-Z])|([A-Z][A-HJ-Y][0-
9]?[A-Z])))) [0-9][A-Z]{2})"/>
  </restriction>
</simpleType>
```

Figure 2-14 The pattern facet.

The pattern specified in Figure 2-14 allows only values that match the British postal code standard, such as SW1A 1AA (the Prime Minister's residence in 10 Downing Street) or W1A 1AE (the American Embassy in London). Formally, these rules are defined by the British Post Office[5] as:

1. The first part of the code before the space character (known as the outward code) can be 2, 3 or 4 alpha-numeric characters followed by a space and the second part of the code (the inward code), which is 3 characters long and is always 1 digit followed by 2 alpha-characters. Permitted combinations according to the `PostcodeType` type are: `AN NAA`, `ANN NAA`, `AAN NAA`, `AANN NAA`, `ANA NAA`, `AANA NAA`, (where `A`=alpha character and `N`=numeric character).
2. The letters I and Z are not used in the second alpha position (except GIR 0AA which is an historical anomaly in the British postal system).
3. The second half of the code never uses the letters C, I, K, M, O, and V.

Any divergence from this form will mean that the element is not a valid `PostcodeType` instance.

Similarly, we might want to create an enumeration where only specific values are allowed within a type, such as those for currencies. An example of this is shown in Figure 2-15, where the XML Schema `string` type is restricted to allow only certain values that represent a number of world currencies:

```
<xs:simpleType name="CurrencyType">
  <xs:restriction base="xs:string">
    <xs:enumeration value="GBP"/>
    <xs:enumeration value="AUD"/>
    <xs:enumeration value="USD"/>
    <xs:enumeration value="CAD"/>
    <xs:enumeration value="EUR"/>
    <xs:enumeration value="YEN"/>
  </xs:restriction>
</xs:simpleType>
```

Figure 2-15 The pattern facet.

5. http://www.govtalk.gov.uk/gdsc/schemaHtml/BS7666-v1-xsd-PostCodeType.htm

The `CurrencyType` declared in Figure 2-15 would validate elements such as `<my-currency>GBP</my-currency>`, but would not validate `<your-currency>DM</your-currency>` since the string DM is not part of this `simpleType` restriction (nor for that matter are Deutsch Marks any longer legal tender).

Continuing in a monetary theme, we can create `StockPriceType` type where we specify that the number of digits after the decimal point is at the most 2. In Figure 2-16 we restrict the XML Schema decimal type such that the maximum number of digits after the decimal point in a stock price is 2. This type can then be used to validate elements that have the form `<msft>25.52</msft>` and `<sunw>3.7</sunw>`:

```
<xs:simpleType name="StockPriceType">
  <xs:restriction base="xs:decimal">
    <xs:fractionDigits value="2"/>
  </xs:restriction>
</xs:simpleType>
```

Figure 2-16 The fractionDigits facet.

To specify sizes of allowed values, we use the `length`, `maxLength` and `minLength` facets. For instance, a sensible precaution to take when creating computer passwords is to mandate a minimum length for security and a maximum length for ease of use (and thus indirectly for security). In XML Schema, we can use `maxLength`, and `minLength` facets to create a `PasswordType` as shown in Figure 2-17:

```
<xs:simpleType name="PasswordType">
  <xs:restriction base="xs:string">
    <xs:minLength value="6"/>
    <xs:maxLength value="10"/>
  </xs:restriction>
</xs:simpleType>
```

Figure 2-17 maxLength and minLength facets.

When applied to an element in a document, the `PasswordType` in Figure 2-17 allows values like `<password>kather1ne</password>`, but does not allow for values such as `<password>carol</password>` based on the number of characters contained in the element. Of course if a particularly overbearing system administration policy was put into place, we could end up having passwords of a long, fixed length using the `length` facet instead of `minLength` and `maxLength`.

In much the same way that we set the maximum and minimum number of characters with the `maxLength`, `minLength` and `length facets`, we can also specify the maximum and minimum values. Specifying a range of values is achieved with the `maxInclusive`, `minIn-`

clusive, minExclusive and maxExclusive facets. For instance, we may wish to define the range of seconds in a minute for timing purposes. A simpleType called SecondsType is shown in Figure 2-18, where the int type from XML Schema is constrained to accept the values from 0 (inclusive) to 59 (60 exclusive):

```
<xs:simpleType name="SecondsType">
  <xs:restriction base="xs:int">
    <xs:minInclusive value="0"/>
    <xs:maxExclusive value="60"/>
  </xs:restriction>
</xs:simpleType>
```

Figure 2-18 minInclusive and maxExclusive facets.

Similarly we might want to define the years in a particular century, as we see in Figure 2-19, where the years that are part of the 20th century are captured as being positive integers (which have the range from 1 upward) from 1901 (1900 exclusive) through to 2000 (inclusive):

```
<xs:simpleType name="TwentiethCenturyType">
  <xs:restriction base="xs:positiveInteger">
    <xs:minExclusive value="1900"/>
    <xs:maxInclusive value="2000"/>
  </xs:restriction>
</xs:simpleType>
```

Figure 2-19 minExclusive and maxInclusive facets.

The totalDigits facet puts an upper limit on the number of digits that a number-based type can contain. For example a year number, for around the next 8000 years, contains a total of four digits. Thus, we can create a simple year type using the totalDigits facet to constrain the number of digits to four, as shown in Figure 2-20 where the positiveInteger type from XML Schema is restricted to those positive integers which have at most 4 digits:

```
<xs:simpleType name="YearType">
  <xs:restriction base="xs:positiveInteger">
    <xs:totalDigits value="4"/>
  </xs:restriction>
</xs:simpleType>
```

Figure 2-20 The totalDigit facet.

The final facet for restricting the value space of simple types is `whiteSpace`. This facet allows a simple type implementer to specify how any white spaces (tabs, spaces, carriage returns, and so on) are handled when they appear inside elements. There are three options for the `whiteSpace` facet which are: `preserve` (the XML processor will not remove any white space characters), `replace` (the XML processor will replace all white space with spaces), and `collapse` (same as replace, with all preceding and trailing white space removed).

Often the `whiteSpace` facet is applied along with other facets to deal with extraneous white space. For instance if we add a `whiteSpace` facet to the `YearType` from Figure 2-20, the XML processor that processes instances of this type can deal with any unimportant white space in it. This is shown in Figure 2-21, where the `whiteSpace` facet is set to `collapse`, which effectively rids the value of any unwanted white space after it has been processed:

```
<xs:simpleType name="YearType">
  <xs:restriction base="xs:positiveInteger">
    <xs:totalDigits value="4"/>
    <xs:whiteSpace value="collapse"/>
  </xs:restriction>
</xs:simpleType>
```

Figure 2-21 The whiteSpace facet.

So, if the XML processor receives an element of type `YearType such as:`

```
<moon-landing>
    1969
</moon-landing>
```

, the `whiteSpace collapse` facet will effectively reduce it to `<moon-landing>1969</moon-landing>`.

> The built-in simple type `NormalizedString` will automatically strip line feeds, carriage returns or tabs from any white spaced text.

Simple Type: List and Union

Though restriction is one means of creating new simple types, it is not the only way. XML Schema supports two additional mechanisms for creating new simple types: `union` and `list`.

> Both `union` and `list` are aggregation mechanisms, and so there is no type hierarchy. Therefore we cannot "cast" between base type and union or list type as we can with types derived through `restriction`.

The `list` mechanism is the simpler of the two to understand. In short, simple types created via the `list` mechanism are a white space-delimited list of values from the base type. For example, we can create a list of instances of `YearType` from Figure 2-20 to create the YearsType as shown in Figure 2-22:

```
<xs:simpleType name="YearType">
  <xs:restriction base="xs:positiveInteger">
    <xs:whiteSpace value="collapse"/>
    <xs:totalDigits value="4"/>
  </xs:restriction>
</xs:simpleType>

<xs:simpleType name="YearsType">
  <xs:list itemType="YearType"/>
</xs:simpleType>
```

Figure 2-22 Creating new simple types with list.

The `YearsType` type defined in Figure 2-22 can then be used to validate instances of the `YearsType` such as the `years` element in Figure 2-23.

```
<WWII> 1939 1940 1941 1942 1943 1944 1945 1946</WWII>
```

Figure 2-23 An instance of the YearsType type.

The `union` mechanism is slightly more subtle than the `list`. It allows the aggregation of the value spaces of two types to be combined into the value space of a new single simple type. For instance, imagine we have two simple types that represent fruits and vegetables, respectively, as shown in Figure 2-24:

```
 <xs:simpleType name="FruitType">
  <xs:restriction base="xs:string">
    <xs:enumeration value="ORANGE"/>
    <xs:enumeration value="APPLE"/>
    <xs:enumeration value="BANANA"/>
    <xs:enumeration value="KIWI"/>
  </xs:restriction>
</xs:simpleType>

  <xs:simpleType name="VegetableType">
  <xs:restriction base="xs:string">
    <xs:enumeration value="POTATO"/>
    <xs:enumeration value="CABBAGE"/>
    <xs:enumeration value="TURNIP"/>
    <xs:enumeration value="LEEK"/>
  </xs:restriction>
</xs:simpleType>
```

Figure 2-24 FruitType and VegetableType simple types.

We can use the `FruitType` and `VegetableType` types in Figure 2-24 to create a `FruitAndVegetableType` via a `union` as shown here in Figure 2-25:

```
<xs:simpleType name="FruitAndVegetableType">
  <xs:union memberTypes="FruitType VegetableType"/>
</xs:simpleType>
```

Figure 2-25 Creating a new simple type via a union.

The resulting `FruitAndVegetableType` type can be used to validate elements such as `<organically-grown>BANANA</organically-grown>` and `<menu-item> POTATO</menu-item>` because both `BANANA` and `POTATO` are valid values for the `FruitAndVegetableType` type.

Simple Type Support in Programming Languages

The XML Schema support for simple user-defined types that allow custom value and lexical spaces is a powerful aspect of the technology. However, since most programming languages do not support this feature, typically programmers have had to produce properties/accessors/mutators that constrain the value space by manually checking values and throwing exceptions where constraints have been invalidated. For example, take the Java equivalent of the `YearType` type (from Figure 2-20) shown in Figure 2-26:

```
public class Year
{
  public int getValue()
  {
    return _value;
  }

  public void  setValue(int value)
                         throws InvalidValueException
  {
    if(value >=  1000 &&  value <= 9999)
    {
      _value = value;
    }
    else
    {
      // Invalid year
      throw new InvalidValueException();
    }

  }

  private  int  _value;
}
```

Figure 2-26 Value and Lexical handling with Java's primitive types.

The `Year` class in Figure 2-26 is somewhat lengthier than the equivalent XML Schema simple type since it has to handle the value space imperatively rather than declaratively. To deal with the lexical space of year instances, we need to manually check the possible values and report back to the user when an invalid value is encountered as exemplified in the `Year.setValue(int)` method.

Writing these kinds of classes by hand is long-winded and prone to error. Of course we could provide tool support to deal with these issues (like the `xsd.exe` tool from the .Net platform toolkit), but if we are dealing with schematized XML documents, it happens that we don't necessarily need to. Consider the diagram in Figure 2-27 of a typical XML-enabled software agent (which could be a standalone application, a database, or more likely a Web service) that communicates with its environment through schematized XML documents.

The ability to define custom value/lexical spaces that fit our precise needs means that it is possible to delegate constraint checking of values in an XML document to the XML processor. Once the XML processor has produced an Infoset for the program to consume, the XML document that the Infoset was created from must have passed validation by its schema, and so the value and lexical constraints placed on the documents must be satisfied. Knowing this, the devel-

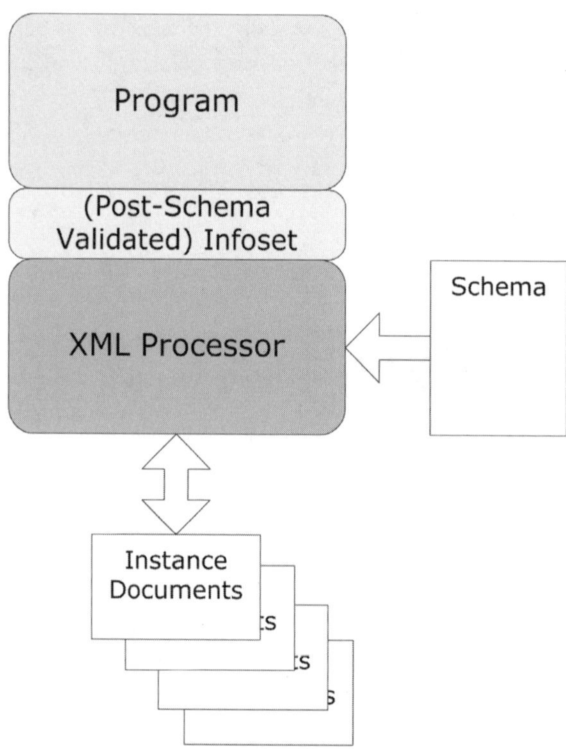

Figure 2-27 Delegating Value/Lexical space error handling to the XML processor.

oper of the consuming program no longer has to write lengthy constraint checking code since this would be a replication of work that the XML processor already undertakes. Thus using schemas can remove some of the burden of manually checking values in our code, though it is not a substitute for failing to program defensively!

Complex Types

As well as creating specialized versions of the XML Schema simple types, we can also create new complex types by aggregating existing types into a structure. XML Schema supports three means of aggregating types with three different complex type compositors: `sequence`, `choice`, and `all` whose semantics are outlined in Figure 2-28.

Compositor	Description
`sequence`	Specifies that the contents of the complex type must appear as an ordered list.
`choice`	Allows a choice of any of the contents of the complex type.
`all`	Specifies that the contents of the complex type appear as a unordered list.

Figure 2-28 complexType compositors.

While the semantics of the compositors vary, the syntax of each is quite similar. To use any of the compositors, we simply declare a new complex type with a compositor as its child element, as shown here in Figure 2-29:

```
<xs:complexType name="AddressType">
  <xs:sequence>
    <xs:element name="number" type="xs:string"/>
    <xs:element name="street" type="xs:string"/>
    <xs:element name="city" type="xs:string"/>
    <xs:element name="state" type="xs:string"/>
    <xs:element name="post-code" type="xs:string"/>
  </xs:sequence>
  <xs:attribute name="business-address" type="xs:boolean"/>
</xs:complexType>
```

Figure 2-29 Declaring a new complexType using the sequence compositor.

In Figure 2-29 we create a new complexType called AddressType by aggregating five elements of type string which represent a mailing address, and a single attribute of type boolean which is used to indicate whether this address is business or residential.

> In the scope of a sequence compositor, each contained element must appear exactly once by default. If more flexibility is needed, then we can add the minOccurs and maxOccurs attributes to each contained element. The minOccurs attribute is set to a value greater than or equal to 0 which then specifies the minimum number of occurrences for its element within the compositor. The maxOccurs attribute specifies the maximum number of elements that should appear in the compositor from 1 to the special value unbounded (which is logically an infinite number of times).

With the AddressType in Figure 2-29, we can now validate elements such as the address element in Figure 2-30:

```
<address>
  <number>221b</number>
  <street>Baker Street</street>
  <city>London</city>
  <state>N/A</state>
  <post-code>NW1 6XE</post-code>
</address>
```

Figure 2-30 A valid instance of the AddressType type.

The all compositor is similar to the sequence compositor except that ordering constraint is relaxed. Therefore while the elements contained within an all compositor must be present, the order in which they appear is unimportant from the point of view of the XML processor.

> The minOccurs and maxOccurs attributes do not make sense in the scope of an all compositor since (for example) it is impossible to specify that an instance document should contain all the instances of a maxOccurs="unbounded" element! Instead, omitting these attributes gives us the default semantics of exactly one element per compositor. The only exception here is that minOccurs="0" can be used to specify optional elements.

An example of the all compositor is shown in Figure 2-31, where the PurchaseOrderType type is presented. The PurchaseOrderType uses the all compositor to create an aggregate structure containing mandatory `order-number` and `item` elements, and an optional `description` element (specified by the `minOccurs="0"` attribute):

```
<xs:complexType name="PurchaseOrderType">
  <xs:all>
    <xs:element name="order-number"
      type="xs:positiveInteger"/>
    <xs:element name="item" type="xs:string"/>
    <xs:element name="description" type="xs:string"
      minOccurs="0"/>
  </xs:all>
</xs:complexType>
```

Figure 2-31 Using the all compositor.

The `PurchaseOrderType` type from Figure 2-31 can be used to validate the instances shown in Figure 2-32, where we see instances both where the description element is missing and where it is present:

```
<purchase-order>
  <order-number>1002</order-number>
  <item>11025-32098</item>
  <description>Personal MP3 Player</description>
</purchase-order>

<purchase-order>
  <item>44045-23112</item>
  <order-number>5290</order-number>
</purchase-order>
```

Figure 2-32 Valid PurchaseOrderType instances.

Using the `choice` compositor, we can force the contents of part of a document to be one of a number of possible options. For example, in Figure 2-33 we see the `UserIdentifier-Type`, which allows a user to supply either a login identifier or Microsoft Passport-style single-signon credentials to log in to a system (this type of arrangement is typical in e-commerce sites).[6]

6. Note that this is a hypothetical example that has been deliberately shortened for clarity, and the types used are not representative of the actual Passport API.

```
<xs:complexType name="UserIdentifierType">
  <xs:choice>
    <xs:element name="login-id" type="xs:string"/>
    <xs:element name="passport" type="xs:anyURI"/>
  </xs:choice>
</xs:complexType>
```

Figure 2-33 Using the choice compositor.

The `UserIdentifierType` can be used to validate elements that contain either a `login-id`, or a `passport` element, but not both. Therefore both the elements shown in Figure 2-34 can be validated against the `UserIdentifierType`:

```
<logon>
  <login-id>chewbacca@wookie.org</login-id>
</logon>

<logon>
  <passport>
    http://passport.example.org/uid/2235:112e:77fa:9699:aad1
  </passport>
</logon>
```

Figure 2-34 Valid UserIdentifierType elements.

The `minOccurs` and `maxOccurs` attributes can be used within `choice` compositor. They allow us to expand the basic exclusive OR operation that `choice` provides, to support selection based on quantity as well as content, as exemplified in Figure 2-35:

```
<xs:complexType name="DrinksMenuType">
  <xs:choice>
    <xs:element name="beer" type="b:BeerType" minOccurs="0"
      maxOccurs="2"/>
    <xs:element name="wine" type="w:WineType" minOccurs="0"
      maxOccurs="1"/>
  </xs:choice>
</xs:complexType>
```

Figure 2-35 Choosing elements based on cardinality.

Using the `DrinksMenuType` type, we can specify using the `minOccurs` and `maxOccurs` attributes that our choice can be either two beers or one drink of wine, as shown in Figure 2-36.

```
<!-- Either two beers… -->
<drinks>
  <b:beer type="bitter"/>
  <b:beer type="lager"/>
</drinks>

<!-- … Or a single drink of wine -->
<drinks>
  <w:wine country="France" grape="Pinot Noir" year="1998"/>
</drinks>
```

Figure 2-36 Instance documents constrained by choice.

Equally, we could select based on quantity of a single item. For example we could envision a `choice` where beer can be sold in four, six and twelve packs by simply setting the `minOccurs` and `maxOccurs` attributes to 4, 6 and 12, respectively, as shown in Figure 2-37:

```
<xs:complexType name="DrinksMenuType">
  <xs:choice>
    <xs:element name="beer" type="xs:string" minOccurs="4"
      maxOccurs="4"/>
    <xs:element name="beer" type="xs:string" minOccurs="6"
      maxOccurs="6"/>
    <xs:element name="beer" type="xs:string" minOccurs="12"
      maxOccurs="12"/>
  </xs:choice>
</xs:complexType>
```

Figure 2-37 Choice based on cardinality.

With `choice`, we have drawn to a close our discussion on compositors. We have seen how we can aggregate existing types into new types in a variety of ways (`sequence`, `choice`, `all`) and some of the variations on those themes (like choice-by-cardinality). However, we can also create new types not only by aggregating existing types, but by aggregating existing types and textual content. For instance, we might wish to mix textual information and structured data to create a letter[7] as shown in Figure 2-38.

7. This example adapted from the W3 Schools example at: http://www.w3schools.com/schema/schema_complex_mixed.asp

```
<letter>
Dear Professor <name>Einstein</name>,
Your shipment (order: <orderid>1032</orderid> )
will be shipped on <shipdate>2003-06-14</shipdate>.
</letter>
```

Figure 2-38 Mixed textual and element content.

In order to mix elements and text, we must create a type that allows such mixtures (and by default types do not). Thus we create a schema such as that shown here in Figure 2-39:

```
<xs:element name="letter">
  <xs:complexType mixed="true">
    <xs:sequence>
      <xs:element name="name" type="xs:string"/>
      <xs:element name="orderid" type="xs:positiveInteger"/>
      <xs:element name="shipdate" type="xs:date"/>
    </xs:sequence>
  </xs:complexType>
</xs:element>
```

Figure 2-39 Schema supporting mixed textual and element content.

The way that we support mixed textual and elemental content is to create a `complexType` with `mixed` content. Thus when the `mixed` attribute is set to `true` (in its absence the default is `false`), the resulting type can mix elements and text as shown in the letter example in Figure 2-38.

The `any` Element

By default, all complex types that we create have closed content models. This means that only the elements that are specified when the type is declared can appear in instances. While this certainly encourages strong typing, it can also be a problem. How do we handle elements within a document that we cannot predict ahead of time? Indeed many of the Web services protocols that we will encounter in later chapters have this requirement, where the content model of schemas for particular protocols has to be extended on a per application basis (in fact, we discuss how WS-Transaction extends WS-Coordination in this way in Chapter 7). Fortunately this kind of extensibility is supported in XML Schema through the `any` element, which allows us to develop an open content model for a type through the use of wildcards.

Using `any` within a complex type means that any element can appear at that location, so that it becomes a placeholder for future content that we cannot predict while building the type. For attributes, there is the `anyAttribute` which defines placeholders for future attribute extensions.

Of course, we might not want to allow completely arbitrary content to be embedded, and so any can be constrained in a number of ways, but don't worry, it will still be generic even after the constraints. The first constraint that we can place on any is how the contents that are substituted will be treated by the XML processor. The processContents attribute has a number of options that can be chosen to set the level of validation of elements specified by an any element. These are:

- strict—This is the default value in the absence of any processContents attribute. The XML processor must have access to the schema for the namespaces of the substituted elements and fully validate those elements against that schema.
- lax—This is similar to strict, with the exception that if no schema can be located for substituted elements, then the XML parser simply checks for well-formed XML.
- skip—This is the least taxing validation method, which instructs the XML processor not to validate any elements from the specified namespaces.

The namespaces against which the contents may be validated are specified by a second optional attribute for the any element called namespace. This attribute specifies the namespace of the elements that it is valid to substitute for an any element within a document, and has a number of possible settings:

- ##any—This is the default setting for the namespace attribute which implies that elements from any namespace are allowed to exist in the placeholder specified by the any element.
- ##other—Specifying this value for the namespace attribute allows elements from any namespace except the namespace of the parent element (i.e., not the targetNamespace of the parent).
- ##local—The substituted elements must come from no namespace.
- ##targetNamespace—Only elements from the namespace of the parent element can be contained.

Finally we are allowed to combine some of the above options to make the available namespaces more configurable. That is, we are allowed to specify a space-separated list of valid namespace URIs (instead of ##any and ##other), plus optionally ##targetNamespace and ##local. Thus we can restrict the namespaces for which it is valid to substitute any element to a list of (one or more) specific namespaces if necessary.

An example of how the any element is used is presented in Figure 2-40.

```
<xsd:complexType name="Notification">
  <xsd:sequence>
    <xsd:element name="TargetProtocolService"
      type="wsu:PortReferenceType"/>
    <xsd:element name="SourceProtocolService"
      type="wsu:PortReferenceType" />
    <xsd:any namespace="##other" processContents="lax"
      minOccurs="0" maxOccurs="unbounded"/>
  </xsd:sequence>
  <xsd:anyAttribute namespace="##other"
    processContents="lax"/>
</xsd:complexType>
```

Figure 2-40 WS-Transaction messages are extensible via any and anyAttribute.

Figure 2-40 shows the `Notification` type from the WS-Transaction protocol schema. A `Notification` in WS-Transaction is a message that is transmitted between actors in the protocol. However, since WS-Transaction is designed to allow different back end transaction systems to operate on the Internet, the messages it exchanges have to be extensible enough to express the semantics of each back end system. This, of course, calls for an open content model to allow third parties to extend the protocol to suit their own systems.

The protocol supports wildcard elements and attributes via the `xsd:any` and `xsd:anyAttribute` elements. In both cases, the wildcard element namespaces must come from any namespace other than the WS-Transaction namespace as its `namespace` attribute is set to `##other`. This is exemplified in Figure 2-41 where we see a SOAP message (see Chapter 3 for a full explanation of SOAP) from one vendor's WS-Transaction implementation (see Chapter 7 for details on Web services transactions) using the wildcard elements to propagate information pertinent to their implementation.[8]

Although the `DialogIdentifier` element from the SOAP message in Figure 2-41 wasn't specified by the schema, it is still a valid message because it matches the constraints of the `<xsd:any namespace="##other" processContents="lax" minOccurs="0" maxOccurs="unbounded"/>` element from the schema. It matches the `##other` constraint since it comes from the namespace http://schemas.arjuna.com/ws/2003/01/wsarjtx which is valid since the WS-Transaction namespace is http://schemas.xmlsoap.org/ws/2002/08/wstx. Since the schema maintains that processing of these elements is lax, it means that the XML processor that receives this message will validate the well-formed XML of the `DialogIdentifier` element. Thus the message conforms to the schema even though the originators of the schema had no idea about the organization that ultimately created the conformant message, let alone the message itself.

8. This SOAP message is from Arjuna Technologies' XTS 1.0 implementation of the WS-Transaction protocol.

```
<?xml version="1.0" encoding="UTF-8"?>
<soapenv:Envelope xmlns:soapenv="http://schemas.xmlsoap.org/soap/
envelope/" xmlns:xsd="http://www.w3.org/2001/XMLSchema"
xmlns:xsi="http://www.w3.org/2001/XMLSchema-instance">
  <soapenv:Body>
    <wstx:OnePhaseCommit xmlns:wstx="http://schemas.xmlsoap.org/ws/
2002/08/wstx">
      <wstx:TargetProtocolService xmlns:wstx="http://
schemas.xmlsoap.org/ws/2002/08/wstx">
        <wsu:Address xmlns:wsu="http://schemas.xmlsoap.org/ws/2002/
07/utility">
http://localhost:5555/jboss-net/services/TwoPCParticipantMSG
        </wsu:Address>
      </wstx:TargetProtocolService>
      <wstx:SourceProtocolService xmlns:wstx="http://
schemas.xmlsoap.org/ws/2002/08/wstx">
        <wsu:Address xmlns:wsu="http://schemas.xmlsoap.org/ws/2002/
07/utility">
http://localhost/jboss-net/services/TwoPCCoordinator
        </wsu:Address>
      </wstx:SourceProtocolService>
      <wsarjtx:DialogIdentifier xmlns:wsarjtx=
        "http://schemas.arjuna.com/ws/2003/01/wsarjtx">
        123456
      </wsarjtx:DialogIdentifier>
    </wstx:OnePhaseCommit>
  </soapenv:Body>
</soapenv:Envelope>
```

Figure 2-41 Using Wildcard element to extend a WS-Transaction message.

In addition to the any and anyAttribute elements, XML Schema also provides two special types called anyType and anySimpleType which can be used instead of a specific named type where we need our schemas to be more generic.

The anyType type is the most generic of the two being substitutable for any type in the whole XML Schema type system, including user-derived types. The anySimpleType is more constrained and supports only types that are from the set of forty-four XML Schema simple types or types derived from them.

These special types provide the same kind of generality when creating type-based content models as the any element provides for document structure. It is not unusual to see attributes like type="xs:anyType" or type="xs:anySimpleType" in element declarations where the type of such elements is expected to be determined by the application that consumes the schema, and not by the schema developer.

Inheritance

While the ability to constrain instance documents is essential for interoperability, harnessing the type system exploits the real power of XML Schema. The inheritance features in XML Schema allow us to create type hierarchies that capture the data models of the underlying software systems that XML is designed to support.

In fact, we have already seen one form of inheritance when we used the `restriction` feature to create new simple types with differently constrained value and lexical spaces. However, XML Schema also supports a mechanism called `extension` that allows us to augment (rather than constrain) the capabilities of an existing type. Using this facility we can begin to create hierarchies of complex types just as we can in object-oriented programming languages.

When using complex type extension, we have two options for creating subtypes. We can create subtypes that contain only simple content (text and attributes only), or subtypes that contain complex content (other elements as well as text and attributes).

An example of extending a complex type with additional simple content is shown in Figure 2-42:

```
<xs:complexType name="MonitorType">
  <xs:simpleContent>
    <xs:extension base="xs:string">
      <xs:attribute name="flatscreen" type="xs:boolean"/>
    </xs:extension>
  </xs:simpleContent>
</xs:complexType>
```

Figure 2-42 Complex Type `extension with simpleContent.`

The `MonitorType` complex type in Figure 2-42 uses the `simpleContent` element to add a single attribute to its content, which is defined as being the `string` built-in type. The base type of the `MonitorType (string)` is specified by the `base` attribute in the `extension` element. The additional simple content is specified as the only child of this `extension` element. The new subtype we have defined can now be used to validate elements such as `<monitor flatscreen="true">HP P4831D</monitor>`.

Figure 2-43 shows an example of how we can use the `extension` mechanism to create subtypes with additional elements using the `complexContent` construct.

```
<xs:complexType name="PersonType">
  <xs:sequence>
    <xs:element name="forename" type="xs:string"/>
    <xs:element name="surname" type="xs:string"/>
  </xs:sequence>
</xs:complexType>

<xs:complexType name="FootballerType">
  <xs:complexContent>
    <xs:extension base="PersonType">
      <xs:sequence>
        <xs:element name="team" type="xs:string"/>
        <xs:element name="goals" type="xs:int"/>
      </xs:sequence>
    </xs:extension>
  </xs:complexContent>
</xs:complexType>
```

Figure 2-43 Complex Type `extension with complexContent.`

The `PersonType` type in Figure 2-43 can be used to validate instances such as that shown here in Figure 2-44:

```
<person>
  <forename>Alan</forename>
  <surname>Turing</surname>
</person>
```

Figure 2-44 An Instance of the `PersonType` Type.

The `FootballerType` in Figure 2-43 has `complexContent`, allowing the elements and attributes to appear within the body of the type. It capitalizes on that fact by adding the `team` and `goals` elements to extend on the base `PersonType` to allow the validation of such elements as shown in Figure 2-45:

```
<footballer>
  <forename>Alan</forename>
  <surname>Shearer</surname>
  <team>Newcastle United</team>
  <goals>145</goals>
</footballer>
```

Figure 2-45 A `FootballerType` Type Instance.

As we see in Figure 2-45, instances of the `FootballerType` type have a similar structure to instances of the `PersonType` type, because the `FootballerType` subtype inherits the forename and surname elements from the `PersonType`, but adds the elements team and goals.

From this example, we can see that it is possible to use the `extension` mechanism to build type hierarchies in XML Schema, just as we can in object-oriented programming languages. However, to be able to exploit such hierarchies (e.g. to "cast" between types) we need to use another XML Schema mechanism: substitution groups.

Substitution Groups

Substitution groups are a feature that allows us to declare that an element can be substituted for other elements in an instance document. We achieve this by assigning an element to a special group—a substitution group—that is substitutable for the element at the *head* of that group, effectively creating an equivalence relation between document elements of the same type (or subtype).

> Elements in a substitution group must have the same type as the head element, or a type that has been derived from the head element's type.

While this isn't exactly like polymorphic behavior in object-oriented programming languages since the base-type/derived type relationship isn't implicit, this feature is immensely useful for creating extensible schemas with open content models.

To illustrate this point, consider the schema shown in Figure 2-46. This schema demonstrates how to use substitution groups to deal with element-level substitutions—a kind of polymorphic behavior for instance documents. The substitution group consists of the elements `cast-member` and `crew-member` declaring themselves to be substitutable for a person element through the `substitutionGroup="person"` attribute declaration. Note that this is a valid substation group because both `cast-member` and `crew-member` are types derived from the `PersonType` type.

The definition of the `cast-and-crew` element references the `person` element from within a `sequence`, setting the `maxOccurs` attributes to allow any number of `person` elements to exist within an instance. However, since person is an abstract element (and thus cannot appear as an element in its own right), this schema actually supports the substitution of `person` elements for any other element declared to be in the same substitution group. Therefore, this schema will validate instance documents such as that shown in Figure 2-47.

```
<?xml version="1.0" encoding="UTF-8"?>
<xs:schema xmlns:xs="http://www.w3.org/2001/XMLSchema">
  <xs:complexType name="PersonType">
    <xs:sequence>
      <xs:element name="firstname" type="xs:string"
        minOccurs="0"/>
      <xs:element name="surname" type="xs:string"/>
    </xs:sequence>
  </xs:complexType>
  <xs:complexType name="CastMemberType">
    <xs:complexContent>
      <xs:extension base="PersonType">
        <xs:sequence>
          <xs:element name="character" type="xs:string"/>
        </xs:sequence>
      </xs:extension>
    </xs:complexContent>
  </xs:complexType>
  <xs:complexType name="CrewMemberType">
    <xs:complexContent>
      <xs:extension base="PersonType">
        <xs:sequence>
          <xs:element name="function" type="xs:string"/>
        </xs:sequence>
      </xs:extension>
    </xs:complexContent>
  </xs:complexType>
  <!-- Declare substitution group and head element -->
  <xs:element name="person" type="PersonType"
    abstract="true"/>
  <xs:element name="cast-member" type="CastMemberType"
    substitutionGroup="person"/>
  <xs:element name="crew-member" type="CrewMemberType"
    substitutionGroup="person"/>
  <!-- Now define the actual document -->
  <xs:element name="cast-and-crew">
    <xs:complexType>
      <xs:sequence>
        <xs:element ref="person" maxOccurs="unbounded"/>
      </xs:sequence>
    </xs:complexType>
  </xs:element>
</xs:schema>
```

Figure 2-46 Using substitution groups.

```
<?xml version="1.0" encoding="UTF-8"?>
<cast-and-crew>
  <crew-member>
    <firstname>Lucas</firstname>
    <surname>George</surname>
    <function>director</function>
  </crew-member>
  <cast-member>
    <firstname>Ewan</firstname>
    <surname>McGregor</surname>
    <character>Obi Wan Kenobi</character>
  </cast-member>
</cast-and-crew>
```

Figure 2-47 Supporting polymorphic behavior with substitution groups.

The instance document in Figure 2-47 shows how types from the `person` substitution group can be used in places where the original schema has specified a `PersonType` element. In this case since both `cast-member` and `crew-member` are part of the `person` substitution group, the document is valid.

> Like the `any` and `anyAttribute` elements, substitution groups are a useful mechanism for creating schema types which are extensible. Again like the `any` and `anyAttribute` elements, substitution groups are widely found in various Web services standards. WSDL (see Chapter 3) makes extensive use of substitution groups to allow other protocols (such as BPEL, see Chapter 6) to extend its basic features to more complex problem domains.

Global and Local Type Declarations

Just like classes in object-oriented programming, we need to create instances of XML Schema types in order to do real work like moving XML encoded messages between Web services. In this section, we examine two means for creating instances of types: using global types and declaring local types.

We have already seen examples of both of global (schema-scoped) and local (element-scoped) type declarations throughout the previous sections. A global type definition occurs where we embed a type directly as a child of the `<schema>` element of a schema. Conversely, a local type is declared as the child an `<element>` element, which is a direct child of the `<schema>` element. This is exemplified in Figure 2-48.

```
<?xml version="1.0" encoding="UTF-8"?>
<xs:schema xmlns:xs="http://www.w3.org/2001/XMLSchema"
elementFormDefault="qualified"
attributeFormDefault="unqualified">
  <!-- A Global Type -->
  <xs:complexType name="CardType">
    <xs:sequence>
      <xs:element name="card-type">
        <xs:simpleType>
          <xs:restriction base="xs:string">
            <xs:enumeration value="Visa"/>
            <xs:enumeration value="MasterCard"/>
          </xs:restriction>
        </xs:simpleType>
      </xs:element>
      <xs:element name="expiry">
        <xs:simpleType>
          <xs:restriction base="xs:string">
            <xs:pattern value="[0-9]{2}-[0-9]{2}"/>
          </xs:restriction>
        </xs:simpleType>
      </xs:element>
      <xs:element name="number">
        <xs:simpleType name="CardNumberType">
          <xs:restriction base="xs:string">
            <xs:pattern
              value="[0-9]{4} [0-9]{4} [0-9]{4} [0-9]{4}"/>
          </xs:restriction>
        </xs:simpleType>
      </xs:element>
      <xs:element name="holder" type="xs:string"/>
    </xs:sequence>
  </xs:complexType>
  <!-- A local type -->
  <xs:element name="debit-card">
    <xs:complexType>
      <xs:complexContent>
        <xs:extension base="CardType">
          <xs:attribute name="issue"
            type="xs:positiveInteger"/>
        </xs:extension>
      </xs:complexContent>
    </xs:complexType>
  </xs:element>
  <!-- Another local type -->
  <xs:element name="wallet">
    <xs:complexType>
      <xs:sequence>
        <xs:element name="credit-card" type="CardType"
          minOccurs="0" maxOccurs="unbounded"/>
        <xs:element name="debit-card" ref="debit-card"
          minOccurs="0" maxOccurs="unbounded"/>
      </xs:sequence>
    </xs:complexType>
  </xs:element>
</xs:schema>
```

Figure 2-48 Global and Local type declarations.

The distinction between the two is important. Global types such as `CardType` in Figure 2-48 are globally visible and so are available within the namespace in which they are declared and in other namespaces, can be extended and generally behave as we would expect classes to behave in an object-oriented programming language. Instances of global types are created by constructing an element whose `type` attribute refers to that particular global type's name. This is shown in Figure 2-48 where we see this element:

```
<xs:element name="credit-card" type="CardType"
  minOccurs="0" maxOccurs="unbounded"/>
```

that defines that an instance of the `CardType` type can be present any number of times in a wallet element.

On the other hand, local types are declared inline with an element (like `debit-card` and `wallet` in Figure 2-48). While the element itself is visible to other elements and types, its implementing type is not and therefore is not extendable by other types—in fact, the implementing type doesn't even have a name so that it can be referred to.

When we declare local types, they can subsequently be referred to only by their enclosing element name and their content cannot be extended. In programming terms, this is similar to a component whose API is known, but whose type is anonymous and internal structure is a black box. This is shown in Figure 2-48 where the `wallet` (itself a local type) is defined as containing any number of instances of the `debit-card` local type via the `ref` attribute, like this:

```
<xs:element name="debit-card" ref="debit-card"
          minOccurs="0" maxOccurs="unbounded"/>.
```

> Instances of local types are specified by the ref attribute, e.g., `<xs:element name="credit-card" ref="debit-card" ... />` Instances of global types are specified by type attribute, e.g., `<xs:element name="credit-card" type="CardType" ... >`

Whether to declare types globally or locally depends on our intended use for those types. If we intend for those types to form part of a type hierarchy, then they should be declared globally so they can be extended at will. If, however, we intend for a type to only support instances within XML documents, then it should be declared locally.

A good rule of thumb for developing content models is to type hierarchies with global types, but to create local type declarations at the leaf nodes of those hierarchies. Thus within the hierarchy we have the full flexibility supplied by global types, yet the "interface" presented to users of that hierarchy is a collection of element declarations against which XML documents can be validated.

Managing Schemas

While most of the schemas we have seen in this chapter have been short, it is possible for schemas that serve particularly complicated problem domains to become long and difficult to manage. XML Schema helps to solve this problem by providing the `include` mechanism that allows us to partition a single logical schema (i.e., the set of types from a single `targetNamespace`) across a number of physical schema documents. For instance, we could choose to create type hierarchies in one physical document and create the document layout in another physical document for ease of management. These two separate physical documents can then be made into a single logical schema by including the type hierarchy document in the document structure schema, as shown in Figure 2-49 and Figure 2-50.

```
<?xml version="1.0" encoding="UTF-8"?>
<xs:schema
targetNamespace="http://wallet.example.com"
xmlns:xs="http://www.w3.org/2001/XMLSchema"
elementFormDefault="qualified"
attributeFormDefault="unqualified">
  <xs:complexType name="CardType">
    <xs:sequence>
      <xs:element name="card-type">
        <xs:simpleType>
          <xs:restriction base="xs:string">
            <xs:enumeration value="Visa"/>
            <xs:enumeration value="MasterCard"/>
          </xs:restriction>
        </xs:simpleType>
      </xs:element>
      <xs:element name="expiry">
        <xs:simpleType>
          <xs:restriction base="xs:string">
            <xs:pattern value="[0-9]{2}-[0-9]{2}"/>
          </xs:restriction>
        </xs:simpleType>
      </xs:element>
      <xs:element name="number">
        <xs:simpleType name="CardNumberType">
          <xs:restriction base="xs:string">
            <xs:pattern
              value="[0-9]{4} [0-9]{4} [0-9]{4} [0-9]{4}"/>
          </xs:restriction>
        </xs:simpleType>
      </xs:element>
      <xs:element name="holder" type="xs:string"/>
    </xs:sequence>
  </xs:complexType>
</xs:schema>
```

Figure 2-49 The Type hierarchy part of the Wallet schema.

```
<?xml version="1.0" encoding="UTF-8"?>
<xs:schema
targetNamespace="http://wallet.example.com" xmlns:tns="http://
wallet.example.com"
xmlns:xs="http://www.w3.org/2001/XMLSchema"
elementFormDefault="qualified"
attributeFormDefault="unqualified">
  <xs:include schemaLocation="CreditCard.xsd"/>
  <xs:element name="debit-card">
    <xs:complexType>
      <xs:complexContent>
        <xs:extension base="tns:CardType">
          <xs:attribute name="issue"
            type="xs:positiveInteger"/>
        </xs:extension>
      </xs:complexContent>
    </xs:complexType>
  </xs:element>
  <xs:element name="wallet">
    <xs:complexType>
      <xs:sequence>
        <xs:element name="credit-card" type="tns:CardType"
          minOccurs="0" maxOccurs="unbounded"/>
        <xs:element name="tns:debit-card" ref="debit-card"
          minOccurs="0" maxOccurs="unbounded"/>
      </xs:sequence>
    </xs:complexType>
  </xs:element>
</xs:schema>
```

Figure 2-50 The Document-Structure part of the Wallet schema.

The schema shown in Figure 2-49 effectively becomes the container for all of the types that might be used in the XML documents that conform to the schema (which at the moment is only a single type, `CardType`). The schema in Figure 2-50 uses the include mechanism to create a single logical schema containing itself and the included schema from Figure 2-49. This gives access to all of the types defined in the included schema, allowing the `wallet` to be constructed in the same way as it was when the two schemas were physically one (in Figure 2-48), with the advantage that because the individual schemas are smaller, maintaining them is easier.

While the `include` mechanism is fine for partitioning a single schema across multiple physical schema documents, it is limited to schema documents which share the same `targetNamespace`. It is easy to see the limitation of this mechanism if we imagine for a moment that the definition of the `CardType` had not been developed by the same in-house team that created the wallet, but had instead been created by an outside consortium of credit card companies. In this case the `targetNamespace` will be different from that of the wallet schema and so `include` will not work. Instead, we use the `import` mechanism, which allows us to combine types and elements from different namespaces into a single schema.

```
<?xml version="1.0" encoding="UTF-8"?>
<xs:schema
targetNamespace="http://card.example.com"
xmlns:xs="http://www.w3.org/2001/XMLSchema"
elementFormDefault="qualified"
attributeFormDefault="unqualified">
  <xs:complexType name="CardType">
  <!-- Card implementation omitted for brevity -->
  </xs:complexType>
</xs:schema>
```

Figure 2-51 The Credit Card schema.

```
<?xml version="1.0" encoding="UTF-8"?>
<xs:schema
targetNamespace="http://wallet.example.com" xmlns:tns="http://
wallet.example.com" xmlns:cc="http://card.example.com"
xmlns:xs="http://www.w3.org/2001/XMLSchema"
elementFormDefault="qualified"
attributeFormDefault="unqualified">
  <xs:import namespace="http://card.example.org"
    schemaLocation="CreditCard.xsd"/>
  <xs:element name="debit-card">
    <xs:complexType>
      <xs:complexContent>
        <xs:extension base="cc:CardType">
          <xs:attribute name="issue"
            type="xs:positiveInteger"/>
        </xs:extension>
      </xs:complexContent>
    </xs:complexType>
  </xs:element>
  <xs:element name="wallet">
    <xs:complexType>
      <xs:sequence>
        <xs:element name="credit-card" type="cc:CardType"
          minOccurs="0" maxOccurs="unbounded"/>
        <xs:element name="debit-card" ref="tns:debit-card"
          minOccurs="0" maxOccurs="unbounded"/>
      </xs:sequence>
    </xs:complexType>
  </xs:element>
</xs:schema>
```

Figure 2-52 The Wallet schema.

The schema in Figure 2-51 declares a single type (`CardType`) in the namespace http://card.example.com. The schema containing the `CardType` type is then exposed to the schema shown in Figure 2-52 via the `import` mechanism, which involves specifying both the namespace that is being imported and the location of the schema which is attributed with that targetNamespace.

The imported namespace is given a prefix (so that it can be referenced within the wallet schema) via the `xmlns:cc` attribute in the root element of the wallet schema document. Now the components of the credit card schema (including `CardType`) are accessible to the wallet schema by referencing its qualified name (`QName`) via the prefix `cc`.

Once we have imported a schema, we can freely reference its contents. In the wallet schema, we use the contents of the credit card schema to create a new type of card (`debit-card`) by extending the credit card schema's `CardType`. We also create a `wallet` element that declares instances of both the global `CardType` and instances of the local `debit-card` type. As we have seen, the `import` declaration works just like an `import` declaration in the Java programming language or using a declaration in C#, which simply exposes the types from a foreign namespace to the current namespace.

Schemas and Instance Documents

Until this point we have largely focused on either XML documents or constructing portable type systems with XML Schema. However, it is only when these two aspects of XML intersect that we actually have a usable technology for moving structured data between systems. That is, we need to be able to communicate the abstract notions defined in schemas via concrete XML documents and on receipt of an XML document, be able to translate it back into some form suitable for processing within the receiving system—which is generally an Infoset or native object model, not a mass of angle brackets and text. The relationship between types, elements and instance documents is captured in Figure 2-53.

Schema-aware XML processors (like Apache's Xerces and the .Net System.XML classes) use an instance document's namespace to match against the corresponding namespace of a schema. However, the XML Schema specification doesn't mandate how the XML processor should locate that schema in the first place. Typically, an XML processor will be programmatically or administratively configured with the locations of any required schemas before undertaking any processing. However, this can be restrictive in that the schemas of all possible instance documents must be known ahead of time if they are to be validated by the XML processor.

While the XML Schema specification doesn't provide a means of mandating the location of a schema, it does provide a means of *hinting* at its location by placing and `xsi:schemaLocation` attribute into the instance document, as shown in Figure 2-54.

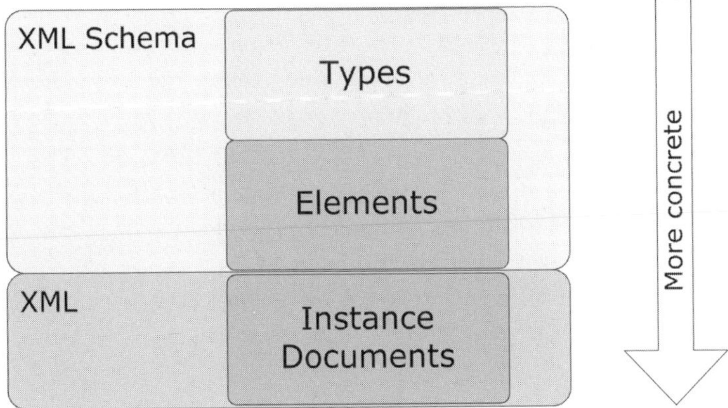

Figure 2-53 Relationship between Types, Elements and Documents.

```
<ptr:printer xmlns:p="http://printer.example.org"
  xmlns:xsi="http://www.w3.org/2001/XMLSchema-instance"
  xsi:schemaLocation="http://printer.example.org
file:/home/local/root/schemas/printer.xsd">
  <!-- rest of schema omitted for brevity -->
```

Figure 2-54 Using the `xsi:schemaLocation` attribute to locate a schema.

The `xsi:schemaLocation` attribute specifies a set of space-delimited namespace-location pairs indicating the location of schemas for particular namespaces. Upon finding the `xsi:schemaLocation` attribute, the XML processor *may* (since it is only a hint) try to obtain the specified schema from the suggested location. Of course, the processor may not try to obtain this information from the `xsi:schemaLocation` attribute, especially if it already has the necessary document-schema mappings through other means.

XML Schema Best Practices

We've now seen a great deal of XML Schema, and over time we have built up a set of informal best practices based on the notion of defining important global types and their interrelations first and document structure later. However, it is useful to condense these details down to their barest bones for quick reference:

1. Always use `elementFormDefault="qualified"` and `attributeFormDefault="unqualified"` to ensure that elements are namespaced by default and attributes are not.
2. Declare all types globally; declare elements (apart from the document root) locally.

3. Use types to express content models, use elements to dictate the structure of documents.
4. Use the XML Schema features that most closely match your object model. Do not map the object model onto a different model in Schema just because it makes writing schemas easier.

These best practices are intended as guidelines. Over time you will develop your own practices that more accurately match the kinds of solutions you are working on. However, the fact remains that no matter what style we ultimately develop for Web services projects, we still need to use XML to move data around systems.

Processing XML

To round off this discussion on XML technology, it is worth taking a brief look at some of the means of processing the XML documents and schemas that we have so far examined to see how we traverse from the XML level to the application level. There are a number of standard, cross-platform tools available that perform much of the hard work involved in processing XML. In this section we concentrate on three of the most prevalent XML processing technologies: SAX, DOM, and XSLT.

The examples we have chosen to illustrate the technologies are necessarily simple. In each example we simply harvest the character information from a simple DVD document as shown Figure 2-55.

With each XML processing tool, we take the XML shown in Figure 2-55 and present it as an XML fragment such as:

```
<d:character xmlns:d="http://dvd.example.org">
        Qui Gon Jin
    </d:character>
    <d:character xmlns:d="http://dvd.example.org">
        Queen Amidala
    </d:character>
    <d:character xmlns:d="http://dvd.example.org">
        Obi Wan Kenobi
    </d:character>
    <d:character xmlns:d="http://dvd.example.org">
        Anakin Skywalker
    </d:character>
    <d:character xmlns:d="http://dvd.example.org">
        Senator Palpatine
    </d:character>
```

which could then be used as the basis for other processing.

```
<?xml version="1.0" encoding="utf-8"?>
<d:dvd xmlns:d="http://dvd.example.org" region="2">
  <d:title>The Phantom Menace</d:title>
  <d:year>2001</d:year>
  <d:language>
    <d:audio>English</d:audio>
    <d:subtitle>Danish</d:subtitle>
    <d:subtitle>Norwegian</d:subtitle>
    <d:subtitle>Swedish</d:subtitle>
    <d:subtitle>English</d:subtitle>
  </d:language>
  <d:actors>
    <d:actor firstname="Liam" surname="Neeson">
      <d:character>Qui Gon Jin</d:character>
    </d:actor>
    <d:actor firstname="Natalie" surname="Portman">
      <d:character>Queen Amidala</d:character>
    </d:actor>
    <d:actor firstname="Ewan" surname="McGregor">
      <d:character>Obi Wan Kenobi</d:character>
    </d:actor>
    <d:actor firstname="Jake" surname="Lloyd">
      <d:character>Anakin Skywalker</d:character>
    </d:actor>
    <d:actor firstname="Ian" surname="McDiarmid">
      <d:character>Senator Palpatine</d:character>
    </d:actor>
  </d:actors>
  <d:directors>
    <d:director firstname="George" surname="Lucas">
      <d:favorite-film>
                The Empire Strikes Back
            </d:favorite-film>
    </d:director>
  </d:directors>
  <d:barcode>5039036007375</d:barcode>
  <d:price currency="sterling">19.99</d:price>
</d:dvd>
```

Figure 2-55 A complex XML document.

SAX: Simple API for XML

The SAX model is based on the notion of a fast, forward-only and low memory footprint method of processing XML documents. To achieve these goals, the SAX parsers read through an XML document firing events whenever they encounter certain interesting parts of the document (in addition to having the ability to check documents against schemas). As it happens, those parts which the SAX parser seeks are wide-ranging and consist of everything from finding the beginning of a document (and its end) through to catching the occurrence of every open and close tag, and any textual data in between those tags.

To work with SAX, the application code must register for events that it is specifically interested in. For example, we might be particularly interested in extracting the details of a DVD from one of our `dvd` documents in order to store those details in some database. To achieve that, we would need to register the features of the document that we are interested in with the SAX parser. Then when the SAX parser parses the document, it will then inform us each time one of those features is encountered and our application code can use those signals to build up its own object model.

To use a SAX implementation within an application, as developers we must write code that subscribes to SAX events and pieces together a set of objects (or other structured data) from the events that the parser generates. The burden on the developer is to create a document handler capable of listening for the salient events being issued by the SAX parser and write a suitable object model to encapsulate data exposed by the SAX events.

If the object model developed to deal with the SAX events is lightweight, the SAX-oriented aspects of an application can be made lightning fast since SAX itself is also lightweight. The downside is, of course, that the document handler might be non-trivial to develop, especially for complex documents.

To illustrate, let's write some code to harvest the character information from a `dvd` document using the Java program shown in Figure 2-56. This is an undeniably long piece of code for essentially stripping out a few elements. Its length is due to the fact that the SAX parser only deals with creating events and not with the structured data associated with those events. In fact, the overwhelming size of this document is pared down to handling the various events that the SAX parser will issue as it parses a `dvd` document.

The `startElement` and `endElement` methods are called by the SAX parser when an element is entered or exited, respectively, and we use that event to determine whether we have found a character element. If we have found a `character` element, we simply set the `_characterFound` flag to `true`, whereas if we have not found a character element or if we are leaving an element altogether, then the flag is set to `false`.

The `characters(...)` method is called by the SAX parser whenever character data is encountered. If we are within a character element, i.e., the `_characterFound` flag is `true`, then we simply store the character data. All other character data is ignored. The main method simply sets up the parser and parses the document before pretty-printing the resulting characters to standard output.

On a positive note, the SAX approach offers good performance since we tailor the object model exactly to our needs (in this case it's just a linked list of characters). On a less positive note, SAX can be a complex tool to implement with due to the large number of possible events that we might have to write handlers for.

```
import java.io.*;
import java.util.*;
import org.xml.sax.*;
import org.xml.sax.helpers.*;

public class SAXExample extends DefaultHandler
{
    // Constants
    private static final String _MY_DVD_NAMESPACE_URI =
                                    "http://dvd.example.com";
    private static final String _CHARACTER_ELEMENT_NAME =
                                                "character";

    // Flag to remember if we are dealing with character
    // data while parsing
    private boolean   _characterFound = false;

    // The data we're looking for in the document
    private LinkedList _characters    = new LinkedList();

    /**
     * The method called when the start of a new element is
     * found.
     */
    public void startElement(String namespaceURI,
                             String localName,
                             String qualifiedName,
                             Attributes attributes)
                            throws SAXException
    {
        // If the element is called "character" and is in the
    // namespace "http://dvd.example.com" we've found one.

        _characterFound =
         namespaceURI.toLowerCase()
         .equals(_MY_DVD_NAMESPACE_URI) &&
         localName.toLowerCase()
         .equals(_CHARACTER_ELEMENT_NAME);
    }

    /**
     * The method called when the end of an element is found.
     */
    public void endElement(String namespaceURI,
                           String localName,
                           String qualifiedName)
                          throws SAXException
    {
        _characterFound = false;
    }
```

Figure 2-56 Creating a SAX-based application in Java.

```
    /**
     * The method called when character data is found.
     */
    public void characters(char[] ch, int start, int length)
                         throws SAXException
    {
        if(_characterFound)
        {
            _characters.add(new String(ch, start, length));
        }
    }

    /**
     * A convenience method to pretty-print the characters
     * found.
     */
    public StringWriter outputCharacters()
    {
        StringWriter sw = new StringWriter();
        for(int i = 0; i < _characters.size(); i++)
        {
            sw.write("<character xmlns=\"" +
                      _MY_DVD_NAMESPACE_URI  + "\">");
            sw.write((String)_characters.get(i));
            sw.write("</character>\n");
        }
        return sw;
    }

    /**
     * The starting point of the application.
     */
    public static void main(String[] args) throws Exception
    {
        // Check to see that we have a single URI argument
        if(args.length != 1)
        {
            return;
        }

        SAXExample saxExample = new SAXExample();
        XMLReader parser = null;

        // Create parser
        try
        {
             parser = XMLReaderFactory.createXMLReader(
                       "org.apache.xerces.parsers.SAXParser");
```

Figure 2-56 Creating a SAX-based application in Java (continued).

```
            // Tell the parser which object will handle
            // SAX parsing events
            parser.setContentHandler(saxExample);
        }
        catch (Exception e)
        {
            System.err.println("Unable to create Xerces SAX
                                   parser - check classpath");
        }

        try
        {
            // The URL that sources the DVD goes here
            //(i.e. perform a GET on some remote Web server).
            parser.parse(args[0]);

            // Dump the character information to screen.
            System.out.println(
                saxExample.outputCharacters().toString());
        }
        catch (Exception e)
        {
            e.printStackTrace();
        }
    }
}
```

Figure 2-56 Creating a SAX-based application in Java (continued).

DOM: Document Object Model

DOM goes one step further than SAX and actually provides a simple tree-based object model on top of the basic XML processing and schema validation capabilities, usually built on top of an underlying SAX parser. When programming with a DOM parser, our application code interacts with an in-memory tree representation of the XML document. As such, DOM parsers are usually more heavyweight processors than their SAX equivalents since irrespective of the complexity or length of the XML document being processed, the same type of tree-based hierarchy is built.

Though this might not be the best data structure for any given application, the fact that DOM provides a simple object model "out of the box" is enticing and because of its simplicity, DOM has gained popularity. Indeed, we would generally only use SAX in preference to DOM where we have stringent performance requirements that rule out creating copies of documents in-memory, or where the tree-like mode of DOM is entirely unsuitable for the actual characteristics of the intended object model. Of course, it is possible to layer our own object model on top of that provided by DOM, thus providing both a natural fit for our application and leveraging DOM's ease-of-use. However, when using DOM as the basis for our own object models, we should be aware that we are consuming memory twice over—once for our own objects and once for DOM.

Like SAX, the DOM API is well planned and straightforward to understand. To show some of features of DOM, we shall revisit the same DVD example that we previously tackled with SAX and illustrate the differences between the two approaches via the C# example shown in Figure 2-57.

```
using System;
using System.Xml;

public class DOMExample
{
    private string getXMLDocument(string url)
    {
        // Grab the dvd document from its source
        System.Net.WebClient wc = new System.Net.WebClient();
        byte[] webData = wc.DownloadData(url);

        // Get the downloaded data into a form suitable for
        // XML processing
        char[] charData = new char[webData.Length];
        for(int i = 0; i < charData.Length; i++)
        {
            charData[i] = (char)webData[i];
        }

        string xmlStr = new String(charData);

        // Clean up the document (first "<" and last ">" and
        // everything in between)
        int start = xmlStr.IndexOf("<", 0,
                                   xmlStr.Length - 1);
        int length = xmlStr.LastIndexOf(">") - start + 1;

        // Return only the XML document parts
        return xmlStr.Substring(start, length);
    }

    public static void Main(string[] args)
    {
    // Check to see that we have a single URI argument
    if(args.Length != 1)
    {
        return;
    }
```

Figure 2-57 Creating a DOM-Based application in C#.

```
    string url = args[0];
        DOMExample domExample = new DOMExample();

        System.Xml.XmlDocument xmlDoc =
                                new System.Xml.XmlDocument();
        xmlDoc.LoadXml(domExample.getXMLDocument(url));

        // Search DOM tree for a set of elements with
        // particular name and namespace
        XmlNodeList xmlNodeList =
                    xmlDoc.GetElementsByTagName("character",
                                   "http://dvd.example.com");

        for(int i = 0; i < xmlNodeList.Count; i++)
        {
            // Dump the contents of the elements we've found
            // to standard output.
            Console.WriteLine(xmlNodeList.Item(i).OuterXml);
        }
    }
}
```

Figure 2-57 Creating a DOM-Based application in C# (continued).

The simple DOM-based application presented in Figure 2-57 is somewhat shorter than the previous SAX-based application. This simplicity does not stem from a different programming language or platform since (even platform zealots must agree) there is little difference between Java and .Net for simple XML processing. The gain in simplicity stems from the DOM processing model which automatically builds a data-structure to hold the contents of the XML document, and provides a simple API for searching and manipulating structure.

In fact the overwhelming majority of this application is spent checking that we have a clean XML document to deal with before we put it into our XML processing components. Since we chose to deal with the results of our remote call as an array of bytes returned via HTTP, we had to convert those bytes to characters and those characters to string, and then ensure that string did not contain any extraneous characters (such as the HTTP header information).

Once we are satisfied that we have our document in a clean form, we then submit it to the .Net DOM infrastructure. Internally, the infrastructure builds the DOM tree for us, and then to extract the character data it is simply a matter of searching for the element name (`character`) in the correct namespace (`http://dvd.example.com`). This search results in a list of possible answers, which we then dump to standard output.

While this is a suitable approach for a trivial example, this DOM-based method might not scale well in production environments. We are paying the price for the ease of use we have enjoyed in terms of memory and processing overhead. So while working with DOM is ultimately easier than SAX programmatically, it is always helpful to think about performance metrics and worth bearing in mind that SAX may be a better choice for some problems.

Extensible Stylesheet Transformation (XSLT) and XML Path Language (XPATH)

XSL is the acronym the W3C has assigned to the "Extensible Stylesheet Language." It consists of a language for transforming XML documents (XSLT) and an expression language used to access or reference parts of an XML document (XPath). It also refers to a formatting language called XML Formatting Objects (or XML-FO), but when most people talk about XSL what they are really talking about is XSLT and XPath. It is this subset of XSL technology that we investigate in this section.

The idea behind XSLT is to provide a declarative, rule-based XML scripting language that can be used to specify transformations on documents—that is, to turn a document from one form into another based on some transformation rules. The benefit of this approach is that we can apply commodity XML processing tools to the processing of XML itself—a recursive and inventive way of bootstrapping XML with XML. XPath supports XSLT by allowing parts of documents undergoing transformations to be referenced. Interestingly enough, XPath is *not* an XML-based syntax since its originators saw the value in being able to embed XPath expressions inside URIs and other non-XML identifiers. The canonical use of XPath is shown in Figure 2-58 where a trivial example of XSLT (with similarly simple XPath expressions) is presented.

> XPath 1.0 has become perhaps the most important of the XSL technologies in the Web services arena and is now heavily used in other technologies like BPEL (see Chapter 6).

The stylesheet presented in Figure 2-58 is straightforward—mainly because we haven't tried to do anything too ambitious—and it is far shorter than either the SAX or even DOM versions of the code. The opening line of the document introduces some namespaces and defines what the result of the transformation will be without the prefix `d`. The subsequent six declarations tell the XSLT processor to do nothing with each of the elements that are named. For example, when the XSLT engine encounters a `year` element as a child of a `dvd` element, it triggers the execution of the matching `template`, which performs no processing. The end result of this "empty" `template` is that no output appears for the given element.

The template matching the element expressed in XPath as `/d:dvd/d:actors/d:actor/d:character` (i.e., the `character` element under the `actor` element, contained within the `actors` and `dvd` elements) does something slightly more ambitious. We create a new element in our output that has the same name as the current element we are examining (`character`), which is achieved by assigning the result of the XSLT `name()` function to the value held by the `name` attribute. We also give the newly created element a namespace (which, again, we borrow from the element currently under scrutiny) by referencing its namespace declaration (`namespace-uri()`) and assigning that value to the default namespace attribute for this element in our output.

```
<xsl:stylesheet version="1.0"
    xmlns:d="http://dvd.example.com"
    xmlns:xsl="http://www.w3.org/1999/XSL/Transform"
    exclude-result-prefixes="d">

    <!-- We are not creating a document, so remove the
           document declaration -->
    <xsl:output method="xml" omit-xml-declaration="yes"/>

    <!-- Do nothing with these elements -->
    <xsl:template match="d:dvd/d:title"/>
    <xsl:template match="d:dvd/d:year"/>
    <xsl:template match="d:dvd/d:language"/>
    <xsl:template match="d:dvd/d:directors"/>
    <xsl:template match="d:dvd/d:barcode"/>
    <xsl:template match="d:dvd/d:price"/>
    <!-- Extract the value held by and character elements
          encountered -->
    <xsl:template match=
        "d:dvd/d:actors/d:actor/d:character">
        <xsl:element name="{name()}"
            namespace="{namespace-uri()}">
            <xsl:value-of select="."/>
        </xsl:element>
    </xsl:template>
</xsl:stylesheet>
```

Figure 2-58 A simple XSLT stylesheet.

The `value-of` element is then used in combination with the `select="."` attribute to select the value held within the current matching element—where the axis "." is defined as "current context" in XPath. The net result of applying this template is to place the character information for each character encountered into the output from the XSLT engine and wrap that character data inside an appropriately namespaced XML element.

Although the example here has been necessarily trivial (since our goals were similarly trivial), XSLT is a powerful means of transforming XML documents. However, even this basic knowledge of what XSLT (and XPath) is and how it can be applied to XML documents will stand us in good stead as we finally venture out into the Web services world.

Summary

XML is the fundamental technology that underpins everything else in Web services. Of paramount importance to the XML suite of technologies is XML Schema, which provides a meta-level description of XML content. XML Schema can, in the simplest sense, be thought of as a means of dictating the format and content of XML documents. However, XML Schema's real power lies in the fact it can be used as a platform independent type description language, where XML documents are then used to transport data in accordance with those type descriptions.

XML technology is already well supported in terms of standard tools. In particular, the XML tools introduced here are widely available across platforms. While the specifics of using most XML tools may vary from platform-to-platform, the models are consistent which means that any experience with such tools is widely applicable.

The sum of these technologies means that XML is not only eminently expressive, but platform independent in the way it is written and processed. As we shall see, this is indeed a rich base on which to build interoperable systems. This is why Web services are based so heavily on XML.

Architect's Note

- XML is the single fundamental technology in Web services on which everything else is predicated. A good working knowledge of it will help you in the long run—where tools and toolkits fall short, you will be able to jump into the breach.
- Everything in the Web services architecture is governed by schemas. Every self-respecting architect and developer should understand XML Schemas, at least to the level presented here.
- XML Schemas are best used to describe type systems first and document layout second.
- When using XML within your own applications, make it a natural part of development to write schemas to accompany the documents. A good rule of thumb is: *A document is useless without its schema.*
- XML processing technologies are a commodity—don't reinvent the wheel unless you specifically cannot achieve your goals with off-the-shelf components.

CHAPTER 3

SOAP and WSDL

Web services are software components that expose their functionality to the network. To exploit that functionality, Web service consumers must be able to bind to a service and invoke its operations via its interface. To support this, we have two protocols that are the fundamental building blocks on which all else in the Web services arena is predicated: SOAP[1] and WSDL[2]. SOAP is the protocol via which Web services communicate, while WSDL is the technology that enables services to publish their interfaces to the network. In this chapter we cover both SOAP and WSDL in some depth and show how they can be used together with rudimentary tool support to form the basis of Web services-based applications.

The SOAP Model

Web services are an instance of the service-oriented architecture pattern that use SOAP as the (logical) transport mechanism for moving messages between services described by WSDL interfaces. This is a conceptually simple architecture, as shown in Figure 3-1, where SOAP messages are propagated via some underlying transport protocol between Web services.

---

1. In this chapter, unless otherwise explicitly stated, all references to SOAP and the SOAP Specification pertain to the SOAP 1.2 recommendation.
2. In this chapter, unless otherwise explicitly stated, all references to WSDL and the WSDL specification pertain to WSDL 1.1; see http://www.w3.org/TR/wsdl. The W3C's WSDL effort is less advanced than the latest SOAP work, though where possible we highlight new techniques from the WSDL 1.2 working drafts.

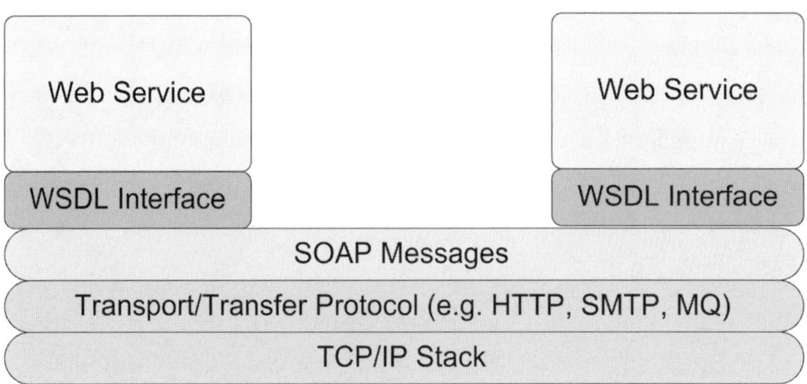

Figure 3-1 The logical Web services network.

A SOAP message is an XML document whose root element is called the *envelope*. Within the envelope, there are two child elements called the header and the body. Application payloads are carried in the body, while the information held in the header blocks usually contains data from the various Web services protocols that augment the basic SOAP infrastructure (and which is the primary subject of this book). The structure of a SOAP message is shown in Figure 3-2.

The SOAP message shown in Figure 3-2 provides the conceptual basis on which the whole SOAP model is based. Application payload travels in the body of the message and additional protocol messages travel in header blocks (which are optional, and may not be present if only application data is being transported). This permits a separation of concerns at the SOAP processing level between application-level messages and higher-level Web services protocols (e.g., transactions, security) whose payload travels in the SOAP header space.

The split between application and protocol data within SOAP messages allows the SOAP processing model to be a little more sophisticated than was suggested by the simple architecture shown in Figure 3-1. SOAP's distributed processing model outlines the fundamentals of the Web services architecture. It states (abstractly) how SOAP messages—including both the header and body elements—are processed as they are transmitted between Web services. In SOAP terms, we see that an application is comprised of *nodes* that exchange messages. The nodes are free to communicate in any manner they see fit, including any message-exchange pattern from one-way transmission through bilateral conversations. Furthermore, it is assumed in SOAP that messages may pass through any number of intermediate nodes between the sender and final recipient.

More interestingly however, the SOAP specification proposes a number of *roles* to describe the behavior of nodes under certain circumstances, which are shown in Figure 3-3. As a message progresses from node to node through a SOAP-based network, it encounters nodes that play the correct role for that message. Inside message elements, we may find role declarations that match these roles (or indeed other roles produced by third parties), and where we find a node and message part that match, the node executes its logic against the message. For example,

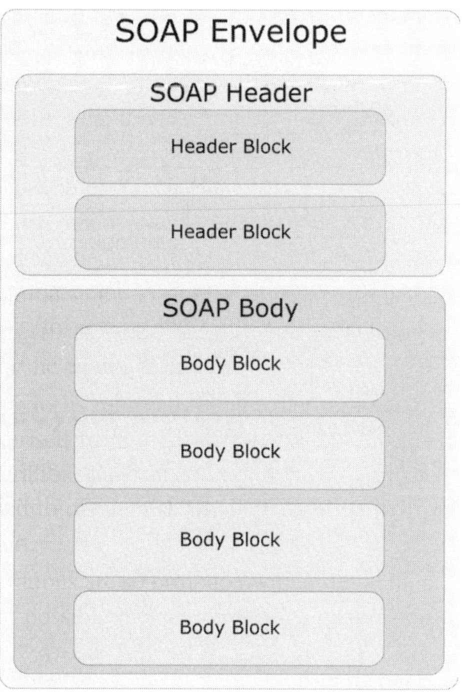

Figure 3-2 The structure of a SOAP message.

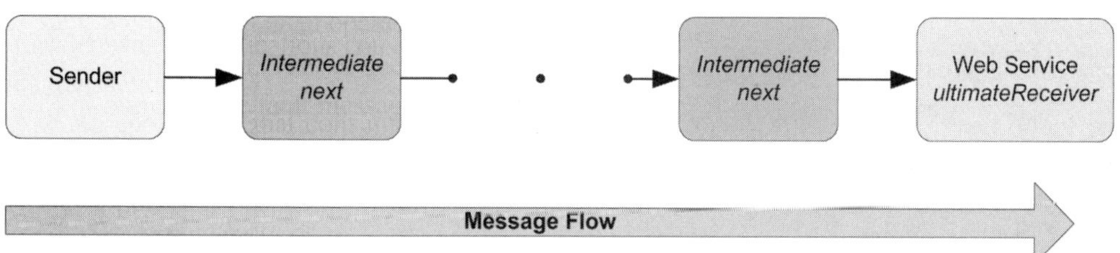

Figure 3-3 SOAP node roles.

where a node receives a message that specifies a role of `next` (and every node except the sender is always implicitly `next`), the node must perform the processing expected of that role or fault. In Figure 3-3, we see that the nodes labeled "intermediate" all play the role `next`. The Web service that finally consumes the message plays the role `ultimateReceiver`, and so each processes only the parts of the SOAP message which are (either implicitly or explicitly) marked as being for that role.

The processing model shown in Figure 3-3 is supported in software by SOAP servers. A SOAP server is a piece of middleware that mediates between SOAP traffic and application components, dealing with the message and processing model of the SOAP specification on a Web service's behalf. Therefore, to build Web services, it is important to understand how a SOAP server implements the SOAP model.

While it is impossible to cover every SOAP server platform here, we will examine the architecture of a generalized SOAP server (whose characteristics are actually derived from popular implementations such as Apache Axis and Microsoft ASP.Net) so that we have a mental model onto which we can hang various aspects of SOAP processing. An idealized view of a SOAP server is presented in Figure 3-4. This shows a generic SOAP server architecture. Inbound messages arrive via the physical network and are translated from the network protocol into the textual SOAP message. This SOAP message passes up the SOAP request stack where information stored in SOAP headers (typically context information for other Web services protocols like security, transactions and so forth) are processed by handlers that have been registered with the Web service. Such handlers are considered to be intermediate nodes in SOAP terms.

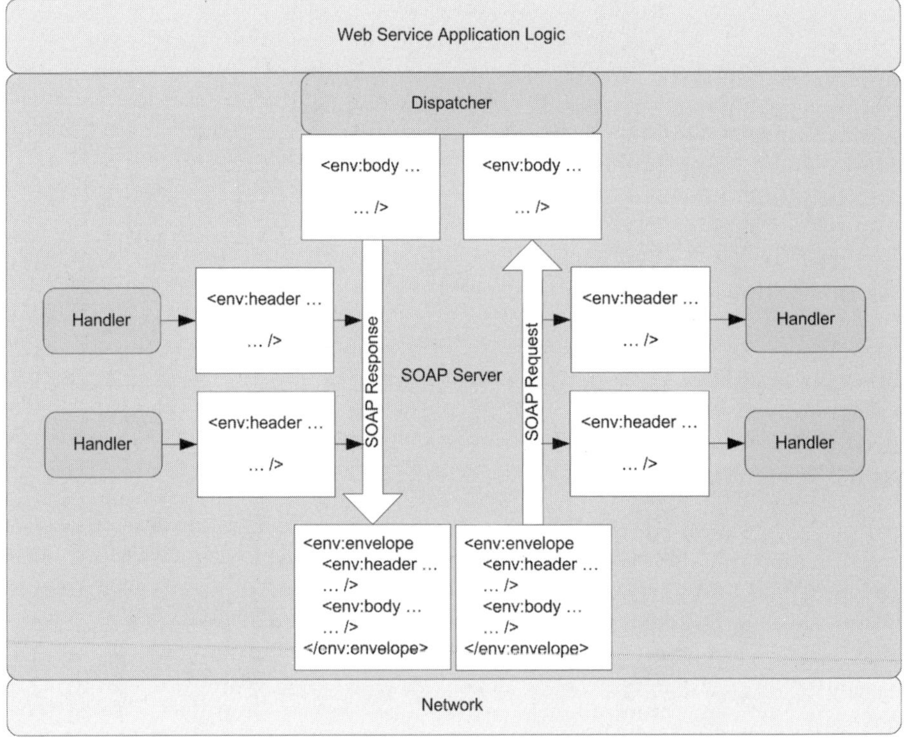

Figure 3-4 The architecture of a generalized SOAP server.

> The handlers that operate on the headers are not generally part of the SOAP server by default, but are usually third-party components registered with the server to augment its capabilities. This means that SOAP servers are themselves extensible and can be upgraded to include additional protocol support over their lifetime as Web services' needs evolve.

At some later point, provided the header processing has not caused the service invocation to fail, the application payload of the message (carried in the SOAP body) reaches a dispatch mechanism where it causes some computation to occur within the back-end service implementation. The application logic then performs some computation before returning data to the dispatcher, which then propagates a SOAP message back down the SOAP response stack. Like the request stack, the response stack may have handlers registered with it which operate on the outgoing message, inserting headers into messages as they flow outward to be consumed by other Web services. Again, these handlers are considered to be nodes in SOAP terms.

Eventually, the outgoing message reaches the network level where it is marshaled into the appropriate network protocol and duly passes on to other SOAP nodes on the network, to be consumed by other SOAP nodes.

SOAP

Having understood the SOAP model and seen how this model is supported by SOAP servers, we can now begin to discuss the details of SOAP itself. SOAP is the oldest, most mature, and the single most important protocol in the Web services world. The SOAP specification defines this protocol as "[an] XML-based protocol that consists of three parts: an envelope that defines a framework for describing what is in a message and how to process it, a set of encoding rules for expressing instances of application-defined datatypes, and a convention for representing remote procedure calls and responses."[3]

> In its earlier incarnations, the acronym SOAP used to stand for "Simple Object Access Protocol," though that meaning has ceased to exist in the SOAP 1.2 specification. This is undoubtedly a good thing since SOAP isn't especially simple, it's not exclusively designed for object access and it is more a packaging mechanism than a protocol per se.

In the following sections, we examine SOAP in some depth—from its basic use pattern and XML document structure, encoding schemes, RPC convention, binding SOAP messages, transport protocols, to using it as the basis for Web services communication.

3. http://www.w3.org/TR/SOAP/

SOAP Messages

We have already seen the overall structure of a SOAP message, as defined by the SOAP `Envelope`, in Figure 3-4. All SOAP messages, no matter how lengthy or complex, ultimately conform to this structure. The only caveat is there must be at least one body block within the SOAP body element in a message and there does not necessarily have to be a SOAP header or any SOAP header blocks. There is no upper limit on the number of header or body blocks, however. A sample SOAP message is presented here in Figure 3-5:

```
<?xml version="1.0" encoding="UTF-8"?>
<env:Envelope
    xmlns:env="http://www.w3.org/2002/06/soap-envelope" >
 <env:Header>
    <tx:transaction-id
        xmlns:tx="http://transaction.example.org"
     env:encodingStyle="http://transaction.example.org/enc"
        env:role=
"http://www.w3.org/2002/06/soap-envelope/role/ultimateReceiver"
        env:mustUnderstand="true">
           decd7461-4ef2138d-7b52e370-fed8a006-ca7ea17
    </tx:transaction-id>
 </env:Header>
 <env:Body xmlns:bank="http://bank.example.org">
    <bank:credit-account env:encodingStyle=
                   "http://www.w3.org/2002/06/soap-encoding">
        <bank:account>12345678</bank:account>
        <bank:sort>10-11-12</bank:sort>
        <bank:amount currency="usd">123.45</bank:amount>
    </bank:credit-account>
    <bank:debit-account>
        <bank:account>87654321</bank:account>
        <bank:sort>12-11-10</bank:sort>
        <bank:amount currency="usd">123.45</bank:amount>
    </bank:debit-account>
 </env:Body>
</env:Envelope>
```

Figure 3-5 A simple SOAP message.

The structure of all SOAP messages (including that shown in Figure 3-5) maps directly onto the abstract model shown in Figure 3-2. Figure 3-5 contains a typical SOAP message with a single header block (which presumably has something to do with managing transactional integrity), and a body containing two elements (which presumably instructs the recipient of the message to perform an operation on two bank accounts). Both the `Header` and `Body` elements are contained within the outer `Envelope` element, which acts solely as a container.

SOAP Envelope

The SOAP `Envelope` is the container structure for the SOAP message and is associated with the namespace `http://www.w3.org/2002/06/soap-envelope`. An example is shown in Figure 3-6 where the namespace is associated with the prefix `env`:

```
<?xml version="1.0" encoding="UTF-8"?>
<env:Envelope
    xmlns:env="http://www.w3.org/2002/06/soap-envelope" >
  <!-- Optional header blocks -->
  <env:Header>
    ...
  </env:Header>
  <!-- Single mandatory body element -->
  <env:Body xmlns:bank="http://bank.example.org">
    ...
  </env:Body>
</env:Envelope>
```

Figure 3-6 The SOAP `envelope` element.

The `Envelope` contains up to two child elements, the `Header` and the `Body` (where the `Body` element is mandatory). Aside from acting as a parent to the `Header` and the `Body` elements, the `Envelope` may also hold namespace declarations that are used within the message.

SOAP Header

The `Header` element provides a mechanism for extending the content of a SOAP message with out-of-band information designed to assist (in some arbitrary and extensible way) the passage of the application content in the `Body` section content through a Web services-based application.

> The SOAP header space is where much of the value in Web services resides, since it is here that aspects like security, transactions, routing, and so on are expressed. Every Web services standard has staked its claim on some part of the SOAP header territory, but in a mutually compatible way. The fact that SOAP headers are extensible enough to support such diverse standards is a major win, since it supports flexible protocol composition tailored to suit specific application domains.

A SOAP header has the local name `Header` associated with the `http://www.w3.org/2002/06/soap-envelope` namespace. It may also contain any number of namespace qualified attributes and any number of child elements, known as *header blocks*. In the absence of any such header blocks, the `Header` element itself may be omitted from the `Envelope`. A sample header block is shown in Figure 3-7.

```
<?xml version="1.0" encoding="UTF-8"?>
<env:Envelope
    xmlns:env="http://www.w3.org/2002/06/soap-envelope" >
  <!-- Optional header blocks -->
  <env:Header>
    <tx:transaction-id
        xmlns:tx="http://transaction.example.org"
     env:encodingStyle="http://transaction.example.org/enc"
        env:role=
"http://www.w3.org/2002/06/soap-envelope/role/ultimateReceiver"
        env:mustUnderstand="true">
           decd7461-4ef2138d-7b52e370-fed8a006-ca7ea17
    </tx:transaction-id>
  </env:Header>

  <!-- Single mandatory body element -->
  <env:Body xmlns:bank="http://bank.example.org">
    ...
  </env:Body>
</env:Envelope>
```

Figure 3-7 A SOAP `header` element.

If present, each header block must be namespace qualified (according to the rules set out in the SOAP schema), may specify how it has been encoded (i.e., which schema constrains it) through the `encodingStyle` attribute, may specify its consumer through the `role` attribute, and may demand that it is understood by SOAP infrastructure that encounters its message through the `mustUnderstand` attribute. The SOAP specification stipulates that it is illegal for the `role` and `mustUnderstand` attributes to appear anywhere other than in header block declarations.

The sender of a SOAP message should not place them anywhere else, and a receiver of such a malformed message must ignore these attributes if they are out of place. These attributes are of fundamental importance to SOAP processing (and thus Web services) and warrant further discussion. The vehicle for this discussion is the example SOAP message shown in Figure 3-5 where we see a header block called `transaction-id` that provides the necessary out-of-band information for the application payload to be processed within a transaction (using a hypothetical transaction processing protocol).

The `role` Attribute

The `role` attribute controls the targeting of header blocks to particular SOAP nodes (where a SOAP node is an entity that is SOAP-aware). The `role` attribute contains a URI that identifies the `role` being played by the intended recipient of its header block. The SOAP node receiving the message containing the header block must check through the headers to see if any of the declared roles are applicable. If there are any matches, the header blocks must be processed or appropriate faults generated.

Although any URI is valid as a role for a SOAP node to assume, the SOAP specification provides three common roles that fit into the canonical SOAP processing model as part of the standard:

- `http://www.w3.org/2002/06/soap-envelope/role/none`: No SOAP processor should attempt to process this header block, although other header blocks may reference it and its contents, allowing data to be shared between header blocks (and thus save bandwidth in transmission).
- `http://www.w3.org/2002/06/soap-envelope/role/next`: Every node must be willing to assume this role since it dictates that header block content is meant for the next SOAP node in the message chain. If a node knows in advance that a subsequent node does not need a header block marked with the "next" role, then it is at liberty to remove that block from the header.
- `http://www.w3.org/2002/06/soap-envelope/role/ultimateReceiver`: The ultimate receiver is the final node in the message chain. Header blocks referencing this `role` attribute (or equivalently referencing no `role` attribute) should be delivered to this last node. It always implicitly plays the role of "next" given that the last node always comes after some other node—even in the simplest case where the last node comes immediately after the initiator.

Figure 3-8 highlights the role attribute from our example SOAP message in Figure 3-5:

```
<env:Header>
  <tx:transaction-id
      xmlns:tx="http://transaction.example.org"
    env:encodingStyle="http://transaction.example.org/enc"
      env:role=
"http://www.w3.org/2002/06/soap-envelope/role/ultimateReceiver"
      env:mustUnderstand="true">
         decd7461-4ef2138d-7b52e370-fed8a006-ca7ea17
  </tx:transaction-id>
</env:Header>
```

Figure 3-8 The `role` attribute.

The `role` attribute in Figure 3-8 has the value `http://www.w3.org/2002/06/soap-envelope/role/ultimateReceiver`, which means the contents of the header block are intended for the final SOAP processing node in this interaction (i.e., the recipient Web service). According to the SOAP processing model, this Web service must be capable of processing the application payload (in the SOAP body) in accordance with the transaction processing specification in the header block.

The mustUnderstand Attribute

If the `mustUnderstand` attribute is set to true, it implies that any SOAP infrastructure that receives the message containing that header block must be able to process it correctly or issue an appropriate fault message. Those header blocks that contain the `mustUnderstand="true"` attribute are known as *mandatory header blocks* since they must be processed by any nodes playing the matching roles. Header blocks missing their `mustUnderstand` attribute should still be examined by nodes that play the appropriate role. If a failure to act on a role occurs, it is not deemed to be critical and further processing may occur since by missing the `mustUnderstand` attribute they are not considered mandatory, as shown in Figure 3-9.

```
<env:Header>
  <tx:transaction-id
      xmlns:tx="http://transaction.example.org"
    env:encodingStyle="http://transaction.example.org/enc"
      env:role="http://www.w3.org/2002/06/soap-envelope/role/
ultimateReceiver"
      env:mustUnderstand="true">
        decd7461-4ef2138d-7b52e370-fed8a006-ca7ea17
  </tx:transaction-id>
</env:Header>
```

Figure 3-9 The `mustUnderstand` attribute.

> The SOAP specification states that SOAP senders *should not* generate, but SOAP receivers *must* accept the SOAP `mustUnderstand` attribute information item with a value of "false" or "0". That is, a SOAP message should contain the literal values "true" and "false" in `mustUnderstand` attributes, not the characters "1" and "0".

In our example shown in Figure 3-9, the `mustUnderstand` attribute is set to `true` because it is imperative that the processing node must perform the account debit-credit within a transaction. If it cannot support transactional processing, then we would prefer that it leaves the accounts well alone—particularly if it is our money being transferred.

The encodingStyle Attribute

The `encodingStyle` attribute is used to declare how the contents of a header block were created. Knowing this information allows a recipient of the header to decode the information it contains. SOAP allows many encoding schemes and provides one of its own as an optional part of the spec. However, we will not dwell on such matters since this attribute is used not only in header blocks but in the body as well, and is covered in much more depth later in this chapter.

SOAP Body

In contrast to the intricacies of the SOAP header space, the body section of a SOAP envelope is straightforward, being simply a container for XML application payload. In fact the SOAP specification states "[T]his specification mandates no particular structure or interpretation of these elements, and provides no standard means for specifying the processing to be done." In our example in Figure 3-5, the application content housed by the SOAP `Body` consists of two elements that are interpreted as commands to debit and credit a bank account, which collectively amount to a funds transfer. The only constraints the SOAP specification places on the SOAP body are that it is implicitly targeted at the `ultimateRecipient` of the application content and that the ultimate recipient must understand its contents.

SOAP Faults

By contrast to its standard role as the simple carrier of application payload, the SOAP Body also acts in a far more interesting way as the conduit for propagating exceptions between the parties in a Web services application. The SOAP `Fault` is a reserved element predefined by the SOAP specification whose purpose is to provide an extensible mechanism for transporting structured and unstructured information about problems that have arisen during the processing of SOAP messages or subsequent application execution. Since the fault mechanism is predefined by the SOAP specification, SOAP toolkits are able to use this mechanism as a standard mechanism for distributed exception handling.

The SOAP `Fault` element belongs to the same namespace as the SOAP `Envelope` and contains two mandatory child elements: `Code` and `Reason`, and three optional elements: `Node`, `Role`, and `Detail`. An example of a SOAP Fault is shown in Figure 3-10 below. The fault is generated in response to the message shown in Figure 3-5 where the message conveyed information on a bank account cash transfer. To understand precisely what has caused the fault, we must understand each of the elements of which it is composed.

The first child element of the `Fault` is the `Code` element, which contains two subelements: a mandatory element called `Value` and an optional element called `Subcode`. The `Value` element can contain any of a small number of fault codes as qualified names (some-

```
<?xml version="1.0" ?>
<env:Envelope
     xmlns:env="http://www.w3.org/2002/06/soap-envelope"
     xmlns:bank="http://bank.example.org">
    <env:Body>
        <env:Fault>
            <env:Code>
                <env:Value>env:Receiver</env:Value>
                <env:Subcode>
                    <env:Value>bank:bad-account</env:Value>
                </env:Subcode>
            </env:Code>
            <env:Reason lang="en-UK">
             The specified account does exist at this branch
            </env:Reason>
            <env:Detail>
                <err:myfaultdetails
                  xmlns:err= "http://bank.example.org/fault">
                    <err:invalid-account-sortcode>
                        <bank:sortcode>
                            10-11-12
                        </bank:sortcode>
                        <bank:account>
                            12345678
                        </bank:account>
                    </err:invalid-account-sortcode >
                </err:myfaultdetails>
            </env:Detail>
        </env:Fault>
    </env:Body>
</env:Envelope>
```

Figure 3-10 An example SOAP fault.

times abbreviated to QName) from the http://www.w3.org/2002/06/soap-envelope namespace, as per Figure 3-11, where each QName identifies a reason why the fault was generated.

In Figure 3-10 the contents of the env:Value element is env:Receiver (shown in Figure 3-12), which tells us that it was the SOAP node at the end of the message path (the receiver) that generated the fault and not an intermediate node dealing with the transaction header block.

As shown in Figure 3-13, the Subcode element contains a Value element that gives application-specific information on the fault through the qualified name bank:bad-account. This QName has significance only within the scope of the application that issued it, and as such the Subcode mechanism provides the means for propagating finely targeted application-level exception messages.

Fault Code	Description
`VersionMismatch`	Occurs when SOAP infrastructure has detected mutually incompatible implementations based on different versions of the SOAP specification.
`MustUnderstand`	Issued in the case where a SOAP node has received a header block has with its `mustUnderstand` attribute set to true, but does not have the capability to correctly process that header block – that is, it does not understand the protocol with which that header block is associated.
`DataEncodingUnknown`	Arises when the content of either a header or body block is encoded according to a schema that the SOAP node reporting the fault does not understand.
`Sender`	Occurs when the sender propagated a malformed message, including messages with insufficient data to enable the recipient to process it. It is an indication that the message is not to be resent without change.
`Receiver`	Generated when the recipient of the SOAP message could not process the message content because of some application failure. Assuming the failure is transient, resending the message later may successfully invoke processing.

Figure 3-11 SOAP fault codes.

```
<env:Fault>
  <env:Code>
    <env:Value>env:Receiver</env:Value>
```

Figure 3-12 Identifying the faulting SOAP node.

```
<env:Subcode>
  <env:Value>bank:bad-account</env:Value>
</env:Subcode>
```

Figure 3-13 Application-specific fault information.

Though it isn't used in this fault, the Subcode element also makes the SOAP fault mechanism extensible. Like the Code element, the Subcode element also contains a mandatory Value child element and an optional Subcode element, which may contain further nested Subcode elements. The Value element of any Subcode contains a qualified name that consists of a prefix and a local name that references a particular QName within the application-level XML message set.

The Reason element associated with a Code is used to provide a human readable explanation of the fault, which in Figure 3-10 tells us that "The specified account does not exist at this branch". SOAP toolkits often use the contents of the Reason element when throwing exceptions or logging failures to make debugging easier. However, the Reason element is strictly meant for human consumption and it is considered bad practice to use its content for further processing.

The optional Node element provides information on which node in the SOAP message's path caused the fault. The content of the Node element is simply the URI of the node where the problem arose. In Figure 3-10 we do not have a Node element because it is the ultimate recipient of the message that caused the fault, and clearly the sender of the message already knows the URI of the recipient. However if, for example, an intermediate node dealing with the transactional aspects of the transfer failed, then we would expect that the Node element would be used to inform us of the intermediary's failure (and as we shall see, we would not expect a Detail element).

The Node element is complemented by the also optional Role element that provides information pertaining to what the failing node was doing at the point at which it failed. The Role element carries a URI that identifies the operation (usually some Web services standard) and that the party resolving the fault can use to determine what part of the application went wrong. Thus, the combination of Node and Role provides valuable feedback on exactly what went wrong and where.

The SOAP Detail element, as recapped in Figure 3-14, provides in-depth feedback on the fault if that fault was caused as a by-product of processing the SOAP Body.

```
<env:Detail>
  <err:myfaultdetails
    xmlns:err= "http://bank.example.org/fault">
    <err:invalid-account-sortcode>
      <bank:sortcode>
        10-11-12
      </bank:sortcode>
      <bank:account>
        12345678
      </bank:account>
    </err:invalid-account-sortcode >
  </err:myfaultdetails>
</env:Detail>
```

Figure 3-14 Fault detail in an application-specific form.

The presence of the Detail element provides information on faults arising from the application payload (i.e., the Body element had been at least partially processed by the ultimate recipient), whereas its absence indicates that the fault arose because of out-of-band information carried in header blocks. Thus we would expect that if a Detail block is present, as it is in Figure 3-10 and Figure 3-11, the Node and Role elements will be absent and vice versa.

The contents of the Detail element are known as *detail entries* and are application-specific and consist of any number of child elements. In Fault detail in an application-specific form. we see the invalid-account-sortcode element which describes the fault is some application specific fashion.

SOAP Encoding

The encodingStyle attribute appears in both header blocks and the body element of a SOAP message. As its name suggests, the attribute conveys information about how the contents of a particular element are encoded. At first this might seem a little odd since the SOAP message is expressed in XML. However, the SOAP specification is distinctly hands-off in specifying how header and body elements (aside from the SOAP Fault element) are composed, and defines only the overall structure of the message. Furthermore, XML is expressive and does not constrain the form of document a great deal and, therefore, we could imagine a number of different and mutually uninteroperable ways of encoding the same data, for example:

```
<account>
    <balance>
        123.45
    </balance>
</account>
```

and `<account balance="123.45"/>`

might both be informally interpreted in the same way by a human reader but would not be considered equivalent by XML processing software. Ironically, this is one of the downfalls of XML—it is so expressive that, given the chance, we would all express ourselves in completely different ways. To solve this problem, the encodingStyle attribute allows the form of the content to be constrained according to some schema shared between the sender and recipient.

One potential drawback is that senders and receivers of messages may not share schemas—indeed the senders and receivers may be applications that do not deal with XML at all—and thus the best intentions of a SOAP-based architecture may be laid to waste. To avoid such problems, the SOAP specification has its own schema and rules for converting application-level data into a form suitable for embedding into SOAP messages. This is known as SOAP Encoding, and is associated with the namespace env:encodingStyle="http://www.w3.org/2002/06/soap-encoding".

The rules for encoding application data as SOAP messages are captured in the SOAP specification as the SOAP Data Model. This is a straightforward and concise part of the specification that describes how to reduce data structures to a directed, labeled graph. While it is outside of the scope of this book to detail the SOAP Data Model, the general technique is shown in Figure 3-15. This SOAP encoding example, highlights the fact that there are two aspects to the encoding. The first of these is to transform a data structure from an application into a form suitable for expressing in XML via the rules specified in the SOAP Data Model. The other aspect is to ensure that all the data in the subsequent XML document is properly constrained by the SOAP schema. It is worth noting that SOAP provides low entry point through SOAP encoding since a SOAP toolkit will support the serialization and deserialization of arbitrary graphs of objects via this model, with minimal effort required of the developer. In fact, coupled with the fact that SOAP has a packaging mechanism for managing message content, and a means (though SOAP encoding) of easily creating message content we are close to having an XML-based Remote Procedure Call mechanism.

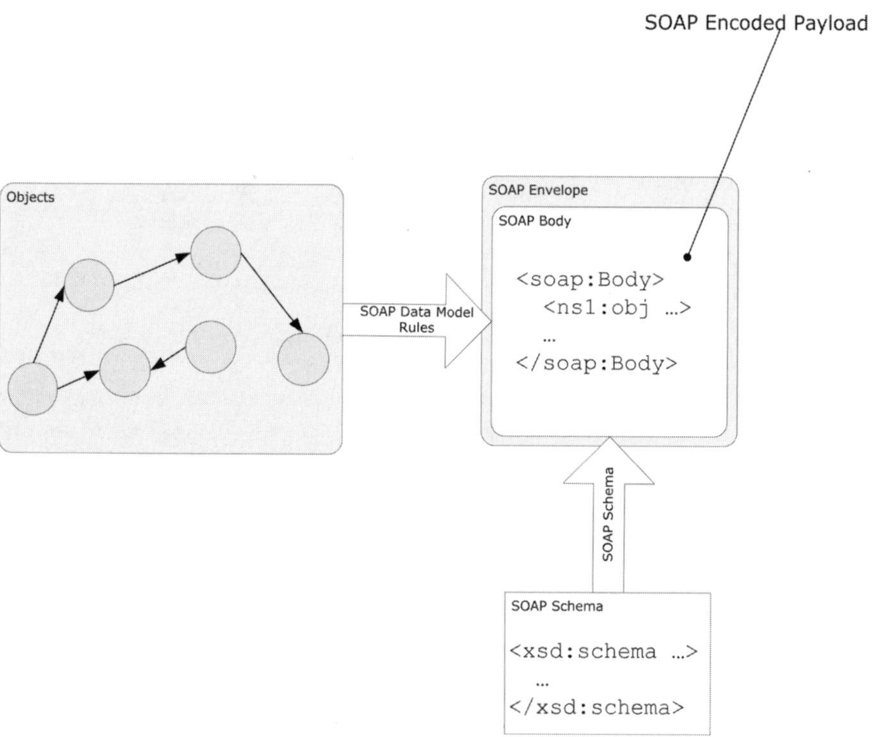

Figure 3-15 SOAP encoding application-level objects.

SOAP RPC

As it happens, the SOAP specification is useful straight "out of the box." The fact that it provides both a message format and marshalling naturally supports RPC, and indeed millions of developers worldwide will by now have seen how easy it is to run SOAP RPC-based Web services on a myriad of platforms. It's probably not the case that SOAP RPC will be the dominant paradigm for SOAP in the long term, but it is easy to achieve results with SOAP RPC quickly because all the major toolkits support it and RPC is a pattern many developers are familiar with.

> Note that although SOAP RPC has enjoyed some prominence in older Web services toolkits, there is a majority consensus of opinion in the Web services community that more coarse-grained, document-oriented interactions should be the norm when using SOAP.

SOAP RPC provides toolkits with a convention for packaging SOAP-encoded messages so they can be easily mapped onto procedure calls in programming languages. To illustrate, let's return to our banking scenario and see how SOAP RPC might be used to expose account management facilities to users. Bear in mind throughout this simple example that it is an utterly insecure instance whose purpose is to demonstrate SOAP RPC only.

Figure 3-16 shows a simple interaction between a Web service that offers the facility to open bank accounts and a client that consumes this functionality on behalf of a user. The Web service supports an operation called `openAccount(…)` which it exposes through a SOAP server and advertises as being accessible via SOAP RPC (SOAP does not itself provide a means of describing interfaces, but as we shall see later in the chapter, WSDL does). The client inter-

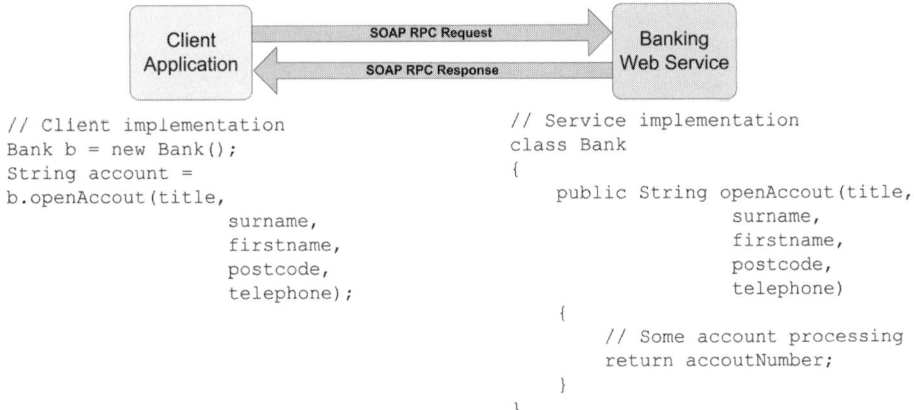

Figure 3-16 Interacting with a banking service via SOAP RPC.

acts with this service through a stub or proxy class called `Bank` which is toolkit-generated (though masochists are free to generate their own stubs) and deals with the marshalling and unmarshalling of local variables into SOAP RPC messages.

In this simple use case, the SOAP on the wire between the client and Web service is similarly straightforward. Figure 3-17 shows the SOAP RPC request sent from the client to the Web service:

```
<?xml version="1.0" encoding="UTF-8"?>
<env:Envelope
    xmlns:env="http://www.w3.org/2002/06/soap-envelope">
    <env:Body>
        <bank:openAccount env:encodingStyle=
         "http://www.w3.org/2002/06/soap-encoding"
         xmlns:bank="http://bank.example.org/account"
         xmlns:xs="http://www.w3.org/2001/XMLSchema"
          xmlns:xsi="http://www.w3.org/2001/XMLSchema-instance">
            <bank:title xsi:type="xs:string">
                Mr
            </bank:title>
            <bank:surname xsi:type="xs:string">
                Bond
            </bank:surname>
            <bank:firstname xsi:type="xs:string">
                James
            </bank:firstname>
            <bank:postcode xsi:type="xs:string">
                S1 3AZ
            </bank:postcode>
            <bank:telephone xsi:type="xs:string">
                09876 123456
            </bank:telephone>
        </bank:openAccount>
    </env:Body>
</env:Envelope>
```

Figure 3-17 A SOAP RPC request.

There is nothing particularly surprising about the RPC request presented in Figure 3-17. As per the RPC specification, the content is held entirely within the SOAP body (SOAP RPC does not preclude the use of header blocks, but they are unnecessary for this example), and the name of the element (`openAccount`) matches the name of the method to be called on the Web service. The contents of the `bank:openAccount` correspond to the parameters of the `openAccount` method shown in Figure 3-16, with the addition of the `xsi:type` attribute to help recipients of the message to convert the contents of each parameter element to the correct kind of variable in specific programming languages. The response to the original request follows a slightly more intricate set of rules and conventions as shown in Figure 3-18.

```
<?xml version="1.0" encoding="UTF-8"?>
<env:Envelope
     xmlns:env="http://www.w3.org/2002/06/soap-envelope">
    <env:Body>
        <bank:openAccountResponse env:encodingStyle=
         "http://www.w3.org/2002/06/soap-encoding" xmlns:rpc=
         "http://www.w3.org/2002/06/soap-rpc" xmlns:bank=
         "http://bank.example.org/account" xmlns:xs=
         "http://www.w3.org/2001/XMLSchema" xmlns:xsi=
          "http://www.w3.org/2001/XMLSchema-instance">
            <rpc:result>bank:accountNo</rpc:result>
            <bank:accountNo xsi:type="xsd:int">
                10000014
            </bank:accountNo>
        </bank:openAccountResponse>
    </env:Body>
</env:Envelope>
```

Figure 3-18 A SOAP RPC response.

The SOAP RPC response is slightly more complex and interesting than the request, and there are two noteworthy aspects of the SOAP RPC response. The first is that by convention the name of the response element is the same as the request element with *Response* appended (and toolkits make use of this convention so it's practically standard now).

The second interesting aspect is that the response is capable of matching the procedure call semantics of many languages since it supports in, out, and in/out parameters as well as return values where an "in" parameter sources a variable to the procedure call; an "out" parameter sources nothing to the procedure but is populated with data at the end of the procedure call. An "in/out" parameter does both, while a return value is similar to an out parameter with the exception that its data may be ignored by the caller.

In this example, we have five "in" parameters (title, surname, first name, post code, and telephone number) which we saw in the SOAP request and expect a single return value (account number) which we see in the SOAP response. The return value is also interesting because, due to its importance in most programming languages, it is separated from out and in/out parameters by the addition of the `rpc:result` element that contains a `QName` that references the element which holds the return value. Other elements which are not referenced are simply treated as out or in/out parameters. This behavior is different from previous versions of SOAP where the return value was distinguished by being first among the child elements of the response. This was rectified for SOAP 1.2 because of the inevitable ambiguity that such a contrivance incurs—what happens when there is no return value?

Of course in a textbook example like this, everything has worked correctly and no problems were encountered. Indeed, you would be hard pressed to find a reader who would enjoy a book where the examples were a set of abject failures. However, like paying taxes and dying, computing systems failures seem inevitable. To cover those cases where things go wrong, SOAP

RPC takes advantage of the SOAP fault mechanism with a set of additional fault codes (whose namespace is http://www.w3.org/2002/06/soap-rpc), which are used in preference to the standard SOAP fault codes in RPC-based messages shown in Figure 3-19, in decreasing order of precedence.

Fault	SOAP Encoding for Fault
Transient fault at receiver (e.g. out of memory error).	Fault with value of env:Receiver should be generated.
Receiver does not understand data encoding (e.g. encoding mechanism substantially different at sender and receiver)	A fault with a Value of env:DataEncodingUnknown for Code should be generated.
The service being invoked does not expose a method matching the name of the RPC element.	A fault with a Value of env:Sender for Code and a Value of rpc:ProcedureNotPresent for Subcode may be generated.
The receiver cannot parse the arguments sent. There may be too many or too few arguments, or there may be type mismatches.	A fault with a Value of env:Sender for Code and a Value of rpc:BadArguments for Subcode must be generated.

Figure 3-19 SOAP RPC faults.

Finally, in Figure 3-20 we see a SOAP RPC fault in action where a poorly constructed client application has tried to invoke an operation on the bank Web service, but has populated its request message with nonsense. In this figure, the bank Web service responds with a SOAP RPC fault that identifies the faulting actor (the sender) as part of the Code element. It also describes what the faulting actor did wrong (sent bad arguments) by specified the QName rpc:BadArguments as part of the subcode element. It also contains some human-readable information to aid debugging (missing surname parameter), in the Reason element.

```
<?xml version="1.0"?>
<env:Envelope
    xmlns:env="http://www.w3.org/2002/06/soap-envelope"
    xmlns:rpc="http://www.w3.org/2002/06/soap-rpc">
  <env:Body>
    <env:Fault>
      <env:Code>
        <env:Value>env:Sender</env:Value>
        <env:Subcode>
          <env:Value>rpc:BadArguments</env:Value>
        </env:Subcode>
      </env:Code>
      <env:Reason>
        Missing surname parameter
      </env:Reason>
    </env:Fault>
  </env:Body>
</env:Envelope>
```

Figure 3-20 A SOAP RPC fault.

Using Alternative SOAP Encodings

Of course some applications already deal with XML natively, and there are currently XML-based vocabularies in use today supporting a plethora of B2B applications. SOAP-based messaging can take advantage of the pre-existence of schemas to craft message exchanges that compliment existing systems using so-called document-style SOAP.

The way in which alternative SOAP encodings are handled is straightforward. Instead of encoding header or body content according to the SOAP Data Model, we simply encode according to the rules and constraints of our data model and schema. In essence, we can just slide our own XML documents into a SOAP message, providing we remember to specify the `encodingStyle` attribute (and of course ensuring that the intended recipients of the message can understand it). This style of SOAP encoding is known as literal style and naturally suits the interchange of business-level documents based on their existing schemas.

This is a definite boon to SOAP use and by our estimation, the future dominant paradigm for SOAP use. Its plus points include not only the ability to re-use existing schemas, but by dint of the fact that we are now dealing with message exchanges and not remote procedure calls, we are encouraged to design Web service interactions with much coarser granularity. In essence, we are changing from a fine-grained model that RPC encourages (you send a little bit of data, get a little bit back and make further calls until your business is completed), to a much coarser-grained model where you send all the data necessary to get some business process done at the recipient end, and expect that the recipient may take some time before he gets back to you with a complete answer.

One particularly apt view of the fine- versus coarse-grained view of Web services interactions is that of a phone call versus a facsimile transmission.[4] Where we interact with a business over the phone there is a great deal of back-and-forth between ourselves and the agent of the business to whom we are talking. We both have to establish contexts and roles for each other, and then enter into a socially and linguistically complex conversation to get business transacted. Small units of data are exchanged like "color" and "amount" that are meaningless without the context, and if the call is lost we have to start over. This is fine-grained interaction.

While we would not seek to undermine the value of good old human-to-human communication, sometimes we just don't have time for this. It's even worse for our computing systems to have to communicate this way since they don't get any of the social pleasures of talking to each other. A better solution is often to obtain a catalog or brochure for the business that we want to trade with. When we have the catalog, we can spend time pouring over the contents to see what goods or services we require. Once we are certain of what we want, we can just fill in and fax the order form to the company and soon our products arrive via postal mail.

This system is eminently preferable for business processes based on Web services. For a start, complex and meaningful data was exchanged that does not rely on context. A catalog and an order form are descriptive enough to be universally understood and the frequency of data exchange was low, which presents less opportunity for things to go astray. This system is also loosely coupled when the systems are not directly communicating (which only happens twice: once for catalog delivery and once while the order is being faxed). They are not affected by one another and do not tie up one another's resources—quite the contrary to the telephone-based system.

Of course, we don't necessarily get something for nothing. The price that we must pay as developers is that we must write the code to deal with the encoding schemes we choose. In the SOAP RPC domain where the encoding is fixed and the serialization from application-level data structure to XML is governed by the SOAP Data Model, toolkits could take care of much of this work. Unfortunately, when we are working with our own schemas, we cannot expect SOAP toolkits to be able to second-guess its semantics and, thus, we have to develop our own handler code to deal with it, as shown in Figure 3-21.

4 See "The 7 Principles of Web Services Business Process Management" at http://www.iona.com/white-papers/Principles-of-Web-Services-and-BPM.pdf

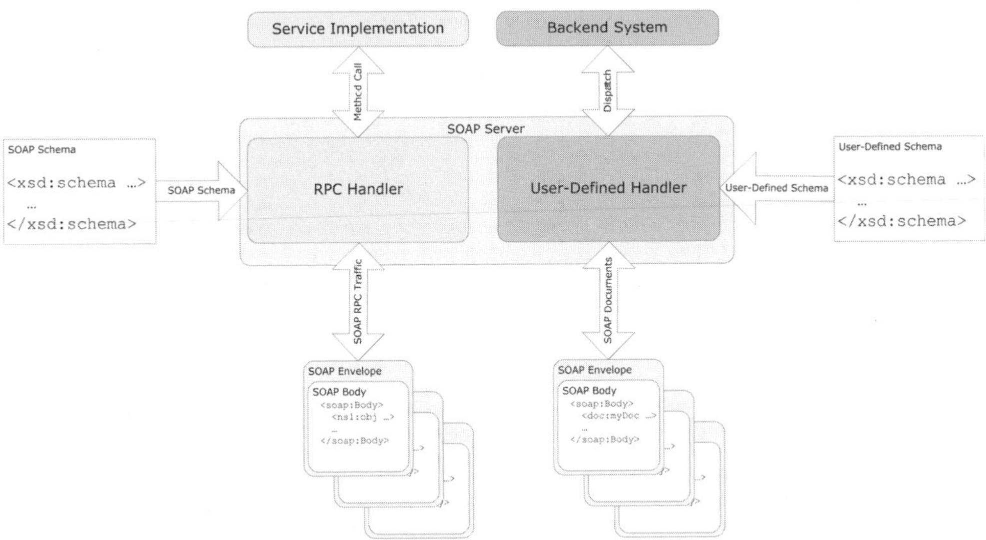

Figure 3-21 Document-oriented SOAP processing.

The user-defined handler in Figure 3-21 is one of potentially many handlers deployed onto the SOAP server to provide the functionality to deal with SOAP messages encoded with arbitrary schemas. Where the SOAP RPC handler simply dispatches the contents of the SOAP RPC messages it receives to appropriate method calls, there are no such constraints on a Web service which uses document-style SOAP. One valid method would be to simply pick out the important values from the incoming document and use them to call a method, just like the SOAP RPC handler. However, as more enterprises become focused on XML as a standard means for transporting data within the enterprise boundary, it is more likely that the contents of the SOAP body will flow directly onto the intranet. Once delivered to the intranet, the messages may be transformed into proprietary XML formats for inclusion with in-house applications, or may be used to trigger business processes without the need to perform the kind of marshalling/unmarshalling required for SOAP RPC.

Note that irrespective of whether the application payload in SOAP messages is SOAP-encoded, or encoded according to a third-party schema, the way that header blocks are used to convey out-of-band information to support advanced Web services protocols is unaffected. Headers are an orthogonal issue to the application-level content.

Document, RPC, Literal, Encoded

Much of the confusion in understanding SOAP comes from the fact that several of the key terms are overloaded. For example, both SOAP RPC (meaning the convention for performing remote procedure calls via SOAP) and RPC style are both valid pieces of SOAP terminology. In this section we clarify the meaning of each of these terms so they do not cause further confusion as we begin discussing WSDL.

Document

Document-style SOAP refers to the way in which the application payload is hosted within the SOAP `Body` element. When we use document style, it means the document is placed directly as a child of the `Body` element, as shown on the left in Figure 3-22, where the application content is a direct child of the `<soap:Body>` element.

Literal — Document

```
<soap:Body>
  <inv:invoice ...>
    <inv:orderNo ...
  </inv:invoice>
</soap:Body>
```

Literal — RPC

```
<soap:Body>
  <m:purchase>
    <inv:invoice ...>
      <inv:orderNo ...
    </inv:invoice>
  </m:purchase>
</soap:Body>
```

Encoded — Document

```
<soap:Body>
  <ns1:invoice>
    <ns1:orderNo...
  </ns1:invoice>
</soap:Body>
```

Encoded — RPC

```
<soap:Body>
  <m:purchase>
    <ns1:invoice>
      <ns1:orderNo...
    </ns1:invoice>
  </m:purchase>
</soap:Body>
```

Figure 3-22 Document, RPC, Literal, and Encoded SOAP messages.

RPC

RPC-style SOAP wraps the application content inside an element whose name can be used to indicate the name of a method to dispatch the content to. This is shown on the right-hand side of Figure 3-22, where we see the application content wrapped `<m:purchase>` element.

Literal

Literal SOAP messages use arbitrary schemas to provide the meta-level description (and constraints) of the SOAP payload. Thus when using literal SOAP, we see that it is akin to taking an instance document of a particular schema and embedding it directly into the SOAP message, as shown at the top of Figure 3-22.

Encoded

SOAP-encoded messages are created by transforming application-level data structures via the SOAP Data Model into a XML format that conforms to the SOAP Schema. Thus, encoded messages tend to look machine-produced and may not generally resemble the same message expressed as a literal. Encoded messages are shown at the bottom of Figure 3-22.

SOAP RPC and SOAP Document-Literal

The SOAP specification provides four ways in which we could package SOAP messages, as shown in Figure 3-22. However, in Web services we tend to use only two of them: SOAP encoded-rpc (when combined with a request-response protocol becomes the SOAP RPC convention) and SOAP document-literal.

Document-literal is the preferred means of exchanging SOAP messages since it just packages application-level XML documents into the SOAP `Body` for transport without placing any semantics on the content.

As we have previously seen, with SOAP RPC the implied semantics are that the first child of the SOAP `Body` element names a method to which the content should be dispatched.

The remaining two options, document-encoded and rpc-literal, are seldom used since they mix styles to no great effect. Encoding documents is pointless if we already have schemas that describe them. Similarly, wrapping a document within a named element is futile unless we are going to use that convention as a remote procedure call mechanism. Since we already have SOAP RPC, this is simply a waste of effort.

SOAP, Web Services, and the REST Architecture

The World Wide Web (WWW) is unquestionably the largest and, by implication, the most scalable distributed system ever built. Though its original goal of simple content delivery was modest, the way that the Web has scaled is nothing short of miraculous.

Given the success of the Web, there is a body of opinion involved in designing the fundamental Web services architecture (that includes the SOAP specification) for which the means to achieving the same level of application scalability through Web services mirrors that of content scalability in the WWW.

The members of this group are proponents of the REST (*REpresentational State Transfer*) architecture, which it is claimed is "Web-Friendly." The REST architecture sees a distributed system as a collection of named resources (named with URIs) that support a small set of common verbs (GET, PUT, POST, DELETE) in common with the WWW.

> The REST idea of defining global methods is similar to the UNIX concept of pipelining programs. UNIX programs all have three simple interfaces defined (STDIN, STDOUT, STDERR) for every program, which allows any two arbitrary programs to interact. The simplicity of REST as compared to custom network interfaces is analogous to the simplicity of UNIX pipelines vs. writing a custom application to achieve the same functionality. REST embraces simplicity and gains scalability as a result. The Web is a REST system, and the generic interfaces in question are completely described by the semantics of HTTP.[5]

What this means to the SOAP developer is that certain operations involving the retrieval of data without changing the state of a Web resource should be performed in a manner that is harmonious with the Web. For example, imagine that we want to retrieve the balance of our account from our bank Web service. Ordinarily we might have thought that something like that shown in Figure 3-23 would be ideal. If this message was sent as part of a HTTP POST, then it would be delivered to the SOAP server, which would then extract the parameters and deliver the results via the `getBalanceResponse` message.

```
<?xml version="1.0" ?>
<env:Envelope
     xmlns:env="http://www.w3.org/2002/06/soap-envelope" >
  <env:Body>
    <bank:getBalance
  env:encodingStyle="http://www.w3.org/2002/06/soap-encoding"
  xmlns:bank="http://bank.example.org/">
      <bank:accountNo>
           12345678
      </bank:accountNo>
    </bank:getBalance>
  </env:Body>
</env:Envelope>
```

Figure 3-23 A "Web-Unfriendly" message.

5. See RESTwiki, http://internet.conveyor.com/RESTwiki/moin.cgi/FrontPage

However, this is now discouraged by the SOAP specification and instead we are encouraged to use HTTP directly to retrieve the information, rather than "tunneling" SOAP through HTTP to get the information. A "Web-friendly" equivalent of Figure 3-23 is shown in Figure 3-24 where the HTTP request directly identifies the information to be retrieved and informs the Web service that it wants the returned information delivered in SOAP format.

```
GET /account?no=12345678  HTTP/1.1
Host: bank.example.org
Accept: application/soap+xml
```

Figure 3-24 A "Web-Friendly" message.

Figure 3-24 is certainly Web friendly since it uses the Web's application protocol (HTTP). However, there are a number of obstacles that have not yet been overcome at the time of writing that may prove detrimental to this approach:

1. A service may be exposed over other protocols than HTTP (e.g., SMTP that does not support the GET verb).
2. This scheme cannot be used if there are intermediate nodes that process SOAP header blocks.
3. There is no guidance yet provided by the SOAP specification authors on how to turn an RPC definition into its Web-friendly format.
4. Too much choice for little gain since we have to support the "Web-Unfriendly" approach anyway for those interactions that require the exchange of structured data.

While these techniques may yet come to fruition, it may be a long time before resolution is reached. When architecting applications today, the best compromise that we can offer is to be aware of those situations where you are engaged in pure information retrieval, and ensure that your architecture is extensible enough to change to a Web-friendly mechanism for those interactions tomorrow. Make sure the code that deals with Web services interactions is modular enough to be easily replaced by Web-friendly modules when the W3C architectural recommendations become more specific.

Looking Back to SOAP 1.1

While Web services will migrate toward SOAP 1.2 in the near future, the most prevalent Web services technology today is the now deprecated SOAP 1.1. Although there isn't a great deal that has changed between the two revisions, there are some caveats we must be aware of when dealing with SOAP 1.1-based systems. To ensure that the work we've invested in understanding

SOAP 1.2 isn't lost on SOAP 1.1 systems, we shall finish our coverage of SOAP with a set of notes that should make our SOAP 1.2 knowledge backwardly compatible with SOAP 1.1.[6]

Syntactic Differences between SOAP 1.2 and SOAP 1.1

- SOAP 1.2 does not permit any element after the body. The SOAP 1.1 schema definition allowed for such a possibility, but the textual description is silent about it. However, the Web Services Interoperability Organization (WS-I) has recently disallowed this practice in its basic profile and as such we should now consider that no elements are allowed after the SOAP body, since any other interpretation will hamper interoperability.
- SOAP 1.2 does not allow the `encodingStyle` attribute to appear on the SOAP Envelope, while SOAP 1.1 allows it to appear on any element.
- SOAP 1.2 defines the new `Misunderstood` header element for conveying information on a mandatory header block that could not be processed, as indicated by the presence of a `mustUnderstand` fault code. SOAP 1.1 provided the fault code, but no details on its use.
- In the SOAP 1.2 infoset-based description, the `mustUnderstand` attribute in header elements takes the (logical) value `true` or `false` while in SOAP 1.1 they are the literal value `1` or `0`, respectively.
- SOAP 1.2 provides a new fault code `DataEncodingUnknown`.
- The various namespaces defined by the two protocols are different.
- SOAP 1.2 replaces the attribute `actor` with `role` but with essentially the same semantics.
- SOAP 1.2 defines two new roles, `none` and `ultimateReceiver`, together with a more detailed processing model on how these behave.
- SOAP 1.2 has removed the dot notation for fault codes, which are now simply of the form `env:name`, where `env` is the SOAP envelope namespace.
- SOAP 1.2 replaces `client` and `server` fault codes with `Sender` and `Receiver`.
- SOAP 1.2 uses the element names `Code` and `Reason`, respectively, for what is called `faultcode` and `faultstring` in SOAP 1.1.
- SOAP 1.2 provides a hierarchical structure for the mandatory SOAP `Code` element, and introduces two new optional subelements, `Node` and `Role`.

---

6. These notes are abridged from the SOAP 1.2. Primer document which can be found at: http://www.w3.org/TR/2002/WD-soap12-part0-20020626/

Changes to SOAP-RPC

Though there was some feeling in the SOAP community that SOAP RPC has had its day and should be dropped in favor of a purely document-oriented protocol, the widespread acceptance of SOAP RPC has meant that it persists in SOAP 1.2, but with a few notable differences:

- SOAP 1.2 provides a `rpc:result` element accessor for RPCs.
- SOAP 1.2 provides several additional fault codes in the RPC namespace.
- SOAP 1.2 allows RPC requests and responses to be modeled as both structs as well as arrays. SOAP 1.1 allowed only the former construct.
- SOAP 1.2 offers guidance on a Web-friendly approach to defining RPCs where the method's purpose is purely a "safe" informational retrieval.

SOAP Encoding

Given the fact that SOAP RPC is still supported in SOAP 1.2 and that there have been some changes to the RPC mechanism, some portions of the SOAP encoding part of the specification have been updated to either better reflect the changes made to SOAP RPC in SOAP 1.2, or to provide performance enhancements compared to their SOAP 1.1 equivalents.

- An abstract data model based on a directed edge-labeled graph has been formulated for SOAP 1.2. The SOAP 1.2 encodings are dependent on this data model. The SOAP RPC conventions are dependent on this data model, but have no dependencies on the SOAP encoding. Support of the SOAP 1.2 encodings and SOAP 1.2 RPC conventions are optional.
- The syntax for the serialization of an array has been changed in SOAP 1.2 from that in SOAP 1.1.
- The support provided in SOAP 1.1 for partially transmitted and sparse arrays is not available in SOAP 1.2.
- SOAP 1.2 allows the inline serialization of multi-ref values.
- The `href` attribute in SOAP 1.1 of type `anyURI`, is called `ref` in SOAP 1.2 and is of type `IDREF`.
- In SOAP 1.2, omitted accessors of compound types are made equal to NILs.
- SOAP 1.2 provides several fault subcodes for indicating encoding errors.
- Types on nodes are made optional in SOAP 1.2.

While most of these issues are aimed at the developers of SOAP infrastucture, it is often useful to bear these features in mind for debugging purposes, especially while we are in the changeover period before SOAP 1.2 becomes the dominant SOAP version.

WSDL

Having a means of transporting data between Web services is only half the story. Without interface descriptions for our Web services, they are about as useful as any other undocumented API—very little! While in theory we could simply examine the message schemas for a Web service and figure out for ourselves how to interoperate with it, this is a difficult and error-prone process and one which could be safely automated if Web services had recognizable interfaces. Fortunately, WSDL provides this capability and more for Web services.

The Web Service Description Language or WSDL—pronounced "Whiz Dull"—is the equivalent of an XML-based IDL from CORBA or COM, and is used to describe a Web service's endpoints to other software agents with which it will interact. WSDL can be used to specify the interfaces of Web services bound to a number of protocols including HTTP GET and POST, but we are only interested in WSDL's SOAP support here, since it is SOAP which we consider to support the (logical) Web services network. In the remainder of this chapter we explore WSDL and show how we can build rich interfaces for Web services that enable truly dynamic discovery and binding, and show how WSDL can be used as the basis of other protocols and extended to other domains outside of interface description.

WSDL Structure

A WSDL interface logically consists of two parts: the abstract parts that describe the operations the Web service supports and the types of messages that parameterize those operations; and the concrete parts that describe how those operations are tied to a physical network endpoint and how messages are mapped onto specific carrier protocols which that network endpoint supports. The general structure of a WSDL document is shown in Figure 3-25.

The foundation of any WSDL interface is the set of messages that the service behind the interface expects to send and receive. A `message` is normally defined using XML Schema types (though WSDL allows other schema languages to be used) and is partitioned into a number of logical parts to ease access to its contents.

Messages themselves are grouped into WSDL `operation` elements that have similar semantics to function signatures in an imperative programming language. Like a function signature, an operation has input, output, and fault messages where WSDL supports at most a single input and output message, but permits the declaration of an arbitrary number of faults.

The `portType` is where what we think of as a Web service begins to take shape. A `portType` is a collection of operations that we consider to be a Web service. However, at this point the operations are still defined in abstract terms, simply grouping sets of message exchanges into operations.

The `binding` section of a WSDL interface describes how to map the abstractly defined messages and operations onto a physical carrier protocol. Each `operation` from each `portType` that is to be bound to a specific protocol (and thus ultimately be made available to the net-

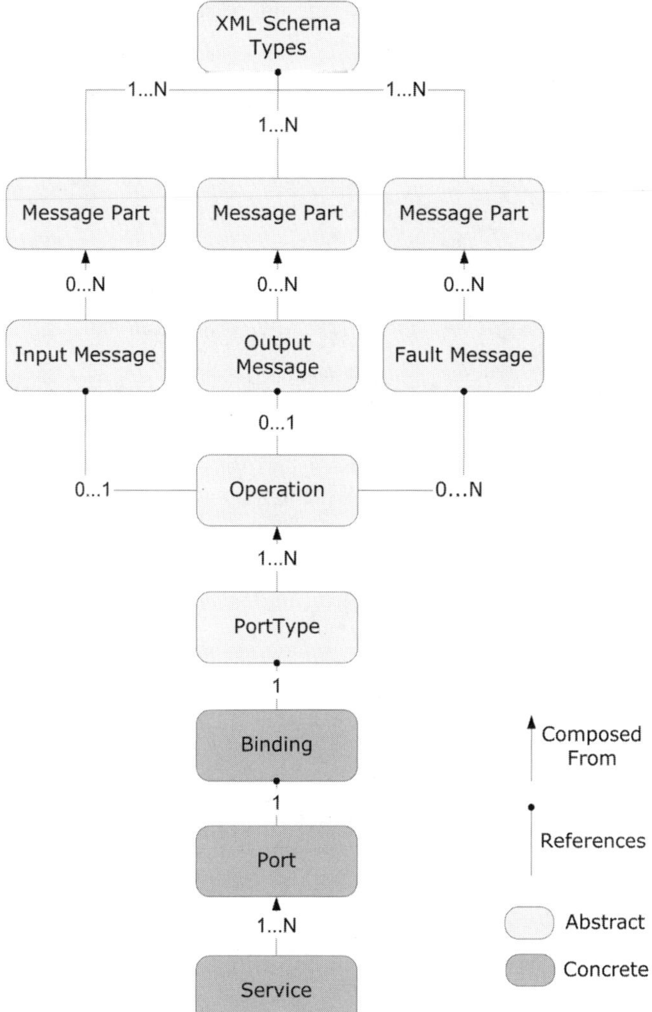

Figure 3-25 WSDL structure.

work) is augmented with binding information from the binding part of the WSDL specification—WSDL supports SOAP, HTTP GET and POST, and MIME—to provide a protocol-specific version of the original `portType` declaration.

Finally, a `port` is declared that references a particular `binding`, and along with addressing information is wrapped together into a `service` element to form the final physical, network addressable Web service.

As we saw in Figure 3-25, the abstract components of a WSDL description are the `types`, `message`, and `portType` elements, while the concrete elements are `binding` and `service`.

The split between abstract and concrete is useful, because it allows us to design interfaces in isolation from eventual deployment environments, using only the abstract definitions in WSDL. Once we are happy with the abstract aspects of the Web service interface, we can then write the concrete parts to tie the service down to a specific location, accessible over a specific protocol.

The Stock Quote WSDL Interface

Having seen WSDL from a theoretical perspective, we can concretize that theory by considering a specific example. The classic Web services application is the stock ticker example where a Web service provides stock quotes on request. Throughout the remainder of this discussion, we shall use a simple Web service which supports a single operation that has an equivalent signature to the following C# code:

```
double GetStockQuote(string symbol);
```

We examine WSDL stage by stage and show how we can turn this simple method signature into a true Web service interface.

Definitions

The opening element of any WSDL document is `definitions`, which is the parent for all other elements in the WSDL document. As well as acting as a container, the `definitions` element is also the place where global namespace declarations are placed.

```
<wsdl:definitions
  targetNamespace="http://stock.example.org/wsdl"
  xmlns:tns="http://stock.example.org/wsdl"
  xmlns:stockQ="http://stock.example.org/schema"
  xmlns:wsdl="http://www.w3.org/2003/02/wsdl">
  <!-- Remainder of WSDL description omitted -->
</wsdl:definitions>
```

Figure 3-26 The WSDL `definitions` element.

A typical WSDL `definitions` element takes the form shown in Figure 3-26, where the element declares the target namespace of the document, a corresponding prefix for that namespace, and a namespace prefix for the WSDL namespace (or alternatively it is also common to use the WSDL namespace as the default namespace for the whole document). Other namespaces may also be declared at this scope, or may be declared locally to their use within the rest of the document. Good practice for declaring namespaces to WSDL documents is to ensure the namespaces that are required for the abstract parts of the document are declared at this level, while namespaces required for the concrete parts of a WSDL document (like the bindings section) are declared locally to make factoring and management of WSDL documents easier.

The Types Element

The `types` element is where types used in the interface description are defined, usually in XML Schema types, since XML Schema is the recommended schema language for WSDL. For instance in our simple stock quote Web service, we define types that represent traded stocks and advertise those types as part of its WSDL interface as illustrated in Figure 3-27.

```
<wsdl:definitions … >
  <wsdl:import namespace="http://stock.example.org/schema"
    location="http://stock.example.org/schema"/>
  <wsdl:types xmlns:xs="http://www.w3.org/2001/XMLSchema">
    <xs:element name="stock-quote">
      <xs:complexType>
        <xs:sequence>
          <xs:element name="symbol" ref="stockQ:symbol"/>
          <xs:element name="lastPrice" ref="stockQ:price"/>
        </xs:sequence>
      </xs:complexType>
    </xs:element>
    <!-- Other schema type definitions -->
  <wsdl:types>
</wsdl:definitions>
```

Figure 3-27 Defining `types` in a WSDL interface.

Before writing the `types` section, we first `import` some types declared by an external schema that make the types within that schema available to this WSDL document to build on. Those schema types (symbol and price) are used to create a new complex type (`stock-price`) which the WSDL interface will use to advertise its associated Web service.

The orthodox view is to use XML Schema to provide constraints and type information in Web services-based applications. However it is not necessarily the case that XML Schema is the right choice for every application domain, particularly those domains that have already chosen a different schema language on which to base their interoperability infrastructure. Recognizing this requirement, WSDL 1.2 supports the notion of other schema languages being used in place of the recommended XML Schema. Although the WSDL 1.2 specification does not provide as wide coverage for other schema languages, it does allow for their use within WSDL interfaces.

Message Elements

Once we have our types, we can move on to the business of specifying exactly how consumers can interact with the Web service. The message declarations compose the types that we have defined (and those that we are borrowing from other schemas) into the expected input, output and fault messages that the Web service will consume and produce. If we take our simple stock ticker Web service as an example, we can imagine a number of messages the Web service would be expected to exchange as shown in Figure 3-28.

```
<wsdl:message name="StockPriceRequestMessage">
  <wsdl:part name="symbol" element="stockQ:symbol"/>
</wsdl:message>
<wsdl:message name="StockPriceRespnseMessage">
  <wsdl:part name="price" element="stockQ:StockPriceType"/>
</wsdl:message>
<wsdl:message name="StockSymbolNotFoundMessage">
  <wsdl:part name="symbol" element="stockQ:symbol"/>
</wsdl:message>
```

Figure 3-28 The message elements.

As we see in Figure 3-28, a WSDL message declaration describes the (abstract) form of a message that a Web service sends or receives. Each message is constructed from a number of (XML Schema) typed part elements—which can come from the types part of the description or an external schema that has been imported into the same WSDL document—and each part is given a name to ease the insertion and extraction of particular information from a message. The name given to a part is unconstrained by WSDL but it is good practice to make the part name descriptive as one would when naming programming language variables.

In this example we have three possible messages: StockPriceRequestMessage, StockPriceResponseMessage, and StockSymbolNotFoundMessage, each of which carries some information having to do with stock prices and, because it is good practice to do so, whose name is indicative of its eventual use in the Web service.

PortType Elements

A portType defines a collection of operations within the WSDL document. Each operation within a portType combines input, output, and fault messages taken from a set of messages like those defined in Figure 3-28.

In the example shown in Figure 3-29, the StockBrokerQueryPortType declares an operation called GetStockPrice which is designed to allow users' systems to ask for the price of a particular equity.

The input to this operation is provided by a StockPriceRequestMessage message. The contents of this message are understood by the implementing Web service, which formu-

```
<wsdl:portType name="StockBrokerQueryPortType">
  <wsdl:operation name="GetStockPrice">
    <wsdl:input message="tns:StockPriceRequestMessage"/>
    <wsdl:output message="tns:StockPriceResponseMessage"/>
    <wsdl:fault name="UnknownSymbolFault"
      message="tns:StockSymbolNotFoundMessage"/>
</wsdl:portType>
```

Figure 3-29 Defining `portType` elements.

lates a response in an `output` `StockPriceRequestMessage` message that contains the details of the stock price for the equity requested.

Any exceptional behavior is returned to the caller through a fault called `UnknownSymbolFault` which is comprised from a `StockSymbolNotFoundMessage` message. Note that `portType` fault declarations have an additional `name` attribute compared to input and output messages, which is used to distinguish the individual faults from the set of possible faults that an operation can support.

Of course not all operations are so orthodox with a single input, output, and fault message, and so we have a variety of possible message exchange patterns described by the `operation` declarations within a `portType`, as follows:

- Input-Output: When the input message is sent to the service, either the output message is generated or one of the fault messages listed is generated instead.
- Input only: When a message is sent to the service, the service consumes it but does not produce any output message or fault. As such no output message or fault declarations are permitted in an operation of this type.
- Output-Input: The service generates the output message and in return the input message or one of the fault messages must be sent back.
- Output-only: The service will generate an output message, but does not expect anything in return. Fault messages are not allowed in this case.

Note that WSDL 1.2 changes the syntax of the `portType` declaration, renaming it `interface`. It also supports a useful new feature in the form of the `extends` attribute, which allows multiple `interface` declarations to be aggregated together and further extended to produce a completely new `interface`. For example, consider the situation where our simple stock Web service needs to evolve to support basic trading activities in addition to providing stock quotes. Using the `extends` mechanism, a new `interface` can be created which possesses all of the operations from each `interface` that it extends, plus any additional operations the developer chooses to add to it as exemplified in Figure 3-30.

The only potential pitfall when extending an `interface` is where names clash. For instance, an extending `interface` should take care not to call its operations by the same name

```
<wsdl:message name="BuyStockRequestMessage">
  <wsdl:part name="symbol" element="stockQ:symbol"/>
  <wsdl:part name="amount" element="xs:positiveInteger"/>
  <wsdl:part name="bid" element="stockQ:StockPriceType"/>
</wsdl:message>
<wsdl:message name="BuyStockResponseMessage">
  <wsdl:part name="symbol" element="stockQ:symbol"/>
  <wsdl:part name="amount" element="xs:positiveInteger"/>
  <wsdl:part name="price" element="stockQ:StockPriceType"/>
</wsdl:message>
<wsdl:message name="BidRejectedMessage">
  <wsdl:part name="symbol" element="stockQ:symbol"/>
  <wsdl:part name="amount" element="xs:positiveInteger"/>
  <wsdl:part name="bid" element="stockQ:StockPriceType"/>
  <wsdl:part name="asking" element="stockQ:StockPriceType"/>
</wsdl:message>

<wsdl:interface name="StockBrokerQueryPurchaseInterface"
  extends="tns:StockBrokerQueryInterface" >
  <wsdl:operation name="BuyStock">
    <wsdl:input message="tns:BuyStockRequestMessage"/>
    <wsdl:output message="tns:BuyStockRequestMessage"/>
    <wsdl:fault name="UnknownSymbolFault"
      message="tns:StockSymbolNotFoundMessage"/>
    <wsdl:fault name="BidRejectedFault"
      message="tns:BidRejectedMessage"/>
</wsdl:interface>
```

Figure 3-30 Extending `interface` definitions.

as operations from any `interface` that it extends unless the operations are equivalent. Furthermore, the designer of a new `interface` that extends multiple existing `interface` declarations must take care to see that there are no name clashes between any of the `interface` declarations as well as with the newly created `interface`.

Bindings

The `bindings` element draws together the `portType` and `operation` elements into a form suitable for exposing to the network. Bindings contain information that dictates how the format of the abstract messages is mapped onto the features of a particular network-level protocol.

While WSDL supports bindings for a number of protocols including HTTP GET and POST, and MIME, we are primarily interested in the SOAP binding for our simple stock quote `portType` from Figure 3-29, which is presented in Figure 3-31.

```
<wsdl:binding name="StockBrokerServiceSOAPBinding"
  type="tns:StockBrokerQueryPortType">
<soap:binding  styleDefault="document"
  transport="http://www.w3.org/2002/12/soap/bindings/HTTP/"
  encodingStyleDefault="http://stock.example.org/schema" />
  <wsdl:operation name="GetStockPrice">
    <soap:operation
      soapAction="http://stock.example.org/getStockPrice"/>
    <wsdl:input>
      <soap:body use="literal"/>
    </wsdl:input>
    <wsdl:output>
      <soap:body use="literal"/>
    </wsdl:output>
    <wsdl:fault>
      <soap:fault name="StockSymbolNotFoundMessage"/>
    </wsdl:fault>
  </wsdl:operation>
</wsdl:binding>
```

Figure 3-31 A SOAP binding.

The binding shown in Figure 3-31 binds the abstract `portType` defined in Figure 3-29 to the SOAP. It states how each of the message components of the operation defined in the `StockBrokerQueryPortType` is mapped onto its SOAP equivalent.

Starting from the top, we see a name for the binding (which is later used to tie a binding to a physical network endpoint) and the `portType` for which this binding is specified.

We then use elements from the WSDL SOAP binding specification to declare a binding for SOAP document-style exchanges, which is expressed as the default mode for this binding through the `styleDefault="document"` attribute. The encoding of the documents exchanged is defined by the stock broker schema `encodingStyleDefault="http://stock.example.org/schema"`. The fact that the service uses document-style SOAP and has its own schema means that it is a document-literal Web service.

Finall,y we see that the binding is for SOAP over the HTTP protocol as specified by the `transport="http://www.w3.org/2002/12/soap/bindings/HTTP/"` attribute. Each of these options is set as the default for the entire binding though both the style and encoding can be changed, if necessary, on a per-message basis.

This binding contains a single operation, namely `GetStockPrice`, which maps each of the input, output, and fault elements of the `GetStockPrice` operation from the `StockBrokerQueryPortType` to its SOAP on-the-wire format. The `soapAction` part of the operation binding is used to specify the HTTP SOAPAction header, which in turn can be used by SOAP servers as an indication of the action that should be taken by the receipt of the message at runtime—which usually captures the name of a method to invoke in a service implementation.

The soap:body elements for both the wsdl:input and wsdl:output elements provide information on how to extract or assemble the different messages inside the SOAP body. Since we have chosen literal encoding and document style for our messages (via the use="literal" and styleDefault="document" attribute), each part of a corresponding message is simply placed as a child of the soap:body element of the SOAP envelope. Had we been using RPC-style SOAP, then the direct child of the soap:body would be an element with the same name as the operation, with each message part as a child, as per SOAP RPC style, as contrasted with document style in Figure 3-32.[7]

```
<!-- RPC style -->
<soap:body>
  <GetStockPrice xmlns:gsp="http://stock.example.org/wsdl"
    xmlns:stockQ="http://stock.example.org/schema">
    <stockQ:symbol>MSFT</stockQ:symbol>
  </GetStockPrice>
</soap:body>

<!-- Document style -->
<soap:body>
  <stockQ:symbol
    xmlns:stockQ="http://stock.example.org/schema">
      MSFT
  </stockQ:symbol>
</soap:body>
```

Figure 3-32 Example SOAP RPC-style “Wrapping” element.

> Note that the WS-I basic profile has mandated that only messages defined with element can be used to create document-oriented Web services, and messages defined with type cannot.

Of course, the value of SOAP is not only that it provides a platform-neutral messaging format, but the fact that the mechanism is extensible through headers. To be of use in describing SOAP headers, the WSDL SOAP binding has facilities for describing header content and behavior. For example, imagine that the query operation for which we have already designed a SOAP binding in Figure 3-31 evolves such that only registered users can access the service and must authenticate by providing some credentials in a SOAP header block as part of an invocation. The WSDL interface for the service obviously needs to advertise this fact to users' applications or no one will be able to access the service.

7. Note: this is not SOAP-encoded, just RPC-style (i.e., wrapped in an element that is named indicatively of the method that the message should be dispatched to).

The WSDL fragment shown in Figure 3-33 presents a hypothetical `soap:header` declaration within the `wsdl:input` element which mandates that a header matching the same namespace as the `userID` message (as declared earlier in the document) is present, and will be consumed by the ultimate receiver of the incoming SOAP message.

```
<wsdl:message name="UserID"
  targetNamespace="http://security.example.org/user">
  <wsdl:part name="signature" type="xs:string"/>
  <wsdl:part name="session" type="xs:anyURI"/>
</wsdl:message>

<wsdl:input>
  <soap:body use="literal"/>
  <soap:header use="literal" message="tns:UserIDMessage"/>
</wsdl:input>

<wsdl:output
  xmlns:sec="http://security.example.org/user">
  <soap:body use="literal"/>
  <soap:headerfault message="sec:UserID" part="signature"/>
</wsdl:output>
```

Figure 3-33 Describing SOAP headers.

Correspondingly, a `soap:headerfault` element is present in the `wsdl:output` element to report back on any faults that occurred while processing the incoming header. If a fault does occur while processing the header, this `soap:headerfault` element identifies the user's signature that caused the problem. This information, which amounts to a "user unknown" response, can then be used at the client end to perhaps prompt the end user to re-enter a pass phrase.

Note that an error such as an incorrect signature is propagated back through the header mechanism and not through the body, since the SOAP specification mandates that errors pertaining to headers must be reported likewise through header blocks.

Services

The services element finally binds the Web service to a specific network-addressable location. It takes the bindings declared previously and ties them to a `port`, which is a physical network endpoint to which clients bind over the specified protocol.

Figure 3-34 shows a service description for our stockbroker example. It declares a service called `StockBrokerService`, which it defines in terms of a port called `StockBrokerServiceSOAPPort`. The port is itself defined in terms of the `StockBrokerServiceSOAPBinding` binding, which we saw in Figure 3-31, and is exposed to the network at the address `http://stock.example.org/` to be made accessible through the endpoint specified at the `soap:address` element.

```
<wsdl:service name="StockBrokerService">
  <wsdl:port name="StockBrokerServiceSOAPPort"
   binding="tns:StockBrokerServiceSOAPBinding">
    <soap:address
        location="http://stock.example.org/"/>
  </wsdl:port>
</wsdl:service>
```

Figure 3-34 A `service` element declaration.

Managing WSDL Descriptions

While the service element is the final piece in the puzzle as far as an individual WSDL document goes, that's not quite the end of the story. For simple one-off Web services, we may choose to have a single WSDL document that combines both concrete and abstract parts of the interface. However, for more complex deployments we may choose to split the abstract parts into a separate file, and join that with a number of different concrete bindings and services to better suit the access pattern for those services.

For example, it may be the case that a single abstract definition (`message`, `portType`, and `operation` declarations) might need to be exposed to the network via a number of protocols, not just SOAP. It might also be the case that a single protocol endpoint might need to be replicated for quality of service reasons or perhaps even several different organizations each want to expose the same service as part of their Web service offerings. By using the WSDL import mechanism, the same abstract definition of the service functionality can be used across all of these Web services irrespective of the underlying protocol or addressing. This is shown in Figure 3-35 where MIME, HTTP, and SOAP endpoints all share the same abstract functionality yet expose that functionality to the network each in their own way. Additionally, the SOAP protocol binding has been deployed at multiple endpoints which can be within a single administrative domain or spread around the whole Internet and yet each service, by dint of the fact that they share the same abstract definitions, is equivalent.

If a WSDL description needs to include features from another WSDL description or an external XML Schema file, then the `import` mechanism is used. It behaves in a similar fashion to the XML Schema `include` feature where it can be used to include components from other WSDL descriptions. We have already seen how the WSDL import mechanism is used in Figure 3-27 where the XML Schema types from the stockbroker schema were exposed to the stock broking WSDL description, as follows:

```
<wsdl:import namespace="http://stock.example.org/schema"
  location="http://stock.example.org/schema"/>
```

The `import` feature of WSDL means that a WSDL description can leverage existing XML infrastructure—previously defined schemas for in-house documents, database schemas, existing Web services, and the like—without having to reproduce those definitions as part of its own description.

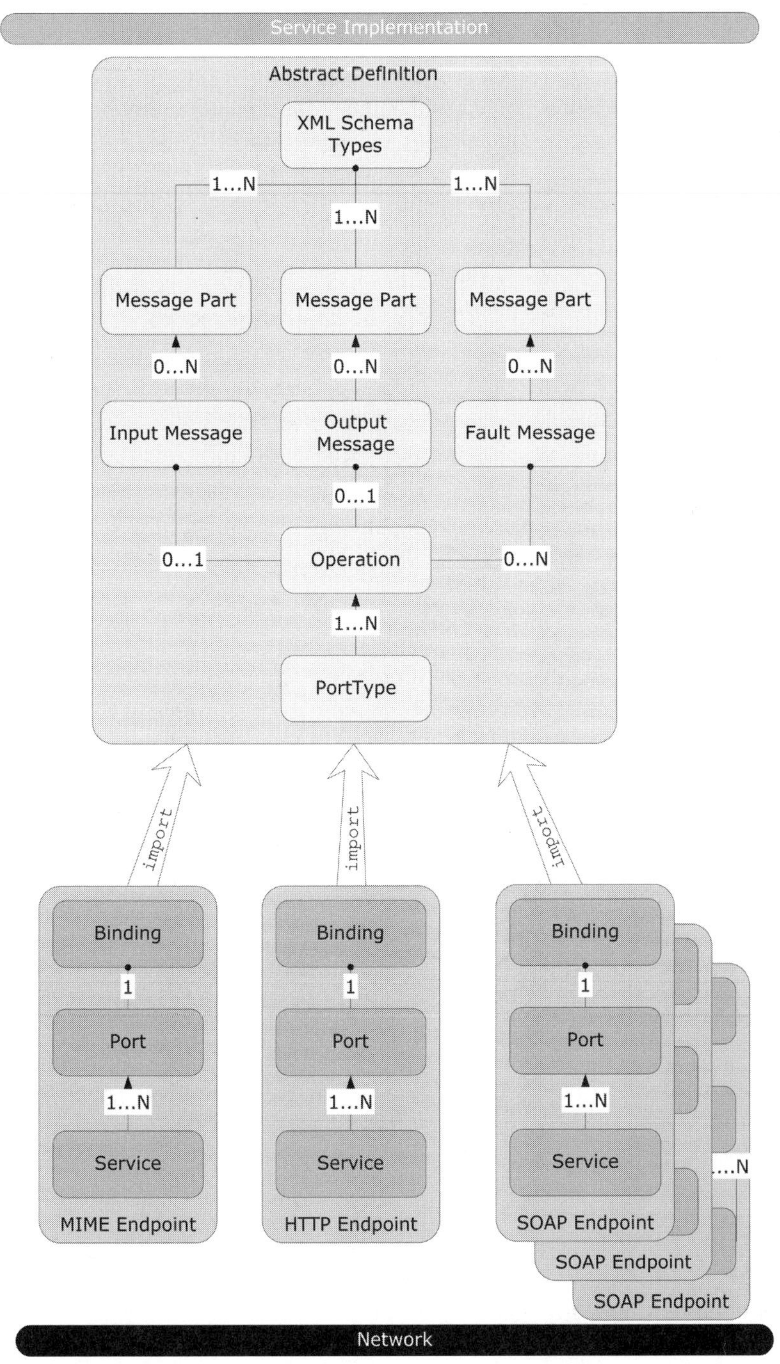

Figure 3-35 Including abstract WSDL descriptions for concrete endpoints.

Extending WSDL[8]

As Web services technology has advanced and matured, WSDL has begun to form the basis of higher-level protocols that leverage the basic building blocks that it provides, to avoid duplication of effort. Many of the technologies that we are going to examine throughout this book extend WSDL via such means to their own purpose. However, where SOAP offers header blocks as its extensibility mechanism for higher-level protocols to use, WSDL offers extension elements based on the XML Schema notion of substitution groups (see Chapter 2).

In the WSDL schema, several (abstract) global element declarations serve as the heads of substitution groups. In addition, the WSDL schema defines a base type for use by extensibility elements as a helper to ensure that the necessary substitution groups are present in any extensions. While it is outside the scope of this book to present the WSDL schema in full, there exists in the schema extensibility elements which user-defined elements can use to place themselves at *any* point within a WSDL `definition`. There are extensibility elements that allow extensions to appear at global scope, within a `service` declaration, before the `port` declaration, in a `message` element before any `part` declarations and any other point in a WSDL description, as shown in Figure 3-36.

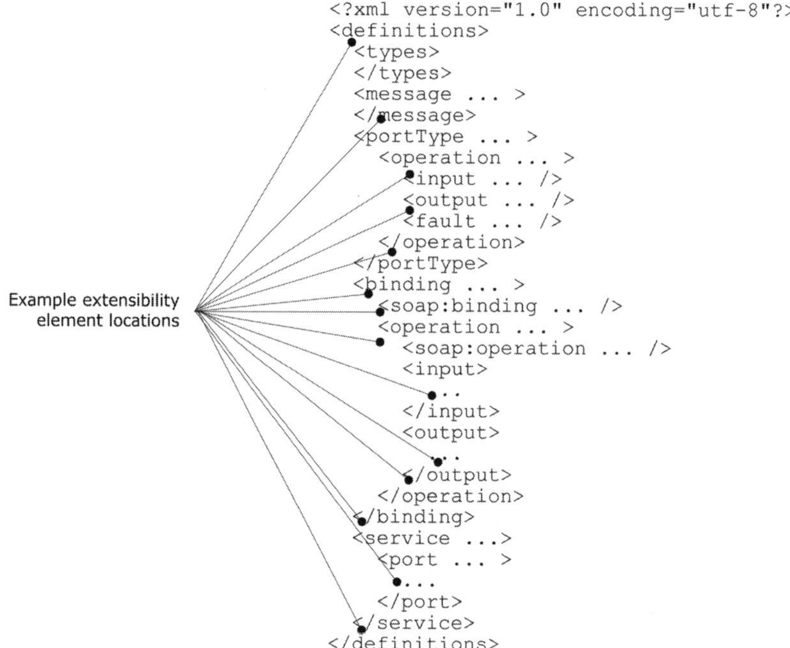

Figure 3-36 WSDL substitution group heads.

8. This section based on a draft version of the WSDL 1.2 specification.

For example, the `soap` elements that we have seen throughout the bindings section of our WDSL description are extensibility elements. In the schema for those elements, they have been declared as being part of the substitution group `bindingExt` which allows them to legally appear as part of the WSDL `bindings` section.

Additionally, third-party WSDL extensions may declare themselves as mandatory with the inclusion of a `wsdl:required` attribute in their definitions. Once a `required` attribute is set, any and all validation against an extended WSDL document must include the presence of the corresponding element as a part of the validation.

> Extensibility elements are commonly used to specify some technology-specific binding. They allow innovation in the area of network and message protocols without having to revise the base WSDL specification. WSDL recommends that specifications defining such protocols also define any necessary WSDL extensions used to describe those protocols or formats.[9]

Using SOAP and WSDL

While many of the more advanced features of the emerging Web services architecture are still being built into many of the platforms, support for SOAP and WSDL in most vendors' Web services toolkits is widespread and makes binding to and using Web services straightforward. In this section, we investigate how a typical application server and can be used to deploy our simple banking example, and how it can be later consumed by a client application. The overall architecture can be seen in Figure 3-37.

The architecture for this sample is typical of Web services applications that routinely combine a variety of platforms. In Figure 3-37, we use Microsoft's .Net and Internet Information Server to host the service implementation, but we use the Java platform and the Apache AXIS Web service toolkit to consume this service and drive the application.

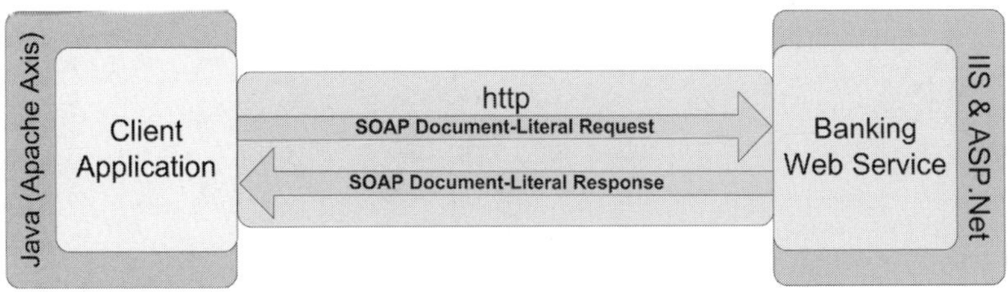

Figure 3-37 Cross-platform banking Web service example.

9. From WSDL 1.2 specification, http://www.w3.org/TR/wsdl12/.

Service Implementation and Deployment

The implementation of our banking service is a straightforward C# class, and is shown in Figure 3-38.

```
using System;
using System.Collections;
using System.ComponentModel;
using System.Data;
using System.Web;
using System.Web.Services;

[WebService(Namespace="http://bank.example.org")]
public class BankService : System.Web.Services.WebService
{
  [WebMethod]
  public string openAccount(string title,
                            string surname,
                            string firstname,
                            string postcode,
                            string telephone)
  {
    BankEndSystem bes = new BackEndSystem();
    string accountNumber = bes.processApplication(title,
                                                   surname,
                                                   firstname,
                                                   postcode,
                                                   telephone);
    return accountNumber;
  }
}
```

Figure 3-38 A simple bank Web service implementation.

Most of the work for this service is done by some back-end banking system, to which our service delegates the workload. Our service implementation just acts as a kind of gateway between the Web service network to which it exposes our back-end business logic, and the back-end systems themselves to which it delegates work it receives from Web services clients. This pattern is commonplace when exposing existing systems via Web services, and makes good architectural sense since the existing system does not have to be altered just to add in Web service support.

The key to building a successful Web service, even one as simple as our bank account example, is to ensure that the orthogonal issues of service functionality and deployment are kept separate. That is, do not allow the implementation of your system to change purely because you intend to expose its functionality as a Web service.

It is a useful paradigm to treat your Web services as "user interfaces" through which users (in most cases other computer systems) will interact with your business systems. In the same way that you would not dream of putting business rules or data into human user interfaces, then you should not place business rules or data into your Web service implementations. Similarly, you would not expect that a back-end business system would be updated simply to accommodate a user interface, and you should assume that such mission-critical systems should not be altered to accommodate a Web service deployment.

When deployed into our Web services platform (in this example, Microsoft's IIS with ASP.Net), the associated WSDL description of the service is generated by inspection of the implementation's interface and made available to the Web. The resultant WSDL[10] is shown in Figure 3-39.

It is important to bear in mind, that although the WSDL shown in Figure 3-39 is intricate and lengthy for a simple service, the effort required to build it is practically zero because of tool support. The only issue that this should raise in the developer's mind is that their chosen platform and tools should handle this kind of work on their behalf. WSDL should only be hand-crafted where there a specific need to do something intricate and unusual that tool support would not facilitate.

Binding to and Invoking Web Services

Once the service has been deployed and its endpoint known by consumers, clients can bind to it by using their client-side Web services toolkits to create proxies. A proxy is a piece of code that sits between the client application and the network and deals with all of the business of serializing and deserializing variables from the client's program into a form suitable for network transmission and back again. The client application, therefore, never has to be aware of any network activity and is simpler to build.

10. The WDSL description generated by ASP.Net is richer than that shown here since it also includes HTTP GET and HTTP POST bindings. However, we are predominantly interested in SOAP as the Web services transport, and so the HTTP bindings have been removed.

```
<?xml version="1.0" encoding="utf-8"?>
<definitions
  xmlns:soap="http://schemas.xmlsoap.org/wsdl/soap/"
  xmlns:xs="http://www.w3.org/2001/XMLSchema"
  xmlns:bank="http://bank.example.org"
  targetNamespace="http://bank.example.org"
  xmlns="http://schemas.xmlsoap.org/wsdl/">
  <types>
    <xs:schema elementFormDefault="qualified"
       targetNamespace="http://bank.example.org">
      <xs:element name="openAccount">
        <xs:complexType>
          <xs:sequence>
            <xs:element minOccurs="0" maxOccurs="1"
               name="title" type="xs:string"/>
            <xs:element minOccurs="0" maxOccurs="1"
               name="surname" type="xs:string"/>
            <xs:element minOccurs="0" maxOccurs="1"
               name="firstname" type="xs:string"/>
            <xs:element minOccurs="0" maxOccurs="1"
               name="postcode" type="xs:string"/>
            <xs:element minOccurs="0" maxOccurs="1"
               name="telephone" type="xs:string"/>
          </xs:sequence>
        </xs:complexType>
      </xs:element>
      <xs:element name="openAccountResponse">
        <xs:complexType>
          <xs:sequence>
            <xs:element minOccurs="0" maxOccurs="1"
               name="openAccountResult" type="xs:string"/>
          </xs:sequence>
        </xs:complexType>
      </xs:element>
      <xs:element name="string" nillable="true"
         type="xs:string"/>
    </xs:schema>
  </types>
  <message name="openAccountSoapIn">
    <part name="parameters" element="bank:openAccount"/>
  </message>
  <message name="openAccountSoapOut">
    <part name="parameters"
     element="bank:openAccountResponse"/>
  </message>
  <portType name="BankServiceSoap">
```

Figure 3-39 Bank service auto-generated WSDL description.

```
    <operation name="openAccount">
      <input message="bank:openAccountSoapIn"/>
      <output message="bank:openAccountSoapOut"/>
    </operation>
  </portType>
  <binding name="BankServiceSoap"
   type="bank:BankServiceSoap">
    <soap:binding
         transport="http://schemas.xmlsoap.org/soap/http"
         style="document"/>
    <operation name="openAccount">
      <soap:operation
           soapAction="http://bank.example.org/openAccount"
           style="document"/>
      <input>
        <soap:body use="literal"/>
      </input>
      <output>
        <soap:body use="literal"/>
      </output>
    </operation>
  </binding>
  <service name="BankService">
    <port name="BankServiceSoap"
     binding="bank:BankServiceSoap">
      <soap:address
          location="http://localhost/dnws/BankService.asmx"/>
    </port>
  </service>
</definitions>
```

Figure 3-39 Bank service auto-generated WSDL description (continued).

In our example, the serialization and deserialization is to SOAP from Java and back again, and is handled by a proxy generated by the Apache AXIS `WSDL2Java` tool. This tool parses WSDL at a given location and generates a proxy class which allows client code to communicate with that service. For example, the proxy code generated by this tool when it consumed our bank example service is shown in Figure 3-40.

```
/**
 * This file was auto-generated from WSDL
 * by the Apache Axis WSDL2Java emitter.
 */

package org.example.bank;
import java.lang.String;

public class BankServiceSoapStub
                extends org.apache.axis.client.Stub
                implements org.example.bank.BankServiceSoap {

  // Data members removed for brevity

  public BankServiceSoapStub()
                          throws org.apache.axis.AxisFault {
     this(null);
  }

  // Other constructors removed for brevity

  private org.apache.axis.client.Call createCall()
                            throws java.rmi.RemoteException {
      // Implementation removed for brevity
      return _call;
    }
    catch (java.lang.Throwable t) {
      throw new org.apache.axis.AxisFault("Failure trying" +
                                 " to get the Call object", t);
    }
  }

  public String openAccount(String title, String surname,
                            String firstname,
                            String postcode,
                            String telephone)
                            throws java.rmi.RemoteException {
     // Implementation removed for brevity
  }
}
```

Figure 3-40 Apache AXIS auto-generated proxy for the bank Web service.

The proxy class shown in Figure 3-40 allows the client of the Web service to call its functionality with a call as simple as the likes of:

```
bankAccountService.openAccount("Mr", "Aneurin", "Bevan",
                               "ABC 123", "0207 123 4567")
```

without having to worry about the fact that on the wire, the proxy has sent a SOAP message that looks like that shown in Figure 3-41 below:

```
<?xml version="1.0" encoding="utf-8" ?>
<soap:Envelope xmlns:soap="http://schemas.xmlsoap.org/soap/
envelope/" xmlns:xsi="http://www.w3.org/2001/XMLSchema-
instance" xmlns:xsd="http://www.w3.org/2001/XMLSchema">
  <soap:Body>
    <openAccount xmlns="http://bank.example.org">
      <title>Mr</title>
      <surname>Bevan</surname>
      <firstname>Aneurin</firstname>
      <postcode>ABC 123</postcode>
      <telephone>0207 123 4567</telephone>
    </openAccount>
  </soap:Body>
</soap:Envelope>
```

Figure 3-41 Proxy generated SOAP message.

At the receiving end, the bank service's SOAP server will retrieve this SOAP from the network and turn it into something meaningful (in our case C# objects) before passing it to the service implementation. The service implementation grinds away at its task, producing some result in its own proprietary format before passing it back to the underlying Web services platform to serialize its results into the appropriate network format (i.e., a SOAP message) and return it to the caller. At this point the service invocation has finished and the resources used during the execution of that service can be freed.

Where's the Hard Work?

For simple interactions, there isn't any hard work for the developer to do because SOAP toolkits are sufficiently advanced enough to automate this. For example, we didn't have to worry about the style of SOAP encoding or how the marshalling occurred in any of our bank account examples, even though we crossed networks, servers, and even languages and platforms.

Though it may seem from these examples that Web services is an automation utopia, it is not. While it is true that for the majority of cases, simple interactions can be automated (though auto-generation of WSDL from service implementation code and auto-generation of proxies from WSDL descriptions), this is about as far as toolkits have advanced.

Given that this book extends beyond this third chapter, it is safe to assume that we're going to have to roll up our shirt sleeves at some point and patch the gaps that the current set of Web services toolkits inevitably leaves. It is in these subsequent chapters where we will find the hard work!

Summary

SOAP is the protocol that Web services use to communicate. It is an XML-based protocol that specifies a container called an Envelope, which stores application payload in a second container, called the Body, and additional (usually contextual) information inside a third container called the Header. The SOAP specification describes a processing model where application messages (and their associated headers) can pass through intermediary processing nodes between the sender and receiver, where the information stored in the SOAP header blocks can be used by those intermediaries to provide various quality of service characteristics. For example, the headers may contain routing information, transaction context, security credentials, or any other protocol information.

WSDL is an interface description language for Web services and like SOAP, WSDL is currently popularized by its 1.1 version, which is due to be superseded by WSDL 1.2. A WSDL interface is composed from a number of elements, each building on the previous, from simple type and message declarations, culminating in a network addressable entity which uses the defined types and messages to expose operations onto the Web.

Though SOAP and WSDL are undoubtedly important protocols in their own right, when drawn together through tool support, their potential is significantly enhanced. Web services toolkits can consume the WSDL offered by a service and automatically generate the code to deal with messages in the format that the service expects, while providing a straightforward API to the developer.

Architect's Note

- SOAP 1.1 is the most widely adopted version of the SOAP specification. However, SOAP 1.2 has now reached W3C recommendation status and thus SOAP 1.1 is now considered deprecated.
- SOAP RPC is quick and easy, but may lead to applications with too tight a level of coupling. Exchanging larger documents is preferable, even if it means writing handler code to deal with them.
- XML-Native applications should not use SOAP-RPC; they should use the XML vocabularies that they have already developed, and use those vocabularies as the basis of their communication via document-oriented SOAP.
- Be prepared for a shift in the Web services architecture, and ensure your services can support "Web-friendly" access where appropriate.
- Do not deploy a Web service without its WSDL description—a service is naked without it.
- Use tool support—it is wasted effort to do for yourself what a tool can do more easily, more quickly, and more accurately.

CHAPTER 4

UDDI—Universal Description, Discovery, and Integration

When UDDI came on the scene, its champions positioned the new technology as the savior of e-business. Businesses along a value chain would use UDDI registries to dynamically and automatically select new business partners, locate the electronic services implemented by those partners and start executing e-commerce transactions with them. This would revolutionize how businesses operate: wipe out the need for human interaction in many business tasks, reduce overheads and middleman costs, and fundamentally enable a dynamic and fluid e-business environment.

Today, it is difficult to find companies that are truly using UDDI, and UDDI registries boast a relatively small number of entries. Does this mean that UDDI is DOA (dead on arrival)? By just looking at the list of some of the companies that are backing the UDDI project, one would conclude probably not.

So, how will UDDI pan out? What will enterprises do with UDDI? What do enterprise architects have to know about UDDI? In this chapter, we delve into these issues and take a practical approach to UDDI and its fit within the enterprise Web services picture. We look at the latest release of the UDDI specification—Version 3—and take a closer look at some of the key architectural changes.

UDDI at a Glance

The UDDI is a registry and a protocol for publishing and discovering Web services. As Web services are a standards-based, open, and platform-independent means of accessing the functional capabilities of other companies, UDDI is the associated standards-based, open, and platform-independent means of publishing and locating these services. The latest information about UDDI and the UDDI community can be found at http://www.uddi.org.

As more and more companies start driving toward a services-oriented architecture, and Web services in particular, for their enterprise application infrastructure, the issue of *locating* Web services becomes increasingly important. When companies initially began experimenting with Web services behind the firewall, there was no question of locating or discovering services as each company controlled everything—both the services and the consuming applications.

As these experimental applications were migrated across the firewall, the services they consumed were augmented to include Web services from a handful of partner companies. All of the necessary information about these services was known *a priori*, and still the need to discover services was unnecessary.

As these applications were further scaled, there emerged a need to answer questions such as: Which business partners have this service? What types of services do these partners offer? As more business partners adopted Web services, the process of obtaining these answers became difficult, not to mention time consuming. The old methods of jointly agreeing on services and their interfaces were no longer feasible. Neither was manually calling up business partners to get a list of their latest service offerings.

There emerged a need for a registry where service providers could publish not only a list of their services but also information necessary to use the services. At the same time, businesses could search through the registry to discover these service providers and their services. These are the underpinnings of UDDI.

Analogies with Telephone Directories

UDDI shares some striking similarities with telephone directories (e.g., yellow pages). As such, the analogy is an effective vehicle for describing the capabilities and usefulness of UDDI.

A phone book allows people to search for other people and businesses, get their contact information, and then directly contact the person or business. Phone books allow various modes of searching, whether it be an alphabetical listing of people or business names (as in the white pages) or through categories of businesses.

Anyone can view the listings of a phone directory; in fact, the more people who view and use the phone book, the more valuable it is. However, only the phone company or its authorized agent publishes the phone book. When adding or updating entries, the requester must validate his or her identity and provide evidence that he or she has the right to add or change the information.

The importance of phone books grows as the need to locate more people and businesses increases. When there are just a handful of people and businesses and few new additions, phone books are not as important. It is easy to keep track of contact information, or gather the information when necessary. However, as the base of people and businesses becomes large and there are continuous changes—both in people and businesses being added or removed from the listings or their contact information changes—phone books become critical. They provide a centralized source for contact information.

UDDI is quite similar. Instead of a directory of telephone numbers, UDDI is a directory of Web services that are available from different vendors. UDDI provides a means of adding new services, removing existing services, and changing the contact (i.e., endpoint) information for services.

Most UDDI implementations also have some of the same constraints as phone books. Only authenticated users (e.g., service providers) can add or change their information on the UDDI registry. Non-authenticated users are not allowed to change any information on a UDDI registry, and only authenticated users can change their own information. This policy prevents maliciously motivated changes to UDDI entries. Any user can access a UDDI registry for read-only purposes.

Both telephone directories and UDDI registries provide a means to locate a vendor or provider of a particular service. For telephone directories, contact information is basically a phone number and perhaps may also include an address. Contact information in a UDDI registry consists of information about the service provider as well as technical information about the Web service itself. Conceptually, the information available in an UDDI registry is similar to that in the white, green, and yellow pages of the phone book. In UDDI, the segmentation of information that is available and searchable can be thought of as follows:

- White Pages: Contact information about the service provider company. This information includes the business or entity name, address, contact information, other short descriptive information about the service provider, and unique identifiers with which to facilitate locating this business.
- Yellow Pages: Categories (taxonomies) under which Web services implementing functionalities within those categories can be found.
- Green Pages: Technical information about the capabilities and behavioral grouping of Web services.

How are people supposed to use an UDDI registry? First, let's look at how people use telephone books. When using the phone book to contact a business, the user has a product or service in mind. From her past purchases, she may also have a few businesses in mind that sell that product. The user looks up these business names to find their contact information. Otherwise, the user searches through product categories to locate a vendor. Once she has identified a suitable vendor, she looks up the corresponding phone number and contacts the vendor.

What if there are multiple possible vendors? How does a user determine the winner? The winning vendor may be chosen based on price. The user may prefer to do business with a particular vendor if she has done a lot of business with the vendor in the past. The user may shy away from a vendor because the vendor has been unreliable or has delivered shoddy product.

Using a UDDI registry is similar to using a standard telephone directory. Users will search through the UDDI registry for an appropriate Web service that meets their needs. The search may involve a straightforward name lookup, or may involve searching through the taxonomies (service provider categories) provided by the UDDI registry. What do you do when there are multiple Web services that may potentially meet your needs? You have to pick a winner based on whatever metrics are important to you. These may be cost, personal preferences, or other business relationships.

Figure 4-1 depicts the similarities between telephone directory books and UDDI registries.

Although there are strong similarities between these, there are some places where the analogy breaks down. First, each Web service implements a unique API. Although this is not by specification, it is statistically unlikely that two independent programmers will define and implement the same programmatic interface. Unlike different phone numbers that merely provide unique identification or routing information for phone calls, different Web service APIs are more analogous to using a different and unique phone number for communicating with each person or business.

Second, people will not typically interact directly with UDDI registries as they do with phone books. This is because the information available on UDDI is not people-friendly. Instead, portals and software tools facilitate access to UDDI registries. Many of the same middleware and application development tools that support Web service development allow users to easily add new services to the UDDI registry. These and other tools also allow browsing through the services on UDDI, and many augment the information available on UDDI with their own analysis. This analysis may include quality-of-service information and additional information helpful in using the Web services.

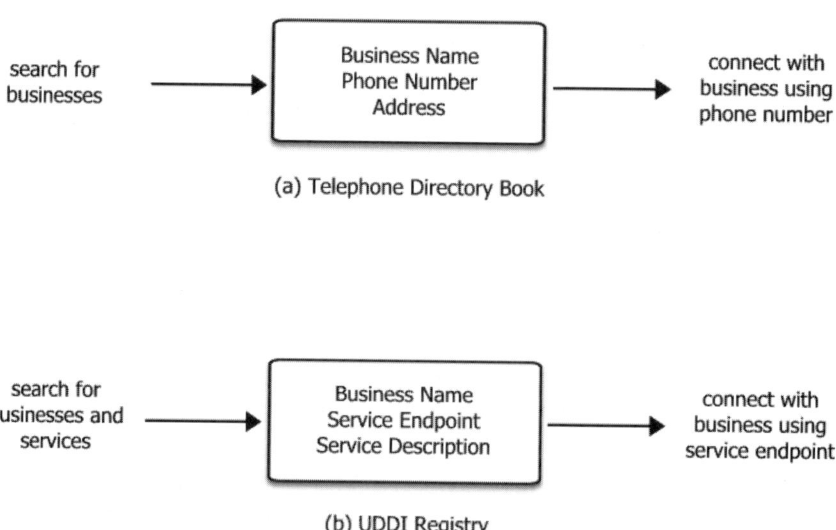

Figure 4-1 Similarities between (a) telephone directory books and (b) UDDI registries.

Another key difference is that within organizations, UDDI will probably be accessed by two different groups of people. Unlike phone books, interactions with UDDI require an understanding of more issues. For example, which Web service to use for a particular application is not only based on technical needs and QoS requirements, other strategic and business issues also come into the mix. There may be existing relationships between two companies that require the use of a particular company's Web service over that of another. Or, it may make strategic sense for a company to use a particular Web service, even if other technically superior Web services exist. As such, a unique interaction of business issues together with technical issues comes together to determine which Web service to use for a particular application. Since most technical programmers are usually not party to such information, business analysts with an understanding of strategic business issues typically will select Web services by searching through UDDI registries and other related information portals. A programmer will then search the UDDI registry for that particular Web service's API, and implement the communications between the application and that Web service, as depicted in Figure 4-2.

A critical point to remember is that business issues are quite fluid. The dynamics of most business environments result in rapidly changing relationships. This, in turn, results in continuously changing or at least evolving business-driven requirements. Flexibility in selecting and consuming Web services is important.

It is a common misconception that applications can themselves dynamically select and consume Web services. Although one day software may become sufficiently smart to do this,

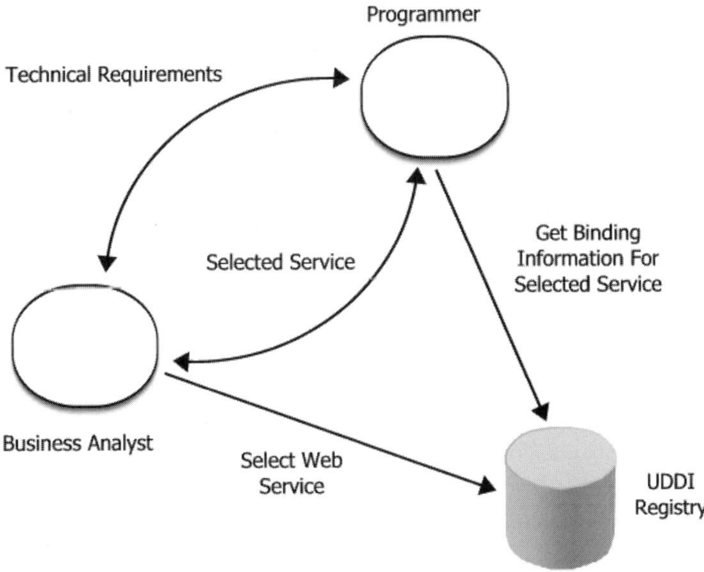

Figure 4-2 The typical roles played while interacting with an UDDI registry.

today selecting and consuming Web services requires some degree of human intervention. Some simple cases of automation do certainly exist, but automating the process in a general sense is not available today. Why not? Because each Web service implements a unique API that requires programmatic and perhaps architectural changes to the consuming application. Moreover, automating the process of selecting the appropriate Web service to consume is difficult and dynamic. Some newer tools support the use of business rules to automate (at a higher level) the process of service selection. Nonetheless, some level of human intervention is necessary.

The UDDI Business Registry

The UDDI Business Registry (UBR) is a global implementation of the UDDI specification. The UBR is a single registry for Web services. A group of companies operate and host UBR nodes, each of which is an identical copy of all other nodes. New entries or updates are entered into a single node, but are propagated to all other nodes.

The UBR is a key element of the deployment of Web services and provides the following capabilities:

- A centralized registration facility at which to publish and make others aware of the Web services a company makes available.
- A centralized search facility at which companies that require a particular service can locate businesses that provide that service as well as relevant information about that service.

A small group of companies operate and manage a set of UBR nodes. In July 2002, the UBR was updated to support version 2 of the UDDI specification. Initially, IBM, Microsoft, and SAP comprised the UBR V2, operating 3 UBR nodes. NTT Communications later launched an UBR node to become the fourth UBR V2 node. More than 10,000 businesses are registered with the initial three UBR nodes, publishing over 7,000 Web services. NTT expects to add another 1,000 businesses within the first operational year of the fourth UBR node.

Each UBR node provides a Web home page for human-friendly navigation of the registry as well as information about the use of the registry. Today, most searches for available Web services are done through human-friendly means: phone conversations between existing business partners, the home pages of the UBR, Web service aggregator portals such as www.xmethods.com, or standard Web search engines such as Google. UBR node home pages also provide other information pertaining to UDDI or to that particular UBR node. This information includes policies on data replication, publishing restrictions, and other administrative or usage issues.

UBR nodes also implement a simple API for direct electronic (computer-to-computer) access to the contents of the registry. The two most important and relevant features of the APIs are inquiry and publication.

The inquiry API allows searching through the registry for information about businesses, the Web services the business makes available, as well as implementation and interface information for each service.

The publication API allows adding, changing, and deleting business and service information within the registry.

Figure 4-3 depicts some typical means of accessing and interacting with an UDDI registry.

The URL access endpoint information of the home page, inquiry API, and publication API of each UBR node is different, and the information for each of the UBR V2 nodes is listed in Table 4-1. The publication API endpoint requires authentication and uses the HTTPS protocol, while the inquiry API and home page use standard HTTP.

The UBR operators also provide fully functional test environments where companies can develop and test their offerings without affecting other users. Some of these test nodes do not support version 2 of the UDDI specification as yet. Table 4-2 lists the endpoint access information for the test nodes of the UBR.

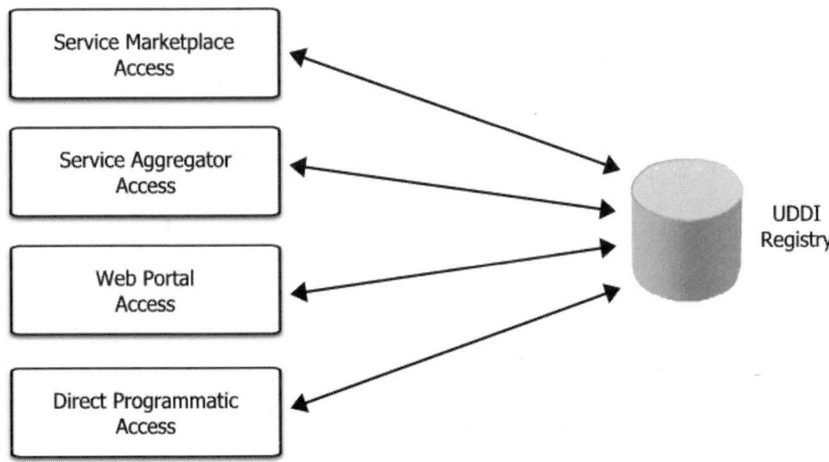

Figure 4-3 The various means of accessing an UDDI registry.

Table 4-1 The operator node URLs for the UDDI Business Registry (UBR).

UBR Operator Node		URL
IBM	Home Page	http://uddi.ibm.com/
	Inquire API	http://uddi.ibm.com/ubr/inquireapi
	Publish API	https://uddi.ibm.com/ubr/publishapi
Microsoft	Home Page	http://uddi.microsoft.com/
	Inquire API	http://uddi.microsoft.com/inquire
	Publish API	https://uddi.microsoft.com/publish
SAP	Home Page	http://uddi.sap.com/
	Inquire API	http://uddi.sap.com/uddi/api/inquiry
	Publish API	https://uddi.sap.com/uddi/api/publish
NTT Com	Home Page	http://www.ntt.com/uddi/
	Inquire API	http://www.uddi.ne.jp/ubr/inquiryapi
	Publish API	https://www.uddi.ne.jp/ubr/publishapi

Table 4-2 The test node URLs for the UDDI Business Registry (UBR).

UBR Test Operator Node		URL
IBM	Home Page	http://uddi.ibm.com/testregistry/registry.html
	Inquire API	http://uddi.ibm.com/testregistry/inquiryapi
	Publish API	https://uddi.ibm.com/testregistry/publishapi
Microsoft	Home Page	http://test.uddi.microsoft.com/
	Inquire API	http://test.uddi.microsoft.com/inquire
	Publish API	https://test.uddi.microsoft.com/publish
SAP	Home Page	http://udditest.sap.com/
	Inquire API	http://udditest.sap.com/UDDI/api/inquiry
	Publish API	https://udditest.sap.com/UDDI/api/publish

Later in the chapter we look at how to programmatically access the information at these UBR nodes to locate the latest information about a particular Web service.

UDDI Under the Covers

In the remainder of this chapter, we discuss how to add entries to a UDDI registry as well as how to search for available services and build applications that consume those services. We will also briefly touch on the major sections of the UDDI specification.

The UDDI Specification

Version 3 is the most recent incarnation of the UDDI specification. Version 3 builds on and expands the foundations laid by versions 1 and 2 of the UDDI specification, and presents a blueprint for flexible and interoperable Web services registries. Version 3 also includes a rich set of enhancements as well as additional features, including improved security and new APIs. The entire UDDI specification can be found at http://www.uddi.org.

The major documents of the UDDI Version 3 specification are listed in Table 4-3.

Table 4-3 The major documents of the UDDI Specification version 3.

UDDI Version 3 Specification Documents	Synopsis
Features List	Brief overview of the key features in version 3.
Specification	The actual specification document.
XML Schemas	A set of XML Schema files that formally describe UDDI data structures.
WSDL Service Interface Descriptions	A set of files that describe the UDDI Version 3 WSDL interface definitions.

Unlike in previous versions, UDDI Version 3 consolidates the entire specification into a single document entitled the UDDI Version 3 Published Specification. This single document contains everything related to UDDI, and also contains all information necessary for developing a UDDI node, the Web services that are called by a UDDI node, or a client application that directly interacts with a UDDI registry.

UDDI Core Data Structures

Information representation within UDDI consists of instances of persistent data structures that are expressed in XML. It is these data structures that are persistently stored and managed by UDDI nodes. The UDDI specification refers to these as entities, and defines four core entity types as listed in Table 4-4.

Table 4-4 The different entity types defined by the UDDI Information Model.

Entity Type Name	Description
businessEntity	A business that provides a Web service.
businessService	A collection of related services offered by a business.
bindingTemplate	Technical information about a particular Web service.
tModel	Technical model information about a Web service that is used to determine whether a service is compatible with the client's needs.

Whether you intend to programmatically connect to a UDDI registry or manually browse through one, it is necessary to understand these core data structures. Central to the purpose of UDDI is the representation of information about Web services so they can be easily registered and classified by publishers as well as searched and consumed by client applications. As such the data structures used by UDDI provide not only technical interface information about a service itself, but also information necessary to classify, manage, and locate services. Figure 4-4 depicts the interrelationships between the core UDDI data structures.

The `businessEntity` entity type represents information about service providers within UDDI. This information includes detailed data about the name of the provider, contact information, and some other short descriptions of the provider. This information may also be

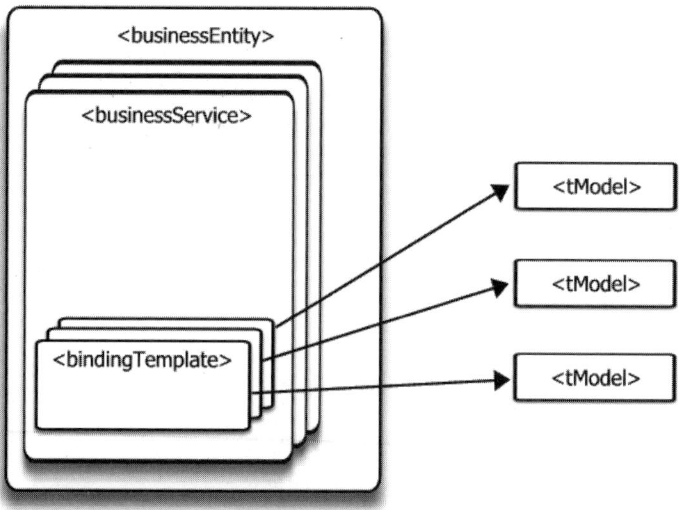

Figure 4-4 The interrelationship between the UDDI core data structures.

provided in multiple languages. The businessEntity structure does not necessarily have to refer to a business, but to any type of service provider, such as a department within an organization or a group.

One or more of the businessService entity types are contained within a businessEntity structure and represents information about the services offered by that businessEntity. The businessService entity type does not provide implementation or technical details, but instead is a logical grouping of Web services and provides information about the bundled purpose of a set of contained Web services.

One or more of the bindingTemplate entity types are contained within a businessService structure and provides technical information about a particular Web service. The bindingTemplate structure directly or indirectly provides descriptive technical information about an instance of a Web service, and includes a network location or endpoint of the service. The network location (access point) is usually a URL, but can be other network access points such as email addresses. The bindingTemplate structure also includes information about the type of Web service located at that access point through references to tModel entities as well as other parameters.

tModels, which are short for technical models, provide more detailed information about a Web service. tModels are reusable entities that are referenced from bindingTemplate structures and denote compliance with a shared concept or design. tModels are not contained within bindingTemplates, but instead are referenced. Distinct tModels exist for different interfaces and contracts that a Web service can comply with including specifications, transports, protocols, and namespaces. The set of tModels that a bindingTemplate refers to makes up a Web service's technical fingerprint. The actual documents and information identified by a tModel are not located within the UDDI registry itself, but instead the tModel provides pointers to the location where such documents can be found.

Two more UDDI entity types that are important are subscription and publisherAssertion. The subscription entity type describes the request to keep track of the evolution or changes to particular entities. The publisherAssertion entity type describes the relationship between one businessEntity and another businessEntity. There are many instances where multiple divisions within a large organization or a group of organizations want to make the relationship between them known in order to facilitate discovery of the services they provide. The individual divisions or organizations each have their own businessEntity, and the entity type publisherAssertion describes the relationship between two businessEntity structures. It is important to note that two organizations must assert the same relationship through the publisherAssertion for that relationship to be publicly available. This disallows the situation where one organization claims a relationship with another where in fact there is none.

Accessing UDDI

UDDI is itself a Web service and as such, applications can communicate with an UDDI registry by sending and receiving XML messages. This makes the access both language and platform independent.

Although it's possible, it is unlikely that programmers will deal with the low-level details of sending and receiving XML messages. Instead, client-side packages for different languages and platforms will emerge that facilitate programmatic access to UDDI.

Two such packages are UDDI4J and Microsoft's UDDI SDK, which are client-side APIs for communicating with UDDI from Java and .Net programs, respectively. UDDI4J was originally developed by IBM and released in early 2001 as an open source initiative. Later, HP joined and contributed to the initiative, developing much of the version 2 release. With the support of IBM and HP (as well as others), UDDI4J has become the de facto standard Java package for communicating with UDDI registries. More information about UDDI4J, including the latest releases and download bundles, can be found at the UDDI4J Project Web site at http://www-124.ibm.com/developerworks/oss/uddi4j/.

Figure 4-5 shows how UDDI4J facilitates programmatic access to an UDDI registry. With UDDI4J, programmers don't have to concern themselves with either the UDDI API or with forming and parsing XML messages. Instead, a new Java object, `UDDIProxy`, is instantiated to act as a proxy and represent the actual UDDI registry. Using setter methods, the proxy object is configured with the URLs of the actual registry location, as well as optional transport information. Essentially, using UDDI4J and just a few, simple lines of code, a Java application can open a communications channel to any UDDI registry.

```
// Create a new UDDIProxy object to connect to a registry
UDDIProxy proxy = new UDDIProxy ();

// Set the inquiry and publish URLs
proxy.setInquireURL (INQUIRE_URL);
proxy.setPublishURL (PUBLISH_URL);
```

Figure 4-5 Opening a connection to an UDDI registry using UDDI4J.

Once we've created the proxy object and set its inquire and publish URLs to the desired UDDI registry locations, we can use the methods that are defined for the `UDDIProxy` object to access and set various elements within the registry. Usually, programmers will use the `find_business`, `find_service`, and `find_tModel` methods to locate service providers, services, and `tModels`, respectively, based on search criteria, such as name (including partial names with wildcards) and categories.

Figure 4-6 shows a complete application using UDDI4J to connect to Microsoft's UDDI Business Registry (UBR) inquiry node and locate service providers whose name includes the string "abc". After an `UDDIProxy` proxy object for Microsoft's UBR inquiry node is set up, the `find_business` method is invoked to search for available business names that contain the substring "abc". The wildcard character '%' is used to specify that the substring may occur anywhere in the business name. Qualifiers, such as case-sensitive string matching, could have been added to the `find_business` method to further limit the search.

```
/**
 * The AccessUDDI class implements a simple application
 *  that connects to Microsoft's UBR inquiry node,
 *  searches for service providers that have the string
 *  "abc" in their name and displays to the standard
 *  output the business name, the business description,
 *  and the names of all services provided by that
 *  business.
 */

import org.uddi4j.client.UDDIProxy;
import org.uddi4j.datatype.Name;
import org.uddi4j.response.BusinessInfo;
import org.uddi4j.response.BusinessList;
import org.uddi4j.response.ServiceInfo;
import java.util.Vector;

public class AccessUDDI
{
   public static void main ( String[] args )
   {
      int i = 0;
      int j = 0;

      UDDIProxy proxy = new UDDIProxy ();
      try
      {
         // Set the inquiryURL
         proxy.setInquiryURL
            ( "http://uddi.microsoft.com/inquire" );

         // Look for names that include "abc"
         Vector names = new Vector ();
         names.add ( new Name ( "%abc%" ) );
```

Figure 4-6 Using UDDI4J to access an UDDI Registry to print out 21 providers that include the string "abc" in their names.

```
         // Search the UDDI registry
         BusinessList results =
            proxy.find_business (
               names,
               null,
               null,
               null,
               null,
               null,
               21 );

         Vector businessInfoVect = results.getBusinessInfos
().getBusinessInfoVector ();

         System.out.println ( "Results are:" );

         for ( i = 0 ; i < businessInfoVect.size () ; i++ )
         {
            BusinessInfo businessInfo = ( BusinessInfo )
businessInfoVect.elementAt ( i );

            System.out.println ( "\nName: " +
businessInfo.getNameString () );
            System.out.println ( " ... Description: " +
businessInfo.getDefaultDescriptionString () );

            Vector serviceInfoVect =
businessInfo.getServiceInfos ().getServiceInfoVector ();
            for ( j = 0 ; j < serviceInfoVect.size () ; j++ )
            {
               ServiceInfo servInfo = ( ServiceInfo )
serviceInfoVect.elementAt ( j );
               System.out.println ( " ... Service Name: " +
servInfo.getNameString () );
            }
         }
      }
      catch ( Exception e )
      {
         e.printStackTrace ();
      }
   }
}
```

Figure 4-6 Using UDDI4J to access an UDDI Registry to print out 21 providers that include the string "abc" in their names (continued).

Once the results of the search are returned from the UDDI registry, additional method calls are used to extract the business name, business description, and service names for all matching businesses. This information is then displayed on the standard output. Figure 4-7 shows a selected subset of the output of the application shown in Figure 4-6.

```
Results are:

Name: abc
 ... Description: null

Name: ABC Corporate Services
 ... Description: A travel services company serving the agent
and hotel segments of the industry.
 ... Service Name: Traveler's Emergency Service System (TESS)
 ... Service Name: Premier Hotel Program (PHP)
 ... Service Name: Global Connect

Name: abc Enterprise
 ... Description: test object
 ... Service Name: Deutsche Telekom Productshow
 ... Service Name: Deutsche Telekom Shopping
 ... Service Name: Deutsche Telekom T-Mobil
 ... Service Name: Deutsche Telekom T-Online

Name: abc inc
 ... Description: test desc

Name: ABC Insurance
 ... Description: null

Name: ABC Microsystems
 ... Description: ?~~ ?? ?? ??...???...
 ... Service Name: <New Service Name>

Name: ABC Music
 ... Description: null
 ... Service Name: List Instruments

Name: ABC travel agency
 ... Description: travel buses for goa,bombay,delhi.

Name: abc123
 ... Description: null
 ... Service Name: bogus service

Name: CompanyABC
 ... Description: null

Name: IntesaBci Sistemi e Servizi
 ... Description: IntesaBci Sistemi e Servizi co-ordinate all of
Bank IntesaBci's operations with regard to the development and
management of IT and telecommunication systems
 ... Service Name: Home Page
```

Figure 4-7 A subset of the result of running the application shown in Figure 4-6.

Looking at the output of Figure 4-7, we can see some of the positive as well as some of the negative points of using the UDDI UBR. First, there are many service providers available within the UBR providing an even larger number of services. These are global providers, and some only offer their services in certain locations. Many of the fields of service providers or services are either unfilled or filled inappropriately. Moreover, many of these service providers or services are either non-existent or simply test deployments.

The UBR is a powerful resource that brings together thousands of providers and services in one easy-to-access location. Sifting through this large (and constantly growing) list to weed out useful providers and services from those that are less than useful (or completely useless) is the difficult part. Although client-side packages such as UDDI4J make developing programs to access and interact with UDDI registries easier, the more important difficulty still remains: how to select the right service and service provider for a given task.

How UDDI Is Playing Out

Now that we have an understanding of the need that UDDI aims to fill, some of the core data structures of UDDI, as well as the variety of the means of communicating with an UDDI registry, it's worth taking a step back to see how UDDI is really playing out. How UDDI will truly be used by companies will determine how, when, where, and why businesses will register their Web services.

Up until now our discussion of UDDI has focused on its analogous behavior with standard telephone directory books: UDDI provides a listing of businesses and the services each business offers as well as a means of searching and discovering Web services to use within consuming applications. Since this usage of UDDI is during the design of applications, it can be referred to as the *design-time* use.

But, will people really use the UDDI APIs during design time? Are people using it today? The answer is not really, and it does not look like it'll change any time in the foreseeable future. Most developers don't programmatically search UDDI for Web services to consume.

Will this change in the future? Most likely not, because selecting which service to consume is difficult. It's not technical issues, but instead business and strategic issues that make the selection process difficult.

In selecting a Web service to use, there may exist business relationships and legal agreements that have to be honored. This may sometimes involve selecting a technically inferior service in order to meet such obligations. There may be pending customer deals that can be closed by using a particular vendor's Web services. A company may attempt to pressure another company by withholding patronage of the latter company's Web services.

Basically business, strategic, and sometimes political issues come into the service selection process. Replacing human intervention through a programmatic API is usually insufficient, and oftentimes grossly so. Because of the wide mix of issues that are often involved, technologists alone will also be insufficient. Accordingly, business analysts, consultants, and other such people (possibly in conjunction with technologists) will usually be responsible for the Web services selection process. These business analysts and consultants will not use the direct programmatic interface of UDDI to search for available services, but instead will use more human-friendly means. These include Web services portals, the home pages provided by some of the UBR node operators, and standard search engines. Of course, word-of-mouth and other such non-technical means will also be prevalent. So, for all intents and purposes, UDDI's programmatic API will probably play a minor role during the design of applications.

If not in the design of applications, where will UDDI play a larger and more prominent role? Although seldom mentioned and even less understood, UDDI has a role larger than just at design time; UDDI is also useful at run time.

UDDI and Lifecycle Management

To understand the usefulness of UDDI at run time, consider the issues that developers and companies have to grapple with after they have developed a Web service or an application that consumes Web services.

Once a Web service has been developed and deployed, it not only has an interface specification but also a network location (usually a URL) associated with it. Over time, the deployment that had sufficed when the service was new and relatively under used, may require changes. This could include migration of the service to a new server. Multiple geographical mirror servers may also be deployed as the need to scale the service increases, or a new server location may be launched while the original one is taken offline for maintenance. The organization or division maintaining the Web service may be relocated or sold, thereby necessitating an update to its access endpoint information. How can these changes be propagated to applications that have already been designed to consume the original Web service? Without appropriate dissemination of such changes, applications consuming the original service can malfunction or produce erroneous transactions.

An application that consumes Web services has to contend with similar issues. Once an application has been written to use a specific Web service for a particular part of its functionality, the application's capability with respect to that part of its functionality is dependent on the Web service. If the Web service goes down or is unavailable for some time, that part of the application will also not function, possibly causing erroneous behavior throughout the application.

Applications based on Web services need a mechanism to stay updated with the latest access endpoint information, including changes to older endpoints, for a particular Web service. It is precisely in this need for lifecycle management of applications and Web services where UDDI can play a critical role. Web services need to disseminate changes to applications that call them. Applications need to be made aware of these changes. UDDI can play the runtime broker or middleman in handling and propagating these changes. The steps in this lifecycle management scenario proceed as follows:

1. Locate a Web service that fulfills the application's needs using whatever means that are useful, including portals, service aggregators, or programmatically with an UDDI registry directly.
2. If the Web service was not initially discovered within an UDDI registry, locate the same service within an UDDI registry and save (e.g., in a database) the `bindingTemplate` information.
3. Develop the application to consume the Web service using the information from the saved `bindingTemplate` information.
4. If the Web service call fails or exceeds an application-specified time-out, query the UDDI registry for the latest information on that Web service.
5. In case the original Web service call failed, compare the latest binding information for that Web service with the saved information. If the latest binding information for the Web service is different from the saved information, then save the new binding information, and retry the Web service call.
6. In the case that the original Web service call exceeded a time-out, compare the latest binding information for that Web service with the saved information. If the information is different or newer access endpoints are available, select another endpoint. The selection procedure may be manual in which the application allows the user to manually choose, or it may be automatic.

In this scenario, UDDI plays a critical role in maintaining the reliability and quality-of-service of both applications and the Web services they consume throughout their lifecycle.

The subset of a simple application that demonstrates the use of UDDI at runtime is shown in Figure 4-8. This code snippet uses the UDDI4J client-side Java API, does not do any error checking and also assumes a simple binding described by the UDDI registry.

Once a Web service invocation fails, the application tries to determine whether the binding information for the service has changed. If it has changed, the new binding information can be incorporated into the Web service call and the service can be retried. Otherwise, an error has to be thrown notifying the user that the service is unavailable.

The application begins by retrieving the binding information for the saved binding key by using the `get_bindingDetail` method. From the `BindingDetail` object, the program extracts the latest access point URL for the Web service. By comparing the latest access point information stored in `newAccessPoint` with the original access point information stored in `accessPoint`, the program is able to determine whether the cause of the service invocation failure was due to a change in the service's binding information. If new binding information is available, the program updates the `accessPoint` variable with the latest information and sets the `retryService` to true indicating that the service call can now be retried. If no new binding information is available, then the service is unavailable and there is no need to retry the service call. The program sets `retryService` to false.

```
// The Web service invocation failed, so check to see
//  whether new binding information is available. If so,
//  retry the Web service call.

BindingDetail bd = proxy.get_bindingDetail ( bindingKey );

Vector btvect = bindingDetail.getBindingTemplateVector ();
BindingTemplate bt = ( BindingTemplate )
                                 btvect.elementAt ( 0 );
newEndpoint = bt.getAccessPoint ().getText ();

if ( thisEndpoint.equalsIgnoreCase ( newEndpoint ) )
{
   // In this case, the endpoint information has changed
   //  so we should retry the Web service invocation with
   //  with the new endpoint

   thisEndpoint = newEndpoint;
   retry = true;
}
else
{
   // In this case, the endpoint information has not
   //  changed so there no reason to retry the Web
   //  service invocation

   retry = false;
}
```

Figure 4-8 Retrying Web service invocations based on dynamic UDDI information.

UDDI and Dynamic Access Point Management

As we've already alluded to, UDDI at runtime can be used not only to get an updated access point URL, but also to dynamically manage and select the most appropriate access point. Oftentimes, a Web service will be deployed on multiple machines that have different characteristics. These characteristics can differ by geographical locations and amount of server resources, including type of network connectivity.

Usually, this variety of service deployments is dynamic, that is, the Web service is initially deployed on a single server. Later, as the service becomes more popular and demand increases, additional access points are deployed. These deployments may be a cluster of servers in close proximity to each other, a geographically distributed set of servers, or both.

A client application that consumes the Web service may have been developed before the additional access points were deployed. Or the best service at the time the application was developed is no longer the best or the most appropriate. For example, the client application may have been developed in one country and later used in another country. Hardwiring the service access point to the one that was selected at design time (in a country other than where the application is being used) will needlessly increase the latency of the service invocation. Mobile applications are most vulnerable to this situation as the application may be best suited to a different access point as the mobile user moves from location to location.

Managing the Web service access points used by a client application becomes increasingly important. It's not that the application will not work with a hardwired access point (assuming the access point remains operational for the life of the application). Instead, the application may potentially work better.

Selecting and managing access points is analogous to downloading files from different mirror sites. A user can certainly download all her content from a single site. But, by judicious selection of different mirror sites, the user can achieve improved performance. The selection of Web service access points can be manual in which the application user is given the ability to choose the actual access point, or the application may automatically select an access point by consulting an UDDI registry. Alternately, the user may specify the high-level characteristics and metrics that are most important to him, with the application using those characteristics as hints in determining the most appropriate service access points. Refer to Chapter 10 for a more in-depth discussion of quality-of-service issues and Web services.

The careful reader will have recognized that some of the benefits of UDDI at run time can also be obtained from alternate means. Using databases, configuration files and other registries are some obvious alternatives. Although other solutions are possible, using UDDI is preferable as it is a standards-based solution with tremendous support from the software industry. The most important benefit of using a standards-based solution with industry-wide support such as UDDI is that almost all Web services can be used. With non-standard solutions, the Web service vendor must also publish its information using the same means used by the application vendor. In cases where a single vendor owns and has administrative control over both the services and the applications, such a solution is manageable. When the service vendors and application vendors are different, a standard solution fosters the use of a variety of Web services.

Figure 4-9 summarizes the use of UDDI at both the design time as well as the run time of Web services-based applications. As the figure depicts, interactions with UDDI at design time will usually include manual intervention from a variety of sources, such as business analysts, consultants, strategists, and technologists to determine the most appropriate Web service. It is important to note that the "most appropriate" service may not be the highest performance service. At run time, however, there is plenty of opportunity to leverage the direct programmatic access of UDDI to build applications that dynamically select the "best" service deployment (from the "most appropriate" service that was determined in the design phase).

In this section, we have discussed just a few uses of UDDI at application run time. Many more uses are possible. In particular, as UDDI matures and more information is made available through UDDI registries, additional opportunities to build more robust and flexible applications will emerge. When developing applications that consume Web services, if developers find themselves hardwiring information particular to a specific service into their applications, alarm bells

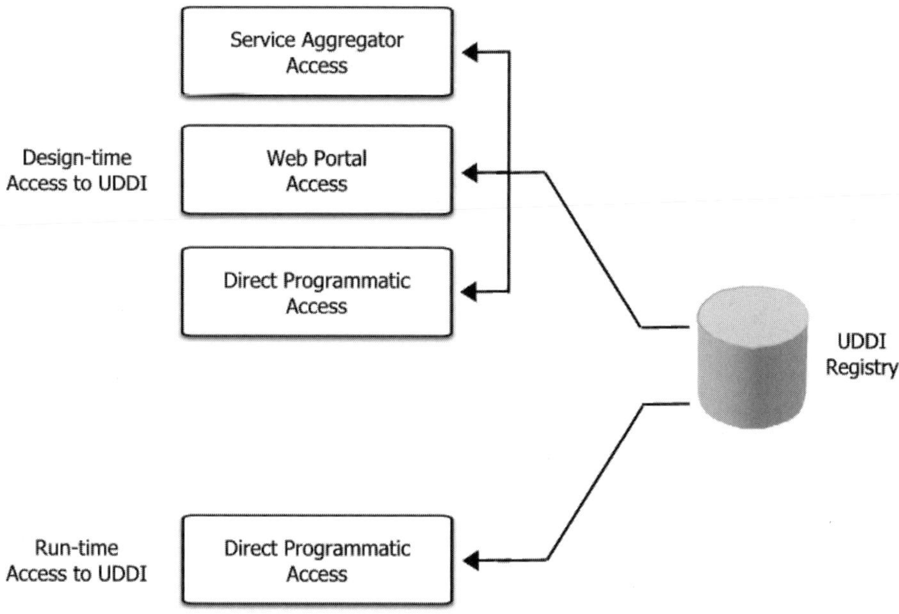

Figure 4-9 The use of UDDI at both design time and run time.

should immediately sound. They must ask themselves whether it is possible to eliminate the direct dependency on a particular service with an indirect and flexible "brokered" access through UDDI.

Summary

UDDI is an industry standard for a platform-independent and flexible means of describing, discovering and integrating services as well as the businesses that provide the services. As we have seen, UDDI has many similarities to telephone books, and provides users a means to search for Web services as well as service provider businesses.

The UBR is a global implementation of the UDDI specification and provides a publicly accessible registry of Web services. Currently, IBM, Microsoft, SAP, and NTT provide UBR nodes where users can register their Web services and make them available to a global market.

Although the UDDI specification provides a programmatic API to publish Web services to a UDDI registry and also to inquire about which services and service providers are available, most service selection issues at design time will require human intervention, thus reducing the usefulness of an automatic, programmatic interface. The business, strategic, and sometimes political issues that come into the service selection process will usually require business analysts and strategic consultants to play a critical role in the service selection process. Accordingly, during the design of an application, more human-friendly means to service selection including aggregation portals such as XMethods, Internet search engines such as Google, word of mouth, and UBR home pages, will be critical.

Instead of its much-hyped role at application design time, UDDI plays a more useful role at application runtime. Applications based on Web services need a mechanism to stay updated with the latest access endpoint information for a particular Web service. Conversely, Web services need a means to broadcast to applications that are already consuming them additional capabilities and resources. UDDI registries and the global UBR implementation provide such capabilities, and can play a critical role in the lifecycle of Web services and the applications that consume them.

UDDI is an important technology with useful capabilities. These capabilities must be properly positioned within the limitations of businesses and the usual operations of partner interactions. As we have discussed, with the right positioning, UDDI forms a core piece of the enterprise Web services platform.

Architect's Notes

- Today, most Web services are discovered through non-programmatic means using manual, human intervention. Similar to the way companies scrutinize potential partner companies prior to committing to a strategic relationship, selecting services to use within enterprise applications requires significant due diligence. Manual intervention by business analysts, consultants, and others familiar with the company's business and strategic needs will almost always be required for selecting services. The most common sources of locating Web services are existing business partners, UBR home pages, service aggregators such as XMethods, or standard Web search engines such as Google.
- The UDDI Business Registry (UBR) is a distributed, public registry containing thousands of service providers and even more services. Sifting through this large (and constantly growing) list to weed out useful providers and services from those that are less than useful (or completely useless) is the biggest drawback and the major difficulty of using such public resources.
- Enterprise UDDIs and other such private (or semi-private) UDDIs that support and facilitate easy access to Web services and other resources within an organization will provide direct value. Typical use cases for UDDI within organizations will be to support and manage reuse of programmatic resources throughout an extended enterprise, as well as to dynamically configure and customize an application by changing attributes within the UDDI.
- Using client-side API packages such as UDDI4J and Microsoft's UDDI SDK facilitate developing programs that access UDDI registries, and also insulate applications from specification changes and differences between various registries.

- UDDI plays a critical and potentially larger role during the run time of applications. Typically, UDDI is seen as a means of discovering services at design time. UDDI also provides a convenient means to manage the lifecycle of Web services as well as the applications that consume them. Changes to information about a Web service can be pushed onto an UDDI registry, and applications that consume that service can be developed to be more reliable and robust by simply querying the UDDI registry for changes upon any invocation failures or other unexpected behavior.

PART 2

Advanced Web Services Technologies and Standards

The plain vanilla Web services technologies we have seen in Part 1 allow us to take disparate applications on a multitude of platforms written by a plethora of vendors and provides a simple, elegant solution to the kinds of problems that engineers and IT professionals encounter on a daily basis. However, up until now we have only seen the tip of the iceberg. And, each of these technologies really *can* do all that they promise. The problem is that once you cut through the hype, they actually don't promise a great deal.

Certainly, we are told that we can link systems together, and we can. We are also told that heterogeneous platforms aren't a problem any longer, and that is largely true, too. However, what the wave of Web services hyperbole manages to evade is the fact that plain vanilla Web services technology does not support the kinds of requirements that enterprises demand. Luckily, the plain vanilla Web services model can be extended to support these enterprise requirements.

In Part 2 of this book, we look at how to support the requirements placed on robust, enterprise-class applications. Although the Web services world is still settling into its groove, there are already a set of front-running technologies that can be used to address many of the enterprise requirements for Web services and Web services-based applications. Over the course of this section, we explore those technologies and show how they can be put to use today. We also describe the key Web service technologies and standards that can be used to address the following enterprise requirements:

Chapter 5: Conversations. WSDL is sufficient for describing the static aspects of a Web service's interface, but it does little in the way of prescribing the ordering of its operations. Many enterprise systems have both a static and an interactive aspect to their system interface. In this chapter we look at how to implement such system interfaces within the context of a Web services environment. More specifically, we look at how to "converse" with a Web service over successive invocations.

Chapter 6: Workflow. If a business is the sum of its processes, the orchestration and refinement of those processes is critical to an enterprise's continued viability in the marketplace.

Those businesses whose processes are agile and flexible will be able to adapt rapidly to and exploit new market conditions, while those businesses whose processes are poorly managed and inflexible will fall by the wayside. In this chapter we show how the application of workflow technology to Web services can support the creation of adaptive enterprise systems to support rapidly evolving business requirements.

Chapter 7: Transactions. A transaction, a critical component of dependable computing systems, is a unit of work that either succeeds completely or fails without leaving any side effects. A common example of a transaction use-case is where money is to be moved between bank accounts. In this case the goal is to ensure that the money both leaves the sender's account and is received by the recipient's account, or if something fails, for it to appear as if the transaction itself logically *never occurred*. In this chapter, we describe technologies that support transactions within a Web services environment, and develop schemes for supporting different levels of transactional integrity for loosely coupled and untrusted systems.

Chapter 8: Security. Security is a cornerstone of enterprise systems. Companies have confidential information and data that simply cannot be accessible—either maliciously or accidentally—by an unauthorized third-party. In this chapter we look at the security issues and attacks that are common to enterprises, including those security attacks that are in many ways facilitated within Web service environments. Then we describe the key technologies that can be used to address these security issues and prevent attacks.

Chapter 9: Quality-of-Service. Exposing a piece of business logic as a Web service is not difficult; architecting the system so that it meets the needs of potential users with respect to latency, performance, reliability, and so on is the hard part. In this chapter, we discuss quality-of-service (QoS) and how it pertains to Web services. We define the specific QoS metrics that are most often important in Web services, techniques to measure performance, and describe best practices and architectures for building Web services that support various QoS guarantees.

Chapter 10: Mobile and Wireless. Mobile and wireless devices have moved away from just a novelty within corporations to be critical tools within the arsenal of 24x7 enterprise operations. Many challenges exist in the development of mobile systems that are usually not an issue in the development of non-mobile systems. Issues such as application energy consumption, network bandwidth utilization, limited computational resources, and small form factor user interfaces all come together to make the design of mobile applications very difficult. In this chapter, we look at the issues that are inherent to the development of mobile systems, discuss the impact of Web services on mobile enterprise environments, and describe best practices for developing mobile Web service systems.

Chapter 11: Portals and Services Management. In this chapter, we look at two technologies that further position Web services as a critical foundation on which to build enterprise systems. Each of these two technologies is related to systems that exist today, but address issues arising from the use of Web services within those systems. The first one addresses how to build user-facing portals by simply aggregating back-end Web services, while the second addresses how to manage a growing number and type of Web services within enterprise environments.

After reading Part 2, you will have a strong understanding of many of the key requirements of enterprise systems and how to meet those requirements within a Web services environment using advanced technologies that are layered on top of the vanilla Web services platform. Refer to Section Three for a detailed, step-by-step guide and lots of sample source code to actually develop Web services and client applications using these higher-level technologies.

CHAPTER 5

Conversations

While WSDL is a capable technology for describing the static aspects of a Web service's interface, it does little in the way of prescribing the ordering of its operations. For a Web service to be truly self-describing, it requires both static and interactive aspects of the interface to be understood by its consumers—that is, how to "converse" with the service over successive invocations.

In the Web services arena, the first technology submitted to a standards body for describing the interactive behavioral aspects of a Web service is the Web Services Conversation Language (or WSCL). WSCL captures the conversation pattern that a Web service is expecting to engage in by describing the order in which its WSDL-described operations should be invoked.

In this chapter we explore the notion of a conversation and based on that experience, drill down into the features that WSCL provides. We demonstrate how WSCL constructs can be aggregated to build rich conversational patterns for Web service interactions. The chapter is drawn to a close with a discussion on how WSCL and WSDL can be used together to support truly automatic binding to Web services.

Conversations Overview

The notion of a conversation is not new in distributed computing systems (or for that matter to human society). Every day we engage in both structured, contextualized conversations such as negotiating for a beer at a bar, and unstructured ad hoc conversations such as asking a work colleague about his plans for the weekend. We are also quite used to having conversations with machines in the form of ATM transactions and similar things (shouting at the monitor when the computer "misbehaves" does not count as a conversation). Take for example a typical barroom scene as shown in Figure 5-1. This is a typical pub situation where a customer orders a drink and goes through a relatively structured conversation with a server. Although the context is well established, a computer system would not be able to cope well with such a scenario because of the wide range of mannerisms that people use when ordering drinks, nor would a computer system be able to help the "customer" that just popped into the bar for directions.

While it is impossible for an unintelligent computer system to partake in unstructured conversations, using an ATM shows that it is quite possible for a computer system to understand structured conversations within a particular context. While we could yell at the ATM until it did what we wanted, we might be in for a long wait since such an ad hoc, unstructured, and out-of-context conversation is unlikely to be understood. Conversely, yelling at our friendly barman, though usually uncalled for and running the risk of a punch in the nose, will result in a continuation of the conversation.

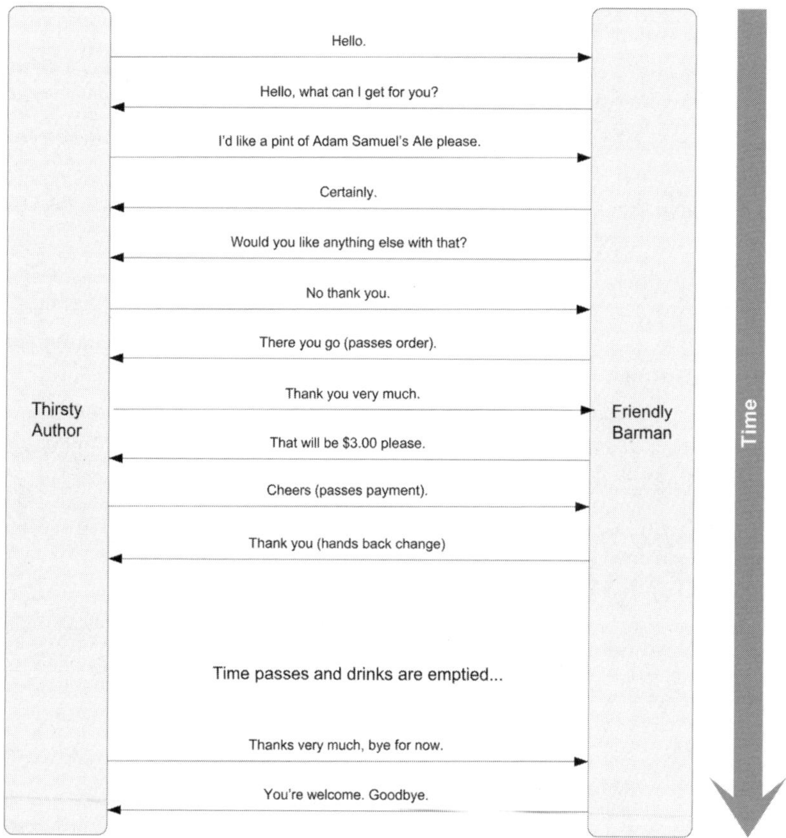

Figure 5-1 A simple inter-human conversation.

From these scenarios we can deduce that conversations are only meaningful in a computing system where the context is well established, and the number, type, and semantics of possible exchanges are known in advance by both parties involved. If either party digresses from the agreed conversation format, then the conversation simply falls apart.

Conversational Requirements for B2B Interactions

While SOAP and WSDL (see Chapter 3) are fine for single-shot exchanges between a client and a Web service, most B2B and B2C interactions of any real value involve multiple message exchanges. Indeed even the simple process of ordering a beer (as shown in Figure 5-1) involves several well-orchestrated message exchanges in order to succeed. It is precisely because typical Web services interactions are multi-phased that we need a mechanism to accurately orchestrate which party is required to send what message and when.

For an analogy to help understand Web services conversations, consider a typical soda vending machine such as that shown in Figure 5-2. While we are all, of course, implicitly familiar with how these kinds of machines work and take for granted the sequence of actions that are necessary to buy a drink from them, it is useful to think about just how this is actually achieved.

A typical vending machine actually has a number of buttons—coin/note slots, trays and so forth—that can be accessed by the user. In fact, the number of possible combinations of interactions with these machines is actually staggering, and only a few of them will result in a drink being dispensed.

This is rather like a Web service where we have operations exposed to the network that are analogous to the buttons and coin slots and so forth on the vending machine. A typical Web service will require its operations to be invoked in a certain order to progress the interaction through to completion. While on the vending machine we will often have a set of instructions that detail in which order money should be inserted, drink selected (or money reclaimed), and drink removed, our Web service's WSDL interface does not provide this additional meta-data (though it may well provide human-readable comments). To provide as rich an interface to Web services clients as vending machines do to their human clients, Web services must expose computer-readable descriptions of how they should be used, just like the human-readable descriptions posted on vending machines.

Of course to support conversations in Web services, we need a standard way of describing dependencies between operations in a standard, structured way. While natural languages might be implemented in user documentation or embedded as comments in a WSDL interface to aid a developer, this is generally not an approach that favors automation (which is ironic given the amount of tool support that exists to solve exactly this problem for WSDL interfaces). However, one proposed technology that seeks to redress the balance between static and dynamic descriptions of a Web service and thus enable conversations is the Web Services Conversation Language.

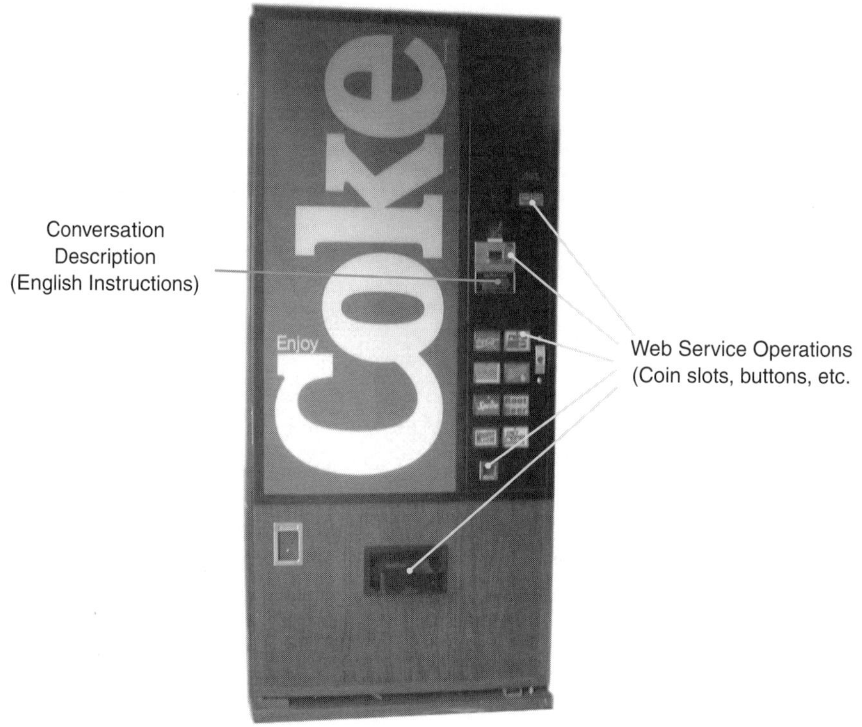

Figure 5-2 Rich interfaces consist of operations plus descriptive metadata.

Web Services Conversation Language

The rationale behind WSCL is that it captures the "time" dimension of Web services conversations and allows Web services to declare the conversation pattern through which they can be driven. WSCL is, at the time of writing, a W3C note submitted by the Hewlett-Packard Company. In January 2003, along with the process modeling language WSCI,[1] WSCL became one of the inputs for the W3C's Choreography working group.

1. See Chapter 6 for a detailed discussion of workflow and business process modeling.

Although WSCL is now providing a basis for future conversation standards, it remains in use today in its current form. For example, UDDI.org uses WSCL as its first proposed language for describing the interfaces of conversational Web services.[2]

The interaction between the consumer and provider of a service is achieved through XML document exchange where WSCL is used to orchestrate the various message exchanges that occur at each stage of the conversation. In fact, WSCL provides a means for declaring the types of messages that are exchanged, specifying the type of interaction that a message is used in (e.g. a one-way message from client-to-server, or a bilateral exchange), and the transition conditions that allow the conversation to progress from one interaction to the next.

Consuming WSCL Interfaces

Like WSDL, WSCL is an interface language designed to be consumed by Web services toolkits. Using both WSDL and WSCL, it is possible for toolkits to create proxies for Web services that not only encapsulate the remote operations and SOAP serialization aspects, but also provide structured help on the order in which operations should be invoked. That is, while WSDL provides message format and operation information, the WSCL description supports the creation of a conversation state machine that can guide the consumer of a Web service through its use. For example, consider the Java interfaces shown in Figure 5-3 and Figure 5-4.

```
public boolean login(String user, String pass);
public boolean buySong(String title, String artist);
public File pay(CreditCard cc);
```

Figure 5-3 A "Static" interface

Figure 5-3 shows the Java interface produced by consuming the WSDL of a simple MP3 vending service. For developers looking at this interface (or indeed the original WSDL interface), its use seems intuitively obvious. The user logs in, then tentatively buys a song which results in a unique token being presented, and then that token is used with credit card details to retrieve a file.

However, there is no way that an automatic system could have made the assumptions that we made to compile the interaction that is so simple for a human to undertake. Since humans are blessed with intuition and can deal well with ad hoc structures and arbitrary contexts, it is straightforward for us to reconstruct the state machine that represents this conversation—we are uniquely privileged insofar as even if we cannot second guess what this state machine is, we can simply read the documentation!

On the other hand, even if a computer system made guesses until it got the interactions correct, it would require on average 7.5 guesses to reach a correct guess for this simple interface (given there are 15 possible use combinations). If the number of methods increases, then the number of guesses needed skyrockets.

2. See http://www.uddi.org/pubs/wscl_TN_forUDDI_5_16_011.pdf for UDDI.org guidelines on using WSCL.

```
public boolean login(String user, String pass);
public boolean buySong(String title, String artist)
                      throws NotLoggedInException;
public File pay(CreditCard cc)
                      throws NoSongBoughtException;
```

Figure 5-4 A more "Conversational" interface.

Figure 5-4 is a much richer interface since with the exception declarations it is possible for the proxy that the toolkit generated from the WSCL description of the service to take care of much of the error handling of the conversation. A simple example of a conversation-aware proxy can be seen in Figure 5-5.

```
public boolean login(String user, String pass)
{
  // Login to service...

  _loggedIn = // The result of logging into the service
  return _loggedIn;
}

public boolean buySong(String title, String artist)
                                  throws NotLoggedInException
{
  if(!_loggedIn)
  {
    throw new NotLoggedInException();
  }

  // Buy song logic

  _token = // The token from the remote service
  return true;
}

public File pay(CreditCard cc) throws NoSongBoughtException
{
  if(_token == null)
  {
    throw new NoSongBoughtException();
  }

  // Retrieve the file

  return file;
}
```

Figure 5-5 A simple WSCL-based proxy implementation.

Although the approach adopted in the example of Figure 5-5 is simple, it does serve to show that a conversational interface can be used to guide the consumer's side of a conversation toward the correct interaction pattern for that service. Given a toolkit that supports WSCL and a service that describes itself with WSCL, we are already a significant way toward using conversations as part of our everyday Web services development.

At this point we can pause for breath, knowing that once again toolkits will make the consumption and application of WSCL straightforward. However, if we're developing rather than consuming a service, things aren't so simple. Given an arbitrary interface, it is highly unlikely that a piece of software can guess its conversation pattern and so, at some point, we will have to actually write WSCL (or at least provide assistance to a tool that creates valid WSCL for us). That means we have to drill down into the WSCL syntax and semantics and see for ourselves exactly how it works.

WSCL Interface Components

A WSCL interface is both complimentary and similar in spirit to its associated WSDL description. Like WSDL, a WSCL interface starts off simple and gradually builds up its description stage by stage until a whole conversation pattern is formed, ready for consumption on the Web. Our discussion on WSCL will follow the same pattern. Using the bar scenario as our example, we will start at the abstract sections of the WSCL interface and work our way through to a full-fledged conversation.

Interactions

An interaction with a conversational Web service is modeled as an XML document exchange whose flow is seen from the point of view of the service being invoked. WSCL supports four distinct message exchange patterns.

- `Send`—The service creates a one-way message that is sent to the consumer and expects no correlated response from that consumer.
- `Receive`—The service expects to receive a message from the consumer, while the consumer expects no message back in return.
- `SendReceive`—The service initiates a bilateral message exchange with the consumer, for which it expects a correlated response.
- `ReceiveSend`—The service expects to receive a message from the consumer to which it will respond.

In our bar scene example there are seven interactions that comprise no fewer than 13 exchanged messages, as we see in Figure 5-6. Even though 13 messages is not a small number of exchanges just to order a beer, this situation can be much more complicated if, for example, the drink that the customer wants is out of stock, or the customer tenders insufficient money to pay for the drinks.

The diagram shown in Figure 5-6 separates the conversation between the "thirsty author" and "friendly barman" endpoints into seven distinct interactions. In addition, those parts of the conversation where further progression is conditional on past execution have been highlighted where:

- The customer has selected a drink the barman cannot offer and until that situation is resolved, the barman is unable to accept further drink requests.
- The customer and the barman are unable to wish each other farewell until all drinks have been paid for.

Although the conversation represented in Figure 5-6 is necessarily simple, it shows all forms of possible interactions supported by WSCL. The interactions have been specifically fac-

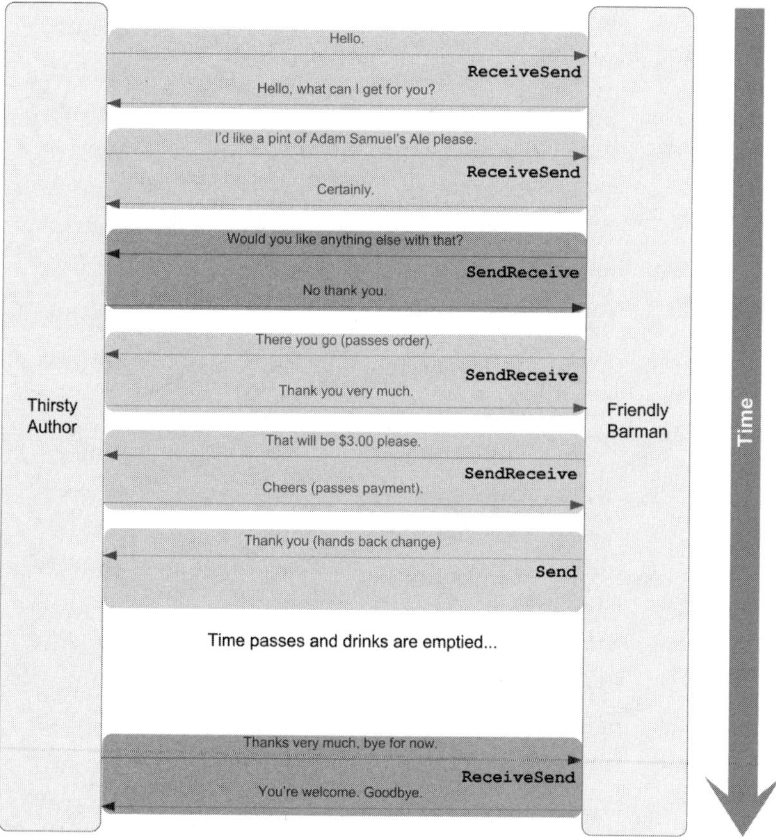

Figure 5-6 Determining the interaction types of the conversation.

tored this way to allow iteration within the conversation should it be necessary. For instance, during the sendReceive interaction where the "friendly barman" asks whether the "thirsty author" would like anything to extend his order, we reached a natural point in the conversation where the previous interactions could be repeated to order several drinks.

Using Figure 5-6 as the basis for our conversation, we can now progress to designing the messages exchanged by the parties and ordering those messages within interactions. In our bar scenario, the messages within the conversation deal with two types, namely beer and money, where broadly speaking messages are passed between the two conversation participants which amount to the fact that beer is exchanged for money. Figure 5-7 and Figure 5-8 show the implementations of the beer and money types as XML Schema schemas that are referenced within the messages exchanged during the interactions of the conversation.

```
<?xml version="1.0" encoding="UTF-8"?>
<xs:schema xmlns:xs="http://www.w3.org/2001/XMLSchema"
  elementFormDefault="qualified"
  xmlns:b="http://drinks.example.org/beer"
  targetNamespace=" ">
  <xs:complexType name="beer">
    <xs:sequence>
      <xs:element name="name" type="xs:string"/>
      <xs:element name="brewer" type="xs:string"/>
    </xs:sequence>
    <xs:attribute name="domestic" type="xs:boolean"
      use="required"/>
  </xs:complexType>
  <xs:element name="beer" type="b:beer"/>
</xs:schema>
```

Figure 5-7 Defining the "Beer" schema.

```
<?xml version="1.0" encoding="UTF-8"?>
<xs:schema xmlns:xs="http://www.w3.org/2001/XMLSchema"
  elementFormDefault="qualified"
  xmlns:m="http://money.example.org"
  targetNamespace="http://money.example.org">
  <xs:complexType name="money">
    <xs:sequence>
      <xs:element name="currency" type="xs:string"/>
      <xs:element name="value" type="xs:decimal"/>
    </xs:sequence>
  </xs:complexType>
  <xs:element name="money" type="m:money"/>
</xs:schema>
```

Figure 5-8 Defining the "Money" schema.

Once the XML schema types involved in the conversation are declared and hosted at a URI addressable location, we can move on to designing the messages exchanged within the interactions. A subset of the messages for this conversation (enough to give a flavor of the full message set) are presented in the subsequent set of figures, starting with the initial CustomerGreetingMessage (Figure 5-9) and ending with the BillMessage (Figure 5-12) toward the end of the conversation, with some of the more interesting intermediate messages in between. It is assumed for the purposes of this example that the targetNamespace attribute of each schema also resolves to the location where that schema resides (and thus can be accessed by any WSCL interfaces through their hrefSchema attributes).

```
<?xml version="1.0" encoding="UTF-8"?>
<xs:schema targetNamespace=
"http://conversations.example.org/bar/CustomerGreetingMessage"
xmlns:xs="http://www.w3.org/2001/XMLSchema"
elementFormDefault="qualified"
attributeFormDefault="unqualified">
  <xs:element name="CustomerGreetingMessage">
    <xs:simpleType>
      <xs:restriction base="xs:string">
        <xs:enumeration value="Hello"/>
      </xs:restriction>
    </xs:simpleType>
  </xs:element>
</xs:schema>
```

Figure 5-9 The CustomerGreetingMessage schema.

Figure 5-9 shows the schema for the customer's initial message to the bar service. The content of the message is simply the string Hello (which is aimed at helping any human readers of the message understand its intent, rather than any WSCL-aware software agent since for those components the message type is sufficient for its purpose).

Figure 5-10 is the response to the CustomerGreetingMessage, the StaffGreetingMessage which contains string content that helps any human readers of the message to understand its intent in the form of "Hello, how may I help you?" On receipt of this message, both parties are effectively agreed that they are both engaged in the conversation.

Since the primary goal of using the bar service is to order a drink, it is satisfying to see the message exchange that achieves this conversation goal. The order message, called CustomerOrderMessage is shown in Figure 5-11. It uses the previously declared beer type from Figure 5-7 to convey to the bar service the type of drink required.

Toward the end of the conversation, the bar service must account for any drinks dispensed and issues a bill to the consumer. Figure 5-12 shows the message sent from the bar service to the consumer to request payment for the ordered drinks. In this case, the message makes use of the

```
<?xml version="1.0" encoding="UTF-8"?>
<xs:schema targetNamespace=
"http://conversations.example.org/bar/StaffGreetingMessage"
xmlns:xs="http://www.w3.org/2001/XMLSchema"
elementFormDefault="qualified"
attributeFormDefault="unqualified">
  <xs:element name="StaffGreetingMessage">
    <xs:simpleType>
      <xs:restriction base="xs:string">
        <xs:enumeration value="Hello, how may I help you?"/>
      </xs:restriction>
    </xs:simpleType>
  </xs:element>
</xs:schema>
```

Figure 5-10 The `StaffGreetingMessage` schema.

```
<?xml version="1.0" encoding="UTF-8"?>
<xs:schema targetNamespace=
"http://conversations.example.org/bar/CustomerOrderMessage"
xmlns:xs="http://www.w3.org/2001/XMLSchema"
xmlns:b="http://drinks.example.org/beer"
elementFormDefault="qualified"
attributeFormDefault="unqualified">
  <xs:element name="CustomerOrderMessage" type="b:beer"/>
</xs:schema>
```

Figure 5-11 The `CustomerOrderMessage` schema.

```
<?xml version="1.0" encoding="UTF-8"?>
<xs:schema targetNamespace=
    "http://conversations.example.org/bar/BillMessage"
    xmlns:xs="http://www.w3.org/2001/XMLSchema"
    xmlns:m="http://money.example.org"
    elementFormDefault="qualified"
    attributeFormDefault="unqualified">
  <xs:element name="BillMessage" type="m:money"/>
</xs:schema>
```

Figure 5-12 The `BillMessage` schema.

externally defined type `money`, which we defined previously in Figure 5-8. The corresponding message that conveys payment back to the service has a similar structure, but a different name of `BillPaymentMessage`.

Once we are happy with the messages that will be exchanged, we can begin to group these messages into the constituent interactions for the conversation. Each interaction in a WSCL message consists of a parent `Interaction` element that has attributes `interactionType` (one of those permitted interaction types: `Send`, `Receive`, `SendReceive`, and `ReceiveSend`) and a unique identifier. Within the `Interaction` element, a number of `InboundXMLDocument` and `OutboundXMLDocument` elements are embedded that define the messages to be sent or received. Within any individual `Interaction` element at most one `InboundXMLDocument` and one `OutboundXMLDocument` will be sent/received. The `InboundXMLDocument` and `OutboundXMLDocument` elements each contain a unique identifier and a `hrefSchema` attribute which references the schema that constrains the message. The attribute `hrefSchema` is optional, which allows the schema definition to be omitted in case of binary payload. This generic form can be seen in Figure 5-13.

```
<Interaction interactionType="<send, receive, etc>"
      id="<unique id for the interaction>" >
  <InboundXMLDocument hrefSchema="<schema URI>"
      id="<unique id for the inbound document>" />
  <OutboundXMLDocument hrefSchema="<schema URI>"
      id="<unique id for the outbound document>" />
</Interaction>
```

Figure 5-13 The general form of a WSCL interaction.

One significant limitation of the current WSCL W3C note is that the `hrefSchema` attribute is specified by the WSCL schema as `anyURI`, which means that messages can only be defined by directly Web-addressable resources. Therefore there is no way in which the messages defined in a WSDL document can be reused in a WSCL document since they are not addressable through a URI (though they are addressable through a `QName` or even could be made addressable through an XPath expression). Working within this limitation means that each of the messages that may be exchanged in a WSCL conversation, and indeed any XML Schema types used by those messages have to be accessible through a URI (which is likely to share its root path with the WSDL document of the service).

The interactions between the endpoints are specified in terms of the message we previously defined. Where in our human conversation we might expect the exchange along the lines of:

```
Thirsty author: Hello.

Friendly barman: Hello, what can I get you?
```

We would now expect their (rather less personal) WSCL interaction equivalents:

```
<Interaction interactionType="ReceiveSend" id="Greeting">
  <InboundXMLDocument hrefSchema=
      "http://conversations.example.org/bar/
CustomerGreetingMessage"
      id="CustomerGreetingMessage"/>
  <OutboundXMLDocument hrefSchema=
      "http://conversations.example.org/bar/
StaffGreetingMessage"
      id="StaffGreeting"/>
</Interaction>
```

Similarly, instead of the human interaction:

```
Friendly barman: That will be $3.00 please.

Thirsty author: Cheers (passes money to barman)
```

we have the WSCL interaction that captures this action:

```
<Interaction interactionType="SendReceive" id="Bill">
  <OutboundXMLDocument hrefSchema=
      "http://conversations.example.org/bar/BillMessage"
      id="BillMessage"/>
  <InboundXMLDocument hrefSchema=
      "http://conversations.example.org/bar/
BillPaymentMessage"
      id="Payment"/>
</Interaction>
```

which describes the barman service demanding payment from the customer service (the outbound `BillMessage` message), to which the customer service responds with payment (via the inbound `BillPaymentMessage` message).

> The fact that billing occurs after goods have been delivered is because the conversation takes place in a trusted environment (a pub in which if the customer leaves without paying, he will encounter an angry bouncer at the exit). Similarly, in trusted Web services-based trading environments where a system interacts with the systems of a partner, this approach also works (since businesses are used to sending invoices first and receiving payments later). However, in untrusted B2C and B2B conversations, it makes sense to take payments before releasing goods!

Although the interactions have been presented in an abbreviated form, the other interactions in this conversation are similar to those shown (all interactions are shown in the complete WSCL example at the end of this chapter). Knowing what interactions occur in the conversation, we can now move on to developing the transitions that dictate the overall flow of interaction between parties in this conversation.

Transitions

Having implemented our conversation types, its message set and its set of interactions, we can now go one stage further with our implementation and actually design the transitions that implement the state machine for this conversation—that is, actually get down to the business of ordering the interactions into a full-fledged conversation. For this, we use the communication pattern derived from Figure 5-6, which we have redrawn for clarity as a UML Activity Diagram in Figure 5-15. The activity diagram shows the possible states of the conversation and highlights the message exchanges at each state, along with the interaction patter. We have also taken the opportunity to tighten up the error handling aspects of the conversation so that no transitions permit the conversation to go wrong. This means that both orders that the barman cannot fulfill and any payment discrepancies (at least from the barman's perspective) will prevent the conversation from progressing until such matters are rectified.

Codifying such rules in WSCL is straightforward. Each `Transition` element in a WSCL document has the following form:

```
<Transition>
  <SourceInteraction href="{some interaction}"/>
  <DestinationInteraction href="{another interaction}"/>
  <SourceInteractionCondition href="{some message}"/>
    ... more conditions
</Transition>
```

Where the `Transition` element is a container for the following items:

- A previous interaction that has occurred referenced by a `SourceInteraction` element.
- The next interaction to occur references by the `DestinationInteraction` element.
- A number of `SourceInteractionCondition` elements that only allow this transition to occur if the referenced message was the last document sent (by the Web service) during the interaction.

While the concept of specifying the source and destination of a transition in WSCL is both obvious and straightforward to implement, the guarding against particular transitions with the

SourceInteractionCondition element is a little more tricky and subtle, allowing the conversation to constrain its transitions to arbitrary paths through the possible set of state transitions for particular conversations. Although there may be many legal paths through a conversation at first, the choices made as to which states we have been to may be used to constrain those that we may move to.

Figure 5-14 shows how the SourceInteractionCondition element can be used to guard against taking particular transitions in a conversation. The SourceInteractionCondition element that references an OutboundXMLDocument from an Interaction which must previously have been sent to allow the transition to occur and thus the use of SourceInteractionCondition is predicated on the existence of more than one possible OutboundXMLDocument for an Interaction. Note that the OutboundXMLDocument part of an interaction is used as opposed to the InboundXMLDocument part because the sender is implicitly aware of something that it sends, and may not be aware of something that it was intended to receive (for instance in a failure case).

In this example, the execution of future interactions InteractionX and InteractionY are guarded by the sending of specific OutboundXMLDocument messages, MessageA and MessageB respectively. Given the constraints specified by the SourceInteractionCondition, it is now illegal in this example conversation to move from InteractionX to InteractionY if InteractionX sent a MessageB message (and the same holds for InteractionZ and MessageA messages).

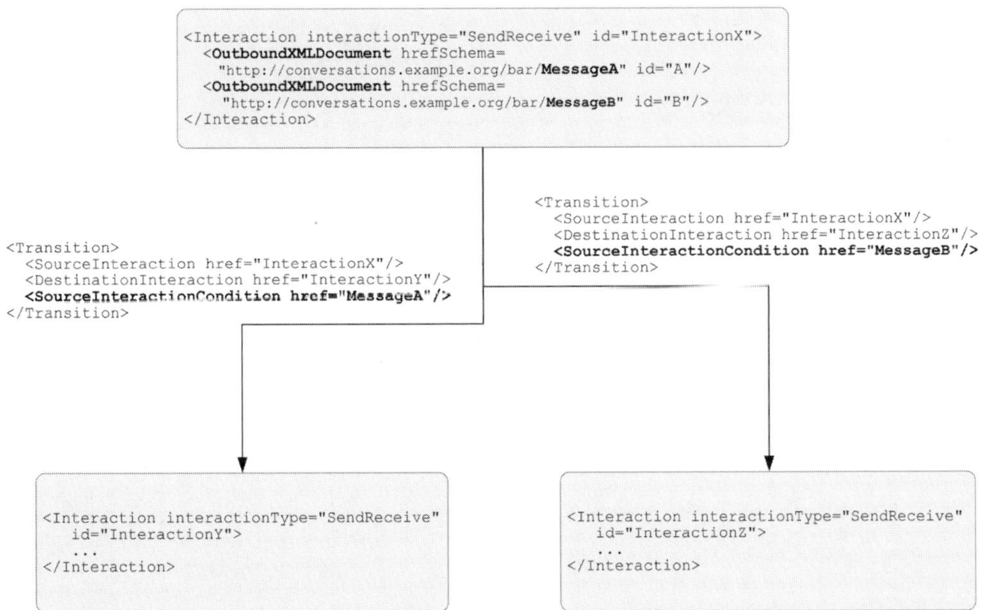

Figure 5-14 Guarding state transitions with SourceInteractionCondition elements.

Having understood the notion of an individual transition, we can now begin to build up a pattern of transitions which collectively define the conversation. For each transition identified in the conversation, an individual `Transition` element is declared in the WSCL interface, as is exemplified by the direct correspondence between each Transition element in our WSCL interface with each arrow in the activity diagram shown in Figure 5-15.

The conversation shown in Figure 5-15 moves from the (empty) `Start` state, to the `Greeting` state, to the `Order` state, after which time the customer is given a chance to augment the order on reaching the `ExtendOrder` state. Once the final order has been created, the conversation moves into the `Serve` state followed by the `Bill` state where drinks are paid for. Once a single order has been paid for, the customer has another chance to order drinks when the conversation moves to the `ReOrder` state. The conversation draws to an end when it moves from the `ReOrder` state to the `Goodbye` state, which results in the farewell messages being exchanged and the conversation ends in the (empty) `End` state.

Although the `Start` and `End` states do not appear in the human level conversation since the start and end of human conversations are implicit within the social protocols that we use, they are a feature of WSCL transitions which allows computing systems to understand the significance of the beginning and end of conversations in the same way. The upshot of this is that

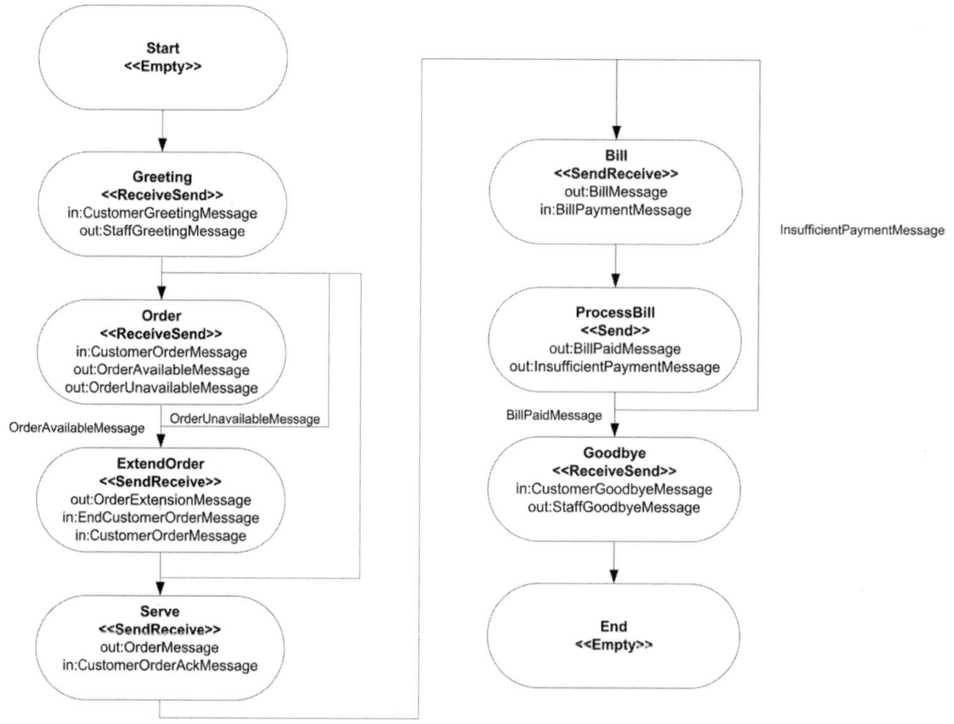

Figure 5-15 A UML activity diagram for the bar conversation.

every WSCL conversation should have at least one possible transition from the `Start` state into the actual conversation and, similarly, at least one transition from some state in the conversation to the `End` state.

> The WSCL specification does not mandate `Start` and `End` interactions, but as we shall see, it is good practice to use them to delineate the boundaries of conversations.

Having grasped the basics of WSCL `Transitions`, let's tackle the parts of the WSCL description that implement this simple UML activity. In Figure 5-15 we see that the interaction begins with a `ReceiveSend` operation that accepts a customer message and responds with a greeting from the barman. This transition causes the state to move from the special `Start` state to the `Greeting` state. The WSCL for this is shown below, and simply declares a source interaction and a destination interaction for this transition.

```
<Transition>
  <SourceInteraction href="Start"/>
  <DestinationInteraction href="Greeting"/>
</Transition>
```

Following the `Greeting` state, we transit to the `Order` state, which allows the transition to the part of the activity where the customer orders a drink.

```
<Transition>
  <SourceInteraction href="Greeting"/>
  <DestinationInteraction href="Order"/>
</Transition>
```

And so the conversation progresses until we arrive at the `Bill` state whose behavior is a little different since we have to deal with the constraint that a customer may not be billed without first having received the drinks. In our simple scenario, there is in fact no other way that the bill state can be reached without the customer having received the drinks. However in large, complex conversations, the ability to constrain access to a state based on activity in other parts of the conversation without having to contrive intricate transition paths is indeed a blessing. As such, the `SourceInteractionCondition` stays, not just as an example of its use, but as a means of increasing the robustness of the conversation in the face of future extensions.

```
<Transition>
  <SourceInteraction href="Serve"/>
  <DestinationInteraction href="ReOrder"/>
  <SourceInteractionCondition href="OrderMessage">
</Transition>
```

There is one important limitation to specifying transitions without SourceInteractionCondition: If there exists a transition from SourceInteraction A to DestinationInteraction B that specifies a SourceInteractionCondition, then it is not possible to also specify a transition from SourceInteraction A to DestinationInteraction B without a SourceInteractionCondition.[3] That is, if there is a SourceInteractionCondition present which guards the execution of a transition, that SourceInteractionCondition cannot be bypassed by clever "routing" of other transitions, which prevents our constraints from being undone by future extensions to the conversation.

Although it is the set of transitions which ultimately defines the set of permissible orders of interactions within a conversation, where there are choices in messages exchanged to trigger a transition, those choices are made by the logic residing in the application endpoints and are not expressed in WSCL. For instance, at the point in our example conversation where the customer decides whether to order another drink, the resulting message is produced as the result of some logic occurring in the customer's system (i.e., the thought, "Am I still thirsty?" is considered). Although the WSCL interface constrains the responses, it is not semantically rich enough to help with that decision. At the end of the day, a human programmer still has to understand any choices that can be made during the conversation.

Conversations

The Conversation part of the WSCL description draws together the messages, interactions, and transitions into the final conversation description. Our discussion of the conversation part of WSCL begins with its endpoints, how conversations are begun and ended.

The first and last interactions of the conversation are given special identifiers in the WSCL specification such that a software agent consuming a WSCL interface can readily determine how to start a conversation and figure out when it has finished. If we examine the conversation element that supports our bar example, we see the following (abbreviated) opening tag for the Conversation element:

```
<Conversation name="BarConversation"
  initialInteraction="Start"
  finalInteraction="End">
```

At this point it is worth pointing out that instead of the Start and End element being identified as the source and sink for the conversation, that the Greeting and Goodbye interactions could have been used. However, owing to the syntax of WSCL, it is only possible to specify a single initialInteraction and finalInteraction attribute for a conversation, though clearly it is possible to start and end a conversation in more than one way. In those cases where conversations can be struck up in a variety of ways, the Start and End interac-

3. This is taken from the WSCL 1.0 note at http://www.w3.org/TR/wscl10/.

tions can in effect act as a "multiplexer" between the possible paths in the conversation, and the single source/sink syntax of WSCL. Although our conversation can, at the moment, only be begun or ended in one way, using the `Start` and `End` element provides that comfortable level of indirection should the conversation be extended in the future.

This strategy can work because the `Start` and `End` interactions are of type `Empty`. An `Empty` interaction is one that does not send or receive any messages, and acts as a "silent" intermediate state between two or more other states. In an `Empty` interaction, the XML form of the interaction is devoid of any `InboundXMLDocument` or `OutboundXMLDocument` child elements, like so:

```
<Interaction interactionType="Empty" id="Start"/>
```

A possible conversation graph that shows this multiplexing behavior is presented in Figure 5-16.

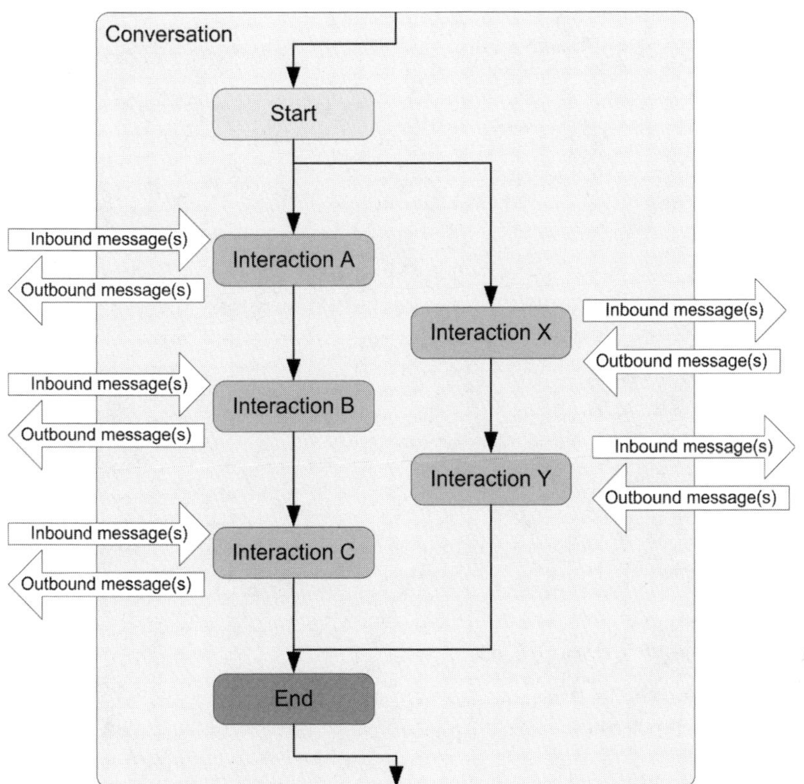

Figure 5-16 Multiplexing endpoints with empty `Start` and `End` interactions.

Figure 5-16 shows two possible starting and ending points for the conversation, and shows how the empty interactions "Start" and "End" (i.e., the two that have no inbound or outbound messages) are used to multiplex the two possible conversation streams. In the declaration for the conversation, only the "Start" and "End" interactions are referenced, while the other more sophisticated interactions remain encapsulated away from the root conversation. This provides two ways of starting and two of ending the conversation, while remaining consistent with the `Conversation` element's syntax.

Having understood the role of the empty interactions, we are now ready to see how the conversation itself is represented in WSCL, as shown in Figure 5-17.

```
<wscl:Conversation
  xmlns:wscl="http://www.w3.org/2002/02/wscl10"
  name="BarConversation" initialInteraction="Start"
  finalInteraction="End"
  targetNamespace="http://example.org/conversations/bar"
  description="Simple bar conversation" >
    <!--The rest of the conversation omitted -->
</wscl:Conversation>
```

Figure 5-17 The `Conversation` element.

The `Conversation` element for our bar example provides attributes that identify (`name`), optional version (`version`), and an optional annotation (`description`) for the conversation interface. In addition it declares the target namespace (`targetNamespace`) of the interface just like WSDL does, and identifies the schema (`hrefSchema`) which can be used to validate the document. The `name` attribute is a shared piece of information that both parties in the conversation use to ensure they both use the same conversation type. The value of the `name` attribute will also be propagated as part of a SOAP header in any of the messages exchanged within the context of the conversation to ensure correlation of conversation messages at both sides of the conversation. Of course, the root element's attributes also declare the entry and exit points of the conversation as we saw earlier.

The Bar Scenario Conversation

At this point we are ready to tackle an entire WSCL interface. Accordingly, the bar conversation is presented in full in Figure 5-18.

We've already covered all of WSCL, so the interface shown in Figure 5-18 doesn't hold any significant surprises. However, there are a number of elements whose function is interesting, particularly those `Interaction` elements that have multiple possible `OutboundXMLMessages` and the corresponding `Transition` elements which possess a `SourceInterac-`

```
<?xml version="1.0" encoding="UTF-8"?>
<wscl:Conversation
  xmlns:wscl="http://www.w3.org/2002/02/wscl10"
  name="BarConversation" initialInteraction="Start"
  finalInteraction="End"
  targetNamespace="http://example.org/conversations/bar"
  description="Simple bar conversation" >
  <!-- Declare the possible interactions that can occur.
  This effectively creates the arcs between the nodes in the
  conversation state machine. -->
  <wscl:ConversationInteractions>
    <wscl:Interaction id="Start" interactionType="Empty"/>
    <wscl:Interaction
         interactionType="ReceiveSend" id="Greeting">
      <wscl:InboundXMLDocument
           hrefSchema="http://conversations.example.org/bar/
CustomerGreetingMessage"
              id="CustomerGreeting"/>
      <wscl:OutboundXMLDocument
            hrefSchema="http://conversations.example.org/bar/
StaffGreetingMessage"
           id="StaffGreeting"/>
    </wscl:Interaction>
    <wscl:Interaction interactionType="ReceiveSend" id="Order">
      <wscl:InboundXMLDocument
             hrefSchema="http://conversations.example.org/bar/
CustomerOrderMessage"
           id="CustomerOrder"/>
      <wscl:OutboundXMLDocument
            hrefSchema="http://conversations.example.org/bar/
OrderUnavailableMessage"
         id="OrderUnavailable"/>
      <wscl:OutboundXMLDocument
             hrefSchema="http://conversations.example.org/bar/
OrderAvailableMessage"
           id="OrderAvailable"/>
    </wscl:Interaction>
    <wscl:Interaction interactionType="SendReceive" id="ExtendOrder">
      <wscl:OutboundXMLDocument
             hrefSchema="http://conversations.example.org/bar/
OrderExtensionMessage"
           id="OrderExtensionQuestion"/>
      <wscl:InboundXMLDocument
            hrefSchema="http://conversations.example.org/bar/
EndCustomerOrderMessage"
          id="EndCustomerOrder"/>
      <wscl:InboundXMLDocument
             hrefSchema="http://conversations.example.org/bar/
CustomerOrderMessage"
           id="AnotherCustomerOrder"/>
    </wscl:Interaction>
    <wscl:Interaction interactionType="SendReceive" id="Serve">
```

Figure 5-18 The complete WSCL bar conversation.

```
      <wscl:OutboundXMLDocument
              hrefSchema="http://conversations.example.org/bar/
OrderMessage"
           id="Drinks"/>
      <wscl:InboundXMLDocument
             hrefSchema="http://conversations.example.org/bar/
CustomerOrderAckMessage"
          id="Cheers"/>
    </wscl:Interaction>
    <wscl:Interaction interactionType="SendReceive" id="Bill">
      <wscl:OutboundXMLDocument
              hrefSchema="http://conversations.example.org/bar/
BillMessage"
           id="RequestPayment"/>
      <wscl:InboundXMLDocument
              hrefSchema="http://conversations.example.org/bar/
BillPaymentMessage"
           id="Payment"/>
    </wscl:Interaction>
    <wscl:Interaction interactionType="Send" id="ProcessBill">
      <wscl:OutboundXMLDocument
              hrefSchema="http://conversations.example.org/bar/
BillPaidMessage"
           id="BillSettled"/>
      <wscl:OutboundXMLDocument
           hrefSchema="http://conversations.example.org/bar/
InsufficentPaymentMessage"
        id="BillUnpaid"/>
    </wscl:Interaction>
    <wscl:Interaction interactionType="SendReceive" id="ReOrder">
      <wscl:OutboundXMLDocument
              hrefSchema="http://conversations.example.org/bar/
RepeatOrderMessage"
           id="MoreDrinksQuestion"/>
      <wscl:InboundXMLDocument
          hrefSchema="http://conversations.example.org/bar/
RepeatOrderDecisionMessage"
        id="MoreDrinksResponse"/>
    </wscl:Interaction>
    <wscl:Interaction interactionType="ReceiveSend" id="Goodbye">
      <wscl:InboundXMLDocument
              hrefSchema="http://conversations.example.org/bar/
CustomerGoodbyeMessage"
           id="CustomerGoodbye"/>
      <wscl:OutboundXMLDocument
              hrefSchema="http://conversations.example.org/bar/
StaffGoodbyeMessage"
           id="StaffGoodbye"/>
    </wscl:Interaction>
    <wscl:Interaction id="End" interactionType="Empty"/>
  </wscl:ConversationInteractions>
  <!-- Declare the conditions under which transitions can occur.
```

Figure 5-18 The complete WSCL bar conversation (continued).

```
  This effectively creates the guards which allow/prevent
  arcs from being traversed in the conversation state machine. -->
  <wscl:ConversationTransitions>
    <wscl:Transition>
      <wscl:SourceInteraction href="Start"/>
      <wscl:DestinationInteraction href="Greeting"/>
    </wscl:Transition>
    <wscl:Transition>
      <wscl:SourceInteraction href="Greeting"/>
      <wscl:DestinationInteraction href="Order"/>
    </wscl:Transition>
    <wscl:Transition>
      <wscl:SourceInteraction href="Order"/>
      <wscl:DestinationInteraction href="ExtendOrder"/>
      <wscl:SourceInteractionCondition href="OrderAvailable"/>
    </wscl:Transition>
    <wscl:Transition>
      <wscl:SourceInteraction href="Order"/>
      <wscl:DestinationInteraction href="Order"/>
      <wscl:SourceInteractionCondition href="OrderUnavailable"/>
    </wscl:Transition>
    <wscl:Transition>
      <wscl:SourceInteraction href="ExtendOrder"/>
      <wscl:DestinationInteraction href="Order"/>
    </wscl:Transition>
    <wscl:Transition>
      <wscl:SourceInteraction href="ExtendOrder"/>
      <wscl:DestinationInteraction href="Serve"/>
    </wscl:Transition>
    <wscl:Transition>
      <wscl:SourceInteraction href="Serve"/>
      <wscl:DestinationInteraction href="Bill"/>
    </wscl:Transition>
    <wscl:Transition>
      <wscl:SourceInteraction href="Bill"/>
      <wscl:DestinationInteraction href="ProcessBill"/>
    </wscl:Transition>
    <wscl:Transition>
      <wscl:SourceInteraction href="ProcessBill"/>
      <wscl:DestinationInteraction href="Bill"/>
      <wscl:SourceInteractionCondition href="BillUnpaid"/>
    </wscl:Transition>
    <wscl:Transition>
      <wscl:SourceInteraction href="ProcessBill"/>
      <wscl:DestinationInteraction href="Goodbye"/>
      <wscl:SourceInteractionCondition href="BillSettled"/>
    </wscl:Transition>
    <wscl:Transition>
      <wscl:SourceInteraction href="Goodbye"/>
      <wscl:DestinationInteraction href="End"/>
    </wscl:Transition>
  </wscl:ConversationTransitions>
</wscl:Conversation>
```

Figure 5-18 The complete WSCL bar conversation (continued).

tionCondition. Take for example the billing aspect of the conversation, which involves the following interactions:

```
<wscl:Interaction interactionType="SendReceive" id="Bill">
  <wscl:OutboundXMLDocument
         hrefSchema="http://conversations.example.org/bar/
BillMessage"
       id="RequestPayment"/>
  <wscl:InboundXMLDocument
         hrefSchema="http://conversations.example.org/bar/
BillPaymentMessage"
       id="Payment"/>
</wscl:Interaction>
<wscl:Interaction interactionType="Send"
       id="ProcessBill">
  <wscl:OutboundXMLDocument
         hrefSchema="http://conversations.example.org/bar/
BillPaidMessage"
       id="BillSettled"/>
  <wscl:OutboundXMLDocument
  hrefSchema="http://conversations.example.org/bar/
InsufficentPaymentMessage"
  id="BillUnpaid"/>
</wscl:Interaction>
```

These interactions show the back-and-forth of paying for drinks (with the possible error condition that the wrong amount is tendered) and are joined together by this transition:

```
<wscl:Transition>
  <wscl:SourceInteraction href="Bill"/>
  <wscl:DestinationInteraction href="ProcessBill"/>
</wscl:Transition>
<wscl:Transition>
  <wscl:SourceInteraction href="ProcessBill"/>
  <wscl:DestinationInteraction href="Bill"/>
  <wscl:SourceInteractionCondition href="BillUnpaid"/>
</wscl:Transition>
<wscl:Transition>
  <wscl:SourceInteraction href="ProcessBill"/>
  <wscl:DestinationInteraction href="Goodbye"/>
  <wscl:SourceInteractionCondition href="BillSettled"/>
</wscl:Transition>
```

These transitions describe the fact that the barman and the customer are allowed to go their separate ways once the bill has been settled. Importantly, the final transition from Process-Bill to Goodbye is guarded by a SourceInteractionCondition which declares that the `BillSettled` message must have been issued by the barman before the transition could occur.

Relationship Between WSCL and WSDL

The three main aspects of a Web service's interface are:

- Abstract interfaces: The application payload (in the form of messages) being exchanged and the order in which they are exchanged (which is known as choreography).
- Protocol bindings: The protocols used to enable the sending and receipt of messages.
- Services: The concrete service implementation that provides a network accessible address for a particular protocol at which the given message set is understood—i.e., the location of an instance of the Web service.

If we reflect on our experience with WSCL and our previous experience with WSDL, then it is clear (as we might expect from two technologies that are both Web service interface languages) that there is some overlap, as shown in Table 5-1:[4]

Table 5-1 WSDL and WSDL Complimentary Features

Aspect	Function	WSDL	WSCL
Abstract Interfaces	Choreography	N/A	Transition
	Messages	Operation	Interaction
Protocol Bindings		Binding	N/A
Concrete Services		Service	N/A

Where WSDL and WSCL overlap, we can map the different terminology used as shown in Table 5-2.

4. The following tables are taken from the W3C WSCL Note at http://www.w3.org/TR/wscl10/.

Table 5-2 Mapping WSDL to WSCL

WSDL	WSCL
Port Type	**Conversation**
Operation • One-way • Request-response • Solicit-response • Notification	Interaction • `Receive` • `ReceiveSend` • `SendReceive` • `Send`
Input	`InboundXMLDocument`
Output, Fault	`OutboundXMLDocument`
Operation name	`ID` attribute of `Interaction` element
Operation input	`ID` attribute of `InboundXMLDocument`
Operation output	`ID` attribute of `OutboundXMLDocument`
Message	URI (which references an external schema)

The WSCL specification suggests that there are three possible approaches for combining WSDL and WSCL into a single Web service interface, depending on which stage the development of the Web service interface has reached. These are:

1. Where only abstract aspects of the WSDL interface exist, a conversational binding can be added to the WSDL interface.
2. Where existing `portType` declarations have been written, a cut-down WSCL description consisting of `transition` elements which reference existing operations can be added.
3. If a fully-formed WSDL description has already been written, a separate, full WSCL interface can be created which simply references the messages from the original WSDL document.

If the abstract parts of the WSDL interface have been completed, then we are able to provide WSCL functionality simply by adding a protocol binding. This is shown in Figure 5-21 where a conversational binding is provided where the operations in that binding reference the interactions of a WSCL interface, in accordance with the mapping shown in Figure 5-19.

In Figure 5-19, the attribute `type="conv:BarServiceConversation"` binding element references the name of the conversation in our example WSCL document presented in Figure 5-18, while the names of each of the operations refers to the `ID` of the interactions, thus exposing the conversation as WSDL operations.

```
<?xml version="1.0" encoding="UTF-8"?>
<definitions name="BarService"
  xmlns="http://schemas.xmlsoap.org/wsdl/"
  targetNamespace=" http://example.org/wsdl/bar"
  xmlns:conv="http://example.org/conversations/bar" >
  <binding name="BarServiceConversationBinding"
    type="conv:BarServiceConversation">
    <soap:binding style="document"/>
    <operation name="conv:Greeting">
      <soap:operation soapAction="Greeting">
    </operation>
    <operation name="conv:Order">
      <soap:operation soapAction="Order">
    </operation>
  <!—Other operations omitted -->
  </binding>

  <service name="BarService">
    <port name="BarServicePort"
      binding="BarServiceConversationBinding">
      <soap:Address location="http://example.org/bar"/>
    </port>
  </service>
</definitions>
```

Figure 5-19 WSDL binding to WSCL conversation.

If the WSDL is already formed to the point where is has a `portType` definition, then we can bolt on the choreography aspects of the service with a cut-down WSCL description containing only the `Transition` elements. In this case we can simply map the `SourceInteraction` and `DestinationInteraction` elements of the `Transition` elements to the names of operations in the WSDL document, while any `SourceInteractionConditions` map to output or fault elements. Of course for this to work, WSCL would have to be equipped to reference elements in other documents (via `QNames` as we saw earlier). An example of this is shown in Figure 5-20.

The third and final method of combining WSCL and WSDL according to the WSCL specification is to simply provide full specifications for both, but where both interfaces share common messages. For instance the message declaration for Order in WSDL could simply refer to the same (externally defined) Order message that the WSCL interface uses, like so:

```
<message name="Order"
     xmlns:msg="http://conversations.example.org/bar/
CustomerOrderMessage">
     <part name="body" element="msg:OrderMessage" />
 </message>
```

```
<wsdl:definitions name="BarService"
  targetNamespace="http://example.com/bar/wsdl"
  xmlns:msg="http://example.org/conversations/bar">
<wsdl:portType name="OrderDrinkPortType">
  <wsdl:operation name="CustomerOrder">
    <wsdl:input name="Order"
         message="msg:CustomerOrderMessage"/>
    <wsdl:output name="OrderAvailable"
         message="msg:OrderAvailableMessage"/>
    <wsdl:fault name="Orderunavailable"
                    message="msg:OrderUnavailableMessage"/>
  </wsdl:operation>
</wsdl:portType>
...
</wsdl:definitions>

<wscl:Conversation
    ...
  targetNamespace="http://example.org/conversations/bar"
  xmlns:wsdl="http://example.com/bar/wsdl">

<wscl:Interaction interactionType="ReceiveSend"
  id="Order">
  <wscl:InboundXMLDocument name="wsdl:CustomerOrder"
       id="CustomerOrder"/>
  <wscl:OutboundXMLDocument name="wsdl:OrderAvailable"
       id="OrderUnavailable"/>
  <wscl:OutboundXMLDocument name="wsdl:OrderUnavailable"
       id="OrderAvailable"/>
</wscl:Interaction>
```

Figure 5-20 Combining WSCL and WSDL via `portType` `QNames`.

This is also used in the corresponding WSCL interface (where we see a matching `hrefSchema` attribute for our previously declared namespace):

```
    <wscl:InboundXMLDocument
      hrefSchema="http://conversations.example.org/bar/
CustomerOrderMessage"
     id="CustomerOrder"/>
```

Assuming a client of the Web service can access both interfaces, it is a straightforward task to marry the operations to the choreography based on their common messages.

What WSCL Doesn't Do

The WSCL specification contains the smallest possible set of elements and attributes to describe conversations. This set is thought sufficient to model many of the conversations needed for Web services. However, there are more complex interactions that may need additional capabilities from a conversation definition language. Such additional requirements include the following:[5]

- Defining document types that have non-XML content (e.g., binary attachments). This is different from omitting the `hrefSchema` attribute because it supports constrained arbitrary data, whereas the absence of `hrefSchema` allows unconstrained data.
- Explicit description of the roles of participants (the only role that WSCL implicitly supports is that of the Web service itself).
- Multi-party conversations with more than two participants or roles. (Once we begin to coordinate multiparty conversations, we are in effect in the territory of business process management and outside of the scope of conversations per se. See Chapter 6 for a detailed discussion of workflow and business process management.)
- Expressing timeouts and other quality of service characteristics of individual interactions.
- Expressing more complex `SourceInteractionCondition` elements (e.g., listing several documents, excluding documents, or even referencing the content of documents).
- Events (interactions that can occur at any time within a conversation instance).
- Recursive conversations, aggregating conversations into larger conversations.
- Subtyping and extending existing conversation definitions.

Summary

Conversation technology is not yet mature in the Web services world. While WSCL is the forerunning technology in this arena, it has not yet reached the heights of being *the* conversations standard.

However, WSCL is a capable, if minimal interface description language. It is based on the notion of being able to represent a conversation as a state machine, which is then itself represented in an XML form. This XML form consists of `Interactions`, which declare the messages exchanged between parties in a conversation and `Transitions`, which govern the ordering of those interactions. These are then wrapped within a `Conversation` element that deals with the initialization and finalization of the conversation, as well as naming, documentation, and namespace issues.

5. This summary is abridged from the WSCL Note available at http://www.w3.org/TR/wscl10/.

While at the time of writing there is little in the way of software support for WSCL, we have informally shown how it is relatively straightforward to automate conversational interactions with Web service technology. Furthermore, if WSCL is used simply as human-readable documentation for a Web service, then it provides an unambiguous means of specifying that service's use, which compliments and demystifies any natural language description.

However, with the advent of newer business process technologies like BPEL and WSCI (see Chapter 6), technologies like WSCL are being subsumed into the larger business process arena. While the deployment of Web service metadata in the form of WSCL interfaces is undoubtedly useful, we may yet see newer standards provide their own means of describing conversational state. It still remains to be seen whether WSCL will emerge relatively intact from the process, though one thing is for sure: we will be seeing much more of conversational interfaces in the future.

Architect's Notes

- WSCL is the leading candidate for a standard single-party conversation language in the Web services arena today.
- WSCL is not yet a standard for Web services (it is a W3C Note), and there are currently no publicly available toolkits that support WSCL creation or consumption.
- Any complex Web service that requires multiple interactions to execute a process should advertise a conversational interface (as much for human documentation as future machine consumption).

CHAPTER 6

Workflow

If a business is the sum of its processes, the orchestration and refinement of those processes is critical to an enterprise's continued viability in the marketplace. Businesses whose processes are agile and flexible will be able to adapt rapidly to and exploit new market conditions, while those businesses whose processes are poorly managed and inflexible will fall by the wayside.

In this chapter we examine the fundamentals of business process management, and show how workflow systems that automate business processes can be a valuable enterprise tool. Following the discussion on the theoretical aspects of workflow, we cover in depth the likely standard for Web services-based workflow: Business Process Execution Language for Web Services or BPEL. We discuss BPEL's roots in proprietary workflow systems and examine other Web services workflow proposals (like WSCI), which will serve to highlight other possible approaches. We also spend some time on BPEL examples and show how it can be readily applied to typical supply chain/value network scenarios. But before we drill down into the details of BPEL, we need to first understand a little background on business process management.

Business Process Management

The model of a business as the sum of its processes is a useful abstraction from which to begin understanding a business. For example, a supermarket is the summation of processes that buy and sell produce and a handful of other processes that keep the shop running. Similarly, but on a grander scale, an airline consists of processes for flight sales, plane maintenance, and so on right down to the processes that ensure that passengers receive meals on board the aircraft.

A classic example of a business process (which has the added advantage of being both familiar and ostensibly linear since it is based on a production-line pattern) is the manufacturing of motor vehicles—being one of the processes that a typical motor manufacturer will engage in as part of its business. Let us consider a typical, though somewhat simplified, view of manufacturing a family car, as shown in Figure 6-1.

The business process shown in Figure 6-1 is perhaps typical of many real-world processes where there are dependencies between some tasks (e.g., the installation of the transmissions system is predicated on the chassis being fabricated) that imply serialized execution, and parts of the system where there are no such interdependencies (e.g., on a sophisticated production line, the installation of suspension and wheels can proceed independently of the installation of seats and windows) where parallel execution can occur. Additionally, as the "Assemble Car" process is divided into its constituent subprocesses, those subprocesses themselves can be split, and so on, until a suitably grained process is arrived at.

In a traditional enterprise, most of the activities are performed in-house. For example, it used to be the case that vehicle manufacturers would build for themselves every important component of their vehicles from the gearbox through to the engine and everything in between. For example, the "add engine" process from Figure 6-1 obviously depends on the engine shop in our business being able to produce engines to install. If we examine that aspect of the business process in more detail, we see that a pattern like that shown in Figure 6-2 emerges.

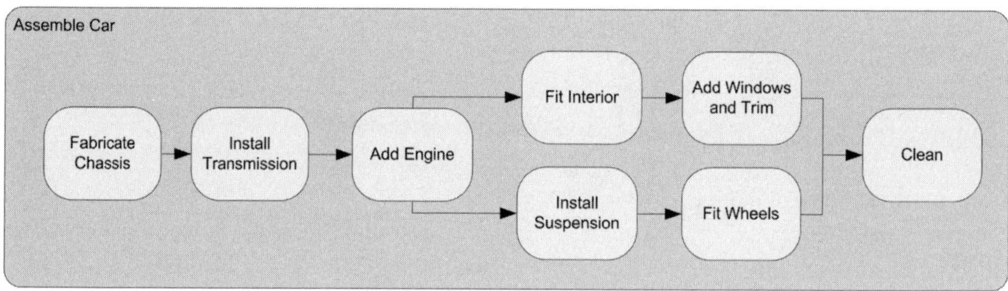

Figure 6-1 A motor vehicle construction business process.

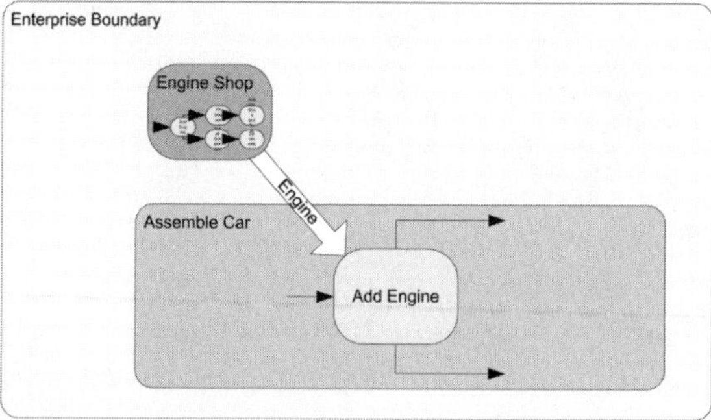

Figure 6-2 Add engine process dependencies.

While this might seem like an eminently sensible arrangement at first (especially since it decouples the internals of building engines from the internals of assembling cars), some thought reveals that in fact it hampers business agility since any change in this practice has to be capitalized up front. For instance, consider the situation where our traditional business has decided to offer a range of hybrid hydrogen fuel cell/gasoline-based cars. Under normal circumstances our business would need to find the capital and expertise to begin to produce its new engine configurations in-house, which is an expensive and labor-intensive process.

However, let us assume for argument's sake that there exist other companies whose own core competencies are not in building cars, but in building hybrid engines for cars. Given the fact that our vehicle assembly and engine construction processes are decoupled, it should be possible to simply source the new engines from a third-party supplier rather than from our own in-house stock (provided the two types of engine are, of course, physically compatible). This leads to a situation shown in Figure 6-3 where the processes of our suppliers are linked into those of the vehicle manufacturer to form a "virtual enterprise." In this arrangement, the ultimate source of the engine for a particular vehicle can either be in-house or third-party, depending on the requirements of that vehicle, without upsetting the vehicle assembly process and thus allowing the company to continue to manufacture cars and add value. Of course some of the processes within the "engine shop" may need to change a little to accommodate purchasing of complete engines (as opposed to previously purchasing raw materials or simple components) but, as a whole, the changes to the overall process are relatively confined in scope to the engine shop's systems and are (hopefully) painless.

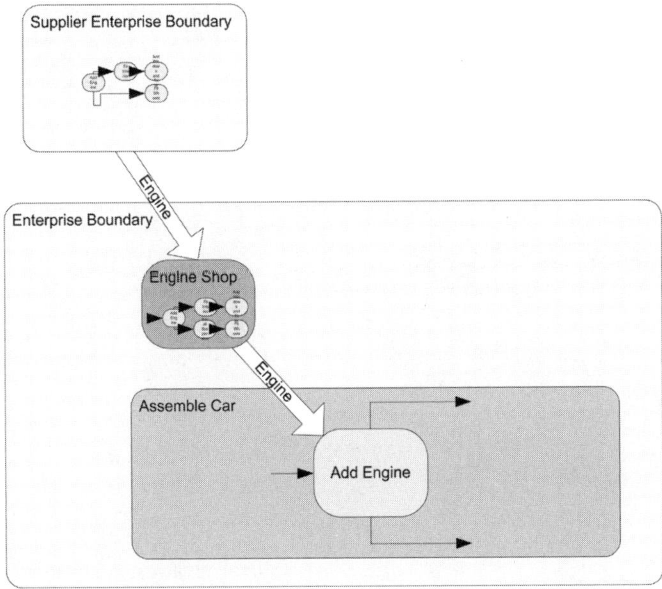

Figure 6-3 The virtual enterprise.

A virtual enterprise consists of both a business's own processes, as well as those of its partners, suppliers, and customers as single system. Taking such a holistic view generally allows the whole system to function seamlessly from a business perspective (though as we shall come to appreciate this does present certain technical challenges from a software point of view). The kinds of changes made to business processes characterized in Figure 6-3 and the ability to manage change within those processes are the hallmark of an agile business. It is a simple truth that businesses with good processes succeed while those with poor processes fail, and that high-quality processes only remain as long as they are able to change rapidly in response to market conditions. The use of computerized business process management systems is attractive because it supports the notion of rapidly evolvable business processes based on a powerful and flexible IT infrastructure. Such systems are known as *Workflow Management Systems* and it is these systems that take the abstractly defined business process and turn it into a computer-coordinated reality.

Workflows and Workflow Management Systems

Information technology is seen as a means by which a business can achieve agility and competitiveness. Although information technology has numerous beneficial effects on a typical enterprise, perhaps the most potent means of applying information technology is to use it to directly manage business processes through workflow management systems.

A workflow management system provides the business analyst with a view of the processes that the business currently operates, and allows the analyst to manage those processes according to the enterprise's business direction and changing market conditions. Under the covers, the workflow system is a dependable (and usually distributed) computing system that ensures the proper flow of information and resources to people or infrastructure that undertakes the actual work.

Workflow systems have been in existence for some time now and have generally served the enterprises in which they have been deployed well, though they have never been widely deployed across enterprises to build the much-vaunted virtual enterprise. The lack of virtual enterprises can be attributed in part to the fact that the underlying technology has failed to deliver the kind of interoperability needed to successfully run such an endeavor. However, with the advent of Web services, the kind of interoperability issues that prevented previous workflow systems from scaling up to inter-enterprise scenarios will disappear and will thus open the opportunity for inter-enterprise workflows.

Workflows

In the absence of a workflow management system, coordinating the interactions between resources in a business is often a task which an application developer must choreograph. The developer understands which systems need to be controlled by the application and in what order, and writes code accordingly. Once complete, this piece of software constitutes a whole or a part of a business process, and its behavior can (in theory at least) be executed time and again to produce the same result.

While this is fine in a static, unchanging world it is not an approach that adapts well to changing business conditions. The manual development of new application code each time a new business process has to be created, or an existing business process refined, means that a business-level analyst will have to seek the assistance of a software developer to help codify the new scenarios. Even from this common scenario, it is clear that there are business benefits to be had by deploying workflow management systems, and there may be significant penalties in terms of human labor and agility to not deploying those systems.

To alleviate such difficulties and to ensure that business processes can evolve rapidly as conditions change, many enterprises have deployed workflow management systems that business-level analysts can use to create and maintain processes with a business (not technology) focus. When a business process has been captured in a form suitable for processing by a workflow management system, it becomes known as a *workflow*.

In effect, a workflow management system is a computing system that allows business processes to be automated by encoding them as workflows (adding value in terms of efficiency) and makes it easier to codify rules for when things go wrong (adding value in terms of reliability and ease of management). In the most abstract sense, these workflow systems tie together three orthogonal aspects of enterprises, namely business processes, human resources and information technology as we see in Figure 6-4 below.[1]

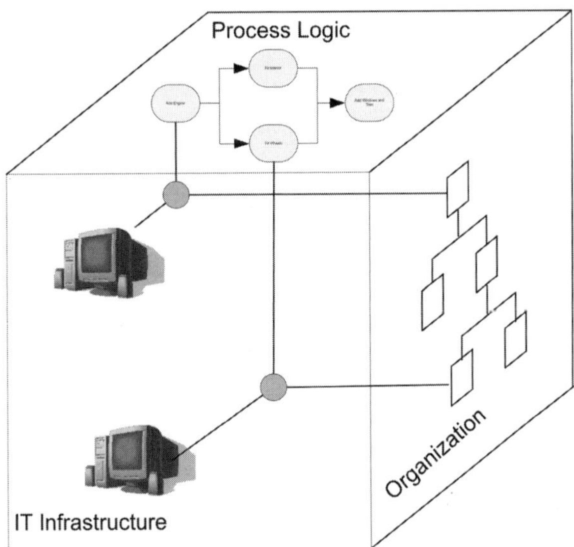

Figure 6-4 The workflow matrix.

1. Adapted from "Production Workflow: Concepts and Techniques" by Frank Leymann and Dieter Roller, Prentice-Hall 2000.

The process logic aspect of the workflow matrix is the codification (in a means suitable for the underlying workflow management system) of the underlying business process into a workflow. This workflow is a logical representation of the physical business process that will be executed to produce some end result (e.g., a motor vehicle, an answered telephone query, a sale of an item of merchandise).

The process layer is supported by the human resource side of the matrix that allocates people to certain aspects of the process, in accordance with the company's organization (which takes into account the availability and skills of its workforce). Individuals with the correct skills and roles for a particular part of a process are selected by the workflow to help perform that part of the process (e.g., a fitter to glaze vehicle windows is allocated during the fit windows part of vehicle assembly).

The third aspect of the workflow matrix is the information technology resource associated with each part of a workflow—in our domain, the Web service that provides the functionality for a particular task. This may include almost anything from individual programs (like word processing) required to complete a task the right way to sophisticated computer-aided engineering systems in high-end manufacturing plants.

The union of these three aspects determines the schedule a specific person or persons may use to complete a specific part of the process using specific resources at some time determined by the workflow management system. When we bear in mind that the workflow management system may be coordinating several hundred or even thousands of such tasks simultaneously, we can begin to get an idea of just how complex and robust such systems must be.

Workflow Management Systems Drawbacks

Though it might seem that modern workflow management systems are at the core of many enterprise information systems, there is a downside. Since most workflow management systems were developed before the advent of Web services, each workflow management system tended to be built on proprietary and largely non-interoperable technology.

While this isn't a drawback within the confines of an individual enterprise, if we recall the notion of the virtual enterprise where processes span companies with apparent ease, we begin to unearth a less enticing side to current systems. Given their proprietary nature, and the fact that there are a number of vendors in the market space each with its own distinct offering, it is entirely possible that two enterprises that would like to create a virtual enterprise to execute some business process will find a stumbling block in the integration of their two different workflow management systems. Of course, you will find protagonists of these systems claiming that it can be done using traditional middleware technology and some goodwill and effort on both sides. However, there is no guarantee that this will be economical, since by their very nature virtual enterprises are temporary, and if an enterprise's gain in partnering is overshadowed by its costs in setting up that partnership, then there is a compelling argument to be made against putting the necessary investment in place. If you happen to be a powerful and important enough customer to your suppliers, you may be able to mandate which workflow management system they install and use to ensure interoperability with your own systems. However, this tends to make for long-lived virtual enterprises and may reduce business agility as a result.

Web Services and Workflow

Web services are the industry's prime candidate for enabling interoperability. Given the broad acceptance of Web services standards and their widespread support by vendors, they have become a natural choice for integration work both within and between enterprises. This platform has set the scene for truly dynamic virtual enterprises where partners can interact with one another's systems via standard protocols without having to worry about the underlying (and possibly completely different) systems that implement the functionality.

The notion of running workflows over such an interoperable system is clearly attractive. We can benefit from all of the useful features that workflow management systems provide but gain (compared to traditional workflow management systems) interoperability with pretty much any party that we want to do business with. The computing vendors have themselves been quick to notice this market opportunity and a number of proposed Web services workflow standards have made their way into the public domain, with the front runner being Business Process Execution Language or BPEL from IBM, Microsoft and BEA.

Business Process Execution Language for Web Services (BPEL)

BPEL is a specification jointly authored by IBM, Microsoft, and BEA that formed part of a trio of specifications which also included application Web service coordination and transactions to support the development of reliable, inter-enterprise workflows. The central tenet of BPEL is the ability to capture both the constituent activities of a workflow and relationships between partners involved in that workflow in a platform-neutral format (XML), and support the highest possible level of interoperability by basing the technology on commonly adopted Web services standards. BPEL is grounded on the WSDL 1.1 specification, where stateless Web service interfaces are augmented with state management and message correlating features which in turn are consumed within workflow processes. This is not dissimilar in its approach to WSCL (as discussed in Chapter 5), which extends WSDL to provide conversation support for Web services.

In this section we work with the BPEL 1.0 standard since it is well known and has a reasonable level of tool support, though BPEL 1.1 has recently been released at the time of writing. The differences between the 1.0 and 1.1 versions are small enough that anyone with a good grasp of BPEL 1.0 will find BPEL 1.1 a straightforward extension.

The BPEL Stack

The BPEL model is built on a number of layers, with each layer building on the facilities of the previous. Figure 6-5 shows the fundamental components of the BPEL architecture, which consists of the following:

- A means of capturing enterprise interdependencies with partners and associated service links (the "type" of the partner based on its WSDL `portType`) and service references (a typed "pointer") to an active partner at runtime.
- Message correlation layer that ties together messages and specific workflow instances, based on messages properties which expose parts of a message as a unique "key."
- State management features to maintain, update and interrogate parts of the process state as a workflow progresses.
- Scopes where individual activities (workflow stages) are composed to form actual algorithmic workflows.

This workflow stack is ultimately supported by an execution engine (there are several available from companies like IBM, Microsoft, and Collaxa). The engine interprets the enterprise interdependencies in order to bind to partners' remote Web services, and also executes the activities that drive those Web services. It is also a useful mental framework to bear in mind while we drill down into BPEL and develop our sample BPEL workflow. Over the next sections we begin to fill in that abstract framework with concrete examples from BPEL, starting with the algorithmic components of a workflow—its *activities.*

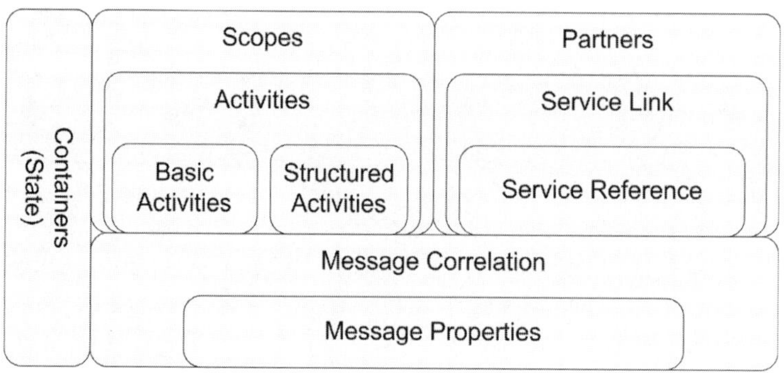

Figure 6-5 BPEL logical view.

Activities

In order to execute a process, we must have some means of describing the algorithmic behavior of that process. We need to understand the features that the workflow language provides to manipulate data, iterate, call external functions, and so on, and how to compose these primitives into meaningful workflows. To support this, the BPEL specification defines a number of types of fundamental activities that are the building blocks of algorithms which it classifies as *basic* and *structured* types. Basic activities deal with state management, communication, and exception handling, while structured activities deal with process control-flow issues. We further classify the activities[2] as shown in Table 6-1:

Table 6-1 Activity Types in BPEL

Structuring Activates	Communication Activities
• `<sequence>` • `<flow>` • `<switch>` • `<pick>` • `<while>` • `<scope>`	• `<receive>` • `<reply>` • `<invoke>`
Miscellaneous Activities	**Exception Handling Activates**
• `<assign>` • `<wait>` • `<empty>`	• `<throw>` • `<terminate>` • `<compensate>`

In the following sections, we take each of the groups of activities from Table 6-1 and examine the syntax and semantics of them.

Structuring Activities

The BPEL structuring activities manage control flow dependencies in a workflow. They are responsible for serializing and parallelizing activities (`sequence`, `flow`), choosing from alternative paths in a workflow (`switch`, `pick`), iterating parts of a workflow (`while`), and declaring activity scopes (`scope`).

---

2. In all examples after this point, all BPEL-specific XML elements will be prefixed with the XML prefix `bpws` which is associated with the namespace http://schemas.xmlsoap.org/ws/2002/07/business-process/.

Sequence

Imposing ordering on activities with a sequence is straightforward. Using a sequence activity, the order of activity is simply the order in which the enclosed activities appear (this is *lexical* order). For instance, the workflow that undertakes the reservation process for a hotel will first receive a sales call, check availability, take a security deposit, and confirm the order in strict sequence. The BPEL process representation for this is shown in Figure 6-6.

```
<bpws:sequence>
  <!-- Wait for reservation call -->
  <bpws:invoke … />
  <!-- Check availability -->
  <bpws:invoke … />
  <!-- Take deposit -->
  <bpws:invoke … />
  <!-- Confirm reservation -->
  <bpws:invoke … />
</bpws:sequence>
```

Figure 6-6 The `sequence` activity.

Flow

Similarly, parallelizing activities that have no dependencies is achieved by enclosing the parallel activities within a `flow` element. For example, the same customer's computing system that initiated the hotel reservation sequence may also have been organizing flights and car rental simultaneously. If we assume these activities are to some degree independent, we can execute them in parallel and develop the `flow` activity shown in Figure 6-7.

```
<bpws:flow>
  <!—Book hotel -->
  <bpws:invoke partner="Hotelier" … />
  <!-- Hire care -->
  <bpws:invoke partner="CarRentalAgency" … />
  <!-- Book flight -->
  <bpws:invoke partner="AirlineReservationDesk" … />
</bpws:flow>
```

Figure 6-7 The canonical form of `flow` activities.

However, activities within a `flow` may not be completely parallel and may require some degree of synchronization. In BPEL, this is achieved with `links` which establish control relationships, or synchronization dependencies, between activities nested within a `flow` and other activities outside of the `flow`.

> The only caveats to using `link` declarations to create dependencies between activities are that a `link` cannot cross the boundary of a `while` activity, that links which cross fault-handling activities must have their sources and never their targets within the fault handler, and that links should never form cycles since this causes deadlock.

At the beginning of the execution of a `flow` activity, all links are inactive and only those activities with no dependencies (those that are not declared as the `target` of any links) can execute. This is shown in Figure 6-8 where only Activity A and Activity B are executing from the start of the workflow, as they are the only activities without dependencies.

As time goes by, the execution of activities completes and on completion each activity evaluates its `transitionCondition` to determine the status of its (previously inactive) outgoing links. This results in each `link` being given a positive or negative state, which it carries forward to its target activity.

Once all incoming links to an activity are active (that is, they have been assigned either a positive or negative state), the activity's `joinCondition` is evaluated. A `joinCondition` is a guard that each activity nested within a `flow` possesses which allows conditional execution within a `flow`. Where a `joinCondition` isn't explicitly specified for an activity, the default value of a `joinCondition` is the result of performing a logical OR operation on the status of all incoming links into an activity.

The effect of both `transitionCondition` and `joinCondition` are shown in Figure 6-9, where we see that the `transitionCondition` for the links from Activity A and Activity B to Activity C has evaluated to true, and as such both links have been activated and have both been set to positive. Based on its links from Activity A and Activity B, Activity C's `join-`

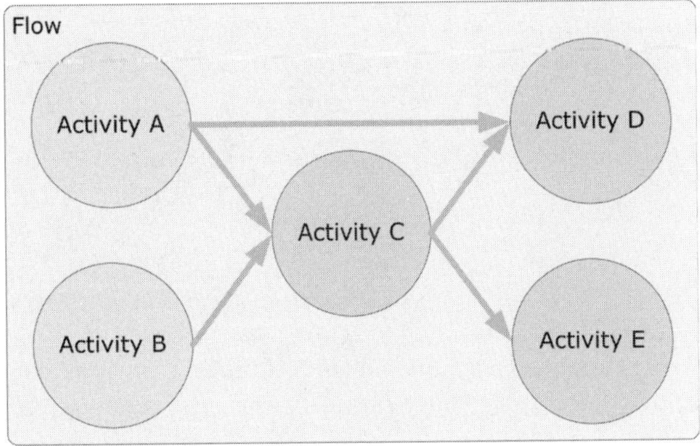

Figure 6-8 Initial execution stages of a `flow` activity.

`Condition` has evaluated to true, and so Activity C has become active. The link from Activity A to Activity D has evaluated to false, but since the link from Activity C to Activity D has not yet become active, Activity D has not executed its `joinCondition` and remains inactive.

The final stage is to execute, or not, Activity D and Activity E. If we imagine a scenario like that shown in Figure 6-10, where we do not use the default `joinCondition` and instead mandate a logical AND for Activity D, then since the link between Activity C and Activity D is set to positive, Activity D will not execute. If we assume no transition condition has been specified for Activity E, we see that Activity E will execute since the default `joinCondition` (logical OR of all incoming links) is present even for activities with only a single incoming `link`.

The fact that not all activities within a `flow` have executed may or may not be a problem. For instance, if it is critical that all activities in the `flow` shown in Figure 6-10 complete, then it is important that an error caused when Activity D cannot execute is propagated to the parent of

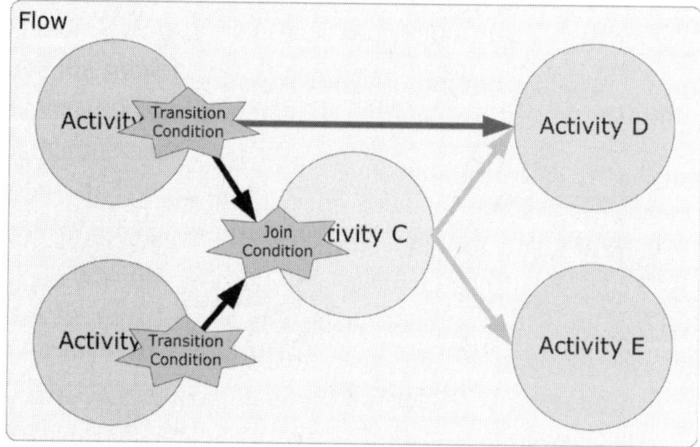

Figure 6-9 `transitionCondition` and `joinCondition` guards.

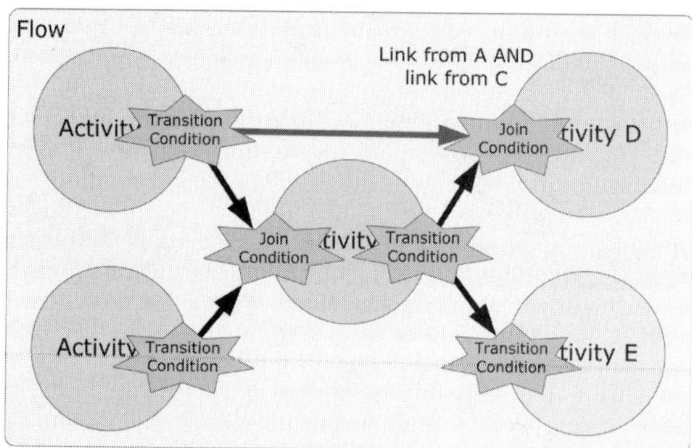

Figure 6-10 Evaluating `joinCondition` guards.

the `flow` activity. On the other hand it may be the case in a highly parallel workflow that control flow will be largely determined by the network of links that constrain execution, and that failure to execute whole branches of activities within a flow is not necessarily a fault but a natural by-product of the design of the workflow. A case in point here are the numerous branches of a `switch` activity which are not executed, yet whose dormancy does not indicate a fault.

Whether or not to flag `joinCondition` failures as a fault to the scope of the `flow` is determined by the setting of the `suppressJoinFailure` attribute in the opening element of the `flow`. Where join failures are a natural by-product of the parallel-by-default workflow design, the `suppressJoinFailure` attribute should be set to "`yes`" which then ensures that unexecuted paths through the workflow do not cause the `flow` activity to throw a fault. Conversely, where all activities within a flow need to be executed and links provide synchronization not choices, the `suppressJoinFailure` attribute is set to "`no`" which means that any `joinCondition` that evaluates to false will cause a `joinFailure` (a standard BPEL fault) to be thrown, and the parent scope can instigate appropriate error-handling activities.

To illustrate the use of `links` in a real business case, imagine the scenario, as shown in Figure 6-11, where a more fully formed workflow includes managerial authorization for the business trip and expense claims in addition to the (parallel) booking of hotel, flights, and rental car.

The workflow shown in Figure 6-11 has distinct authorization, booking, and expense phases where each of the booking and expense claim activities are potentially parallel. This parallelism is constrained by the addition of synchronization dependencies. The corresponding BPEL code is shown in Figure 6-12 where the `flow` activity is used encourages parallel activity during the booking phase, while the `links` are used to constrain that activity to the extent that the logical ordering of the task—authorize, book, expense—is maintained.

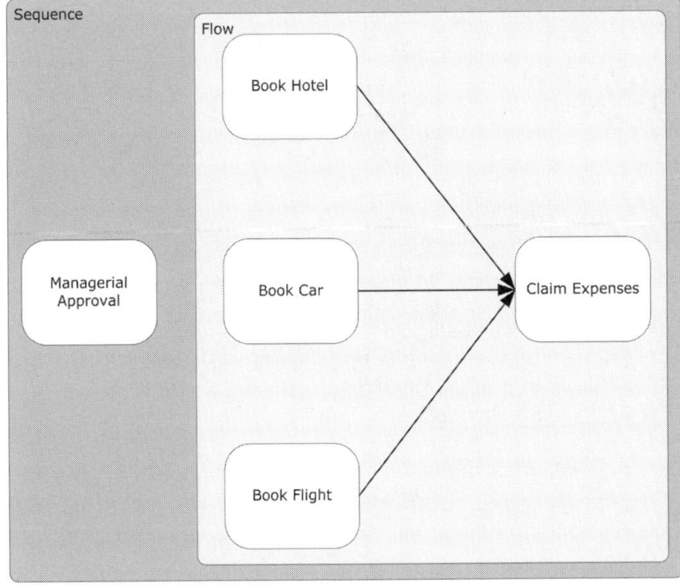

Figure 6-11 A Parallelized Booking Workflow.

```
<bpws:sequence>
  <bpws:invoke name="ManagementInvocation"
    partner="Boss">
    …
  </bpws:invoke>
  <bpws:flow>
    <bpws:links>
      <bpws:link name="HotelExpenses"/>
      <bpws:link name="CarExpenses"/>
      <bpws:link name="FlightExpenses"/>
    </bpws:links>
    <bpws:flow>
      <!-- Book hotel -->
      <bpws:sequence>
        <bpws:invoke name="HotelInvocation"
          partner="Hotelier">
          …
        </bpws:invoke>
        <bpws:receive name="HotelResponse" … >
          <bpws:source link="HotelExpenses"
            transitionCondition="bpws:getContainerProperty
                   ("HotelBookings", "costPerNight") < 300"/>
        </bpws:receive>
      </bpws:sequence>

      <!-- Hire care -->
      <bpws:invoke name="CarHireInvocation"
        partner="CarRentalAgency">
        <bpws:source link="CarExpenses"/>
        …
      </bpws:invoke>

      <!-- Book flight -->
      <bpws:invoke name="AirlineInvocation"
        partner="AirlineReservationDesk">
        <bpws:source link="FlightExpenses"/>
        …
      </bpws:invoke>

    <!-- Claim expenses -->
    <bpws:invoke name="ExpenseClaimInvocation"
      partner="Cashier"
      joinCondition="bpws:getLinkStatus("HotelExpenses") AND
                     bpws:getLinkStatus("CarExpenses") AND
                     bpws:getLinkStatus("FlightExpenses")">
      <bpws:target link="HotelExpenses"/>
      <bpws:target link="CarExpenses"/>
      <bpws:target link="FlightExpenses"/>
      …
    </bpws:invoke>
  </bpws:flow>
</bpws:sequence>
```

Figure 6-12 A typical `flow` activity with `links` describing dependencies.

Figure 6-12 shows the skeleton of a typical flow activity. In this flow, we see four invocation activities which are ordered according to dependencies described by links where the booking activities are parallelized, while the expense claim invocation depends on the outcome of previous booking invocations, as per Figure 6-11. These dependencies are encoded into the workflow as follows:

- A set of links for the flow is declared.
- Each activity within the flow that is involved in a dependency with another activity declares either a source element or a target element depending on whether they are the source of a dependency or the dependent activity.
- Each source and target element names a link to bind its dependency.

For instance, in Figure 6-12 we see that the AirlineInvocation invoke activity is the source of a dependency described by the FlightExpenses link: <bpws:source link="FlightExpenses"/>. The ExpenseClaimInvocation invoke activity is declared as the target of the FlightExpenses link and thus is dependent on the AirlineInvocation activity (along with some other links) as shown by the declaration: <bpws:target link="FlightExpenses"/>.

However, there is more to Figure 6-12 than simple dependencies described by links. We have also specified a number of guards in the form of transitionCondition and joinCondition expressions as part of the HotelInvocation and ExpenseClaimInvocation activities. Specifically, we have added a transitionCondition to the HotelInvocation activity so that only if the price of the hotel is less than $300 per night will the HotelExpenses link be set to a positive state. In those cases where the chosen hotel is charging more than $300 per night for accommodation, this link will be set to carry a negative token. Thus at the end of the HotelInvocation activity, the following expression is evaluated: transitionCondition="bpws:getContainerProperty ("HotelBookings", "costPerNight") < 300" to determine whether the outgoing link should be set to positive or negative.

> Expressions including bpws:getContainerProperty are explained fully in later sections. For now just assume that they work on state contained within a workflow process, but don't worry too much about exactly where that state is held.

The importance of the HotelExpenses link becomes apparent when we consider the joinCondition of the ExpenseClaimInvocation activity. Instead of using the default logical OR on each incoming link, this joinCondition performs a logical AND on the status of each incoming link and will, therefore, only allow the ExpenseClaimInvocation activity to execute if each link carries a positive token—that is only once all preceding activities have completed their execution and each transitionCondition has been evaluated to true, like this:

```
joinCondition="bpws:getLinkStatus("HotelExpenses") AND
bpws:getLinkStatus("CarExpenses") AND
bpws:getLinkStatus("FlightExpenses")>
```

If a `joinCondition` fails, we essentially have two options. Usually in workflows like this one where all paths through a parallel execution have to be taken, we would set the `suppressJoinFailure` attribute of the surrounding scope to be "`no`" so that any `joinCondition` that evaluates to false will cause a `joinFault` to be thrown. This `joinFault` can then be handled by the parent scope, which might perform compensation or other error handling. On the other hand, and specifically in those parallel-by-default cases where it is quite normal for activities not to execute because of runtime conditions, we might want to ignore any thrown `joinFault` faults as a by-product of inherently parallel execution. In those cases, we set the `suppressJoinFailure` attribute of the surrounding scope to "`yes`".

Switch

The `switch` activity allows branches in a workflow to be navigated, based on conditions defined in case elements, or to follow a specific branch in the case where no such conditions have been met. Thus the BPEL `switch` activity is similar in both name and nature to the C, C++, Java, and C# switch statement.

A simple `switch` activity is presented in Figure 6-13, where based on the cost of an air ticket (less than $200, less than $400, or otherwise) different activities are executed to authorize the payment, where presumably as the cost increases so does the level of scrutiny of each check increase.

```
<bpws:switch>
  <bpws:case condition="bpws:getContainerProperty(finances,
                                          flightCost) < 200" >
    <!-- budget bracket authorization -->
  </bpws:case>
  <bpws:case condition="bpws:getContainerProperty(finances,
                                          flightCost) < 400" >
    <!-- intermediate bracket authorization -->
  </bpws:case>
  <bpws:otherwise>
    <!-- higher bracket authorization -->
  </bpws:otherwise>
</bpws:switch>
```

Figure 6-13 A `switch` activity.

Pick

The pick activity is akin to an asynchronous event-driven switch activity. A pick activity declares events that it will trigger on, and corresponding activities to execute once those events occur. Events can take the form of either the receipt of a message or a time-based event including both duration (time relative from now) and deadline (fixed future time).

It is also possible for a pick activity to provide the entry point into a workflow. In this case the pick activity acts very much like a receive activity (which we discuss in the next section), with the key difference that it can initiate a workflow based on a number of messages rather than the single message that receive supports. Like the receive activity, when a pick is used to instantiate a workflow it is annotated with a createInstance="yes" attribute. If this attribute is specified, alarms (of either form) are not permitted.

Every pick activity contains at least one onMessage event. The onMessage events dictate when the activity becomes active—that is, when a matching message is received. Additionally a pick activity can contain a time-based alarm, either time relative from the time the pick activity is first encountered or an absolute value in the future. This is particularly useful when we need to timeout after an event has transpired (or failed to transpire) in our workflow.

An example pick activity is shown in Figure 6-14, where the activity waits on a response message from the airline booking system via its onMessage declaration. However, where that response is not been quick enough—we specify a three-day limit on the response with an XML Schema duration value—a timeout is triggered through its onAlarm declaration and some fault handling logic is executed. Note that in this case we specify a timeout relative to the activation of the pick activity using the for attribute. Had we wanted to use a fixed future deadline (perhaps where all flights must be booked by close of business on Friday), then we would have used the until form in conjunction with an XML Schema dateTime value.[3]

```
<bpws:pick createInstance="no">
  <bpws:onMessage partner="AirlineReservationDesk"
    portType="ent:BookingPortType"
    operation="bookingResponse" container="BookingResponses">
    <bpws:correlations>
       <bpws:correlation set="BookingsCorrelationSet"
          initiation="no"/>
    </bpws:correlations>
    <!-- Continue with booking -->
  </bpws:onMessage>
  <bpws:onAlarm for="P0Y0M3DT0H0M">
    <!-- Airline not responded, deal with problem -->
  </bpws:onAlarm>
</bpws:pick>
```

Figure 6-14 A pick activity.

3. For a useful quick reference to the forms of possible dates, times, and durations available in XML Schema, see http://www.xml.dvint.com/docs/SchemaDataTypesQR-2.pdf.

While

Activities are iterated by nesting them within a `while` activity. In BPEL, the while activity evaluates a condition expressed in XPath 1.0 and if that expression evaluates to `true`, another iteration of the enclosed activities is executed. We cover BPEL expressions later in this chapter, but for now think of them as something akin to SQL statements for BPEL.

In Figure 6-15 we see a simple `while` activity that allows flights to be booked only if the number of flights already booked in the current month is less than some threshold figure (in this case we have chosen 20 as being a reasonable value). If this condition evaluates to true, then further bookings will be possible, otherwise the booking activities will not be executed and presumably some further authorization will be sought.

```
<bpws:while condition=
 "bpws:getContainerProperty(monthlyFlightDetails,noOfFlights)
  < 20">
  <!-- flight booking activities -->
</bpws:while>
```

Figure 6-15 A `while` activity.

Scope

The final structuring activity is `scope`. A `scope` is a means of explicitly packaging activities together—providing activity context—such that they can share common error handling and compensation routines. The full structure for a `scope` is shown in Figure 6-16 and consists of a set of optional fault handlers, a single optional compensation handler and the primary activity of the scope that defines its behavior. In the absence of a `scope` declaration the scope of an activity is itself, with the exception of correlation sets and containers, which exist implicitly at global scope.

In the absence of a `scope` declaration, each activity is implicitly associated with its own scope which shares the same name and delimiters as the activity. An example scope is shown in Figure 6-17, where the booking process for an individual ticket is shown enclosed in a scope.

The normal behavior for the scope shown in Figure 6-17 is for the booking activity near the bottom of the example to be executed and for flight tickets to be reserved. However, this scope declares a number of exception handlers with `catch` activities that allow a variety of faults that might occur while booking tickets to be rectified before they cause further problems. For instance, these `catch` activities deal with such matters as a flight number being incorrectly specified, a flight already being fully booked, or a fault in the payment method used to purchase the tickets. We will assume that these fault handlers are able to correct any problems so that the scope can complete normally. The `catchAll` handler is a little different in that it handles any faults other than those that are explicitly handled by the preceding `catch` activities. Since the

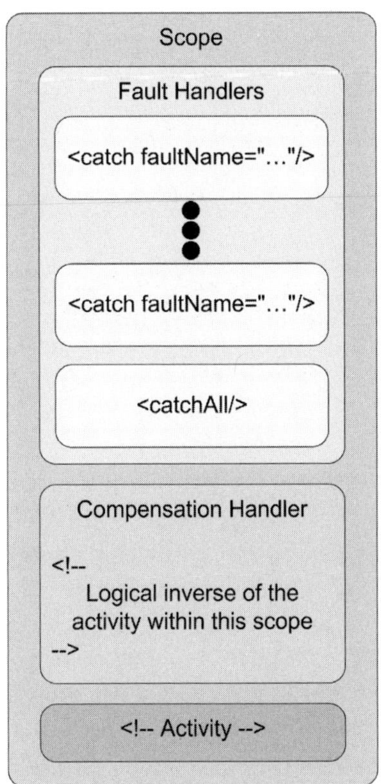

Figure 6-16 BPEL `scope` structure.

```
<bpws:scope containerAccessSerializable="no">
  <bpws:faultHandlers>
    <bpws:catch faultName="FlightFullFault" … />
    <bpws:catch faultName="UnknownFlightFault" … />
    <bpws:catch faultName="UnauthorizedPaymentFault" … />
    <bpws:catchAll>
      <bpws:compensate/>
    </bpws:catchAll>
  </bpws:faultHandlers>
  <!-- Booking activity -->
</bpws:scope>
```

Figure 6-17 A `scope` activity.

nature of the fault is unknown, the designer of this scope has decided that the safest thing to do would be to `compensate` the inner scopes, by calling the logic held in their `compensationHandler` activities to restore the system to the same state (or a logically equivalent state) as it was before the top-level scope executed. The skeleton for a `compensationHandler` is shown in Figure 6-18.

```
<bpws:process>
  <!-- Process definition omitted for brevity -->
  <bpws:compensationHandler>
    <!-- Application specific compensation -->
  </bpws:compensationHandler>
</bpws:process>
```

Figure 6-18 A `compensationHandler`.

Compensation handlers are a fundamental component of BPEL workflows to support reliable, long-lived business processes. During the execution of a workflow, data in the various systems that the workflow encompasses changes. Normally such data is held in mission-critical enterprise databases, queues and so forth which have ACID transactional properties to ensure data integrity.[4] This leads to the possible situation whereby a number of valid commits to such databases could have been made during the course of a workflow, but where the overall workflow might fail, leaving its work partially completed. In such situations the reversal of partial work cannot rely on backward error recovery mechanisms (rollback) supported by the databases since the updates to the database will have been long since committed. Instead we are forced to *compensate* at the application level by performing the logical inverse of each scope that was executed as part of our workflow, from the most recently executed scope back to the earliest executed scope. This model is known as a saga, and is the only default compensation model supported by BPEL.

> In addition to the saga model, BPEL supports the creation of user-defined compensation patterns for situations where the default saga model is unsuitable, which forms part of the discussion on error handling activities in the next section.

The general concept of a saga is shown in Figure 6-19 whereby each activity A_1, A_2, A_3, and A_4, have corresponding compensating activities C_1, C_2, C_3, and C_4. In the case where an activity faults and invokes its compensation handler C_n, then compensation handlers C_{n-1}, C_{n-2}, C_{n-3} and so on back to C_1 (which is the compensation handler for the activity A_1) must be invoked.

4. See Chapter 7 for a discussion of transactions and ACID properties.

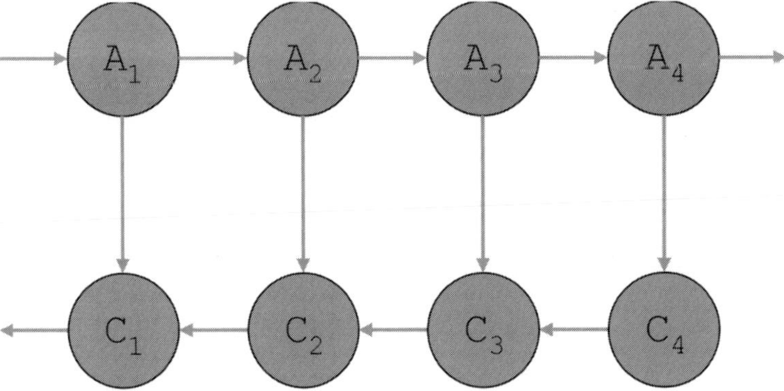

Figure 6-19 Sagas.

Where fault handlers provide alternative forward execution paths through a `scope`, compensation handlers, when invoked, undo the work performed by a `scope`. Since a `compensationHandler` for a specific `scope` reverses that scope's work, the handler can potentially be as complex and intricate as the scope's normal original activity.

> A `compensationHandler` can be set to compensate an entire business process after its normal completion (instead of individual scopes). If an entire process is to be compensated, the `enableInstanceCompensation` attribute of the `compensationHander` is set to "`yes`" to indicate its process, as opposed to scope, affiliation.

When a `compensationHandler` is executed, either through the explicit use of a `compensate` activity or where it is instigated by the underlying BPEL engine in response to some external stimulus, it operates on a snapshot of the state of the workflow process at the time of execution. This means that an executing `compensationHandler` does not update the state of the executing process, though it can manipulate its own snapshot data. This is both a blessing and a curse, since the nature of the environment within which compensating activities are executed is often difficult to predict in advance, and it may be shortsighted to assume that compensating and concurrent normal activities should be oblivious to one another. Fortunately, the BPEL specification notes this problem and proclaims that future versions will allow compensating activities to take account of the current state of live workflow activities and vice versa.

In the absence of a `compensationHandler` for a `scope`, the `scope` implicitly contains the default `compensationHandler`, and the presence of this `compensationHandler` ensures that the compensation handlers in any nested scopes are activated. Thus, when a top-level scope is compensated, all contained scopes are also compensated, starting with the most recently executed. Each of those scopes' nested scopes will also be compensated starting with the most recently executed, and the same will happen over again until all nested scopes have been compensated, in the order of those most recently executed first.

For example, if a particularly disastrous fault developed during the execution of a workflow instance that changed a user's password on all systems the user has access to (a somewhat crude version of centralized computer management), we might have no recourse other than to compensate that workflow, thus reversing all of its work including changing any altered passwords back to their original form so the user is not locked out of any individual system.

A compensation handler is limited to the particular workflow instance within which it was invoked. Given the possibility—or indeed likelihood—that workflows will be composed from workflows and span enterprises, a means of consistently undoing related work across enterprise boundaries is required. Typically this kind of situation is handled with a distributed transaction protocol whereby activities across enterprises can be associated with the same logical unit of work (a transaction) and every scope in that transaction will undo any work (compensate) if any of the other scopes in that transaction find that they must compensate.

The BPEL specification suggests WS-Transaction (see Chapter 7) as the protocol of choice for managing transactions that support the interactions of workflow instances running within different enterprise systems. In short, the WS-Transaction protocol is used both as the means of grouping distributed scopes together into a single logical unit of work and as the dissemination of the outcome of that unit of work—whether all scopes completed successfully or whether they need to be compensated.

Exception Handling Activities

Following our discussion on `scope`, it is useful at this point to elaborate further on the basic syntax and semantics of the error handling activities. There are three fundamental error handling activities supported by BPEL—`throw`, `terminate`, and `compensate`, where `throw` is used to flag an error, and `terminate` and `compensate` are reactions to errors thrown by a workflow instance or by the underlying process engine.

Throw

The `throw` activity is simple to understand, since it bears close resemblance to the `throw` keyword in the Java programming language. To illustrate, we can borrow from a simple Web services-based login and authentication system that uses `throw` to indicate that a login attempt failed, as we see in Figure 6-20.

```
<bpws:throw faultName="login:LoginFailure"
            faultContainer="LoginFailureContainer"/>
```

Figure 6-20 A `throw` activity.

In this case the execution of the throw activity populates a container—being a place where BPEL workflows store state, which for now we can assume are akin to variables in a programming language—with fault data so that the workflow process dealing with the login can create the corresponding login failure message and send it to the user, though in those cases where fault data is not required, then no container need be specified.

Catch

Handling faults also follows a similar pattern to common programming languages such as C++, Java, and C#. A catch declaration is used to handle specific faults occurring within a scope, and a catchAll declaration within the activity's scope faultHandlers declarations will handle any faults not handled by a more specific catch at the same scope.

The catch and catchAll activities are exemplified in Figure 6-21, where specific faults LoginFailure and LoginServerNotRespondingFailure are handled explicitly. If, however, another kind of fault arises that cannot be handled by these two explicitly typed fault handlers, then the fault propagates to the catchAll activity, which in this case has been written to cease the process using the <terminate/> activity.

```
<bpws:faultHandlers>
  <bpws:catch faultName="LoginFailure">
    <!-- Handle the fault -->
  </bpws:catch>
  <bpws:catch faultName="LoginServerNotRespondingFailure">
    <!-- Handle the fault -->
  </bpws:catch>
  <bpws:catchAll>
    <!-- Unexpected fault, shutdown -->
    <bpws:terminate/>
  </bpws:catchAll>
</bpws:faultHandlers>
```

Figure 6-21 BPEL catch and catchall fault handlers and terminate activity.

Terminate

Terminating a workflow is just as simple as throwing a fault. When executed, the terminate activity unconditionally stops any running activities as soon as possible, without executing any compensating or fault-handling behavior. In our example shown in Figure 6-21, the terminate activity is used to close the workflow instance in the event of an unhandled fault.

Compensate

The final fault handling activity type, `compensate`, is more subtle and powerful than simple faults and termination activities, and builds on the `compensationHandler` activity associated with a `scope` to provide application-controlled error handling. The `compensate` activity is used to invoke compensation on a scope that has already completed its execution without faulting, and can only be invoked from within a fault handler or another compensation handler, as shown in Figure 6-22.

```
<!-- Execute default compensation handler -->
<bpws:compensate/>
<!-- Execute named compensation handler -->
<bpws:compensate scope="RemoveUserCredentials"/>
```

Figure 6-22 Possible `compensate` activities.

When a workflow instance has explicitly initiated is own application-controlled compensation, there are two possible approaches that it might choose. The first is to use the default `compensationHandler` as invoked by the `<compensate/>` form, in which the scope name is omitted. A default `compensationHandler` may be empty, in which case invoking it through a `<bpws:compensate/>` activity simply causes all inner scopes to execute their default compensation handlers as per the saga model and shown on the left in Figure 6-23. It is also possible to construct the default `compensationHandler` to perform additional work, such as updating workflow state or sending notifications to external Web services prior to performing default compensation for inner scopes if necessary.

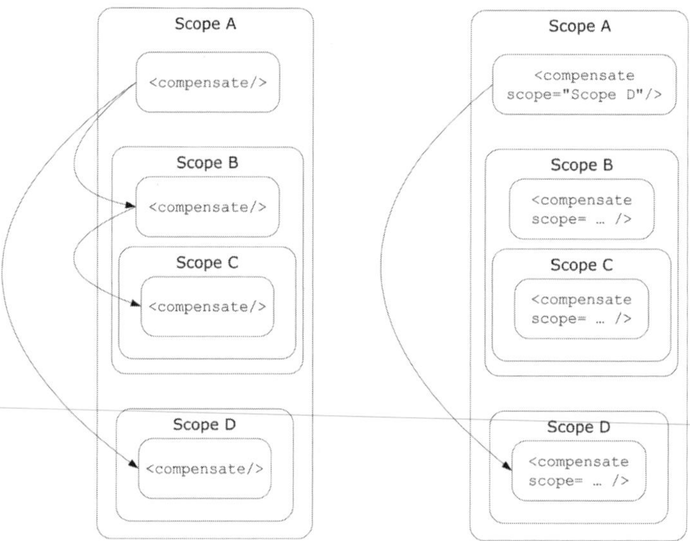

Figure 6-23 Default and explicitly named `compensate` activities.

The second approach is to explicitly call the compensation handlers for specific activities rather than follow the default reverse order of completion. Parameterized `compensate` activities describe the compensation path entirely by the scopes that each executed `compensate` activity references, as shown on the right in Figure 6-23. This allows for more intricate patterns of compensation than the simple recursive pattern used by the default `compensate` activity, and allows workflow designers to build smart compensation strategies into their workflows that minimize the required work and disruption in the event of compensation being initiated.

> There are caveats that must be borne in mind when using compensation. First, if a scope being explicitly compensated by name was executed within a loop, the compensation handlers for the successive iterations of that loop are executed in reverse order; and second, the default compensate activity cannot be mixed with named compensation activities within a single scope: `<compensate/>` and `<compensate scope="some-scope"/>` is illegal if the named scope is an inner scope of the default compensate activity—you can compensate all inner scopes, or selected inner scopes but trying to mix both is wrong.

Communication Activities

The set of communication activities deals with the sending and receiving of messages so that a workflow process instance can communicate with other Web services hosting other resources, including other workflow process instances. BPEL provides three activities—`invoke`, `receive`, and `reply`—each of which handles a different type of interaction between partners in a workflow. Partners are discussed in-depth in later sections. However, it suffices for now to understand that a partner is effectively mapping to a WSDL `portType` description of a physical partner's Web service.

Invoke

The `invoke` activity allows a workflow instance to call a synchronous or asynchronous operation on a remote Web service. An asynchronous one-way operation is the simplest form of `invoke` since it only requires a single input container to send messages. To illustrate, examine the example shown in Figure 6-24 where a request for additional cable TV channels is sent from a set-top box to a cable operator's system. In this example the `invoke` activity calls the `addChannel` operation from the `ChannelManagementPortType` `portType` exposed by its `CableOperator` partner, sending a message from the `RequestedChannels` container to request additions to the subscriber's package. The subscription update is sent asynchronously under the assumption that the cable company will have some non-interactive batch-mode process for updating all subscriber's hardware periodically to make the best use of network resources.

```
<bpws:invoke partner="CableOperator"
      portType="co:ChannelManagementPortType"
      operation="addChannel"
      inputContainer="RequestedChannels"/>
```

Figure 6-24 An asynchronous `invoke` activity.

A synchronous invocation is slightly more complicated since it also needs to deal with any response messages or faults that invoking an operation may produce. A cable operator may accept synchronous invocations for queries from set-top boxes for customers wanting to know their subscription details.

A set-top box would invoke that service as shown in Figure 6-25, where the `invoke` activity requires both an `inputContainer` from which to extract the request message and an `outputContainer` to deposit the response message from the cable operator's service.

```
<bpws:invoke partner="CableOperator"
      portType="co:ChannelManagementPortType"
      operation="getSubscriptionStatus"
      inputContainer="SubscriberDetails"
      outputContainer="PackageDetails"/>
```

Figure 6-25 A aynchronous `invoke` activity.

Receive

Web service operations are exposed to the outside world by a `receive` activity. The `receive` activity is the workflow entity onto which a WSDL operation maps. It specifies the `partner` it expects that will invoke the corresponding operation, and `portType` and `operation` that it expects the partner to invoke. In Figure 6-26 we show the `receive` activity that the cable operator exposes as its `addChannel` operation (the operation invoked by customers in Figure 6-24). The cable operator uses a container called `addChannelOrders` to hold incoming `AddChannelMessage` messages from customers. When the `receive activity` is activated by the arrival of an `AddChannelMessage` from a customer, a new instance of the cable operator's channel adding workflow is created and executed.

A `receive` activity is blocking and does not allow the workflow graph that it precedes to progress until the messages that it requires have been received. Furthermore, it may be the case (as it is in Figure 6-26) that a `receive` activity initiates a workflow process instance on receipt of a message. In such cases (as in that of Figure 6-26), the activity is annotated with the `createInstance="yes"` attribute to indicate that it is the initial process of the workflow. In this case it is not allowed for any other type of activity to precede the `receive` activity.

In those cases where one of a set of messages, whose order of arrival cannot be predicted, needs to be received before a workflow instance can execute, it is permissible to have multiple

```
<bpws:containers>
  <bpws:container name="addChannelOrders"
       messageType="co:AddChannelMessage"/>
</bpws:containers>
<bpws:receive partner="customer"
     portType="co:ChannelManagementPortType"
     operation="addChannel"
     container="addChannelRequest">
  <!-- Add a channel -->
</bpws:receive>
```

Figure 6-26 A `receive` activity.

receive activities declared with `createInstance="yes"` attributes. The BPEL implementation will determine which of the arriving messages actually triggers the instantiation of the workflow, usually based on a first-come, first-served rule. Messages arriving later will simply be routed to an existing workflow instance and will not cause the creation of a new instance where the message can be correlated with an existing instance.

BPEL does not support the declaration of multiple `receive` activities for the same `partner`, `portType`, and `operation` since it is the sum of these three components which provides a unique key matching the `receive` activity to its WSDL counterparts. Similarly, this constraint cannot be circumvented by declaring a `pick` activity since a `pick` effectively is a `receive`, albeit one with useful timing features.

Reply

A `reply` activity is used for sending synchronous responses to messages received through a `receive` activity. Correlation between a `receive` and a `reply` is handled by the underlying BPEL implementation.

To draw to a close this description of communication activities, we present the cable company's synchronous response to the customer's request for subscription details from Figure 6-25. This is shown in Figure 6-27, where the `customer` partner is sent a message from the `CustomerSubscriptionDetails` container (which contains messages whose contents are the details of subscriptions), as a result of invoking the `getSubscriptionStatus` operation.

```
<bpws:reply partner="customer"
     portType="co:ChannelManagementPortType"
     operation="getSubscriptionStatus"
     container="CustomerSubscriptionDetails"/>
```

Figure 6-27 A `reply` activity.

Miscellaneous Activities

The final three activities available to the BPEL workflow developer are the `assign`, `wait`, and `empty` activities. These activities encapsulate data-handling, unconditional timing, and no-op behavior respectively.

Assign

The `assign` activity is used to copy data (messages, parts of messages and service references) between containers. `Assign` activities follow one of several patterns, depending on what is being assigned, but in all forms type compatibility between the source and destination of the assignment must be maintained. Thus valid assignments can occur where both the `from` and `to` elements reference containers hold the same message types; or where both endpoints of an assignment are the same (XPath-friendly) XML Schema types, or compatible sub-types. Any deviation from these three forms will cause the underlying workflow engine to throw a fault which our process will have to handle.

A typical example of assignment is where (some of) the contents of one message are copied into another. This assignment is shown in Figure 6-28, where the address details of a customer, as supplied by that customer as part of a purchase order, are copied to a dispatch note prior to shipping the customer's order.

> It is noteworthy here that where the contents of a container are only partly initialized through assignments, the container cannot be used as the input container to any invoke activities. Before a container can be used in this way, it must have all of its fields filled in, either through piecemeal assignments or through the assignment of a whole message from another identical container.

```
<bpws:assign>
  <bpws:copy>
    <bpws:from container="PurchaseOrders"
         part="customerAddress"/>
    <bpws:to container="dispatchNotes"
         part="customerAddress"/>
  </bpws:copy>
</bpws:assign>
```

Figure 6-28 An `assign` activity.

Of course other forms of assignment are used on our workflow, and the BPEL specification offers a useful taxonomy of possible assignment styles as shown in Figure 6-29. However, with the caveat is that the opaque form of the `from` element is only available in abstract processes, where the data contained in the opaque section is populated by some agent in the workflow system's back end.[5]

```
<from container="ncname" part="ncname"?
      query="queryString"?/>
<from partner="ncname"
      serviceReference="myRole|partnerRole"/>
<from container="ncname" property="qname"/>
<from expression="general-expr"/>
<from> ... literal value ... </from>
<from opaque="yes">

<to container="ncname" part="ncname"? query="queryString"?/>
<to container="ncname"/>
<to container="ncname" property="qname"/>
```

Figure 6-29 Permitted assignment styles in BPEL.

In all variants the `container` attribute provides the name of a container, and the `part` attribute provides the name of a part within that container. In the first `from` and `to` variants, the value of the query attribute is a query string (expressed in XPath 1.0 by default), which identifies a single value within a source or target container part.

The second `from` and `to` variants allow dynamic manipulation of the service references associated with partners, where the value of the `partner` attribute matches the name of a `partner` declared in the process. In the case of `from` elements, the role must be specified to highlight whether the assignment is passing on its own role or that of a partner. The value `myRole` indicates that the service reference of the process with respect to that partner is the source, while the value `partnerRole` means that the partner's service reference is the source. For the `to` element, the assignment is only possible to the `partnerRole`, hence there is no need to specify the role. The type of the value used in partner-style `from` and `to` elements is always a service reference. This style of assignment permits endpoint details for services to be propagated between partners—something akin to the passing of a pointer-to-pointer as an argument to a function in C.

The third form of the `from` and `to` elements allow explicit manipulation of message properties, while the fourth `from` variant allows assignment from a literal or computed value.

The fifth `from` element allows a literal value to be given as the source value to assign to a destination. The type of the literal value has to match that of the destination specified by the `to` element, and type-checking may be strengthened by the optional inclusion of an `xsi:type` attribute to make explicit the types being assigned (this is useful when, for

5. The remainder of this section is based on the assignment section of the BPEL specification. See: http://www-106.ibm.com/developerworks/library/ws-bpel/#Assignment.

instance, the string "123" is to be assigned where that string may be equally and validly interpreted as a number).

The sixth from pattern (<from opaque="yes">) allows an opaque value to be assigned based on non-deterministic choice—a value produced by a private back-end system. The value held in the from element must be capable of being mapped onto XML Schema string-compatible type to preserve compatibility with XPath 1.0.

Wait

The wait activity introduces an unconditional pause into a workflow, where that pause may be relative (i.e., pause for a fixed amount of time) or absolute (pause until a certain date and time). It is, in some respects, similar to a pick activity though it lacks the message-oriented aspects and is much simpler to declare. There are also fewer subtleties to trap the unwary workflow designer.

A typical use for this feature is shown in Figure 6-30, where an enterprise's inventory process waits for 24 hours (as defined by the string serialized XML Schema dateTime type: PT24H) hours in between runs.

```
<bpws:while condition="true">
  <!-- XML Schema string form 24 hours -->
  <bpws:wait for="PT24H"/>
  <!-- Inventory process -->
</bpws:while>
```

Figure 6-30 A wait activity.

Empty

The final activity type in BPEL is the <empty/> activity that does nothing. A typical use for the empty activity is where a specific fault is to be suppressed, like an empty catch block in programming languages that supports structured exception handling. This is shown in Figure 6-31 where an InvalidPostcode fault is suppressed on the basis that it is likely, though more troublesome, to correctly dispatch the order to the customer without a correct postcode.

```
<bpws:catch faultName="wm:InvalidPostcode">
  <bpws:empty/>
</bpws:catch>
```

Figure 6-31 An empty activity.

We have now covered all of the activities supported by BPEL and touched on a couple of other features like state management and message correlation. However, before we can dive into creating full workflows from scratch, we will need a little more understanding of the features that BPEL offers for capturing the static relationships between enterprises and workflow instances. These are introduced in the sections that follow.

Service Linking, Partners, and Service References

In order to create workflows that span enterprises, we must build into our workflows knowledge of how those enterprises are interrelated. BPEL provides a means of capturing the roles played by business partners in a Web services-based workflow through *Service Linking, Partners*, and *Service References* whose relationships are shown in Figure 6-32.

Service links are the most abstract form of relation supported in BPEL and serve to link two parties by specifying the roles of each party and the (abstract) interface that each provides. The `serviceLinkType` definitions can either be part of a service's WSDL interface, or it can be defined separately and referenced by the WSDL. Embedding this definition directly in a WSDL description leverages WSDL's extensibility mechanism, allowing `serviceLinkType` elements to become a direct child of the `wsdl:definitions` element. This style has certain advantages over separating the WSDL and `serviceLinkType` definitions insofar as it allows `serviceLinkType` definitions to share WSDL namespaces, and more importantly its import mechanism for importing `wsdl:portType` elements.[6]

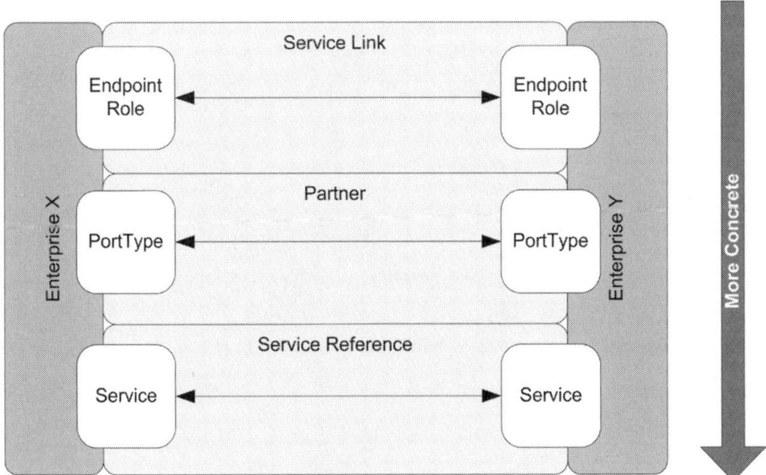

Figure 6-32 Abstract and concrete enterprise relationship.

6. See BPEL specification, http://www-106.ibm.com/developerworks/library/ws-bpel/.

The actual content of a `serviceLinkType` is straightforward. It defines a service link usually between two services, qualified by the `targetNamespace` of the WSDL document, and then exposes that relationship as two roles to the rest of the workflow. In some instances, a `serviceLinkType` may specify a single role, which indicates that the workflow is willing to bind to any other service without placing any requirements on that service.

In Figure 6-33, two sample `serviceLinkType` elements are defined. The first defines a link between a `WidgetSeller` and a `WidgetBuyer` service. Thus when a `WidgetBuyerSellerLinkType` is used in a workflow, it will implicitly associate a `WidgetSellerPortType` with a `WidgetBuyerPortType` and enforce the appropriate operation and message constraints. The second defines an `InquiryLinkType`, which is used to model the link between the widget manufacturer and a third-party making widget-related enquiries. Note that in this case, there is only one role specified, `WidgetAuthority`, which indicates that the widget manufacturing service is willing to link to any other service without placing any further constraints the interface exposed by that service.

```
<slnk:serviceLinkType name="WidgetBuyerSellerLinkType"
   xmlns:slnk="http://schemas.xmlsoap.org/ws/2002/07/service-
link/">
  <slnk:role name="WidgetSeller">
    <slnk:portType name="WidgetSellerPortType"/>
  </slnk:role>
  <slnk:role name="WidgetBuyer">
    <slnk:portType name="WidgetBuyerPortType"/>
  </slnk:role>
</slnk:serviceLinkType>
<slnk:serviceLinkType name="WidgetInquiryLinkType"
   xmlns:slnk="http://schemas.xmlsoap.org/ws/2002/07/service-
link/">
  <slnk:role name="WidgetAuthority">
    <slnk:portType name="WidgetInquirerPortType"/>
  </slnk:role>
</slnk:serviceLinkType>
```

Figure 6-33 A `serviceLink` relation.

A BPEL `partner` refines a `serviceLinkType` declaration by defining the roles played by actual partners at the endpoints of the relationship. A `partner` is declared within the workflow script itself (as opposed to the WSDL interface) because it forms part of the behavior of that workflow.[7] A sample `partner` declaration for a user authentication system is presented in Figure 6-34.

---

7. Partnerships only make sense within the scope of the workflow where business partners interact (and indeed where partners may be located as part of the computation of a workflow). Conversely, since `serviceLinkType` declarations specify the required interface and role of partner services binding to the current service, they are part of the static interface of the services and are correspondingly located within the WSDL interface.

```
<bpws:partners
    xmlns:sl="http://widgets.example.org/serviceLinkTypes">
  <bpws:partner name="customer"
      serviceLinkType="sl:WidgetBuyerSellerLinkType"
      myRole="WidgetSeller"
      partnerRole="WidgetBuyer"/>
  <bpws:partner name="enquirer"
      serviceLinkType="sl:WidgetInquiryLinkType"
      myRole="WidgetAuthority" />
</bpws:partners>
```

Figure 6-34 Partner declarations.

The root element for `partner` declarations within a BPEL workflow is `partners`. Inside that element we have individual partner declarations that specify the role of our enterprise and its partners on a per `serviceLinkType` basis. Of the two partners defined in Figure 6-34, `customer` specifies roles for both ends of the corresponding `serviceLinkType` declaration, in preparation for the bilateral exchanges that purchasing widgets necessitates. However, while inquiring about widgets, the manufacturer is not particularly fussy about who binds to and uses it, and so the partner declaration is unilateral. It specifies only the `myRole` attribute as `WidgetAuthority`, which confirms that entities placing inquiries effectively play no role in this area.

At this point we have effectively determined the types of service we are interacting with (through `serviceLinkType` declarations) and the roles of the enterprises that are going to provide the necessary functionality (through `partner` declarations). The final step in concretizing our business interrelationships is to specify the network locations of our partners so we can discover and consume their Web services.

Of course physical network address locations change over time (and indeed sometimes change quite rapidly) and WSDL has a means of supporting this through a separation of `port-Type` (abstract network interface) and `port` (physical, protocol-bound interface on the network), which are mapped through `bindings` and later exposed as `services`. The consumer of a service must understand the `portType` section of a WSDL document before it can consume a service, though the binding to an actual `port` can be delayed right up until a client needs to invoke that service at runtime. The information needed to create the runtime binding can be accessed in a number of ways, including out-of-band communication between users and directory services like UDDI. The point is, given the distinction between abstract and concrete in WSDL, BPEL has to have a means of bridging the same gap between abstract partner declarations and exchanging messages over the network with real services at runtime. This is addressed by `ServiceReference` elements, which are part of a workflow and act as typed references to a specific service. `ServiceReferences` allow consuming services to bind abstractly defined partners to physical network endpoints and communicate to expose those endpoints (with other useful data such as object or process ids) to workflow activities.

```
<sref:serviceReference
      xmlns:sref="http://schemas.xmlsoap.org/ws/2002/07/
service-reference/"
      xmlns:ws="http://widgets.example.org/ ">
  <sref:service name="ws:WidgetService"/>
</sref:serviceReference>
```

Figure 6-35 A minimal `ServiceReference` declaration.

Figure 6-35 shows a minimal `ServiceReference` declaration where the service provided by a particular partner is statically embedded. In this case the `wsdl:service` element defined in a service's WSDL interface is used to create a "Web pointer" that can be used within the activities of a single workflow and passed among collaborating services as part of their message exchanges.

However, the real potency of `ServiceReference` comes to light when we dynamically compute or discover the endpoint or business process instance that we want to communicate with. We can thus augment the minimal `ServiceReference` shown in Figure 6-35 with specific instance information, such as the `ws:existingCustomer` shown in Figure 6-36.

```
<sref:serviceReference
      xmlns:sref="http://schemas.xmlsoap.org/ws/2002/07/
service-reference/"
      xmlns:ws="http://widgets.example.org/ ">
  <sref:service name="ws:WidgetService"/>
  <sref:referenceProperties>
    <sref:property name="ws:existingCustomer">
         Johnny.Widget@widget-u-like.com
    </sref:property>
 </sref:referenceProperties>
</sref:serviceReference>
```

Figure 6-36 Identifying process/object instances with `ServiceReference`.

The `ServiceReference` shown in Figure 6-36 has additional information held by `property` elements within the `referenceProperties` element that identifies a specific resource managed by a Web service. In BPEL, that resource is likely to be an instance of a workflow. However, it may be a process or object identifier, or other identifier that has significance to both ends of the interaction. It is important to understand that while the computational aspects of BPEL provide the ability to obtain and utilize such properties, BPEL does not place any semantics on them. That is, any information appearing inside a `property` element is opaque to any BPEL infrastructure and is understood only by the endpoints sending and receiving the `ServiceReference`. Although the sender or recipient may be BPEL workflows, those workflows must have been designed explicitly to understand such information—BPEL cannot second-guess its semantics.

Fortunately, the reference data is always associated with globally named properties. It is safe to say that the recipient, understanding the global properties, will also understand the `ServiceReference`. However, for us mere humans to understand the implications of this, we have to understand what a BPEL property is.

Message Properties and Property Aliases

Once we have captured the relationships between our enterprise and its partners, we can begin to exchange messages through the conduits defined by those relationships. Indeed, every business already engages in this kind of activity, exchanging purchase orders, invoices, goods (with their associated documents), and even payments. It should not come as a surprise that the next item in our BPEL investigation concerns itself with messages.

Whether we are dealing with an invoice or a dispatch note, there is often a field or set of fields within that note that can be used to unambiguously differentiate that note from piles of other similar looking ones. For instance, an invoice number is usually used in correspondence in preference to the date and address of the sender of the invoice since it is both simpler and more likely to resolve in a unique result. This notion of "distinguished" data is supported in BPEL through *message* properties. Simply put, a message property is a unique name (within the workflow) which has a specific type from XML Schema (e.g., `xs:postiveInteger`) and whose name has significance to the workflow (e.g., invoice number). An example is shown in Figure 6-37.

```
<bpws:property name="invoice-number"
      type="ins:InvoiceNumberType"/>
<bpws:property name="phone" type="xs:postiveInteger"/>
<bpws:property name="website" type="xs:anyURI"/>
<bpws:property name="email" type="ens:EmailAddressType"/>
```

Figure 6-37 Message property examples.

Having a friendly name and type information for our property is somewhat akin to having object references in traditional programming languages. However, just as object references need to be bound to objects before we can use them, we need to bind properties to values before workflow scripts can access those values. In BPEL we have a way of binding typed-friendly names to values that we can use within our workflows, called *property* aliases. A property alias is used to bind the value of a property to the value of an element in a message using an XPath query to expose elements from those messages. For instance, we may be interested in the invoice number from a purchase order and wish to expose that value to the workflow as per Figure 6-38.

```
<bpws:propertyAlias propertyName="tns:InvoiceNumber"
   messageType="tns:PurchaseOrderMessage" part="invoice"
   query="/invoice-number"/>
```

Figure 6-38 Defining a `propertyAlias`.

Figure 6-38 shows how we can bind properties to values through `propertyAlias` declarations. The attributes in the element declare the property name that we are binding to (`InvoiceNumber`), the message (`PurchaseOrderMessage`) and specific message part (`invoice`) where the value that we wish to bind to is located. The final step to complete the binding is to specify the XPath query (specified in the `query` attribute) that returns the value from the specified message part. In Figure 6-38 this is calculated by the expression `/invoice-number`, which evaluates the contents of the first `invoice-number` element from the root context where the context is provided by the preceding `messageType` and `part` attributes. Now when `PurchaseOrderMessage` messages are processed, the property `InvoiceNumber` will be assigned the value of the corresponding `invoice-number` in the message, or conversely may be used to assign such a value to the `invoice-number` element, just as an object reference can be used in an object-oriented programming language.

Correlating Messages

Through message properties and their corresponding property aliases we are able to manipulate and inspect the contents of messages. However, we also need to be able to relate incoming and outgoing messages to each other and to specific business process instances. While in a typical Web services environment, messages are generally delivered to a particular WDSL port. In BPEL we not only need to deliver messages to the correct port, but to the correct instance of the business process behind that port. Given WSDL's stateless model, developers usually contrive their own methods of accessing resources "behind the port," usually by adding resources identifiers (like GUIDs) into messages, or by encoding the resource into a URI. However, to save developers the burden of having to create ad hoc (and non-interoperable) message routing schemes, BPEL provides message correlation features to support such routing in a generic and reusable fashion.

> The requirement for a BPEL workflow to correlate messages for itself is lessened if the messaging infrastructure for an application is built using some sophisticated conversational transport protocol that can handle message correlation at a lower level. However, in a Web services environment this is generally not the case (at least not currently) and so application-level constructs are still needed. Application-level correlation can, however, be significantly reduced in cases where it is known that more sophisticated transport protocols will be used to transfer network messages. In such cases, correlation declarations in BPEL can be abbreviated to those activities that establish conversations.

The generic routing mechanism supported by BPEL is based on a declarative mechanism called *correlation sets*. To use a correlation set, the developer defines a number (>= 1) of message properties which, when taken together, form a unique key that can be used to distinguish that message from all other instances of that message from other process instances. Once correlation sets are declared, the BPEL implementation then looks after matching this unique key to a particular process instance.

In order to declare a correlation set for the message, we first need to decide what it is about the contents of one instance of that message that differentiates it from another. Or more precisely, which subset of the message properties declared for a message can uniquely identify a message? It is this set of message properties that forms the correlation set.

The first step in setting up correlation for a workflow is to ensure that sufficient message properties are declared to allow the unique identification of messages. For a hypothetical message in the cable TV domain, we expose some of the content of the `AddChannelMessage` message through the following message properties and bind them through their corresponding aliases, as demonstrated in Figure 6-39.

```
<bpws:property name="customer-id" type="co:CustomerIDType"/>
<bpws:property name="channel" type="co:ChannelIDType"/>
<bpws:propertyAlias propertyName="tns:customer-id"
     messageType="tns:AddChannelMessage"
     part="uid"/>
<bpws:propertyAlias propertyName="tns:channel"
     messageType="tns:AddChannelMessage"
     part="order" query="/new-channel"/>
```

Figure 6-39 The `AddChannelMessage` message properties and aliases.

Figure 6-39 declares two properties, `customer-id` and `channel`, which are sufficient to uniquely identify an individual workflow process instance. These properties are bound to elements from the `AddChannelMessage` through `propertyAlias` declarations expose the values held by individual messages in their `uid` and `new-channel` elements respectively. Where the `customer-id` property is bound to the `uid` part of the `AddChannelMessage`, while the `channel` property is bound to the contents of the `new-channel` element of the order part of the `AddChannel` message through the addition of the XPath query `"/new-channel"`.

The correlation set that uses the property elements declared in Figure 6-39 is shown in Figure 6-40. References to this correlation set may be used whenever there is interaction between the customer and the cable operator's Web services. This enables routing to the correct process instances since it ties together a number of message properties (in this case `uid` and `new-channel`) into a unique key. It is then a simple matter for the workflow system to look up the instance associated with this unique key and deal with message routing accordingly.

```
<bpws:correlationSets>
  <bpws:correlationSet properties="tns:uid
                                   tns:new-channel"
       name="AddChannelCorrelationSet"/>
</bpws:correlationSets>
```

Figure 6-40 Correlation set declaration.

Correlating Web Services Invocations

Correlation sets can be used by both senders and receivers of messages, though the way they are used differs depending on whether a message is being sent or received. To make use of a correlation set for a particular Web service invocation, `Correlation` declarations are added to the `invoke`, `receive`, and `reply` activities that handle synchronous and asynchronous Web service invocations. In the case where a message is used to initialize a correlation set, the activity is called an *initiator,* where in the case where an activity uses a pre-initialized correlation set it is said to be a *follower.* It is important to note that whether a message is being sent or received is an orthogonal issue as to how correlation is used since both senders and receivers can be initiators and followers.

Figure 6-41 shows four distinct possibilities for correlated asynchronous communication between Web services, which are the outgoing initiator, outgoing follower, incoming initiator, and incoming follower. We can see each of these roles in a simple cable television scenario as shown in Figure 6-42 and in the subsequent BPEL examples. Note that the following examples are abbreviated versions of the full BPEL syntax that focus specifically on the role of correlation sets during invocation. WSDL, BPEL and other pieces of XML are presented together for convenience and would be factored into different locations (e.g., WSDL file, BPEL script file) in an actual deployment.

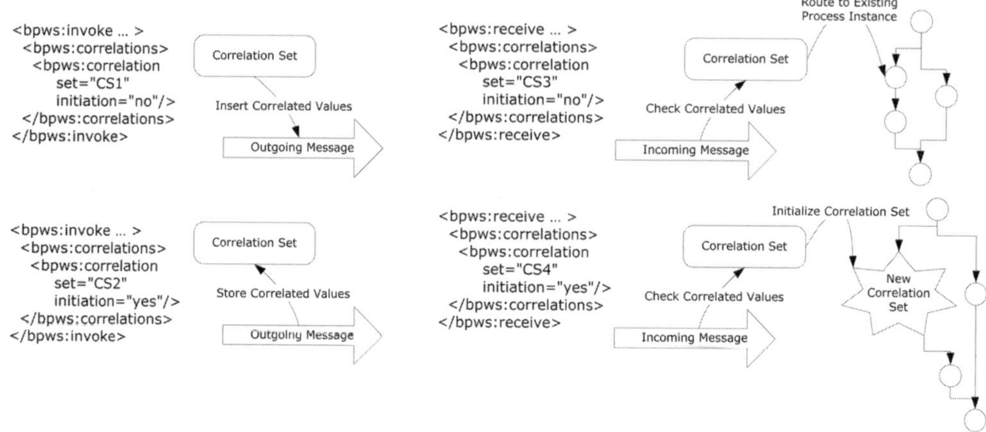

Figure 6-41 Initiators and followers of correlation sets.

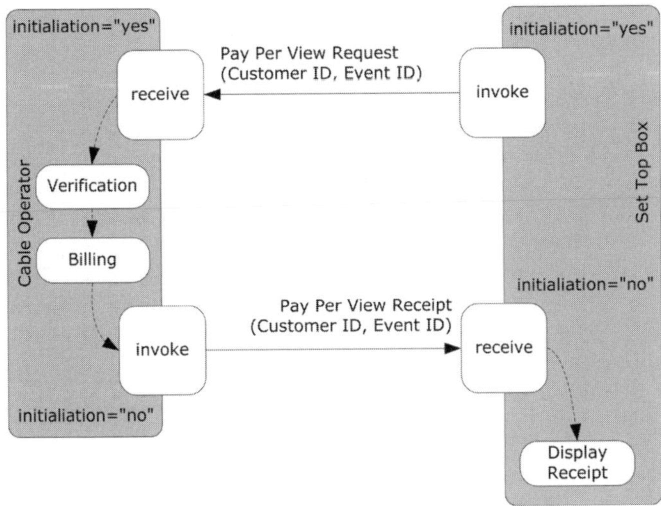

Figure 6-42 Purchasing a Pay Per View event for cable television subscribers.

Figure 6-42 shows a simplified cable TV scenario where a customer (via a set-top box) orders a pay-per-view event. At the system level this translates into running a set-top box workflow that invokes the cable operator's Web services with the request for the pay-per-view event, and then waits for the response from the cable operator before displaying a confirmation message.

The first step in this process is where the set-top box invokes the cable company's Web service to request the pay-per-view event. This is shown in Figure 6-43.

```
WSDL
<!-- Message -->
<wsdl:message name="PayPerViewRequestMessage">
  <wsdl:part name="customer" type="co:CustomerID"/>
  <wsdl:part name="event" type="co:EventID" />
</wsdl:message>

<!-- Message properties -->
<bpws:property name="eventProperty" type="co:EventID"/>

<!-- Property Aliases -->
  <bpws:propertyAlias propertyName="co:eventProperty"
    messageType="co:PayPerViewRequestMessage" part="event"
  />
```

Figure 6-43 Initializing a Correlation Set within an `invoke` activity.

```
BPEL Script
<!-- Correlation Set -->
<bpws:correlationSets>
  <bpws:correlationSet properties="co:eventProperty"
     name="PayPerViewEventCorrelationSet"/>
</bpws:correlationSets>

<!-- Invocation -->
<bpws:invoke partner="CableOperator"
    portType="co:CableOperatorPortType"
    operation="requestPayPerViewEvent"
    inputContainer="PayPerViewRequests">
  <bpws:correlations>
    <bpws:correlation set="PayPerViewEventCorrelationSet"
        initiation="yes"/>
  </bpws:correlations>
    </bpws:invoke>
```

Figure 6-43 Initializing a Correlation Set within an `invoke` activity (continued).

The invocation shown in Figure 6-43 sends a simple message consisting of the customer ID and the event ID to the cable operator to request the particular pay-per-view event. At the same time that the invocation occurs, the correlation set `PayPerViewEventCorrelationSet` is initialized and so the value of the event ID is stored. Once a correlation set has been initialized, whenever messages are sent for which there is a `propertyAlias` specified, the value stored in the correlation set will be inserted into that message. The message then wings its way over the network to the cable operator's systems, where it is consumed by the receive activity shown in Figure 6-44.

```
WSDL
<!-- Message properties -->
<bpws:property name="customerProperty" type="co:CustomerID"/>
<bpws:property name="eventProperty" type="co:EventID"/>

<!-- Property Aliases -->
  <bpws:propertyAlias propertyName="co:customerProperty"
    messageType="co:PayPerViewRequestMessage" part="customer"
  />
  <bpws:propertyAlias propertyName="co:eventProperty"
    messageType="co:PayPerViewRequestMessage" part="event"
  />
```

Figure 6-44 Initializing a correlation set within an `receive` activity.

```
BPEL Script
<!-- Correlation Set -->
<bpws:correlationSets>
  <bpws:correlationSet properties="co:customerProperty
                                   co:eventProperty"
     name="PayPerViewEventCorrelationSet"/>
</bpws:correlationSets>

<!-- Receive message -->
<bpws:receive partner="SetTopBox"
    portType="co:CableOperatorPortType"
    operation="requestPayPerViewEvent"
    container="IncomingPayPerViewRequests"
    createInstance="yes">
  <bpws:correlations>
    <bpws:correlation set="PayPerViewRequestsCorrelationSet"
        initiation="yes"/>
  </bpws:correlations>
</bpws:recieve>
```

Figure 6-44 Initializing a correlation set within an `receive` activity (continued).

The `receive` activity in Figure 6-44 consumes the message produced by the `invoke` activity in Figure 6-43 and creates a new workflow instance on the cable company's workflow system. Once the workflow is instantiated, the `PayPerViewRequestsCorrelationSet` correlation set is initialized and the verification and billing aspects of the workflow proceed.

At some point later when the cable company is satisfied that it can source the event to the customer, and that the customer has paid for those rights, the workflow instance at the cable company finishes by invoking an operation on the customer's set-top box with a message that informs the customer that the pay-per-view transaction has been completed, as we see in Figure 6-45.

```
WSDL
<!-- Message -->
<wsdl:message name="PayPerViewResponseMessage">
  <wsdl:part name="customer" type="co:CustomerID"/>
  <wsdl:part name="event" type="co:EventID" />
  <wsdl:part name="authorized" type="xs:boolean"/>
</wsdl:message>

<!-- Property Aliases -->
  <bpws:propertyAlias propertyName="co:customerProperty"
    messageType="co:PayPerViewResponseMessage"
    part="customer"
  />
  <bpws:propertyAlias propertyName="co:eventProperty"
    messageType="co:PayPerViewResponseMessage" part="event"
  />
```

Figure 6-45 Following a Correlation Set within an `invoke` activity.

```
BPEL Script
<!-- Invocation -->
<bpws:invoke partner="SetTopBox"
    portType="co:SetTopBoxPortType"
    operation="payPerViewEventOutcome"
    inputContainer="PayPerViewResponses">
  <bpws:correlations>
    <bpws:correlation set="PayPerViewEventCorrelationSet"
        initiation="no"/>
  </bpws:correlations>
</bpws:invoke>
```

Figure 6-45 Following a Correlation Set within an `invoke` activity (continued).

The `invoke` activity in Figure 6-45 constitutes the last part of the workflow that was originally started in Figure 6-44, and as such the necessary containers and correlation sets are in scope. Of particular interest is the `PayPerViewEventCorrelationSet` correlation set that populates the outgoing message with the correct customer and event ID details for this workflow—that is, the customer who made the original request and the event originally requested. The only difference with the way in which the cable operator's system responds compared to the set-top box's original request is that the response message has an additional part which declares whether the purchase of the event was successful (as defined in the `PayPerViewResponseMessage` message). This message then makes its way over the network to the customer's set-top box where it is received via a receive activity as shown in Figure 6-46.

In this final `receive` activity, the message has been routed to the correct workflow instance on the set-top box via the `PayPerViewEventCorrelationSet` correlation set and the contents of the incoming message (which are bound to the message through the corresponding `propertyAlias` declarations). Note that the correlation plays a particularly important role here since the customer may have requested many pay-per-view events. It is important to get the correct acknowledgement back to the right process, otherwise the customer will not know which events have been bought and which purchases have failed.

```
<!-- Property Aliases -->
  <bpws:propertyAlias propertyName="co:customerProperty"
    messageType="co:PayPerViewResponseMessage"
    part="customer"
  />
  <bpws:propertyAlias propertyName="co:eventProperty"
    messageType="co:PayPerViewResponseMessage" part="event"
  />
```

Figure 6-46 Following a correlation set within an `receive` activity.

```
BPEL Script
<!-- Receive message -->
<bpws:receive partner="SetTopBox"
    portType="co:SetTopBoxPortType"
    operation="payPerViewEventOutcome"
    container="IncomingPayPerViewResponses"
    createInstance="no">
  <bpws:correlations>
    <bpws:correlation set="PayPerViewEventCorrelationSet"
        initiation="no"/>
  </bpws:correlations>
</bpws:recieve>
```

Figure 6-46 Following a correlation set within an `receive` activity (continued).

Up until this point, we have only considered the correlation of asynchronous services. Synchronous services may also require correlation, though because synchronous requests and responses are implicitly correlated at the transport level, there is less work to do. However, since the messages exchanged across a synchronous transport form part of a larger workflow, their contents may well be correlated to other messages, whether they are synchronous or not. So, we do not avoid understanding the role of a message simply because it travels over HTTP! The standard pattern for correlating synchronously exchanged messages is shown in Figure 6-47, where we see a simple stock check request being sent to a widget manufacturer.

```
<bpws:invoke partner="widget-manufacturer"
     portType="StockCheckPortType"
     operation="checkStockAvailability"
     inputContainer="OutOfStockWidgets"
     outputContainer="StockCheckedWidgets">
  <bpws:correlations>
    <bpws:correlation
         set="StockedWidgetsCorrelationSet"
         pattern="out-in" initiation="yes"/>
  </bpws:correlations>
  <bpws:catch faultName="bw:PaymentUnauthorized"
       faultContainer="UnauthorizedPaymentResponses">
    <bpws:empty/>
  </bpws:catch>
</bpws:invoke>
```

Figure 6-47 Synchronous message correlation.

The correlation pattern used when communicating synchronously is a little different from the asynchronous version. In Figure 6-47, we have declared a correlation using the `Stocked-`

WidgetsCorrelationSet. This specifies that the interaction is synchronous using the attribute pattern="out-in" and is an initiator since the invoke activity populates the values of the correlation set and initializes the values of messages stored in containers once the synchronous operation returns.

In this case the same criteria are used to correlate the outgoing request and later response, since we know that that both messages contain the manufacturers' standard widget codes in identically named elements. However, in the general case, we need to consider the two correlations separately and use one for the pattern="out" leg of the message exchange and a different correlation with pattern="in" for the return leg where the format of the request and response messages are different.

The final point of interest for correlation sets in general is that a single set may be valid for multiple different messages. For example, we may have a number of different messages in a workflow which, although different in structure, element names, attribute names, and so forth, may contain semantically and type-equivalent data.

In Figure 6-48, three propertyAlias declarations each bind a different element from a different message onto the same message property, wm:widgetID. Then whenever one of the particular type of messages is in-scope, the propertyAlias is automatically bound to the right data element in that message and the corresponding messageProperty is set. The construction of correlation sets is thus simplified since the set can be reduced to a single property, albeit a single property which has multiple potential propertyAlias bindings, as opposed to the canonical form, which would use multiple properties each with its own propertyAlias.

```
<bpws:propertyAlias propertyName="wm:widgetID"
  messageType="wm:PurchaseOrderMessage"
  part="WidgetID"/>
<bpws:propertyAlias propertyName="wm:widgetID"
  messageType="stock:StockCheckRequestMessage"
  part="PartNumber"/>
<bpws:propertyAlias propertyName="wm:widgetID"
  messageType="stock:StockCheckResponseMessage"
  part="PartNumber"/>
```

Figure 6-48 Binding a single property to the contents of multiple messages.

Containers and Data Handling

When dealing with Web services-based workflows, we encounter a significant philosophical difference between the two technologies. Workflows are inherently stateful applications, whereas Web services are inherently stateless. Of course, many Web services do actually maintain state between invocations, but do so in a proprietary manner in databases, files, statically allocated program variables and so forth, all of which requires programmer effort and is likely to be inaccessible to the business analyst. BPEL has abstracted these proprietary approaches and replaced them with a generic state management facility based on *containers*.

A BPEL container is a typed data structure that stores messages associated with a workflow instance. The underlying notion of containers is that in a workflow, the state of the application is simply a function of the messages that have been exchanged. Containers begin their lives uninitialized, and are populated over time by the arrival of messages or computations being executed which populate them.

A container cannot be used in an invocation operation until it is fully initialized, which means that a container cannot be used until all of the properties associated with the message type of the container have themselves been initialized.

In Figure 6-49 we present a simple container declaration that could be used by a cable operator to store requests for package updates. This container is used for holding incoming channel addition requests from customers while our workflow process goes about the business updating the customer's billing details and set-top box software accordingly.

```
<bpws:containers>
  <bpws:container name="AddChannelRequests"
       messageType="co:AddChannelMessage"/>
  <!-- Other containers ommitted for brevity -->
</bpws:containers>
```

Figure 6-49 Declaring a container to hold channel addition messages.

Declaring a container is straightforward. It consists of a name for the container that is unique within the scope of the workflow process definition, and the type of message as defined in the corresponding WSDL document. For this example the WSDL interface identified by the `co` prefix resolves to `http://cableoperator.example.org/wsdl`, which is the address at which our fictitious cable operator resides.

Generally, the messages stored in containers are those same messages that are exchanged with partners. However, there is nothing preventing a programmer from concocting a message type purely to store local variables during computations. Such messages are never exchanged with partners, and are usually declared inline with their associated containers, where true message containers reference their message types from published WSDL interfaces. For example, a workflow designer might need to count the number of customer channel addition requests before launching the batch process that updates the software on those customers' set-top boxes. In that case a container may be constructed to hold counter "messages," as shown in Figure 6-50.

```
<bpws:container name="UpdateCounter">
   <bpws:message name="CounterMessage">
      <wsdl:part name="counter" type="xs:int"/>
   </bpws:message>
</bpws:container>
```

Figure 6-50 Using containers to hold temporary variables.

Of course having containers to hold state is only useful if we have ways of accessing and manipulating that state. BPEL supports *expressions* for computing state and *assignments* for updating state, both of which are based on XPath.

BPEL Expressions

The default language for expressions in BPEL is XPath 1.0. Though the specification allows other query languages to be used, the specific reference and use of XPath 1.0 is likely to sway most implementations to also adopt XPath as the de facto query language for BPEL. This means that calculations, of some relatively basic form constrained by XPath's own abilities, can be performed as part of an activity. Such calculations may be trivial, such as incrementing an order number, or may be more complex like calculating a service reference based on the result of interrogating a UDDI service. Generally speaking, BPEL supports four kinds of expressions:

1. Boolean—XPath `EXPR` production where the evaluation results in a Boolean expression. Such expressions are used to manage process control flow.
2. Deadline—XPath `EXPR` production where the evaluation results in a string that is compatible with the format of either XML Schema `date` or `dateTime` types. Such expressions are used in timed `wait` and `pick` activities with a fixed deadline.
3. Duration—XPath `EXPR` production where the evaluation results in a string that is compatible with the format XML Schema `duration`. These expressions are used in timed wait situations with a relative deadline.
4. General—XPath `EXPR` production where any of the XPath types (string, number, or Boolean) can be the result. Such expressions are used for assignment and, depending on the type of the result, may use different operators. Numbers use the <, <=, =, !=, >=, > operators, while integer arithmetic is supported through the +, -, *, / operators. For strings, XPath only supports the equality and inequality operators =, !=.

In addition to the standard XPath 1.0 functions, BPEL also declares three additional XPath functions to enable XPath expressions to access process-specific data (such as elements of messages held in containers). The first of these functions, `getContainerData`, is shown in Figure 6-51.

```
bpws:getContainerData ('containerName', 'partName',
                                        'locationPath'?)
```

Figure 6-51 XPath function referencing data based on container, part and location.

The function shown in Figure 6-51 extracts values held in containers. The first parameter for the function specifies the name of the container in which the data is stored. The second parameter is the part of the message in which the required data is stored, and the optional third parameter is the path within the message where the required data is held. Where the third parameter is not present, the function will return the whole message part element, though the BPEL specification points out that this function is strictly not allowed in abstract processes.

The function shown in Figure 6-52 also retrieves data from containers, but instead of being based on message parts and paths like the function shown in Figure 6-51, it uses properties to reference data elements stored in a particular container. The first parameter for the function specifies the name of the container in which the data is stored, and the second parameter is the name of a global property for a message, given as a `QName`. The return value of this function is the value of the data item referenced by the `propertyName` parameter.

```
bpws:getContainerProperty ('containerName', 'propertyName')
```

Figure 6-52 XPath function referencing data based on container and property.

The final BPEL XPath function is shown in Figure 6-53. This function returns either true or false depending on the status of the link passed as a parameter into the function. If the link status is positive then the function returns true, otherwise it returns false. This function is different from the others that BPEL declared insofar as its argument has to be specified statically—that is, it must be the name of a `link` that appears within a flow activity within the statically defined process and absolutely is not allowed to be computed at runtime.

```
bpws:getLinkStatus ('linkName')
```

Figure 6-53 XPath function for interrogating links.

In addition to extracting data from containers, in the course of a business process we are likely to need to update data held in containers by assigning values to them. This type of activity occurs when we are building up messages to send out to partners or performing calculations based on process variables. The assign activity is used to copy data between containers, update existing data, and construct new data items and insert them into a container as part of a logically atomic operation. The assign activity can be applied equally well to messages, properties and literals, and can even be applied to copy service references to and from partner links.

Workflow Example: Online Shop

Having seen the array of features that BPEL provides, it is now time for us to apply some of those features to building a real workflow. For our example, we shall consider the abstract process of a simple online shop selling toasters, whose computing systems interact with those of its customers and financial partner in a simple arrangement, as shown in Figure 6-54.

Our toaster store is a simple e-business. It has dealings with a number of customers and a bank that provides necessary financial services for processing customer purchases. Additionally our store keeps a small inventory of toasters to be able to respond quickly to any customer, or to keep afloat in times of toaster shortage. However, the core value process of this business is the one that enables customers to purchase toasters and have them delivered to the comfort of their own homes. This involves a number of activities to be coordinated in order to fulfill the customer's requirements, including inventory, payment, and shipping issues. A pictorial representation of this workflow is given in Figure 6-55, Figure 6-56, and Figure 6-57.

Figure 6-55 shows a simple top-level view of the workflow that consists of payment authorization that verifies the financial robustness of the particular customer. Then the payment authorization activity is followed by the stock picking activity. If for some reason the requested item is not available for sale, the customer is informed of the delay or the fact that the order has to be cancelled. At this point the customer is also given the opportunity to cancel the order if the delay is deemed unacceptable. The customer may be informed of further delays, and throughout

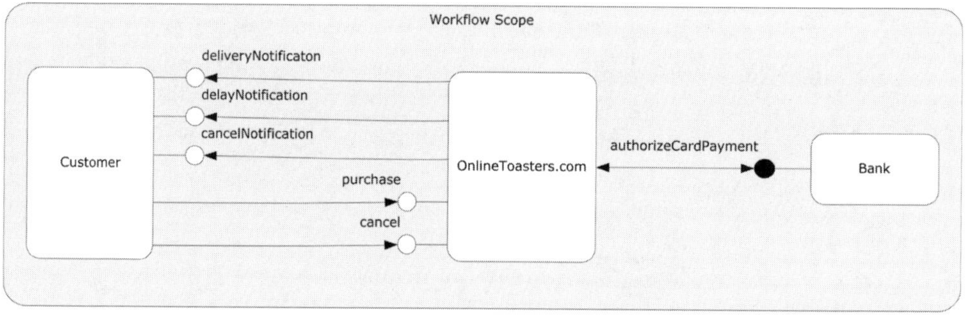

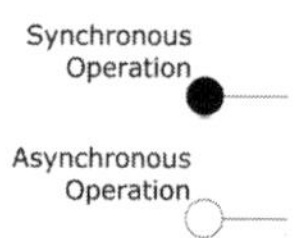

Figure 6-54 Online toaster store partners and interactions.

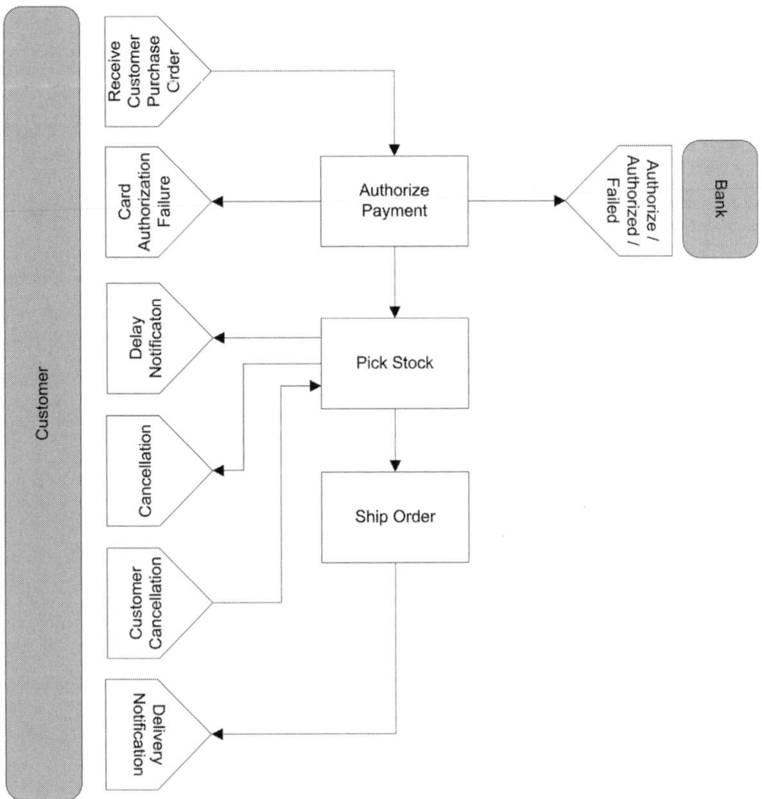

Figure 6-55 The Toaster-Purchase process.

the process has the opportunity to cancel. The final stage in this workflow is the shipping, which is where the packaged goods are posted to the customer.[8]

The payment authorization process is further elaborated on in Figure 6-56. In the normal case, the bank authorizes the credit card payment and the workflow continues to the next stage. If, however, the credit card authorization fails, the customer is informed that the payment has been rejected and the workflow terminates immediately.

Figure 6-57 shows the stock picking and shipping parts of the workflow. The stock picking process is straightforward when the item is in stock since that item is simply sent on to the dispatch part of the process for delivery to the customer. If, however, the item is not in stock, things

8. At this point we should emphasize that this workflow is purely a vehicle through which we will exemplify BPEL, and is not a production-quality workflow design (which is outside the scope of this book). We make no apologies for the naïve design of the workflow since this enables us to explore BPEL without becoming entangled in the intricacies of a particular workflow problem domain.

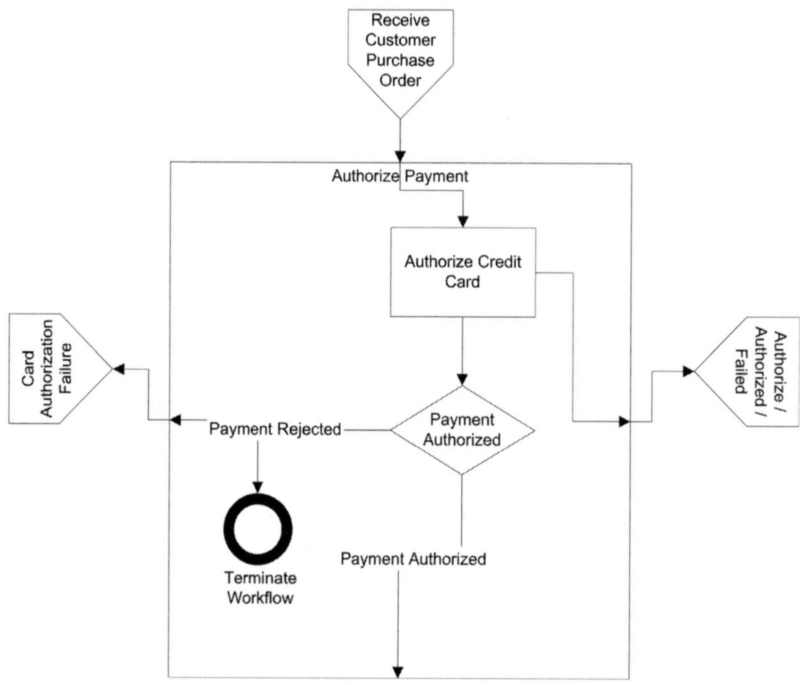

Figure 6-56 Payment authorization sub-process.

get more interesting. The part of the workflow where stock is obtained from a supplier is executed, and the customer is informed of the delay while a supplier is located to source the item. While the item is being tracked down, the customer will receive a delay notification, in response to which the customer is free to cancel the order up until the time that the goods are obtained and dispatched. If the customer decides to cancel the order, it results in the workflow being rolled back, and the customer's credit card being credited. If eventually stock is located, then the workflow progresses to its dispatch phase and the items are posted to the customer, who is informed by the arrival of a delivery notification generated by the workflow instance when the item leaves the store's premises.

Having understood this simple workflow scenario, we can now begin to codify the application protocol that supports the interactions between the parties. There is a shared vocabulary defined by the online toaster store that forms the basis for this protocol as captured in its WSDL schema shown in Figure 6-58.

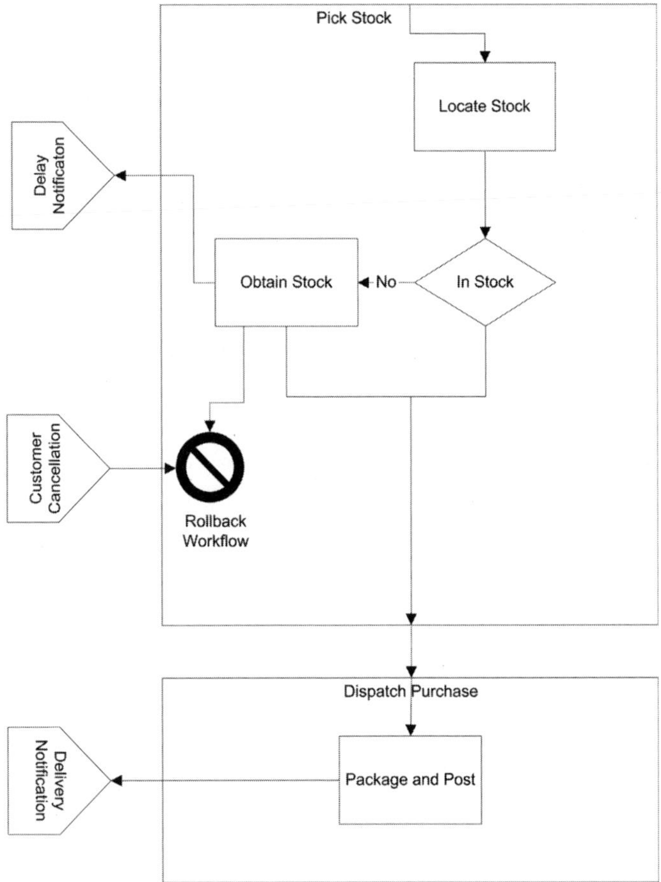

Figure 6-57 Stock allocation and shipping subprocess.

```
<wsdl:definitions
  targetNamespace="http://toaster.example.org/definitions"
  xmlns:tns="http://toaster.example.org/definitions"
  xmlns:wsdl="http://schemas.xmlsoap.org/wsdl/"
  xmlns:xs="http://www.w3.org/2001/XMLSchema">
  <wsdl:types>
    <xs:schema elementFormDefault="qualified"
     attributeFormDefault="unqualified">
      <xs:complexType name="ToasterType">
        <xs:sequence>
          <xs:element name="name" type="xs:string"/>
          <xs:element name="manufacturer" type="xs:string"/>
          <xs:element name="cost">
            <xs:simpleType>
              <xs:restriction base="xs:double">
                <xs:fractionDigits value="2"/>
              </xs:restriction>
            </xs:simpleType>
          </xs:element>
          <xs:element name="SKN">
            <xs:simpleType>
              <xs:restriction base="xs:string">
                <xs:pattern value="[0-9]{3}-[0-9]{3}"/>
              </xs:restriction>
            </xs:simpleType>
          </xs:element>
        </xs:sequence>
      </xs:complexType>
      <xs:complexType name="CustomerType">
        <xs:sequence>
          <xs:element name="title">
            <xs:simpleType>
              <xs:restriction base="xs:string">
                <xs:enumeration value="Mr"/>
                <xs:enumeration value="Mrs"/>
                <xs:enumeration value="Ms"/>
                <xs:enumeration value="Dr"/>
                <xs:enumeration value="Prof"/>
              </xs:restriction>
            </xs:simpleType>
          </xs:element>
          <xs:element name="firstname" type="xs:string"/>
          <xs:element name="surname" type="xs:string"/>
          <xs:element name="house" type="xs:string"
            minOccurs="0"/>
          <xs:element name="street" type="xs:string"/>
          <xs:element name="city" type="xs:string"/>
          <xs:element name="postcode" type="xs:string"/>
        </xs:sequence>
      </xs:complexType>
```

Figure 6-58 The online toaster store schema.

```
      <xs:complexType name="CreditCardType">
        <xs:sequence>
          <xs:element name="card-type">
            <xs:simpleType>
              <xs:restriction base="xs:string">
                <xs:enumeration value="Visa"/>
                <xs:enumeration value="MasterCard"/>
              </xs:restriction>
            </xs:simpleType>
          </xs:element>
          <xs:element name="expiry">
            <xs:simpleType>
              <xs:restriction base="xs:string">
                <xs:pattern value="[0-9]{2}-[0-9]{2}"/>
              </xs:restriction>
            </xs:simpleType>
          </xs:element>
          <xs:element name="number">
            <xs:simpleType name="CardNumberType">
              <xs:restriction base="xs:string">
                <xs:pattern value="[0-9]{4} [0-9]{4} [0-9]{4} [0-9]{4}"/>
              </xs:restriction>
            </xs:simpleType>
          </xs:element>
          <xs:element name="holder" type="xs:string"/>
        </xs:sequence>
      </xs:complexType>
    </xs:schema>
  </wsdl:types>
</wsdl:definitions>
```

Figure 6-58 The online toaster store schema (continued).

Having the schema, we can begin to construct the WSDL interface for our Web services, and begin to see just how we can turn this from a flow-diagram idea into an actual Web services reality.

Customer Web Service

In a typical interaction between a customer's system (which will be something like a shopping portal) and our online toaster shop's systems, we might expect a set of message exchanges looking something like that shown in Figure 6-59.

The first thing to notice about the interaction shown in Figure 6-59 is that the messages are not synchronous, though there are obvious pairings. There is no notion of request-response in this interaction since the process started by the buyer sending a purchase message to the seller may take an arbitrarily long time to complete and, thus, a request-response style interaction is unjustifiable from both performance and reliability viewpoints. Instead, the seller receives the purchase message and at some point later, if all goes well, sends a message back to the buyer

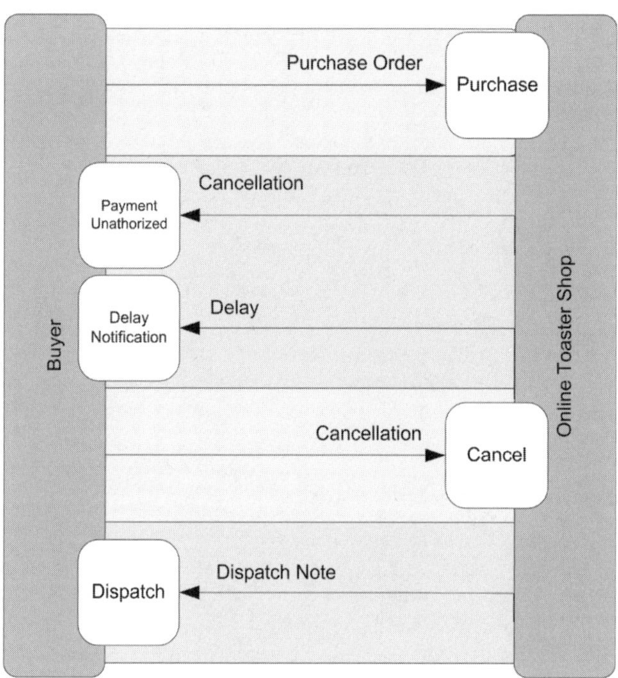

Figure 6-59 Buyer/seller message exchanges.

indicating that the purchase has been successful. If the customer's credit card cannot be authorized for the sale price, then the seller sends a cancellation message. If there are delays in the purchase, then the customer may send a cancellation message. If, however, the workflow isn't terminated by a customer cancellation message, the workflow terminates successfully by sending a dispatch note to the customer.

The customer's service has a WSDL interface designed to allow the toaster store to keep it abreast of the workflow as it progresses, as shown in Figure 6-60.

The WSDL in Figure 6-61 exposes three one-way operations that will be invoked by the toaster-vending service (and that are often referred to as *callback* operations) as the purchase workflow proceeds. Normally, the toaster-vending service will at some point send a `DeliveryNotificationMessage` message to invoke the `notifyDelivery` operation, but in the case where there has been a problem with the purchase, it may instead respond with an `OrderCancelledMessage` message. In the event of a delay in shipping the customer's purchase, the online store can call back the customer with a `DelayNotificationMessage` message to invoke the `delayDelivery` operation. This informs the customer of the delay and gives that customer a chance to cancel the order.

```
<?xml version="1.0" encoding="utf-8"?>
<wsdl:definitions
  xmlns:wsdl="http://schemas.xmlsoap.org/wsdl/"
  xmlns:xs="http://www.w3.org/2001/XMLSchema"
  targetNamespace="http://customer.example.org/wsdl"
  xmlns:tns="http://customer.example.org/wsdl"
  xmlns:df="http://toaster.example.org/definitions"
  xmlns:soap="http://schemas.xmlsoap.org/soap/envelope/">
  <wsdl:import
    namespace="http://toaster.example.org/definitions"
    location="http://toaster.example.org/definitions.wsdl"/>
  <wsdl:message name="DeliveryNotificationMessage">
    <wsdl:part name="toaster" type="df:ToasterType"/>
    <wsdl:part name="customer" type="df:CustomerType"/>
    <wsdl:part name="dispatchDate" type="xs:dateTime"/>
  </wsdl:message>
  <wsdl:message name="DelayNotificationMessage">
    <wsdl:part name="toaster" type="df:ToasterType"/>
    <wsdl:part name="customer" type="df:CustomerType"/>
    <wsdl:part name="orderDate" type="xs:dateTime"/>
    <wsdl:part name="delayedBy" type="xs:positiveInteger"/>
  </wsdl:message>
  <wsdl:message name="OrderCancelledMessage">
    <wsdl:part name="toaster" type="df:ToasterType"/>
    <wsdl:part name="customer" type="df:CustomerType"/>
    <wsdl:part name="reason" type="xs:string"/>
  </wsdl:message>
  <wsdl:portType name="CustomerPortType">
    <wsdl:operation name="notifyDelivery">
      <wsdl:input message="tns:DeliveryNotificationMessage"/>
    </wsdl:operation>
    <wsdl:operation name="delayDelivery">
      <wsdl:input message="tns:DelayNotificationMessage"/>
    </wsdl:operation>
    <wsdl:operation name="cancelDelivery">
      <wsdl:input message="tns:OrderCancelledMessage"/>
    </wsdl:operation>
  </wsdl:portType>
</wsdl:definitions>
```

Figure 6-60 Customer service's WSDL interface.

Decoupling services by allowing them to communicate asynchronously is a sensible design decision in most enterprise-class Web services. If services communicate asynchronously, then they can fail (and recover) without compromising other services (clients of a service are not rudely interrupted by a connection failing, since there is no connection present most of the time). Then network resources are not wasted by keeping alive connections for large amounts of time.

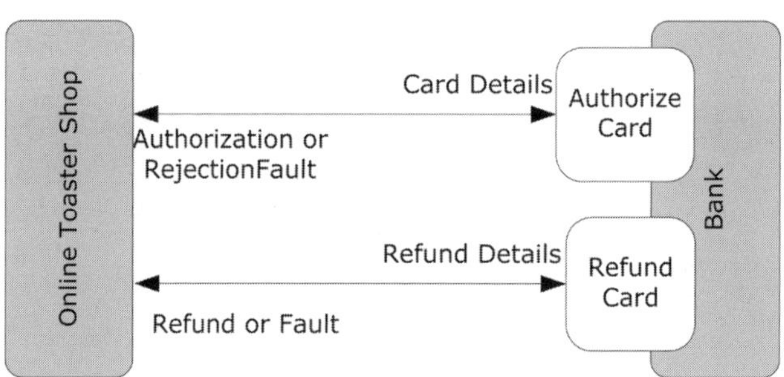

Figure 6-61 Payment authorization message exchange pattern.

The interaction between the online toaster shop and its partner bank is a little different from the interaction between a customer and the store in two main ways. First, the relationship between the toaster store and its bank is likely to be far more permanent than the transitory relationship struck up for a particular customer purchase. Second, since (at least within the scope of this workflow) the interaction with the partner is short-lived, we can afford to more closely couple the two systems. Practically, this means that we are able to use synchronous communications between the two services because we are satisfied of the high availability of the bank systems, the fact that its systems' interfaces are unlikely to change a great deal over time, and the fact that authorizing a credit card payment is a short-lived process. As such, the bank defines its WSDL to accommodate this style of interaction as shown in Figure 6-62, where the infrastructure to support the simple synchronous credit card authorization is exposed to a request-response operation called `authorizeCreditCard`, along with a similar synchronous refund operation called `refundPayment`.

```
<?xml version="1.0" encoding="utf-8"?>
<wsdl:definitions
  xmlns:wsdl="http://schemas.xmlsoap.org/wsdl/"
  xmlns:xs="http://www.w3.org/2001/XMLSchema"
  targetNamespace="http://bank.example.org/wsdl"
  xmlns:tns="http://bank.example.org/wsdl"
  xmlns:df="http://toaster.example.org/definitions"
  xmlns:soap="http://schemas.xmlsoap.org/soap/envelope/">
  <wsdl:import
    namespace="http://toaster.example.org/definitions"
    location="http://toaster.example.org/definitions.wsdl"/>
  <wsdl:message name="CreditCardAuthorizationRequestMessage">
    <wsdl:part name="creditCard" type="df:CreditCardType"/>
    <wsdl:part name="amount" type="xs:float"/>
  </wsdl:message>
```

Figure 6-62 Bank service WSDL.

```
  <wsdl:message name="CreditCardAuthorizedMessage">
    <wsdl:part name="creditCard" type="df:CreditCardType"/>
    <wsdl:part name="amount" type="xs:float"/>
  </wsdl:message>
  <wsdl:message name="UnauthorizedPaymentMessage">
    <wsdl:part name="creditCard" type="df:CreditCardType"/>
    <wsdl:part name="amount" type="xs:float"/>
    <wsdl:part name="reason" type="xs:string"/>
  </wsdl:message>
  <wsdl:message name="RefundRequestMessage">
    <wsdl:part name="creditCard" type="df:CreditCardType"/>
    <wsdl:part name="amount" type="xs:float"/>
  </wsdl:message>
  <wsdl:message name="PaymentRefundedMessage">
    <wsdl:part name="creditCard" type="df:CreditCardType"/>
    <wsdl:part name="amount" type="xs:float"/>
  </wsdl:message>
  <wsdl:message name="RefundFailedMessage">
    <wsdl:part name="creditCard" type="df:CreditCardType"/>
    <wsdl:part name="amount" type="xs:float"/>
    <wsdl:part name="reason" type="xs:string"/>
  </wsdl:message>
  <wsdl:portType name="BankPortType">
    <wsdl:operation name="authorizeCreditCard">
      <wsdl:input
        message="tns:CreditCardAuthorizationRequestMessage"/>
      <wsdl:output
        message="tns:CreditCardAuthorizedMessage"/>
      <wsdl:fault name="unathorizedPaymentFault"
        message="tns:UnauthorizedPaymentMessage"/>
    </wsdl:operation>
    <wsdl:operation name="refundPayment">
      <wsdl:input message="tns:RefundRequestMessage"/>
      <wsdl:output message="tns:PaymentRefundedMessage"/>
      <wsdl:fault name="refundFault"
        message="tns:RefundFailedMessage"/>
    </wsdl:operation>
  </wsdl:portType>
</wsdl:definitions>
```

Figure 6-62 Bank service WSDL (continued).

The final piece of WSDL for our example is that of the OnlineToasters.com Web service, as shown in Figure 6-63.

Figure 6-63 contains a single `portType` declaration to allow customers to place orders with the OnlineToasters.com system. It also declares a number of message `property` elements and a number of bindings to a number of messages for each of those property elements through the `propertyAlias` declarations. As we shall see, these `property` declarations are used

```
<?xml version="1.0" encoding="utf-8"?>
<wsdl:definitions
  xmlns:wsdl="http://schemas.xmlsoap.org/wsdl/"
  xmlns:xs="http://www.w3.org/2001/XMLSchema"
  targetNamespace="http://toaster.example.org/wsdl"
  xmlns:tns="http://toaster.example.org/wsdl"
  xmlns:df="http://toaster.example.org/definitions"
  xmlns:soap="http://schemas.xmlsoap.org/soap/envelope/"
  xmlns:bpws="http://schemas.xmlsoap.org/ws/2002/07/business-
process/">
  <wsdl:import
    namespace="http://toaster.example.org/definitions"
    location="http://toaster.example.org/definitions.wsdl"/>
  <wsdl:message name="PurchaseMessage">
    <wsdl:part name="toaster" type="df:ToasterType"/>
    <wsdl:part name="customer" type="df:CustomerType"/>
    <wsdl:part name="creditCard" type="df:CreditCardType"/>
    <wsdl:part name="timestamp" type="xs:dateTime"/>
  </wsdl:message>
  <wsdl:message name="CancelMessage">
    <wsdl:part name="customer" type="df:CustomerType"/>
    <wsdl:part name="timestamp" type="xs:dateTime"/>
  </wsdl:message>
  <wsdl:message name="StockCheckRequestMessage">
    <wsdl:part name="toaster" type="df:ToasterType"/>
  </wsdl:message>
  <wsdl:message name="StockCheckResponseMessage">
    <wsdl:part name="daysToDelivery"
      type="xs:postiveInteger"/>
  </wsdl:message>
  <wsdl:message name="CurrentTimeMessage">
    <wsdl:part name="currentTime" type="xs:dateTime"/>
  </wsdl:message>
  <wsdl:message name="OrderPostedMessage">
    <wsdl:part name="customer" type="df:CustomerType"/>
    <wsdl:part name="timestamp" type="xs:dateTime"/>
    <wsdl:part name="now" type="xs:dateTime"/>
  </wsdl:message>
  <wsdl:portType name="ToasterVendorPortType">
    <wsdl:operation name="purchaseToaster">
      <wsdl:input message="tns:PurchaseMessage"/>
    </wsdl:operation>
    <wsdl:operation name="cancelToaster">
      <wsdl:input message="tns:CancelMessage"/>
    </wsdl:operation>
    <wsdl:operation name="stockCheck">
      <wsdl:input message="tns:StockCheckRequestMessage"/>
      <wsdl:output message="tns:StockCheckResponseMessage"/>
    </wsdl:operation>
```

Figure 6-63 OnlineToasters.com WSDL interface.

```
    <wsdl:operation name="registerPostedOrder">
      <wsdl:output message="tns:OrderPostedMessage"/>
    </wsdl:operation>
  </wsdl:portType>


  <!-- BPEL message properties and propertyAliases -->
  <bpws:property name="OrderCustomerProperty"
    type="df:CustomerType"/>
  <bpws:property name="OrderTimestampProperty"
    type="xs:dateTime"/>
  <bpws:propertyAlias
    propertyName="tns:OrderCustomerProperty"
    messageType="tns:PurchaseMessage" part="customer"/>
  <bpws:propertyAlias
    propertyName="tns:OrderCustomerProperty"
    messageType="tns:CancelMessage" part="customer"/>
  <bpws:propertyAlias
    propertyName="tns:OrderCustomerProperty"
    messageType="tns:OrderPostedMessage" part="customer"/>
  <bpws:propertyAlias
    propertyName="tns:OrderTimestampProperty"
    messageType="tns:PurchaseMessage" part="timestamp"/>
  <bpws:propertyAlias
    propertyName="tns:OrderTimestampProperty"
    messageType="tns:CancelMessage" part="timestamp"/>
  <bpws:propertyAlias
    propertyName="tns:OrderTimestampProperty"
    messageType="tns:OrderPostedMessage" part="timestamp"/>
</wsdl:definitions>
```

Figure 6-63 OnlineToasters.com WSDL interface (continued).

throughout the workflow to identify and correlate messages (bound to them through `propertyAlias` declarations) and workflow instances that logically belong to the same customer order using BPEL's correlation set features.

More importantly, Figure 6-63 is also the starting point of the interface for our enterprise, and it is this interface that we will augment as we dig down further into BPEL. At this point OnlineToasters.com is (theoretically) up and running. All we need now is to work out how to integrate our bank and customers into our workflow. The first step in this process is to model our business processes in relation to those of our partners. In our example scenario, we capture the abstract roles of the enterprises with a number of `serviceLinkType` declarations as shown in Figure 6-64.

Each role in a BPEL service link is defined by a name for that role and a number of `portType` declarations that an entity playing that role has to support. For example, in Figure

```
<wsdl:definitions
  targetNamespace="http://toaster.example.org/slinks"
  xmlns:wsdl="http://schemas.xmlsoap.org/wsdl/"
  xmlns:slnk="http://schemas.xmlsoap.org/ws/2002/07/service-
link/"
  xmlns:xs="http://www.w3.org/2001/XMLSchema"
  xmlns:toast="http://toaster.example.org.wsdl"
  xmlns:cust="http://customer.example.org/wsdl"
  xmlns:bank="http://bank.example.org/wsdl">
  <wsdl:import namespace="http://toaster.example.org/wsdl"
    location="http://toaster.example.org/wsdl "/>
  <import namespace="http://customer.example.org/wsdl"
    location=" http://customer.example.org/wsdl "/>
  <import namespace="http://bank.example.org/wsdl"
    location=" http://bank.example.org/wsdl "/>
  <slnk:serviceLinkType name="CallBackLink">
    <slnk:role name="self">
      <portType name="toast:ToasterVendorPortType"/>
    </slnk:role>
  </slnk:serviceLinkType>
  <slnk:serviceLinkType name="CustomerVendorLink">
    <slnk:role name="customer">
      <portType name="cust:CustomerPortType"/>
    </slnk:role>
    <slnk:role name="vendor">
      <portType name="toast:ToasterVendorPortType"/>
    </slnk:role>
  </slnk:serviceLinkType>
  <slnk:serviceLinkType name="CardAuthorizerLink">
    <slnk:role name="authorizer">
      <portType name="bank:BankPortType"/>
    </slnk:role>
  </slnk:serviceLinkType>
  <wsdl:service name="toasterServiceBusinessProcess"/>
</wsdl:definitions>
```

Figure 6-64 Service link declarations.

6-65, any Web service playing the role of a `customer` must support the `CustomerPortType` portType.

Usually each `portType` specified by a role originates in a different namespace, since partners are usually physically separate enterprises. However we can also define relationships where a service link is declared with `portType` declarations from the same namespace. In Figure 6-64, this is exemplified by the role `self` indicating that the implementing service must expose a `ToasterVendorPortType` `portType` which, as we saw in Figure 6-64, is within the namespace of the online toaster store's WSDL interface (and as we shall see in workflow process itself is used to allow our enterprise to invoke other services within its own enterprise boundary).

The final form of serviceLinkType is the one where one role is specified instead of the usual two. This indicates that a service is willing to bind to any other service without the requirement that the binding service has any particular interface characteristics. A good example of this in Figure 6-65 is the CardAuthorizerLink where the bank service is described as one that is quite unconcerned about who binds to it (at least as far as their interfaces are concerned). It is important to remember that unilateral role declarations are only useful in one-way or synchronous message exchanges since by definition an asynchronous bilateral exchange of messages requires a known portType (and address) to call back to.

At this point we have captured the relational aspects of the system. We know which enterprises are involved and we understand their interfaces, roles, and interrelations. The final stage in taking this forward to a workflow is to write the algorithm that performs the necessary computation and coordination between these parties to get a customer's order delivered. This workflow is shown split into logical units in Figure 6-65 through Figure 6-75.

```
<bpws:process name="toasterPurchaseProcess"
 targetNamespace="http://toaster.example.org/purchaseProcess"
 suppressJoinFailure="yes"
 xmlns:bpws="http://schemas.xmlsoap.org/ws/2002/07/business-
process/"
 xmlns:slinks="http://toaster.example.org/slinks"
 xmlns:df="http://toaster.example.org/definitions"
 xmlns:toast="http://toaster.example.org/wsdl"
 xmlns:cust="http://customer.example.org/wsdl"
 xmlns:bank="http://bank.example.org/wsdl"
 xmlns:wsdl="http://schemas.xmlsoap.org/wsdl/">
 <bpws:correlations>
   <!-- The customer details and timestamp are sufficient to
        uniquely identify a purchase -->
   <correlationSet name="OrderCorrelationSet"
     properties="toast:OrderCustomerProperty,
     toast:OrderTimestampProperty"/>
 </bpws:correlations>
```

Figure 6-65 Correlation set declaration.

Figure 6-65 shows the opening declarations of the workflow process where the various namespace affiliations of the elements in the process are introduced. More interestingly, it also introduces a correlation set which defines a unique key based on the CustomerOrderProperty and OrderTimestampProperty properties defined in Figure 6-63. When activated, this correlation set can be used to route messages to a particular process instance (or create a new process instance) based on the contents of the matching fields in those messages and the activity waiting for that message. In our workflow, the correlation set is initialized in Figure 6-71 by the receipt of a customer order, and is later used to correlate with a possible customer cancellation message for that order as in Figure 6-74.

```
<bpws:containers>
    <!-- For receiving messages from customers -->
    <bpws:container name="PurchaseOrders"
      messageType="toast:PurchaseMessage"/>
    <bpws:container name="Cancellations"
      messageType="toast:CancelMessage"/>
    <!-- For sending messages to customers -->
    <bpws:container name="DispatchNotifications"
      messageType="cust:DeliveryNotificationMessage"/>
    <bpws:container name="DelayNotifications"
      messageType="cust:DelayNotificationMessage"/>
    <bpws:container name="CancellationNotifications"
      messageType="cust:OrderCancelledMessage"/>
    <!-- For authorizing credit card payment with
         the bank -->
    <bpws:container name="PaymentAuthorizationRequests"

messageType="bank:CreditCardAuthorizationRequestMessage"/>
    <bpws:container name="AuthorizedPayments"
      messageType="bank:CreditCardAuthorizedMessage"/>
    <bpws:container name="UnauthorizedPayments"
      messageType="bank:UnauthorizedPaymentMessage"/>
    <bpws:container name="RefundRequests"
      messageType="bank:RefundRequestMessage"/>
    <bpws:container name="RefundedPayments"
      messageType="bank:PaymentRefundedMessage"/>
    <bpws:container name="RefusedRefunds"
      messageType="bank:RefundFailedMessage"/>
    <!-- For performing stock checks -->
    <bpws:container name="StockCheckItem"
      messageType="toast:StockCheckRequestMessage"/>
    <bpws:container name="ItemAvailability"
      messageType="toast:StockCheckResponseMessage"/>
    <!-- For creating dispatch notes -->
    <bpws:container name="PostedOrders"
      messageType="toast:OrderPostedMessage"/>
  </bpws:containers>
```

Figure 6-66 Container declarations.

The container declarations for this process shown in Figure 6-66 are used to hold incoming messages while they are being processed, and as a placeholder for the construction of outgoing messages as their contents are being populated.

The `partner` elements shown in Figure 6-67 build on the previous `serviceLinkType` declarations, to create friendly-named entities with which our workflow algorithm engages in communication. Each partner declaration also specifies which role of the associated `serviceLinkType` will be played by our enterprise and which by a particular partner's.

```
<!-- The entities involved in this workflow -->
<bpws:partners>
  <bpws:partner name="backEndService"
    serviceLinkType="slinks:CallBackLink"
    partnerRole="self"/>
  <bpws:partner name="customer"
    serviceLinkType="slinks:CustomerVendorLink"
    myRole="vendor" partnerRole="customer"/>
  <bpws:partner name="bank"
    serviceLinkType="slinks:CardAuthorizerLink"
    partnerRole="authorizer"/>
</bpws:partners>
```

Figure 6-67 Partner declarations.

```
<bpws:faultHandlers>
  <bpws:catchAll>
    <!-- If an unexpected fault happens at this level,
         reverse the whole business transaction -->
    <compensate/>
  </bpws:catchAll>
</bpws:faultHandlers>
```

Figure 6-68 Top-level fault handler declarations.

The fault handler shown in Figure 6-68 is designed to allow the workflow to shutdown gracefully in the event of an unexpected and otherwise unhandled fault propagating to the top level. In the event of any unhandled fault reaching this level, the `catchAll` activity is activated which forces the workflow to compensate, as per the compensation routine in Figure 6-69. This causes the compensation activity at this level to be executed, followed by recursive compensation on all subactivities.

The compensation activity shown in Figure 6-69 first defines that any faults arising during compensation are suppressed by having a `catchAll` fault handler contain an `empty` activity. In this case it is a safe thing to do because the only fault we expect is that the bank will fault if we try to refund a card from which it has not extracted a payment. However, in more industrial strength workflows, it is entirely plausible that compensation activities will contain their own sophisticated fault handling routines to ensure that compensation progresses even in the presence of faults.

In the unexceptional execution case, the compensation activity builds a refund request message by copying the details of the transaction from the `PurchaseOrders` container, which contains the details of the current order, into the `RefundRequests` container, which holds (at this point empty) messages suitable for sending to the bank to request a credit card refund. Once this message is constructed, it is sent to the bank through an `invoke` activity

```
<bpws:sequence>
  <bpws:scope containerAccessSerializable="no">
    <!-- The inverse of this activity is to refund the
         customer's credit card and send a cancellation
         message -->
    <bpws:compensationHandler>
      <!-- Fault handler to deal with transient network
           faults when communicating with the bank -->
      <bpws:faultHandlers>
        <!-- Do nothing if the bank faults, because there's
             no refund to process -->
        <bpws:catch faultName="refundFault"
          faultContainer="RefusedRefunds">
          <bpws:empty/>
          <!-- Surpress the fault -->
        </bpws:catch>
      </bpws:faultHandlers>
      <!-- Build refund request message -->
      <bpws:assign>
        <bpws:copy>
          <bpws:from container="PurchaseOrders"
            part="creditCard"/>
          <bpws:to container="RefundRequests"
            part="creditCard"/>
        </bpws:copy>
      </bpws:assign>
      <bpws:assign>
        <bpws:copy>
          <bpws:from container="PurchaseOrders"
            part="toaster" query="/cost"/>
          <bpws:to container="RefundRequests"
            part="amount"/>
        </bpws:copy>
      </bpws:assign>
      <!-- Instruct bank to process refund -->
      <bpws:invoke partner="bank"
        portType="bank:BankPortType"
        operation="refundPayment"
        inputContainer="RefundRequests"
        outputContainer="RefundedPayments"/>
    </bpws:compensationHandler>
```

Figure 6-69 Top-level compensation handler for the workflow.

which specifies that the `refundPayment` operation is to be invoked on the bank partner using the message in the `RefundRequests` container as the input message to that operation and storing the results of that invocation in the `RefundedPayments` container. In the case where a fault is returned because the bank cannot refund the card (since there was no corresponding previous debit), the fault handler is invoked and the fault suppressed.

The net result of this handler being activated is that any order being processed is dropped, and any credit card payments that have been taken are cancelled.

```
<!-- Handle possible faults (and possibly cancel
     purchase)-->
<bpws:faultHandlers>
  <bpws:catch faultName="bank:unauthorizedPaymentFault"
    faultContainer="UnauthorizedPayments">
    <!-- Build the contents of the cancellation
         notification message from the authorization
         fault and customer's original purchase
         order -->
    <bpws:assign>
      <bpws:copy>
        <bpws:from container="UnauthorizedPayments"
          part="reason"/>
        <bpws:to container="CancellationNotifications"
          part="reason"/>
      </bpws:copy>
    </bpws:assign>
    <bpws:assign>
      <bpws:copy>
        <bpws:from container="PurchaseOrders"
          part="customer"/>
        <bpws:to container="CancellationNotifications"
          part="customer"/>
      </bpws:copy>
    </bpws:assign>
    <bpws:assign>
      <bpws:copy>
        <bpws:from container="PurchaseOrders"
          part="toaster"/>
        <bpws:to container="CancellationNotifications"
          part="toaster"/>
      </bpws:copy>
    </bpws:assign>
    <!-- Send the cancel message to the customer -->
    <bpws:invoke partner="customer"
      portType="cust:CustomerPortType"
      operation="cancelDelivery"
      inputContainer="Cancellations"/>
    <!-- Terminate the workflow -->
    <bpws:terminate/>
  </bpws:catch>
</bpws:faultHandlers>
```

Figure 6-70 Fault handlers for the credit card authorization subprocess.

Figure 6-70 shows the fault handler for those situations where a customer order provides credit card details for which authorization and payment are subsequently denied by the bank, as signified by the return of an unauthorizedPaymentFault message in response to a authorizeCreditCard operation invocation on the bank Web service. This fault handler responds to that eventuality by building a CancellationNotificationMessage message, copying the reason element from the fault produced by the faulting invocation, and the customer and item details from the original purchase order into the CancellationNotifications container. This container is used as input for the one-way invoke activity on the customer's cancelDelivery operation to inform the customer that the order has been cancelled and why. The handler then terminates this workflow instance, which it is safe to do since at this point no billing has occurred nor have any items been shipped.

```
<!-- Receive Customer Order and  Payment -->
<bpws:receive partner="customer"
  portType="toast:ToasterVendorPortType"
  operation="purchaseToaster"
  container="PurchaseOrders" createInstance="yes">
  <bpws:correlations>
    <bpws:correlation set="OrderCorrelationSet"
      initiation="yes"/>
  </bpws:correlations>
</bpws:receive>
```

Figure 6-71 Receiving a customer order.

The receive activity shown in Figure 6-71 is the entry point to this workflow. It accepts the invocation from a customer on our enterprise's purchaseToaster operation and stores the contents of the message in the PurchaseOrders container ready to be used in the workflow. The receive activity also initializes the OrderCorrelationSet correlation set with the customer and timestamp parts from the incoming PurchaseMessage message, forming a unique key that identifies this instance of the process from now onward. New messages arriving that contain these fields can now be automatically routed to the correct instance by the underlying BPEL engine.

The first thing that our workflow does when it receives a purchaseMessage message is to check whether the customer is good for payment! It does this by building a CreditCardAuthorizationRequestMessage message in the PaymentAuthorizationRequests container, which it populates with the credit card details and the cost of the order as shown in Figure 6-72. The credit card details are extracted directly from the purchaseMessage message through an assignment from the creditCard part of the purchaseMessage message to the creditCard part of the PaymentAuthorizationRequests container. The amount being charged is extracted from the toaster part of the purchaseMessage message, with the

```
    <!-- Build the message to send to the credit card
         authorization service -->
    <bpws:assign>
      <bpws:copy>
        <bpws:from container="PurchaseOrders"
          part="creditCard"/>
        <bpws:to container="PaymentAuthorizationRequests"
          part="creditCard"/>
      </bpws:copy>
    </bpws:assign>
    <bpws:assign>
      <bpws:copy>
        <bpws:from container="PurchaseOrders"
          part="toaster" query="/cost"/>
        <bpws:to container="PaymentAuthorizationRequests"
          part="amount"/>
      </bpws:copy>
    </bpws:assign>
    <!-- Invoke the credit card authorization service -->
    <bpws:invoke partner="bank"
      portType="bank:BankPortType"
      operation="authorizeCreditCard"
      inputContainer="PaymentAuthorizationRequests"
      outputContainer="AuthorizedPayments"/>
  </bpws:scope>
  <!-- End of authorization, from here on in we know
       the customer has paid -->
```

Figure 6-72 Authorizing a credit card payment.

query string `/cost` being used to extract to particular piece of data from that message part. Once the message has been constructed, the bank is asked to take payment on the credit card via a synchronous `invoke` activity, which receives confirmation of the payment via a message delivered back to the `AuthorizedPayments` container. If the payment is not authorized, then the bank returns a fault which is handled by the fault handler shown in Figure 6-70 that terminates the purchase process.

Once payment has been taken, the goods the customer has ordered are made ready for dispatch. The first step in this task is to check stock availability for the ordered item, which involves invoking a Web service within our own enterprise. This is shown in Figure 6-73 where a synchronous `invoke` activity is used to query our inventory for the customer's item. Figure 6-73 shows how the `toaster` part of the original `PurchaseMessage` message is used to build a `StockCheckRequestMessage` message in the `StockCheckItem` container, which is then used to invoke the `stockCheck` operation on the inventory Web service. The result of that invocation is placed in the `ItemAvailability` container, which is then subsequently used to determine how to respond to the customer as shown in Figure 6-74.

```
<!-- Pick Stock -->
<!-- Build stock check request message -->
<bpws:assign>
  <bpws:copy>
    <bpws:from container="PurchaseOrders"
      part="toaster"/>
    <bpws:to container="StockCheckItem" part="toaster"/>
  </bpws:copy>
</bpws:assign>
<!-- Call stock check and look at availability date -->
<bpws:invoke partner="backEndService"
  portType="toast:ToasterVendorPortType"
  operation="stockCheck" inputContainer="StockCheckItem"
  outputContainer="ItemAvailability"/>
```

Figure 6-73 Obtaining stock from inventory or partner.

```
<bpws:switch>
     <!-- If we can't get the toaster in 3 days or less,
          then we have to inform the customer of the delay
          and give them a chance to cancel-->
     <bpws:case
   condition="bpws:getContainerData(ItemAvailability,
daysToDelivery) > 3">
       <!-- Build the delay notification message -->
       <bpws:assign>
         <bpws:copy>
           <bpws:from container="PurchaseOrders"
             part="toaster"/>
           <bpws:to container="DelayNotifications"
             part="toaster"/>
         </bpws:copy>
       </bpws:assign>
       <bpws:assign>
         <bpws:copy>
           <bpws:from container="PurchaseOrders"
             part="customer"/>
           <bpws:to container="DelayNotifications"
             part="customer"/>
         </bpws:copy>
       </bpws:assign>
       <bpws:assign>
         <bpws:copy>
           <bpws:from
      expression="bpws:getContainerData (ItemAvailability,
daysToDelivery)"/>
```

Figure 6-74 Dealing with possible stock delays.

```
          <bpws:to container="DelayNotifications"
            part="delayedBy"/>
        </bpws:copy>
      </bpws:assign>
      <bpws:assign>
        <bpws:copy>
          <bpws:from container="PurchaseOrders"
            part="timestamp"/>
          <bpws:to container="DelayNotifications"
            part="orderDate"/>
        </bpws:copy>
      </bpws:assign>
      <!-- Tell the customer about the delay -->
      <bpws:invoke partner="customer"
        portType="cust:CustomerPortType"
        operation="delayNotification"
        inputContainer="DelayNotifications"/>
      <!-- And wait for them do cancel, if it is
           their volition -->
      <bpws:pick>
        <bpws:onMessage partner="customer"
          portType="toast:ToasterVendorPortType"
          operation="cancelToaster"
          container="Cancellations">
          <!-- Correlate the received message with the
               current process -->
          <bpws:correlations>
            <bpws:correlation set="OrderCorrelationSet"
              initiation="no"/>
          </bpws:correlations>
          <!-- If the customer cancels during the delay
               time, then compensate the whole workflow -->
          <bpws:compensate/>
        </bpws:onMessage>
        <bpws:onAlarm
         for="bpws:getContainerData (ItemAvailability,
daysToDelivery)">
          <!-- If the delay time has expired and the
               customer hasn't cancelled then continue with
               workflow (do nothing extra) -->
          <bpws:empty/>
        </bpws:onAlarm>
      </bpws:pick>
    </bpws:case>
  </bpws:switch>
  <!-- End of stock picking, we know now that we have the
       item ready to ship -->
```

Figure 6-74 Dealing with possible stock delays (continued).

Depending on the results of the stock check operation shown in Figure 6-73, the behavior of the section of the workflow shown in Figure 6-74 has two mutually exclusive paths that it can take. In the case where the stock is readily available (which our workflow defines as being ready to send in less than three days), then the activities shown in Figure 6-74 are effectively skipped and the workflow progresses to Figure 6-75 where the customer's items are shipped. If, however, the order will take three or more days to be ready to ship, then a more intricate protocol with the customer is initiated.

This is decided on in the `case` element of the `switch` activity in Figure 6-75, which uses a `condition` to determine whether the result of the stock check indicate the order will be ready within the internal three-day deadline. It checks the `ItemAvailability` container for the `daysToDelivery` part and compares that to the number 3 (remembering, of course, that we are dealing with XPath 1.0 where the only supported types are `Boolean`, `string`, and `number`). If the value in the `daysToDelivery` field is greater than 3, then the workflow builds a `DelayNotificationMessage` message in the `DelayNotifications` container and invokes the customer's `delayNotification` operation using this container as the input.

At this point the ball is in the customer's court. The customer may decide that the delay is simply unacceptable and will therefore cancel the order by invoking the `cancelToaster` operation on the online toaster shop, which activates the `onMessage` part of the `pick` activity. This `onMessage` is correlated with the `OrderCorrelationSet` correlation set so that only messages bound for an existing order will be routed to this activity, as is clear from its status as a follower marked by the `initation="no"` attribute. Finally, if the customer does decide to cancel and the `onMessage` part of the `pick` activity is activated, then the whole workflow instance is compensated, which means the customer's credit card will be refunded and no goods will be shipped.

Conversely, the customer may be willing to accept the delay advertised in the `delayNotificationMessage` message they received and after the delay has finished, the `onAlarm` part of the `pick` activity is activated. In this case executing the `onAlarm` activity causes an `empty` activity to be executed, before the workflow continues to the final order dispatch aspect shown in Figure 6-75.

The final part of our workflow simply informs the customer that the order has been dispatched and when it was sent. As the customer's order leaves the toaster vendor's premises, it is scanned by a barcode reader, which then invokes the `registerPostedOrder` operation on the toaster vendor's Web service. This operation is supported by a `receive` activity in the workflow script shown in Figure 6-75. That `receive` blocks until the arrival of an `OrderPostedMessage` message correlated to this process instance by its `customer` and `timestamp` properties as per the `OrderCorrelationSet`.

Once an appropriate message has been received, a `DeliveryNotificationMessage` message is created in the `DispatchNotifications` container through a number of assignments from the original `PurchaseMessage` and `OrderPostedMessage` messages.

```
    <!-- Ship Order -->
    <!-- Wait for barcode reader to scan outgoing box -->
<bpws:receive partner="backEndService"
    portType="toast:ToasterVendorPortType"
    operation="registerPostedOrder"
    container="PostedOrders" createInstance="no">
    <bpws:correlations>
      <bpws:correlation set="OrderCorrelationSet"
        initiation="no">
    </bpws:correlations>
    <!-- Fill order details in dispatch note -->
    <bpws:assign>
      <bpws:copy>
        <bpws:from container="PurchaseOrders"
          part="toaster"/>
        <bpws:to container="DispatchNotifications"
          part="toaster"/>
      </bpws:copy>
    </bpws:assign>
    <bpws:assign>
      <bpws:copy>
        <bpws:from container="PurchaseOrders"
          part="customer"/>
        <bpws:to container="DispatchNotifications"
          part="customer"/>
      </bpws:copy>
    </bpws:assign>
    <bpws:assign>
      <bpws:copy>
        <bpws:from container="PostedOrders"
          part="now"/>
        <bpws:to container="DispatchNotifications"
          part="dispatchDate"/>
      </bpws:copy>
    </bpws:assign>
    </bpws:receive>
    <!-- Send dispatch note to customer -->
    <bpws:invoke partner="customer"
      portType="cust:CustomerPortType"
      operation="notifyDelivery"
      inputContainer="DispatchNotifications"/>
    <!-- End of order shipping, the customer has
         their toaster -->
  </bpws:sequence>
</bpws:process>
```

Figure 6-75 Shipping the order and ending the workflow instance.

This container is then used as the input to an `invoke` activity that calls the customer's `notifyDelivery` operation, at which point the workflow instance ends.

BPEL 1.1 and OASIS WSBPEL

The original BPEL specification that we have considered so far in this chapter has been superceded as part of the original vendor's efforts to standardize the technology. As such, as their submission to OASIS under the WSBPEL (Web Services Business Process Execution Language) Technical Committee, IBM, Microsoft, BEA and partners have updated the specification to version 1.1 with a number of changes.

The most obvious changes in BPEL 1.1 is that the term "container" has been replaced with the more traditional term "variable," though its type is still considered in terms of messages. These variables are now supported at arbitrary scope, unlike BPEL 1.0 which only supported containers at the global process scope.

In addition to variables, the authors of the specification have added event handlers into the activity set by introducing the `<eventHandlers>` activity. An `eventHandlers` activity is similar to a `pick` activity insofar as it contains a number of `onMessage` or `onAlarm` activities. Where it differs from the standard `pick` activity is that an `eventHandler` can be executed concurrently with the currently running scope. This allows concurrent processing within a single scope where previously concurrent "threads" of control were not permitted. There are some standard caveats with the use of an `eventHandler`, like the fact that one cannot be used to call a `compensate` activity, but these are minor and will be easily handled by tool support.

While these changes aren't particularly earth shattering in themselves, now that BPEL is being standardized it is probable that further evolution may occur. Nonetheless, BPEL is already a second-generation language and as such is less likely to be subject to change than any of its possible competitors.

BPEL and Its Relation to BPML, WSCI, WSFL, Xlang, and Others

In a domain with such a perceived widespread need as business process management for Web services, it is not surprising that several efforts outside of BPEL have proposed alternative solutions. Indeed, work is still ongoing with such efforts as it is with BPEL itself.

One alternative approach, BPML (Business Process Modeling Language), considers e-business processes as made of a common public interface and of many private implementations as process participants. This enables the public interface of BPML processes to be described as ebXML business processes or RosettaNet Partner Interface Processes, independently of their private implementations.

In much the same way XML documents are usually described in a specific XML Schema, BPML processes can be described in a specific business process modeling language layered on top of the BPML XML Schema. BPML represents business processes as the interleaving of control flow, data flow, and event flow, while adding orthogonal design capabilities for business rules, security roles, and transaction contexts.[9]

Another alternative, WSCI (Web Services Choreography Interface), is somewhat of a half-way house between WSCL and BPEL since it concentrates on the details of the ins and outs of a specific endpoint and scales this out to multiparty choreography by the use of *connectors* that link the outputs from service invocations to the inputs of others. In common with BPEL, WSCI can handle message correlation, properties and so forth automatically. However, its strength in describing the behavior of individual endpoints is reflected in the fact that it supports such notions as transaction and compensation boundaries.

> WSCL (see Chapter 5) is also sometimes thought of as a choreography language, though it is considered separately since it deals with choreographing individual service endpoints, which is an orthogonal issue (and complementary) to business process orchestration.

IBM's WSFL and Microsoft's Xlang have similar goals to BPEL and indeed it is the convergence of these two technologies that ultimately yielded the BPEL specification. Xlang in particular has a good heritage since it is widely deployed in B2B scenarios, being the lingua franca of Microsoft's BizTalk server B2B platform.

Although the world of business process choreography for Web services is still in a state of flux, BPEL is the clear leader, having come from the most eminent Web services vendors and due to the fact that it is a second generation technology while others remain in their first iteration. Though there may be convergence over time, the general principles, if not the majority of the syntax and language constructs, set out by BPEL are likely to be pervasive within this domain.

Summary

Workflow is a technique of managing the coordination of resources over time in some business process, ensuring the right resources (people, materials) are in the right place (manufacturing facility, database) at the right time (inventory, just-in-time). With the advent of Web services as the likely means of tying enterprises together in the future, the prospect of creating truly virtual enterprises may become a reality. There is a real requirement for the development of workflow technologies that can bridge enterprises using the underlying Web services-based network as a basis. The current leader in this field, in terms of both heritage and implementation support, is BPEL.

9. From http://www.bpml.org.

The BPEL model logically consists of two distinct components. The first is a process description language with support for performing computation, synchronous and asynchronous operation invocations, control-flow patterns, structured error handling, and saga-based long-running business transactions. The second is an infrastructure layer that builds on WSDL to capture the relationships between enterprises and processes over a Web services-based infrastructure. Together these two layers allow the orchestration of Web services in a business process where the infrastructure layer exposes Web services to the process layer, which then drives the Web services infrastructure as part of its workflow activities.

The ultimate goal of business process languages is to completely abstract underlying Web services so that a business process language such as BPEL effectively becomes the Web services API. While such an abstract language may not be suitable for every possible Web services-based scenario, it will certainly be useful for many. If tool support evolves, it will be able to deliver on its ambition to provide a business analyst-friendly interface with which to choreograph enterprise Web services.

Architect's Notes

- BPEL is set to be the dominant Web services choreography language. It may change over time as standards in the area mature, but given the fact that it is a second generation effort, it is more immune to change than the other first-generation contenders in this area.
- Developing BPEL workflows by hand is difficult and error-prone. Tool support is essential, especially if control of mission-critical workflows is to be given to non-specialist programmers. Writing code in XML does not magically make it simple.
- If you are modeling an existing process with a view to automation, approach development in three stages. First understand your algorithm (that is, the necessary activities and the control flow dependencies). Then decompose the relationships between your enterprise and your partners into BPEL-friendly interface code (`partners`, `serviceLinks` and so forth). Finally, progress to connecting your workflow to your partner's services.
- If you are starting from a blank slate, it might be more useful to start from your partner interrelations and work "inward" toward your process script.
- BPEL will be the "API" for business analysts developing and deploying workflows into enterprises.

CHAPTER 7

Transactions

Transactions are a fundamental abstraction in dependable computing systems. Put simply, a transaction is a unit of work which either succeeds completely or fails without leaving any side effects. To illustrate, a commonly cited example of a transaction use-case is where an amount of money is to be moved between bank accounts. In this case the goal is to ensure that the money both leaves the sender's account and is received by the recipient's account, or if something fails, for it to appear as if the transaction itself logically *never occurred*.

This is the inherent value of transactional systems; if something goes wrong, they allow us as programmers to make it appear as if it never happened in the first place. In an inherently unreliable world, transactions can truly be a godsend, especially when we consider the amount of computing infrastructure involved in something apparently as simple as moving money between accounts. Any aspect of that computing system from the network cables through to the software and everything in between has a small yet significant chance of failing—something we'd rather it didn't do while it's processing our money! The point is that using transactions to safeguard against failures allows us to reverse any partial work performed during a failed transaction and, thus, prevent our money from disappearing into a banking black hole.

ACID Transactions

The field of transaction processing is by no means a new discipline. Transaction processing infrastructures such as CICS and Tuxedo, OTS/JTS and MS DTC have been around for decades, and much innovative and interesting work continues in the field today. However, underlying the development of transaction technology over the decades has been one pervasive notion: ACID.

ACID is the acronym used to describe the classical form of all-or-nothing transactions, which are *Atomic*, *Consistent*, *Isolated*, and *Durable*. These properties are of such fundamental importance to transaction processing systems that they warrant further elaboration, even in a Web services book. The ACID characteristics are:

- *Atomic*—The transaction executes to the end, or logically appears to not have executed at all. This is particularly important when executing business logic (such as the bank account debit-credit) that involves the updating of multiple underlying data sources, where the atomicity property turns a set of operations into a single indivisible logical operation.
- *Consistent*—Any data that has been updated during the lifetime of the transaction is left in a consistent state at the end of the transaction (provided it was, of course, consistent to begin with), irrespective of any failures that have occurred during that transaction. This usually means that database primary keys remain unique and the database has referential integrity (everything that a record refers to actually exists), or that the conditions set by certain business rules are met (for instance, ensuring an overdraft status is less than the total permissible overdraft that an account will grant).
- *Isolated*—Any running transaction believes that it has exclusive access to the resources associated with it. The classical case for the isolation property stems from a situation where several debtors each chase the last $50 from an account. If the two transactions to transfer money from the debtor's account to the creditor's are allowed to run un-isolated, then they will both claim the remainder of the money, though clearly it is impossible for them to withdraw $100 when there is only $50 available! Thus for the isolation property to be met, the outcome of running the transactions must be equivalent to if the individual transactions had run one at a time. Ensuring isolation is usually achieved through locking of shared data. In this case, the balance of a bank account would be locked to prevent concurrent access and maintain isolation.
- *Durable*—A durable transaction system ensures that even in the event of failure, the work of the transaction will not be lost, but will instead be persisted on some form of storage (like disk or a database) that will typically survive any failures. Durability is usually implemented by the transaction engine writing an *intentions log* to persistent storage throughout the work of the transaction, and by carrying through the results of its intentions to the durable data source once the transaction is successfully brought to an end. Conversely, if the transaction fails for some reason, then the intentions log can be discarded (ensuring that none of the operations logically ever occurred) or used to replay the transaction up to its point of failure and re-try the partially finished work.

Having established the fundamental properties of ACID transactions, it is worthwhile taking a look at how such abstractions are used within today's enterprise before we move up to running transactions at the Web services level. As we discussed earlier, in the simplest form, a transaction is a logically undoable unit of work. For illustrative purposes, we shall return to the bank account example since it is well known and relatively straightforward to comprehend. It is important to remember that we're dealing with principles in this section, and that industrial-strength transaction processing systems have vastly more sophisticated implementations than the mechanisms we're going to examine. However, the principles remain valid and with that caveat in mind we can examine the simple debit/credit transaction shown in Figure 7-1.

Figure 7-1 shows the classical transaction example where one bank account is debited and another is credited. In this example there are no failures while the work is being undertaken, and the flow of work through the transaction is therefore straightforward.

1. The transaction is started and the database records that are involved in the transaction are locked (so that the isolation property is maintained).
2. The transaction then enters its work phase where a check is made to see whether there are sufficient funds available to continue with the transfer. In this case, we can assume that such funds do exist. (Where funds aren't available, the transaction may finish now and unlock the records early, freeing them up for use by other transactions).
3. The intention to withdraw funds from the debtor's account is recorded with a *shadow write* (a write that updates a temporary copy of the actual data) but, importantly, the changes to the debtor's account are not yet made—the changes are in the show copy only.
4. The intention to credit the creditor's account is also recorded with a shadow write, though again the actual account is not updated.
5. The transaction reaches its termination phase where the intended outcome for the transaction (i.e., to commit or abort—to make durable or not the effects of the shadow writes) is synchronously recorded in an intention log, which then becomes the definitive source for finding the outcome of the transaction.

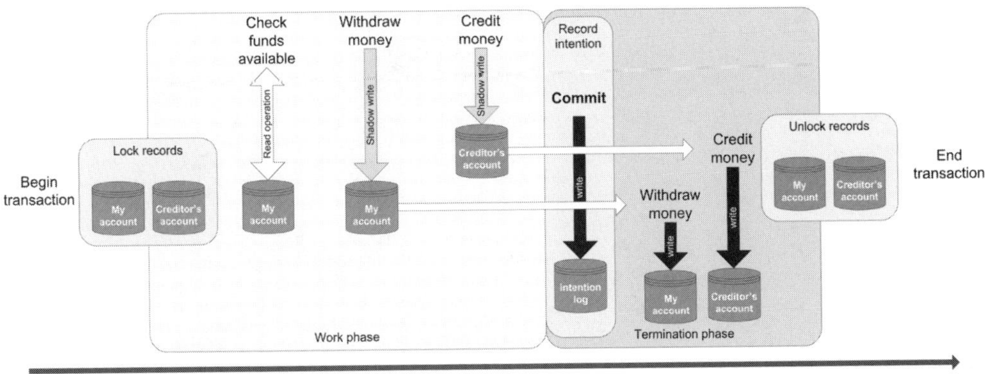

Figure 7-1 A successful debit/credit transaction.

6. As the intention is to commit the transaction, the effects of the shadow writes are committed to the actual records in persistent storage.
7. Once the termination mechanism is satisfied that the effects of the intentions log have indeed been committed to persistent storage (e.g., through strictly synchronous disk writes), then the transaction can terminate and the intentions log can be discarded and locks released.

In a typical transaction we operate on copies of the actual online data and only when we are satisfied that the work has come to a successful conclusion do we allow the copies to replace that original data. While successful transactions are interesting enough, it is far more entertaining to look at what happens when a system failure causes the transaction itself to fail, and show how such system failures can be masked by transactions. In the example shown in Figure 7-2, a system failure causes some difficulty for the executing transaction with the worst possible timing—the debtor's account has been provisionally debited, while no monies have yet made their way to the creditor's account.

Assuming the system that supports the transaction shown in Figure 7-2 can be re-started, the system must then recover any transactions that were in progress prior to the crash. In our example case, this is relatively straightforward since it is a matter of aborting the transaction simply by discarding shadow writes and unlocking any resources (database records in our case) that were associated with the transaction, as shown in Figure 7-3. This has the effect of completely reversing the transaction with no side affects, other than the fact that processing the payment will have been delayed by the amount of time that the system takes to rerun the work.

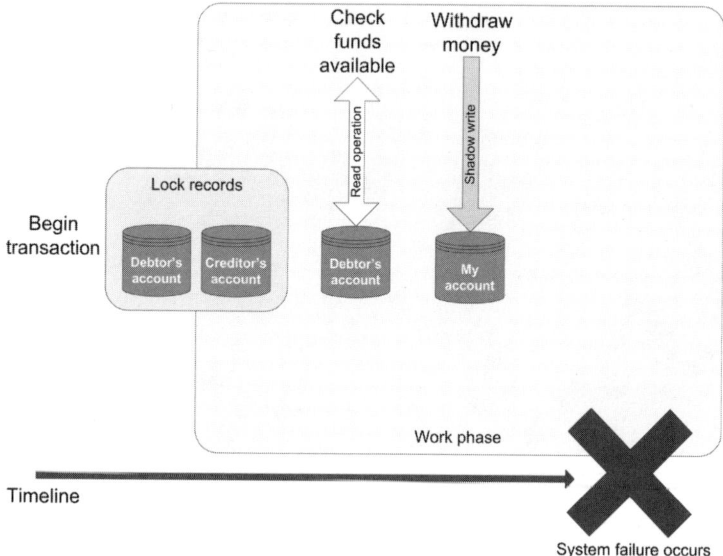

Figure 7-2 An unsuccessful debit/credit transaction.

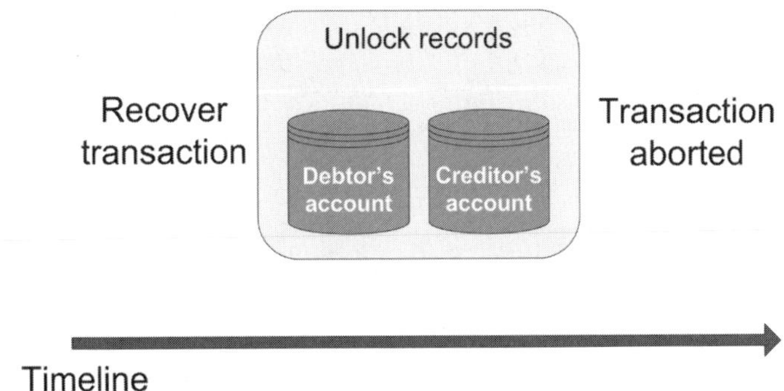

Figure 7-3 Recovering an unsuccessful debit/credit transaction.

Failure during the termination phase presents a different problem, but one which can be solved nonetheless. Imagine a situation such as that depicted in Figure 7-4, where the transaction has successfully progressed to termination, but where a system failure has caused the transaction to fail before the termination phase has completed.

In the situation portrayed in Figure 7-4, once the system has started its recovery process, it is a relatively simple matter to read the intention log and to effectively replay the termination phase to completion. Since no records have yet been unlocked, the data remains inaccessible to other transactions, which although it may cause inconvenience is perfectly safe. Using the decisions recorded in the intentions log, with the stored shadow writes recorded during the work phase, the recovery process can simply rerun the procedure, as we can see in Figure 7-5.

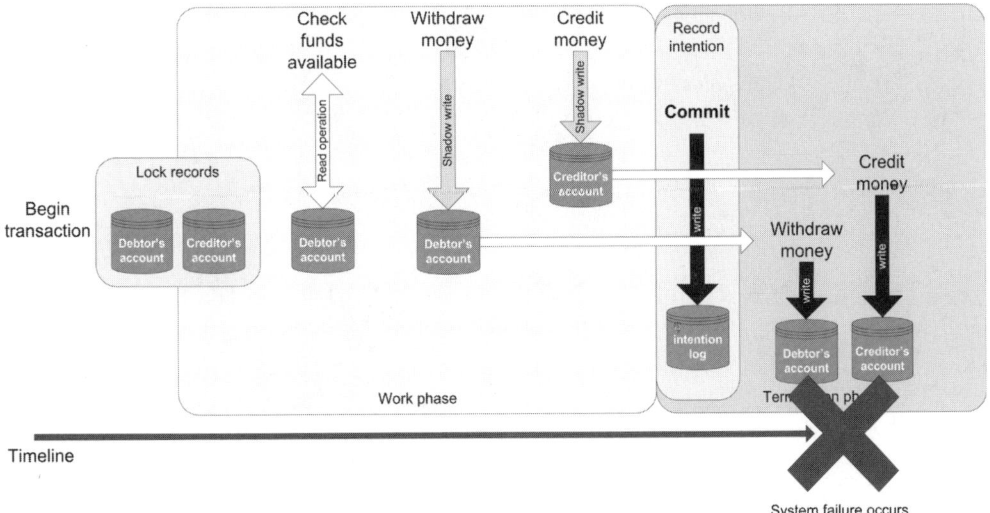

Figure 7-4 A transaction failing during the termination phase.

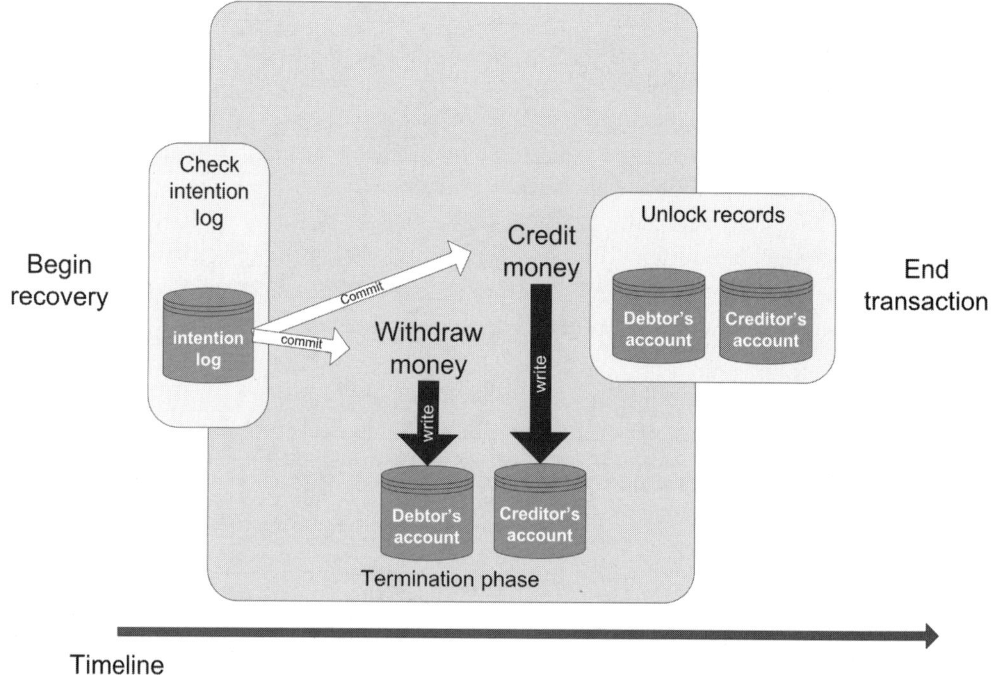

Figure 7-5 Recovery from a failed transaction during the termination phase.

Though the implementations are admittedly naïve, the concepts we've examined here are generic enough to provide a basic understanding of what a transaction is and how it provides its dependable unit-of-work abstraction. However, the examples we've considered have been centralized—the transactions have executed with a single program and operated on locally available records. This is clearly not the ideal architecture on which to base Web services transactions, but fortunately there is a precedent and known techniques for running ACID transactions in a distributed environment.

Distributed Transactions and Two-Phase Commit

The evolution of transactions from centralized to distributed systems has followed the evolution of computing from a centralized resource model to its modern day distributed and federated architectures. The underlying goals in distributed transaction processing are the same as in the traditional centralized model: to ensure a unit of work either successfully completes or logically appears to have never been run at all.

To achieve these goals, distributed transaction processing systems have attempted to keep the notion of ACID transactions as their dominant paradigm. While this might at first seem a tough goal to coordinate multiple systems through a transaction, the key algorithm which enables ACID across systems is well known: *Two-Phase Commit.*

Two-phase commit (or simply 2PC) is an algorithm that tries to achieve consensus between all parties that are participating in a transaction before allowing the transaction to fully terminate. 2PC does this by first gathering consensus among the distributed parties as to whether they should commit the transaction, and then relaying the group decision to all of those parties. Again the canonical example is the debit/credit problem, which in its distributed form can be extended across multiple systems. In this case we will assume that the creditor's and debtor's bank accounts are held by different divisions of the bank (e.g., personal and commercial sectors) and as such are hosted by different computing systems.

The Two-Phase Commit Approach

The two-phase commit protocol is the absolute bedrock of the transaction processing world, even, as we shall see, fundamental to executing transactions over Web services. Given its importance, it's a worthwhile exercise to understand the model and assumptions on which 2PC is based.[1] The assumptions on which 2PC is founded are relatively straightforward and common sense, simply stating up front the standard operating conditions which we would expect for a transaction to be able to make headway. These assumptions are:

1. During its work phase, a transaction accesses some underlying resources (such as databases, queues, or messaging systems) from time to time. If a fatal error occurs at any point while using these resources, the transaction is aborted immediately; otherwise it proceeds to run the two-phase protocol at the termination phase.
2. The underlying resources that the transaction touches have control only over the state to which they have direct access—resources cannot coerce one another into taking a particular decision as to whether to commit or abort the transaction, and it is usually the case that the resources are mutually unaware of one another.
3. There is one and only one program that issues the instruction to commit the transaction.
4. All underlying resources that are participating in the transaction must have completed their work before the termination phase can begin.
5. Any failures in the system result in the failed component halting completely and remaining silent for the remainder of the transaction. This algorithm does not allow for so-called "Byzantine" failures where a component can fail in such a way that it sends out erroneous and misleading messages to other components rather than failing silently.

1. This is a much simplified and shortened description of the two-phase algorithm. For an in-depth explanation, see "Principles of Transaction Processing" by Philip Bernstein and Eric Newcomer—(Morgan-Kaufmann, ISBN 1-55860-415-4).

The protocol itself is straightforward. Each of the two phases has a specific task to perform. The first phase gathers consensus among the participating resources as to whether they agree to proceed with the transaction by asking each to cast a vote to indicate whether they are *prepared* to proceed. The second phase simply informs each of the participating resources whether the outcome of the vote was to commit (where every single resource signaled that it was prepared) or to abort (where at least one resource signaled that it was not prepared).

The question then arises, "How does this apply to our debit/credit example?" The answer is that from the point of view of the transaction's work, everything is business as usual with the caveat that the underlying resources may be less performant since they are no longer co-located with the transactional program itself with transaction coordination and application messages being sent across the network.

The high-level architecture of the distributed scenario is shown in Figure 7-6 and Figure 7-7. Figure 7-6 simply shows the work aspect of the transaction, where the debit and credit operations are delimited by a transaction begin/end pair. The application-level messages involved in performing the work now travel outside of the application that hosts the work and onto other systems, in this case System A and System B.

Correspondingly, Figure 7-7 shows the transaction coordination messages that are exchanged to facilitate the desired consistent outcome. Notice that in this scenario, a (trusted) third party, in the form of a transaction coordinator, appears whose function is to mediate the exchange of transaction control messages in accordance with the two-phase commit protocol.

If we now re-examine the debit/credit scenario, we can see how the two-phase commit protocol can help to maintain the same ACID guarantees that we had in the centralized transaction processing engine. Starting with the client application (the party that performs the actual

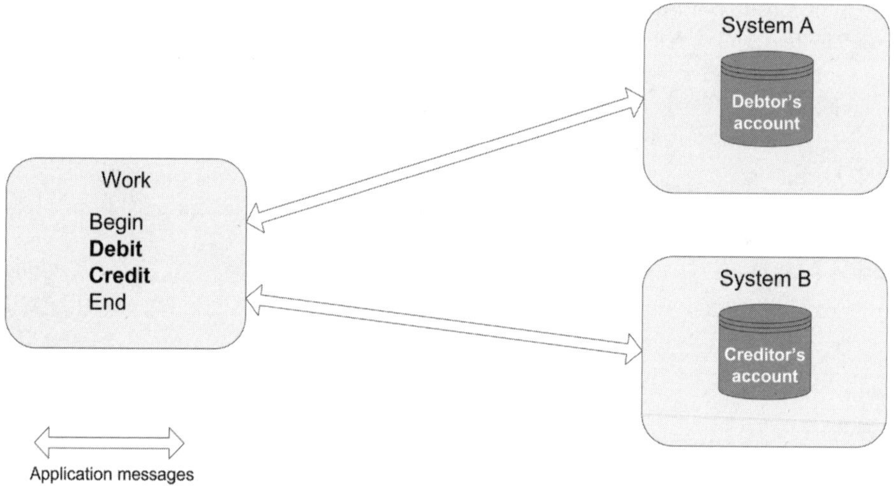

Figure 7-6 The application message paths in a distributed transaction.

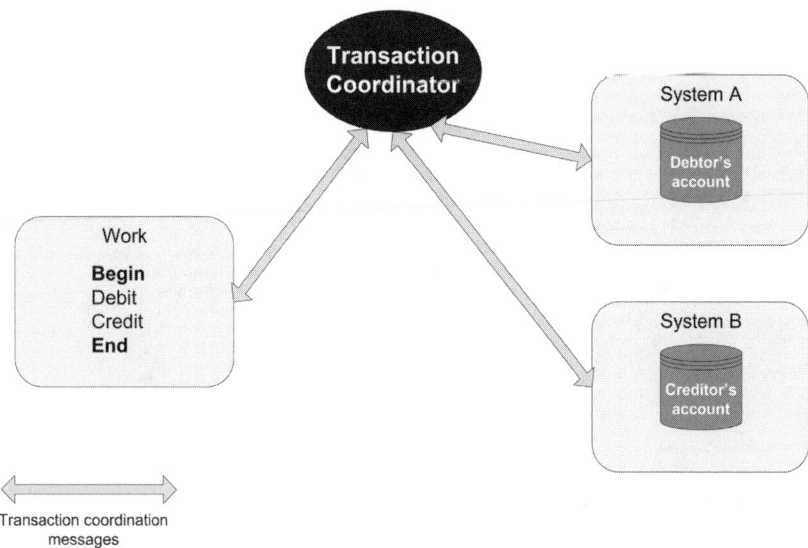

Figure 7-7 The transaction coordination message paths in a distributed transaction.

work associated with the transaction) initiating a transaction through a *begin* imperative (from the underlying transaction API) that, instead of being a local call, is sent across the network transaction coordinator which initializes a transaction on behalf of the client. This initialization also returns a message to the client application containing details that the client will pass on to other resources that will participate in the transaction. This information, known as the context, ensures that all parties have a reference to the transaction and the coordinator that is managing it. This start-up phase is shown in Figure 7-8.

Once the transaction has started and we have a context within which we can undertake the work, the client then interacts with the resources performing the necessary business logic. The application message sent from the client to System A that causes the debit to occur also carries the transaction context, which the transaction-aware resource knows how to deal with. In this case it is the first time that the resource has seen the context so it uses the information to *enlist* itself with the transaction coordinator, which is shown in Figure 7-9. From now on when System A receives messages about this transaction from the coordinator, it will be required to respond with messages indicating its intent or action. Once the enlist operation has finished, the remainder of the operations in our example follow the same pattern as the centralized example, whereby the debit operation locks the data and performs a shadow write (or equivalent) at the database, but it will not yet cause the online data itself to be updated.

A similar set of operations happens with the creditor's account where System B also enlists itself with the transaction coordinator, as shown in Figure 7-10, and has updates written to some persistent store but has not yet merged with the main online data.

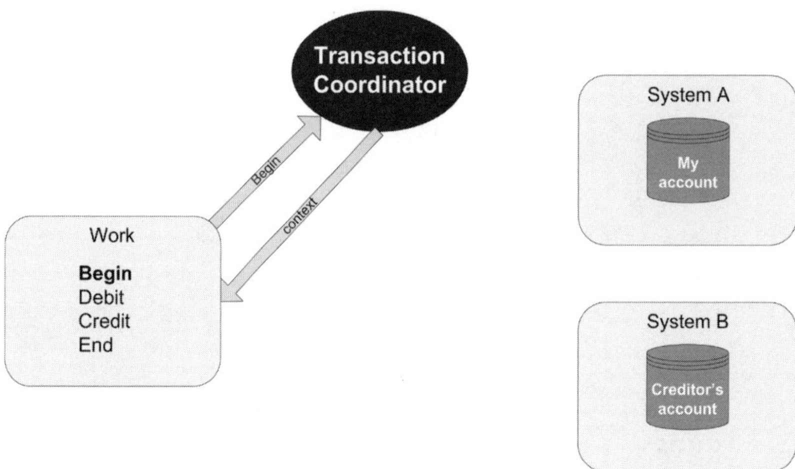

Figure 7-8 Beginning a distributed transaction.

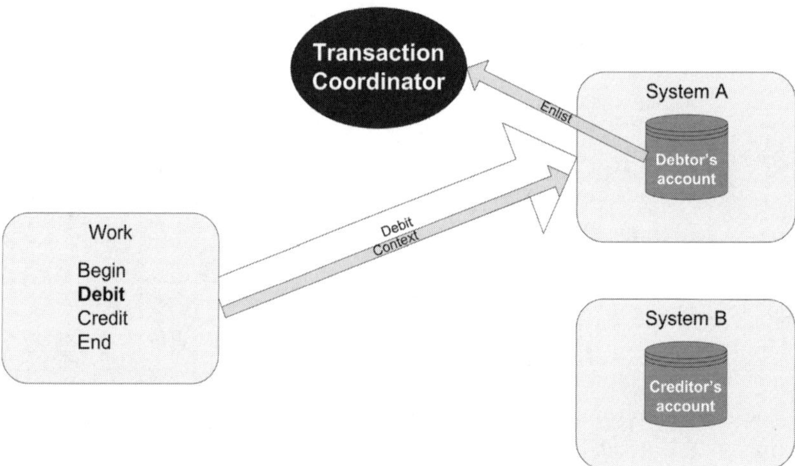

Figure 7-9 The work phase: Debit.

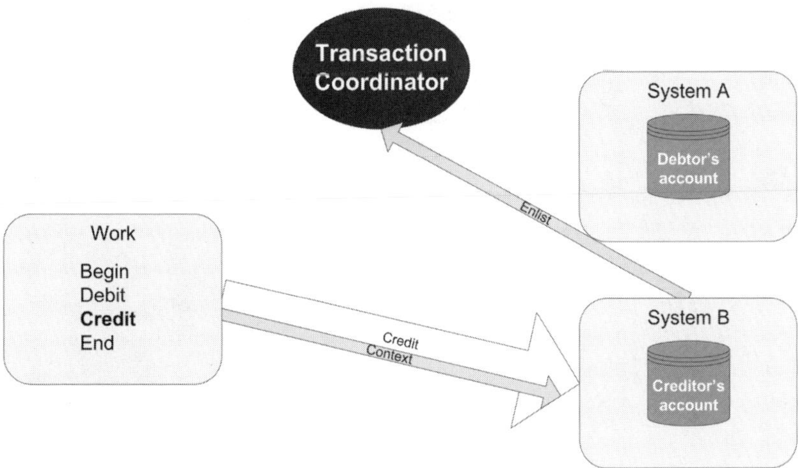

Figure 7-10 The work phase: Credit.

Once the work phase of the transaction is complete, the termination phase is started. In this case the client reaches the end of its work and issues a *commit* message to the transaction coordinator to start the two-phase commit protocol, which is then completed entirely under the auspices of that coordinator. The first of the two phases is voting where each participating resource is asked whether it is prepared to proceed through to completion with the transaction. The message exchanges performed during the voting process are shown in Figure 7-11 and Figure 7-12.

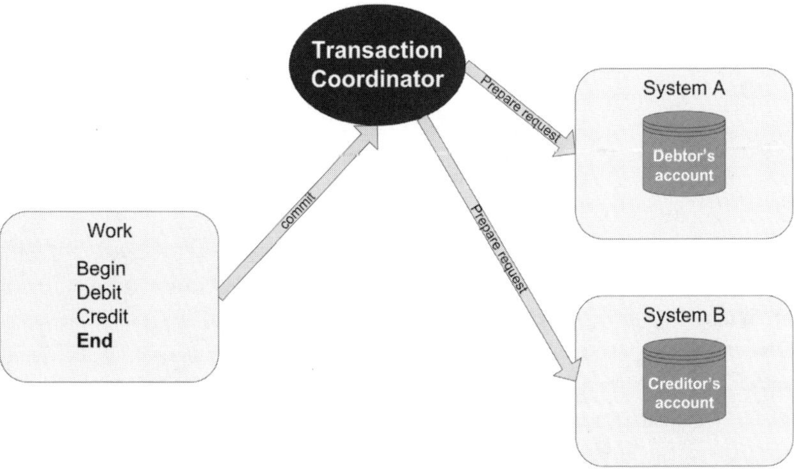

Figure 7-11 The two-phase commit: Phase 1, Soliciting Votes.

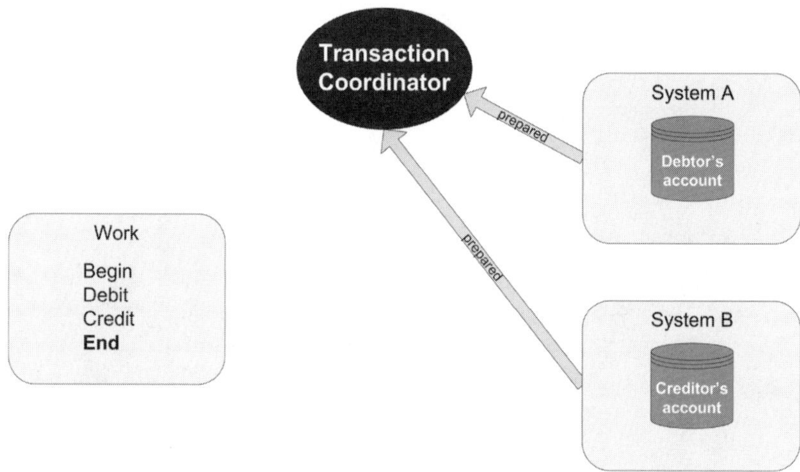

Figure 7-12 The two-phase commit: Phase 1, Reconciling Votes.

Once participants have cast their votes, they are bound to follow their decision, even if they fail. So if System A fails after it has cast a positive vote but before it has made the changes to my account, it must ensure that when it recovers, it honors its pre-crash commitments in the same way that a centralized system would. In the case shown in Figure 7-12, both of the participants have voted positively (they have stated that they are *prepared*) and so the transaction manager relays the information to all participants that they should make any changes to their state durable by issuing a commit message to them. The second phase is shown in Figure 7-13 where the participants receive commit messages, on receipt of which they must update their online data and remove any locks held to allow the progression of other transactions.

The final step in the completion of the transaction is for the coordinator to report back to the client that the work has been successfully completed, thus allowing the client to safely terminate. The message exchange underpinning this simple last step is presented in Figure 7-14.

Up until now things have gone rather well, at least from the point of view of the banks that have suffered no system failures and the creditor who has received his money. However, transactions exist to mask system failures and we would feel cheated if we hadn't seen how a transaction-based infrastructure can maintain data consistency across systems even in the presence of failures. Let's revisit the same scenario, but this time add a sprinkling of mayhem into the system to create a few failures along the way.

The easiest of the failure cases to deal with is when a failure occurs during a transaction's work phase where no state changes have been made. In such cases the transaction is simply aborted, and any locks are released by live systems. Any locks still held by failed systems will be released on recovery. In such cases we simply try the work again, once all of the systems are up and stable.

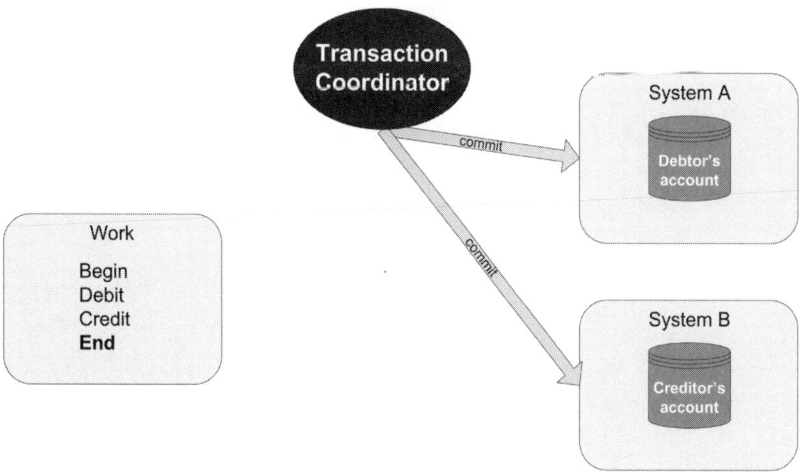

Figure 7-13 The two-phase commit: Phase 2, Committing Resources

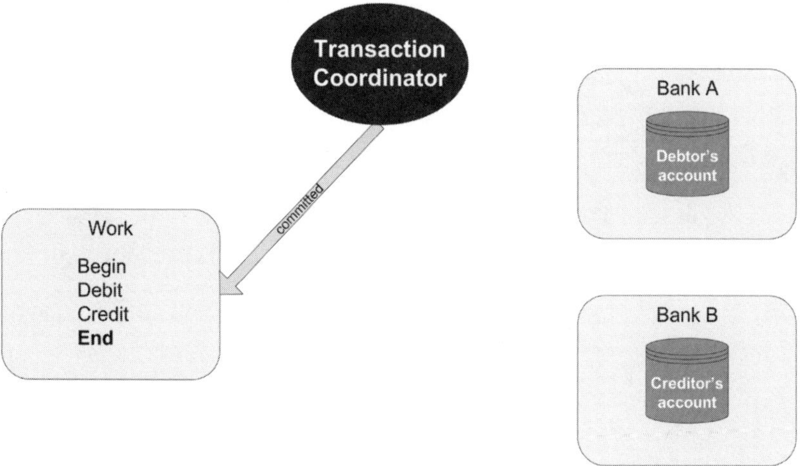

Figure 7-14 The two-phase commit: Phase 2, Returning Successfully to the Client.

The more devious and interesting scenarios crop up when failures occur during the termination phase of the transaction. Let's consider the scenario where one of the participants for some reason (usually a failure of some description) refuses to progress the transaction to completion, such as the example in Figure 7-15.

In Figure 7-15, System B has suffered some kind of failure (or for some reason has made a unilateral decision to abort), which has resulted in it responding negatively to the voting request. In this case the transaction coordinator has no choice but to insist that both the parties in the

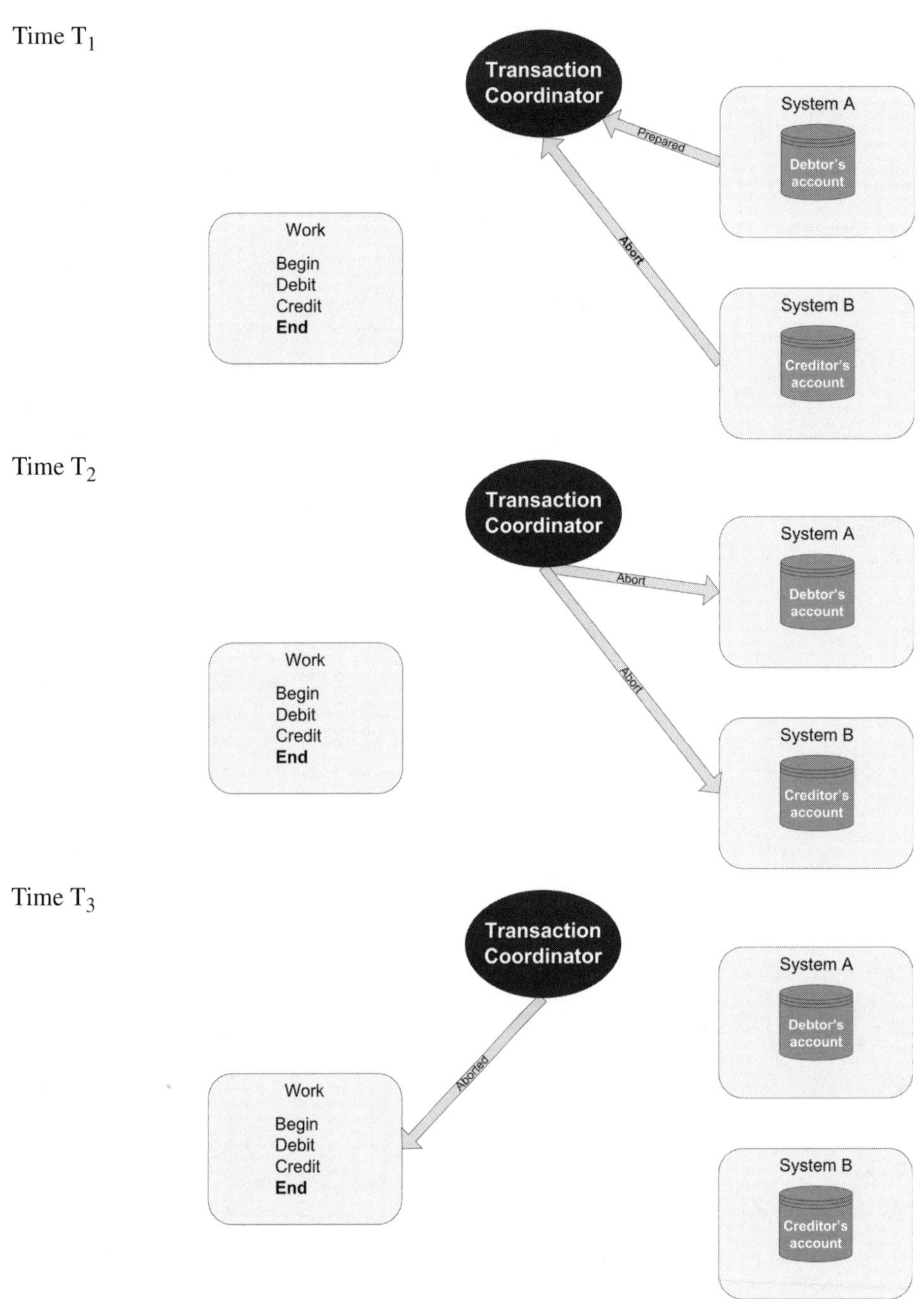

Figure 7-15 Inconsistent outcome to voting.

transaction *abort* any work that they have done, which it communicates to the participants with an abort message. The participants then discard any partial updates to the data and release any locks. Having ensured that the data will be left in a consistent state, the coordinator returns a message to the client application to indicate that the transaction aborted.

It is easy to imagine variations on this theme such as when no response is forthcoming from a participant that has suffered a catastrophic failure during the first phase or when the transaction manager itself crashes (or even when the network connection between transaction manager and participant has been lost). In cases where a participant hangs indefinitely before the second phase, the transaction manager will not keep its patience and may choose to abort the transaction to release locks at some given time in the future, or to proceed to completion in those cases where assurances, in the form of positive votes, have been given. In any case, once the crash participant recovers it will have to ask the transaction coordinator for the outcome of the transaction. Where the transaction manager suffers a failure, the participants and client are simply left waiting for it to recover, at which point it will simply pick up where it left off. There is, however, a particular variant of this problem that exposes a negative aspect of two-phase commit where in between the first and second phases a participant is in effect left dangling, uncertain as to what the final outcome will be. The period of uncertainty is a nuisance since the longer it is, the longer resources will be locked, potentially delaying other work and increasing the likelihood that a participant will be forced to make a unilateral decision. Therefore, there is always a danger where a transaction coordinator crashes and does not recover in a timely fashion that the whole transaction may have to be aborted and rerun, with the risk of non-atomic behavior having occurred.

Nonetheless, transaction coordinator and participant failures, although irksome at times, are handled reasonably well by the two-phase commit approach. The two-phase algorithm is not, however, without its more serious drawbacks. In particular there is one aspect of the algorithm that can be of particular nuisance and that usually falls to a party outside of the transaction system to correct: *heuristic outcomes*.

Dealing with Heuristic Outcomes

An heuristic outcome to a transaction is simply the worst thing that can arise during a 2PC-based transaction system. They may occur where a participant in the transaction reneges on its promise to either commit or abort and instead does the exact opposite. This means that the ACIDity of the transaction is compromised, since changes to data in some participants will have been made durable, while changes to data managed by other participants will have been discarded. As was alluded to earlier, the chances of such an outcome occurring are significantly increased if the period of uncertainty (the gap between prepare and commit phases) is too long, and we may arrive at a situation where participants in a transaction start to guess at outcomes for themselves (that is, they may make *heuristic* decisions).

There is a glimmer of hope with a potential heuristic outcome since it's not always the case that mixed responses during the second phase and will ultimately cause an actual heuristic end to the transaction. Even though some heuristic outcomes can be handled by the transaction manager, the best rule of thumb is simply to try to avoid them altogether. Sometimes if the events leading up to potential heuristic outcomes happen early enough in the second phase, the remainder of the phase can be automatically brought into line. This is, however, a special case. More often than not an heuristic outcome cannot be avoided and it is left to mechanisms outside of the system (including good old human-to-human communication) to deal with the aftermath. Given the gravity of heuristics, it's important to understand exactly how they can arise and be dealt with. Consider the example shown in Figure 7-16, which depicts the second phase of the two-phase protocol. The first participant (System A) responds to its commit message (Message 2) with an abort response. That response may have been caused because of a failure or perhaps because the period of uncertainty was so long that System A decided to unilaterally abort the transaction to free up resources. This is clearly a violation of what it originally must have agreed to undertake in the first phase or the transaction coordinator would not have issued a commit to it. However, in this case the transaction coordinator can leap into the breach knowing, as it does, that no other participants have yet been contacted, and that it can alter the messages that it would have originally sent from commit messages to abort messages as shown by Message 4. In this case none of the other (hopefully better behaved) participants will be any the wiser about the close shave with the heuristic outcome, and will instead be instructed to discard any changes to their state.

If the contradictory responses from a badly-behaved participant do not occur early enough in the second phase, then we inevitably end up with an heuristic outcome, and potentially a

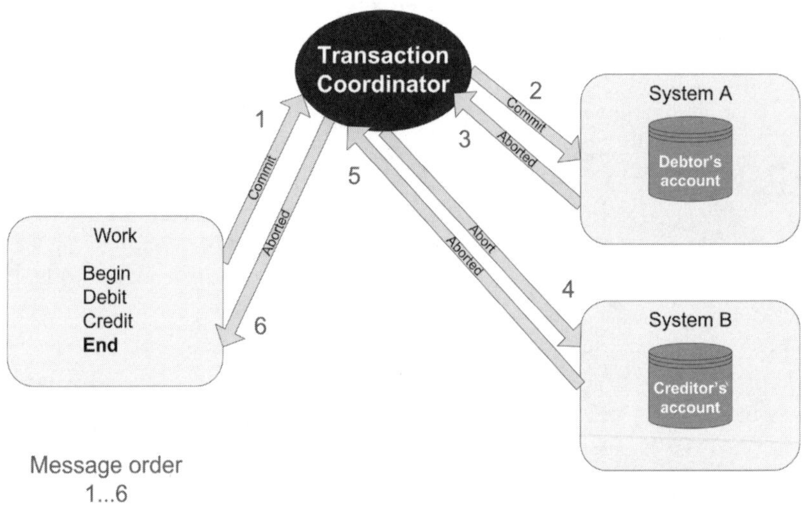

Figure 7-16 Automatically avoiding a heuristic outcome.

whole lot of work poring over logs trying to piece together what actually happened. The kinds of situation that will eventually lead to a heuristic outcome are seen in Figure 7-17 and Figure 7-18, where the *heuristic commit* and *heuristic abort* scenarios are shown.

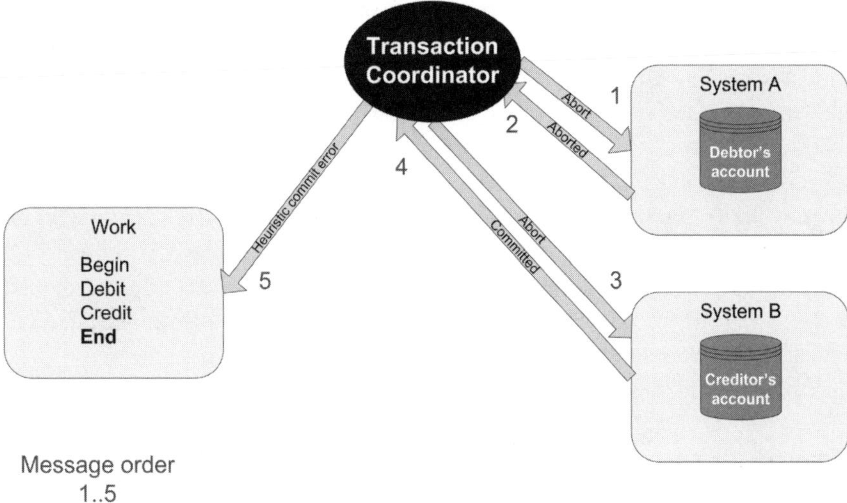

Figure 7-17 Heuristic Commit.

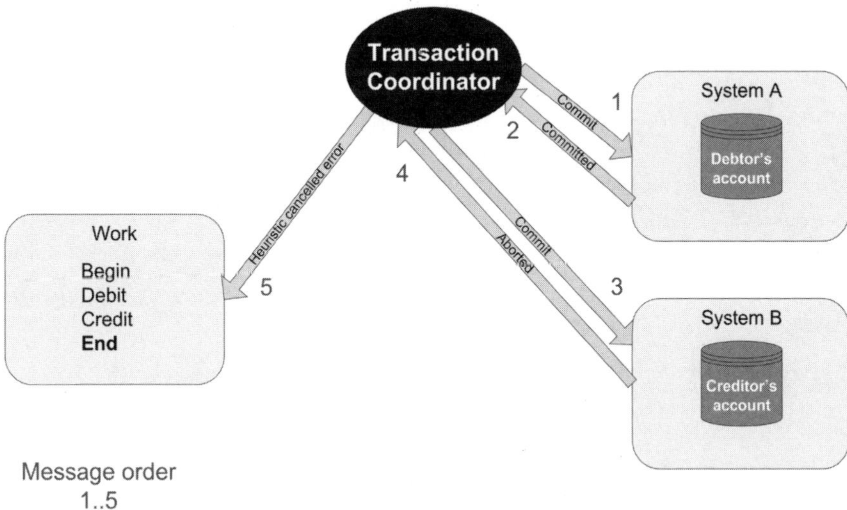

Figure 7-18 Heuristic Abort.

The heuristic commit outcome shown in Figure 7-17 has arisen because System B has decided to unilaterally commit the changes to its data even though the transaction coordinator has specified otherwise. Figure 7-18 shows an almost identical situation where a participant that should have committed decided instead to unilaterally roll back. The ultimate cause of either heuristic outcome, from the point of view of the transaction coordinator, is Message 4, which is the contrary message to that which the transaction coordinator was expecting (commit vs. abort or vice versa). The coordinator cannot retroactively recover from this situation by re-contacting the participants it contacted earlier because as far as they are now concerned the two phases are complete, and thus the transaction itself has finished. It therefore has only one choice: to report the error back to the client application and let a third party resolve any inconsistencies that have arisen.

There is simply no way that the two-phase protocol can internalize the problems caused by heuristics—it simply does not have enough attempts at communicating (having only one chance per phase) with participants to let them know of any heuristic decisions which have arisen. This begs the question, "Why not simply add an extra phase to communicate any heuristic decisions to participants?" In theory this is a good idea insofar as it would solve the heuristic problems we've encountered while using the two-phase algorithm, because we would always have a phase where we could warn unwary participants about heuristics and let them take the appropriate restorative action. If we were using a three-phase commit protocol, an additional set of message exchanges would occur after the normal commit/abort messages to propagate the details of any heuristics. In practice, a three-phase approach is used in some transaction systems for use in large-scale and lossy environments. However, we have now introduced an opportunity for the third phase to cause an heuristic outcome, which in turn would have to be handled by a fourth phase. Of course, the fourth phase is not immune to mixed outcomes and so we would require a fifth phase and so on.

To be entirely sure about the validity of the Nth phase of a transaction, we always need an $N+1^{th}$ phase—it's just a matter of how big we are realistically going to let N grow to. There is clearly a trade-off between the number of phases required and the performance of our system (in terms of the number of message exchanges required), which is mediated by the architectural characteristics of the underlying system that required transactional support. In general two-phase commit is a good trade-off between reliability and performance, which is why it has been the fundamental algorithm of choice in most commercial transaction-processing software.

Advanced Topics: Nesting and Interposition

In our whistle-stop tour of transactions so far, we've tackled a majority of the fundamental concepts. However, this isn't yet the end of the transactions story. Before we can delve into how transactions can be applied in a Web service environment, we need to tackle two more advanced transaction concepts: *nesting* and *interposition*. Don't be too intimidated. Although these are considered advanced topics in terms of their deployments and the benefits they provide, they're actually not incredibly difficult to understand.

In a Web services world, we are generally trying to tie together coarsely-grained business processes that typically take significant periods of time to execute and, thus, there are plenty of opportunities for a piece of work to fail along the way. Nesting transactions is a useful means of structuring a piece of work to provide *failure isolation*. What this actually means is that a transaction can contain smaller subtransactions that can fail and be retried without having to necessarily abort the whole transaction. In a long-running piece of work this can be especially valuable, as is apparent in Figure 7-19, where an especially long-running piece of work has been split into a number of smaller units. While there is a cost associated with the management of each individual transaction (so more transactions means more cost), in this case that cost has been more than worthwhile since the final subtransaction has failed. Had this failure and subsequent abort caused the abortion of a week's, a day's, or even an hour's worth of work, then it would be annoying to say the least, and potentially quite costly. Once the failure that caused subtransaction E to abort has subsided, it can simply be replayed (avoiding the replay cost of the whole parent transaction) and allow the parent transaction itself to reach completion.

On the other hand, interposition is a more subtle transaction structuring strategy through which we may improve performance and offer better encapsulation by allowing additional transaction coordinators to become involved in the management of a single transaction. This is shown in Figure 7-20, where Enterprise B, instead of enrolling its back end systems directly in the top-level transaction, has enrolled its own interposed coordinator instead.

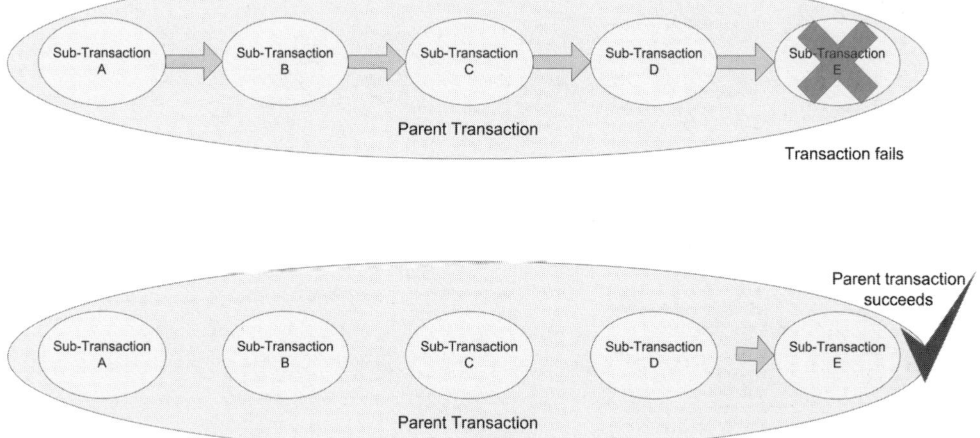

Figure 7-19 Nested transactions to provide failure isolation.

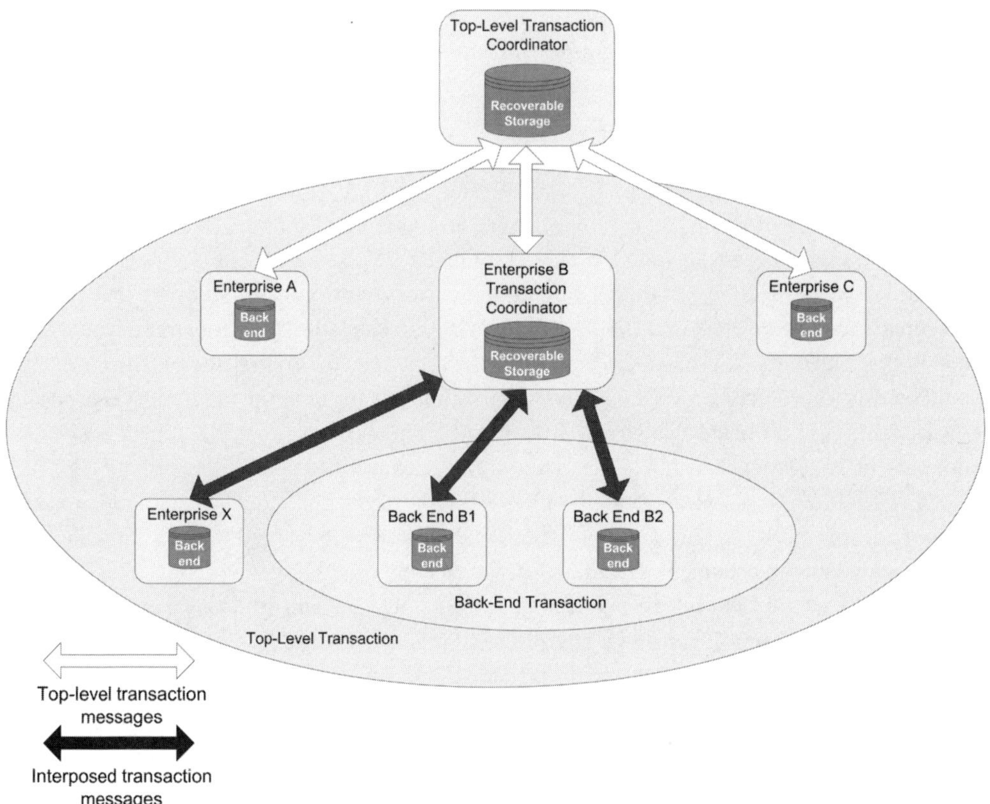

Figure 7-20 Interposed transactions for performance and encapsulation.

At first glance it might appear that this interposed scheme complicates matters rather than provides benefits. However, there are a number of reasons why, in certain circumstances, it makes sense to utilize this scheme, such as:

- Security/trust reasons where a back-end system may not trust, nor wish to be exposed to any coordinator outside of its own enterprise or other domain of trust.
- Network issues where the back-end systems may not even be visible to the top-level coordinator (e.g., in the case where the back-end systems are hosted on a private network, while the transaction coordinator is hosted on the Internet).
- Performance whereby the number of messages exchanged over highly latent wide-area networks are reduced because most messages are exchanged with the local interposed coordinator, which relays only the outcomes of those messages to the top-level coordinator.

In this case Enterprise B becomes a subcoordinator for Enterprise X (and for any of its own locally enlisted participants), and the messages exchanged between Enterprise B and Enterprise X will identify Enterprise B, not the top-level transaction manager, as the coordinator. The fact that the coordinator has changed is transparent to Enterprise X, and the top-level coordinator does not even see Enterprise X at all.

The work that Enterprise B must now do when it receives the termination message from the top-level coordinator is different from when it was just a "plain" participant. It must act as a coordinator, running its own local first- and second-phase messages exchanges, and relaying the aggregation of these messages to the top-level transaction coordinator.

As with nesting, interposition provides a really useful abstraction for transactions, especially in the Web services architecture. Since trust is fundamentally lacking between arbitrary hosts on the Web, then the ability for a service to work with its own trusted coordinator is compelling, and where services are not mutually visible, the case is vital.

Scaling Transactions to Web Services

ACID transactions in their centralized or distributed variations are especially suited to the bank account credit-debit type of problem, and offer the kinds of guarantees on which truly dependable back-end computing systems can be built. There is, however, a practical limitation to how far ACID transactions can be applied to the Web services world, even with advanced mechanisms like nesting and interposition.

To preserve the ACID properties, locks must be maintained on data throughout the duration of a transaction. While maintaining locks for the duration of a transaction is a reasonable thing to do within your own organization, it becomes less so when third parties are given access to your systems through Web services. The last thing that we would want to happen is for a mischievous party to run and never terminate a transaction. This would hold locks on data for extended periods, with the upshot that the holding of such locks would prevent actual business from being conducted through a denial of service attack.

It would seem, therefore, that we have a paradox. We need Web services to be able to conduct business from an interoperation point of view, but we need transactions if we are going to conduct business of any real value. If we decide to apply ACID transactions directly to the Web, then this paradox becomes a reality and our systems will grind to a halt. If, however, we take the general concepts of prior transaction models and re-cast them into a Web services-friendly model, then it is possible to overcome that paradox, albeit at the cost of relaxing the ACID properties. The underlying assumptions about the environment in which the two-phase algorithm is executed remain the same for Web service transactions as they do for regular distributed transactions. We must assume that work finishes before the transaction can terminate, there are no Byzantine failures, and so forth. Without such assumptions the two-phase model could not safely be applied to Web services transactions, just as it could not safely be applied to regular distributed transactions. Thus we can re-cast the original ACID properties to be more suitable for Web services as follows:

- *Atomic*—This aspect is not relaxed in the Web services model, since its exclusion would reduce the value of using transactions at all.
- *Consistent*—Since Web services effectively demarcate the boundaries of a system to which external users have no visibility, it is impossible to mandate that data remains consistent (since there is no possibility of direct control of that data). However, it is reasonable to mandate that Web services participating in a transaction receive consistent outcomes. That is, if the decision is to abort the transaction, all Web services involved with a particular transaction receive an abort message (and similarly, a commit message in the case of commit). One useful twist on this consistent outcome philosophy is to allow subsets of Web services (as defined by the application) to receive consistent outcomes. As we shall see later, the Business Transaction Protocol uses such a mechanism to provide flexibility in transaction structure.
- *Isolated*—Ensuring isolation is usually achieved through locking of shared data. Given the fact that Web services expose data to potentially unknown and untrusted third parties, it may be unwise to lock data since it provides an opportunity for denial of service (though there is no reason why we would not lock data provided we had a limited trusted domain). Since there may be no strict locking involved in a Web service transaction, the level of isolation may not be as high as a traditional back-end transaction processing system.
- *Durable*—Web services participating in a transaction must be supported by some recoverable infrastructure (as must any transaction coordinator), so that in the event of failure they can rejoin the transaction on recovering. Again, since the actual implementation of a Web service is not available, transaction users of that Web service have no system-level guarantees that the service *will* be recoverable, only that if it exposes transaction endpoints that it *should* be.

Given the Web services (or for that matter any other loosely-coupled) architecture, it's clear that we simply aren't going to utilize ACID transactions in the general case. Though we may still hope for all-or-nothing semantics, consistent outcomes and some level of durability, we cannot realistically hope for isolation unless we are operating within a specific domain of trust. What is needed is a twist on the classic two-phase algorithm for ACID transactions to turn it into a two-phase-based algorithm for Web services transactions. Fortunately, candidates for just such a protocol do exist.

OASIS Business Transaction Protocol

The OASIS Business Transaction Protocol (or simply BTP) is a protocol for coordinating loosely coupled systems like Web services. BTP was the product of more than a year's work from several major vendors including BEA, Hewlett-Packard, Sun Microsystems, and Oracle, which set out to reconcile transactionality with systems consisting of loosely coupled autonomous parties. In short, the result of this collaboration has been to produce a specification which, although based on the traditional two-phase approach, is still suitable for supporting transactions on the Web.

The BTP Model

To facilitate transactional coordination for Web services, the first challenge that has to be overcome is establishing exactly what transactions mean in a Web services world. It's clear from our earlier observations on relaxing the ACID properties that the BTP model could not itself lay claim to ACID semantics (and as such simply become an XML-based re-cast of existing transaction systems). Instead, BTP derived precisely the level of transactionality that could be maintained without imposing semantics (e.g., strict two-phase locking, compensating actions) behind Web services endpoints. It also addressed how transactional coordination could be done in harmony with the general philosophy of today's Web services architecture.

From this general philosophy, a three-pronged attack on the problem was formed:

1. BTP is an interoperation protocol that deals only with wire-level message exchanges, and the expected behavior of the senders and recipients of those messages. It does not presuppose any implementation details or architecture behind a service endpoint; it simply tries to coordinate those services via its messages using a two-phase approach (which importantly does *not* imply two-phase locking).
2. BTP extends the traditional transaction model with additional transaction types (known as the *atom* and the *cohesion*) that are better suited to the autonomous, distributed, and unreliable nature of the Web.
3. The coordinating party is no longer the exclusive decision-making body. BTP permits all parties involved in a transaction to specify their own qualification criteria within the scope of the transaction. This allows choices to be made up front as to a service's participation in a transaction, graceful retirements from running transactions, and a plethora of other useful features that all add up to reducing unnecessary and costly (in fact quite costly if we scale to the Web) network message exchanges between parties in a transaction.

Let's take these issues one at a time. First we must understand that BTP concerns itself only with message exchanges (and thus only implies the behavior at the message endpoints and does not specify its implementation). Since it is designed to deal with autonomous third parties that do not answer to a single design authority or even belong to the same trust domain, it can, of course, only have the authority to specify these message exchanges as we see in Figure 7-21.

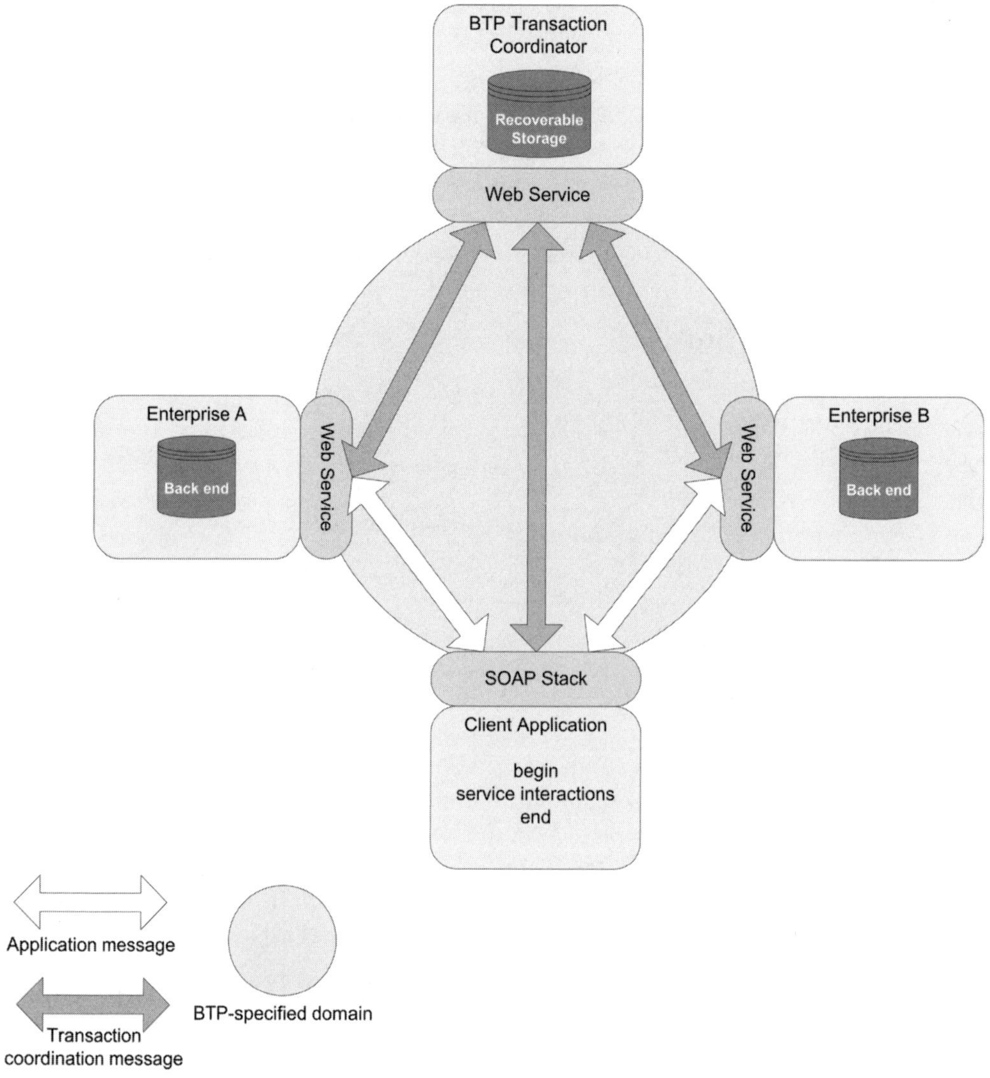

Figure 7-21 Business transaction protocol: An interoperation protocol.

The upshot of this approach is that any underlying technology can be used to build BTP infrastructure, and to build BTP-aware Web services. Provided the correct XML is sent on the wire, there is no prejudice against any back-end system. However, since there is no prejudice about the capabilities of any back-end system, we cannot second-guess the semantics, of the back-end transactional infrastructure. Since we do not know the back-end semantics we cannot absolutely guarantee ACID semantics with BTP. This is itself reflected in the choice of language used by BTP. Where a traditional ACID transaction processing system might use commit and abort, BTP uses *confirm* and *cancel*. Such language has been deliberately used to decouple the notion of two phases being equated to "ACID on the Web."

Second, although BTP cannot guarantee true ACID semantics through a true atomic transaction abstraction (because it has no knowledge of back-end semantics), it can guarantee consistency of the outcome messages sent to Web services participating in a transaction. In BTP, there is an abstraction that supports these semantics, called the *atom*. Any participants that are conducting work within the scope of an atom are guaranteed to see the same outcome (i.e. to confirm or cancel the transaction) as all other participants in the same atom (see Figure 7-22 where a uniform confirm is sent to all participants).

In addition to the atom, BTP also supports a second transaction type known as the *cohesion*, which allows the consistency of the outcome to be applied to specific distinct subsets of participants in a transaction, according to some business logic. This might at first seem a little strange, especially since there is a premium bestowed on traditional transaction processing systems that each participant in a transaction will see the same outcome. However, in an e-business environment, the ability to solicit interest from a number of parties and then proceed to complete a deal with a subset of those parties is commonplace. The BTP cohesion simply provides a means of operating under such a model in the Web services world, where we might interact with a number of partners' and customers' systems from the start of the transaction but ultimately as

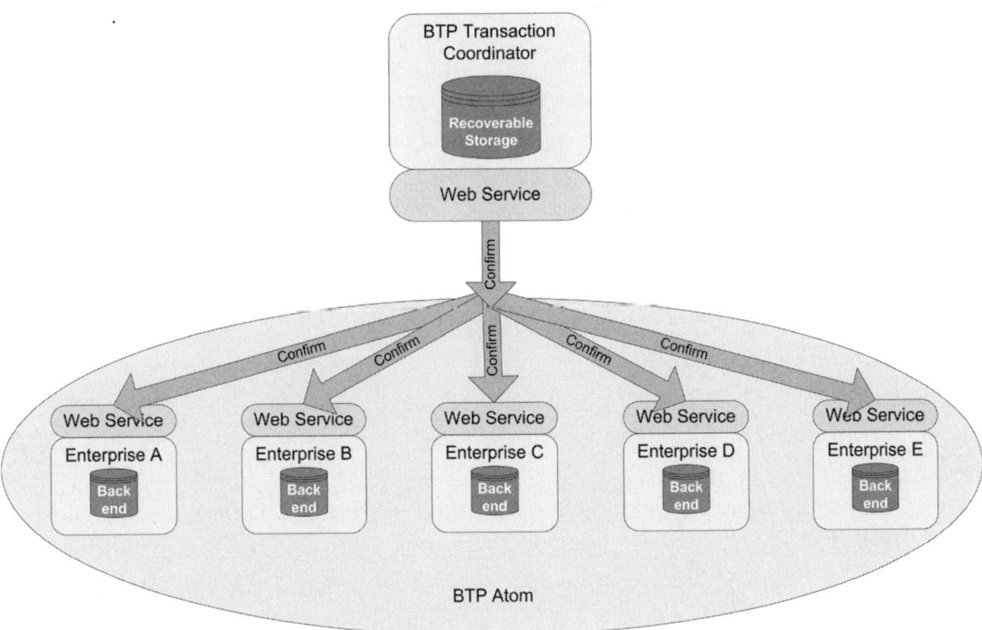

Figure 7-22 Atoms provide consistent outcomes.

the work progresses only choose to carry our business forward with a subset of those systems. Those systems with which we eventually choose to do business will all receive messages to confirm their part of the transaction (known as the confirm-set), while those systems which our business decisions lead us to exclude from the transaction will receive cancel messages. This kind of use-case is demonstrated in Figure 7-23 where according to some business logic, a subset of the available participants is chosen to form part of the confirm set (and thus will ultimately make their work durable) while the other participants are cancelled.

Finally, unlike traditional transaction processing systems, the transaction coordinator ventures but one of many opinions voiced while the outcome decision for a transaction is being decided. In a traditional system this would be nothing short of heresy since the transaction coordinator is effectively godlike. In BTP, since we have no real level of control over the systems with which we're transacting, it makes sense for them to have their say and even more sense to listen. In a Web services world, because we have no real control over the services with which we interact, these services will have their own way in any case, so BTP does the sensible thing and at least listens to them and tries to accommodate their whims!

In BTP, this exchange of additional "small print" is achieved through the use of *qualifiers*, which are additional information that may be sent with each and every BTP message. There is a standard set of BTP qualifiers that mostly govern timing issues and this set is extensible for others to apply to their own particular application domains. Perhaps the most interesting and useful

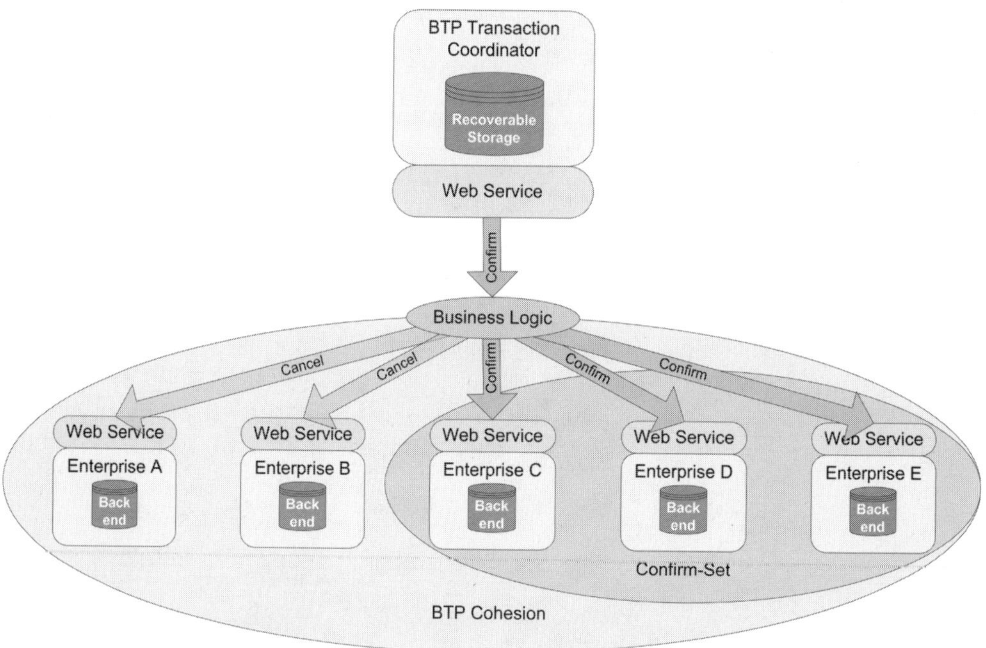

Figure 7-23 Using a cohesion to create a narrow confirm set.

of the qualifiers that form part of a standard BTP implementation are those through which the transaction manager and participants can further decouple themselves from one another based on timeouts. The BTP specification provides three such mechanisms:

1. *Transaction Time Limit*—The client application suggests the length of time that the work phase of a transaction is likely to take. A participant can use this information to determine a situation where the transaction coordinator has become unresponsive and therefore where it might be reasonable to begin unilateral cancellation of work. This is exemplified in Figure 7-24.

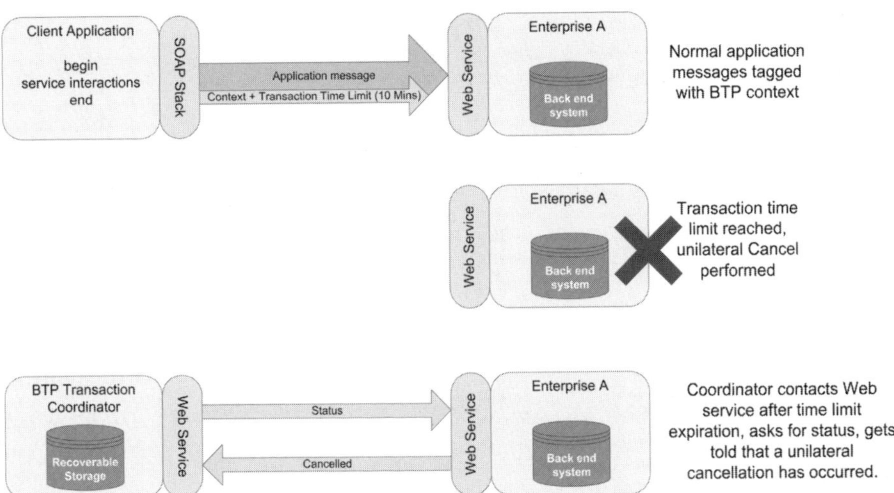

Figure 7-24 Transaction time limit qualifier.

2. *Inferior Timeout*—A participant can relay this qualifier to the transaction coordinator along with a positive vote (i.e., when it votes to prepare) during the first phase, as shown in Figure 7-25. This qualifier tells the coordinator how long the participant will remain prepared, and what action it will take when this period has expired.

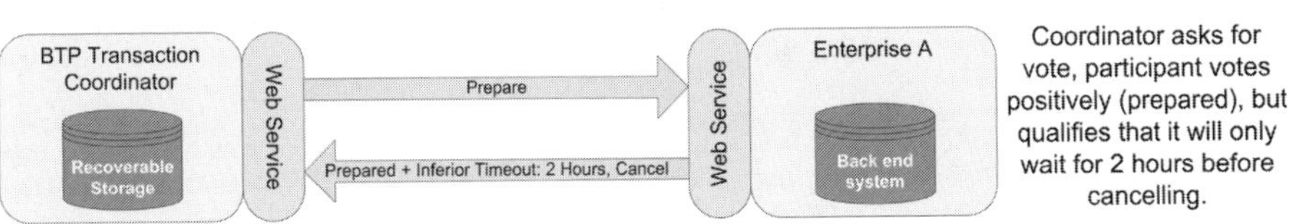

Figure 7-25 Inferior timeout qualifier.

3. *Minimum Inferior Timeout*—As per the example in Figure 7-26, the transaction coordinator specifies to a participant that it must agree to participate in the transaction for a certain period of time. If the participant knows that it cannot or will not do so, then it will respond negatively to any request to join the transaction.

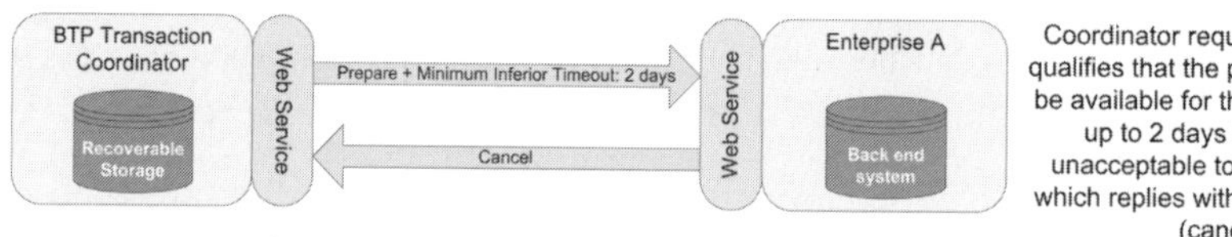

Figure 7-26 Minimum inferior timeout qualifier.

In short what BTP provides are transaction abstractions suited to B2B interactions with loose coupling, and it is deliberately non-prescriptive about what happens behind Web service endpoints. This all sounds rather good, but unless we can actually put it into practice it will remain a fine-sounding pipedream. Fortunately, there are BTP implementations available today, which means that we can implement transactional support for our Web services.

Implementing with BTP

Now that we understand the basics of transaction processing and the ins and outs of the BTP model, we're ready to look at how to implement applications and services with a BTP toolkit.

There are a number of BTP toolkits available on the market today. Although we use HP's software in this chapter, it is now being developed and marketed by Arjuna Technologies. See http://www.arjuna.com to download and get a free 30-day license. Choreology (http://www.choreology.com) also offer a BTP implementation via its Web site.

In this section, we're going to use one of the vendor toolkits (we've used HP's toolkit,[2] but the underlying principles are similar with other vendors' software) to build and consume transaction-aware Web services. But before we do, let's remind ourselves of the architecture in the context of a simple transactional scenario through which we'll build up our implementation.[3]

2. All of the code samples in this article are written with HP's Web Services Transactions 1.0, though the general concepts embodied within the code are generic and should span most BTP APIs.
3. Much of the following information is adapted from "Building Transactional Web Services with OASIS BTP," Webber, J., Web Services Journal, Vol. 2, Issue 10, October 2002, continued Vol. 2, Issue 11, November 2002. It is reprinted with permission of Sys-Con Media.

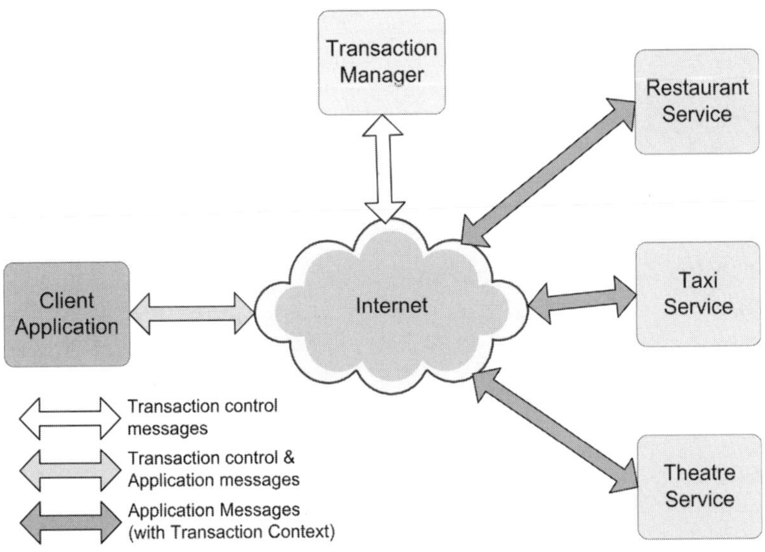

Figure 7-27 Architecture of a simple transactional Web service-based application.

The diagram shown in Figure 7-27 is similar to many high-level Web services architectures. The only differences here are that one service, the transaction manager, has been singled out as being distinct from the other Web services (which we assume are responsible for some aspects of a business process), and the fact that we have chosen to identify two distinct categories of messages: control messages (used to control transactions) and application messages (which propagate application data around the system). Of course, now armed with our background in transactions, this shouldn't come as too much of a shock.

However, if it really were as simple as deploying a transaction manager service into the architecture, then this chapter really wouldn't be necessary. Unfortunately it's not that simple, or at least not *quite* that simple, as we shall see. To illustrate, it's convenient to use Figure 7-27 as a point of reference as we work through the architecture filling in the details. We'll work from left to right, from the client through to the Web services, and cover everything in between.

Consuming Transactional Web Services

Though Web services are a hot technology, we shouldn't lose sight of the fact that they exist to support business processes. With that in mind, the right place to start our investigation is most definitely at the client end of a system—where the results of Web services interactions are brought together and ultimately where the value of a business process is focused. To place this in the proper context, it's useful to see an exploded view of the client-side infrastructure as per Figure 7-28.

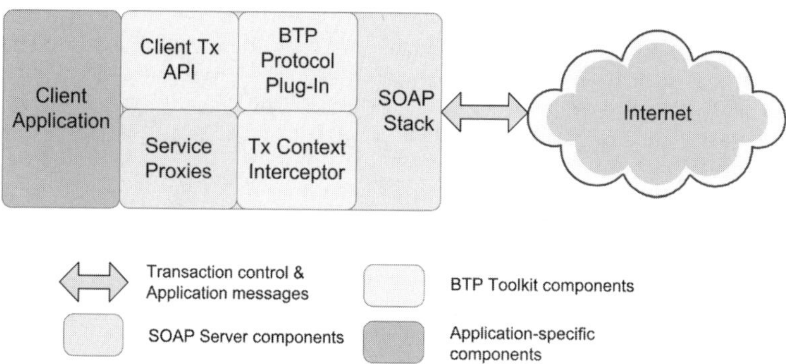

Figure 7-28 BTP client-side infrastructure.

In a non-transactional Web services-based application, the client process can be something as simple as a collection of calls (via proxies) to services that are involved in the business process. In a transactional Web services-based application, the same is, surprisingly enough, true with the caveat that the developer must demarcate any transactions that support business logic, as well as deal with application-specific calls. In this case the transaction demarcation is supported by the transaction API (the *Client Tx API* in Figure 7-28), whereas the business methods supported by service proxies remain (logically) free of any transactional infrastructure from the point of the client application developer. In fact, under the covers there is a mechanism that performs context associations with local threads of control within the client and messages passed between the client and (transactional) Web services. In Figure 7-28, this is the purpose of the *Tx Context Interceptor.*

Client API

The API provides the developer with the necessary tools with which to structure and control transactions within the application. The commands available to a developer in a transactional Web services environment are quite familiar to anyone who has used other transaction APIs in the past, with the caveat that BTP supports full control over both phases of the commit process and thus has a larger command set than we might otherwise envision. The common verbs (and by implication the methods that enact those verbs) for transaction demarcation are supported by the *UserTransaction* API:

- *Begin*—creates a new top-level transaction (or interposed transaction—BTP does not natively support nesting) for either atomic or cohesive transactions.
- *Prepare*—instructs an atomic transaction to prepare its associated participating services when the transaction is to terminate.
- *Prepare Inferiors*—instructs a cohesive transaction to prepare one or more of its participating services at transaction termination time.
- *Confirm*—instructs an atomic transaction to confirm all of its participating services, confirms all participating services that voted to confirm in the case of a cohesive transaction.

- *Cancel*—instructs all participating services in an atomic transaction, or those services specified in the parameter to the method call in a cohesive transaction, to cancel.

In addition to these demarcation verbs, there are a number of other commands through which we can inquire about a transaction:

- *Status*—asks the transaction manager to return the state (e.g., *committed*, *preparing*) of the current transaction.
- *Transaction type*—exposes the type of the current transaction (i.e., *atom* or *cohesion*).
- *Transaction name*—exposes the name of the current transaction in string form.

There are two verbs that allow advanced manual transaction management, which are:

- *Suspend*—disassociates the current thread from the current transaction.
- *Resume*—(re)associates the current thread with the current transaction.

Anyone who has previously worked with transactions will immediately find himself or herself at home with this API, since it is in the same spirit as other transaction APIs, as we can see by considering an example such as the code fragment shown in Figure 7-29.

```
// obtain a UserTransaction object (assume it is previously
// initialized)
userTransaction = UserTransactionFactory.getTransaction();

// obtain references to the web services we are going to use:
restaurant = new RestaurantService();
taxi = new TaxiService();
theatre = new TheatreService();

// Start a new transaction, using a simple Atom
userTransaction.begin(com.hp.mw.xts.TxTypes.ATOM);

// now invoke the business logic
restaurant.bookSeats(3);
theatre.bookSeats(3, 2);
taxi.bookTaxi();

// prepare the transaction (1st phase of two phase
// coordination)
userTransaction.prepare();

// confirm the transaction (2nd phase of two phase
// coordination)
userTransaction.confirm();
```

Figure 7-29 Controlling atoms from a Java Web service client.

In the code shown in Figure 7-29, we see a Java client driving an atom being used to ensure a consistent outcome across calls to the Web services shown in Figure 7-27. Initially we obtain a reference to an instance of `UserTransaction` from a (previously initialized) `UserTransactionFactory`, which we then use to delimit the scope of the single transaction in our application. Our atomic transaction is started by calling the `begin(...)` method on the user transaction API and specifying the type of transaction as an `atom`. From now on, the business logic is straightforward and contains no further transaction control primitives; we simply go ahead and make the bookings that we want for our night out through the `book (...)` methods of the service proxies we created. Once the business logic has completed, we can terminate the transaction by calling `prepare(...)` and `confirm(...)` which, in the absence of failures, should confirm to all parties that they should henceforth honor all of our booking requests. If there are failures, then all parties are informed and should take the necessary steps to undo any work undertaken on our behalf, while the client application will receive an exception that details what exactly has gone wrong.

The most interesting aspect of this example is that is shows just how simple and non-invasive it can be to wrap work with Web services within a transaction. In fact the business logic aspects of the code would be the same regardless of whether or not transactions are used.

Under the Covers: BTP's Two-Pipe Model

To support transactional Web services-based applications, BTP utilizes two distinct types of messages that the client application exchanges with Web services. The first of these messages is exchanged exclusively within the transaction infrastructure. The other type consists of messages that the client exchanges with business Web services onto which BTP messages might be piggybacked.

The messages that the application exchanges with the transaction infrastructure are encapsulated by the primitives supported by the client API. For example, a *begin(...)* method being executed by the client causes a corresponding BTP begin message to be sent to a transaction manager via the SOAP server, and for response messages from the transaction manager to be processed in the reverse order. This is shown in Figure 7-30, and a sample BTP message (begin) is shown in Figure 7-31. The only slightly unusual aspect to this example is that the response to begin messages (and it is only begin messages this occurs with) is cached for later use so that local threads of execution can be associated with the BTP transaction under which its work is being executed.

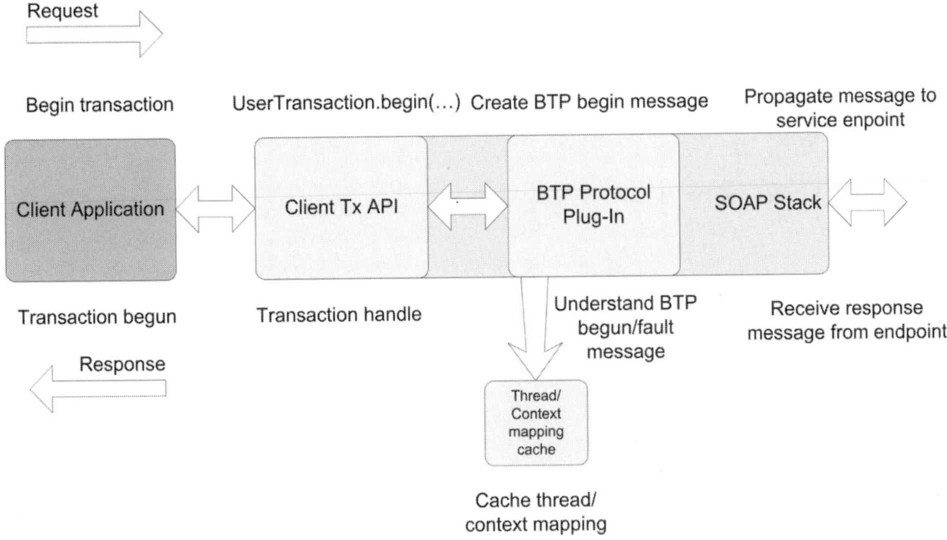

Figure 7-30 Creating and consuming BTP messages at the client side.

```
<?xml version="1.0" encoding="UTF-8" ?>
<SOAP:Envelope SOAP:encodingStyle="http://schemas.xmlsoap.org/
soap/encoding/" xmlns:SOAP="http://schemas.xmlsoap.org/soap/
envelope/">
  <SOAP:Body>
    <btp:begin transaction-type="atom"
      xmlns:btp="urn:oasis:names:tc:BTP:1.0:core" />
  </SOAP:Body>
</SOAP:Envelope>
```

Figure 7-31 A BTP Begin message.

With application messages, the situation is a little different. Unlike BTP messages where the message contents travels in the body of the SOAP envelope, when application messages are sent application-specific content travels in the body while any BTP content is relegated to the header part of the envelope. We can see this in Figure 7-32 where the SOAP body carries the application payload, while the header is used to carry the BTP context.

This scheme works well since most SOAP stacks are well equipped to perform efficient header processing, and placing the BTP content, including the transaction context, in the header means that SOAP actors can pick out the parts of the header space of interest without having to parse the whole application payload. From a development point of view, most SOAP servers support pluggable header processors, which means that building BTP context processing into

```
<?xml version="1.0" encoding="UTF-8" ?>
<SOAP:Envelope SOAP:encodingStyle="http://schemas.xmlsoap.org/
soap/encoding/"
  xmlns:SOAP="http://schemas.xmlsoap.org/soap/envelope/">
  <SOAP:Header>
    <btp:messages xmlns:btp="urn:oasis:names:tc:BTP:1.0:core">
      <btp:context>
        <btp:superior-address>
          <btp:binding-name>soap-http-1</btp:binding-name>
            <btp:binding-address>
              http://example.com/btpservice
            </btp:binding-address>
          </btp:superior-address>
          <btp:superior-identifier>
            12fa6de4ea3ec
          </btp:superior-identifier>
        <btp:superior-type>atom</btp:superior-type>
      </btp:context>
    </btp:messages>
  </SOAP:Header>
  <SOAP:Body>
    <ns:booking xmlns:ns="http://btp.restaurant.org/">
      <seats xsi:type="xsd:int">99</seats>
    </ns:booking>
  </SOAP:Body>
</SOAP:Envelope>
```

Figure 7-32 An application message with BTP context.

your infrastructure should be straightforward, and any BTP toolkit should provide useful components to ease the process. To demonstrate that point, let's take a look at the general client-side architecture (which is based on Apache Axis in the toolkit we've used), as per the examples in Figure 7-33 and Figure 7-34.

Figure 7-33 shows the outward path of a call to a Web service, starting from the left with the local method call onto a service proxy. The call then follows the logical path of being converted to the appropriate SOAP body that contains the application payload before it progresses to the outgoing context handler. The context handler takes advantage of the fact that the information supplied in response to the BTP begin message was recorded, and is able to produce a BTP context from that data which it duly inserts into the SOAP envelope's header. If there is no contextual data stored for the current thread (i.e., it isn't part of a transaction or the transaction has been deliberately suspended), then the context insertion is simply bypassed.

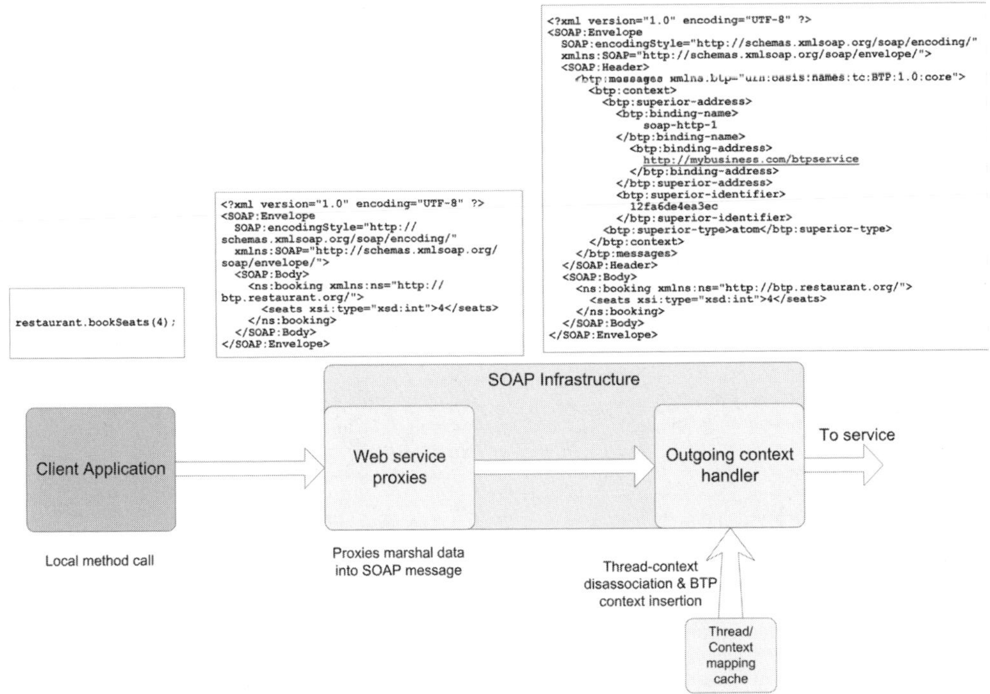

Figure 7-33 Client-side request processing.

For return messages, the strategy is simply the reverse as shown in Figure 7-34 where the flow is from right to left. Responses are quickly scanned to see if they contain any BTP context entries in their headers. If context data is present, it is stripped out of the message and may be used to resume the transaction locally by associating the current thread, while the rest of the message passes through to the service proxies. Once at the service proxies, the local method call returns control to the client, which is unaware of all of the additional processing that has occurred on its behalf.

Having reached the point where we can send application messages with BTP contexts, as well as BTP messages themselves, we're able to follow the messages as they travel across the wire. As we follow the cables, we are inevitably led to yet more Web services.

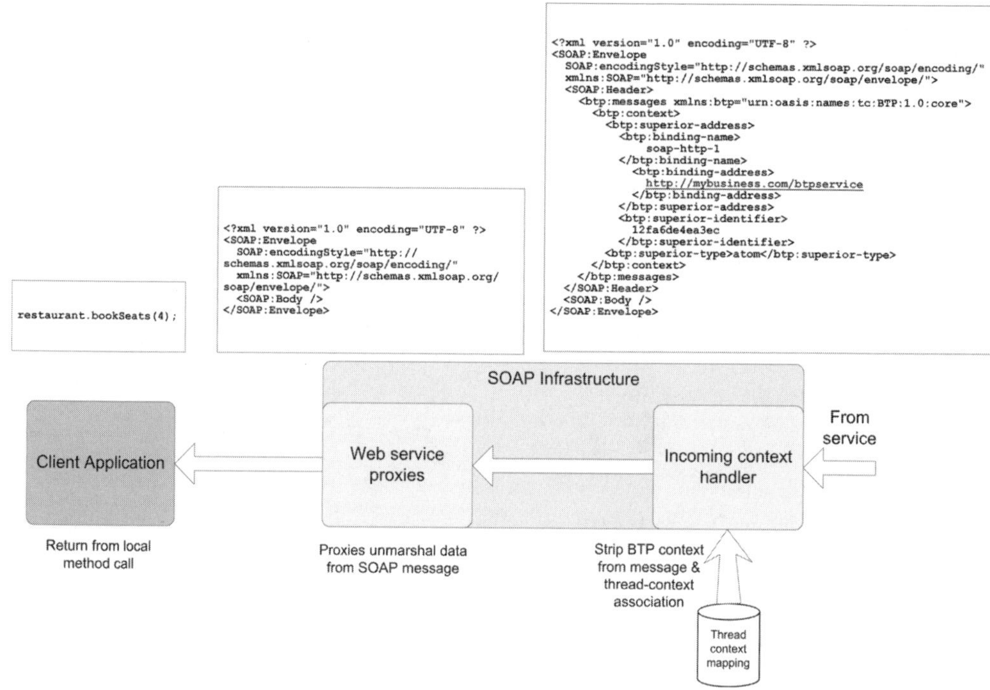

Figure 7-34 Client-side response processing.

Transactionalizing Web Services

To transactionalize a Web service with BTP is perhaps something of a misnomer, since BTP does not deal with transactional Web services per se. It chooses instead to partition Web services into two distinct types to enable clear separation of business services and their associated transaction-oriented *participants*. Business services are similar to client applications in that there is no inherent transactionality directly associated with them—they simply exist to host and expose business logic. On the other hand, the participants associated with business services are essentially business logic agnostic and deal only with the transactional aspects of service invocations. This dichotomy turns out to be quite useful since it means that existing services can be given transactional support without necessarily performing any invasive procedures on them. The fact that non-transactional Web services can be given transactionality without having to rebuild the service is a real plus, which also means that the transactional and business aspects of a system can be evaluated and implemented independently. Having added some more pieces of the puzzle, we can now reshape the global BTP architecture, resulting in Figure 7-35.

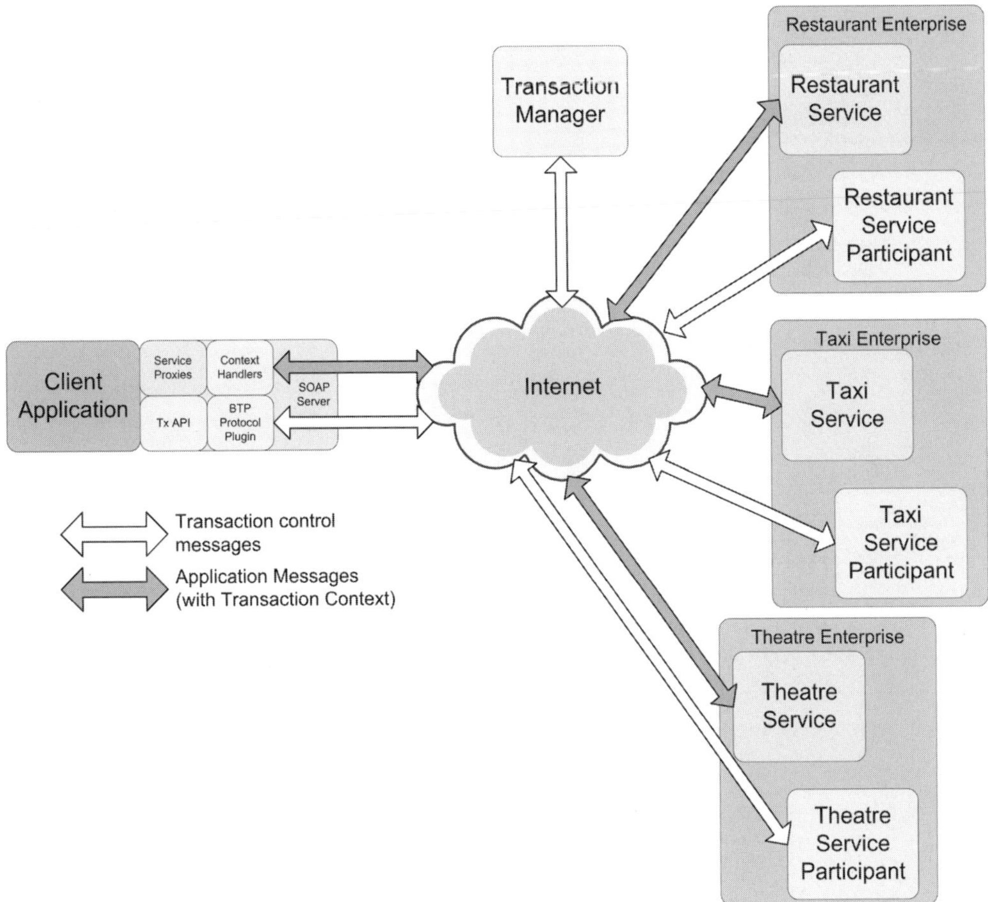

Figure 7-35 Booking a night out with BTP-enabled infrastructure.

Figure 7-35 typifies a BTP rollout, showing how the endpoint of each BTP actor fits into the global model. Here we see the services that expose business logic to the Web are supported by other services, the BTP participants, which deal with the transaction management aspects of business Web services and, most importantly, how there is a clean separation between the two kinds of service. However, there is clearly some overlap even at this level since application messages carry BTP contexts whenever service invocations are being made within the scope of a transaction. It is here that the business logic and transaction domains collide, albeit gently.

Supporting Infrastructure

For business Web services, most of the interesting work from a transactional perspective happens under the covers. Like the client application, Web services benefit from advances in SOAP server technology that support header processing before the application payload of a SOAP message is delivered. For BTP-aware Web services, SOAP header processing can be utilized to insert and extract BTP contexts on behalf of Web services in a reciprocal fashion to the way header processing is performed at the client side. Since header processing is non-invasive to the service-level business logic, we can see that the impact of making a service transactional with BTP being minimal. A typical transactional infrastructure for a Web service stack is presented in Figure 7-36 and Figure 7-37.

Figure 7-36 depicts what happens when a Web service receives a SOAP request. If the request doesn't carry a BTP context, then it is simply passed through the incoming context handler to other registered handlers (if there are any) and will eventually deliver its payload to the service. If, however, the request carries a BTP context, then the context is stripped out of the header of the incoming message and is associated with the thread of execution within which the service's work will be executed. To achieve this, the handler *resumes* the transaction, using elements from the *Transaction Manager* part of the API we saw earlier, which effectively associates (or re-associates if this is not the first time the same context has been received) the work performed by the service with a BTP transaction.

When returning from a service invocation, the reverse process occurs as shown in Figure 7-37. The message from the service passes through the outgoing context handler that checks to

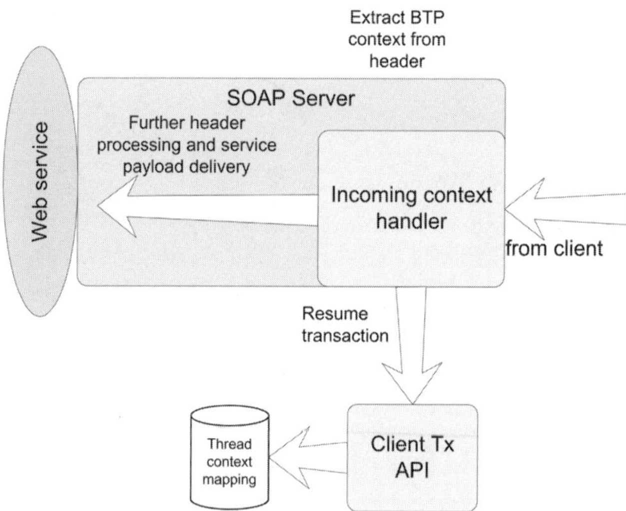

Figure 7-36 Web service incoming context handler.

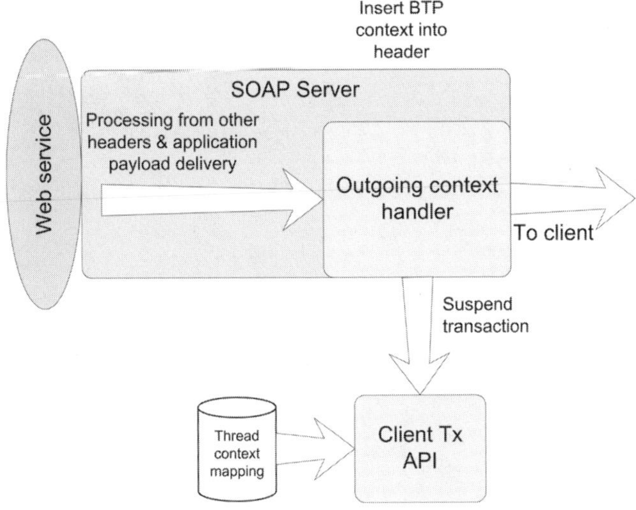

Figure 7-37 Web service outgoing context handler.

see if there is a transaction associated with the work that took place to produce the message. If the work was performed by a thread within the scope of a transaction, then the BTP context is inserted into the header of the message and the transaction is *suspended*, which effectively pauses its work for the service until further messages with a matching context are received.

While none of this is especially rocket science or brain surgery, it does serve to reiterate that BTP-enabling Web services is a non-invasive procedure. However, at some point every BTP deployment has to interact with existing infrastructure, and it is here that we enter a more intricate phase of Web service development.

Participants

Participants are the last piece of implementation in our BTP architecture. Although the high level view of how participants fit into the global BTP architecture has been discussed, we haven't yet studied the anatomy of a participant, which is an oversight we are about to correct.

Participants are the entities that act on behalf of business Web services in matters regarding transactionality. From a Web services point of view, they are equipped to deal with message exchanges with the transaction manager, whereas from an enterprise's perspective they are implemented to propagate transaction messages and outcomes to back-end systems. While that sounds like hard work, a toolkit will simplify matters by offering an interface that your participant will implement to become part of the participant stack. The participant stack is shown in Figure 7-38, and (a cut down view of) the interface which constitutes the API for the participant stack from the developer's point of view is shown in Figure 7-39.

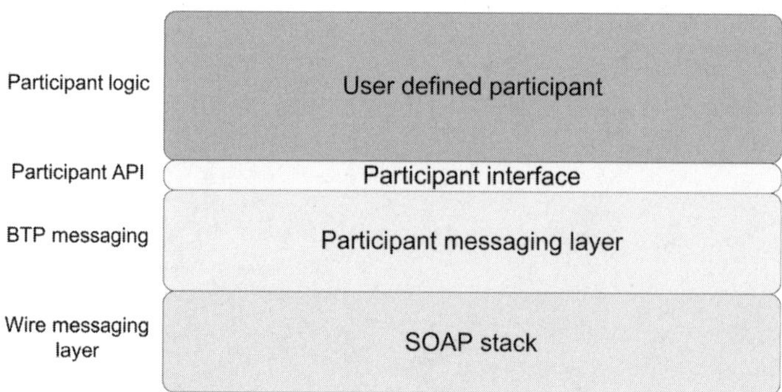

Figure 7-38 The participant stack.

Figure 7-38 shows the conceptual view of a participant (minus the back-end plumbing that we shall see later). It's conceptually a straightforward document exchange-based Web service where the messaging layer understands BTP messages and invokes methods on the user-defined participant (which has a known interface) in accordance with the type and content of the messages it receives. Any returns from the participant are shoehorned into BTP messages and sent back through the SOAP infrastructure.

```
public interface Participant
{
    public Vote prepare (Uid id, Qualifier[] qualifiers)
        throws GeneralException, InvalidInferiorException,
            WrongStateException, HeuristicHazardException,
            HeuristicMixedException;

    public void confirm (Uid id, Qualifier[] qualifiers)
        throws GeneralException, InvalidInferiorException,
            WrongStateException, HeuristicHazardException,
            HeuristicMixedException,
            InferiorCancelledException;

    public void cancel (Uid id, Qualifier[] qualifiers)
        throws GeneralException, InvalidInferiorException,
        WrongStateException, HeuristicHazardException,
        HeuristicMixedException, InferiorConfirmedException;

    public void contradiction (Uid id,
                               Qualifier[] qualifiers)
        throws GeneralException, InvalidInferiorException,
            WrongStateException;

    // Other methods...
}
```

Figure 7-39 The (Java) participant interface.

The participant API effectively shields participant developers from having to understand the BTP messages that participants consume, though this shielding is not entirely "bullet proof" since some understanding of how and when the methods in a participant are called is still required. Figure 7-39 shows the more important methods that an implementer has to write in order to create a participant. As we might expect, these methods correspond to the messages that are exchanged between transaction manager and participant (which is itself identified by a unique ID or *Uid* in the API). As such if we have an understanding of BTP (which we *should* have to write a decent participant), then the methods are quite self-explanatory. However, here is a brief overview:

- `prepare(...)`—The prepare method begins BTP's two-phase confirm protocol. During this method a participant typically checks with its back end to see whether it can proceed with a transaction on behalf of the service it is representing, and returns a *Vote* which causes an appropriate response to be propagated down the stack and ultimately to the transaction manager. Note if the participant votes to cancel, it may not receive further messages from the transaction manager from here on, and its back end may take suitable abortive action.
- `confirm(...)`—Confirming a participant causes the second phase of the two-phase confirm to occur. At confirm time the participant relays to its back end that any updates to state should be made durable.
- `cancel(...)`—Cancel is the opposite of confirm, whereby a participant will typically relay to its back end that it should undo, forget, or otherwise reverse any changes that have been made to system state by the business logic residing in the associated Web service either by traditional locking strategies in a trusted domain or by a compensative strategy otherwise.
- `contradiction(...)`—Contradictions are the BTP terminology for what are traditionally known as heuristics. If a service back end finds itself in a situation where it has done the opposite of what it has been asked to do by the transaction manager (e.g., it has cancelled when it should have confirmed or vice versa), and cannot mask the fault, it will send an exception to the transaction manager. The transaction manager will evaluate the situation from a global perspective and may need to inform other participants of the contradiction that has occurred. If that is the case, then a participant will learn about contradictions that have occurred when its contradiction method is invoked. At that point a participant typically tries to instigate compensative action, though to fully recover from a contradictory situation help from outside the system (even human help) may be required as per traditional heuristic outcomes.

One final intricacy for participants is the sending and receiving of *qualifiers*. As was discussed earlier in the chapter, qualifiers are a neat feature from BTP which derive from the fact that the BTP transaction manager is not godlike, as are its equivalents in other transaction management models, but instead accepts the possibility that other parts of the system might justifiably want to help out in the decision making process. In the API, qualifiers are delivered to the participant implementation through the *Qualifier[] qualifiers* parameter (where the transaction manager gets the chance to state its additional terms and conditions) and are returned from the *prepare(...)* method as part of the *Vote* (where the participant then gets to respond with its own terms and conditions). Qualifiers are a real help when it comes to Web services transactions because in a loosely coupled environment, it is invaluable information to know from the client side that the party you're communicating with will only be around for so long, or to be able to specify from the participant side that your party won't hang around while others procrastinate. The downside is, of course, that as the developer of a participant you will be expected to write code that handles any qualifiers and propagates them onto the equivalent mechanisms in your back-end systems—but the reward in terms of integration with the Web services architecture is worth the effort.

Compensating Actions: A Strategy for Participant Implementation

The overriding theme of Web services transaction is that locking for any significant period of time simply is not suitable for Web-scale architecture. Therefore the strategies that we choose to provide to the abort facility of a participant should not (outside of a specific trusted domain) involve the use of locking and shadow writes because of the potential denial of service consequences.

If we accept that we will not hold long-lived locks on data, then we also accept that we cannot simply discard shadow updates and release locks (known as *backward error recovery*) to implement our cancel operation.

Since we cannot hold locks for an extended period, we must only hold locks for that instant at which we update a piece of state, and to update that state directly rather than update a shadow copy. Now in the event of a cancel request reaching our participant, we must use a *forward error recovery* strategy to reverse the changes that we optimistically committed to durable storage—that is, we execute a *compensating action*.

A compensating action is in effect the reciprocal function to the original business logic, which has the effect of returning the system to the same state as before the business logic. For example, in our debit-credit system, a compensating action would durably record the intended debits and credits for each account, and in the event of a cancel would simply run a debit where there was a credit, and a credit where there was a debit, as shown in Figure 7-40.

Although compensation does provide a solution to the problem of exposing long-term lockable resources to the Web, it is not itself without drawbacks:

- Compensation may not always be able to return the system to a state completely identical to the system state before the transaction ran. For example, if the debit-credit operation had been executed by placing checks in the mail, it may not be able to fully compensate for this action within the system itself.

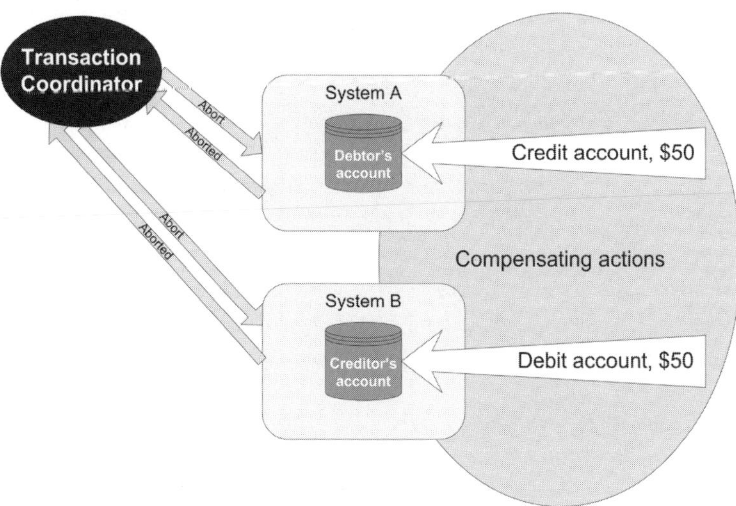

Figure 7-40 A compensative Cancel for the debit-credit example.

- Since running a compensating action is actually running a piece of business logic, compensations may be as computationally expensive to execute as any other piece of business logic which may place a heavy burden on any underlying infrastructure.
- Forward error recovery is more expensive to design and implement than backward error recovery mechanisms since the compensating actions will have to be developed for each permissible operation, rather than using a generic mechanism. Furthermore, compensating actions may generally not be as trivial as those seen in the debit-credit example.

Thus the cost of adopting a forward error recovery strategy with compensating actions is, in terms of additional analysis and implementation, compared with backward error recovery mechanisms. The benefits though are clear, insofar as without such a strategy our transactional Web services can only safely be advertised to and consumed by our trusted infrastructure, which very much limits scope for real B2B interactions over Web services.

Integrating Participants and Services

Context-work association is not the only place where there is overlap between BTP infrastructure and the Web services that it supports. In fact it is the integration of BTP participants with service back ends that is the most important and intricate aspect of a BTP deployment. Unlike service-side context handling, sadly there are no stock answers to the problem of participant-service integration, because the strategy adopted will depend on the existing transactional back-end infrastructure that the service itself relies upon. However, we can mitigate this to some degree by using tools provided to the back-end developer in the form of an API that takes care of the common back-end tasks. In the same spirit as the client API, two further verbs that deal with enlisting and removing participating services from a transaction are supported by the TransactionManager API and may be used from the service's back-end. They are:

- *Enrol*—Enlists a specific participant with the current transaction.
- *Resign*—Removes a specific participant from the current transaction.

Using this service-side API and in keeping with the theme of non-invasiveness that is so much in the spirit of BTP, we would ideally like to deploy systems that do not disturb existing (working) Web services. Fortunately, there are means and ways of doing just that, as shown in Figure 7-41.

Figure 7-41 depicts the back end of a Web service, and is simply the continuation of the diagrams shown in Figure 7-36 and Figure 7-37. We can assume there will be some kind of transactional infrastructure in the back end of most enterprise-class Web services, and for the sake of simplicity here we can assume it is something like a database.

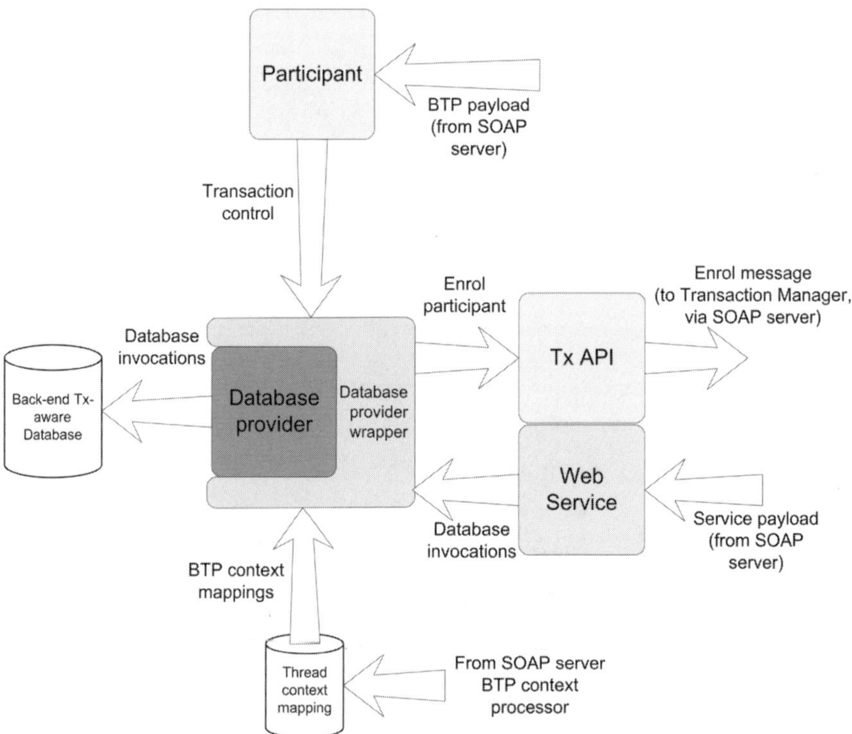

Figure 7-41 Integrating services, back-end infrastructure, and participants.

The good news is that even without BTP transactions thrown into the mix, the exposed Web service will still need to talk to its own back-end systems. It is therefore possible to intercept the interactions between the service and the back end to suit our own purposes. A useful strategy in this situation is to wrap the service's database provider within our own provider that supports the same interface, but is also aware of the BTP infrastructure.

In this example, our database provider wrapper has access to BTP context information from the header processing logic embedded in the service's stack, and is aware of the participant service that performs BTP work on behalf of the business service. Armed with such knowledge, the database wrapper can enroll a participant into the BTP transaction through the *enroll* operation supported by the API, which causes a BTP Enroll message exchange to occur with the transaction manager. When there are no upsets during the enrollment of the participant, BTP messages can now be exchanged between the transaction manager and the participant, ensuring that the participant knows exactly what's happening in the BTP transaction at all times. Having that knowledge allows the participant to mediate between the transactional semantics (if any) of the service's database access and the activity in the BTP transaction. Such arbitration may not be trivial and will certainly require some domain expertise, since the participant implementation will have to reconcile BTP semantics with those of the service's own back-end transaction processing model. For example, a participant implementation might choose to perform a simple mapping of BTP messages to its native database, queue, or workflow system equivalents, or the participant might choose to take an optimistic approach and immediately commit all changes to the database and perform a compensating action in the event of a failure. What implementers must remember is that there is no absolute right or wrong, just participant implementations that work well for a given system and those that don't, and that time spent analyzing use-cases up front will pay dividends in the long run.

When two or more participants from a single organization are enrolled within the scope of the same transaction, they can collude with one another and use the knowledge of the transaction to alter the business-level outcomes. For instance, if a participant for a nut-vending service and a bolt-vending service from the same organization are both enrolled within the scope of the same atom, they know that nuts *and* bolts will be purchased. This allows the business logic to offer more competitive pricing based on the knowledge that either both will be purchased or neither. Conversely, if the participants are enrolled within the scope of a cohesion, there are no such guarantees and pricing may be altered accordingly.

The Transaction Manager

It might seem a little strange to mention the transaction manager at such a late stage and with so little detail given its importance in the architecture. This is especially apparent given that the transaction manager is, after all, the component on which all other components depend. The paradox is that the transaction manager is simply the least interesting part of the architecture from an application or Web service developer's point of view. It is simply a SOAP document exchange-based Web service that implements the BTP state machine and suitable recovery mechanisms so that transactions are not compromised in the event of failure. From a development point of view, a BTP transaction manager is simply a black box, deployed somewhere on the network to enable the rest of the infrastructure to work, and it falls only to those who have chosen to implement BTP toolkits to worry about its internals.

Bringing It All Together: A Cohesive Example

We've seen the BTP architecture, the SOAP plumbing and have touched on the transaction model that BTP supports. Now we can draw together the many different aspects into a more powerful illustration. For this example, we're going to revisit the night out application whose architecture we developed earlier in Figure 7-35. That code interacted with a number of Web services within the context of a BTP atom, thus ensuring a consistent outcome for the services in the transaction. We use a similar pattern for this cohesion-based example, though since cohesions are more flexible than atoms, we have to work just a little harder. We use approximately the same use-case except we'll spice things up a little by allowing either the theatre or the restaurant service to fail, with the intention being that as long as we get a night out, we don't care much what we actually do. The code that shows how to program with cohesions is in Figure 7-42.

```
// obtain a UserTransaction object (assume the factory is
// initialized)
UserTransaction userTransaction =
  UserTransactionFactory.getTransaction();

// Obtain references to the web services we are going to use:
RestaurantService restaurant = new RestaurantService();
TaxiService  taxi = new TaxiService();
TheatreService = new TheatreService():

// In a cohesion, we have to make an application-level mapping of
// services to participants (outside of BTP scope). Our example
// services support this.
String restaurantParticipantID = restaurant.getParticipantID();
String theatreParticipantID = theatre.getParticipantID();
String taxiParticipantID = taxi.getParticipantID();

// Start a new transaction, using a Cohesion
userTransaction.begin(com.hp.mw.xts.TxTypes.COHESION);

// Now invoke the business logic
restaurant.bookSeats(3);
theatre.bookSeats(3, 2);
taxi.bookTaxi();
```

Figure 7-42 Using cohesions from a Web service client.

```
// Prepare (all of) the participants (i.e. with null parameter)
StatusItem[] statusItems = userTransaction.prepare_inferiors(null);

// Iterate over the statuses, and make sure the taxi's pledged to
// honor the booking
boolean restuarantOK = false;
boolean taxiOK = false;
boolean theatreOK = false;
for(int i = 0; i < statusItems.length; i++)
{
    if(statusItems[i].inferiorName().equals(restaurantParticipantID))
    {
        if(statusItems[i].status() == TwoPhaseStatus.PREPARED)
        {
            restaurantOK = true;
        }
    }

    else if(statusItems[i].inferiorName().equals(taxiParticipantID))
    {
        if(statusItems[i].status() == TwoPhaseStatus.PREPARED)
        {
            taxiOK = true;
        }
    }

    else if(statusItems[i].inferiorName().equals(theatreParticipantID))
    {
        if(statusItems[i].status() == TwoPhaseStatus.PREPARED)
        {
            theatreOK = true;
        }
    }
}

// If we can't get a taxi, then we have to call the whole event off.
if(!taxiOK)
{
    ut.cancel(null); // Cancel everything
}
else if(restaurantOK || theatreOK)
{
    ut.confirm(); // Confirm whatever is available
}
else
{
    ut.cancel(null); // Can't get anywhere to go, cancel everything.
}
```

Figure 7-42 Using cohesions from a Web service client (continued).

The code in Figure 7-42 follows a similar pattern to the atom example shown in Figure 7-29. We start our transaction and interact with the services via proxies as usual. The important difference in the cohesion scenario compared to the atom example is that the application must deal directly with the participants that support the services, whereas with atoms the details of any service's participants are encapsulated by the transaction manager.

There are various ways in which we might obtain the names of the participants that the services enroll into the transaction, but unfortunately the BTP specification does not provide any definitive means of obtaining that information (though it does allow participants to be given "friendly names" through the use of a qualifier called *Inferior Name* to help out in such situations). In this example, we allow the services themselves to report on the names of their participants through their `participantID()` operations, though any form of a priori knowledge via human or automated means (like UDDI-based discovery) could be feasibly substituted. With time and experience, patterns for this kind of work will emerge and become commonplace.

Once we have the names under which the participants are enrolled into the cohesion, we can then use them to ascertain what decisions the services' participants make when we terminate the transaction. In this example, we iterate over the decisions that were returned by the `prepare_inferiors(…)` call to find out if the taxi and at least one other service are prepared to make forward progress. If our conditions are met, we confirm the transaction with the `confirm()` method which confirms all those services' participants that agreed that they could meet our requirements (those that voted to confirm) and cancels any services that could not meet our requirements (those that voted to cancel). Conversely, if our overall requirements cannot be met, then we can immediately cancel the transaction and the participants will all be instructed to undo the work of their associated Web services.

The power of cohesions arises from the fact that we are at liberty to make choices about who will participate in our transaction right up until the point that we try to confirm it. In fact, we could have used several taxi services in this example to ensure that we have at least one travel option and simply cancelled those that we didn't want before we came to confirm the cohesion.

Using cohesions, as implementers of the client application we are at liberty to structure our transactions as we see fit to suit the problem domain. For instance, if we knew that we absolutely had to take a taxi to meet friends at the restaurant, but were not sure whether we wanted to go to a show afterward, we could wrap the taxi and restaurant booking operations within an atom (or indeed wrap several independent taxi and restaurant bookings into several atoms) and enroll that atom into a cohesion along with the participant for the theater Web service. In this case we are guaranteed to get the taxi and restaurant bookings together (or not at all), while we have some leeway in terms of whether we decide to go to the theater.

BTP: In a Nutshell

Though BTP itself is a sophisticated protocol, from the point of view of an implementer much of its detail is handled by supporting toolkits. Creating applications that drive BTP transactions is straightforward because of the traditional-looking and intuitive API. Though making Web services transactional is a little trickier, BTP toolkits will help to simplify things to a great extent by providing much of the Web service-side infrastructure. The only tough challenge for implementers is the construction of participants, which does require a more thorough understanding of transactional architectures to get right.

Other Web Services Transaction Protocols

Though BTP is the predominant transaction protocol for Web services today, it is by no means the only proposed solution. Even now, there are other implementation options that we can use to build transactions into Web services and there are other specifications that are being proposed as supplicants or replacements for BTP. While the new specifications are interesting, let's first delve into the other practical, implemented alternatives we can use today.

Microsoft .Net

Microsoft's .Net platform provides a rich set of building blocks from which developers can build Web services through its ASP.Net technology. Using ASP.Net, developers can create Web services and hook those services directly into back-end technologies developed on the same .Net platform.

What this means to the Web services developer is that, if it is appropriate, protocols like BTP can be forsaken and instead the facilities of the underlying platform can be applied to support Web services. This is possible because Microsoft's Transaction Server, COM+, and the .Net common language runtime all support the same transaction model, to which ASP.Net Web services have access, as shown in Figure 7-43.

In ASP.Net, we can apply almost the same declarative transaction demarcation attributes to Web services that we can to standard .Net components. We do this by providing the option to run the service within the context of what Microsoft refers to as an *Automatic Transaction*, where distributed transaction management is automatically delegated to the underlying OS platform.

While the process of adding transaction support to an ASP.Net Web service is straightforward, from a Web services perspective there is an important limitation inherent in this model in that it effectively exposes lockable resources to the Web because the transactions it runs are classical two-phase commit and possess the ACID properties. However, if the Web services that we are going to expose are to work within a particular domain of trust (and not the public Web) then we might be prepared to use this technology, trading off simplicity for scalability, as pictured in Figure 7-44.

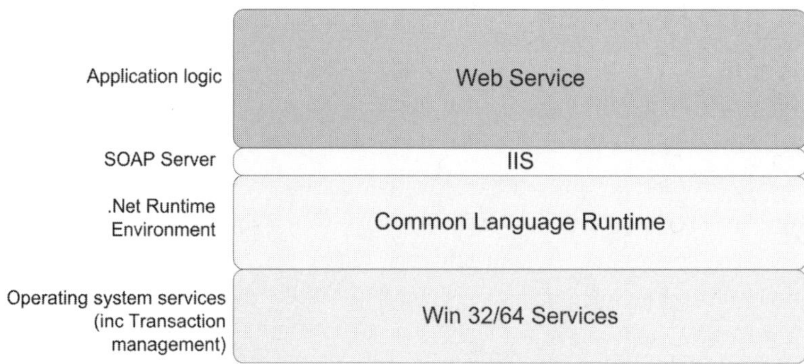

Figure 7-43 Microsoft.Net Stack: A transaction-oriented perspective.

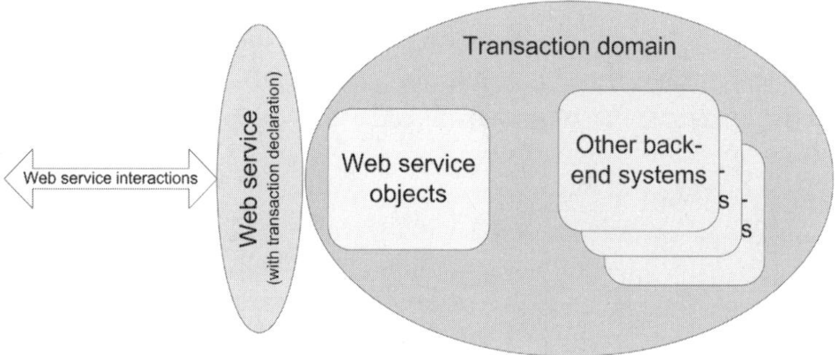

Figure 7-44 ASP.Net transactions.

For a Web service the possible transaction semantics that we can apply are as follows:

- *Disabled*—Transaction context will be ignored by ASP.Net and the Web service will not under any circumstances itself create work within the scope of a transaction.
- *Not Supported*—Indicates that the service does not execute within the scope of a transaction. When a service invocation is processed, it is not associated with a transaction, regardless of whether there is a transaction active at the time.
- *Supported*—Indicates that a service will run in the context of an existing transaction, but if no transaction exists then no transaction will be created and the service's work will run outside of the scope of a transaction.
- *Required*—Indicates that a service will run within the context of an existing transaction, or if no transaction currently exists, a new one will be created.
- *Requires New*—A new transaction will be created for each service invocation.

In order to use these declarations and therefore take advantage of the underlying transaction processing infrastructure, it is simply a matter of adding the appropriate attributes to your source code, as shown in Figure 7-45.

```
using System;
using System.Web.Services;
using System.Web.Util;

public class TaxiService : WebService
{
  [WebMethod
    (TransactionOption=TransactionOption.RequiresNew)]
  public bool BookTaxi(string from, string to, int month,
                       int day, int hour, int mins)
  {
        // Business logic and database interactions
  }
}
```

Figure 7-45 A .Net Taxi Service Implemented in C#.

In the C# class shown in Figure 7-45, the skeleton of a sample taxi booking service is shown, and the `TransactionOption` field of the `WebMethod`[4] attribute is set to `RequiresNew` indicating that a new back-end transaction will be created for each service invocations which will be used to scope the work that the service will undertake across its back-end databases.

J2EE and Enterprise Java Beans

The Enterprise Java Beans or EJB part of the J2EE specification provides a rich component model where various aspects of component management can be delegated to the server within which the EJBs are hosted. Of particular interest to us here is the fact that, like the .Net framework, the EJB container provides ACID transactional support to its hosted components in a similar declarative fashion, but on a per Bean basis.

When working with EJBs exposed via a SOAP server, it simply becomes a matter of delegating work from the front-end Web service to the back-end EJBs and allowing the EJB infrastructure to manage transactionality on behalf of those components, as shown in Figure 7-46.

The pattern exemplified in Figure 7-46 is somewhat crude and has the effect of exposing an EJB, or parts of an EJB, to the Web services network. Once again, like the .Net solution, this

4. The WebMethod attribute is a simple means of exposing a method via ASP.Net.

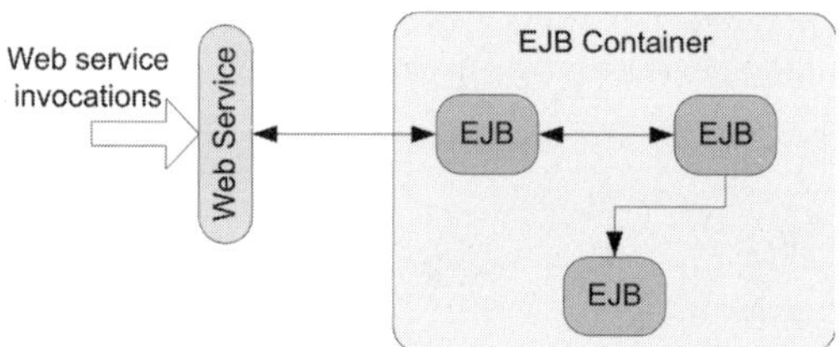

Figure 7-46 Delegating transactional work to EJBs from a Web service.

approach effectively exposes lockable resources to the Web and is a pattern that should only be used within trusted domains[5].

WS-Coordination and WS-Transaction

Web Services Coordination (WS-Coordination) and Web Services Transactions (WS-Transaction) are part of a recent trio specifications published jointly by BEA, IBM, and Microsoft as an alternate way of addressing the problems of generic coordination, and transacting over Web services. The proposed architecture is interesting since it relies on a generic coordination mechanism (whose behavior is specified in WS-Coordination) on which specific coordination protocols are layered. An architectural of this coordination stack overview is presented in Figure 7-47.[6]

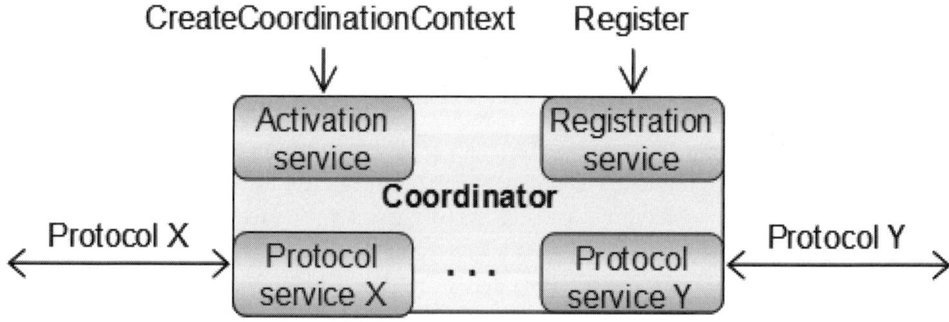

Figure 7-47 WS-Coordination architecture.

5. It is noteworthy that a similar delegation pattern can also be used to expose other J2EE components like Message Driven Beans over SOAP.
6. Source: WS-Coordination specification, http://dev2dev.bea.com/techtrack/ws-coordination.jsp

Web services can use the Activation service part of the coordinator to create the coordination context for a particular activity using a specific supported protocol (like WS-Transaction). Once a coordination context has been received by an application, it can then be propagated around that application's Web services, in much the same way as BTP-aware Web services propagate transaction contexts. The context contains the necessary information to register with the activity and dictate how the application will immediately be coordinated.

Though WS-Coordination defines a generic and reusable Web services coordination architecture, at the moment the only such coordination protocol that has been suggested is WS-Transaction. WS-Transaction in some respects shares many of the same goals and the same general style as BTP.

WS-Transaction is built on two distinct transaction models that the authors of the specification believe to be suitable for the kinds of situations that will arise when transacting across a Web services environment. The two transaction models it supports (based on the transaction model developer for Microsoft's BizTalk server) are:

- Atomic Transaction
- Business Activity

An atomic transaction is essentially an XML marked-up version of the classical all-or-nothing atomic transaction. Atomic transactions are meant to underpin activities that last for short periods of time, where the locks necessary to maintain consistency will not be held for so long that performance will not be degraded, and should be run in trusted environments to prevent denial-of-service. The WS-Transaction specification is quite clear in the fact that it should be used in conjunction with the WS-Security specification to ensure that transactions only span trusted domains.

An atomic transaction essentially consists of five distinct activities that various actors in the system may instigate:[7]

- *Completion*—One the application that created the transaction registers for the completion protocol, so it can tell the coordinator to either try to commit the transaction or force a rollback. A status is returned to indicate the final transaction outcome.
- *CompletionWithAck*—Same as Completion, but the coordinator must remember the outcome until receipt of an acknowledgment notification.
- *PhaseZero*—The Phase Zero message is sent to interested participants to inform them that the two-phase commit protocol is about to begin. This message allows those participants to synchronize any persistent data to a durable store prior to the actual two phase commit algorithm being executed.

7. Based on the WS-Transaction specification, http://dev2dev.bea.com/techtrack/ws-transaction.jsp#ws-transaction__toc16503456.

- *2PC*—A participant registers for these messages for a particular transaction, so that the coordinator can manage a commit-abort decision across all the participants (i.e., this is analogous to the BTP enroll). If more than one participant is involved, both phases of 2PC are executed. If only one participant is involved, a One Phase Commit (a 2PC performance optimization used in the case of a single participant) is used to communicate the commit-abort decision to the participant.
- *OutcomeNotification*—A participant that wants to be notified of the commit-abort decision registers to receive this "third-phase" message. Applications use outcome notifications to release resources or perform other actions after commit or abort of a transaction.

Although some of the language used to describe atomic transactions differs from that used to describe BTP atoms because of WS-Transaction's reliance on the underlying coordination framework, the semantics of many of the messages are similar.

On the other hand, business activities bear little resemblance to any mechanism in BTP. Business actions are designed for use in long-running transactions and ensure that any updates to state in a system are made immediately, thus significantly reducing the period of time for which locks need to be held (and reducing the window of opportunity for denial-of-service). That is, there is no notion of a two-phase commit for a business action because updates are committed immediately on receipt of their associated messages, and it is only in the case where a failure occurs later in an activity that participants are re-contacted. In the failure case, compensating actions are run to restore the data housed within a participant to a consistent form.

Of course, the identification of what constitutes a "short-lived" transaction from one with greater longevity is subjective, and opinions and practices will differ from architecture to architecture. The WS-Transaction spec offers a possible taxonomy[8] to clarify to developers which kind of transaction should be used in a particular use-case, as shown in Figure 7-48.

To date, there are no available implementations of the WS-Coordination or WS-Transaction specifications, and so at best we can only imagine its deployment and use patterns. However, WS-Coordination and WS-Transaction have the backing of several important Web services vendors and it will only be a matter of time before implementations are made available to the developer community.

8. Source: WS-Transaction specification, http://dev2dev.bea.com/techtrack/ws-transaction.jsp#ws-transaction__toc16503466.

categories	example faults	exception handling techniques
loosely-coupled business activity	order cancellation; reservation update	business-logic fault handlers
tightly-coupled business task	service temporarily unavailable; system crash	atomic transaction abort and retry

Figure 7-48 WS-Transaction atomic transaction/business activity taxonomy.

Summary

Transactions are a fundamental abstraction for fault-tolerant computing and provide the bedrock on which reliable B2B interactions can be built. At the moment choices for transactional Web service deployment are less than abundant, with BTP being the only Web services transaction protocol with implementations that we can use today. Another option is to create our own back-end only based Web services transactions by leveraging the transaction support in our back end .Net and J2EE platforms. However, the WS-Transaction specification will gather momentum since it is backed by some of the biggest vendors in the Web services arena, and will certainly be backed by implementations soon enough.

Architect's Notes

- You must use transactions if your Web services are to conduct business of any significant value.
- Your choice of which transaction technology to adopt should be based on your own internal needs, and the technologies used by your business partners. It is not sensible to adopt BTP if your business partners have adopted WS-Transaction.
- Transactions (like security) are one of those things that appear simple to implement and deploy, and whose development effort is usually grossly underestimated. Give serious consideration to buying or outsourcing transaction processing that you require, unless you have sufficient manpower and specialized knowledge of the area.

CHAPTER 8

Security

The most critical issue limiting the widespread deployment of Web services by organizations is the lack of understanding of the security risks involved as well as the best practices for addressing those risks. Development and IT managers want to know whether the security risks and the types of attack common for Web sites will be the same for Web services. Will existing enterprise security infrastructure already in place, such as firewalls and well-understood technologies like Secure Sockets Layer (SSL), be sufficient to protect their companies from Web service security risks?

Much of the experience companies have with security is with Web sites and Web applications. Both Web sites and Web applications involve sending HTML between the server and the client (e.g., Internet browser). Web services involve applications exchanging data and information through defined application programming interfaces (APIs). These APIs can contain literally dozens of methods and operations, each of which presents hackers with potential entry points to compromise the security and integrity of a system.

The decentralized and heterogeneous nature of Web services presents challenges in building and maintaining system-wide security. Not only is the architecture of Web services decentralized, but also the administration of the overall system. Moreover, monitoring and enforcing security policies across heterogeneous services, many of which are Web service-wrapped legacy applications that were not originally developed to be available over a shared public network, is increasingly challenging. These inherent characteristics of Web services present many opportunities for security lapses, and also make their detection more complex and lengthy.

As with other security measures, Web services security must address the issues around malicious intruders as well as non-malicious or unintentional attackers. Since Web services involve programmatic access and APIs, the potential for unintentional or accidental security breaches increases. Nonetheless, both forms of intruders are equally damaging and costly, and must be addressed through coherent security mechanisms.

In this chapter, we discuss security within the context of Web services and Web service-based applications. We begin by describing the critical security threats of Web services. Then, we move on to discuss best practices for addressing potential threats in the development of Web services as well as for detecting and eliminating intruders within deployed systems.

Everyday Security Basics

The issues underlying security on the Internet are not that different from security issues we face when making everyday transactions. These issues are not just about monetary transactions that involve the exchange of money during purchases, but any transaction where there is dissemination of critical information—such as social security or other uniquely identifying numbers, or of limited resources, such as money.

Transactions rely on a level of trust between the parties involved in the transaction. The person disseminating information must prove to the person receiving information that she is who she claims to be. The person receiving the information must also prove to the person disseminating the information that he will hold the information in confidence and use it responsibly and appropriately. In many situations, the second person may also have information to disseminate based on the received information. In this case, both parties must prove their identities to the other.

As an example, imagine that Person A is trying to get a Personal Identification Number (PIN) and password for using a calling card from Person B. Before issuing the PIN and password, Person B requests Person A's credit card number to which it will charge the cost of the calls. Before giving out the credit card number, Person A must be sure that Person B is who he says he is, e.g., a legitimate representative of the phone company. Person A must also prove to Person B that she is who she says she is and the legitimate owner of the credit card. Otherwise, if Person A is not the legitimate owner of the credit card, the credit card company may not release funds to the phone company even though Person A has used the calling card to make calls. Figure 8-1 illustrates this conversation between the two people and shows the importance of trust in the transaction.

Every transaction involves risks, whether the transaction is an online Internet-based transaction or a standard face-to-face interaction-based transaction. These risks can be classified into four broad categories:

- Identity risks: The party with whom you are transacting is not who he says he is; the party is an imposter. The imposter could be an individual or a retail merchant. A retailer may use the exact or similar name of a trusted brand to deceive its customers. Although this is more difficult to do (at least for very long) for merchants that have a physical presence (e.g., brick-and-mortar companies), it is easier and more prevalent with online, mail order, and telephone-based businesses.

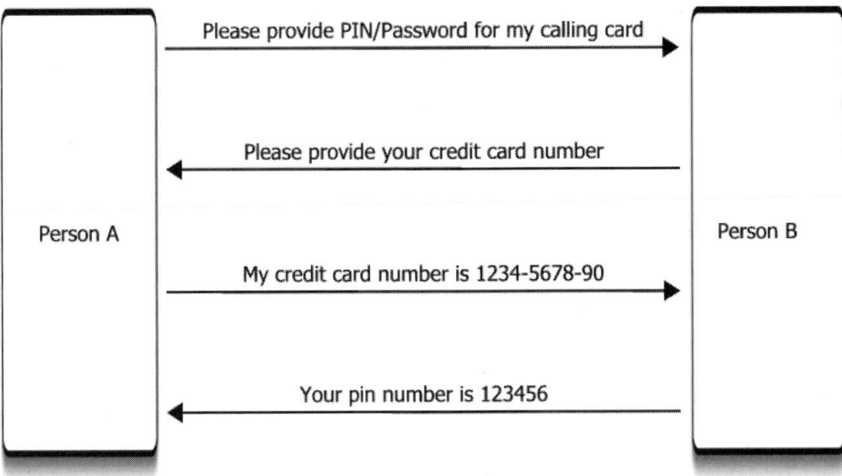

Figure 8-1 The importance of trust between transacting parties.

- Information theft: The person to whom you gave your critical personal information uses it not only for the current transaction, but also for subsequent unauthorized transactions. A personal credit card number may be given to a retailer for a legitimate purchase. Later, the retailer may use the credit card number to make transactions on his own behalf that are unknown to and unauthorized by the credit card holder.
- Information interception: A person different from the person to whom you legitimately gave your personal information intercepts the information and uses it to his benefit. Interception of personal information such as credit card numbers can occur through others overhearing your telephone conversation with phone-based businesses, looking over your shoulder at checkout counters and automatic teller machines (ATMs), or by simply going through your personal mail.
- Negligence: A person who is both legitimate in his identity and to whom you legitimately provided your personal information may carelessly make that information available or easier to access by others. A call center operator of a telephone-based business may write down your name and credit card number on a piece of paper and then later enter the information into the computer for a legitimate transaction. She may negligently forget to destroy or shred the paper and instead simply discard it. A third-party may locate that piece of paper and use the information for his personal gain.

These categories of risks are all around us throughout our everyday lives. As some of the examples described, even if one were to completely avoid computers and the Internet, the potential for risk in doing transactions is very much present.

But, the increasing use of computers for electronic transactions increases the potential for security breaches. At the same time, electronic transactions provide more opportunities to identify, document, and trap security breaches. In the next section, we discuss the importance of looking at security from an end-to-end perspective, and not just a point-to-point one.

Security Is An End-to-End Process

Contrary to popular belief, security is important not only during data transport between one computer and another computer, but also after transport. In the process of doing a transaction the path that data follows is oftentimes complex and long, involving multiple hops. If a small section of this path is insecure, the security of the entire transaction and the system is compromised.

Today, many systems that are seemingly secure are in fact insecure. Designers and architects usually focus on the security issues relating to the transmission of data between the client and the server, while other segments of the data transmission value chain are assumed to be secure and do not get much attention. Many of today's Web site and Web application vulnerabilities are directly applicable to Web services as these and other legacy systems are oftentimes just being wrapped and made available as Web services. Figure 8-2 illustrates the security lapses of many of today's otherwise secure systems.

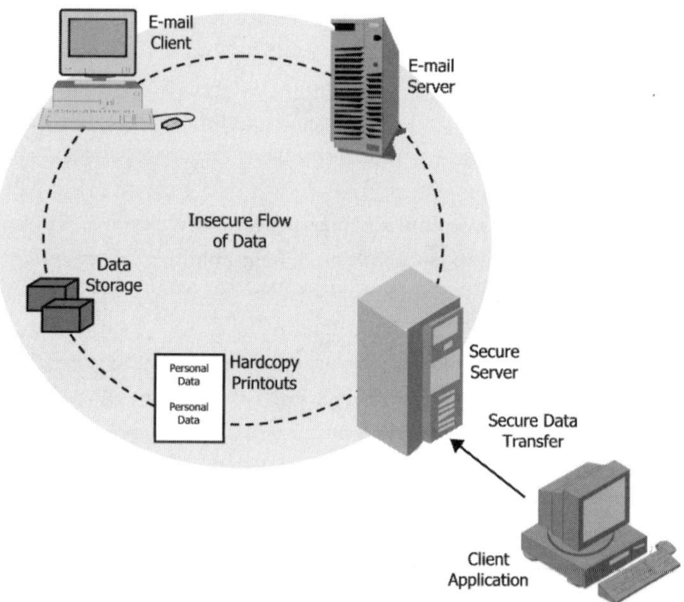

Figure 8-2 The security lapses of many of today's seemingly secure systems.

In this section, we describe some of these security holes in more detail and discuss how to address them.

Data Handling and Forwarding

Consider filling out a Web-based form for purchasing goods online. Typically, such online forms say that information entered into the form is secure. That is usually sufficient for the user to enter sensitive and personal information into the form and send it off over the network. The information is usually encrypted and secure as it is transferred between the client application (e.g., a browser) and the server. Once the data reaches the server, it is decrypted and is no longer secure. How companies handle and forward this open data creates potential security vulnerabilities.

Many businesses forward this data via electronic mail to the appropriate representative who can handle the customer's request. The transmission of this data, which is now in the clear, from the server to the representative's electronic mailbox as well as from the electronic mailbox to the representative's e-mail client presents many opportunities for this personal data to be misappropriated. Someone running a packet-sniffing program can easily access the data. Moreover, any administrators of the e-mail server can also access the decrypted data.

Worse yet, some companies take the decrypted data from the server and forward it to the appropriate representative to handle the customer request as a hardcopy printout, a fax, or a voice phone call. Each of these modes of data handling and forwarding present numerous opportunities to steal the customer's personal information.

There are many means to address these types of data handling and forwarding problems. The first is simply to re-encode and encrypt the data before the server forwards it. Another solution is to encrypt the data so that it can be partially decrypted by the receiving server. The partial decrypt allows only routing information to be gathered so the information can be forwarded to the appropriate representative as encrypted data. We take a closer look at this type of technology later in this chapter.

Finally, it is important to realize that security issues and transaction risks cannot be eliminated through technology alone. Security is a process and set of policies that must be adhered to not only by computers, but also by people who come into contact with sensitive information. Clear policies must be instituted, and people must be trained, monitored and held accountable.

Data Storage

Many businesses routinely backup their data, including customers' personal information, to a disk drive or magnetic tape. Continuing with the above example, the server that receives and decrypts the information from the client may backup the data for some time period just in case the e-mail or hardcopy becomes lost prior to fulfilling the request. Many sites simply store all of the decrypted information as a flat text file on another hard disk drive.

All of this personal information is aggregated as decrypted in-the-clear information into a single place for a malicious user to access. Any administrator with access to the hard disk drive can potentially misappropriate the personal data. If, by mistake or by malicious intent, an administrator sets the access permissions of this data to be readable by others, even more people can steal the information. The situation is worse for sites that are hosted by a hosting company. In this case, the administrators and users of other sites that are co-located on the same server can also misappropriate personal data.

Errors in Identity

There are many assumptions made in the process of securing a system. One of these assumptions is that the identity of a person or an entity is in fact correct. Identities are usually validated through digital certificates that prove to others that an entity is in fact who it claims to be. Digital certificates are granted to companies by a number of companies who are responsible for verifying the identity of a company. The assumption that most make is that the company responsible for verifying each entity and granting a digital certificate has properly done its job. Through breaches of process, human error, and sometimes malicious intent, this assumption is not valid.

In this case, there are limited options. And, thankfully, these situations are rare. Nonetheless, it is important to be aware of these situations and to question these and other assumptions that underlie modern security techniques and technologies.

Implementing secure systems is difficult. Architects and designers charged with such tasks must not only look at the exchange of data between the client and the server, but the entire end-to-end path that data takes. This includes analyzing not only the technologies that are used but also the business processes that are used once the server receives the data from the client. As more and more Web applications and Web sites are simply repackaged, wrapped, and exposed as Web services, these security risks and issues will pervade Web services environments as well.

Web Service Security Issues

Before we can address Web services security, we must first understand the areas where potential threats may occur as well as how they may occur. In this section, we look at the issues surrounding Web services security flow of a Web service invocation starting from the client application through the actual business logic implementation of the service and back to the client again. Throughout this flow, we analyze the possible threats and best practices to address those threats.

Data Protection and Encryption

Data protection refers to the management of transmitted messages so that the contents of each message arrives at its destination intact, unaltered, and not viewed by anyone along the way. The concept of data protection is made up of the sub-concepts of data integrity and data privacy:

- Data integrity: When data is transmitted from one entity to another entity, the receiving entity must have faith that the data is in fact what the sending entity transmitted. The concept of data integrity assures the recipient that the data was neither damaged nor intercepted by a third-party and altered while in transit.
- Data privacy: Data integrity assures the recipient that the data has been received unaltered and intact. Data privacy builds on this and assures the recipient that the contents of the data have not been viewed by any third-party.

Data protection is critical within a Web services environment as personal information, such as credit card numbers, and competitive organizational information, such as customer contacts and employee names, will be exchanged between Web services.

Encryption techniques are used to implement data integrity and data privacy. The most commonly used of such solutions is the Secure Sockets Layer (SSL) protocol. The SSL protocol creates a secure tunnel between the origination and destination computers based on public-key encryption techniques. The protocol also supports authentication of the origination computer to the destination computer, and optionally supports authentication of the destination computer.

However, SSL provides only point-to-point data protection. In many instances the Web service provider may itself forward the request to be ultimately handled by another computer or even a person. A legacy mainframe may actually fulfill requests that are forwarded to it from another computer that simply "wraps" the application running on the mainframe's capabilities as a Web service. As shown in Figure 8-3, after the termination of the SSL connection (at the Web services server) all the data is left insecure.

The inability to provide end-to-end security among multiple parties is a major drawback of the SSL protocol within Web services environments where it is routine for multiple entities to be involved. Consider purchasing a book from an online merchant using a credit card. The purchase

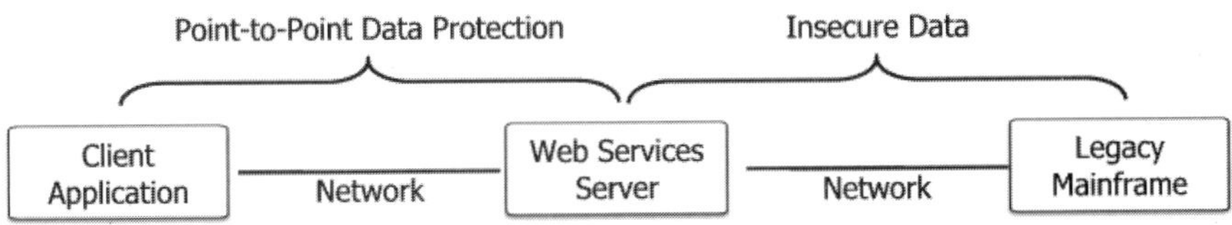

Figure 8-3 SSL provides point-to-point data protection, leaving forwarded data insecure.

order for a book is sent from the user to the merchant, who then forwards the credit card information to a bank. Only information about the book, e.g., book title and quantity ordered, must be viewable by the online merchant, not by both the merchant and the bank. Similarly, the credit card information must be viewable only by the bank. The ability to selectively encode various parts of a message using different keys is a critical requirement for Web services.

Moreover, SSL involves a large amount of overhead in encrypting and decrypting an entire message. Oftentimes, a message is comprised of a mixture of both secure and insecure information. Returning to our book purchase order, information about the book can be sent as clear text, while the credit card number must be encrypted. For these types of messages, encrypting the entire message using SSL adds needless overhead.

The SSL protocol provides point-to-point data protection between two parties but has the following weaknesses:

- It does not provide end-to-end data protection between multiple parties.
- It does not support selectively encrypting segments of a message.

XML Encryption builds on SSL and provides end-to-end security that addresses these two weaknesses. To understand how XML Encryption works, consider the following XML code fragment representing our purchase order for a book:

```
<?xml version='1.0'?>
<PurchaseOrder>
  <Cart>
    <Item>
      <Title>Developing Enterprise Web Services</Title>
      <Quantity>21</Quantity>
    </Item>
  </Cart>
  <Payment>
    <PaymentType>VISA</PaymentType>
    <Number>123456789000</Number>
    <Expiration>01-23-2024</Expiration>
  </Payment>
</PurchaseOrder>
```

The purchase order is comprised of XML elements that specify the contents of the shopping cart as well as the payment details. The `<Cart>` element contains items to be purchased. Each `<Item>` element contains the title of the book as well as the desired quantity. The `<Payment>` element contains subelements that specify the type of credit card, the credit card number, and the credit card expiration date.

Using XML Encryption, we can selectively encrypt an entire element or the contents of an element. In the above book purchase order, the only element that must be encrypted is the credit card number denoted by the `<Number>` element. The resulting document after using XML Encryption to encrypt the credit card number is as follows:

```
<?xml version='1.0'?>
<PurchaseOrder>
  <Cart>
    <Item>
      <Title>Developing Enterprise Web Services</Title>
      <Quantity>21</Quantity>
    </Item>
  </Cart>
  <Payment>
    <PaymentType>VISA</PaymentType>
    <EncryptedData xmlns='http://www.w3.org/2001/04/xmlenc#'
           Type='http://www.w3.org/2001/04/xmlenc#Element'>
        <CipherData>
    <CipherValue>A23B45C56</CipherValue>
        </CipherData>
    </EncryptedData>
   <Expiration>01-23-2024</Expiration>
  </Payment>
</PurchaseOrder>
```

The encrypted data is specified within the `<EncryptedData>` element. The `Type` attribute specifies that an element has been encrypted, and the `xmlns` attribute specifies the namespace used. The actual encrypted data appears as the contents of `<CipherValue>`.

In some cases, it is advantageous to encrypt only the contents of the element and not the element itself. Using XML Encryption to do thisresults in the following encrypted document:

```
<?xml version='1.0'?>
<PurchaseOrder>
  <Cart>
    <Item>
      <Title>Developing Enterprise Web Services</Title>
      <Quantity>21</Quantity>
    </Item>
  </Cart>
  <Payment>
    <PaymentType>VISA</PaymentType>
    <Number>
      <EncryptedData
            xmlns='http://www.w3.org/2001/04/xmlenc#'
            Type='http://www.w3.org/2001/04/xmlenc#Content'>
        <CipherData>
    <CipherValue>A23B45C56</CipherValue>
        </CipherData>
      </EncryptedData>
    </Number>
    <Expiration>01-23-2024</Expiration>
  </Payment>
</PurchaseOrder>
```

Again, the encrypted data is specified within the <EncryptedData> element. This time, the Type attribute specifies that the contents of an element have been encrypted and the element tags, <Number> and </Number>, appear as clear text. The actual encrypted data still appears as the contents of <CipherValue>.

Finally, we can also use XML Encryption to encrypt the entire message as follows:

```
<?xml version='1.0'?>
  <EncryptedData xmlns='http://www.w3.org/2001/04/xmlenc#'
       Type='http://www.isi.edu/in-notes/iana/assignments/
             media-types/text/xml'>
    <CipherData>
      <CipherValue>A23B45C56</CipherValue>
    </CipherData>
  </EncryptedData>
```

This time, the entire document, including all the tags and their values, are encrypted and appear as the value of the <CipherValue> element. The value of the attribute Type (of <EncryptedData>) is now set to http://www.isi.edu/in-notes/iana/assignments/media-types/text/xml since the encrypted data prior to encryption was XML—the official type definition by the Internet Assigned Numbers Authority (IANA) for XML.

Interestingly enough, XML Encryption can also be used to encrypt non-XML documents. For instance, encrypting a JPEG image file using XML Encryption results in this document:

```
<?xml version='1.0'?>
  <EncryptedData xmlns='http://www.w3.org/2001/04/xmlenc#'
       Type='http://www.isi.edu/in-notes/iana/assignments/media-
types/jpeg'>
    <CipherData>
      <CipherValue>A23B45C56</CipherValue>
    </CipherData>
  </EncryptedData>
```

There is little difference between the entire XML document that was encrypted and the encrypted JPEG image. The only difference is the value of the Type attribute of EncryptedData. For the XML document, the value of Type was set to http://www.isi.edu/in-notes/iana/assignments/media-types/text/xml while in this case the value of Type is set to http://www.isi.edu/in-notes/iana/assignments/media-types/jpeg—the official IANA type definition for JPEG images. Of course, the actual data will also be different.

Toolkits are available that facilitate the process of encrypting documents using XML Encryption. Implementations of XML Encryption are included within IBM's XML Security Suite and Baltimore Technologies' KeyToolsXML.

More information about XML Encryption can be found in the W3C's technical report XML Encryption Syntax and Processing at http://www.w3.org/TR/xmlenc-core/.

Authentication and Authorization

Authentication refers to verifying that the identity of an entity is in fact that which it claims to be. The entity trying to have its identity authenticated is known as the *principal*. The evidence used to prove the principal's identity is known as the *credentials*. If the correct credentials are used, the principal is assumed to be who it claims to be.

Credentials can be misappropriated. Passwords, for example, are easy to steal, while retinal scan data and thumbprints are more difficult.

In a Web services environment, a Web service provider may need to be authenticated by the Web service requester before the service is invoked and personal information is sent. The requester may also need to be authenticated by the provider before the service is rendered and critical information is sent back in the reply.

In many simple service invocations that do not involve the exchange of personal information or where there is no charge for the service invocation, authentication is unnecessary. For example, a client application that queries a free weather report Web service neither needs to authenticate the provider nor does the provider need to authenticate the requester.

After a principal's identity has been authenticated, authorization mechanisms are used to determine what the user (or application) will be allowed to access. Information about the user, such as subscription levels, is used to allow the appropriate level of access. For example, a Web service may have twenty operations, of which only five are available for access by some users while all twenty are available for other users. Or, particular endpoints of a Web service may be made available for premier customers, while standard customers must share just a single endpoint.

Authorization is increasingly important within Web services environments. Web services expose data as well as processes and operations to programmatic access. For the most part, access to this type of information was previously channeled through humans. These human beings acted as checkpoints that safeguarded the information from unauthorized access. With Web services providing programmatic access, authorization schemes must act as the checkpoints.

A variety of technologies and approaches can be used to implement authentication and authorization for Web services. These approaches can generally be classified as system-level approaches, application-level approaches, or third-party approaches.

System-level approaches do not require custom application (or Web service) programming to implement. Nor does it require any changes to the Web service if the authentication approach is changed. Usually, the operating system or the Web server handles authentication and authorization prior to forwarding the SOAP request to the Web service.

Common system-level approaches to authentication include basic passwords, encrypted passwords, and digital certificates. Digital certificates require that each user obtain a certificate verifying his identity. Since today the use of certificates is limited, this approach does not present a viable mass-market authentication scheme. In Microsoft Windows-based systems, both password and certificate credentials are checked against valid user accounts, which necessitate creating accounts before users can access a Web service.

Application-level approaches to authentication require custom development, and usually have to be modified with changes to the authentication mechanism. Sometimes, system-level approaches are insufficient or require too much overhead. For example, the overhead of creating and maintaining individual Windows user accounts may outweigh the benefits of using system-level passwords.

Application-level authentication approaches can pass credentials as part of the SOAP message. In this case, the Web service must parse the credentials as well as implement authentication and authorization mechanisms itself. The credentials can be transmitted as part of the SOAP header or the SOAP body. In the case where credentials are passed as part of the SOAP header, a service other than the called Web service may parse and authorize the invocation. Such a modularized solution allows the development of system-level schemes, and ensures that the Web service consumes computer cycles processing only valid and authorized requests.

SOAP on top of HTTP exposes the credentials as clear text, and facilitates misappropriation of this information. SSL can be used to encrypt the data for all SOAP messages sent to the other operations of the Web service. Unfortunately, SSL imposes significant performance overhead compared with just HTTP alone.

For operations where security can be loosened a bit, alternatives that are less of a performance drain are available. For instance, an authentication operation may be added to the Web service itself. SSL can be used to send SOAP messages to this operation so the credentials are not in the clear. Once a user has been authenticated, the Web service can return a token or a session key that can be used for subsequent SOAP messages. Although the session key can be stolen, the credentials (username and password) are not available and it is not critical to encrypt the session key. Accordingly, HTTP alone can be used. Another method is to use HTTP cookies for the session information instead of the SOAP header or body.

Figure 8-4 depicts a SOAP envelope that uses the optional SOAP header specification to pass username and password credentials. Before the SOAP body, the SOAP header is defined that includes `UserName` and `Password` elements. SOAP messages that either lack a header or present incorrect credentials will not be allowed to invoke the `GetRealTimeQuote` method.

```
<soap:Envelope
     xmlns:soap="http://schemas.xmlsoap.org/soap/envelope/">
  <soap:Header>
    <AuthHeader xmlns="http://tempuri.org/">
      <UserName>MyUserName</UserName>
      <Password>MyPassword</Password>
    </AuthHeader>
  </soap:Header>
  <soap:Body>
    <GetRealTimeQuote xmlns="http://tempuri.org/">
      <symbol>HPQ</symbol>
    </GetRealTimeQuote>
  </soap:Body>
</soap:Envelope>
```

Figure 8-4 Passing username-password credentials as part of the SOAP header.

Integrated development environments (IDEs), Web services platforms and tools facilitate generating and parsing SOAP headers and bodies so that developers do not have to write the parsing code themselves.

Third-party authentication services may also be available. Single sign-on capabilities are of particular interest to Web services environments, which are comprised of a large number of heterogeneous services, each of which may use different authentication mechanisms. Requiring the service requester to maintain and manage a large number of credentials for the variety of authentication schemes used by the different Web services within the environment is difficult and impractical.

With a single sign-on scheme, service requesters need only maintain a single credential. The third-party single sign-on service manages and maps the single credential held by service requesters to each of the service providers. The complexities of maintaining, managing, and revoking authentication credentials and authorization access list are handle by the third-party service provider. Two examples of single sign-on services are Microsoft Passport and the Liberty Alliance.

Non-Repudiation and Signatures

Protecting the confidentiality of messages is important within any secure environment. But, data privacy is just one piece of the security puzzle. Alongside privacy are the following related and equally important issues:

- Data authenticity: This verifies the identity of the sender of a message. The concept of data authenticity answers the question: *Who sent this message?*
- Data integrity: This verifies that the message data that was received was in fact the same data that was sent by the sender, and the information was not modified in any way in transit. The concept of data integrity answers the question: *Is this data really what the sender sent?*
- Non-repudiation: It provides a means to prove that a sender sent a particular message, and does not allow the sender to later disavow having sent it. The concept of non-repudiation answers the question: *Can the sender deny having sent this message?*

The means to support the important issues of authenticity, integrity, and non-repudiation are not provided by standard security mechanisms, such as SSL and passwords that we have already discussed.

These issues are addressed by the concept of digital signatures. Digital signatures are similar to standard handwritten signatures, and allow the receiver of a document to verify that the source from which it came has created (or viewed) and validated the contents of the document. It also supports the ethic of accountability in that the identity of the person who validated the document can be proved and the person can be held accountable for their validation.

Consider the creation of purchase orders within organizations. Purchase orders (POs) are documents that allow an organization to purchase components or services from a vendor. Usually, companies buy components in large volumes and errors in the components purchased, delivery dates, or payment terms may result in potentially large losses either from lost revenue or from increased costs.

The steps necessary to create a PO are usually complex and involve critical decisions made by a number of different people. The process may proceed as follows:

1. An engineer researches the different components that can be used within the system being developed and makes a recommendation for the desired part.
2. A project manager determines when the components must be delivered to allow the proper manufacturing and assembly of the overall system.
3. A vice president (or someone else with the appropriate authority) authorizes the purchase.
4. An accountant specifies the bank account number (or other payment means) by which to pay for the purchase.
5. A purchasing officer takes the information from the engineer and project manager and identifies the vendors and distributors that sell that component. He also negotiates the best price and payment terms.

In each step, different people's areas of expertise are brought to bear. Each of these people must be accountable for their actions only and not for those of others. If the engineer makes a mistake in identifying the appropriate component, only she should be held accountable; the purchasing officer who made the actual purchase should not be liable. Similarly, the purchasing officer must be confident that the component part number specified on the PO is as the engineer specified and has not been modified (either intentionally or accidentally) by someone else.

The XML Signatures specification specifies a technology that meets these needs, and is well suited for use within Web services environments. The key characteristics of the XML Signature technology are:

- XML support: The XML Signatures technology provides a standard means by which the actual signature is represented in XML. Since Web services are based on XML, having a standard mechanism for representing digital signatures within XML environments is important.
- Selective signatures: The XML Signatures technology provides a means to selectively sign different parts of a document with different signatures. As we saw in the example of writing a purchase order, different parts of a document (the purchase order) may need to be signed by different people (or entities). Usually within Web service environments, multiple Web services may coordinate and collaborate to accomplish a unit of work (e.g., create a purchase order). Clearly, the need for selective signatures is critical within Web service environments.

- Simple archiving: Signed documents are important not only during transmission between parties, but also as an archival medium. As demonstrated by the purchase order example, signed documents can be used as a means to prove and enforce accountability and liability. In order to do so, signed documents must be easily archived so that both the contents of a document as well as its signature(s) can be easily retrieved at a later time if needed. Since the XML Signature technology supports signatures that are inlined with the actual XML document (as opposed to separate signature files), it presents a simple means by which signed documents can be archived and later retrieved.
- Supports references: A document to be signed may not directly contain all of its contents, but instead contain references to remote content. For example, in the purchase order example, a photograph of the component to be purchased may be referenced but not directly contained within the document. Even though the image may not be contained within the document, the signature for that part (and other related parts) of the document must include the referenced image. The XML Signature technology supports the use and signing of referenced document content.

Now that we have seen the benefits of digital signatures as well as the unique features of the XML Signature technology, we next turn to the process of signing documents.

The basic technology behind signatures is simple and is based on Public Key Infrastructure (PKI) technologies. The basic process is as follows:

1. The document that is to be signed is transformed using the private key of the sender.
2. When the document is received, the receiver transforms the received document using the public key of the sender. Since only a transformation using the public key of the sender can undo the initial transformation using the private key of the sender, the receiver can be certain that the owner of the private key has signed the document.

For this digital signature to have any validity, the receiver must have confidence in the authenticity of the public key and that it actually belongs to the entity the receiver thinks it belongs to. Otherwise, an imposter can claim to be a different entity, transform the document using his private key, and provide his public key to the receiver. To safeguard against this situation, a certificate issued by a trusted Certificate Authority is used to match a public key with the actual entity.

Now that we have discussed the fundamental concepts underlying digital signatures, the steps in generating a signature using the XML Signature technology are as follows:

1. Identify the resources that are to be signed by using a Uniform Resource Identifier (URI). The resource identified by the URI can be located remotely and available over a

network, or can be located within the signature document itself. Each of these resources is located within `<Reference>` elements.

Figure 8-5 depicts how each of the resources that are to be signed is enumerated. The two resources shown refer to an HTML document (`http://www.example.org/index.html`) and to a data object (`ComponentSuggestionForProjectX`) that is located within the document itself. Other resources such as JPEG images (`http://www.example.org/logo.jpg`), or XML documents (`http://www.example.org/data.xml`) can also be referenced.

```
<Signature xmlns="http://www.w3.org/2000/09/xmldsig#">
  <Reference URI="http://www.example.org/index.html">
  </Reference>
  <Reference URI="ComponentSuggestionForProjectX">
  </Reference>
  <Object id="ComponentSuggestionForProjectX">
    .
    .
    .
  </Object>
</Signature>
```

Figure 8-5 Identifying the resources to be signed.

2. The next step is to calculate the digest of each of the enumerated resources. A digest is a unique thumbprint of the actual resource that is calculated using a digest algorithm such as the Secure Hash Algorithm (SHA-1) or the MD5 algorithm. A digest is similar to a hash and results in a smaller representation of the original data. The transformations using private and public keys are performed on the smaller digest value and not the original data, largely because of the performance implications of transforming large amounts of data. On receiving the signed document, the receiver calculates the digest and uses the sender's public key to transform the digest and verify the signature.

   Figure 8-6 shows how the digests are associated with each resource. Each `<Reference>` element specifies the URI for the actual resource and contains a `<DigestMethod>` element that specifies the algorithm used to calculate the digest, as well as a `<DigestValue>` element that contains the actual calculated digest value.

```
<Signature xmlns="http://www.w3.org/2000/09/xmldsig#">
  <Reference URI="http://www.example.org/index.html">
    <DigestMethod
       Algorithm="http://www.w3.org/2000/09/xmldsig#sha1" />
    <DigestValue>HlSGWGJiTAg4loR1BEI9238H3f3=<DigestValue>
  </Reference>
  <Reference URI="ComponentSuggestionForProjectX">
    <DigestMethod
       Algorithm="http://www.w3.org/2000/09/xmldsig#sha1" />
    <DigestValue>kLsgTYdTIAG4UoB1rt972H48FHR=<DigestValue>
  </Reference>
  <Object id="ComponentSuggestionForProjectX">
    .
    .
    .
  </Object>
</Signature>
```

Figure 8-6 Specifying the digest values for each of the identified resources that are to be signed.

3. The next step is to collect all of the `<Reference>` elements that will be signed together into a `<SignedInfo>` element, then calculate the digest and private key transformations (signature).

   Before the digests and signatures can be calculated, the `<SignedInfo>` element must be canonized. The canonical form of an XML document takes into account the fact that logically identical XML documents can have different physical representations. These differences can stem from such issues including the use of whitespace, the use of quotation marks around element attribute values, the inclusion of default attributes, and the lexicographic ordering of attributes and namespace declarations. As a simple example, consider the following two XML fragments for a hotel room booking:

```
<room bedtype="king" smoking="no">, and
<room smoking="no" bedtype="king">
```

   Although both segments are logically identical and convey the same information, their representations are physically different. That is, the two fragments do not have the same sequence of bytes. This results in differences in the digest values computed by the sender and receiver of signed documents.

   Figure 8-7 illustrates how all of the `<Reference>` and `<SignedInfo>` elements are combined together with the calculated signature inside of a `<Signature>` element.

```
<Signature xmlns="http://www.w3.org/2000/09/xmldsig#">
  <SignedInfo>
    <CanonicalizationMethod
       Algorithm="http://www.w3.org/TR/2001/
                  REC-xml-c14n-20010315" />
    <SignatureMethod
       Algorithm="http://www.w3.org/2000/09/
                  xmldsig#dsa-sha1" />
    <Reference URI="http://www.example.org/index.html">
      <DigestMethod
       Algorithm="http://www.w3.org/2000/09/xmldsig#sha1" />
      <DigestValue>HlSGWGJiTAg4...</DigestValue>
    </Reference>
    <Reference URI="ComponentSuggestionForProjectX">
      <DigestMethod
       Algorithm="http://www.w3.org/2000/09/xmldsig#sha1" />
      <DigestValue>kLsgTYdTIAG4UoB1r...</DigestValue>
    </Reference>
  </SignedInfo>
  <SignatureValue>
    HlSGWGJiTAg41B1rt972H48FHR=
  </SignatureValue>
  <Object id="ComponentSuggestionForProjectX">
     .
     .
     .
  </Object>
</Signature>
```

Figure 8-7 Combining together all of the `<Reference>` elements together into a `<SignedInfo>` element, and calculating the signature.

The digital certificate for the sender may also be provided within the signature. The X.509 digital certificate for the sender including the sender's public key would provide all the information necessary to confidently verify the signature. The certificate information would be placed within a `<KeyInfo>` element as follows:

```
<KeyInfo>
  <X509Data>
     .
     .
     .
  </X509Data>
</KeyInfo>
```

We have now created a digital signature and have successfully signed the resources to be transmitted from the sender to the receiver.

On receiving the signed document, the receiver must simply follow these steps to verify the signature as well as the integrity of the received data:

1. Calculate the digest of the `<SignedInfo>` element using the digest algorithm specified in the `<SignatureMethod>` element.
2. Use the public key of the sender (from the `<KeyInfo>` element or from external sources) to verify the signature of the digest.
3. Calculate the digests of each of the resources (within each `<Reference>` element) using the algorithm specified in the `<DigestMethod>` element. Compare the calculated values with those specified within the `<DigestValue>` of each `<Reference>` element to verify the integrity of the data.

These simple steps are used to create and later verify digital signatures using the XML Signatures specification. Digitally signed documents provide a means to verify the authenticity and integrity of a document as well as a means to implement non-repudiation.

Types of Security Attacks and Threats

In this section we briefly look at the types of security attacks and threats that are possible within a Web services environment. Since Web services leverage much of the infrastructure developed for Web sites, it is understandable that the types of security breaches that are common for Web sites will also be common for Web services. However, since Web services provide an application programming interface (API) for external agents to interact with it and also provides a description of this API (in the form of WSDL files), Web service environments facilitate and in fact attract attacks. These environments also make it more difficult to detect attacks from legitimate interactions.

Malicious Attacks

As we have discussed, Web service traffic shares a lot in common with Web site traffic. Both types of traffic usually flow through the same ports and while many firewalls can recognize SOAP traffic, they usually treat them as standard HTTP traffic.

Although Web site and Web service traffic may be treated in a similar fashion, the potential for security lapses is much greater with Web services. Web services expose critical application interfaces and operations and make them accessible through HTTP traffic. Each of these hundreds and thousands of operations represents a potential security problem.

Instead of hiding information about how to access and use each of these operations, Web services publish this information via WSDL files. Moreover, since the messaging format used by Web services is XML, each of the data fields are self-describing and highlight to hackers the means by which to interact with each service. One technique to lessen the security risks that may stem from exploiting the information on WSDL files is to simply not make WSDL files publically available. Instead of registering a Web service (and its WSDL description) with a public registry such as the Universal Business Registry (UBR) or having your SOAP server automatically generate WSDL descriptions for all (e.g., unauthenticated and unauthorized) users, for some Web services it may make sense to control the distribution of their WSDL descriptions.

Many malicious attacks are software-specific and the potential for attacks can be greatly reduced by simply eliminating any hints as to the type of software infrastructure that is used by a Web service. For instance, since an attack exploits a weakness or a "hole" in a particular piece of software, if an attacker knows that a Web service is run on a certain vendor's SOAP server, potential attacks may be facilitated. It is advisable to eliminate (or even disguise) information that identifies any part of the system infrastructure through headers, fault codes, and stack traces that are returned to client applications. It is also important to rename or even eliminate demo applications and other well-known locations within an infrastructure that may be exploited by attackers.

Although we have discussed security attacks within the context of malicious attacks, Web services also pave the path for accidental attacks. With accidental attacks, legitimate client applications access and interact with Web services, but do so in such a way as to cause harm. This may be a result of not fully understanding a Web service's API, or it may simply be a matter of negligence.

Whether the attack is malicious or accidental, they must be detected, contained, and prevented. Although Web service environments make a lot of information available for potential hackers, they also make a lot of information available for security systems. The interface information available as WSDL files together with SOAP message content and access patterns can be used to build more sophisticated firewalls that block and potentially deter would-be attackers.

Denial of Service Attacks

A denial-of-service (DoS) attack is an attack in which a user is deprived of a service that it normally expects to have available to it. A DoS attack can be as simple as maliciously disconnecting the power or network connection of a server, or it can involve more complex means such as overloading a service by repeatedly sending messages to it.

The most common type of DoS attack is a buffer overflow attack. In a buffer overflow attack, a client application sends data to a service that is longer than it can handle causing the service to go down or causing the service to execute code supplied by the client. Web services are particularly susceptible to buffer overflow attacks as they expose their APIs and a large amount of data is exchanged between them.

Today, many Web services are being created by simply wrapping legacy systems. Many of these systems were designed to be used within tightly controlled, closed environments and are not prepared for ill-formed or unusual requests or messages. Oftentimes, these vulnerabilities are exploited by hackers to transmit quotes, parentheses, and wildcard asterisks that confuse Web services. The lack of error checking and unpreparedness for uncontrolled environments make Web services-wrapped legacy systems ripe for buffer overflow attacks. The key here is to validate all data and ignore any requests containing data that do not pass the validation checks.

Sending extremely large XML documents to a Web service can also be considered a type of DoS attack. The parsing of either a very long or a very deep XML document by DOM-style XML parsers can result in an enormous memory footprint and significantly reduce the computational resources available to service requests. Designing your Web service to not accept arbitrary XML documents (as attachments) or placing size restrictions is one way to avoid incurring these XML-based DoS attacks.

Another common type of DoS attack is a replay attack. With these attacks, a valid message is repeatedly sent to a service. Since the service can only handle a set number of requests per unit time, the service's ability to handle legitimate requests is severely limited or stopped all together. Web services that are CPU-intensive to service a request are especially vulnerable to replay attacks. In these cases, it is critical to authenticate the requester before starting to process the request.

Web services provide more opportunities for replay attacks, and their heterogeneous functionalities and interfaces make it more difficult to distinguish a replay attack from legitimate interaction. On the other hand, Web service (SOAP) messages provide easier visibility into payloads and facilitate the development of monitoring and pattern detection tools that can prevent replay attack messages from reaching the actual service target.

Dictionary Attacks

A dictionary attack is an action in which a client takes advantage of weak passwords or other authentication mechanisms to gain access to a service. Web services use a variety of authentication schemes, including passwords to prevent unauthorized access. Unfortunately, just like personal passwords, many Web service passwords are weak and can easily be cracked. Hackers leverage these vulnerabilities to either programmatically or manually attempt common passwords to gain access.

Today, Web services employ a variety of different means for authentication. In some ways, this heterogeneous nature of Web service authentication presents obstacles for widespread automated dictionary attacks. On the other hand, as Web service security and authentication frameworks mature and standard mechanisms are used across different Web services, this difficulty will be lessened. Password hardening and strengthening rules must be employed to prevent dictionary attacks.

Internal Threats

Security threats and attacks are usually thought of as acts perpetrated by those outside of an organization. However, Web services expose a variety of information and functionality to large numbers of people, including those within the host organization. Moreover, Web service interfaces are well documented and the data is transmitted using XML, which is self-describing and human readable.

Employees or former employees with access to networks behind the enterprise firewall, to administrator passwords or with knowledge of system vulnerabilities can easily acquire confidential information or critical data. A particularly common example of internal attacks on Web services deals with Web service providers that use security but terminate the secure messaging channel at the entry-point of the organization. Once the secure channel is terminated, all data travels in the clear and is accessible by anyone on the local network. Credit card numbers, social security numbers, and maiden names are all available to employees with access to the local network. Since internal employees are most familiar with the systems and environment of their organization and because firewalls do nothing to protect attacks that originate from within the organization, internal threats are usually difficult to detect.

These are just a few of the most common threats and attacks on Web services environments. As Web service technologies mature and their use increases, hackers will come up with new and more innovative ways of comprising and attacking these environments.

Quickly detecting attacks within Web service environments also poses considerable challenges. Since Web service environments are heterogeneous and have decentralized administration, getting good administrative and log information is difficult. Properly cross-referencing the information that can be gathered from different systems also presents difficulties. For instance, each Web service system may follow different log formats, collect different types of data, and even present different timestamp information based on each system's clock settings. Clearly, bringing together the different pieces of the puzzle to recognize and identify an attack is difficult within Web services environments.

In this section, we have explored the various security issues and potential threats that can emerge within a Web services environment. We have also looked at how technologies such as SSL, XML Encryption, and XML Signatures can be used to address some of these issues. In the next section, we look at an extensible framework that builds on these and other security technologies and presents a coherent security model for Web service environments.

Web Services Security Roadmap

A comprehensive security framework is necessary that addresses today's Web service needs and is also sufficiently flexible to support the requirements of future applications. Figure 8-8 depicts a Web services security roadmap that, once fully specified, will provide such a framework. This roadmap is based on a document entitled "Security in a Web Services World: A Proposed Architecture and Roadmap" that was jointly submitted by IBM and Microsoft.

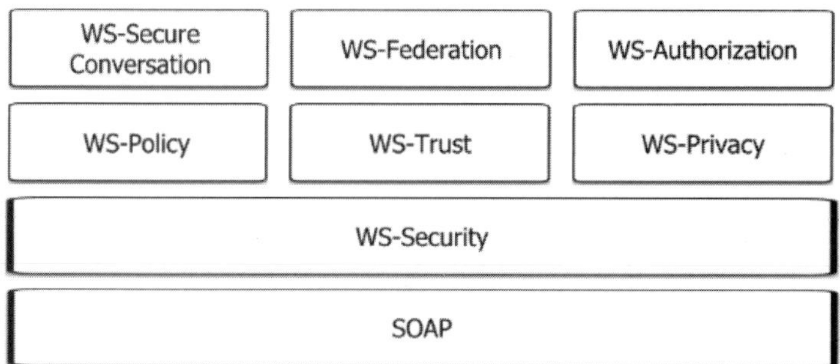

Figure 8-8 Web services security roadmap.

A summary of each specification in Figure 8-8 follows. All of these are forward-looking specifications, with the exception of WS-Security, which is fairly well defined.

- **WS-Security.** This builds on the SOAP specification and specifies how to sign and secure SOAP messages.
- **WS-Policy.** This specifies a generic format through which to describe the security capabilities and requirements for SOAP message senders and receivers. This group includes not only consumers and endpoints, but also intermediaries.
- **WS-Trust.** This specifies and describes the model for establishing and coordinating trust relationships between multiple parties.
- **WS-Privacy**. This builds on WS-Security, WS-Policy, and WS-Trust to specify a model by which organizations using Web services can indicate preferences as well as conformance to particular privacy policies.
- **WS-SecureConversation.** This builds on WS-Security and WS-Trust to specify how Web services can mutually manage and authenticate security contexts. It includes describing how Web services can authenticate messages from service requesters as well as how service requesters can authenticate Web services.
- **WS-Federation.** This builds on WS-Security, WS-Policy, WS-Trust, and WS-SecureConversation to specify how to broker and manage heterogeneous, federated trust contexts.
- **WS-Authorization.** This specifies how access policies for Web services are specified and managed using a flexible and extensible authorization format and language.

The combination of all of these specifications will result in a comprehensive framework that supports and enables securing of many scenarios that are not possible today.

In the next section, we take a more detailed look at WS-Security and how it builds on SOAP to provide message integrity and confidentiality.

WS-Security

WS-Security is a specification that unifies multiple Web services security technologies and models in an effort to support interoperability between systems in a language- and platform-independent manner. More specifically, WS-Security specifies a set of SOAP extensions that can be used to implement message integrity and confidentiality. To this end, the WS-Security specification brings together a number of XML security technologies and positions them within the context of SOAP messages.

The origins of WS-Security are with Microsoft, IBM, and VeriSign submitting a group of security specifications to the Organization for the Advancement of Structured Information Standards (OASIS). Later, Sun Microsystems started to cooperate to further develop the specifications. With such heavyweights behind it, WS-Security is emerging as the de facto standard for Web services security.

WS-Security is a unified model and specification for message protection within a Web services environment. WS-Security specifies standardized means by which the header, body, attachments, or parts of a message can be protected through a combination of encryption and digital signatures.

As we discussed earlier in this chapter, the W3C has developed specifications for XML Encryption and XML Digital Signatures. WS-Security provides message integrity, authentication, and non-repudiation by using security tokens and the W3C's XML Digital Signatures specification. WS-Security provides message confidentiality by using security tokens and the W3C's XML Encryption specification. Essentially, WS-Security builds on these key XML technologies and specifies elements that support these technologies within the context of SOAP messages.

In particular, WS-Security specifies XML structures (within the context of SOAP messages) for security claims and tokens. Security claims are statements that a client (or a user) makes. Claims can include the client's name, identity, key, rights, and privileges. A security token is a collection of security claims. A password and a digital certificate are examples of security tokens.

Security claims can be either endorsed or unendorsed by a trusted third-party. Claims are generally of the following three types:

- Endorsed claim: This is verified and vouched for by a trusted third-party, such as a certificate authority. Endorsed claims are usually represented as a signed security token that is digitally signed by the trusted third-party. A digital certificate granted by a trusted Certificate Authority is an example of a signed token that provides a verified association between a client's identity and a public key.
- Unendorsed claim: This claim is one that is not verified or endorsed by any trusted third-party, but is simply asserted by a client. A username is an example of a security token that asserts an unendorsed claim. An unendorsed claim can be trusted if there

already exists a trust relationship as well as a trusted communications channel exists between the sender and receiver (including any intermediaries).

- Proof-of-possession claim: This is a special type of unendorsed claim that is based on a piece of information that only the rightful claimant should know. A username and password is an example of a security token that asserts such a claim. The correct password for a particular username is a piece of information that only the client with the username should know.

WS-Security provides a flexible and extensible means by which the sender of a message can make security claims by associating security tokens with a SOAP message. Based on the WS-Security specification, Web services should ignore messages with invalid or inappropriate security claims.

In the remainder of this section, we describe the major XML structures of the WS-Security specification and how they are used within SOAP messages. More information about the WS-Security specifications can be found at http://www.verisign.com/wss/wss.pdf.

The Security Header Element

Each SOAP message has a receiver that receives the incoming SOAP message and acts on it. In the WS-Security specification, this receiver is called an actor. The `Security` header element provides information for the receiver of the SOAP message and specifies the actor.

A message may have one or more actors. For example, consider a Web service transaction to purchase a book. The bank must parse the payment information, such as the credit card number, where the bookstore must parse the book title and quantity information. In this case, there are two actors—the bank and the bookstore. The use of multiple actors for security purposes within a single SOAP message is depicted in Figure 8-9.

```
<soap:header>
  <Security actor = "bank.example.org">
     .
     .
     .
  </Security>
  <Security actor = "bookstore.example.org">
     .
     .
     .
  </Security>
</soap:header>
```

Figure 8-9 Multiple `Security` header elements used within a SOAP message.

Security information for different actors must appear in different Security elements. For instance, encryption and signature information for each actor must appear within a Security element.

If the actor is unspecified within a security element, any receiver can use that information. However, since multiple receivers may use the information contained within the security element, the element cannot be deleted until the message reaches its final destination. A Security header element without a specified actor attribute can only appear once within a message, and two Security header elements cannot specify the same actor.

After a receiver processes a message, the Security header for that actor can be deleted before the message is forwarded to its next destination. However, if a subelement within a Security element is referenced by a subelement within another Security element and a receiver deletes the original security element, the receiver must prepend the referenced information.

The UsernameToken Element

The UsernameToken element simply provides a means to associate basic authentication information such as a username and an optional password with a message. Figure 8-10 illustrates the use of this element.

```
<UsernameToken Id="...">
  <Username>...</Username>
  <Password Type="...">...</Password>
  <Nonce EncodingType="...">...</Nonce>
  <Created>...</ Created>
</UsernameToken>
```

Figure 8-10 The UsernameToken element syntax.

The Id attribute of the UsernameToken element is a string label for identifying this security token. The Username subelement specifies the client's username, while the optional Password subelement specifies the password. The optional attribute Type of the Password subelement specifies the type of the password. The pre-defined password types are PasswordText and PasswordDigest. PasswordText, which is the default if no type attribute is specified, indicates that the actual password is given as the value of the Password element, while the PasswordDigest type indicates that the digest of the actual password is given as the value of the Password element.

The optional elements Nonce and Created were added to the specification as extensions for use in those cases where an increased level of protection is necessary and both the sender and the receiver know the plain text password. The optional attribute EncodingType of the Nonce element specifies the encoding type of the nonce, with a default encoding of Base64.

In the case where either the Nonce or the Created elements are used, a Password-Digest can be calculated and transmitted as follows:

```
Password_Digest_Value = SHA1 ( nonce + created + password )
```

The value of the digested password is calculated on the concatenation of the nonce (if present), the created timestamp (if present), and the actual password. This approach provides a means to obscure the actual password as well as to help prevent replay attacks.

The BinarySecurityToken Element

Binary or other non-XML format security tokens are specified with the BinarySecurityToken element. Examples of binary security tokens include X.509 certificates and Kerberos tickets. Figure 8-11 illustrates the use of this element.

```
<BinarySecurityToken Id="..."
                     ValueType="..."
                     EncodingType="...">

  ...

</BinarySecurityToken>
```

Figure 8-11 The BinarySecurityToken element syntax.

The Id attribute of the BinarySecurityToken element is a string label for identifying this security token. The ValueType attribute specifies the value type and value space of the security token. The pre-defined values for ValueType include X509v3 for a X.509 v3 certificate, Kerberosv5TGT for a Kerberos v5 ticket granting ticket, and Kerberosv5ST for a Kerberos v5 service ticket. The EncodingType attribute specifies the encoding format of the binary data of the security token. The pre-defined values for EncodingType include Base64Binary for base-64 encoding and HexBinary for hex encoding.

The SecurityTokenReference Element

The SecurityTokenReference element provides a means to reference a security token instead of the token itself. The security token is accessed and "pulled" by the receiver from a specified URI. Figure 8-12 illustrates the use of this element.

```
<SecurityTokenReference Id="...">
  <Reference URI="..."/>
</SecurityTokenReference>
```

Figure 8-12 The `SecurityTokenReference` element syntax.

The `Id` attribute of the `SecurityTokenReference` element is a string label for identifying this security token. The `URI` attribute of the `Reference` element specifies the location of the security token.

The `SecurityTokenReference` element is also commonly used as a child element of the `KeyInfo` element (see next subsection) to specify the location of a security token containing the key information used for the signature or encryption steps.

The KeyInfo Element

The `KeyInfo` element is used in a similar manner as the `BinarySecurityToken` element, but is used for different types of keys and is specified for future extensibility. For well-defined key types, `BinarySecurityToken` is the preferred element to use.

```
<KeyInfo Id="..."
  <KeyName>...</KeyName>
</KeyInfo>
```

Figure 8-13 The `KeyInfo` Element usage syntax.

The `ID` attribute of the `KeyInfo` element is a string label that specifies the identifier for this key.

The Signature Element

The `Signature` element is used to add a signature that is compliant with the XML Digital Signatures specification for signing one or more elements of the SOAP Envelope or its attachments. Each SOAP message can carry multiple signatures, each of which may reference different or overlapping parts of the message.

Although WS-Security builds on the XML Digital Signatures specification, signatures within a SOAP envelope should not use the Enveloped Signature Transform or the Enveloping Signature of the XML Digital Signatures specification. This is because SOAP headers can legitimately change as SOAP messages are processed by multiple servers en route to their final destination. Instead, each of the signed elements should be explicitly identified.

The extended example at the end of this section illustrates the use of digital signatures within a SOAP message as specified by the WS-Security specification.

The ReferenceList Element

The first of three elements that are defined within the XML Encryption specification and can be used within a `Security` header element for encrypting parts of a SOAP envelope is the `ReferenceList` element. The `ReferenceList` element is essentially used as a manifest of the encrypted portions of the message.

Figure 8-14 illustrates the usage of the `ReferenceList` element within a SOAP message.

```
<S:Envelope
  xmlns:S="http://www.w3.org/2001/12/soap-envelope"
  xmlns:ds="http://www.w3.org/2000/09/xmldsig#"
  xmlns:wsse="http://schemas.xmlsoap.org/ws/2002/
             04/secext"
  xmlns:xenc="http://www.w3.org/2001/04/xmlenc#">
  <S:Header>
    <wsse:Security>
      <xenc:ReferenceList>
        <xenc:DataReference
           URI="#encryptedPartID"/>
      </xenc:ReferenceList>
    </wsse:Security>
  </S:Header>
  <S:Body>
    <xenc:EncryptedData Id="encryptedPartID">
      <ds:KeyInfo>
        <ds:KeyName>...</ds:KeyName>
      </ds:KeyInfo>
      <xenc:CipherData>
        <xenc:CipherValue>...</xenc:CipherValue>
      </xenc:CipherData>
    </xenc:EncryptedData>
  </S:Body>
</S:Envelope>
```

Figure 8-14 The `ReferenceList` Element used within a SOAP message.

The `ReferenceList` element is useful and typically used in situations where the sender and receiver of the SOAP message use a shared key.

The EncryptedKey Element

The EncryptedKey element is useful in situations where encryption is done using a key. This key is, in turn, encrypted using the recipient's key and the encrypted key is embedded within the message. All of the data that is encrypted using the original key must be enumerated within a ReferenceList element.

Figure 8-15 illustrates the usage of the EncryptedKey element within a SOAP message.

```
<S:Envelope
  xmlns:S="http://www.w3.org/2001/12/soap-envelope"
  xmlns:ds="http://www.w3.org/2000/09/xmldsig#"
  xmlns:wsse="http://schemas.xmlsoap.org/ws/2002/
              04/secext"
  xmlns:xenc="http://www.w3.org/2001/04/xmlenc#">
  <S:Header>
    <wsse:Security>
      <xenc:EncryptedKey>
        <xenc:EncryptionMethod Algorithm="..."/>
        <ds:KeyInfo>
          <ds:KeyName>...</ds:KeyName>
        </ds:KeyInfo>
        <xenc:CipherData>
          <xenc:CipherValue>...
          </xenc:CipherValue>
        </xenc:CipherData
        <xenc:ReferenceList>
          <xenc:DataReference
            URI="#encryptedPartID"/>
        </xenc:ReferenceList>
      </xenc:EncryptedKey>
    </wsse:Security>
  </S:Header>
  <S:Body>
    <xenc:EncryptedData Id="encryptedPartID">
      <xenc:CipherData>
        <xenc:CipherValue>...</xenc:CipherValue>
      </xenc:CipherData>
    </xenc:EncryptedData>
  </S:Body>
</S:Envelope>
```

Figure 8-15 The EncryptedKey element used within a SOAP message.

It is important to note that the only difference between Figure 8-14 and Figure 8-15 is in the Header contents. The contents of the Body of both messages are identical.

The `EncryptedKey` element is typically used when the sender of a message creates a randomly-generated symmetric key for encryption. The sender them encrypts the randomly-generated key using the recipient's key to securely communicate the original encryption key.

The EncryptedData Element

The `EncryptedData` element is most useful in situations where non-XML attachments are encrypted as well as in those cases where security information must be provided in a fully encrypted format. For each encrypted attachment, an `EncryptedData` element is added to the `Security` header element and the contents of the attachment are replaced with the encrypted octet string (MIME media type application/octet-stream).

If MIME types are used, the original media type of the attachment is declared within the `MimeType` attribute of the `EncryptedData` element. Moreover, the encrypted MIME part is referenced by a `CipherReference` element (as defined in the XML Encryption specification). The value of the `URI` attribute of the `CipherReference` element points to the MIME type prepended by the `cid:` scheme.

Figure 8-16 illustrates the usage of the `EncryptedData` element within a SOAP message in the communication of an encrypted JPG image attachment.

```
<S:Envelope
  xmlns:S="http://www.w3.org/2001/12/soap-envelope"
  xmlns:ds="http://www.w3.org/2000/09/xmldsig#"
  xmlns:wsse="http://schemas.xmlsoap.org/ws/2002/
             04/secext"
  xmlns:xenc="http://www.w3.org/2001/04/xmlenc#">
  <S:Header>
    <wsse:Security>
      <xenc:EncryptedData MimeType="image/jpg">
        <xenc:EncryptionMethod Algorithm="..."/>
        <ds:KeyInfo>
          <ds:KeyName>...</ds:KeyName>
        </ds:KeyInfo>
        <xenc:CipherData>
          <xenc:CipherReference URI="cid:image"/>
        </xenc:CipherData>
      </xenc:EncryptedData>
    </wsse:Security>
  </S:Header>
  <S:Body>
  </S:Body>
</S:Envelope>
```

Figure 8-16 The `EncryptedData` Element used within a SOAP message to communicate an encrypted JPG image attachment.

Since the function of the SOAP message in Figure 8-16 is simply to transmit the image attachment, the message Body is empty. The Body element tags are kept to maintain the validity of the SOAP envelope.

Putting It All Together

In this section, we analyze an entire SOAP message and illustrate the use of security tokens, signatures, and encryption as defined by the WS-Security specification. The entirety of the SOAP message envelope, including the header and the body, follows together with brief explanations of the key sections.

```
<?xml version="1.0" encoding="utf-8"?>

This is the start of the SOAP envelope, and defines the various
namespaces that are referenced within the envelope.

<S:Envelope
  xmlns:S="http://www.w3.org/2001/12/soap-envelope"
  xmlns:ds="http://www.w3.org/2000/09/xmldsig#"
  xmlns:wsse="http://schemas.xmlsoap.org/ws/2002/
              04/secext"
  xmlns:xenc="http://www.w3.org/2001/04/xmlenc#">
  <S:Header>
```

Following the envelope header, the routing information for this SOAP message specified according to the rules of the WS-Routing specification is enumerated. WS-Security and SOAP in general provide mechanisms to indicate that different parts of a message are for different receivers. WS-Routing provides a means by which to specify the actual routing of a message through a number of receivers. For instance, a SOAP message to purchase a book will first need to travel to the credit card processing Web service of a bank before it can be forwarded to the bookstore for order fulfillment. More information on WS-Routing can be found at http://msdn.microsoft.com/ws/2001/10/Routing/. These header elements are only included for completeness and are not critical to our discussions here on WS-Security.

```
<m:path
  xmlns:m="http://schemas.xmlsoap.org/rp/">
  ...
</m:path>
<wsse:Security>
```

This is the start of the WS-Security Security header element. The BinarySecurityToken element is used to specify an X.509 v3 certificate security token with the identifier CertToken. The EncodingType attribute specifies the encoding as base 64.

```
<wsse:BinarySecurityToken Id="CertToken"
    ValueType="wsse:X509v3"
    EncodingType="wsse:Base64Binary">
    ...
  </wsse:BinarySecurityToken>
```

The following specifies information about the key that is used to encrypt the body of this SOAP message. The actual symmetric key is encrypted and sent as part of the message. The `Algorithm` attribute of the `EncryptionMethod` element specifies the algorithm that is used to encrypt the key, while the `KeyName` subelement of the `KeyInfo` element specifies the key that is used to encrypt the original symmetric key. The value of the `CipherValue` element is the actual encrypted key, while the `DataReference` element specifies the part of the message body that is encrypted using the original symmetric key.

```
<xenc:EncryptedKey>
  <xenc:EncryptionMethod Algorithm="..."/>
  <ds:KeyInfo>
    <ds:KeyName> ... </ds:KeyName>
  </ds:KeyInfo>
  <xenc:CipherData>
    <xenc:CipherValue> ... </xenc:CipherValue>
  </xenc:CipherData>
  <xenc:ReferenceList>
    <xenc:DataReference URI="#encryptedBodyPart"/>
  </xenc:ReferenceList>
</xenc:EncryptedKey>
```

The following specifies the digital signature for this SOAP message. First, the canonicalization and signature algorithms are specified. The contents of the `Reference` element identify the actual parts of the message that are being signed. The `DigestMethod` and `DigestValue` specify the algorithm for calculating the digest of the selected parts of the message and the resultant digest value, respectively. The `SignatureValue` element contains the actual signature, while the `SecurityTokenReference` subelement of the `KeyInfo` element indicate that the key used for the signature is the same one that was specified earlier in the message (with the reference identifier `CertToken`).

```
<ds:Signature>
  <ds:SignedInfo>
    <ds:CanonicalizationMethod Algorithm="..."
      <ds:SignatureMethod Algorithm="..."/>
        <ds:Reference>
          <ds:Transforms>
            <ds:Transform Algorithm="..."/>
            ...
            </ds:Transforms>
          <ds:DigestMethod Algorithm="..."/>
      <ds:DigestValue> ... </ds:DigestValue>
  </ds:Reference>
```

```
      </ds:SignedInfo>
      <ds:SignatureValue> ... </ds:SignatureValue>
        <ds:KeyInfo>
          <wsse:SecurityTokenReference>
            <wsse:Reference URI="#CertToken"/>
          </wsse:SecurityTokenReference>
        </ds:KeyInfo>
      </ds:Signature>
```

The following two lines indicate the end of the WS-Security `Security` header and the SOAP message envelope header, respectively:

```
    </wsse:Security>
  </S:Header>
```

The body of this SOAP message starts by specifying that an XML element value has been encrypted using XML Encryption and replaced with the encrypted data. The encryption algorithm is specified by the `EncryptionMethod` element, while the actual encrypted data is specified by the `CipherValue` element. The key that was actually used for the encryption was specified within the message header.

```
  <S:Body>
    <xenc:EncryptedData
     Type="http://www.w3.org/2001/04/xmlenc#Element"
     Id="encryptedBodyPart">
      <xenc:EncryptionMethod Algorithm="..."/>
      <xenc:CipherData>
        <xenc:CipherValue> ... </xenc:CipherValue>
      </xenc:CipherData>
    </xenc:EncryptedData>
  </S:Body>
</S:Envelope>
```

This SOAP message demonstrates how WS-Security provides mechanisms for data security, including encryption and digital signatures, within the SOAP envelope itself. This secured envelope can be transmitted using any transport protocol as it does not rely on any transport-level security mechanisms, such as SSL over HTTP.

Preventing Replay Attacks

Digitally signing and encrypting SOAP messages provides data protection, integrity, authentication, and non-repudiation. However, vulnerabilities may still exist. One such vulnerability is a replay attack in which a properly signed and encrypted message is repeatedly sent to a Web service. A replay attack is a special type of denial-of-service attack in which the Web service resources are so busy processing each of these repeated messages, that legitimate messages are denied access to the service.

Replay attacks may also have application-specific side effects. Consider a SOAP message that instructs a bookstore Web service to order a book and debit the purchase price from a particular bank account number. This legitimately encrypted and signed message can be saved by a malicious attacker and repeatedly sent to the bookstore Web service. This would have the application-specific side effect of ordering multiple copies of the book and depleting the user's bank account.

To address this serious issue, the WS-Security specification defines the `Timestamp` element for SOAP messages. The Timestamp element provides a means by which to indicate the creation and expiration times of a message, as well as the delays introduced by intermediaries along the message path. Using this information, the receiver of a SOAP message can make a determination as to whether to ignore or process an incoming message.

The `Timestamp` element supports the following three subelements: `Expires`, `Created`, and `Received`. The syntax for each of these subelements is as follows:

```
<Expires ValueType="..." Id="...">...</Expires>
```

The `Expires` element defines the expiration timestamp for the message. The value of the Expires element is in the UTC format as specified by the optional `ValueType` attribute. If the `ValueType` attribute is not specified, the default is assumed to be `xsd:dateTime` The optional attribute `Id` can be used to reference this element.

The syntax for the `Created` element are as follows:

```
<Created ValueType="..." Id="...">...</ Created>
```

The `Created` element specifies the creation timestamp for this message. The semantics and default values for the optional attributes `ValueType` and `Id` are similar to those of the `Expires` element.

The syntax for the `Received` element are as follows:

```
<Received Actor="..." Delay="..." ValueType="..." Id="...">
  ...
</Received>
```

The `Received` element specifies the time that an intermediary server received the message. The required attribute `Actor` specifies which actor received the message. Actor values must match those used within a WS-Routing header. The `Delay` attribute indicates the delay, in milliseconds, of the actor receiving the message. The optional attributes `ValueType` and `Id` are similar to those used by the Expires and Created elements.

Multiple `Timestamp` headers may be used within a message if they are for different actors. Both the Created and Expires subelements are optional but may appear at most once within a Timestamp element. The Received subelement is also optional, but may appear at most once per actor (unless the message path involves a loop).

It is interesting to note that the requestor's clock and the receiver's clock may not be synchronized. An assessment is necessary as to the level of skew to properly interpret the data specified by the `Timestamp` element. The WS-Security specification does not specify a means of synchronization, and any synchronizing mechanism, including an out-of-band, may be used.

Figure 8-17 illustrates the use of the Timestamp header element within a SOAP envelope to prevent replay attacks.

```
<S:Envelope
  xmlns:S="http://www.w3.org/2001/12/soap-envelope"
  xmlns:wsu="http://schemas.xmlsoap.org/ws/2002/07/utility">
  <S:Header>
    <wsu:Timestamp>
      <wsu:Created>2003-08-15T06:27:00Z</wsu:Created>
      <wsu:Expires>2003-08-15T06:37:00Z</wsu:Expires>
      <wsu:Received Actor="http://bookstore.example.org/"
                    Delay="60000">
        2003-08-15T06:30:00Z
      </wsu:Received>
    </wsu:Timestamp>
    ...
  </S:Header>
  <S:Body>
    ...
  </S:Body>
</S:Envelope>
```

Figure 8-17 The use of the `Timestamp` element within a SOAP message to prevent replay attacks.

The `Timestamp` header element specifies a creation time of 6:27 on August 15, 2003, and an expiration duration of ten minutes. The intermediary `bookstore.example.org` specifies that it received the message three minutes after it was created and added a processing delay of one minute.

As we have seen, the WS-Security specification provides a rich set of XML structures to be used within the context of SOAP messages for security and related purposes. By providing security information in a standardized manner within SOAP messages themselves, message data security becomes transport-independent and more interoperable between multiple disparate systems.

Summary

The lack of a coherent security model and policy is the most often cited reason for the slow deployment of externally facing Web services by enterprises. Addressing security issues with vigor will not only make Web services (as well as the applications that consume Web services) more secure, but will also increase the community's confidence in Web service technologies. This improved confidence will likely result in increased numbers and types of available Web services.

In this chapter we took a broad look at security, and then focused on the security issues specific to Web services environments. We described how security is really an end-to-end process, and a secure system cannot be implemented by simply using a few technologies within a service or application.

We went on to discuss some of the XML security technologies that are finding their way into Web service environments. Two of these technologies are XML Encryption and XML Digital Signatures. XML Encryption builds on SSL to provide end-to-end data protection between multiple parties that supports selectively encrypting segments of a message. Different segments may be encrypted using different keys to allow only particular parties along a multi-party chain to access certain information, and certain segments may not be encrypted at all to reduce encryption/decryption processing time and energy consumption.

XML Digital Signatures complements XML Encryption and provides a means for verifying the authenticity (who sent it?) and integrity (was it received as it was sent by the sender or was it modified in transit?) of a message. XML Signature also provides a means for non-repudiation so that the sender of a message cannot disavow having sent the message.

WS-Security is emerging as the de facto standard for Web services security. In essence, WS-Security integrates and unifies multiple security models and technologies under a single umbrella, supporting interoperability across various systems. In particular, WS-Security positions existing XML technologies, including XML Encryption and XML Digital Signatures, within the context of SOAP messages.

Architect's Notes

- Security requires an end-to-end perspective and not just a point-to-point one. It is not simply the exchange of data between the client and the server that is important, but instead the entire path that the data takes. This includes not only technologies, but also operational processes.
- Do not encrypt the entire message. Due to the overhead of encryption and decryption, only encrypt what needs to be encrypted. Encrypt data meant for different people using different keys. The advantage of using XML Encryption is that it supports both of these requirements.

- Inline signatures with the information that they sign. Signed documents are important not only during transmission between parties, but also as a means to prove and enforce accountability and liability. To do so, signed documents must be easily archived so that both the contents of a document as well as its signature(s) can be easily retrieved at a later time. XML Digital Signatures supports inlined signatures and also allows different signatures for different parts of a document.
- WS-Security is emerging as the de facto standard for a comprehensive framework for Web services security.

CHAPTER 9

Quality of Service

As more and more Web services become available, quality of service (QoS) becomes an important differentiating feature that will directly drive the popularity and the overall usefulness of a service. Exposing a piece of business logic as a Web service is not difficult; architecting the system so that it meets the needs of potential users (e.g., other applications invoking the service) is the difficult part.

In this chapter, we discuss what quality of service is and how it pertains to Web services. We define the specific metrics that are most often important in Web services, and describe techniques to measure a Web service's performance. We review how the architecture of Web services, including SOAP and WSDL, affects and sometimes limits Web service performance. With all of this under our belts, we describe best practices and architectures for building Web services and service-oriented architectures that support various QoS needs and guarantees.

What Is QoS?

Quality of service is a broad term encompassing the means by which to predict and manage a variety of system-wide resources that are important to the runtime performance of an application. Since computing resources, such as network bandwidth, are limited, they must be managed so they are useful and predictable to those who use it.

Consider two perpendicular streets that meet at a four-way intersection. If the amount of traffic on each street is light, the flow of traffic on both streets is fast. As traffic increases on the two streets, the flow of traffic comes to a standstill as a result of uncontrolled gridlock at the intersection. As this happens, the amount of time needed to cross the intersection is unpredictable, and the two streets become unreliable and much less useful.

We can manage these resources (in this case, the two streets) by simply installing traffic lights at the intersection. Traffic lights control the flow of traffic and eliminate uncontrolled gridlock at the intersection. Based on the setting of the durations of the traffic lights, we can reliably predict that a minimum of *n* number of automobiles will flow through on the northbound segment of the street every *m* seconds. The traffic lights thus provide quality of service guarantees for the intersection, and guarantee that at least *n* automobiles can cross the intersection every *m* seconds (barring any accidents and other delays after the traffic signal).

We can also implement different levels of quality of service for different travelers traversing the same intersection. For instance, carpools—automobiles with two or more occupants—can be provided a different level of quality of service. Since the timing of the traffic lights cannot be made different for different automobiles, we can assign a separate lane for carpool traffic. Through this scheme we can guarantee that at least *c* carpool automobiles can cross the intersection every m seconds. The development of two levels of quality of service for the northbound-to-southbound lanes is illustrated in Figure 9-1.

In this example, we were able to attain predictable and reliable flow of traffic through the intersection by simply managing the two streets by installing a traffic light at the intersection. The traffic light makes the intersection a more useful resource by making it have predictable and reliable properties.

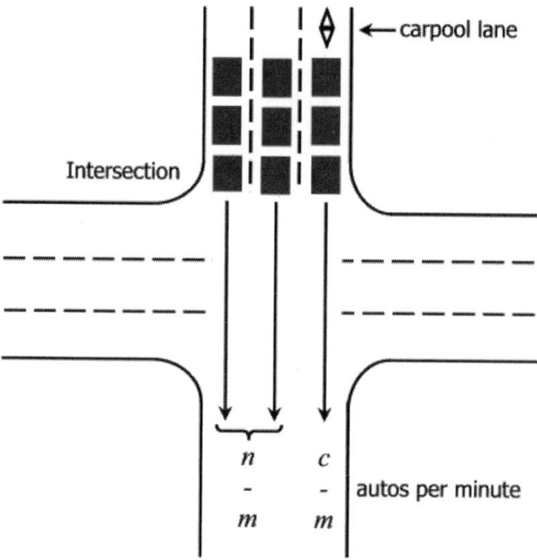

Figure 9-1 Architecting a predictable flow of traffic through an intersection using quality of service to determine when automobiles are allowed to go through the intersection and when they must stop.

QoS is most often associated with network resources and, in particular, network bandwidth. Mission-critical applications as well as multimedia systems vie for limited network resources to transmit packets. As more and more of these temporally-sensitive as well as standard applications are deployed, their growing bandwidth needs are outpacing available network bandwidth. The resulting congestion delays the delivery of packets traversing through the network. The delay affects all applications, but has a more profound effect on mission-critical and temporal applications, which must operate within time constraints and deadlines.

For many applications, the delays would be acceptable if they were predictable. For example, a movie application that requires the delivery of two packets per second works well if the network can provide such a guarantee. Suppose the network cannot accommodate two packets per second, but instead can only guarantee one packet per second. With this QoS guarantee, the movie application can still work quite well by simply buffering half of its required packets beforehand. That is, for a 60-second movie, if the application stores (buffers) 60 packets before it starts playing the movie, the movie can still show two packets every second. The only time the movie application cannot work well is when there are no guarantees on packet delivery whatsoever. With information about the worst-case available bandwidth or packet delay, the application can configure itself to reduce its picture quality, lessen its frame rate, or increase its buffer size so it matches the requirements of the data consumer with those of the data producer. Such a match makes efficient use of limited network bandwidth.

Although typically associated with network resources, QoS is equally applicable to other limited computing resources. Consider a Web server that locates and returns Web pages based on requests from client devices. The Web server can only service a finite number of requests every minute. Even if the network connecting the client device to the Web server is a private network with little traffic (and large bandwidth), the Web server's time to service the request will determine the packet delay (or response time) seen by the client application.

Scaling the number of Web servers available to service each request and balancing the request load over these multiple servers can improve the performance of the Web server. If the Web server cluster provides a predictable time in which a request is serviced, the client application can be optimized based on that information. For example, time-out variables can be set accordingly to minimize retries.

As the over-subscription of limited computing resources continues (and in fact increases), mechanisms are needed to manage these limited resources so that they are available in a predictable manner to potential users of the resources. Users can select or reject resources based on whether the resource's predictable properties meet the users needs. Once selected, users can optimize or configure themselves to best match the properties of the resource, thus efficiently using the resource.

Why Is QoS Important for Web Services?

Web services allow individual components of business logic to be published as building blocks to larger applications and services. Since each Web service is only a small segment of a larger application and not an entire large, monolithic application, there will be a significant number of competitive implementations for each Web service. Quality of service will be one of the most important differentiators between all of these competitive solutions.

Quality of quality of serviceservice encapsulates not only implementation details that affect metrics such as performance, but also deployment issues. For example, an application that is deployed on an application server can automatically scale and create additional instances of itself to handle dynamically changing request loads. The same application that is deployed in a standalone manner cannot automatically scale with increasing load, and thus its response time will linearly increase with increasing load.

As a developer of an application that will consume Web services, QoS is an important design aspect to think about. For some classes of applications, stringent QoS requirements are less important, while for other classes they are critical. For example, an application that uses a weather Web service to display the forecast may not require a set QoS. Instead, the fastest free Web service may suffice. As long as the weather information is reasonably accurate, the QoS of the service call is less important.

On the other hand, a real time stock ticker tape application for an investment bank's top clients requires a stringent set of QoS guarantees from its consumed Web services. Every second of unexpected delay may result in hundreds or thousands of dollars in potential losses in stock price depreciation or unrealized stock price appreciation. In this case, the choice between a Web service with a predetermined and flat response time versus one with a linearly increasing load-based response time is obvious. With everything else the same, the predictable response wins hands down. Predictability is such an important metric that even in situations where everything else is not the same, a Web service with predictable response may still be selected.

Full Control versus Predictable Worst-Case Performance

One of the hallmarks of enterprise computing is control. IT organizations within enterprises have assumed (or have tried very hard to assume) full control over as many software systems as possible. This control allows IT organizations to build processes that facilitate their quick response and solution to any potential issues on any enterprise software or system.

As we have discussed in this book, Web services represent a major departure from this. Since Web services are remotely hosted and managed, applications that consume Web services become dependent on the Web service providers. So, IT organizations lose much of their administrative control over enterprise applications that consume third-party Web services.

In lieu of their traditional control (or attempted control) over all aspects of enterprise software, IT will demand that applications only consume Web services that provide strict QoS guarantees for key metrics. *Predictable worst-case performance* will be the foundation on which IT will build its processes. Only those external resources (e.g., Web services) that provide such predictable behavior will be able to access and interact with internal enterprise applications.

Next, the questions are: What are the QoS metrics that enterprise IT will deem to be critical? How will Web services provide QoS guarantees? How will enterprise applications select the right Web services?

QoS Metrics for Web Services

QoS metrics are a set of qualitative measures of how appealing a Web service is for applications that may potentially consume it. QoS answers a set of "How?" questions, as listed in Table 9-1.

Table 9-1 A listing of the QoS measures that are important for enterprise Web services.

Availability	How often is the service available for consumption?
Accessibility	How capable is the Web service of serving a client'' request now?
Performance	How long does it take for the service to respond?
Compliance	How fully does the service comply with stated standards?
Security	How safe and secure is it to interact with this service?
Energy Efficiency	How energy-efficient is this service for mobile applications?
Reliability	How often does this service fail to maintain its overall service quality?

- **Availability**: The availability aspect of QoS represents the probability that this service is ready for immediate consumption. Smaller values indicate the service may not be a good choice for consumption by an application as it has a high probability of not being available. Low availability of a Web service limits the usefulness of consuming this service.

  Availability can be affected by a variety of issues, including the architecture of the program underlying the Web service, the deployment platform, or the service's overall maintenance.
- **Accessibility**: The accessibility aspect of QoS represents the probability that this service is able to handle a Web service request. A Web service may be available but not accessible by a client application. This can happen if the service is not architected to be scalable in the face of rapidly changing request volumes.

- **Performance**: The performance aspect of QoS represents both the latency and the throughput of a Web service. Latency describes how quickly (roundtrip time in milliseconds) the service responds once invoked by the consuming application. Throughput describes the number of Web service requests that are serviced within an amount of time.

  The performance of a Web service is based on the time necessary to access the service as well as the time necessary to execute the service's business logic. Smaller latency values represent a higher performance service with a speedier response.
- **Compliance**: The compliance aspect of QoS represents how well the service complies with stated features of the service. Since Web services encompass a variety of technologies and standards, compliance measures how fully the implementation of the service complies with those stated technologies. Compliance does not measure whether the service supports the latest standards or versions, but instead how fully it complies with those standards and those versions of standards that it states it supports. The compliance of a Web service is determined by the details of its implementation.
- **Security**: The security aspect of QoS represents the usefulness and strength of the mechanisms the service provides for supporting security and confidentiality throughout an interaction. Security is important for Web services as both the service provider and the service consumer may not be located behind the corporate firewall or communicate over a private network; a significant number of Web service interactions will happen over the public Internet.
- **Energy Efficiency**: The energy efficiency aspect of QoS represents the amount of energy consumed by an application while it interacts with a Web service to accomplish a unit of work. This is usually relevant only for mobile environments where the client device has a limited energy supply (e.g., runs on a battery). The power consumed by a wireless Web services-based application is a combination of the power consumed by the local platform (local software running on the local hardware) and the power consumed by the wireless network (while interacting with the Web service).

  The power consumed while interacting with a remote Web service is dictated by the number of bits communicated (either transmitted to or received by the client application). As mobile devices become a growing part of the computing landscape and as mobile applications increasingly utilize Web services, the power consumption aspect of QoS will become more important. The interface of the service, including choices of data types, encoding and representations, determines a Web service's measure of energy efficiency.
- **Reliability**: The reliability aspect of QoS represents a summary measure of the service's overall ability to maintain its quality. This metric is usually measured in terms of failures per unit time (e.g., day, week, month, or year), and represents the overall reliability of the Web service.

Given these critical enterprise QoS requirements, we next investigate where the potential pitfalls are in developing high-QoS Web services and applications.

Where Are the Holes?

Web services are a broad architectural technology that is built on other point technologies such as SOAP. In turn, SOAP is based on XML and HTTP, and uses networks (including the Internet) for communications. In order to understand quality of service for Web services, we must first understand the inherent limitations and bottlenecks of the underlying technologies and transport systems. Once we have a full grasp of these holes, we will be in a position to craft a Web services architecture that supports QoS.

XML

SOAP messages are encoded in XML. Various aspects of Web services QoS are affected by XML because:

- XML representations of data result in significantly larger documents than their binary counterparts.
- Instantiating an XML parser takes time and increases the memory footprint, especially as these parsers grow increasingly bloated trying to support newer XML features.
- Parsing XML information from within a SOAP envelope is expensive, with respect to processor time and power consumption.
- SOAP data typing information results in larger XML documents.
- Generating XML from the application or service's native data representation adds further overhead in processor time and power consumption.

Given that XML is a human-readable and self-describing language for representing information, it incurs much overhead. In the next section, we see that HTTP also adds to the overall overhead and is another source of "holes" for QoS.

HTTP

HTTP is the most prevalent transport for SOAP. HTTP is a lightweight, stateless protocol for distributed communications. HTTP was chosen because of its near ubiquitous status achieved as the protocol for the World Wide Web. Moreover, SOAP based on HTTP allows Web service messages to traverse enterprise firewalls easily, as many firewalls are already configured to allow HTTP traffic. As such, HTTP is a good choice since it supports near ubiquitous communications, and works with existing enterprise IT configurations.

Communication Networks

As we have already seen, SOAP messages are relatively large, with the actual payload representing just a fraction of the entire message. These weighty messages must traverse communication networks between the client application to the actual Web service and then back again to the client application for each Web service invocations.

Some of these networks will be internal private networks, while others will be public shared networks, such as the Internet. In many cases, the messages will travel over a combination of private and public networks—traveling some parts of its path on a private network and other parts on a public network. No matter what the type of network used, as Web services are used more often and the number of SOAP requests and responses mount, the communications network will be a significant source of latency.

The latency will not simply increase linearly with the increase in network traffic. When the demands placed on the network surpass its bandwidth, packets can simply be dropped. The sender of the packet will resend the packet only after a specified time-out period. For a successful Web service invocation, messages must be transmitted both for the request as well as for the response. So the percentage increase in network traffic that causes a packet to be dropped can result in a many times larger increase in application latency.

Server-Side Infrastructure

Web services do not exist within a vacuum. Instead, they must live in harmony with existing server-side and back-office infrastructure such as Web servers, application servers, databases, as well as legacy systems. Since many initial Web services are simply existing applications, including legacy and mainframe applications, which have been "wrapped" as Web services, server-side infrastructure also has a profound impact on the performance of Web services.

A typical Java 2 Enterprise Edition (J2EE) server-side infrastructure (together with the corresponding client side) is depicted in Figure 9-2.

How this server-side infrastructure may potentially impact a service's QoS measure must be taken into account.

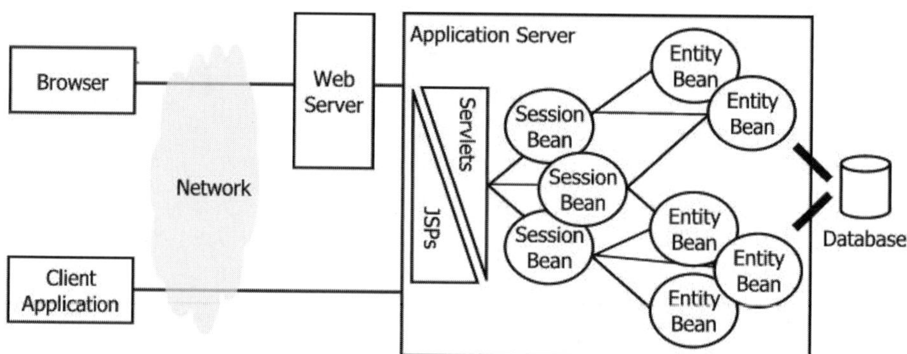

Figure 9-2 Web services exist within and alongside server-side infrastructure.

- Web servers: Are usually the front end of a n-tier architecture for distributed computing. Web servers accept incoming requests and route the requests to the appropriate application server based on load balancing and other techniques. As the front door access to a Web service, the performance, availability, reliability, and other QoS measures of the Web server itself will place a limit on the QoS measures of the Web service. For example, a Web server with high latency (response time) or low reliability will place a lower bound on the overall QoS measure of the actual Web service.
- Application servers: Implement "containers" that host various components of the business logic of an application. For a Java 2 Enterprise Edition (J2EE) application server, these include containers for Enterprise Java Beans (EJBs) and Servlets. The implementation of the application server determines its own QoS measures and, in turn, limits the QoS of the actual Web service.
- Databases: Many classes of applications access information stored in enterprise databases. The mechanisms by which these accesses are made as well as the performance of the database itself will also affect the QoS measures of the actual Web service.

As we have seen, a variety of systems and technologies contribute to the overall quality of a Web service. In the next section, we look at how to address some of these issues and best practices for doing so.

Design Patterns and Best Practices

As application developers, we have control over some aspects of the system and no control whatsoever over other aspects. For example, even though XML introduces a lot of network and processing overhead, a developer cannot unilaterally decide to use another language for data representation and still interoperate with other Web services. On the other hand, the developer is free to use any XML parser (or even implement her own parsing scheme).

In this section, we discuss design patterns and best practices for developing Web services and applications with high measures of QoS. Our intention is not to suggest replacements to the technologies that make up the Web services platform. Instead, our goal is to describe common or recurring issues in the development of Web services and Web services-based applications, as well as the preferred solutions.

Before we begin, one thing to keep in mind is that applications as well as the environments in which they are deployed must be analyzed within the context of an entire end-to-end system before trying to optimize any one subsystem. As we have already seen, a variety of technologies and systems contribute to the overall QoS measures of an application. We must first understand where the problems lie before we can start to address them.

After all, Amdahl's Law holds true for Web services as well. Amdahl's Law states that the amount of speedup achieved by a system by optimizing any one subsystem is bounded by the percentage of time that subsystem is used by the overall system. That is, in developing an application that consumes Web services, do not spend months optimizing the performance of a specific part of the application until you are certain of the need.

One mistake common to developers of Web services is they often assume that the much talked about weighty nature of XML is the source of their performance problems. After spending weeks or months re-architecting their application and incorporating more efficient XML parsers, they find that their application's performance has marginally improved.

When analyzing an application, look at not only the application but also the infrastructure on which the application is deployed (e.g., application server, hardware), the communications network, as well as other systems that are on the critical path, such as the Web server. Optimizing the implementation of one part of an application while neglecting the slow network connection or the overloaded Web server will only have marginal benefit. It is imperative to first understand where the inefficiencies lie.

Having said this, let's now turn to some important design patterns and best practices for developing Web services and applications that have a high QoS measure from the get go.

Use Coarse-Grained Web Services

As we have seen, there is significant overhead to invoking remote Web services using SOAP. Incurring that large amount of overhead to retrieve just a few bits of information is not efficient and results in reduced measures of QoS.

For example, consider the classic example of using Web services to retrieve stock price information. A Web service is first invoked to get the stock ticker symbol from the company name. Then a second Web service is invoked to get the latest stock price of a company given its stock ticker symbol. Ironically, this commonly cited example results in low performance. The large amount of overhead of a SOAP invocation weighed against the relatively small amount of information that is returned by each Web service—simply a single ticker symbol or a single number representing the current stock price—results in reduced application performance.

Mobile applications that consume such fine-grained Web services additionally increase their wireless network usage, resulting in increased network usage cost. Moreover, since the amount of power consumed in wireless communications is proportional to the number of bits transmitted or received, the use of fine-grained Web services results in wasted energy through the overhead of fine-grained Web service invocations.

The consumption of coarse-grained Web services by applications can increase their QoS measures along a variety of metrics, including performance, cost, and power consumption.

A coarse-grained Web service is one that implements an interface with operations, each of which performs considerable work and minimizes the need for other related operation invocations. This could mean that each operation performs a lot of computation or work. Alternately, each operation may return a large amount of relevant information, thus minimizing the need for follow-on calls.

Consider developing a stock price calculator application. The application allows a user to input the name of a company and then displays its current stock price. The application relies on one or more Web services for the actual stock price data.

Figure 9-3 illustrates three different architectures for implementing the stock quote calculator application. The first architecture, depicted in Figure 9-3(a), uses two fine-grained Web services and requires the application to make two separate invocations. The first Web service is needed to map the actual company name to its stock ticker symbol, which the second Web service is required to access the stock price data.

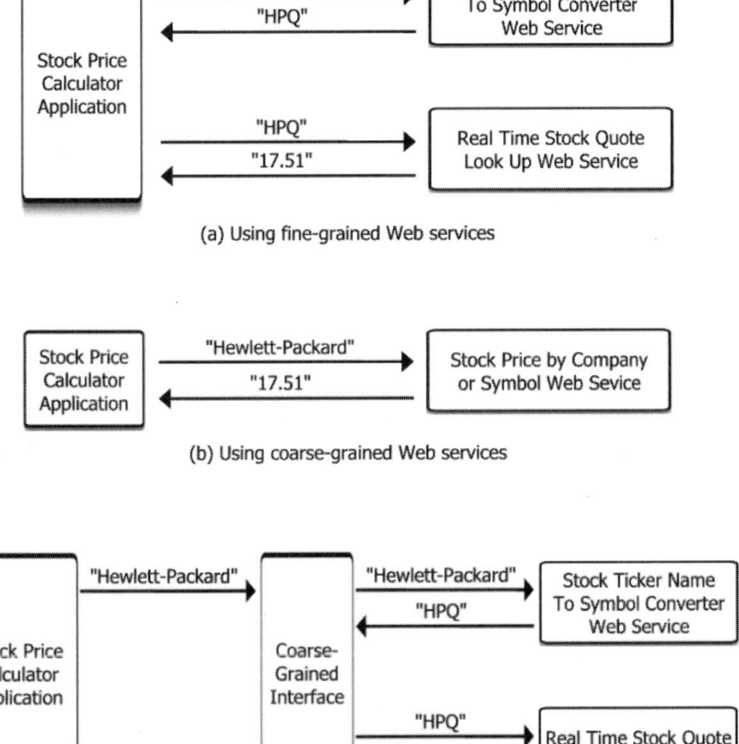

Figure 9-3 Using coarse-grained Web services increases an applications QoS measures along a variety of metrics, including performance, cost, and power consumption.

The second architecture, depicted in Figure 9-3(b), uses a single coarse-grained Web service that only requires a single call by the application. This Web service can handle both company names or the company symbols as input, and removes the need for the company name to company ticker symbol lookup invocation.

Finally, the third architecture, depicted in Figure 9-3(c), again uses two fine-grained Web services but only requires a single call by the application. This is accomplished by using an intermediary server that accepts incoming calls from the application and in turn invokes a number of Web services to fulfill the application's request. The intermediary could be a Web service itself, which is a result of wrapping a number of underlying Web services. Or, it could also be a proxy that calls Web services on behalf of the application. In many cases, this proxy may be a J2EE Servlet that accepts HTML or XML data (not necessarily SOAP), parses the data, calls the required Web services, and then returns the results again as HTML or XML.

This type of intermediary architecture is particularly useful in mobile environments where the connection between the mobile device and the intermediary is over a wireless network, while the connection between the intermediary and the Web services is over wire line networks. By minimizing the data transmitted over the wireless network (by using a coarse-grained interface and by using messaging that is less verbose than SOAP), the power consumed by the mobile application, the application latency, and the network usage costs are all reduced. Chapter 10 has more information on developing efficient mobile systems with Web services.

Do not fall into the pitfall of doing fine-grained remote procedure calls (RPCs).

- As a developer of Web services, do not expose all of your application's methods as Web services.
- Many utilities that take existing applications and make them available as Web services automatically expose all the operations.
- When using an application-to-Web-service utility, configure it to expose only a few of the application's operations. Otherwise, build a "wrapper" application that combines the operations of the underlying application(s) into a few coarse-grained operations and then runs the application-to-Web-service utility on the wrapper application.

Build the Right Client Application

Using Web services within an application is not an excuse to neglect developing any business logic for the client application itself. Web services should be used to augment the application or to provide functionality that is difficult to implement within the client application. Web services should not be used to replace the client application's business logic.

As a first-order analysis, look at the frequency of Web service calls from the client application. A high frequency may suggest that the application is over-utilizing remote Web services instead of local application business logic. For the most frequent Web service invocations, ask yourself whether it is practical to implement the functionality within the application. Can it be implemented correctly? Are the algorithms well known? How long will it take to implement it?

For example, consider an application that uses Web services to calculate the square root of a number. If the application continuously invokes this Web service, it will usually be worthwhile to implement the square root function within the client application itself. If implementing it locally is not possible (for time-to-market reasons or a lack of development resources), then locate a Web service that takes as input a list of numbers and returns another list of the square root of each number of the input list. You will have to re-architect and re-code parts of the client application to support such a Web service. But either way, the frequency of Web service invocations will be reduced.

For Web services that do not provide functionality but instead return data (stock quotes or the latest quarterly sales data), consider using coarse-grained Web services that return a large amount of data, which is cached by the client application. Prior to making subsequent Web service calls, the client application first checks the cached data. If the data is available and is valid (not expired), that data is used. Only if the data is not found locally is a remote Web service invoked. This technique is similar to synchronizing data between the client application and the back-end data store.

Consider a client application that allows a manager to analyze the quarterly sales results for his organization. The application provides multiple views of the data, including graphical illustrations of the percentage of revenue from each vertical market, profit-loss analyses, and so on. Based on what the user wants to see, the application invokes a Web service that returns the appropriate information and the application simply displays it. For instance, if the manager wants to view a pie chart of the percentages of revenue from each vertical market, the application invokes a Web service that returns the vertical names and the percentage contribution to overall revenue. The application simply displays this information as a pie chart.

Alternately, the application can invoke a Web service operation to return all of the latest sales data for the organization. Then, the client application itself can compute the required percentages for each vertical's contribution to overall revenue, as well as additional analyses that the user may want. Each of these additional analyses is completed by the client application itself without accessing any network-based Web service. By using a coarse-grained Web service and accessing a larger amount of data, the application makes more efficient use of the network, reduces application latency, and enables network-disconnected usage of the application (e.g., on an airplane where network connectivity may not be easily available).

Do not use Web services as an excuse to not develop any business logic for the client application.

- A high frequency of Web service calls may suggest that the application is over-utilizing remote Web services instead of local application business logic.
- For Web services that provide functional capabilities, ask yourself whether implementing the functionality locally within the client application is possible. Alternately, look for more coarse-grained Web services that implement a larger functionality within a single service, and build local application business logic to accommodate the new Web service.
- For Web services that provide data, consider using Web services that return a large amount of data, which can be cached by the client application and processed for later use.

Cache Web Service Results

Whether you are consuming coarse- or fine-grained Web services within your application, there is a chance that other applications (or even your application at a later time) will need to make the same Web service call. If the information returned by the Web service is not time-sensitive or only changes after a set time period, the return data from Web services can be cached and reused.

Continuing with our example of stock price information, real-time stock prices fluctuate constantly and are not suitable for caching. However, many stock price Web services only update their stock quotes every fifteen to thirty minutes. This data can easily be cached by a server on the local network and eliminate the need for remote Web service calls. Mutual fund prices are usually calculated and updated daily. Again, this information can be cached somewhere on the local network close to the application.

Caching data from Web service invocations not only increases the performance of Web services-based applications but also improves the performance of already congested networks. This will free valuable network bandwidth for other applications.

Web service caches can be utilized anywhere along the application fulfillment chain. Figure 9-4 illustrates that caches that temporarily store the results from previous Web service invocations can be deployed on the Local Area Network (LAN) where the application resides, on the networks (e.g., the Internet) that connect the application to the Web service, or on the network close to the Web service endpoint.

Caches that are located closer to the application provide increased performance and eliminate unnecessary network traffic. However, such co-located or close-proximity caches are not always available or are cost prohibitive. Caches located on networks with a high volume of traf-

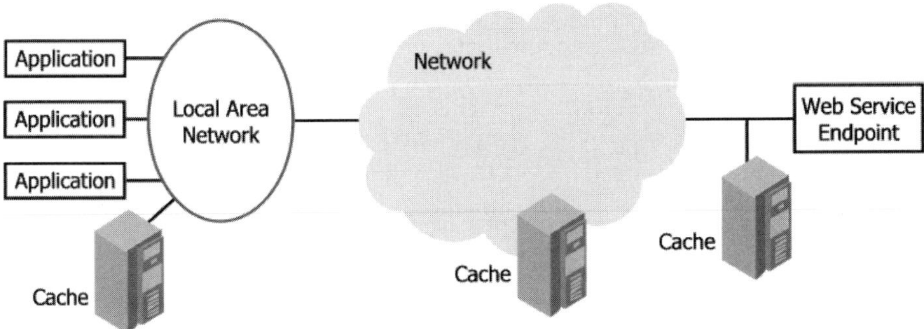

Figure 9-4 Caching can be utilized anywhere along the Web services-based application fulfillment chain to reduce network traffic and application latencies.

fic can cache results from a large number of Web services and can amortize their costs over a high volume of application calls.

Caching for improved performance of Web service invocations is not limited only to the caching of results of Web services. If the business logic underlying the Web service is complex or time-intensive, the results of portions of the business logic or database accesses can be cached. This cached data can be used to rapidly compute the result of a Web service invocation. The caching in this case is not of the results of the Web service, but instead of portions of the *implementation* of the Web service. This approach improves the latency of the Web service, but does not reduce the traffic on the networks.

A Web services caching product that addresses this need is provided by Chutney Technologies. Chutney's Apptimizer product provides caching mechanisms not only for Web services, but also for business logic components, database accesses, as well as HTML documents.

Use Resources Efficiently

It may seem like common sense to use resources efficiently, but a number of QoS measures of an application can be immediately improved by simply using the right infrastructure or the right tool for the job.

When discussing issues surrounding improving the performance of Web services and applications that consume Web services, XML is on the tip of everybody's tongue. But XML used properly and supported with the right infrastructure does not have to significantly reduce the QoS measures of an application.

An XML parser is a key infrastructure component for applications that deal with XML data. A variety of parsers exist today, each of which has different characteristics and application models. The most common flavors of XML parsers are the Document Object Model (DOM) and the Simple API for XML (SAX) types.

The SAX type of parser is based on the notion of a fast, forward-only and low memory footprint method of processing XML documents. SAX parsers traverse an XML document one element at a time and hand the data back to the application through a defined interface. SAX parsers are lightweight and have low memory requirements. As a result of its lightweight nature, applications that use SAX parsers may end up parsing a single document multiple times to access various document nodes.

DOM parses the entire XML document all at once and builds a tree-based object model representation of the entire XML document. When programming with a DOM parser, our application code interacts with an in-memory tree representation of the XML document. As such, DOM parsers only parse the XML document once. After the object representation is in memory, the DOM parsers also allow a tremendous amount of navigational capability throughout the document. As a result of creating the in-memory representation of the entire document as well as the additional navigational facilities, DOM parsers are usually more heavyweight processors than their SAX counterparts and require more memory.

Other important differences between XML parsers are whether the parser supports data validation and the language in which they are implemented. Parsers also differ in their speed and runtime footprint.

Selecting the right XML parser for each application is often a difficult decision. The general rules of thumb that can be used to help the decision process are:

- If the application only needs to locate tags and then extract the tag values, use a non-validating parser.
- If the XML document is large, but your application only needs to access a few elements of the document, use a SAX parser.
- If a large number of the elements of the XML document will be accessed, or if the document itself must be accessed multiple times, use a DOM parser.

Even with DOM and SAX parsers, for some applications and environments an even more stripped down XML parser may be required. For example, consider an application that calculates the real-time value of a mutual fund by repeatedly invoking a single Web service to find the latest price of each stock in the mutual fund portfolio. In this case, a general-purpose XML parsing and document manipulation infrastructure is unnecessary. Since the same SOAP request message (except each company's name) is generated and the same SOAP response message is parsed for each invocation, the XML can be hard coded within the application. The company name, which is the only part of the message that changes, can be generated for each invocation. Similarly, the price of each stock can be extracted from each response message based on a hard-coded pattern.

For those situations where the same or a similar XML document is generated or parsed repeatedly, consider hardcoding the XML elements within the application itself or use a stripped down XML parsing and generation infrastructure that supports your application's needs. This technique is useful not only for client applications but also for Web services. A popular Web service that is the only XML service deployed on a server can use a more bare-bones XML infrastructure (or handle the XML parsing and generation within the application itself). The only caveat here is to architect the system in a modular fashion so the system is easy to maintain and more standard infrastructure can be swapped in if necessary.

For applications that interact with XML, think carefully about your choice of XML handling infrastructure. Some good rules of thumb to remember are:

- Use a SAX type of parser if the XML document is large, but your application only needs to access a few elements and speed is important.
- Use a DOM type of parser if the XML document will be manipulated repeatedly, a large number of the XML elements needs to be accessed, or random access into the XML document is necessary.
- The Java API for XML (JAX) type of XML binding infrastructure provides development convenience, but often at the cost of performance.
- If an application generates or parses the same or similar XML document repeatedly, consider hard coding the XML elements into the application itself.

Large XML documents can be more efficiently transported over networks by simply using compression. The tradeoff is between bloating the network (e.g., power and transmission time) versus bloating the processor (on both the server and client sides) to uncompress the document.

As we discuss in Chapter 10, *Mobile and Wireless*, the amount of energy required to transmit or receive a bit of information over a wireless network is quickly reaching its theoretical minimum. What this means is that over time and with improvements in technology, the amount of energy expended in transmitting or receiving a bit of information will be roughly constant.

On the other hand, improvements in transistor technologies continue to drive down the amount of energy expended per unit work by processors and other integrated circuits. What this means is that over time, the amount of energy used in performing a unit of work (e.g., compressing messages) will continue to decrease. A graphical illustration of this is shown in Figure 10-2 in Chapter 10.

Given that the amount of energy expended by integrated circuits such as processors continues to drop while the amount of energy expended by wireless networks is roughly constant, it behooves mobile application developers to compress messages (even if it is a fast and simple compression scheme) prior to sending them over the network. Based on the actual message as well as the compression technique used, compression ratios of 20% to 70% are not uncommon. One thing to keep in mind is that if the client compresses Web service requests, compression itself and the same compression scheme must also be supported by the Web service.

Although our discussion here about SOAP message compression has dealt with energy efficiency, message compression also affects other QoS metrics. Uncompressed messages transmitted over already overloaded networks can result in decreased performance (increased latency) both from the transmission time of the larger messages and also from retries caused by dropped packets. Accordingly, although compression is useful for mobile applications communicating with Web services over low bandwidth wireless networks, it is also relevant for non-mobile environments as well.

Additional techniques can be employed to further improve QoS measures, including energy efficiency and performance of Web services-based applications. One such technique can be used when Web services are not directly accessed by a client application, but instead are accessed indirectly through an intermediary server. Rather than use XML-based SOAP messaging between the client application and the intermediary server, a more succinct data encoding and representation can be used.

Figure 9-5 illustrates the use of HTTP parameters between the client application and the intermediary server, which in this case is a J2EE servlet. Instead of generating and transmitting a SOAP request message, the client application simply performs an HTTP POST to the URL http://example.org/StockQuoteServiceA/getQuote with the form parameter `sym` and the parameter value `HPQ`.

The servlet simply interprets this as an invocation of the `getQuote` operation of the `StockQuoteService` Web service with the argument `sym` and argument value of `HPQ`. The servlet then maps the unique identifier `StockQuoteService` to an actual Web service (shown in this case as `FastStockQuote`). Then the servlet parses the WSDL description of the `FastStockQuote` Web service to determine the input argument type of the `getQuote`

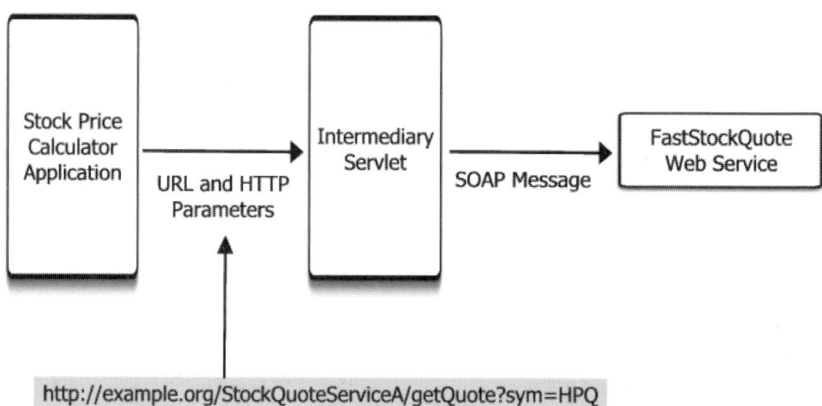

Figure 9-5 Improving QoS by eliminating the use of XML between the client application and an intermediary server, which proxies Web services invocations between the client application and the actual Web service.

operation. Assuming that the required argument type for `getQuote` is String, the servlet processes the argument name and value (`sym` and `HPQ`, respectively) and generates a SOAP request message. The SOAP request message is then sent to the actual endpoint of the `FastStock-Quote` Web service.

By using this technique, we are able to effectively compress the entire SOAP request message (in this case 849 bytes) to a few additional characters appended to the end of the URL. The client application not only saves precious network bandwidth and transmission time, but also does not require infrastructure for XML parsing and generation.

This technique of using an intermediary server between the client application and the remote Web service is quite useful in mobile environments. More information about this and other architectures for indirect access to Web service from mobile application is described in Chapter 10.

For improved measures of QoS for Web services-based application environments, carefully utilize limited resources such as network bandwidth and processor cycles. Key issues to keep in mind are:

- Compress SOAP messages whenever possible, and remember that compression (and the actual algorithm used) must be supported by both the client application as well as the Web service.
- Use intermediary servers to offload processing and network bandwidth utilization by the client application.
- For severely resource-limited applications (e.g., mobile applications), use a servlet as the intermediary server and pass Web service invocation information to the servlet as HTTP parameters.

Building QoS into Web Services and Applications

Now that we have seen why QoS is important for Web services and some of the factors that affect its QoS measure, we next turn to building QoS into Web services. Web services that provide good and predictable QoS will differentiate themselves from competing services and will be more popular for Web services-based applications. As such, when we talk about building QoS into Web services, we must talk about both the provider side and the consumer side.

On the provider side are individual Web services. The questions the architect or developer of a service must answer are:

- How do we build QoS into the services?
- How do we architect the service to achieve acceptable QoS measures?
- How do we support different QoS requirements from multiple applications?
- How do we propagate changes (e.g., access endpoint information) for this service to consuming applications so that they continue to function?

On the consumer side are applications that invoke (or consume) Web services. Applications will select Web services that provide superior QoS. Supporting QoS within applications that consume Web services brings a different mix of issues. Architects and developers charged with implementing Web services-based applications must ask themselves these questions:

- What are my application's QoS requirements?
- Which QoS metrics are "must have" and which are "nice to have"?
- Will these requirements evolve or change over the lifecycle of the application?
- Which Web services address my needs?
- What if this Web service fails to meet my QoS needs in the future (either because my QoS requirements changed or the service's QoS is reduced)?

It is interesting to note that some applications may themselves be made available as Web services, and will have to address issues on both the consumer and the provider side.

QoS-Enabled Web Services

In this section, we look at how to build QoS-enabled Web services. A developer of a QoS-enabled Web service must not only build the actual Web service, but also communicate the QoS measures to potential consumers of the Web service.

We begin by looking at how to communicate Web service QoS to potential consumers of the Web service.

Communicating QoS to Client Applications

When developing an application that consumes Web services, one of the most difficult tasks is to identify the right services to use. Web services are software modules that implement a particular function or capability. Since Web services will typically not be enormous monolithic applications, there will usually be multiple competing implementations for a particular type or class of service functionality. Although the capabilities will be the same or similar, the different Web services will compete based on implementation details such as access latency and interface specification. In addition to technical details, the selection of Web services will also be based on business, strategic, and political issues.

In selecting a Web service to use, there may exist business relationships and legal agreements that have to be honored. This may sometimes involve selecting a technically inferior service in order to meet such obligations. There may be pending customer deals that can be closed by using a particular vendor's Web services. A company may attempt to pressure another company by withholding patronage of the latter company's Web services. Because of the wide mix of issues that are often involved, technologists alone will also be insufficient. Accordingly, business analysts, consultants, and other such people (possibly in conjunction with technologists) will usually be responsible for the Web service selection process. In the remainder of our discussion, we focus on the technical QoS issues in selecting Web services.

An application developer or architect must understand the QoS and other non-functional attributes of Web services before he can determine those Web services that are appropriate. Unfortunately, Web Services Description Language (WSDL) files that are usually used to determine whether to use a particular Web service only specify the service's interface and location. Today answers to the following (and many other) questions are beyond the scope of WSDL files:

- What is the expected latency of this service?
- What specification version does the service support?
- Does the service support transactions?
- What is the average power consumed by interacting with this service?

The answers to these questions lie not only in the actual service implementation but also with the particular Web services platform (the service access point) used. For instance, a Web services platform that supports caching will provide improved average latency for those operations that do not change much with time. Weather information is a good example. Moreover, Web services platforms that support prioritized service requestors will offer better performance for some users and slower response times for others. This means that the same Web service implementation may have different QoS values depending on its access endpoint.

One means of supporting QoS by Web services is to augment service specifications to include QoS information. QoS can be assigned to three levels of granularity:

- Access endpoints
- Individual Web services
- Individual operations or methods of individual Web services

WSDL files can be extended to include this type of information. As we have noted, the same Web service at different endpoints may have different WSDL files to reflect the difference in their QoS or other non-functional attributes.

Figure 9-6 shows a segment of a WSDL file that has been augmented to include QoS information. It is important to note that no industry standard exists to augment WSDL files (or other Web service-specific object) with QoS information as yet. What we discuss in this subsection is simply one way of supporting and communicating Web service QoS to potential consumers of Web services using WSDL files.

```
<wsdl:service name="WeatherService">
  <wsdl:port name="WeatherPort"
             binding="weather:WeatherBinding">
    <soap:address location="http://example.org/weather1"/>
    <QoS group="1"/>
  </wsdl:port>
  <wsdl:port name="WeatherPort"
             binding="weather:WeatherBinding">
    <soap:address location="http://example.org/weather2"/>
    <QoS group="2"/>
  </wsdl:port>
</wsdl:service>
```

Figure 9-6 QoS-annotated WSDL segment showing differentiated service endpoints.

The `<QoS group=n>` tag is used to annotate the WSDL file to specify different service endpoints with different QoS. The semantics of the QoS tag must be predefined so that applications programmatically inspecting WSDL files for various Web services can make a determination of the appropriate group for its needs.

The `QoS` information can be used at application design time or even at runtime to select the appropriate service endpoint. The `QoS` information available to a client application can be further enhanced with more specific information. This information may include the expected response times at different time periods throughout the day. Other information, such as the cost of accessing that Web service endpoint, can also be supported.

A QoS-annotated WSDL segment that specifies not only the different QoS groups but also the expected response times is shown in QoS-annotated WSDL segment showing differentiated service endpoints as well as specific information about expected response times during different time periods throughout the day.

The Timing tag specifies various time-related information about the Web service. The attribute response specifies in milliseconds the expected response time of accessing the Web service. The attribute period specifies the time period within a twenty-four hour day for which the expected response time is valid. For example, from Figure 9-7, we can conclude that if a client application were to access the weather Web service at http://example.org/weather2 (QoS group 2) at 8:30 A.M., the expected response time would be 930 milliseconds.

In some cases, different operations within a Web service may have different expected QoS attributes. Depending on the operation, it may also have other different characteristics, such as the fee required to access the operation. Figure 9-8 shows a segment of a WSDL file that has been augmented to include specific information at the service operation level.

```
<wsdl:service name="WeatherService">
  <wsdl:port name="WeatherPort"
             binding="weather:WeatherBinding">
    <soap:address location="http://example.org/weather1"/>
    <QoS group="1">
      <Timing response="310" period="1900-0659"/>
      <Timing response="740" period="0700-1859"/>
    </QoS>
  </wsdl:port>
  <wsdl:port name="WeatherPort"
             binding="weather:WeatherBinding">
    <soap:address location="http://example.org/weather2"/>
    <QoS group="2">
      <Timing response="590" period="1900-0659"/>
      <Timing response="930" period="0700-1859"/>
    </QoS>
  </wsdl:port>
</wsdl:service>
```

Figure 9-7 QoS-annotated WSDL segment showing differentiated service endpoints as well as specific information about expected response times during different time periods throughout the day.

The operation attribute of the Timing tag specifies the Web service operation name for which the other attribute values are valid. By parsing the WSDL segment in Figure 9-8, a client application can determine that if it were to access the getTemp operation of the weather Web service at http://example.org/weather2 (QoS group 2) at 8:30 A.M., the expected response time would be 870 milliseconds.

In this section, we illustrated a means of communicating QoS information of Web services to potential client applications by annotating WSDL files. Not only can information about expected response times be communicated, but also any QoS measure as well as other information such as access fees. Information such as access fees are fixed by the Web service owner, while QoS information such as response time, reliability, and availability must be monitored and then reported. Web services monitoring and management utilities are available to track this information or, as we will see in a later section, simple applications can be written to track the measure of various metrics.

```
<wsdl:service name="WeatherService">
  <wsdl:port name="WeatherPort"
           binding="weather:WeatherBinding">
    <soap:address location="http://example.org/weather1"/>
    <QoS group="1">
      <Timing operation="getTemp" response="310"
              period="1900-0659"/>
      <Timing operation="getTemp" response="740"
              period="0700-1859"/>
      <Timing operation="getHighTemp" response="110"
              period="1900-0659"/>
      <Timing operation="getHighTemp" response="280"
              period="0700-1859"/>
    </QoS>
  </wsdl:port>
  <wsdl:port name="WeatherPort"
           binding="weather:WeatherBinding">
    <soap:address location="http://example.org/weather2"/>
    <QoS group="2">
      <Timing operation="getTemp" response="420"
              period="1900-0659"/>
      <Timing operation="getTemp" response="870"
              period="0700-1859"/>
      <Timing operation="getHighTemp" response="230"
              period="1900-0659"/>
      <Timing operation="getHighTemp" response="410"
              period="0700-1859"/>
    </QoS>
  </wsdl:port>
</wsdl:service>
```

Figure 9-8 QoS-annotated WSDL segment showing differentiated service endpoints as well as specific information about the expected response times during different time periods throughout the day of individual operations.

Lifecycle Management

Once a Web service has been developed and deployed, it not only has an interface specification but also a network location (usually a URL) as well as other information (such as QoS compliance and specifications) associated with it. Over time, the deployment that had sufficed when the service was new and relatively underused may require changes. This could include migration of the service to a new server. Multiple geographical mirror servers may also be deployed as the need to scale the service increases, or a new server location may be launched while the original one is taken offline for maintenance. The organization or division maintaining the Web service may be relocated or sold, thereby necessitating an update to its access endpoint information. How can these changes be propagated to applications that have already been designed to consume the original Web service? Without appropriate dissemination of such changes, applications consuming the original service can malfunction or produce erroneous transactions.

Applications based on Web services need a mechanism to stay updated with the latest information, including changes to access endpoints, additional endpoints, and updated QoS specifications for a particular Web service. It is precisely in this need for lifecycle management of Web services where UDDI can play a critical role. Web services need to disseminate changes to applications that call them. Applications need to be made aware of these changes. UDDI can play the role of runtime broker or middleman in handling and propagating these changes.

QoS-Enabled Applications

The first step in QoS-enabling an application that consumes Web services is to determine and set the QoS requirements. And the first step in setting the requirements is to be realistic. We would all love to have Web services that respond within a microsecond, but it's just not going to happen for most of them. The response time for many Web services will be measured in hundreds to thousands of milliseconds. As we saw earlier in the chapter, even the simplest of services must incur overhead from server-side middleware and infrastructure, as well as from the technologies such as XML and HTTP which underlie SOAP.

Monitoring QoS Performance

Monitoring various QoS metrics of the Web services consumed by an application is one of the most important means to maintain the quality and reliability of an application. Luckily, it is simple to monitor and measure the performance of the individual consumed Web services.

Web services monitoring and management products usually monitor the response time, availability, as well as other metrics that can be used by client applications in determining whether to consume a particular Web service. If such a monitoring product is not available, the client application, the Web service client proxy stub, or the Web services infrastructure can be augmented to monitor and log various QoS metrics.

Figure 9-9 shows segments of a Web services client proxy stub that has been enhanced to monitor and log the roundtrip time for the Web service invocation.

The `FlightInfoServiceBindingStub` is a client proxy stub used by a client application as a local interface to the remote `FlightInfoService` Web service. Two `java.util.Date` objects are used as a timer. Immediately before the client proxy stub invokes the remote Web service, the current time is recorded in the `startTime` object. Once the remote Web service call returns, another `java.util.Date` object is instantiated, and its time is recorded in the `stopTime` object. The difference between the `stopTime` and `startTime` is used to gauge the roundtrip response time of the Web service invocation.

```
public class FlightInfoServiceBindingStub extends
   javax.xml.rpc.Stub implements FlightInfoServicePortType
{

   .
   .
   .
   // additional methods not shown

public int getDepartureTime ( java.lang.String arg1 ,
                              int arg2 ,
                              java.lang.String arg3 )
    throws java.rmi.RemoteException
{
  if ( call.getProperty
       (org.apache.axis.transport.http.HTTPTransport.URL )
         == null )
  {
    throw new org.apache.axis.NoEndPointException ();
  }
  call.removeAllParameters ();
  call.addParameter ( "arg1" ,
    new org.apache.axis.encoding.XMLType (
      new javax.xml.rpc.namespace.QName (
        "http://www.w3.org/2001/XMLSchema" , "string" ) ) ,
      org.apache.axis.client.Call.PARAM_MODE_IN );
  call.addParameter ( "arg2" ,
    new org.apache.axis.encoding.XMLType (
      new javax.xml.rpc.namespace.QName (
        "http://www.w3.org/2001/XMLSchema" , "int" ) ) ,
    org.apache.axis.client.Call.PARAM_MODE_IN );
  call.addParameter ( "arg3" ,
    new org.apache.axis.encoding.XMLType (
      new javax.xml.rpc.namespace.QName (
        "http://www.w3.org/2001/XMLSchema" , "string" ) ) ,
      org.apache.axis.client.Call.PARAM_MODE_IN );
  call.setReturnType (
    new org.apache.axis.encoding.XMLType (
      new javax.xml.rpc.namespace.QName (
        "http://www.w3.org/2001/XMLSchema" , "int" ) ) );
  call.setProperty (
    org.apache.axis.transport.http.HTTPTransport.ACTION ,
    "http://tempuri.org/" );
  call.setProperty ( call.NAMESPACE ,
                     "http://tempuri.org/" );
  call.setOperationName ( "getDepartureTime" );
```

Figure 9-9 Monitoring the roundtrip response time of a Web service invocation by using a timer within the Web service client proxy stub.

```
    // Start a Timer
    Date startTimer = new Date ();
    long startTime = startTimer.getTime ();

    // Invoke the service
    Object resp = call.invoke (
      new Object[]{arg1, new Integer ( arg2 ), arg3} );

    // Stop the timer
    Date stopTimer = new Date ();
    long stopTime = stopTimer.getTime ();
    long elapsedTime = stopTime - startTime;

    System.out.println ( "Roundtrip time is: " +
      elapsedTime + " ms." );

    if ( resp instanceof java.rmi.RemoteException )
    {
      throw ( java.rmi.RemoteException ) resp;
    }
    else
    {
      return ( ( Integer ) resp ).intValue ();
    }
  }
}
```

Figure 9-9 Monitoring the roundtrip response time of a Web service invocation by using a timer within the Web service client proxy stub (continued).

By simply augmenting the application code directly or each of the invoked Web service stubs, the amount of time for the Web service request-response roundtrip time can be calculated and recorded. These values can then be compared against the specified QoS measures to verify that the monitored performance is within the bounds of the specification.

Figure 9-10 lists the roundtrip response times of the `FlightInfoService` Web service as monitored by the `FlightInfoServiceBindingStub` client proxy stub enhanced with the timer logic. As is clearly seen in the monitored data, each invocation response time varies. The longer initial response time is due to the Web service being dynamically loaded by the SOAP Server in response to receiving the invocation. The other, smaller variations are a result of changing environments of both the application and the Web service, including network congestion and server load.

Although enhancing each client proxy stub with a timer is simple, it is a laborious process. A more architecturally elegant solution would be to place such logic within the Web services (SOAP) Server message handler. The monitored information could be recorded by a central location, returned to the application itself, or fed to an application management utility.

```
Roundtrip time is: 1645 ms.
Roundtrip time is: 792 ms.
Roundtrip time is: 431 ms.
Roundtrip time is: 697 ms.
```

Figure 9-10 Roundtrip latencies for four invocations of a Web service.

Discovering the Right Service

Now that we have seen how QoS information that is annotated within other Web service specification information can be used to answer some critical questions in selecting the appropriate Web service, we next turn to the actual process of locating the right Web service.

Brokers will usually handle the establishment of bindings between applications (service requestors) and Web services (service providers). Brokers are "middleman" programs that facilitate locating the appropriate Web service based on given specifications, parameters, and hints. Since the functionality of these brokers are the same for all service providers and service requestors (only the specifications, parameters, and hints change), infrastructure software such as middleware will most likely provide these capabilities. Brokers (either the entire broker system or parts thereof) may also be remotely located as a Web service, in and of itself.

The steps in the interaction between an application and a QoS broker as the application tries to locate the right Web service to bind to are as follows:

- The application sends a request to the QoS broker with information about the type of service required (or even a UDDI tModel reference to a Web service interface) together with the application's QoS requirements.
- The broker searches a Web services registry, such as UDDI, for potential Web services.
- The broker negotiates with Web services to determine the actual QoS the services offer, and tries to establish an agreed QoS that matches the application's QoS needs and the QoS offered by the Web service.
- If a suitable Web service is found, the broker establishes binding between the application and the Web service.
- The broker informs the application that a suitable service has been located and the binding has been made.

It is important to remember that QoS brokers (or any broker) will not be able to act alone. Instead, all of the needs of the application will have to be taken into account in an effort to determine the best available Web service (or even if a suitable service exists). For instance, most businesses will require the use of a business and strategic broker in addition to a QoS broker. The business and strategic broker will create a subset of those Web service vendors that are appropriate to use based on business issues, while the QoS broker will create a subset based on QoS issues. Today, much of this brokering is done manually through human intervention. In the near future, it is unlikely that all of the required brokering can be automated to a sufficient level, or that automated results will be suitable for use without human intervention.

Recovering from Service Failures

Perhaps the simplest yet one of the most important QoS issues for applications that consume distributed and remote Web services is fault-tolerance and recovering from service failures. Services can fail for a variety of reasons, such as:

- An error in the service caused it to fail.
- The service itself consumed another service that failed.
- Network problems caused the service call to fail.
- Critical infrastructure, such as power, failed and caused the entire server to go down.

Developers often make the assumption that if they consume a Web service provided by a large corporation, the Web service will be 100% reliable. It's certainly true that larger corporations have resources as well as contingencies in place that may minimize potential problems with their Web services, but these services are far from fully reliable. Services may have to be taken offline for maintenance, they may be migrated to different machines, or they may be replicated for scaling purposes. These harmless actions may cause potential issues for applications that are consuming them. Also, problems with resources that are outside of the corporation's control, such as the network, may cause the service to be unavailable (and appear to have failed) to the consuming application.

It is precisely in this need for lifecycle management of applications and Web services where UDDI can play a critical role. Web services need to disseminate changes to applications that call them. Applications need to be made aware of these changes. UDDI can play the runtime broker or middleman in handling and propagating these changes.

The steps in this lifecycle management scenario are:

- Develop the application to consume the Web service using the information from the saved `bindingTemplate` information;
- If the Web service call fails or exceeds an application-specified timeout, query the UDDI registry for the latest information on that Web service;
- In the case the original Web service call failed, compare the latest binding information for that Web service with the saved information. If the latest binding information is different from the saved information, then save the new binding information and retry the Web service call.
- In the case that the original Web service call exceeded a timeout, compare the latest binding information for that Web service with the saved information. If the information is different or newer access endpoints are available, select another endpoint. The

selection procedure may be manual in which the application allows the user to manually choose, or it may be automatic.

In this scenario, UDDI plays a critical role in maintaining the reliability and quality of service of both applications and the Web services they consume throughout their lifecycle.

Summary

As the number of Web services increases and groups of competing Web services that provide the same or similar capability emerge, quality of service (QoS) becomes an important differentiating feature that directly drives a Web service's usefulness and popularity. Exposing a piece of business logic as a Web service is not difficult; architecting the service so that it meets the quality needs of its users and also maintains that level of quality over a sustained period of time is the difficult part.

In this chapter, we took a tour of quality of service as it relates to Web services. We touched on some of the QoS measures that are critical for enterprise applications. We discussed the technologies that underlie Web services as well as related systems and how these technologies and systems contribute positively or negatively to QoS metrics. We then took an in-depth look at architectural and design patterns as well as best practices for developing QoS-enabled Web services and client applications.

Architect's Notes

- In analyzing the performance of a Web service, remember that Web services do not exist in a vacuum. A number of underlying technologies, such as XML and HTTP, as well as associated infrastructure and systems, such as application servers, Web servers, legacy systems, and communication networks, make up the environment in which Web services operate. Look at the performance of a Web service within this larger context, and then identify subsystems to improve.
- In designing Web services, see how closely related operations and functionalities can be combined together into an easy-to-understand coarse-grained interface. In searching for Web services to consume within your application, opt for coarse-grained Web services that do a lot of work or return a lot of information per each invocation.
- Do not use Web services as an excuse not to develop the right client application. Only use Web services to augment the client application's business logic with those functionalities or data that cannot be reasonably implemented or stored locally.
- Use resources efficiently, and look for innovative means of optimizing such use. Choose the XML parsing infrastructure that is right for your application or system (comprising all of the applications running on the device). Compress XML documents

whenever possible. If a Web service does not use compression, use an intermediary server that supports compressed communications with the client application. For additional processor and network efficiency, use non-XML-based encoding that is smaller in size and does not require an XML infrastructure. Using servlets together with HTTP POST parameters is a well-understood and easily implemented choice. This is especially so for mobile applications.

- Track the performance of your Web services and applications by inserting monitoring agents at various points within the application fulfillment path. Use this monitored data to update QoS specifications for your Web service as well as to uncover optimization opportunities.

CHAPTER 10

Mobile and Wireless

Mobile and wireless devices are fast becoming first class citizens of the Internet as well as of corporate enterprises. The device landscape, once dominated by personal computers (PCs), is becoming littered with a variety of different form factors, user interface (UI) paradigms, and vertical market use cases. This is not surprising as we have always shared our homes and offices with a multitude of "things"—alarm clocks, boom boxes, stereo systems, telephones, printers, televisions, and many more.

What is changing, however, is that these "things" are becoming digital and digital platforms that are capable of receiving renewable software, content, and services, which can then be delivered to the user through the device's unique ergonomics and form factors. Not only is there emerging a large number and variety of these digital platforms, but device add-ons, such as bar code scanners and cameras, are further enhancing the capabilities of these digital platforms.

A personal digital assistant (PDA) that was once used for appointment and contact management can now be augmented with a bar code scanner add-on and be used to track and manage inventory. The same PDA can have its abilities further increased with a digital camera add-on to take, edit, and annotate pictures. Add-ons not only enhance the capabilities of each device, but also the number and type of software and services that the device can usefully run.

Many of these devices are being developed to support wireless connectivity because the lack of wires simplifies their configuration and use. With wireless capability, users do not have to worry about having the right connectors or the right cables. There is no need to purchase network hubs or routers as more devices are added. Within homes and offices, there is no need to figure out how to route cables from one machine to another machine, which may be in separate rooms.

It is important to note that wireless and mobile are not the same: wireless does not necessarily mean mobile. As shown in Figure 10-1, the classic example of this is a standard television set. Receiving television programming signals over the air certainly makes televisions wireless, but their one-hundred to two-hundred pound weight does not qualify them as being very mobile.

Mobile devices are those devices that can be easily used anywhere in any situation. They do not require special configurations of their users. Instead, all of the devices' capabilities can be used while the user is "on the go."

In order for devices that support communications with other devices to be considered mobile, they have to use wireless connectivity. Clearly a physical cable cannot tie down a device that can be used while "on the go." Wireless connectivity also allows the user to access any information at any time, thus ensuring that all of the capabilities of the device are available no matter where the user is.

A cellular phone is mobile. A mobile phone can be used wherever there is cellular wireless network coverage. While within these coverage areas, mobile phones allow users to utilize their capabilities while sitting down, walking, or even while driving a car. Voice-based dialing features and hands-free headsets further cement cellular phones' position as mobile devices.

On the other hand, contrary to popular belief, laptop computers are not mobile. At the very least, laptops require their users' laps, thus necessitating that users be sitting or kneeling. Using the laptop's keyboard also requires at a minimum one hand, and ideally two to be more productive. Using a laptop anywhere in any situation, say, while walking, is not practical. Laptop computers, even those with wireless connections, do not fit within the definition and requirements of mobile devices.

Although many of the concepts and issues we discuss herein are relevant for both wireless as well as mobile devices, in this chapter we focus on mobile devices. Their small form factors

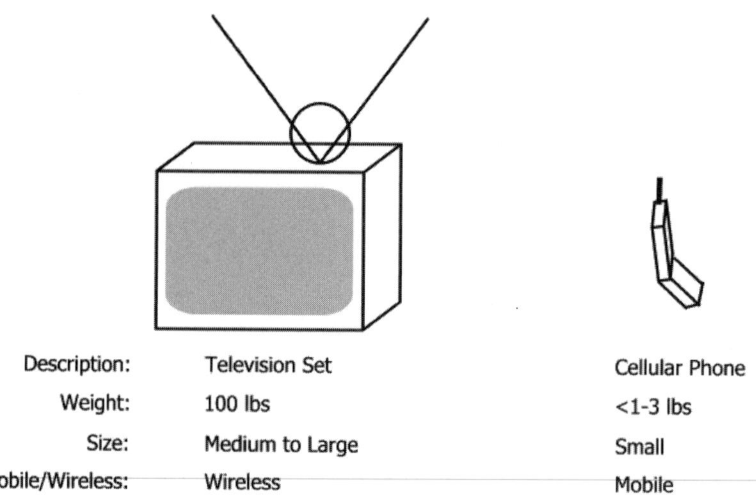

Description:
Television Set
Cellular Phone
Weight:
100 lbs
<1-3 lbs
Size:
Medium to Large
Small
Mobile/Wireless:
Wireless
Mobile

Figure 10-1 Wireless devices are not necessarily mobile.

and simplified usage paradigms allow mobile devices to be used seamlessly in all situations, while pervasive wireless networks enable these devices to access information and communicate from anywhere.

Mobile Web Services

The challenge for architects designing software is to be able to seamlessly support mobile devices. Where a software architect could before count on a keyboard, mouse, and monitor together with a hard disk drive, a reasonable amount of memory and processing power, she can no longer count on such a fixed and well-defined target platform. Instead, the architect must now concern herself with whether a display is available at all, and whether the available processing resources are sufficient to provide a reasonable latency to the application. Moreover, as the number and type of mobile devices increase, architects must think about how the nuances between different devices will affect their software.

Web services are an interesting addition to the technology mix for developing mobile applications. The use of Web services allows some, if not most, of the application's business logic to run on remote servers, which are independent of the mobile device's computational resource limitations. This has the added benefit that a variety of mobile devices can effectively access the same functionality or business logic.

With much of the business logic implemented and executed on remote servers, the developer can focus her time on the application's user interface (UI). It is amazing how little time engineers devote to thinking about and designing an application's UI. The UI is the gateway between the user and the application's business logic. Even the most valuable of applications, if coupled together with an ill-thought-out and ill-presented UI, will have only limited market success. The extra days or weeks spent in thinking about and developing an appropriate, intuitive, and easy-to-use UI for each target device are well worth it.

Since the use of Web services separates some of the business logic and does not require that the entire application be run on the mobile device itself, the time to download (over a wireless network) an application to run it can be greatly reduced. Assuming that most of the business logic is provided by Web services, the only portions of the application that must be downloaded are the user interface and the integration logic necessary to invoke, coordinate, and integrate the various Web services.

If the required functionalities of an application already exist as Web services, the development time and overall time-to-market can be greatly reduced, creating competitive advantages for those who use Web services for mobile applications. Testing and maintenance time and costs can also be reduced through a distributed and modularized Web services architecture.

Table 10-1 enumerates and compares some of the advantages of using Web services for mobile applications. The data provided is for a mobile chess game application. The column labeled Monolithic Chess Game lists data for a monolithic Java application that includes the user interface together with all of the business logic. The column labeled Web Service Chess Game lists data for a distributed application that implements a local (on the mobile device) user interface but relies on a remote Web service to determine the next move for the computer.

Table 10-1 Comparison of download file size, download time, and performance between a monolithic mobile application and a Web service-based mobile application

	Monolithic Chess Game	Web Service Chess Game
Download File Size	621 KB	56 KB
Wireless Network File Download Time	00:07:34	00:00:41
Wireless Network Monthly Data Allowance (10MB plan) Usage	6.2%	0.006%
Application performance (seconds per move)	54 to 720	10 to 81

The file that must be downloaded for the monolithic chess game application is more than eleven times larger than that for the Web services-based application. This results in a download time of more than seven minutes and thirty-four seconds for the monolithic application as compared to just forty-one seconds for the Web services application. Mobile users with a flat-rate monthly data bandwidth billing will use up almost ten percent of their monthly allowance downloading the monolithic application, but less than one percent with the Web services application.

The large file size will dissuade most mobile users from downloading the application over the air, where the forty-one second download time for the Web services-based application will motivate even users unfamiliar with the application to download the application, on an impulse. Of course, the Web services application will use additional bandwidth or time as the user uses the application. However, by this time, the user will have made a determination as to the positive value of the mobile application, and the continued wireless network usage will be justified.

The Web services-based chess game application also shows a lower and more consistent latency than the monolithic application. The latency measured is the amount of time necessary for the chess game application to determine its next move given the user's current move. Since the Web service is running on a powerful server, its latency increases minimally as the game progresses and the next-move computations become increasingly complex. The Web service latency is bounded on the lower end by network delays. The monolithic application runs completely on the mobile device. As the computations become increasingly complex, the latency increases significantly.

Now that we have seen some of the benefits of using Web services for mobile applications, in the next section we take a deeper look at some of the challenges with developing applications for mobile environments and best practices for addressing those challenges.

Challenges with Mobile

Many challenges exist in the development of mobile applications and systems that are usually not an issue in the development of non-mobile systems. For instance, non-mobile developers rarely think about the ramifications that their application architecture will have on a system's energy consumption. Non-mobile developers also do not usually think about how their application's network utilization will affect the user's monthly wireless subscription bill.

In this section, we briefly look at the issues that are inherent to the development of mobile systems. Then, we discuss approaches for addressing these issues and solution best practices.

The Wireless Network

The first obstacle faced in developing mobile applications is the wireless network. A variety of wireless networks are available, including cellular and 802.11 wireless local area network (WLAN). Each of these network technologies has unique characteristics that make them appropriate for different environments.

Recognizing the unique characteristics of each network and their potential synergies, some devices support multiple network technologies. Cellular technologies provide roaming wireless network connectivity, while WLAN technologies provide higher speed wireless connectivity within the enterprise as well as at specific "hot spot" locations.

Notwithstanding supporting multiple networks, mobile applications must address many issues:

- **Network coverage**. Mobile devices do not have network connectivity everywhere at all times. Cellular access is often unavailable under bridges, within buildings, or in remote areas. 802.11 WLAN or Bluetooth simply may not exist at many locations.
- **Latency**. Wireless network connections are slow, and some are slower than others. Few wireless connections achieve their advertised bandwidth, with error correction and retries further increasing the effective latency. High latencies affect applications but, more importantly, frustrate users and may reduce adoption rates.
- **Power**. Wireless networks consume power at a voracious rate. For every bit of information transmitted or received, an amount of power is consumed. As shown in Figure 10-2, the amount of power consumed in transmitting or receiving a bit of information over a wireless link is approaching its theoretical minimum. This means that improvements in wireless technologies will bring only marginal reduction in power consumption. On the other hand, technology advancements for computational resources continue on their downward trend. This means that by using an increased amount of computational resources on a mobile device to reduce the number of bits transmitted or received (e.g., through compression techniques or by simply running more of the application locally) can result in significant power savings.

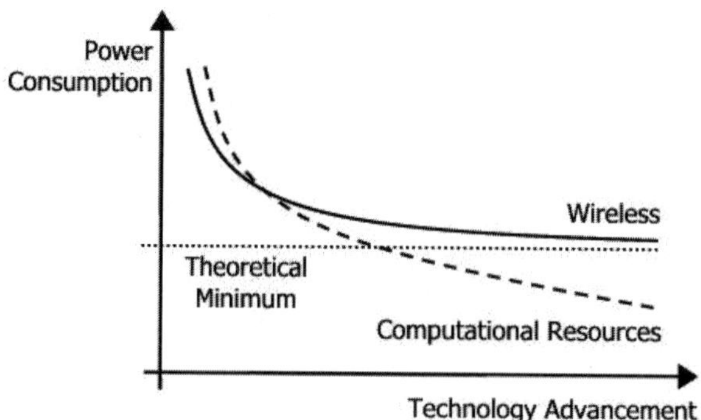

Figure 10-2 The relative power consumption of wireless networks to computational resources.

- **High Costs**. Although they are dropping, wireless usage rates are expensive. Other than fixed costs of an enterprise WLAN, wireless network access involves a service provider who may charge by the minute, by the amount of bandwidth used, or through a flat rate.

Most mobile applications today tend to fall at either end of the two extremes of network usage as shown in Figure 10-3. At one end of this spectrum are applications that require an "always on" network connectivity. At the other end are applications that function properly without the wireless network at all, but simply synchronize their data through a network-connected PC. In general, both sides of these extremes fail to provide their users with intelligent value. Applications based only on offline synchronization capabilities do not leverage wireless connectivity to provide real-time access to the latest information. On the other hand, applications that heavily use the wireless network provide real-time access while decreasing application latency and increasing usage costs. To provide value, mobile applications must intelligently use wireless networks.

These and other issues unique to wireless networks motivate rethinking the information access model for mobile devices. Today, the most widely used mobile information access model combines features of PC browsers together with the notion of write-once-run-anywhere. This model has two critical features:

1. The back-end server is required throughout the transaction. If the connection between the server and the client is broken, the user must start over, as there is no real means of saving information prior to a transaction completing.

Figure 10-3 The spectrum of network usage by mobile applications.

2. The user interface is as simple as possible, further limited by the lowest common denominator that can be supported by all the targeted mobile devices. Device profiling together with a transformation engine is used to dynamically re-target (or transcode) the user interface for any device.

The small form factor of mobile devices demand rich and intuitive user interfaces, not simple, lowest common denominator ones. This, together with the higher rate of disconnects in a wireless network environment, requires a more appropriate model of information access that recognizes the realities of mobile networks and devices.

A mobile information access model is first focused on transactions. The PC browser model of information access is focused on interactions: the user inputs some information, the server responds with some information and requests additional information, then the user again inputs more information and the cycle continues. This sort of interaction is justified when network speeds are reasonably fast and rapid-entry information input devices such as keyboards and mice are available. In mobile environments, the lack of inexpensive, high-speed networks necessitates a focus on transactions, or getting things done.

A transaction-based mobile information access model captures all of the relevant information from the user upfront, and then transmits the information to the back-end server, which then attempts to service the request. The response to the mobile application may include a confirmation request from the user before the transaction is completed. The user may do such a confirmation with a simple voice command or a single-button tap. The interactions by the user are based on disconnected operations that the user can complete at his leisure since the wireless network is not utilized.

A mobile information access model also extensively uses data compression to reduce the number of bits transmitted or received over the wireless network. After the relevant information has been captured, the entire data is compressed (and perhaps also encrypted) before transmission.

Finally, in order to facilitate user input through mobile devices and to capture all of the relevant information from the user at the earliest point, significant thought must be given to designing a rich, easy-to-use user interface for each application. Figure 10-4 depicts the flow for this mobile information access model.

Consider using a typical PC browser to purchase airline tickets. First, the user enters the source and destination airports together with the travel dates. The server responds with a list (often very long) of possible flights. The user then selects the desired outbound and inbound flights, and the server responds with the purchase price. If the price is all right, then the user must select his seat choices. Then, the server finally responds with a form that lets the user purchase the airline tickets by entering his credit card information, home address, and mode of ticket delivery.

In a transaction-focused mobile information access model, the user enters all of the information, including specific flight times, desired seats, price range, and billing information into the application once at the beginning (some information such as home address would be entered

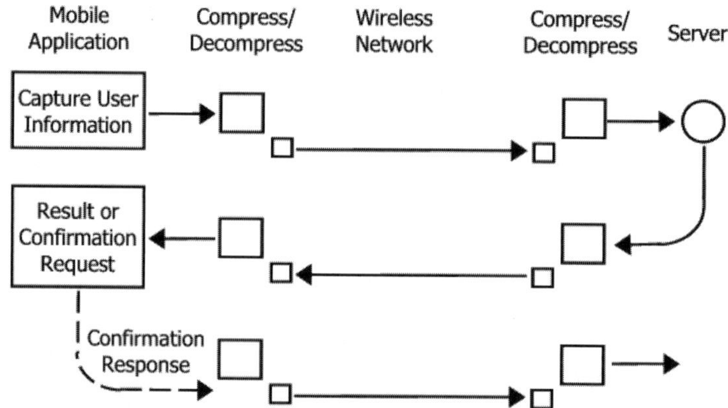

Figure 10-4 A mobile information access model that captures all user information upfront, extensively compresses all wireless network traffic, and uses the back-end server to service the request as best as possible.

just once and be available to all applications). This would allow the user to enter the data, and then continue with whatever else he needed to do. The result would be returned by the server at a later time, and would be a combination outbound-inbound flight that meets the request specifications, or its closest match.

Essentially, with a transaction-focused mobile information access model, mobile client devices and back-end servers communicate with more specific questions, such as "What is the best flight that departs from San Francisco International Airport at 9 P.M. Monday night headed for Washington Dulles International Airport?" instead of "What is the listing of all flights between San Francisco International Airport and Washington Dulles International Airport on Monday," which is more like the interactive model of PC browsers.

Limited Computing Resources

Many mobile devices today have more computing resources than larger systems did just a few years ago. Nonetheless, they do have limited resources dictated by their power and form factor constraints. Different devices have different resources, and the same application running on different devices will have a different performance.

Many applications use eXtensible Markup Language (XML) to represent data. Web services technologies also use XML. The use of XML in mobile environments warrants some discussion, as mobile devices using XML to represent and manipulate data will have to address a number of issues.

Mobile software platforms such as Java 2 Mobile Edition (J2ME) support only limited string manipulation capabilities. Applications that use generic XML parsers and XML APIs may not work.

XML is reasonably verbose as it uses tags to demarcate different data fields in human-readable form. Data represented using XML will require additional network bandwidth to transmit as well as additional processing resources to parse. XML's increased bandwidth and processing needs also result in higher power consumption.

XML's verbose nature and increased resource requirements have long been an issue with mobile application development. Data compression together with more efficient XML parsing and object representation techniques can be used to address these issues.

User Interfaces

The user interface (UI) is perhaps the most important part of an application. If the UI is difficult to use, non-intuitive, or awkward, user frustration will slow or reduce the application's adoption, no matter how compelling or important the underlying application functionality.

Mobile applications have to be easy to use within their use case or context. An application that gives users directions while they are driving a car should not require the driver to stop driving and take both hands off the steering wheel to interact with it. Conversely, educational applications or games, which assume the full attention of the user, can utilize a more hands-on UI.

It is important to remember that a UI is bi-directional: it must facilitate entering information and it must also facilitate the user's comprehension of information. This information includes instructions (both written and contextual) for entering information, as well as specific data that is returned by the application's underlying business logic.

Most mobile platforms support graphical user interface (GUI) components such as buttons, text entry boxes, and selection boxes. Combinations of these and other GUI widgets can be used to effectively build UIs. Most mobile devices also provide physical knobs and buttons that can be combined with GUI components to implement a more intuitive and easier-to-use user interface.

Physical UI components and GUI components together with the contextual basis of the mobile device itself results in complex interactions and it is usually difficult to automate the development or mapping of UIs from one device to another. Transcoding technologies attempt to automate the development of UIs across multiple devices. Transcoding uses a database with information about the characteristics of devices to automatically re-target content and interactivity. Content and interactions that spanned 21-inch screens are reduced to just a few square inches by scaling down rich graphics, reducing colors, repositioning text and GUI components, or simply eliminating segments all together.

Two issues limit the usefulness of transcoding. Developers usually find themselves building least common denominator content and interactions that can be easily transcoded to a number of devices. This approach sacrifices the richness of some devices for the limitation of others.

Secondly, transcoding technologies usually cannot address issues of context of a device or of an application. This often results in non-intuitive interactions or presentation of content.

Transcoding achieves low costs of mobile information access and development, by sacrificing the richness of mobile user interfaces. Although low cost, these user interfaces are often non-intuitive and difficult to use, frustrating users and have led to abysmal adoption rates of mobile information services.

Since the user interface is the customer touch point, it behooves developers to spend additional time (and money) to build appropriate, context-aware, and easy-to-use user interfaces that leverage the richness of different devices and mobile platforms.

Macromedia's Flash is an interesting technology for the development of rich, mobile user interfaces. The mobile version of the Flash player comes pre-installed and bundled on a number of devices, including personal digital assistants (PDAs) and cellular phones.

Flash also has a powerful design environment, Flash MX, as well as additional tools and utilities (available through the Macromedia Web site) that cater to the needs of designers who are not necessarily engineers. That is, a designer who understands the psychological and contextual requirements of building mobile user interfaces can do so without having to write programming code.

Figure 10-5 shows a screenshot of a Flash-based mobile chess game application. Flash also supports scripting through its ActionScript language. Based on JavaScript, ActionScript provides a simple means to control different aspects of a Flash movie. For instance, based on user activity, such as a mouse click, different scenes within the movie can be manipulated and shown. For example, in the mobile smart chess application shown in Figure 10-5, a mouse click over a cell that is occupied by a white chess piece results in the piece being relocated to the cell over which the mouse released. Mouse clicks over cells that are unoccupied or are occupied by black chess pieces are ignored and the movie continues as is.

Figure 10-5 A Flash-based mobile chess user interface.

Now that we have seen some of the challenges and issues in developing mobile applications and systems, in the next section we turn to developing mobile Web services solutions. We also discuss the pros and cons of different systems architectures in implementing such solutions.

Proxy-Based Mobile Systems

When developing mobile Web services-based applications, a variety of different architectures are possible. A mobile systems architecture that is commonly used is a proxy-based one in which the mobile application communicates only with a proxy server. The proxy server in turn communicates with and manages the back-end resources, such as Web services.

Figure 10-6 depicts the block diagram architecture of a proxy-based mobile application. The mobile device is capable of running multiple applications. Each of these mobile applications presents a front-end user interface that presents information to users and captures user input. The application does only enough processing on the user input so that the proxy server can properly interpret the data. Different proxy servers may exist for different applications, or a single server may handle multiple applications. The role of the proxy server is to implement all required business logic to service the needs of the mobile application. The implementation of the business logic may include Web services or other distributed computing resources.

Although each mobile application can directly interact with its proxy server, an intermediary messaging platform can be used to facilitate and manage communications. The messaging platform and the proxy server are the central locations in which to add paired services so that messages encoded on the mobile device are properly decoded by the proxy server (and vice versa). These paired services may include messaging protocols, compression algorithms, and security mechanisms. By locating these services in a distinct layer outside of the applications, both applications and the messaging platform can be more easily developed, maintained, and augmented.

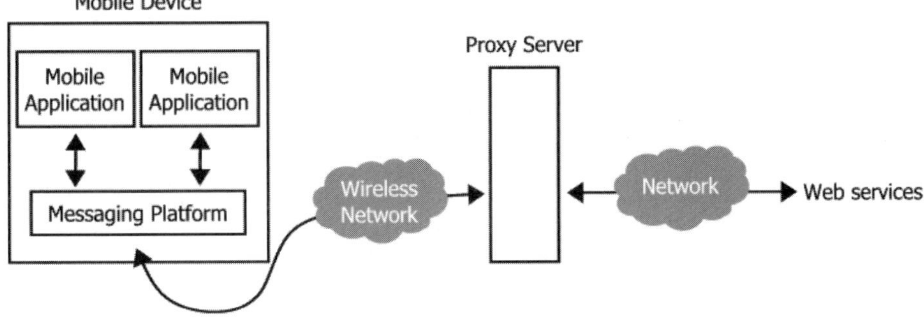

Figure 10-6 A proxy-based mobile Web services application.

Mobile Messaging Platform

We first discuss a simple Java implementation of a mobile messaging platform. The messaging platform has a component that runs locally on the mobile device (client-side) as well as a component that runs on the server. The client-side components consist of:

- MobileMessagingPlatformServer.java
- MobileMessagingPlatformThread.java
- MobileServicesClient.java

While the server-side components consist of:

- ServiceProxyGateway.java
- InvokeService.java

Figure 10-7 illustrates the relationships between the various components of the mobile messaging platform as well as between the mobile messaging platform and each of the mobile applications.

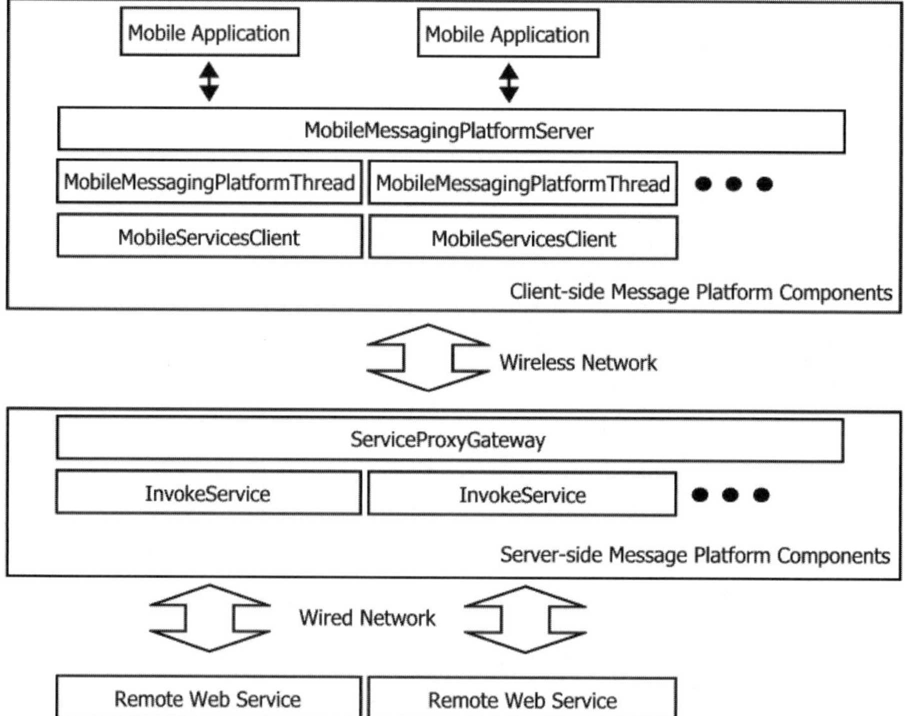

Figure 10-7 The components of the mobile messaging platform.

We first discuss the components that run on the mobile device. What follows is the entire source code of MobileMessagingPlatformServer.java. This class listens for connections from applications running on the local device, and spawns a thread to handle the application requests.

```
/*
 * MobileMessagingPlatformServer.java
 */

import java.io.IOException;
import java.net.ServerSocket;
import java.net.Socket;

public class MobileMessagingPlatformServer
{
   public MobileMessagingPlatformServer ()
   {
      serverStart ();
   }

   private void serverStart ()
   {
      try
      {
```

The messaging platform listens for connections from applications on port 20001. When a new connection is received, the `MobileMessagingPlatformThread` is instantiated and started.

```
         ServerSocket server = new ServerSocket ( 20001 );
         while ( true )
         {
            Socket socketObj = server.accept ();
            MobileMessagingPlatformThread mmpt =
    new MobileMessagingPlatformThread
    ( socketObj );
            mmpt.start ();
         }
      }
      catch ( IOException ioe )
      {
         System.out.println ( "IOException error: " +
        ioe + "." );
      }
   }
```

The main method simply instantiates the `MobileMessagingPlatformServer` object.

```
   public static void main ( String args[] )
   {
      MobileMessagingPlatformServer mmps =
  new MobileMessagingPlatformServer ();
   }
}
```

What follows is the entire source code of MobileMessagingPlatformThread.java. This class parses the incoming messaging requests from each local application, analyzes and formats each request, and then forwards each request to the MobileServicesClient class for transmission to the proxy server.

```
/*
 * MobileMessagingPlatformThread.java
 */

import java.io.BufferedOutputStream;
import java.io.BufferedReader;
import java.io.IOException;
import java.io.InputStreamReader;
import java.io.PrintWriter;
import java.net.Socket;
import java.util.StringTokenizer;

public class MobileMessagingPlatformThread extends Thread
{
   private Socket socket;
   private BufferedReader streamIn;
   private PrintWriter writeOut;

   private String method = null;
   private String rettype = null;
   private String names = null;
   private String types = null;
   private String values = null;
   private String servicename = null;
   private String serviceclass = null;

   public MobileMessagingPlatformThread ( Socket socket )
   {
      this.socket = socket;
```

First, we prepare to read the incoming data as well as prepare to write data back to the local application through the socket connection.

```
      try
      {
         streamIn = new BufferedReader (
new InputStreamReader (
socket.getInputStream () ) );
         writeOut = new PrintWriter (
```

```
socket.getOutputStream () , true );
      }
      catch ( IOException ioe )
      {
         System.out.println ( "IOException error - " +
 ioe + "." );

         try
         {
            socket.close ();
         }
         catch ( IOException e )
         {
            System.out.println ( "IOException error
     while closing." );
         }
      }
   }

   public void run ()
   {
      char cb[] = new char[ 1 ];
      String resultString = null;
      MobileServicesClient mClient =
  new MobileServicesClient ();

      try
      {
```

Now, we read in the incoming data from the socket connection and convert it to a String. Next, the `parseInMsg` method is called on the entire String message to be parsed. As the message is parsed, each attribute name-value pair is written to the corresponding variable. After all of the variables have been updated, the `MobileServicesClient` object is called to actually transmit the data to the proxy server.

```
   while ( streamIn.read ( cb , 0 , 1 ) != -1 )
         {
            StringButter sb = new StringBuffer ( 16384 );
            while ( cb[ 0 ] != '\0' )
            {
               sb.append ( cb[ 0 ] );
               streamIn.read ( cb , 0 , 1 );
            }

            String msgIn = sb.toString ();
            System.out.println ( "Server received message: "
            + msgIn );
            parseInMsg ( msgIn );

            System.out.println ( "Parsed data as
    follows:" );
```

```
            System.out.println ( "servicename=" +
servicename );
            System.out.println ( "serviceclass=" +
serviceclass );
            System.out.println ( "method=" + method );
            System.out.println ( "rettype=" + rettype );
            System.out.println ( "names=" + names );
            System.out.println ( "types=" + types );
            System.out.println ( "values=" + values );

            resultString = mClient.invokeService (
servicename ,
          serviceclass ,
method ,
rettype ,
names ,
types ,
values ).trim ();

            System.out.println ( "Result is: " +
resultString + "." );

            writeOut.write ( resultString + "\0" );
            writeOut.flush ();
         }
      }
      catch ( IOException ioe )
      {
         System.out.println ( "IOException error." );
      }
   }
```

The parseInMsg method parses the incoming message and writes each attribute name-value pair to its corresponding variable. Within the message sent from the local application, each name-value pair attribute, except for the last one, is followed by the delimiter "###".

The StringTokenizer object returns each delimited token, and the string representation of the token is stored in thisToken. The attribute name and value are extracted from each token by calculating the substring of each thisToken string object.

```
   private void parseInMsg ( String inStr )
   {
      StringTokenizer st = new StringTokenizer (
inStr , "###" , false );
      String thisToken = null;

      while ( st.hasMoreTokens () )
      {
         thisToken = st.nextToken ().toString ();

         if ( thisToken.startsWith ( "servicename=" ) )
         {
```

```
            servicename = thisToken.substring ( 12 );
         }
         else if ( thisToken.startsWith ( "serviceclass=" ))
         {
            serviceclass = thisToken.substring ( 13 );
         }
         else if ( thisToken.startsWith ( "method=" ) )
         {
            method = thisToken.substring ( 7 );
         }
         else if ( thisToken.startsWith ( "rettype=" ) )
         {
            rettype = thisToken.substring ( 8 );
         }
         else if ( thisToken.startsWith ( "names=" ) )
         {
            names = thisToken.substring ( 6 );
         }
         else if ( thisToken.startsWith ( "types=" ) )
         {
            types = thisToken.substring ( 6 );
         }
         else if ( thisToken.startsWith ( "values=" ) )
         {
            values = thisToken.substring ( 7 );
         }
         else
         {
            System.out.println ( "Unknown parameter
received." );
         }
      }
   }
}
```

What follows is the entire source code of `MobileServicesClient`.java. This class consists of a single public method, which transmits the Web service call to the proxy server that will in fact invoke the Web service. The message that is transmitted to the proxy server is also formatted such that the proxy server can appropriately invoke the Web service and interpret the results.

The message is sent to the proxy server through a HTTP POST request. On the proxy server side, a J2EE Servlet receives and handles the request.

```
/*
 * MobileServicesClient.java
 */

import java.io.IOException;
import java.io.InputStream;
import java.io.OutputStreamWriter;
```

```
import java.io.PrintWriter;
import java.lang.reflect.Method;
import java.net.HttpURLConnection;
import java.net.MalformedURLException;
import java.net.URL;
import java.net.URLEncoder;
import java.util.StringTokenizer;

public class MobileServicesClient
{
   public static String invokeService ( String serviceName ,
                                        String serviceClass,
                                        String method ,
                                        String retType ,
String argNames , String argTypes , String argValues )
   {
      byte buf[] = new byte[ 2056 ];
      int n;
      String urlString;
      StringBuffer sb = new StringBuffer ();
      String resultStr = "";
      Class classObj = null;
      Class[] argTypeClasses;
      Method methodObj = null;
      Object obj = null;
```

We first form the message that will be sent as part of our HTTP POST request to the proxy server. We append together all of the information such that the proxy server can itself invoke the appropriate Web service.

```
      sb.append ( "service =" );
      sb.append ( URLEncoder.encode ( serviceName ) );
      sb.append ( "&method=" );
      sb.append ( URLEncoder.encode ( method ) );
      sb.append ( "&rettype=" );
      sb.append ( URLEncoder.encode ( retType ) );
      sb.append ( "&names=" );
      sb.append ( URLEncoder.encode ( argNames ) );
      sb.append ( "&types=" );
      sb.append ( URLEncoder.encode ( argTypes ) );
      sb.append ( "&values=" );
      sb.append ( URLEncoder.encode ( argValues ) );
      String formData = sb.toString ();
```

We then transmit our HTTP POST request to the proxy server located at:

```
http://192.168.1.102:9090/ServiceProxyGateway/ServiceProxyGateway
```

The data is transmitted as if it were HTML form data and is not encrypted for security.

```
        try
        {
           URL url = new URL ("http://192.168.1.102:9090/
ServiceProxyGateway/ServiceProxyGateway" );
   HttpURLConnection urlcon = ( HttpURLConnection )
url.openConnection ();
           urlcon.setRequestMethod ( "POST" );
           urlcon.setRequestProperty ( "Content-type" ,
"application/x-www-form-urlencoded" );
           urlcon.setDoOutput ( true );
           urlcon.setDoInput ( true );
           PrintWriter pout = new PrintWriter (
new OutputStreamWriter (
                urlcon.getOutputStream () , "8859_1" ) ,
  true );
           pout.print ( formData );
           pout.flush ();
```

After the HTTP POST request has been sent, we wait for the response. The proxy server responds after it has actually invoked the desired Web service.

Once we receive the response from the proxy server, we concatenate together the response segments to form the entire response message, which is stored in the `resultStr` object. The `resultStr` object is returned as the result of invoking the Web service.

```
           InputStream in = urlcon.getInputStream ();
           while ( ( n = in.read ( buf , 0 , buf.length ) )
!= -1 )
           {
              resultStr = resultStr.concat (
  new java.lang.String ( buf ).trim () );
           }
        }
        catch ( MalformedURLException mue )
        {
           System.out.println ( mue );
        }
        catch ( IOException ioe )
        {
           System.out.println ( ioe );
        }
        return ( resultStr );
    }
}
```

Next, we look at how to develop the proxy server. As we saw earlier, the Web service call is transmitted as a message from the actual mobile application to the mobile messaging platform, which then transmits it to the proxy server. In this mobile messaging platform, we use an HTTP POST request to send the message from the mobile messaging platform to the proxy server. Correspondingly, a J2EE Servlet is used on the proxy server side to receive and handle the HTTP POST request.

The proxy server is comprised of the J2EE Servlet `ServiceProxyGateway` as well as the helper class `InvokeService` that actually invokes the remote Web service. What follows is the entire source code of `ServiceProxyGateway`.java.

```
/*
 * ServiceProxyGateway.java
 */

import javax.servlet.ServletConfig;
import javax.servlet.ServletException;
import javax.servlet.http.HttpServlet;
import javax.servlet.http.HttpServletRequest;
import javax.servlet.http.HttpServletResponse;
import java.io.IOException;
import java.io.PrintWriter;
import java.util.StringTokenizer;

public class ServiceProxyGateway extends HttpServlet
{
   private static final String CONTENT_TYPE = "text/html";

   public void init ( ServletConfig config )
throws ServletException
   {
      super.init ( config );
   }

   /* Handle HTTP GETs and POSTs together */
   public void doGet ( HttpServletRequest request ,
HttpServletResponse response )
      throws ServletException , IOException
   {
      doPost ( request , response );
   }

   public void doPost ( HttpServletRequest request ,
 HttpServletResponse response )
     throws ServletException , IOException
   {
      String paramServiceURL;
      String paramMethod;
      String paramRetType;
      String paramArgNames;
      String paramArgTypes;
      String paramArgValues;
```

First we read the parameters of the HTTP POST request that was sent by the mobile messaging platform.

```
paramServiceURL = request.getParameter ( "service" );
paramMethod = request.getParameter ( "method" );
paramRetType = request.getParameter ( "rettype" );
paramArgNames = request.getParameter ( "names" );
paramArgTypes = request.getParameter ( "types" );
paramArgValues = request.getParameter ( "values" );
```

Once we have read in all of the parameters of the POST request, we print them out to the console as a temporary log of the data that was received.

```
System.out.println ( "Service Proxy Gateway." );
System.out.println ( "Received data:" );
System.out.println ( "    Service URL: " +
paramServiceURL );
System.out.println ( "    Service Method: " +
paramMethod );
System.out.println ( "    Method Return Type: " +
paramRetType );
System.out.println ( "    Method Arg Names: " +
paramArgNames );
System.out.println ( "    Method Arg Types: " +
paramArgTypes );
System.out.println ( "    Method Arg Values: " +
paramArgValues );
System.out.println ( " " );
```

Now that we have all of the parameters necessary to invoke the remote Web service, we instantiate a new `InvokeService` object, and set the various parameters in preparation for the Web service invocation using the object's setter methods.

```
InvokeService callWS = new InvokeService ();
callWS.setMethod ( paramMethod );
callWS.setReturnType ( paramRetType );
callWS.setWSURL ( paramServiceURL );
```

Since a Web service method invocation may have multiple arguments, we parse through each argument token and set its appropriate name, value, and type fields. A comma delimits each of the arguments, and `StringTokenizer` objects are used to extract each token from each of the overall strings.

```
    callWS.clearArgs ();
    StringTokenizer tokenizerNames =
new StringTokenizer ( paramArgNames ,
"," , false );
    StringTokenizer tokenizerTypes =
new StringTokenizer ( paramArgTypes ,
"," , false );
    StringTokenizer tokenizerValues =
new StringTokenizer ( paramArgValues ,
"," , false );
```

```
      int k = 0;
      while ( tokenizerNames.hasMoreTokens () )
      {
         String tokType =
tokenizerTypes.nextToken ().trim ();
         String tokName =
tokenizerNames.nextToken ().trim ();
         String tokVal =
tokenizerValues.nextToken ().trim ();

         callWS.setArgs ( k , tokType , tokName , tokVal );

         k = k + 1;
      }
```

After the `callWS` object has been properly set, the `invokeWSMethod` method of the `callWS` object is called to invoke the actual Web service. `CallRetObj` is the object returned by the Web service invocation. The string representation of the `CallRetObj` is returned as the response of the Servlet to the HTTP POST request sent by the mobile messaging platform running on the mobile device.

```
      Object callRetObj = callWS.invokeWSMethod ();
      String callRetObjString =
   ( String ) callRetObj.toString ();

      response.setContentType ( CONTENT_TYPE );
      PrintWriter out = response.getWriter ();

      out.println ( callRetObjString );
   }

   public void destroy ()
   {
   }
}
```

What follows is the entire source code of InvokeService.java. The `InvokeService` class invokes a Web service method using information about the Web service endpoint, method name, each of the method argument names, values, and types, as well as the method return type.

```
/**
 * InvokeService.java
 */

import org.apache.axis.client.Call;
import org.apache.axis.client.Service;

import java.util.ArrayList;
import java.util.List;
```

```
public class InvokeService
{
   private static String targetWSURL = "";
   private static String mMethodName = "";

   private static Class mReturnType;
   private static String lReturnType = "";
   private static Object retObj;

   private List lArgNames = new ArrayList ();
   private List lArgTypes = new ArrayList ();
   private List lArgValues = new ArrayList ();

   public InvokeService ()
   {
   }
```

The invokeWSMethod method is called to invoke a Web service method as specified using the setter methods.

```
   public Object invokeWSMethod ()
   {
      Object[] mArgValues =
  new Object[ lArgValues.size () ];

      try
      {
         Service service = new Service ();
         Call call = ( Call ) service.createCall ();

         call.setTargetEndpointAddress ( new java.net.URL
    ( targetWSURL ) );
         call.setOperationName ( mMethodName );
         call.setProperty ( Call.NAMESPACE ,
    "http:////tempuri.org//" );

         retObj = call.invoke ( ( Object[] )
      lArgValues.toArray ( mArgValues ) );
      }
      catch ( Exception e )
      {
         System.err.println ( e.toString () );
      }
      return ( retObj );
   }

   // The setWSURL method sets the desired Web service
   //  endpoint location.
   public void setWSURL ( String targetLocation )
   {
      targetWSURL = targetLocation;
```

```
}

// The setMethod method sets the desired Web service
//  method name.
public void setMethod ( String methodName )
{
   mMethodName = methodName;
}

// The setReturnType method sets the desired Web
//  service's return type.
public void setReturnType ( String returnType )
{
   lReturnType = returnType;

   if ( ( lReturnType.compareToIgnoreCase
     ( "integer" ) == 0 ) ||
      ( lReturnType.compareToIgnoreCase ( "int" ) == 0 ))
   {
      mReturnType = int.class;
   }
   else if ( ( lReturnType.compareToIgnoreCase
     ( "string" ) == 0 ) ||
      ( lReturnType.compareToIgnoreCase ( "str" ) == 0 ))
   {
      mReturnType = String.class;
   }
   else
   {
      System.out.println ( "InvokeService:
 Unsupported RetArgType received." );
   }
}

// The clearArgs method clears all of the method
//  argument information: names, types, and values.
public void clearArgs ()
{
   lArgNames.clear ();
   lArgTypes.clear ();
   lArgValues.clear ();
}

// The setArgs method sets the name, value, and
//  type of the kth argument of the desired Web
//  service method, where k equals argNum.
public void setArgs (int argNum ,
      String argType ,
     String argName ,
     String argValue )
{
   lArgNames.add ( argNum , argName );
```

```
        if ( ( argType.compareToIgnoreCase ( "integer" )
    == 0 ) ||
           ( argType.compareToIgnoreCase ( "int" ) == 0 ))
        {
           lArgTypes.add ( argNum , int.class );
           lArgValues.add ( argNum ,
    new Integer (
        Integer.parseInt ( argValue ) ) );
        }
        else if ( argType.compareToIgnoreCase
  ( "string" ) == 0 )
        {
           lArgTypes.add ( argNum , String.class );
           lArgValues.add ( argNum , argValue );
        }
        else if ( argType.compareToIgnoreCase
  ( "boolean" ) == 0 )
        {
           lArgTypes.add ( argNum , boolean.class );
           lArgValues.add ( argNum , argValue );
        }
        else
        {
           System.out.println ( "InvokeService:
    Unsupported ArgType received." );
        }
     }
}
```

Now that we have seen how to develop the mobile messaging platform, we can build applications using any language or platform and simply pass messages to the messaging platform to invoke arbitrary Web services through the proxy server.

Flash ActionScript Mobile Application User Interface

As we discussed earlier, Macromedia Flash is a powerful platform for the development of user interfaces for mobile applications. Not only does Flash support complex graphics and interactions, it comes with a development environment as well as tools that facilitate graphical user interface development. As more and more mobile device manufacturers bundle the Flash player with their products, Flash represents a strong contender as the platform-of-choice for the development of user interfaces for Web services-based mobile applications.

Flash also supports scripting through its ActionScript language. Based on JavaScript, ActionScript provides a simple means to control different aspects of a Flash movie. For instance, based on user activity, such as a mouse click, different scenes within a Flash movie can be manipulated and shown. For example, in the mobile smart chess application shown in Figure 10-5, a mouse click over a cell that is occupied by a white chess piece results in the piece being relocated to the cell over which the mouse released. Mouse clicks over cells that are unoccupied or are occupied by black chess pieces are ignored, and the movie continues as is.

In this section, we look at the code required to invoke Web services from a Flash-based mobile application user interface. The code segment consists of the following four functions:

- `callWS`: This function is called by the Flash-based user interface when the Web service is to be invoked.
- `sendMsg`: This is a helper function that is internally called by the `callWS` function to send the Web service invocation message to the mobile messaging platform.
- `handleIncoming`: This is a callback function that is automatically called when a message from the mobile messaging platform is received.
- `closeXmlSocket`: This is a simple function that closes and terminates the communications channel between the Flash-based user interface and the mobile messaging platform.

The ActionScript source code in its entirety for these four functions follows:

```
function callWS ( )
{
  // If a communications channel to the mobile messaging
  //  platform is already open, use it; otherwise, open
  //  a new socket connection.
  if (connectedToServer == 0)
  {
    objXMLSocket = new XMLSocket ();
    objXMLSocket.onConnect = myOnConnect;

    // Register the handleIncoming function as the
    //  callback function for this socket
    objXMLSocket.onXML = handleIncoming;
    if ( !objXMLSocket.connect ( "localhost" , 20001 ))
    {
      // The communications socket could not be opened
      trace ("Connection failed.")
      connectedToServer = 0;
    }
  }
  else
  {
    // The communications socket either already exists
    //  or a new one was successfully created. Now we
    //  can send the message to the mobile messaging
    //  platform using the sendMsg function.
    sendMsg( "http://192.168.1.102:9090/hpws/soap/
              ChessMaster", "ChessMaster", "makeNextMove",
              "String", "board", "String", boardStr );
  }
}
```

```
function sendMsg ( servicename,
                   serviceclass,
                   method,
                   rettype,
                   names,
                   types,
                   values)
{
  // This function simply forms a message string consisting
  //  of parameter name-value pairs delimited by "###"
  strText = "servicename=" add servicename add "###" add
            "serviceclass=" add serviceclass add "###"  add
            "method=" add method add "###" add
            "rettype=" add rettype add "###" add
            "names=" add names add "###" add
            "types=" add types add "###" add
            "values=" add values;

  // The message string is formed into a XML element
  //  and sent to the mobile messaging platform
  objXml = new XML ();
  objElement = objXml.createTextNode ( strText );
  objXML.appendChild ( objElement );
  objXMLSocket.send ( objXML );
}

function handleIncoming ( objXml )
{
  // Acknowledge that a new message has been received
  trace ( "Incoming message received." );
  trace ( "String value is: " + objXML.toString () );

  // Convert the incoming message to a string and call
  //  the appropriate function to handle the message
  makeComputersMove ( objXML.toString () );
}

function closeXmlSocket ( )
{
  // Close the communications socket
  objXMLSocket.close();
}
```

The mobile device-side console log information that is printed as a result of the Flash-based mobile chess application invoking the ChessMaster Web service using the mobile messaging platform is shown in Figure 10-8.

```
Server received message: servicename=http://
192.168.1.102:9090/hpws/soap/
ChessMaster###serviceclass=ChessMaster###method=makeNextMove#
##rettype=String###names=board###types=String###values=1:1:2:
1:3:1:4:1:5:1:6:1:7:1:8:1:1:2:2:3:3:3:4:2:5:6:6:2:7:2:8:2:1:8
:2:8:3:8:4:8:5:8:6:8:8:6:8:8:1:7:2:7:3:6:4:7:5:7:6:7:7:7:8:7:

Parsed data as follows:
servicename=http://192.168.1.102:9090/hpws/soap/ChessMaster
serviceclass=ChessMaster
method=makeNextMove
rettype=String
names=board
types=String
values=1:1:2:1:3:1:4:1:5:1:6:1:7:1:8:1:1:2:2:3:3:3:4:2:5:6:6:
2:7:2:8:2:1:8:2:8:3:8:4:8:5:8:6:8:8:6:8:8:1:7:2:7:3:6:4:7:5:7
:6:7:7:7:8:7:

Result is: 3,6,3,5,.
```

Figure 10-8 Device-side console log output for a Flash-based mobile chess application user interface invoking the ChessMaster Web service using the mobile messaging platform.

The information following the `Server received message:` label is the actual message received by the mobile messaging platform by the application user interface. The information following the `Parsed data as follows:` label is each of the parameter name-value pairs after they have been parsed and extracted by the mobile messaging platform. Finally, the information following the `Result is:` label is the string representation of the response received by the mobile messaging platform as a result of invoking the ChessMaster Web service.

Now that we have seen how to invoke a remote Web service from a mobile application using a mobile messaging platform, we next see how to invoke a Web service from a mobile application directly, without a messaging platform.

Invoking Web Services Directly Through a Proxy Server

If we do not want to use a messaging platform, we can directly invoke remote Web services by using the `MobileServicesClient` class from earlier in the chapter. TestServiceInvoke.java is a simple Java program that directly invokes the ChessMaster Web service without going through the mobile messaging platform.

```
/*
 * TestServiceInvoke.java
 */
```

```
public class TestServiceInvoke
{
   public static void main ( String args[] )
   {
      MobileServicesClient mClient =
  new MobileServicesClient ();

      String servicename = "http://192.168.1.102:9090/hpws/
        soap/ChessMaster";
      String serviceclass = "ChessMaster";
      String method = "makeNextMove";
      String rettype = "String";
      String names = "board";
      String types = "String";
      String values = "1:1:2:1:3:1:4:1:5:1:6:1:7:1:8:1:
       1:2:2:3:3:3:4:2:5:6:6:2:7:2:8:2:
       1:8:2:8:3:8:4:8:5:8:6:8:8:6:8:8:
       1:7:2:7:3:6:4:7:5:7:6:7:7:7:8:7:";

      String resultString = mClient.invokeService (
        servicename ,
                       serviceclass ,
                              method ,
        rettype ,
        names ,
        types ,
        values ).trim ();

      System.out.println ( "Result is: " + resultString );
   }
}
```

Although the above Web service invocation is hard-coded to a particular Web service endpoint and input values, it can be used as a template and expanded for more dynamic Web service invocations from mobile applications.

Proxy server-based Web service invocations from mobile applications (with or without a mobile messaging platform) incur a variety of side effects—some positive and some not so positive. In the remainder of this section, we discuss these side effects and provide guidance for best practices.

The first side effect of a proxy server-based Web service invocation model for mobile applications is that they are reasonably straightforward to develop if a non-mobile implementation already exists. For example, if the (non-mobile) Web application is built using J2EE servlets, the servlets can be easily modified to serve as the proxy server.

Presumably, each servlet of the original application was designed to accept input parameters, perform business logic (including invoking Web services) based on the input, and finally generate markup output. The existing application can be mobilized through the following steps:

1. Develop an appropriate user interface for the mobile application.
2. Based on user interaction with the user interface, develop business logic that runs on the mobile device and generates the appropriately formatted data to be transmitted to the servlet (proxy server) using HTTP POST.
3. Modify each servlet such that instead of returning presentation-focused markup as its response, it returns data in a concise format.
4. Augment the business logic running on the mobile device so that it can interpret the data returned by each servlet and update the user interface as appropriate.

By following these steps, a Web services-based application can be mobilized within a matter of days instead of months. Much of the development work is simply re-using existing and pre-tested business logic. Only the mobile application user interface and some business logic that runs on the mobile device must be developed and tested.

Techniques to support Web service invocation reliability and failover that are architected into the non-mobile application can be directly used by the mobilized application within a proxy server-based model. Techniques such as searching through an UDDI registry for alternate or more appropriate Web service endpoints can be implemented by the proxy server, instead of requiring that that business logic be implemented by the mobile application itself.

Moreover, within a typical enterprise environment, Web services-based applications utilize multiple Web services instead of just one. In this case, a proxy server-based invocation model effectively creates a single, coarse-grained interface to the multiple, underlying Web services. As illustrated in Figure 10-9, a proxy-based invocation model eliminates the individual Web service calls.

Eliminating individual Web service calls in favor of an effective coarse-grained interface to multiple Web services has numerous benefits for mobile applications as well as for their users. These benefits include:

- **Usage costs**: By reducing the number of individual Web service invocations and using a higher-level, more coarse-grained interface to multiple Web services a proxy server-based Web service model reduces network usage, and thus usage costs.
- **Latency**: By reducing network usage, proxy server-based Web service invocations also potentially lower application latency by reducing the number of messages that must traverse over slower speed wireless networks. Additionally, since there may be lengthy delays between one Web service call and the next call, the connect/disconnect cycles required to access the wireless network increase latency.
- **Energy conservation**: Since transmitting and receiving every bit of data using a wireless network consumes a fixed amount of energy, reducing the amount of wireless network usage has a corresponding reduction in energy consumption. Conserving the energy consumed by mobile applications increases the device's battery life.

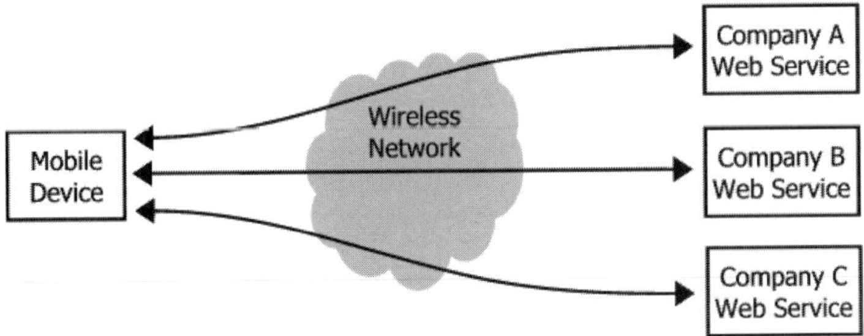

(a) Direct Web service invocation from a mobile device requires that all messages travel over the wireless network.

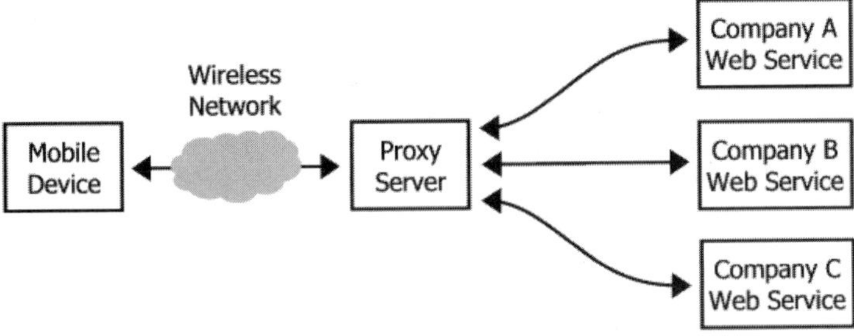

(b) Proxy-based Web service invocation reduces wireless network utilization and the energy consumed for communications.

Figure 10-9 Proxy-based Web service invocations reduce wireless network usage.

These and other related benefits are advantageous for the mobile application itself, as well as for users of the application.

Although they are usually easier to develop and have a plethora of advantages, proxy-based Web service invocation models also suffer from a few shortcomings. The most important of these is that each application has a single point of failure, namely the proxy server. If the proxy server becomes unavailable or experiences a decrease in performance due to increased usage, each mobile application that relies on that proxy will suffer.

Additionally, the proxy server introduces an additional hop along the network that can increase the mobile application's latency. In some cases, the proxy server may be located further away on the network than the actual Web service endpoint. Depending on the relative speeds of the wireless and wireline networks, a direct Web service invocation may introduce less latency than a proxied invocation.

Many of these issues can be addressed or at least reduced by using clusters of servers that are geographically distributed throughout the network for the Web service invocation proxies. If any particular proxy server goes down or becomes slow, the other servers within the distributed cluster can handle proxy requests.

Now that we have seen the implementation of a proxy-based mobile Web services system, in the next section we describe the design of mobile applications that directly access Web services.

Direct Mobile Web Service Access

Mobile applications can directly access Web services without an intermediary proxy server. MobileDirectTestServiceInvoke.java is a simple Java program that uses the InvokeService class we discussed earlier in the chapter and directly calls the ChessMaster Web service without using a proxy server for the invocation.

The Java source code in its entirety for the MobileDirectTestServiceInvoke.java class follows:

```
/*
 * MobileDirectTestServiceInvoke.java
 */

import java.util.StringTokenizer;

public class MobileDirectTestServiceInvoke
{
   public static void main ( String args[] )
   {
```

Each of the hard-coded values for the Web service endpoint, method name, and method arguments can be easily changed to build a dynamic mobile application capable of invoking any Web service with arbitrary input parameters.

```
      String servicename = "http://192.168.1.102:9090/hpws/
            soap/ChessMaster";
      String serviceclass = "ChessMaster";
      String method = "makeNextMove";
      String rettype = "String";
      String names = "board";
      String types = "String";
      String values = "1:1:2:1:3:1:4:1:5:1:6:1:7:1:8:1:
       1:2:2:3:3:3:4:2:5:6:6:2:7:2:8:2:
       1:8:2:8:3:8:4:8:5:8:6:8:8:6:8:8:
       1:7:2:7:3:6:4:7:5:7:6:7:7:7:8:7:";

      // Prepare to invoke the Web service by setting its
      //  endpoint location, method name, return type, and
      //  and arguments.
      InvokeService callWS = new InvokeService ();
      callWS.setMethod ( method );
      callWS.setReturnType ( rettype );
      callWS.setWSURL ( servicename );
```

Go through the name, type, and value tuples for each of the arguments to the Web service method using `StringTokenizers`. Use `callWS.setArgs` to update the `callWS` object with each set of extracted tokens.

```
      callWS.clearArgs ();
      StringTokenizer tokenizerNames =
    new StringTokenizer ( names , "," , false );
      StringTokenizer tokenizerTypes =
    new StringTokenizer ( types , "," , false );
      StringTokenizer tokenizerValues =
    new StringTokenizer ( values , "," , false );

      int k = 0;
      while ( tokenizerNames.hasMoreTokens () )
      {
         String tokType =
      tokenizerTypes.nextToken ().trim ();
         String tokName =
      tokenizerNames.nextToken ().trim ();
         String tokVal =
      tokenizerValues.nextToken ().trim ();

         callWS.setArgs ( k , tokType , tokName , tokVal );
         k = k + 1;
      }
```

After all of the arguments have been properly configured, we invoke the Web service by calling the `invokeWSMethod` method on the `callWS` object.

```
      Object callRetObj = callWS.invokeWSMethod ();
      String callRetObjString =
      ( String ) callRetObj.toString ();

      System.out.println ( "Result is: "
          + callRetObjString );
   }
}
```

Unfortunately, the support infrastructure necessary for this application is not available on many mobile devices. Supporting SOAP parsing requires a rich set of capabilities that is simply not available on many mobile platforms. For instance, the Java 2 Mobile Edition (J2ME) Connected Limited Device Configuration (CLDC) platform provides only limited string manipulation capabilities in an effort to improve runtime performance and reduce the overall footprint size. This lack of full Java string functionalities present significant issues for the underlying XML parsers upon which the SOAP parser is based.

Additionally, most SOAP parsers require that the entire XML document be resident in memory before the SOAP envelope is parsed. Most mobile platforms are based on Simple API for XML (SAX) parsers that never create a complete object model that is resident in memory.

The kSOAP platform addresses the need for a SOAP parser for mobile devices. kSOAP is built on Enhydra's kXML parser, and presents an efficient platform for mobile SOAP-based messaging. More information about kSOAP can be found at http://ksoap.enhydra.org.

The Java source code in its entirety for the MobileDirectKSoapTestServiceInvoke class follows. This class uses kSOAP to directly invoke the ChessMaster Web service on a remote machine.

```
/*
 * MobileDirectKSoapTestServiceInvoke.java
 */

import org.ksoap.ClassMap;
import org.ksoap.SoapObject;
import org.ksoap.transport.HttpTransportSE;
import java.util.StringTokenizer;

public class MobileDirectKSoapTestServiceInvoke
{
   public MobileDirectKSoapTestServiceInvoke ()
   {
   }

   public Object invokeService ( String serviceName ,
                                 String method ,
                                 String argNames ,
                                 String argValues )
   {
      Object resultObj = null;
      HttpTransportSE tse = null;
      SoapObject requestSoapObj;
      ClassMap cm;

      try
      {
         tse = new HttpTransportSE ( serviceName , method );
         tse.debug = true;
         cm = new ClassMap ();
         tse.setClassMap ( cm );

         requestSoapObj =
   new SoapObject ( "http:////tempuri.org//" ,
         method );
```

Since the Web service argument names and values are managed as comma-delimited tokens within larger strings, we must first extract tokens from each string. `StringTokenizer` may not be available on some mobile platforms. In this example, for code simplicity only, we use `StringTokenizer` objects. Depending on how the arguments to the Web service are managed, `StringTokenizer` may not be needed at all, or an alternate means of extracting string tokens can be implemented.

```
         StringTokenizer tokenizerNames =
    new StringTokenizer (  argNames ,
          "," ,
          false );
         StringTokenizer tokenizerValues =
    new StringTokenizer (  argValues ,
          "," ,
          false );

         while ( tokenizerNames.hasMoreTokens () )
         {
            String tokName =
    tokenizerNames.nextToken ().trim ();
            String tokVal =
    tokenizerValues.nextToken ().trim ();

      // Add each argument name and value
            requestSoapObj.addProperty ( tokName , tokVal );
         }
         resultObj = tse.call ( requestSoapObj );
      }
      catch ( Exception e )
      {
         System.out.println ( "InvokeService: Error" );
      }
```

We use the `HttpTransportSE` object's debug capabilities to output the request SOAP message that is sent from the mobile application to the remote Web service, as well as the response SOAP message that is returned by the remote Web service to the mobile application.

```
      System.out.println ( "SOAP Request is:\n" +
           tse.requestDump );
      System.out.println ( "SOAP Response is:\n" +
           tse.responseDump );

      return resultObj;
   }

   public static void main ( String args[] )
   {
      String servicename = "http://192.168.1.102:9090/hpws/
           soap/ChessMaster";
      String serviceclass = "ChessMaster";
      String method = "makeNextMove";
      String names = "board";
      String values = "1:1:2:1:3:1:4:1:5:1:6:1:7:1:8:1:
      1:2:2:3:3:3:4:2:5:6:6:2:7:2:8:2:1:
```

```
        8:2:8:3:8:4:8:5:8:6:8:8:6:8:8:1:7:
        2:7:3:6:4:7:5:7:6:7:7:7:8:7:";

        MobileDirectKSoapTestServiceInvoke mdks =
    new MobileDirectKSoapTestServiceInvoke ();
        String resultString =
    mdks.invokeService (  servicename ,
          method ,
          names ,
          values ).toString ().trim ();

        System.out.println ( "Result from Web service is: " +
              resultString );
    }
}
```

Figure 10-10 shows the SOAP envelope that is generated and sent to the ChessMaster Web service by the `MobileDirectKSoapTestServiceInvoke` class.

```
<SOAP-ENV:Envelope xmlns:xsi="http://www.w3.org/
    2001/XMLSchema-instance"
    xmlns:xsd=http://www.w3.org/2001/XMLSchema
    xmlns:SOAP-ENC="http://schemas.xmlsoap.org/
        soap/encoding/"
    xmlns:SOAP-ENV="http://schemas.xmlsoap.org/
        soap/envelope/">
  <SOAP-ENV:Body
    SOAP-ENV:encodingStyle="http://schemas.xmlsoap.org/
        soap/encoding/">
    <makeNextMove xmlns="http:////tempuri.org//"
        id="o0" SOAP-ENC:root="1">
      <board xmlns="" xsi:type="xsd:string">
          1:1:2:1:3:1:4:1:5:1:6:1:7:1:8:1:1:
          2:2:3:3:3:4:2:5:6:6:2:7:2:8:2:1:8:
          2:8:3:8:4:8:5:8:6:8:8:6:8:8:1:7:2:
          7:3:6:4:7:5:7:6:7:7:7:8:7:
      </board>
    </makeNextMove>
  </SOAP-ENV:Body>
</SOAP-ENV:Envelope>
```

Figure 10-10 The request SOAP envelope for invoking the ChessMaster Web service.

Figure 10-11 shows the SOAP envelope that is returned by the ChessMaster Web service to the `MobileDirectKSoapTestServiceInvoke` class. On receiving the SOAP envelope, the `MobileDirectKSoapTestServiceInvoke` class parses the envelope, and sets the value of `resultString` to "`3,6,3,5,`".

```
<?xml version="1.0" encoding="UTF-8"?>
<SOAP-ENV:Envelope xmlns:SOAP-ENV="http://schemas.
    xmlsoap.org/soap/envelope/">
  <SOAP-ENV:Body SOAP-ENV:encodingStyle="http://schemas.
      xmlsoap.org/soap/encoding/">
    <makeNextMoveResponse xmlns:SOAP-ENC=
        "http://schemas.xmlsoap.org/soap/encoding/"
        xmlns:xsd="http://www.w3.org/2001/XMLSchema"
        xmlns:xsi="http://www.w3.org/2001/XMLSchema-
                   instance">
      <return xsi:type="xsd:string">3,6,3,5,</return>
    </makeNextMoveResponse>
  </SOAP-ENV:Body>
</SOAP-ENV:Envelope>
```

Figure 10-11 The response SOAP envelope sent by the ChessMaster Web service.

In this section, we saw how to directly invoke Web services from mobile devices. Mobile platforms that have sufficient resources can use more traditional XML and SOAP parsers, while more limited devices can use platforms such as kSOAP and kXML.

J2ME Web Services

The Java 2 Micro Edition (J2ME) Web Service specification is an attempt at standardizing programmatic access to Web services from J2ME client applications. Currently, this specification exists as Java Specification Request (JSR) 172 as part the Java Community Process (JCP). More information about JSR-172 can bc found at http://www.jcp.org.

Web services can be accessed by J2ME clients today, but involve low-level network APIs that result in non-standard and proprietary implementations. Other specifications and initiatives, such as Java API for XML Processing (JAXP) and Java API for XML-based RPC (JAX-RPC), have addressed high-level and standardized means of accessing XML-based Web services from Java platforms. However, these initiatives do not sufficiently address the unique requirements and limitations of mobile environments, including footprint, computational resources, and wireless networks.

The goal of JSR-172 is to augment the J2ME platform to support two additional capabilities:

1. Support parsing of XML data.

   As mobile devices are used increasingly within enterprise environments, they will need to access structured data most likely in the form of XML. Instead of requiring individual applications to build XML parsing support themselves, an optional package for the J2ME platform makes sense. The J2ME XML parsing will support a strict subset of JAXP 1.2 such that the API implementation fits within the footprint and performance requirements of target mobile devices.

2. Support easy and standardized programmatic access to XML-based SOAP Web services.

   As an increasing number of useful Web services become available both within the enterprise as well as from third-party vendors, facilitating and standardizing easy programmatic access to these Web services becomes desirable. This optional package will define a standard API for accessing XML Web services from J2ME applications.

   The Web services support within the JSR-172 specification is meant to be independent of the XML parsing support—the Web services optional package is independent of the XML parsing optional package and can be used independently and separately from each other. The JSR-172 Web services specification only supports access to Web services by the mobile client and does not currently address hosting Web services by mobile devices. The Web services API is a strict subset of the JAX-RPC specification such that the API implementation fits within the footprint and performance requirements of target mobile devices.

Since the JSR-172 separates its support of Web services from its support of XML parsing, the remainder of this chapter discusses only the Web services support.

Supported APIs

The JSR-172 specification includes APIs that programmers can use to access remote Web services. The specification does not include any special server-side APIs, but instead specifies only client-side APIs.

The client-side APIs specified by the JSR-172 specification are the following APIs of the JAX-RPC specification:

- The `javax.xml.rpc.Stub` interface
- The javax.xml.rpc.JAXRPCException class

All J2ME Web service runtime system implementations must implement the above APIs.

Programming Model

The current version of the JSR-172 specification requires that developers building mobile applications that directly invoke remote Web services follow these steps:

1. Generate a local stub from the WSDL description of the remote Web service.
2. Instantiate an instance of the generated stub.
3. Invoke methods of the instantiated stub, which correspond to operations of the remote Web service.
4. Package the stub with the mobile application.

These steps are inline with standard Web service invocations using stubs. By following these steps and using an implementation of the JSR-172 specification, J2ME developers can easily build and deploy Web services-based mobile applications.

Summary

This chapter discussed Web services and applications within the context of mobile and wireless environments. The common availability of wireless cellular networks and wireless LANs together with advancements in highly integrated semiconductor components is enabling a wide array of mobile and wireless devices that are extending the reach of enterprise information "into the field."

The development of Web services-based applications that can run on mobile devices requires special thought. Mobile applications can access remote Web services either directly or through a proxy server. Using a proxy server to access Web services effectively creates a higher-level coarse-grained interface to the underlying Web services. This reduces usage of the wireless network and can favorably impact cost, performance, as well as power consumption. In many cases, where a non-mobile implementation of the application already exists, a proxy server-based Web services invocation is reasonably easy and straightforward, thus reducing development costs and time-to-market.

For some situations, direct invocation of Web services from mobile application is warranted. If the mobile platform is sufficiently robust, the application can generate and parse SOAP messages using standard SOAP and XML parsers. Alternately, more efficient and smaller footprint platforms such as kSOAP and kXML can be used.

Architect's Notes

- The steadily increasing number and type of mobile devices that are used within enterprise environments has critical ramifications for enterprise application development. In developing new applications or maintaining existing ones, keep in mind how your architectural decisions will affect how easily the application can be mobilized.
- An architecture well suited for accessing Web services from mobile applications is based on using proxy servers that intermediate between the mobile application and the remote Web services. Any protocol that meets the application's objectives (e.g., minimizing network bandwidth, network usage cost, power consumption, or XML parsing) can be used between the mobile application and the proxy server, even though the remote Web services may only support SOAP messages. In particular, J2EE Servlets present a simple and easy-to-use communications mechanism between the mobile application and the proxy server. Moreover, the use of this (and other) well-understood technology between the mobile application and the proxy server allows the developer to push such complex issues such as security away from the wireless network and onto the wired network between the proxy server and each Web service.
- In those situations where a proxy server is unavailable, resource-limited mobile applications can directly invoke Web services by using SOAP and XML parsers such as kSOAP and kXML, respectively.
- It is important to address security issues within mobile environments as wireless networks facilitate eavesdropping on potentially private conversations between applications and remote Web services.

CHAPTER 11

Portals and Services Management

In this chapter, we look at two technologies that further position Web services as a critical foundation on which to build enterprise systems. Each of these two technologies is related to systems that exist today, but address issues arising from the use of Web services within those systems. The first one addresses how to build user-facing portals by simply aggregating back-end Web services that instead of allowing access to programmatic data allows access to interactive presentation code, e.g., HTML fragments. This supports rapid integration and configuration of Web service portlets within a larger portal site, without custom application development.

The second technology addresses how to manage a growing number and type of Web services within enterprise environments. Managing Web services requires more than simply monitoring whether a particular application is up or down. A Web services management platform allows a company to manage individual Web services as business resources that can be manipulated and used to meet business goals.

We begin by looking at how to build portals that consume Web services as well as some related technologies that facilitate the development, maintenance, and customization of portals.

Portals

A portal is a user-facing aggregation point where multiple, potentially unrelated functionalities and services are housed. More generally, a portal can be thought of as a gateway to a variety of resources. Usually, the user is able to manage these resources by simply adding or removing them. This allows users to customize the portal to fit their needs and interests.

A variety of portal types exist, including consumer portals, corporate employee portals, and business partner portals. They all have the same purpose: to provide a single point-of-entry or gateway to a variety of resources that are important and relevant to their users.

Some well-known portals are yahoo.com, msn.com, and amazon.com. Both yahoo.com and msn.com provide a point of aggregation for mass-market services such as electronic mail, stock prices and news. Instead of having to go to one site to retrieve electronic mail, another site to view the performance of their stock portfolio, and yet another site to read the latest news headlines, users of these portals can simply visit one site to access and use all these services.

Topical or timely resources are also usually made available and highlighted through portals. For instance, when loan interest rates are low and people are thinking about refinancing their home mortgages, having a mortgage refinance calculator available at the same place where users read news about dropping interest rates makes sense.

Figure 11-1 depicts a portal that has been configured to aggregate a stock price tracker, a news headline service, and a home mortgage refinance calculator.

Portals provide a single location that users can turn to when they are looking for information and services. Instead of spending a lot of time searching through multiple locations, portals aggregate the relevant information at a single, easy-to-remember location.

A type of portal commonly found within enterprises is the corporate employee portal. An employee portal aggregates and makes available resources and services that are relevant to employees of a corporation. For example an employee portal may bring together the following information and services: payroll, expense report management, employment agreements and other legal documents, timesheets, 401(k) and other retirement plan information, health and medical plan information, as well as contact information for other employees.

Portals aggregate a lot of information. Not all of the information will be relevant or useful to everybody who uses the portal. Accordingly, portals allow users to configure or personalize

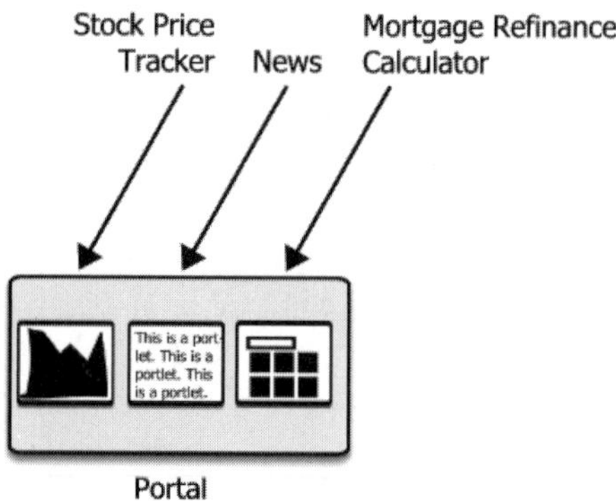

Figure 11-1 A portal is a user-facing aggregation point where multiple, potentially unrelated resources are housed.

the portal to show information and services that are only relevant to them. For example, an employee who does not or cannot participate in retirement plans may not want to clutter her portal with a lot of information and services related to 401(k)s and retirement plans. Of course, in the future, if the employee wants to participate in retirement plans, she can simply configure the portal to again display information and offer services related to the latest retirement plans offered by her company.

Now that we have seen the value and usefulness of portals and their utility as a user-configurable aggregation point, in the next section we look at different means by which to develop portals using Web services.

Programmatic and Interactive Web Service Interfaces

The promise of Web services is to simplify the development of applications by supporting the rapid composition of various software components. Individual service components provide functionalities that are composed together to implement an overall value-added capability. The composition of these service components requires custom programming that ties together the individual functionalities and perhaps includes additional business logic. This custom programming together with the consumed Web services represents the overall business logic of the application. The application user interface allows users to interact with the application's overall business logic. This is depicted in Figure 11-2.

Web services provide a data-centric, programmatic interface that allows general integration with other Web services and with application business logic. These programmatic interfaces consist of individual operations that can be invoked by a client application. To use such Web services to build a portlet—a single service within the larger portal context—requires developers who have expertise in that domain to first fully understand the interface of each Web service, invoke the correct service operations in the correct sequence, and finally design an appropriate user interface.

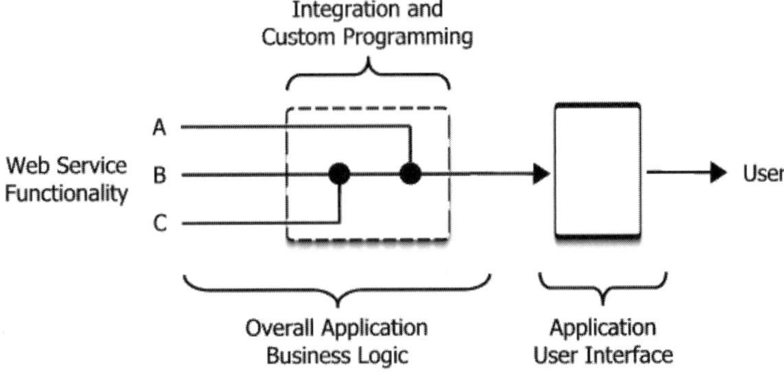

Figure 11-2 Constructing an application by integrating together Web services.

This is an expensive and time-consuming process for building each portlet. This is especially so since each portal will usually have tens of portlets and each portlet will often be used by a large number of portals. Consider the following two use cases:

- **Corporate employee portals** provide a single online location for employees to learn about and access the various services their company makes available to them. Some common examples of such services are expense report filing and management, as well as retirement plans such as 401(k)s. Many of these services are outsourced to third-party companies. Nonetheless, access to these services must be available through the employee corporate portal.

  If the individual services are exposed by third-party providers as Web services, they must be integrated together with custom business logic and user interface development into the corporate portal. This integration requires domain expertise and knowledge of the provider's Web service APIs. The initial customer development and, more importantly, the continuous maintenance reduce much of the cost savings and advantages of outsourcing the service to a third-party provider.

  Alternately, an ideal scenario would be one in which the IT department in charge of the corporate employee portal would simply be able to "plug in" the entire expense report filing and management capabilities including the user interface directly into the portal. The third-party service provider would handle improvements and changes to the individual Web services, integration logic, and user interface directly.
- **Manufactured components retail portals** provide a single online location where complex machinery and components from a large number of manufacturers can be purchased. Customers of the portal may need to consult component specifications and interact with component advisory tools before they are able to select the right parts for their needs. Unfortunately, most retail portals are unable to provide such manufacturer-specific tools and applications, and the portal's customers are forced to jump from the portal site to the Web sites of the individual manufacturers where the tools and applications are available.

  The customer's user experience and satisfaction would be greatly enhanced if all of the information, tools, and applications were available together with the retail portal's ordering and shipment handling capabilities. The customer would be able to access all required information as well as complete the purchase process easily all from a single site.

  Again, an ideal scenario would be one in which the retail portal would simply be able to "plug in" each manufacturers' tools and applications as portlets within the retail portal site. Each manufacturing company, which already has the deep domain expertise necessary to build and maintain not only the business logic but also the required user interface for each such tool, would have full control over each application with the portal being the channel into consumers. All development as well as improvements and changes to the individual Web services, integration logic, and user interface would be handled directly by each manufacturing company.

In these and other similar use cases, the difficulty in implementing a portal is that the end-user application provider is not in a position to understand the intricacies of the business or products of each of its back-end providers. For example, retail portal companies are only in the business of selling. They do not have the time nor the resources to understand the manufacturing process underlying each end product they sell.

When Web services are used to expose the information and services of the back-end provider to be integrated into the front-end portal, the challenges increase further. The data-centric interface of a Web service makes this integration difficult because:

- Front-end application developers must understand the necessary user interface and interactive flow of the back-end provider's application, requiring a significant learning curve and time.
- This interactive flow must be mapped to the individual methods of the Web service interface, necessitating an in-depth understanding of the API.
- As the back-end provider changes or updates its Web service APIs, the front-end application will also require modification and maintenance.
- It is difficult to ensure that the developed front-end application sufficiently uses the capabilities of the Web services and addresses the needs of users.

These issues could be addressed if the specific capabilities of each of the back-end providers could be made available to the front-end application by simply "plugging in" without the need for domain expertise or expensive custom development.

Figure 11-3 graphically compares the architectural differences between building custom portlets based on underlying Web services (as shown in Figure 11-3(a) with simply plugging in back-end Web services as portlets directly into a portal. In the latter case, a third-party (the provider of the Web service) develops the entire application, which is made available through a variety of portals and is directly accessible and useable by each portal's users without any custom development by the portal providers. Each of these applications is developed, managed, and maintained by the respective companies, not the portal provider.

In order to make entire applications, including the user interface and the interactive flow, available as Web services that portals can directly plug in requires a higher-level interface than existing data-centric programmatic Web service interfaces. As shown in Figure 11-4, such an interface will expose not only business logic and database layers, but also the user interface and interactivity layer. These interactive Web service interfaces allow direct and simple integration of individual applications—known as portlets—with the larger portal context through the user interface aggregation layer. By using interactive instead of programmatic interfaces, developers

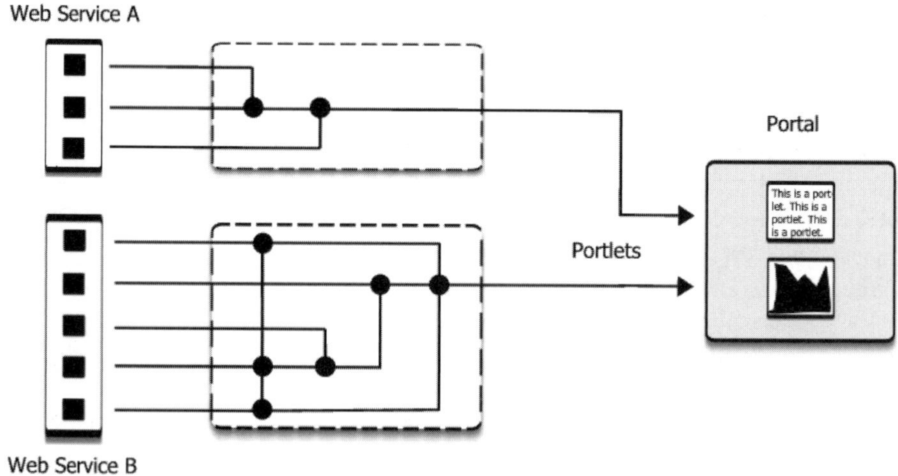

(a) Assembling a portal using Web service programmatic APIs.

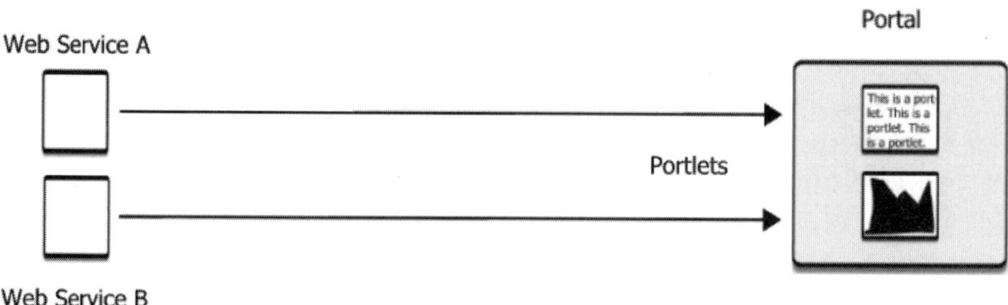

(b) Assembling a portal using interactive APIs.

Figure 11-3 Assembling a portal from individual Web services from (a) using the data-centric interfaces and (b) using interactive interfaces.

can package their applications as portlets and make them available to portals via industry standard Web services technologies.

With interactive Web service interfaces, portal developers and administrators can simply "plug in" individual Web services without custom programming and development. As the back-end Web services change and are modified over time, there is no maintenance to be done by the

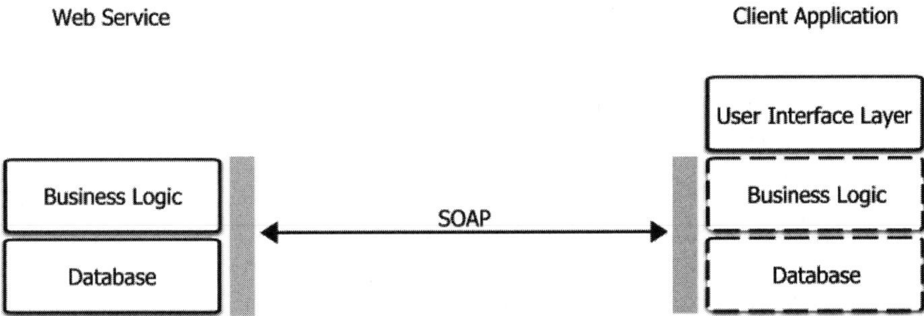

(a) A client application consuming a Web service using programmatic APIs.

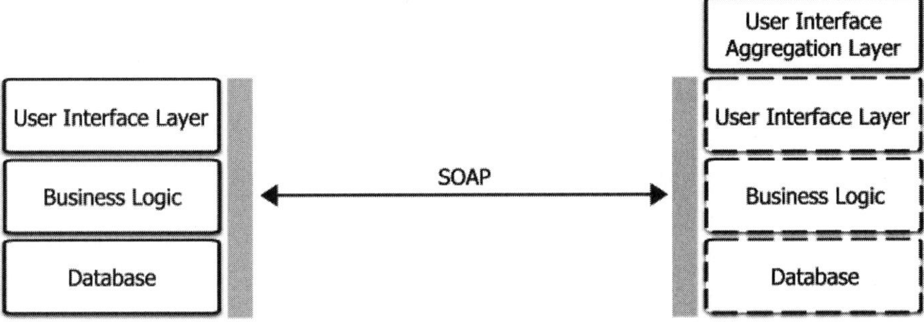

(b) A client application consuming a Web service using interactive APIs.

Figure 11-4 A client application consuming Web services using (a) data-centric programmatic and (b) interactive interfaces.

portal developer; all changes by the Web services provider are automatically made available to the portal users. Similarly, users can manage and personalize their portal by simply plugging in and unplugging the individual interactive Web service portlets.

Now that we have seen the utility of user interaction-centric interactive interfaces to Web services in addition to data-centric programmatic interfaces, we next look at technologies and system specifications to build and consume such interactive Web services.

The WSRP and WSIA Specifications

Web Services for Interactive Applications (WSIA) and Web Services for Remote Portlets (WSRP) are specifications for user interaction-centric interactive Web services based on existing, industry standard Web services technologies.

These technologies specify a means for communication between a client application and a Web service using SOAP in which the response to a Web service invocation is a fragment of presentation code (e.g., HTML) that can be embedded within a larger set of pages, such as a portal. Moreover, links within the original presentation fragment support user actions that communicate with the Web service and returns another presentation fragment, thus enabling multi-page user interactivity.

The WSIA and WSRP specifications evolved out of multiple efforts by different vendors to provide presentation-level interfaces to Web services. Earlier initiatives such as Web Service Expression Language (WSXL) and Web Service User Interface (WSUI) as well as a number of portal integration frameworks were brought together to form the two working groups of WSIA and WSRP within the OASIS standards organization. The WSIA working group was charged with the task of specifying the means to develop and expose presentation-level interfaces to Web services, while WSRP was changed to focus on additional required capabilities specific to portals. More information about the WSIA and WSRP standards can be found at www.oasis-open.org.

In the remaining subsections, we review the WSRP specification, and the issues around building portlets and portals with WSRP.

Building Portlets and Portals with WSRP

Before we continue with the WSRP specification, it is important to define and understand the three actors involved in a flow. The WSRP standard specifies three actors involved in a flow:

- **Producers** are Web services that are made available as WSRP services. An example of a producer is a weather Web service that provides real-time weather information.
- **Consumers** use WSRP services, usually within a larger context such as a portal. An example of a consumer is a portal toolkit or framework that aggregates and manages multiple WSRP services.
- **End users** are actual people who use and interact with a portal that uses WSRP services.

Based on these actor definitions, WSRP specifies the calls that enable a consumer to retrieve presentation code fragments from a Producer. The specification also defines what a valid presentation code fragment is, and how these fragments can be integrated within a larger presentation context.

The WSRP protocol is segmented into four different interfaces:

- **Service Description** interface is implemented by the producer and includes a single, simple operation that allows the consumer to retrieve a description of the Producer.
- **Markup** interface is implemented by the producer and includes operations for embedding producer markup within the consumer.

- **Portlet Entity Management** interface includes operations that allow the consumer to customize portlet entities by setting and configuring properties.
- **Registration** interface includes operations that allow the consumer to register itself with the Producer.

In the remainder of this subsection, we look at the major operations of each of these four interfaces. All of the operations supported by each interface together with their signatures can be found in the WSRP specification at www.oasis-open.org.

The Service Description interface has a single operation:

- **`getServiceDescription`** returns a description as well as metadata for the Producer portlet. The information returned from this operation includes such things as the type of presentation markup, and is used by the consumer to properly manage interactions between the end user and the producer.

The key operations of the Markup interface are:

- **`getMarkup`**: The consumer invokes the `getMarkup` operation to retrieve the current presentation markup.
- **`performInteraction`**: The consumer invokes this operation in response to the end user interacting with the producer's markup. End user interactions can include the end user clicking on a hyperlink or submitting a form.
  End user interaction with the producer markup must pass through the consumer, and hyperlinks URLs and form URLs are referred to as Interaction URLs. Additional information and parameters are passed using these Interaction URLs and allow the consumer to know the call type as well as the parameters to use in the subsequent call to the producer.

The key operations of the Portlet Entity Management interface are:

- **`getPortletEntityPropertyDescription`**: The consumer invokes this operation to retrieve a listing of the properties available for a portlet entity.
- **`getPortletEntityDescription`**: The consumer invokes this operation to retrieve the description of a portlet entity.
- **`setPortletEntityProperties`**: The consumer invokes this operation to set the values of entity properties.
- **`getPortletEntityProperties`**: The consumer invokes this operation to retrieve the values of entity properties.
- **`clonePortletEntity`**: The consumer invokes this operation to create a new configured portlet entity.
- **`destroyPortletEntities`**: The consumer invokes this operation to destroy a created configured portlet entity.

The key operations of the Registration Management interface are:

- **`register`**: The consumer invokes this operation to register itself with the producer. As part of the registration process, the consumer passes information about itself to the producer.
- **`deregister`:** The consumer invokes this operation to deregister and end its relationship with the Producer.
- **`modifyRegistration`:** The consumer invokes this operation to notify the Producer of any changes to the consumer.

Figure 11-5 depicts the steady-state interaction between the three actors: WSRP end users, consumers, and producers. In response to the end user wanting to view a portlet, the consumer invokes the `getMarkup` operation of the producer. The producer generates the appropriate markup fragment and returns it to the consumer. If the end user selects a hyperlink or submits form data, the consumer captures the information and forwards it to the producer by invoking the `performInteraction` operation. The producer returns the updated state to the consumer. The consumer again invokes the `getMarkup` operation of the producer together with the updated state to retrieve the current markup fragment for the portlet.

Now that we have a good idea about the interaction between the end user, consumer, and producer actors within a WSRP environment, we next discuss some of the restrictions that are placed on these interactions so that producer markup fragments can be appropriately embedded and used within the larger portal context.

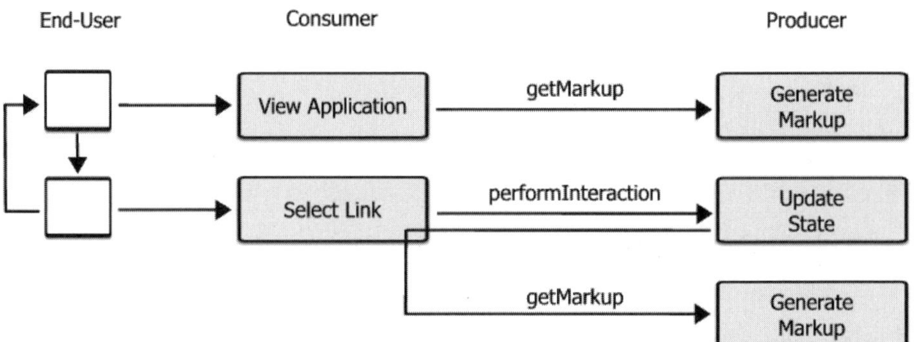

Figure 11-5 Interaction between the three actors : WSRP end users, consumers, and producers.

Restrictions

The presentation code fragments returned by a WSRP service have restrictions that allow a WSRP service Consumer to aggregate the code fragments together into the larger context of the portal.

Fundamentally, the markup fragments generated by each WSRP and returned must be aggregated together into a single markup page, which is then returned to the end user. This disallows the use of all markup language features and instead requires that the markup fragment returned is only a subset of the overall markup language.

For example, in the case of HTML, tags such as <body>, <frame>, <frameset>, <head>, <html>, and <title> are not allowed to be returned by a WSRP service. It is also usually advisable that presentation style information such as the font or color of text is not hard coded into the returned markup. This allows the portal to specify these tags and create a consistent "look and feel" for all of the consumed portlets across the entire portal page.

An additional restriction placed on the markup fragments returned by WSRP services has to do with embedded hyperlinks. Hyperlinks allow interactivity between the End-user and the WSRP Producer. However, since the end-user is interacting with the Producer via the Consumer, hyperlink URLs must be addressed to and resolved by the Consumer and not by the Producer directly.

URL rewriting techniques can be used to modify the link to be returned by the WSRP Producer by a link tag that routes the HTTP GET or HTTP POST requests to the WSRP Consumer. The prefix of the link URL routes the action to the Consumer. The suffix of the URL contains additional information, including the WSRP service, the action, and additional parameters, which can then be used by the WSRP Consumer to access the service and update the entire portal page.

These URL links can be generated in one of two ways. A WSRP Consumer can send a URL template to the WSRP Producer when it invokes the `getMarkup` method. In this case, the Producer returns all final interaction URLs within the markup fragment. Otherwise, the Producer can return interaction URLs that conform to a certain pattern. These URL patterns can then be parsed by the Consumer, and rewritten so that user actions are routed through the Consumer application. The first method of the Producer returning the final interaction URLs is known as Producer URL Writing, while the second method of the Consumer rewriting the URLs returned by the Producer is known as Consumer URL Writing.

Deploying and Locating Services

To use WSRP services within portals, information about the services must first be made known to potential Consumers. Typically, this will be accomplished by publishing information about the service in registries such as UDDI.

All WSRP services implement the same WSDL interface, which ensures that any WSRP service can be consumed and used by any WSRP-compliant portal. Additional information is also provided to portal administrators and end-users to easily select and use WSRP services. This information includes service name, description, and supported markup languages.

Locating WSRP services within registries such as UDDI is simply a matter of querying the registry for all services that implement the WSRP WSDL `tModel`. Subsetting based on particular business names or desired attributes and properties can further narrow the search. Creating, managing, and destroying instances of WSRP services will usually be handled by the Consumer platform, such as a portal toolkit. In the remainder of this section, we briefly review the key interactions supported between WSRP services and WSRP compliant portals.

Putting It All Together

In this subsection, we take a closer look at the interaction between the Consumer and the Producer as well as between the Consumer and the End-user by analyzing the exchanged messages. In this example, the Producer is a simple service that generates two HTML pages that are hyperlinked to each other.

First, the Consumer invokes the `getServiceDescription` operation of the Producer to understand its capabilities. Figure 11-6 shows the response returned by the Producer as a result of this invocation.

```
<getServiceDescriptionResponse
  xmlns="http://www.oasis-
         open.org/committees/wsrp/v1/wsdl/types">
  <offeredEntities>
    <entityHandle>
      thisHandle
    </entityHandle>
    <markupTypes>
      <markupType>text/html</markupType>
      <locales>en</locales>
      <modes>view</modes>
      <windowStates>normal</windowStates>
    </markupTypes>
    <doesUrlTemplateProcessing>
      false
    </doesUrlTemplateProcessing>
  </offeredEntities>
</getServiceDescriptionResponse>
```

Figure 11-6 The response from the invocation of the `getServiceDescription` operation.

The response message gives the Consumer a lot of information about the Producer portlet. The `view` value of the `modes` tag specifies that the markup returned will be pages that the End-user can interact with or it may simple be interaction-free content. Other possible values include `edit`, which specifies that the returned markup will allow the End-user to enter customization data, `help`. This specifies that the returned markup will provide the End-user with context-sensitive help information to explain the usage of the portlet, and `preview`, which specifies that the returned markup will be a sample of how the markup that would be returned under the `view` mode will appear within the current configuration.

The `false` value of the `doesUrlTemplateProcessing` tag specifies that the Producer does not perform URL writing, and instead relies on the Consumer to specify the correct interaction URL. That is, this Producer Web service relies on Consumer URL Writing and does not perform Producer URL Writing.

Figure 11-7 depicts the response message from the Producer after the Consumer invokes the `getMarkup` operation of the Producer.

```
<getMarkupResponse
    xmlns="http://www.oasis-open.org/committees/wsrp/v1/
          wsdl/types"
  <markupContext>
    <markup>
      <![CDATA[
        <div class=portlet-font>
          <p>Hello World! This Is Page One.<p>
          <a href="wsrp-rewrite?
                   wsrp-urlType=render&
                   wsrp-navigationalState=two&
                   wsrp-mode=view&
                   wsrp-windowState=normal/wsrp-rewrite">
          Click Here To Go To Page Two</a>
        </div>
      ]]>
    </markup>
    <locale>en</locale>
    <markupType>text/html</markupType>
    <requiresUrlRewriting>true</requiresUrlRewriting>
  </markupContext>
</getMarkupResponse>
```

Figure 11-7 The response to the invocation of the `getMarkup` operation with `navigationalState` set to "one".

The response message is an XML message that contains the HTML fragment to be displayed as part of this portlet. First, note the Cascading Style Sheet (CSS) class name `portlet-font` that conforms the font of the portlet to be that used throughout the overall portal.

Based on the response message of Figure 11-7, the content that is displayed within the portlet is shown in Figure 11-8.

```
Hello World! This Is Page One.

Click Here To Go To Page Two
```

Figure 11-8 The content displayed within the portlet.

The value of the `href` attribute for the `Click Here To Go To Page Two` link specifies how the state of the portlet should be updated when the user clicks on the link. The current state as represented by `wsrpnavigationalState` is `one`. After the user clicks on the link, the `wsrpnavigationalState` is set to `two`. The states `one` and `two` are used internally by the Producer to represent the two possible portlet content segments. The `wsrp-urlType=render` results in the Consumer invoking the `getMarkup()` operation of the Producer.

Since the value of the `requiresUrlRewriting` tag is `true`, the string that is the value of the `href` attribute must be converted to an actual URL before it is sent to the End-user. In order for the Consumer to generate the appropriate URL, it first locates the delimiters: `wsrp-rewrite?` and `/wsrp-rewrite` within the existing `href` attribute value. The string contained within these delimiters is:

```
wsrp-urlType=render&
wsrp-navigationalState=two&
wsrp-mode=view&
wsrp-windowState=normal
```

Each of these name-value pairs are converted to an actual URL as follows:

```
http://consumer.example.org/portletContainerPath/
render?mode=view&navigationalState=two&windowState=normal
```

Finally, the markup fragment that is embedded within the overall portal is shown in Figure 11-9.

Multiple such markup fragments, each fragment representing the interactive user interface of a WSRP service, comprise a WSRP portal.

```
<div class=portlet-font>
  <p>Hello World! This Is Page One.<p>
  <a href="http://consumer.example.org/
          portletContainerPath/render?mode=view&
          navigationalState=two&windowState=normal">
        Click Here To Go To Page Two</a>
</div>
```

Figure 11-9 The HTML markup fragment that is embedded within the overall portal after the Consumer processes the markup and performs URL rewriting.

Summary

In this section, we looked at technologies that facilitate the development and maintenance of Web services-based portals. A portal is a user-facing aggregation point where multiple, potentially unrelated functionalities and services are housed. Usually, portals are used as a gateway to consumer type of services, such as news, electronic mail, and stock prices, or to corporate employee services, such retirement planning and account information, time cards and payroll, as well as employment agreements and other legal documents.

Many of these portal services are outsourced to or licensed from third-party providers. Since the portal developer will usually be aggregating a large variety of services, he will probably not have deep expertise in all of the domains represented by those services. Accordingly, a data-centric programmatic interface that requires domain expertise to aggregate and use each of the underlying Web services is impractical.

Instead, the WSRP specification defines a higher-level user-interface-based interactive interface to Web services. Rather than invoking fine-grained individual, service-specific operations of each Web service, the consumer makes generic, coarse-grained invocations such as `getMarkup()`, which returns the entire markup fragment for that portlet within the overall portal. By using WSRP-compliant Web services, a portal developer can simply embed the markup fragments returned from each WSRP portlet within the larger portal context. This can be done without having past experience with the domain of the Web service or in-depth knowledge of the specific Web service.

In the next section, we switch gears and look at how the growing development and usage of Web services is requiring an architectural layer to facilitate the management and control of these individual resources.

Web Services Management

As the number of Web services increases and starts to invade the enterprise software environment, a management layer becomes increasingly important. Currently the demand for Web services management products is not very high since most enterprise Web service initiatives are still in their infancy and involve just a handful of services. As more of these initiatives are migrated from pilot projects to deployment rollouts and as the number of consumed Web services increases, Web services management will quickly become a critical capability.

In this section, we briefly explore the concepts and issues underlying Web services management. We discuss what Web services management is, why it is important, and how this technology can be used to build robust and cost-effective enterprise systems. We also discuss the Web Services Distributed Management (WSDM) standard.

The Objectives of Web Services Management

Web services allow individual functional software components to be developed and exposed to other applications and services. This level of fine granularity is leading to an explosion in the number of Web services that are available from different sources and from different vendors. A Web services management platform enables a company to manage individual Web services as business resources that can be manipulated and used to meet business goals. Web services management is not just about monitoring the uptime of software components.

How can Web services management be used to further business goals? Simply put, developing a Web service and making it available for others does not necessarily fulfill any business goal. Neither does building an application that consumes Web services.

Developed Web services can be aligned to business goals by:

- Making the service available as a revenue-generating service that is tied into the company's billing and invoicing system.
- Allowing priority-based access to selected Web services for customers who pay premium prices.
- Reducing duplication of effort and costs by allowing others a view into all available Web services so that the same functionality is not developed again.

Applications that consume Web services can be aligned to business goals by:

- Making available the different vendors that provide the desired Web service functionality.
- Allowing changes to the consumed Web services based on the most competitive pricing or quality.
- Monitoring who within the company is using which services.
- Determining which people or groups should be charged for Web service usage.
- Reporting on the level of service received by applications.

Sometimes architects question the value of adding another architectural layer, instead of just incorporating the required capabilities within the application or service. A few reasons necessitate the Web services management layer. First, the Web services platform is a moving target: new technologies are being added, existing technologies are being changed and some technologies are even being removed all together. The composition of the Web services platform will determine the requirements for services management. Additionally, industry standards for Web services management are under development and are changing. If services management capabilities were to be built into applications themselves, each application would have to be modified and maintained as the Web services management technologies and standards changed. The time and expertise necessary to maintain these applications would be prohibitively expensive. By abstracting out the services management technologies into a distinct architectural layer, we are able to achieve cost-effective application development and maintenance without requiring all application developers to be fluently versed in all services management issues. A distinct management layer also dissuades individual developers or groups from designing and implementing their own management solutions, which may be difficult or expensive to rectify and coordinate with other management solutions.

Web Services Management Modules

The individual modules that comprise and will be required of a Web services management platform will evolve and change over time with the increasing use of Web services. Nonetheless, Figure 11-10 depicts a basic Web services management platform and how this platform fits within a Web services architecture. Different Web services interfaces are available for applications to invoke. Application requests to a Web service interface are routed through the Web services management modules to the actual service implementation. The service implementations can be located on the same machine as the Web services management platform, or they may be remotely located and connected by networks.

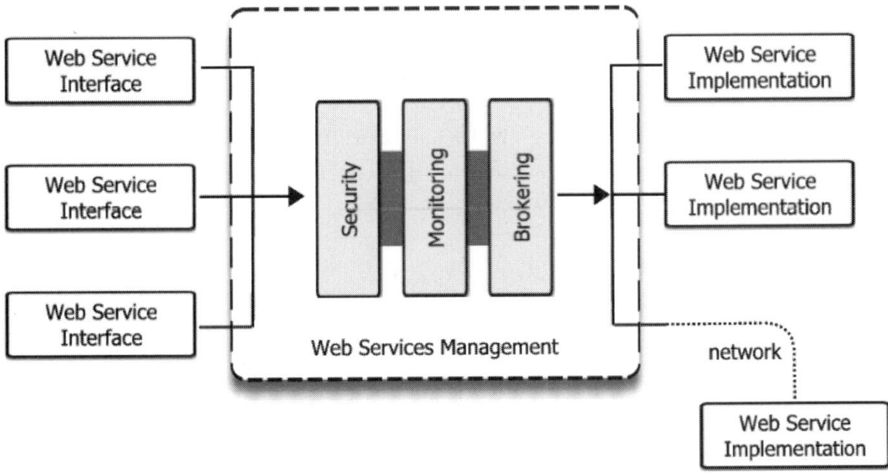

Figure 11-10 The use of Web services management within an enterprise Web services environment.

Security. One of the major hallmarks of Web services management is to allow secure and authorized access to Web services. The Security module of the Web services management platform can be thought of as an XML application firewall that keeps unwanted SOAP traffic out but facilitates and records access by authorized users.

Network firewalls do not sufficiently address the needs of secure Web services. For starters, firewalls enforce policies based on analysis at the packet level. An effective Web services firewall will need to apply policies at the message level, not at the individual packet level. Policies and analysis at the SOAP message layer affords additional opportunities for filtering and security that are not available at simply the packet layer.

Since many Web services will be available to both internal consumers (within the enterprise) as well as external, public consumers, the Security module must provide a variety of capabilities:

- Encryption and decryption
- Authentication and authorization
- Single sign-on
- Intrusion detection and filtering
- Non-repudiation

Even within these individual capabilities, the Security module will have to support a number of mechanisms. For example, consider some of the different means of verifying the identity of Web service users: username and password pairs, certificates, and license keys. Although a username-password pair may work well for a small number of corporate partners who are using a service, such an authentication scheme may not work well for a service that is accessible by the public.

Security solutions such as SSL also may fall short. SSL provides security between two servers, but does not adequately address the scenario in which a SOAP message is routed through multiple servers along the way to its final endpoint destination. Authentication information needs to be forwarded to servers, but a standard mechanism for doing so using SOAP messages does not yet exist. If the secure Web server handles authentication and data decryption, the information sent to the endpoint is insecure. Some of these issues will be addressed by solutions such as the Liberty Alliance and Microsoft's Passport.

Monitoring. Once service requests have been identified and approved for access, they must be monitored and recorded for accounting and performance tracking needs. Web services monitoring involves a variety of steps, including:

- Usage and Performance Logging: A set of applications, each with a number of users, will invoke Web services. For each such invocation, a record is kept of each user as well as the performance of the service for that user. Decreased performance by a Web service may trigger alerts notifying the appropriate managers and decision makers. The statistics gathered are important from a reporting perspective, but also have tremendous value in improving a service or application's performance.

- Accounting: Some services will be available for free, while others will be premium services available only through a subscription or a fee. Various service providers will have diverse rates and may be different depending on the user. The accounting capabilities within the monitoring module support a variety of charging, reporting, and dispute reconciliation mechanisms. Since the access fees to Web services will typically be small, the micro-charges and micro-payments will be aggregated together before being inserted into the corporate accounting software.
- Access Control: Once a user has been properly identified and authenticated, access control mechanisms are used to determine whether that user has access to a particular Web service. In some cases, a single Web service may have different implementations and deployments that are available for different users, perhaps based on subscription or pricing levels.
- Performance and Quality of Service Management: Monitoring the performance of Web services will be critical as many enterprises will not rely on third-party service providers without a contractual obligation with respect to a service level. Such service level agreements (SLAs) will be binding on both service providers and service consumers. The performance management capabilities within the monitoring module are important for both service providers and for service consumers. Providers must make sure that their services are delivering the required performance, and must also monitor that their consumers are adhering to their obligations. Similarly, consumers must monitor that their applications are adhering to their SLAs and must also monitor that their service providers are doing the same.

Brokering. Once it has been authenticated and identified, and it has been monitored, recorded, and access control rules have been applied, a service request is ready for brokering. Brokering involves a number of capabilities, including:

- Service Selection and Routing: Hardwiring an application to use a particular Web service reduces the robustness of the application, and also does not allow it to efficiently take advantage of new services. By brokering service requests, a single request can dynamically select the most appropriate service implementation and automatically route the request to that endpoint. This is important not only for changes to a service's endpoint information, but also as new competing services become available. The service selection can be based on quality of service and performance information, or even by analyzing the contents of the message body.
- Request Transformation: Different service implementations may have different interfaces or format needs. In the process of routing a request to a different service implementation, a service request may need to be transformed to meet the requirements of the dynamically selected service implementation.

- Service Invocation: Not all service implementations may support the same version of a communications protocol, or even the same protocol. The exact messaging requirements of a particular service should be abstracted away, so that applications have access to a wide variety of services to use. Whether a service is a SOAP service or a CORBA service makes no difference to the consuming application; the functional capabilities of the service should be the only relevant issue.

We have discussed some of the key features required of a Web services management platform. By abstracting services management into a separate architectural layer, applications and services can be efficiently developed, even as the Web services management technologies and standards evolve and change.

Web Services Distributed Management

Web Services Distributed Management (WSDM) is the name given to a new technical committee formed within the Organization for the Advancement of Structured Information Standards (OASIS) standards body. The objective of the WSDM technical committee is to define an industry standard specification for Web services management. This includes not only defining a model for Web services as manageable resources of an enterprise, but also using Web services technologies to manage distributed resources.

This process is still in its early stages, and the technical committee expects to release the initial specification in January 2004. The latest information about the WSDM specification and the progress of the technical committee can be found at http://www.oasis-open.org.

Summary

In this chapter, we took a brief look at two different Web services technologies. The first one allows developers to quickly build portals by consuming Web services. Recognizing that the standard data-centric programmatic interface of Web services does not facilitate building portals that may potentially consist of a wide variety of portlets, WSRP specification defines a higher-level interactive interface to Web services. Interactive interfaces do not expose fine-grained service-specific operations, but instead expose the user interface (markup) of the Web service through a set of coarse-grained generic operations. The portal developer does not need in-depth domain knowledge for each consumed Web service. A portal can consume any WSRP-compliant service by using these same operations across all of the Web services.

The second technology addresses the need for an architectural layer for the monitoring and management of Web services. Typical systems management software helps to answer questions such as whether a piece of software or a system is up or down. The systems that are monitored and managed are larger, and the information that is gathered is at a more coarse granularity. The advent of Web services places different and additional requirements for monitoring and management systems. The sheer number of Web services and the enormous transaction volume they will create differentiates Web services management systems from traditional systems management environments. Moreover, Web services will be implemented on heterogeneous platforms and many will be located outside of the enterprise firewall. Given the new and additional requirements placed on management systems by Web services, the WSDM specification is trying to define a set of industry-wide management and monitoring modules. This will provide a standard and well-understood means of offering security, access control, accounting, monitoring and logging, performance and quality of service, as well as brokering across multiple Web services and across multiple organizations.

Architect's Notes

- Data-centric programmatic interfaces provide fine-grained access to Web services, but also require in-depth domain expertise to use.
- Interactive interfaces provide a higher-level access model to Web services in which instead of individual operations being exposed, the user interface markup is exposed to the client application. Interactive Web service interfaces provide a set of standard invocation calls that facilitate retrieving each Web service's markup as well as updating the state of each Web service based on user interactivity.
- The WSRP specification is based on interactive interfaces and defines a framework for using Web services within portals. By using interactive interfaces instead of programmatic interfaces, individual Web service portlets can be easily added or removed from the overall portal without custom programming and knowledge of the Web service or its functional domain.
- Simply developing a Web service and making it available for others does not necessarily fulfill any business goal. A Web services management platform enables a company to manage individual Web services as business resources that can be manipulated and used to meet business goals.

PART 3

Putting It All Together—Building Real World Enterprise Web Services and Applications

In this third and final part of the book, we use the industry standards, technologies, and best practices described in the previous two sections to build real world enterprise Web services and applications. The two chapters in this section are filled with source code and are a detailed step-by-step guide to developing Web services and client applications that use Web services.

Any application can be put together in a haphazard manner, but these applications are almost never appropriate for a real world production environment. Real world enterprise applications must be easy to develop, even easier to customize and maintain, support transactional requirements, allow seamless porting to multiple devices and platforms, and so on. Enterprise Web Services and Web Services-based applications cannot be developed by just reading through the SOAP or WSDL standards. Developers must understand a number of different standards and technologies and, more importantly, their inter-relationships and best practices for their use.

Chapter 12: Real World Web Service Application Development—Foundations. In Chapter 12, we go step-by-step and develop a Web services application as well as the consumed Web services using only the vanilla Web services technologies as described in Section One. We not only describe how to build the system and provide the source code, but we also discuss how to deploy the Web services and application onto the Tomcat application server and the Axis

SOAP server (both of which are freely available). We build the application in this chapter in an effort to illustrate that the core Web services platform is simply a set of enabling technologies for XML-based distributed computing.

Chapter 13: Real World Web Service Application Development—Advanced Technologies. The exchange of XML messages between businesses is only the tip of the iceberg as far as enterprise computing is concerned. To enable true enterprise-level computing with Web services, we must address the enterprise requirements that enable dependable applications to be built. In Chapter 13 we address these requirements by adding security, transactionality, workflow, and mobility into the application we developed in Chapter 12.

Chapter 14: Epilogue. We have seen a number of important concepts in Web services, and in Chapters 12 and 13 we have seen how those concepts can be put into practice. In Chapter 14, we put that knowledge into perspective, summarizing the important points of each technology and offering advice on how these technologies may evolve as Web services practice matures.

After reading Part 3, you will have a thorough understanding of the steps necessary to build and deploy Web services and client applications that meet enterprise requirements.

CHAPTER 12

Real World Web Service Application Development—Foundations

In this chapter we go step-by-step and develop a Web services application as well as the consumed Web services using only the technologies of the core Web services platform—SOAP and WSDL. In the next chapter, we build on and extend this application, using the technologies and standards discussed in the second section of this book, and develop an enterprise-class system.

We build the application in this chapter in an effort to illustrate that the core Web services platform is simply a set of enabling technologies for XML-based distributed computing. Additional technologies and architectural patterns for workflow, mobile, quality-of-service, security, and transactions are necessary to develop Web services and applications that meet enterprise requirements.

For the application that we will develop in this chapter, we have chosen enterprise procurement. The need to procure goods and services from other businesses is required for almost all companies. It is also one of the most difficult, time consuming, and expensive processes. The widespread adoption of Web services opens up the door to an automated procurement process that reduces overhead, operational inefficiencies, and purchasing errors.

Enterprise Procurement

Most companies have to buy goods or services from other companies in the course of doing their business. The procurement can be for physical components such as silicon chips, plastic components, or power modules, as well as for services such as contract manufacturing or overnight courier services.

Procurement within an enterprise environment is extremely complex. Just some of the key issues that must be addressed include:

- There are multiple vendors that provide the same or similar goods or services.
- There may be existing relationships or most-preferred statuses in place with one or more of the vendors to provide preferential pricing, and these change constantly.
- There may be component or service credits due from one or more vendors that motivate purchasing from those vendors, even if the unit price is slightly higher.
- For strategic or political reasons, the company may want to give or withhold business from particular vendors.
- The number and set of vendors depends on what is being procured and may include small-to-medium businesses (including so called "mom-and-pop shops").
- Some vendors may offer a good price, but will not have the required quantity, thus necessitating procuring from multiple vendors.
- The price and quantity available may change, and often may do so rapidly.
- Different vendors may have different means of interacting with their sales offices, including phone, e-mail, and fax.

The person responsible for procuring a particular product or service must analyze these and many more issues. What is worse is that often once the optimal vendor has been identified, by the time the order is ready to be placed the price or quantity available may have changed, requiring complete reanalysis. Moreover, partnerships, most preferred status, and buying policies change quickly, often within hours. Propagating these changes throughout the entire procurement staff (that may be geographically distributed) takes time. The result is inefficient and non-optimal purchasing decisions. Moreover, simple human-error and negligence result in costly purchasing errors such as incorrect part numbers, shipping addresses, or quantities.

Procurement management applications are available. But they have limited value, as the applications themselves cannot always interface with each vendor's inventory and sales processes.

Web services have the potential to change this. The widespread adoption of Web services technologies by companies will allow easy access to enterprise processes and functions, such as inventory and sales. This will enable the development of truly useful enterprise procurement applications.

Figure 12-1 depicts the functionality of an enterprise procurement application. The application essentially acts as a gateway to the inventory and sales processes of vendors, each of which sells the products of manufacturers.

Next, we take an in-depth look at the required functionality for our enterprise procurement application, as well as the desired system architecture.

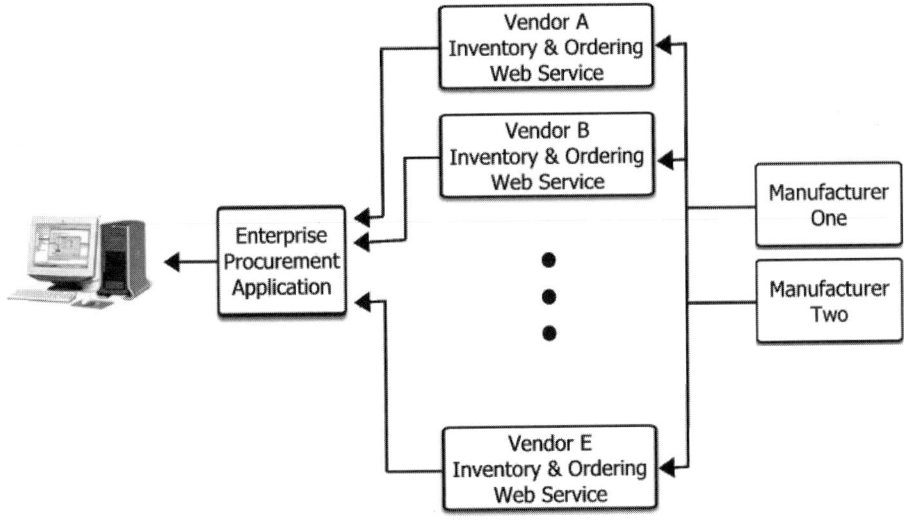

Figure 12-1 An enterprise procurement application acts like a gateway between the procurement administrator and the vendors that sell goods and services.

System Functionality and Architecture

The basic functionality of our Enterprise Procurement System (EPS) application is to:

- Provide a Web-based interface that allows users to browse a catalog of goods and services from which they can select a particular part number.
- Provide a Web-based interface that allows users to enter a part number to be located, the desired quantity, and whether the user is interested in optimizing for cost (if a high-volume product is being built) or for lead time (if a prototype needs to be built rapidly).
- Connect to the Web services of a set of vendors and use the entered part number, quantity, and optimization criteria (cost or lead time) to get a price or lead time quote.
- Analyze the returned values from the vendor Web services, and select the best choice.
- Present the best price or lead-time from the available vendors that meet the user's procurement needs.
- If the part cannot be located, consult another Web service to find alternate part numbers that may have similar functionality to that of the first part.
- Present the alternate part number to the user; otherwise, inform the user that there is no such alternate part.

Figure 12-2 shows a block diagram depicting the overall system architecture of the EPS application.

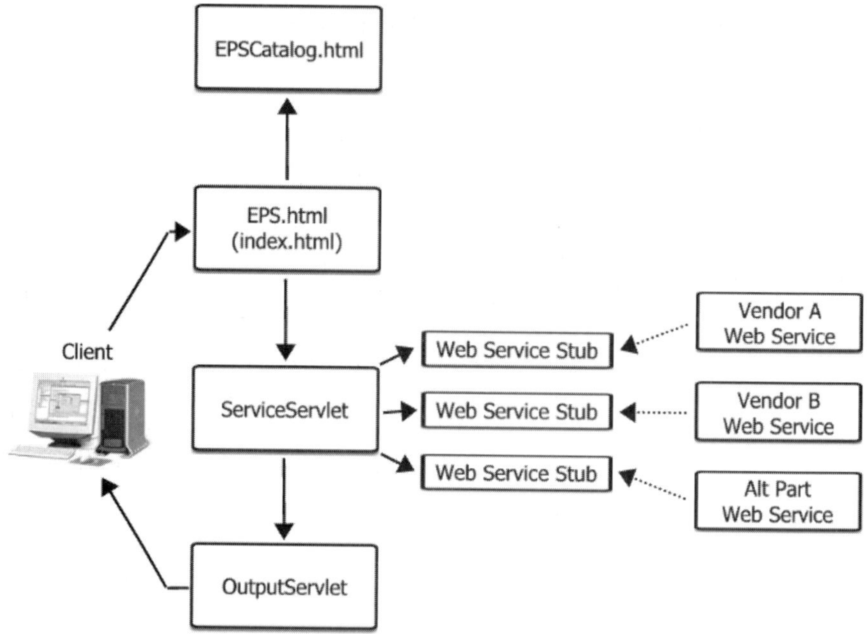

Figure 12-2 Block diagram depicting the overall system architecture of the EPS application.

The Web browser client first accesses the `EPS.html` file, which is a static HTML form where the user enters the desired part number, quantity, and optimization metric. A hyper link on the `EPS.html` page also takes the user to the `EPSCatalog.html`, which is another static HTML page displaying the vendors, part numbers, and product descriptions.

The form data from the `EPS.html` page is sent to a J2EE Servlet, `ServiceServlet`. The Servlet analyzes the form data and connects to the Web services of two vendors—Vendor A and Vendor B—in an effort to locate the best price or lead time for the given part number. If the two vendors do not have the part or do not have it in sufficient quantity, the Servlet then connects to the `AltPart` Web service in an effort to locate alternate part numbers. Based on the information from the Web services, the `ServiceServlet` formulates the information to be returned to the user and forwards it to the `OutputServlet`. The `OutputServlet` takes the information from the `ServiceServlet` and simply formats and presents it to the user.

The EPS application that we implement here is straightforward. Our objective is to demonstrate a real-world, enterprise usage of Web services and not to implement a full-featured procurement system. Additional capabilities such as a dynamic catalog that sources the parts available from each vendor Web service as well as an order placement and delivery management dashboard can be added.

Running the EPS Application

In this section, we briefly look at the flow through the EPS application from the user's perspective. In the next section, we delve into the actual development of the EPS.

Figure 12-3 shows a screenshot of the first page of the EPS application. This static HTML page, generated by the `EPS.html` file, is the main form in which the user enters information about the component to be procured. In the screenshot, information for part number 15151, desired quantity of 4, and optimization criteria of lead-time are specified.

The `EPS.html` form page also provides a hyperlink labeled "Browse the Catalog" that presents to the user the component catalog as shown in Figure 12-4. The EPS component catalog displays the vendor names, the component part numbers they carry, and a brief description of each component.

Based on the information entered into the `EPS.html` form, a response page is generated by the `OutputServlet`. For the form data entered as shown in Figure 12-3, the corresponding response page is shown in Figure 12-5.

As we have seen from the screenshots, the EPS application provides a simple Web-based interface for procuring components from multiple, competing vendors. Given the desired part number and the optimization criteria, the program compares the prices and lead times from the various vendors and reports the best vendor back to the user. Web services facilitate the development and maintenance of this application as any component vendor that provides a Web service for their inventory and ordering processes can be utilized by the EPS application. By virtue of it

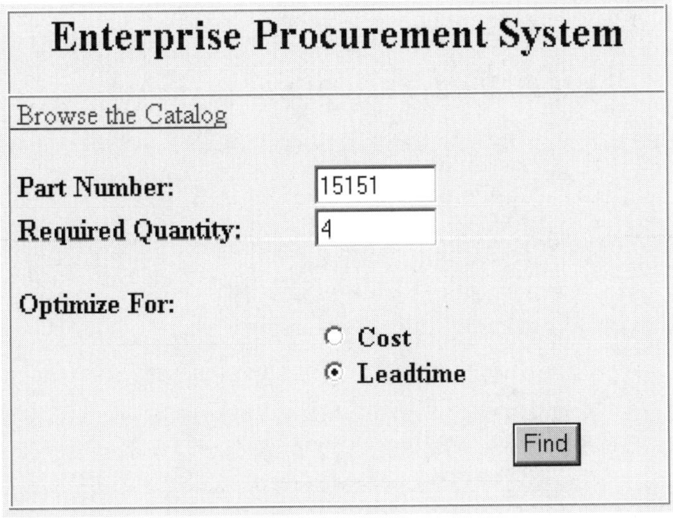

Figure 12-3 Screenshot of the first page of the EPS application that is generated by the EPS.html file.

Enterprise Procurement System Component Catalog	
Manufacturer One Components	
15361	Mfgr One Part # 15361
15362	Mfgr One Part # 15362
14525	Mfgr One Part # 14525
14369	Mfgr One Part # 14369
13204	Mfgr One Part # 13204
12079	Mfgr One Part # 12079
16276	Mfgr One Part # 16276
Manufacturer Two Components	
15151	Mfgr Two Part # 15151
15152	Mfgr Two Part # 15152
15153	Mfgr Two Part # 15153
15148	Mfgr Two Part # 15148
15150	Mfgr Two Part # 15150
15332	Mfgr Two Part # 15332

Figure 12-4 Screenshot of the EPS application component catalog that is generated by the EPSCatalog.html file.

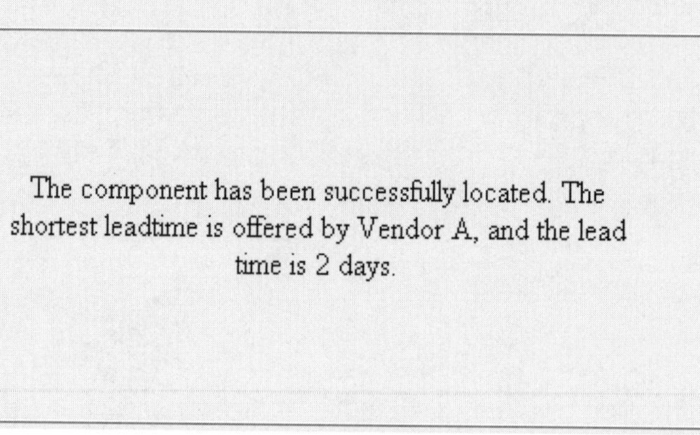

Enterprise Procurement System
The component has been successfully located. The shortest leadtime is offered by Vendor A, and the lead time is 2 days.

Figure 12-5 Screenshot of the results page that is generated by the OutputServlet based on the user entering part number 15151, quantity 4, and optimization metric lead time.

using Web services, the EPS is not a proprietary system capable of only communicating with vendors A and B.

System Implementation

Now that we have seen the user flow for the EPS application, in this section we take a detailed look at each of the implementation source files. We begin by describing how to develop applications and then expose them as Web services. Next, we look at how to implement the client application including the Web service invocations as well as other business logic. And, finally, we describe how to develop presentation code in the form of static HTML pages, J2EE servlets, as well as Java Server Pages (JSPs) that can invoke and leverage Web service functionality.

Figure 12-6 depicts the steps by which a Web service is created, deployed, and registered as well as how a client application access the functionalities of each Web service.

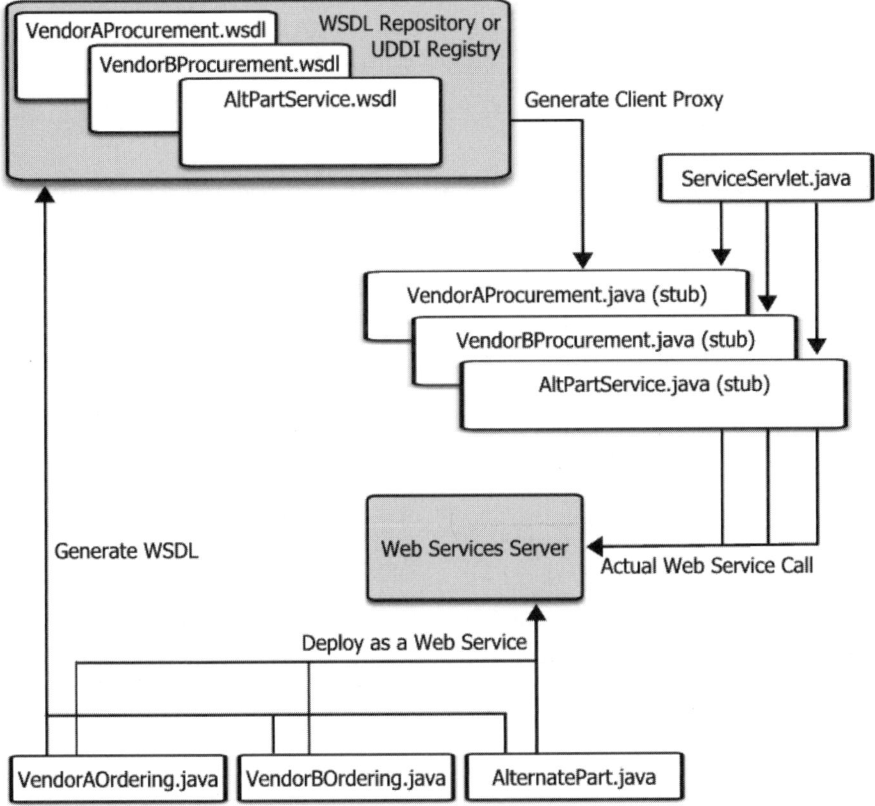

Figure 12-6 Architectural depiction of how a Web service is created and a client application accesses it.

The steps to build and deploy a Web service are:

1. Implement the business logic of the Web service as an application using your favorite language and platform. In this example, we use Java.
2. Use tools (that are part of your Web service platform) to deploy the application as a Web service.
3. Use additional tools (again, that are part of your Web service platform) to generate the WSDL for each deployed Web service.
4. Register each Web service and WSDL so that potential client applications can locate and understand the usage of the Web service.

The steps to build a client application that consumes Web services is as follows:

1. Generate a client proxy for each Web service to be used by the application based on each Web service's WSDL.
2. Within the client application, instantiate each client proxy and call the appropriate methods of the client proxy.

In the next sections, we look at each of these steps in more detail.

VendorAOrdering.java

In this section, we look at the steps involved in developing a Web service. We begin by developing a Java class, which we then expose as a Web service using the tools provided by our Web services platform.

For the sake of brevity, we only discuss the `VendorAOrdering` Java class and the associated `VendorAProcurement` Web service. The steps for developing classes and exposing them as Web services are the same for the other two Web services as well.

The source code for `VendorAOrdering.java` in its entirety follows:

```
public class VendorAOrdering
{
   public VendorAOrdering ()
   {
   }

   public int getPrice ( int partNumber , int quantity )
   {
      int price = -1;

      switch ( partNumber )
      {
         // part pricing business logic deleted
         // for brevity
```

```
        }
        return ( price );
    }

    public int getLeadTime ( int partNumber , int quantity )
    {
        int leadtime = -1;

        switch ( partNumber )
        {
            // part leadtime determination business logic
            // deleted for brevity
        }
        return ( leadtime );
    }

    public int placeOrder ( int partNumber , int quantity )
    {
        int confirmationOrderNumber = -1;

        // order confirmation number generation business
        // logic deleted for brevity
        return ( confirmationOrderNumber );
    }

    public String getOrderShipmentInfo ( int orderNumber )
    {
        String shipDate = "";

        // order shipment information business
        // logic deleted for brevity
        return ( shipDate );
    }
}
```

The code segment is a simple class that implements the following four methods:

- `getPrice`: returns the unit price for a component given its part number and the desired purchase quantity.
- `getLeadTime`: returns the expected leadtime for delivery of a component given its part number and the desired purchase quantity.
- `placeOrder`: returns a confirmation number for an order of the given component part number and purchase quantity.
- `getOrderShipmentInfo`: returns the expected delivery date of an order given its order confirmation number.

The `VendorAOrdering` class is a standard Java class, which can be instantiated and tested within an application. In this case, instead of instantiating it within an application, we wish to expose it as a Web service. There are just a few rules to follow in developing a Java class that will be exposed as a Web service. First, the class must have a public default constructor, and second the methods that will be available as Web service operations must be public.

Once the class file has been tested, deploying it as a Web service is simple. The Web services platform on which the service will be deployed will provide a tool that accepts as input a Java class (or application and fragments implemented in other languages) and deploys it as a Web service. Here we describe the steps required to deploy a Java class as a Web service using Tomcat and Apache Axis. The steps are:

1. Create a Web Service Deployment Descriptor (WSDD) file for the Web service.
   A WSDD file instructs the Axis engine to make that particular class available as a Web service, and incoming requests for that named Web service are handled by the specified class. Although a WSDD file can specify a rich set of instructions to the Axis engine, in many cases the basic Web service deployment is sufficient. The WSDD file for such a basic deployment is as follows:

```
<deployment xmlns="http://xml.apache.org/axis/wsdd/"
  xmlns:java=
    "http://xml.apache.org/axis/wsdd/providers/java">
  <service name="VendorAProcurement" provider="java:RPC">
  <parameter name="className" value=" VendorAOrdering"/>
  <parameter name="allowedMethods" value="*"/>
 </service>
</deployment>
```

   This file deploys a new Web service called `VendorAProcurement` using the RPC style. The Web service is based on the Java class `VendorAOrdering`, and all of the public methods of the class are available as accessible operations of the Web service. Additional information about WSDD files and other parameters supported in the deployment of Web services can be found in the Apache Axis documentation.
2. Deploy the Web service by using the Axis `AdminClient` and the created WSDD file. Assuming the WSDD file is named `VendorA.wsdd`, the Web service is deployed onto Axis by executing the following command:

```
java org.apache.axis.client.AdminClient VendorA.wsdd
```

3. Place the `VendorAOrdering.class` Java class file in the system classpath so that it is accessible to Axis.
4. Verify the deployment by browsing through the WSDL file of the new Web service.
   Upon successful execution of these steps, the VendorAProcurement Web service should be ready for use at the following location:

```
http://localhost:8080/axis/services/VendorAProcurement
```

A simple way to verify that the Web service has been deployed to the server is by checking that its WSDL has been properly created and is available at the expected location. The WSDL for our `VendorAProcurement` Web service should be available at the following URL:

```
http://localhost:8080/axis/services/
VendorAProcurement?wsdl
```

Although we have demonstrated how to deploy a Java class as a Web service on Apache Axis, other Web services platforms also provide similar tools that facilitate the deployment of applications as Web services.

So far, we have made the class available as a Web service, but have not published the WSDL so that client applications can locate and use the service. We demonstrate how to do this in the next section.

VendorAProcurement.wsdl

Figure 12-7 lists the entire WSDL for the `VendorAProcurement` Web service. Each of the operations supported by the Web service are enumerated together with each operation's arguments, the type of each argument as well as the type of the operation's return value. The endpoint location of the Web service is also specified within the address element.

```
<?xml version="1.0" encoding="UTF-8"?>
<wsdl:definitions targetNamespace="http://localhost:8080/axis/services/
VendorAProcurement" xmlns="http://schemas.xmlsoap.org/wsdl/"
xmlns:apachesoap="http://xml.apache.org/xml-soap" xmlns:impl="http://
localhost:8080/axis/services/VendorAProcurement" xmlns:intf="http://
localhost:8080/axis/services/VendorAProcurement" xmlns:soapenc="http://
schemas.xmlsoap.org/soap/encoding/" xmlns:wsdl="http://schemas.xmlsoap.org/
wsdl/" xmlns:wsdlsoap="http://schemas.xmlsoap.org/wsdl/soap/"
xmlns:xsd="http://www.w3.org/2001/XMLSchema">
  <wsdl:message name="getLeadTimeRequest">
    <wsdl:part name="in0" type="xsd:int"/>
    <wsdl:part name="in1" type="xsd:int"/>
  </wsdl:message>
  <wsdl:message name="getOrderShipmentInfoRequest">
    <wsdl:part name="in0" type="xsd:int"/>
  </wsdl:message>
 <wsdl:message name="getOrderShipmentInfoResponse">
    <wsdl:part name="getOrderShipmentInfoReturn" type="xsd:int"/>
  </wsdl:message>
   <wsdl:message name="placeOrderRequest">
    <wsdl:part name="in0" type="xsd:int"/>
    <wsdl:part name="in1" type="xsd:int"/>
  </wsdl:message>
```

Figure 12-7 The WSDL for the VendorAProcurement Web service.

```
<wsdl:message name="getPriceResponse">
  <wsdl:part name="getPriceReturn" type="xsd:int"/>
</wsdl:message>
<wsdl:message name="placeOrderResponse">
  <wsdl:part name="placeOrderReturn" type="xsd:int"/>
</wsdl:message>
<wsdl:message name="getLeadTimeResponse">
  <wsdl:part name="getLeadTimeReturn" type="xsd:int"/>
</wsdl:message>
<wsdl:message name="getPriceRequest">
  <wsdl:part name="in0" type="xsd:int"/>
  <wsdl:part name="in1" type="xsd:int"/>
</wsdl:message>
<wsdl:portType name="VendorAProcurement">
  <wsdl:operation name="getPrice" parameterOrder="in0 in1">
    <wsdl:input message="impl:getPriceRequest" name="getPriceRequest
    <wsdl:output message="impl:getPriceResponse" name="getPriceRespo
  </wsdl:operation>
  <wsdl:operation name="getLeadTime" parameterOrder="in0 in1">
    <wsdl:input message="impl:getLeadTimeRequest"
     name="getLeadTimeRequest"/>
    <wsdl:output message="impl:getLeadTimeResponse"
     name="getLeadTimeResponse"/>
  </wsdl:operation>
  <wsdl:operation name="placeOrder" parameterOrder="in0 in1">
    <wsdl:input message="impl:placeOrderRequest" name="placeOrderReque
    <wsdl:output message="impl:placeOrderResponse"
     name="placeOrderResponse"/>
  </wsdl:operation>
  <wsdl:operation name="getOrderShipmentInfo" parameterOrder="in0">
    <wsdl:input message="impl:getOrderShipmentInfoRequest"
     name="getOrderShipmentInfoRequest"/>
    <wsdl:output message="impl:getOrderShipmentInfoResponse"
     name="getOrderShipmentInfoResponse"/>
  </wsdl:operation>
</wsdl:portType>
<wsdl:binding name="VendorAProcurementSoapBinding"
type="impl:VendorAProcurement">
  <wsdlsoap:binding style="rpc" transport="
  http://schemas.xmlsoap.org/soap/http"/>
  <wsdl:operation name="getPrice">
    <wsdlsoap:operation soapAction=""/>
    <wsdl:input name="getPriceRequest">
      <wsdlsoap:body encodingStyle=
      "http://schemas.xmlsoap.org/soap/encoding/"
       namespace="http://DefaultNamespace" use="encoded"/>
    </wsdl:input>
    <wsdl:output name="getPriceResponse">
      <wsdlsoap:body encodingStyle=
      "http://schemas.xmlsoap.org/soap/encoding/"
      namespace=
      "http://localhost:8080/axis/services/VendorAProcurement"
       use="encoded"/>
```

Figure 12-7 The WSDL for the VendorAProcurement Web service (continued).

```
      </wsdl:output>
    </wsdl:operation>
    <wsdl:operation name="getLeadTime">
      <wsdlsoap:operation soapAction=""/>
      <wsdl:input name="getLeadTimeRequest">
        <wsdlsoap:body encodingStyle=
        "http://schemas.xmlsoap.org/soap/encoding/" namespace=
         "http://DefaultNamespace" use="encoded"/>
      </wsdl:input>
      <wsdl:output name="getLeadTimeResponse">
        <wsdlsoap:body encodingStyle=
        "http://schemas.xmlsoap.org/soap/encoding/" namespace=
        "http://localhost:8080/axis/services/VendorAProcurement"
         use="encoded"/>
      </wsdl:output>
    </wsdl:operation>
    <wsdl:operation name="placeOrder">
      <wsdlsoap:operation soapAction=""/>
      <wsdl:input name="placeOrderRequest">
        <wsdlsoap:body encodingStyle=
        "http://schemas.xmlsoap.org/soap/encoding/" namespace=
         "http://DefaultNamespace" use="encoded"/>
      </wsdl:input>
      <wsdl:output name="placeOrderResponse">
        <wsdlsoap:body encodingStyle=
        "http://schemas.xmlsoap.org/soap/encoding/" namespace=
        "http://localhost:8080/axis/services/VendorAProcurement"
         use="encoded"/>
      </wsdl:output>
    </wsdl:operation>
    <wsdl:operation name="getOrderShipmentInfo">
      <wsdlsoap:operation soapAction=""/>
      <wsdl:input name="getOrderShipmentInfoRequest">
        <wsdlsoap:body encodingStyle=
        "http://schemas.xmlsoap.org/soap/encoding/" namespace=
         "http://DefaultNamespace" use="encoded"/>
      </wsdl:input>
      <wsdl:output name="getOrderShipmentInfoResponse">
        <wsdlsoap:body encodingStyle=
        "http://schemas.xmlsoap.org/soap/encoding/" namespace=
        "http://localhost:8080/axis/services/VendorAProcurement"
         use="encoded"/>
      </wsdl:output>
    </wsdl:operation>
  </wsdl:binding>
  <wsdl:service name="VendorAProcurementService">
    <wsdl:port binding="impl:VendorAProcurementSoapBinding"
    name="VendorAProcurement">
      <wsdlsoap:address location=
       "http://localhost:8080/axis/services/VendorAProcurement"/>
    </wsdl:port>
  </wsdl:service>
</wsdl:definitions>
```

Figure 12-7 The WSDL for the VendorAProcurement Web service (continued).

The WSDL for each deployed Web service is automatically generated by the Web service platform. For example, in the previous section after we deployed and exposed the `VendorAOrdering` Java class as the Web service `VendorAProcurement`, the WSDL file `VendorAProcurement.wsdl` was automatically generated and made available at: `http://localhost:8080/axis/services/VendorAProcurement?wsdl`.

The WSDL from this location can be saved and distributed as a text file to potential consumers of this Web service. The Web service may be registered at a registry such as the Universal Business Registry (see Chapter 4 for more information about UDDI and the UBR), or the WSDL may be deposited in a public or private WSDL repository.

Now that we have seen how to implement a Web service and make it available for others to use, we next turn our focus to the steps involved in building client applications that use Web services. We start by looking at the client application's user-facing presentation that is implemented as a set of static HTML pages.

EPS.html

`EPS.html` is the first touch point for users accessing the EPS application. It is a static HTML page that consists of a single form. Each of the form fields is positioned within various rows and columns of a table structure.

What follows are the key segments of the `EPS.html` source file. The basic parts of the page that are implemented using standard HTML tags are removed for brevity.

```
<HTML>
  <HEAD>
    <TITLE>Enterprise Procurement System</TITLE>
  </HEAD>
  <BODY bgcolor="#CFFFFF">
    <TABLE cellpadding="0" cellspacing="0" border="1">
      <TR>
        <TD width="375" height="30" colspan="3"
       align="center">
          <H2>Enterprise Procurement System</H2>
        </TD>
      </TR>
      <TR>
        <TD width="345">
          <FORM name="form" action=
          "http://localhost:8080/epsdemo/ServiceServlet"
                method="post">
```

The details of the HTML form have also been removed for brevity. A standard HTML form is used to collect information on the part number to be purchased as well as the desired quantity and vendor selection metric (e.g., lowest cost or lowest lead time). This user data is passed as HTML form parameters as a HTTP POST to the J2EE Servlet located at http://localhost:8080/epsdemo/ServiceServlet.

```
            </FORM>
          </TD>
        </TR>
      </TABLE>
    </BODY>
</HTML>
```

The Servlet `ServiceServlet` services the user requests by invoking the `VendorA-Procurement` and `VendorBProcurement` and, if necessary, the `AltPartService` Web services based on the received user input.

As we have seen, the client application, in this case the Web browser, does not access the Web services directly. Instead, the Web service invocations are placed behind an abstraction layer, e.g., a Servlet API. This allows adding Web services to an application without having to modify the entire system. Although this type of abstraction and architecture is useful, there is no reason why a client application could not directly invoke Web services.

EPSCatalog.html

The `EPSCatalog.html` file is a simple, static HTML file that presents all of the components that are available to be procured through the EPS application. A two-column table structure organizes each component part number together with a brief description of the component.

Since the page is simple and can be developed using standard HTML, we do not list the code here. A screenshot of the page is depicted in Figure 12-4.

A more complex but easier to maintain component catalog page can also be developed by using dynamic pages instead of static ones. Assume that each of the vendor Web services support a component query function that returns a list of component part numbers the vendor carries together with brief descriptions. Whether the component is currently available is an orthogonal issue. A dynamic catalog page can be developed by simply querying this method of each vendor's Web service and presenting to the user the response data.

ServiceServlet.java

`ServiceServlet.java` is a J2EE Servlet Java source file. It is a controller Servlet that accepts HTTP POST requests from `EPS.html`, processes the POST parameters, invokes the appropriate Web services, and generates the user response. The response is forwarded to the `OutputServlet`, which prepares the response for user presentation.

Figure 12-8 depicts the three Web services that are used by the EPS application. The Web services of Vendor A and Vendor B are competitive services that allow a client application to inquire about the price or lead time of a particular component, and then order the component. The Alternate Part Web service is used when the desired part is unavailable from both vendors A and B in order to locate a similar or alternate component.

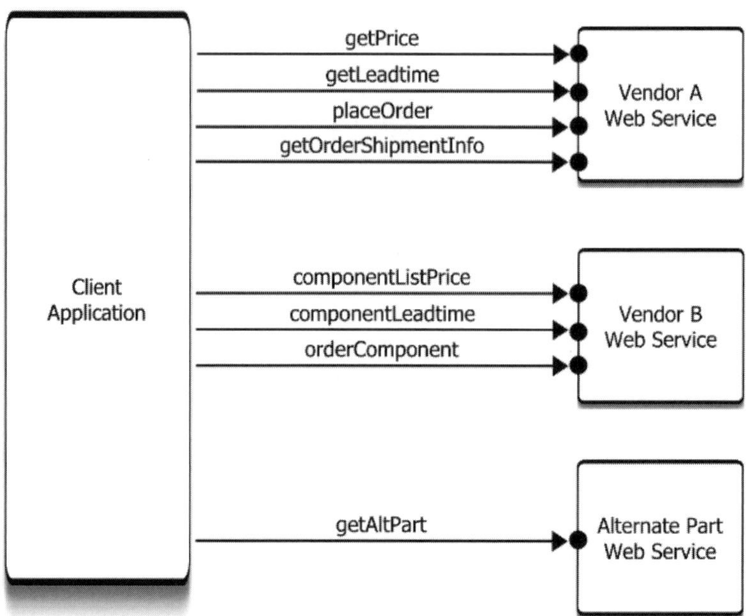

Figure 12-8 Enterprise procurement application architecture that interfaces with vendor Web services.

The first thing we notice about the Web services from Vendor A and Vendor B is that they expose a different number of methods—Vendor A exposes four methods, while Vendor B exposes only three—and the names of each method are different. The number, type, and sequencing of arguments for each method may also be different. Although the two Web services provide almost identical functionality, the interfaces they expose are quite different. This difference in API between competing Web services makes building scalable client applications difficult.

The source code for `ServiceServlet.java` in its entirety with comments and explanations follows:

```
/**
 *   File: ServiceServlet.java
 *   Desc: Controller Servlet that accepts HTTP POSTs from
 *         EPS.html, processes the POST parameters, invokes
 *         the appropriate Web services, and generates the
 *         response, which is forwarded to the
 *         OutputServlet.
 **/

import javax.servlet.ServletConfig;
import javax.servlet.ServletException;
import javax.servlet.http.HttpServlet;
import javax.servlet.http.HttpServletRequest;
```

```
import javax.servlet.http.HttpServletResponse;
import java.io.IOException;
import java.io.PrintWriter;

public class ServiceServlet extends HttpServlet
{
   private static final String CONTENT_TYPE = "text/html";

   // Individual Web service error codes
   private final static int ALTERNATE_PART_ERROR = -1;
   private final static int VENDOR_A_ERROR = -1;
   private final static int VENDOR_B_ERROR = 0;

   public void init ( ServletConfig config ) throws
ServletException
   {
      super.init ( config );
   }

   // Forward HTTP GET requests to the doPost handler
   public void doGet ( HttpServletRequest request ,
HttpServletResponse response ) throws ServletException ,
IOException
   {
      doPost ( request , response );
   }

   // Process the HTTP POST request
   public void doPost ( HttpServletRequest request ,
HttpServletResponse response ) throws ServletException ,
IOException
   {
      // Variables to hold the parameters from the POST
      String paramPartNumber = null;
      String paramQuantity = null;
      String paramOptimizeFor = null;

      // Is the form fully completed by the user and the
      //  form data ready to be processed? Or, are some
      //  fields not completed?
      boolean formReady = true;

      // Message to return to the user
      String responseMessage = null;

      // Name of the selected vendor from which the
      //  procure the components
      String selectedVendorName = null;

      // Variables that hold the cost or lead time
      //  responses from each vendor Web service
      int vendorAResult = 0;
```

```
int vendorBResult = 0;

// Value of the best cost or lead time response
int bestResult = 0;

// Was the specified component located or not
boolean componentNotFound = false;

// if the specified component was not located,
//  what is the part number for an alternate component
int alternatePartNumber = 0;

// The Web service client-side binding stub variables
AltPartServiceService apService;
AltPartService apPort;
VendorAProcurementService vapService;
VendorAProcurement vapPort;
VendorBProcurementService vbpService;
VendorBProcurement vbpPort;

// Get the printwriter for the Servlet
response.setContentType ( CONTENT_TYPE );
PrintWriter out = response.getWriter ();

// Get the parameter values from the POST request
paramPartNumber = request.getParameter (
    "partnumber" );
paramQuantity = request.getParameter ( "quantity" );
paramOptimizeFor = request.getParameter (
    "optimizefor" );

// All of the fields of the HTML form must be filled
//  in. Otherwise, print a message asking the user to
//  fill everything in.
if ( ( paramPartNumber == null ) ||
   ( paramQuantity == null ) )
{
   // Some of the form fields were not properly filled
   //  in. Thus, the form is not ready.
   formReady = false;
}
else
{
   paramPartNumber = paramPartNumber.trim ();
   paramQuantity = paramQuantity.trim ();
   paramOptimizeFor = paramOptimizeFor.trim ();

   if ( ( paramPartNumber.length () == 0 ) ||
      ( paramQuantity.length () == 0 ) ||
      ( paramOptimizeFor.length () == 0 ) )
   {
      // The form fields were properly filled in, and
```

```
            //  the form is ready to be processed.
            formReady = false;
         }
      }

      if ( formReady )
      {
         // Only if the formReady variable is true, do we
         //  invoke the Web services and try to locate the
         //  specified part.
         try
         {
            // Vendor A Procurement service
            vapService =
    new VendorAProcurementServiceLocator ();

            // Now use the service to get a stub which
            //  implements the SDI.
            vapPort = vapService.getVendorAProcurement ();

            // Vendor B Procurement service
            vbpService =
    new VendorBProcurementServiceLocator ();

            // Now use the service to get a stub which
            //  implements the SDI.
            vbpPort = vbpService.getVendorBProcurement ();

            if ( paramOptimizeFor.equalsIgnoreCase (
            "cost" ) )
            {
               // optimize for cost
               vendorAResult = vapPort.getPrice (
     new Integer ( paramPartNumber ).intValue (),
                new Integer ( paramQuantity ).intValue () );
               vendorBResult = vbpPort.componentListPrice (
     new Integer ( paramQuantity ).intValue () ,
                new Integer ( paramPartNumber).intValue() );
            }
            else
            {
               // optimize for lead time
               vendorAResult = vapPort.getLeadTime (
     new Integer ( paramPartNumber ).intValue (),
                new Integer ( paramQuantity ).intValue () );
               vendorBResult = vbpPort.componentLeadtime (
     new Integer ( paramQuantity ).intValue () ,
                new Integer ( paramPartNumber ).intValue());
            }
         }
         catch ( Exception e )
         {
```

```
      System.out.println ( "Error in client proxy." );
   }

   // set bestResult to an error initially
   bestResult = VENDOR_A_ERROR;

   // -1 returned from Vendor A's Web service means
   //  that they do not have the part, or they do not
   //  have it in sufficient quantity
   if ( vendorAResult != VENDOR_A_ERROR )
   {
      // if vendorA returned a value, set this to the
      //  be bestResult
      bestResult = vendorAResult;
      selectedVendorName = "Vendor A";
   }

   // 0 returned from Vendor B's Web service means
   //  that they do not have the part, or they do not
   //  have it in sufficient quantity
   if ( vendorBResult != VENDOR_B_ERROR )
   {
      if ( vendorBResult < bestResult )
      {
         bestResult = vendorBResult;
         selectedVendorName = "Vendor B";
      }
   }

   // if bestResult is a VENDOR_A_ERROR, then no
   //  component was found from any vendor
   if ( bestResult == VENDOR_A_ERROR )
   {
      componentNotFound = true;
   }

   if ( componentNotFound )
   {
      // The specified part could not be found by any
      //  of the vendor Web services. So, now we use
      //  the alternatePart Web service to locate an
      //  alternate part, and provide the alternate
      //  part number.
      try
      {
         // Alt Part service
         apService =
new AltPartServiceServiceLocator ();

         // Now use the service to get a stub that
    //  implements the SDI.
         apPort = apService.getAltPartService ();
```

```
            alternatePartNumber = apPort.getAltPart (
    new Integer ( paramPartNumber ).intValue());
         }
         catch ( Exception e )
         {
            System.out.println
    ( "Error in AltPartService client proxy" );
         }

         if ( alternatePartNumber !=ALTERNATE_PART_ERROR)
         {
            responseMessage =
               "The component could not be located. " +
               "We found an alternate part - " +
               " with part number " +
               alternatePartNumber +
               " -- that may meet your needs.";
         }
         else
         {
            // If no alternate part number is found, then
            //  just say so
            responseMessage =
              "The component could not be located. We
              tried to find an alternate part, but we
              could not. Good luck!";
         }
      }

      if ( !componentNotFound )
      {
         responseMessage =
          "The component has been successfully located.";

         if (paramOptimizeFor.equalsIgnoreCase ("cost") )
         {
            responseMessage = responseMessage.concat (
     "The lowest price is offered by " +
              selectedVendorName +
              ", and the unit price is $ " +
              bestResult + "." );
         }
         else
         {
            responseMessage = responseMessage.concat (
            "The shortest leadtime is offered by " +
            selectedVendorName +
            ", and the lead time is " + bestResult +
            " days." );
         }
      }
```

```
        }
        else
        {
           // If the form is not ready (!formReady) then tell
           //  the user to fill in the form completely
           responseMessage =
            "Please fully complete all of the form fields.";
        }

        // Use forward or redirect to send the responseMessage
        //  data to the OutputServlet - used for simplicity
        response.sendRedirect ("http://localhost:8080/epsdemo/
         OutputServlet?responseMessage=" + responseMessage );

    }

    public void destroy ()
    {
    }
}
```

Now that we have seen how the `ServiceServlet` accepts data from an HTML page and invokes Web services to fulfill the specified requests, in the next section we look at one of the Web service binding stubs and how it facilitates client application development.

Client-Side Binding Stubs

Client-side binding stubs are local programs that facilitate invoking the methods of remote Web services. For instance, as we saw above in our discussion of the `ServiceServlet` servlet, invocations of the remote `VendorAProcurement` Web service are through the local `VendorAProcurement` stub. The `VendorAProcurement` stub is a Java source file that provides the identical API as that of the remote Web service. The client stub is simply a proxy-like means of the application to invoke the methods of a Web service through a local interface. The stub has the same API as that of its corresponding Web service, but the stub does not actually implement any of the business logic of the Web service.

The calling application instantiates the client stub and invokes the appropriate methods. The client stub simply forwards the method invocation using the appropriate protocol to the actual Web service. Upon receiving the request from the client stub, the Web service processes the request and formulates a response. The response is received by the client stub, which then forwards it back to the calling application as the return to the method invocation.

All of the client-side binding stubs are generated based on the Web service's WSDL file. Each Web service platform provides tools that automatically generate these files, further facilitating the job of developers.

Apache Axis provides the tool `WSDL2Java` for generating client-side binding stubs from Web service WSDL files. The basic invocation is as follows:

```
java org.apache.axis.wsdl.WSDL2Java <WSDL filename or URL>
```

If we want to generate the client-side stubs for the `VendorAProcurement` Web service, we execute the following command:

```
java org.apache.axis.wsdl.WSDL2Java
 http://localhost:8080/axis/services/VendorAProcurement?wsdl
```

This command generates the following four files:

- VendorAProcurement.java
- VendorAProcurementService.java
- VendorAProcurementServiceLocator.java
- VendorAProcurementSoapBindingStub.java

Our discussion in the previous section on invoking Web service operations from the `ServiceServlet` servlet demonstrated how these generated files are used as a local proxy for the remote Web service and how each actual Web service operation invocation takes place.

Since each of these files is automatically generated, we do not provide source code listings or describe them in further detail.

Now that we have seen how Web services can be used to fulfill user requests, in the next section we finish the enterprise procurement application by formatting and presenting the results to the user.

OutputServlet.java

The `OutputServlet.java` is a J2EE Servlet Java source file that implements the user's view of the results of the enterprise procurement application. The response generated by the ServiceServlet is presented through the OutputServlet.

The implementation of `OutputServlet` is simple and straightforward. The key steps are:

1. Get the `responseMessage` parameter from the POST request.
2. Check the validity of the parameter.
3. Generate the HTML to return to the client browser, including the data from the `responseMessage` parameter.

The functionality of the Servlet is provided by the `doPost` handler method. `HTTP GET` requests are forwarded to the `doPost` handler as well. The Java source code for the `doPost` method in its entirety together with comments and explanations follows:

```
public void doPost ( HttpServletRequest request ,
          HttpServletResponse response )
  throws ServletException , IOException
{
   response.setContentType ( CONTENT_TYPE );
   PrintWriter out = response.getWriter ();

   String textFieldMessage = request.getParameter
         ( "responseMessage" );

   if (textFieldMessage != null)
   {
      textFieldMessage = textFieldMessage.trim();
   }

   out.println ( "<head>" );
   out.println ( "<title>Enterprise Procurement
      System</title>" );
   out.println ( "</head>" );
   out.println ( "<body bgcolor=#cfffff>" );
   out.println ( "<table cellpadding=\"0\" cellspacing=\"0\"
      border=\"1\">" );
   out.println ( "<tr>" );
   out.println ( "<td width=\"375\" height=\"30\"
      colspan=\"3\" align=\"center\"><h2>
      Enterprise Procurement " );
   out.println ( "System</h2></td>" );
   out.println ( "</tr>" );
   out.println ( "<tr>" );
   out.println ( "<td width=\"345\" height=\"200\" align=
      \"center\"> " );
   out.println ( textFieldMessage );
   out.println ( "</td>" );
   out.println ( "</tr>" );
   out.println ( "</table>" );
   out.println ( "</body>" );
   out.println ( "</html>" );
}
```

This completes our discussion of the implementation details of the Enterprise Procurement System application. In the next sections, we discuss how to deploy and then run the application.

Deploying the Application

In this section, we cover how to deploy the application on the Jakarta Tomcat servlet container and the Apache Axis SOAP server. Both Tomcat and Axis are available for free, and can be downloaded from http://jakarta.apache.org/tomcat/ and http://ws.apache.org/axis/, respectively. In our descriptions, we use Tomcat 4.1 and Axis 1.1.

To fully deploy the EPS application, we must simply deploy the EPS application as a Web application onto Tomcat. This assumes that Axis SOAP server as well as each of the Web services that are consumed by the EPS application have been successfully deployed onto Tomcat. Axis can be easily deployed onto Tomcat by simply copying the folder `%AXIS_HOME%\webapps\axis\` to the folder `%TOMCAT_HOME%\webapps\`. We discussed the steps in deploying a Web service from a Java class in the subsection entitled "VendorAOrdering.java".

Before we can deploy the EPS application to Tomcat, we must first create a Web application, which is a collection of files within specific named folders that can be accessed by the servlet container (e.g., Tomcat) during runtime. The files can be left "unpacked" on the file system, or they may be "packed" into what is known as a Web Archive, or WAR file. Unpacked deployments are preferable during development when constant changes are made, but packed WAR files are more convenient when development is finished and the Web application must be distributed.

A Web application is deployed by placing the files required by the servlet container to run the application in the following standard format and locations:

- `%DOCUMENT_ROOT%\`: Place HTML, JSP, and other associated files, such as images, in this folder. For larger applications, these files can be better organized and put into subfolders (e.g., for images, html, and so on).
- `%DOCUMENT_ROOT%\WEB-INF\web.xml`: This is the Web Application Deployment Descriptor for the application. This file describes all of the components of the Web application.
- `%DOCUMENT_ROOT%\classes\`: Place all of the Java classes used by the application in this folder.
- `%DOCUMENT_ROOT%\lib\`: Place all JAR files, including third-party libraries, in this folder.

We can create a Web application for the EPS application by organizing all of the files as follows:

- `C:\epsdemo\index.html`
- `C:\epsdemo\catalog.html`
- `C:\epsdemo\WEB-INF\web.xml`
- `C:\epsdemo\WEB-INF\classes\AltPartService.class`
- `C:\epsdemo\WEB-INF\classes\`
  `AltPartServiceService.class`
- `C:\epsdemo\WEB-INF\classes\`
  `AltPartServiceServiceLocator.class`
- `C:\epsdemo\WEB-INF\classes\`
  `AltPartServiceSoapBindingStub.class`

- C:\epsdemo\WEB-INF\classes\OutputServlet.class
- C:\epsdemo\WEB-INF\classes\ServiceServlet.class
- C:\epsdemo\WEB-INF\classes\VendorAProcurement.class
- C:\epsdemo\WEB-INF\classes\VendorAProcurementService.class
- C:\epsdemo\WEB-INF\classes\VendorAProcurementServiceLocator.class
- C:\epsdemo\WEB-INF\classes\VendorAProcurementSoapBindingStub.class
- C:\epsdemo\WEB-INF\classes\VendorBProcurement.class
- C:\epsdemo\WEB-INF\classes\VendorBProcurementService.class
- C:\epsdemo\WEB-INF\classes\VendorBProcurementServiceLocator.class
- C:\epsdemo\WEB-INF\classes\VendorBProcurementSoapBindingStub.class
- C:\epsdemo\WEB-INF\lib\axis.jar
- C:\epsdemo\WEB-INF\lib\commons-discovery.jar
- C:\epsdemo\WEB-INF\lib\jaxrpc.jar
- C:\epsdemo\WEB-INF\lib\saaj.jar

Each of the JAR files that are placed within the C:\epsdemo\WEB-INF\lib\ folder is available in the Axis distribution (%AXIS_HOME%\lib\). The contents of the web.xml Web Application Deployment Descriptor is shown in Figure 12-9.

The web.xml Web Application Deployment Descriptor specifies that the EPS Web application consists of two servlets, ServiceServlet and OutputServlet. The Java class that implements the servlet as well as the URL pattern that can be used to access the servlet is specified for each servlet.

We have now created a Web application for the EPS application. To deploy this Web application, we simply have to copy the folder in which the Web application lives (C:\epsdemo\) to the deployment folder of Tomcat (%TOMCAT_HOME%\webapps\).

Upon completing this step, we have successfully deployed the EPS application as a Web application onto the Tomcat servlet container. We can access the application by typing the following URL into any browser:

```
http://localhost:8080/epsdemo
```

The index.html (EPS.html) HTML file should be displayed on typing this URL into your browser. Be sure that Tomcat has successfully started before typing in the URL.

```
<?xml version="1.0" encoding="ISO-8859-1"?>
<!DOCTYPE web-app PUBLIC "-//Sun Microsystems, Inc.//DTD Web
Application 2.3//EN" "http://java.sun.com/dtd/web-
app_2_3.dtd">

<web-app>
<servlet>
  <servlet-name>ServiceServlet</servlet-name>
  <servlet-class>ServiceServlet</servlet-class>
</servlet>
<servlet>
  <servlet-name>OutputServlet</servlet-name>
  <servlet-class>OutputServlet</servlet-class>
</servlet>
<servlet-mapping>
  <servlet-name>ServiceServlet</servlet-name>
  <url-pattern>/ServiceServlet</url-pattern>
</servlet-mapping>
<servlet-mapping>
  <servlet-name>OutputServlet</servlet-name>
  <url-pattern>/OutputServlet</url-pattern>
</servlet-mapping>
</web-app>
```

Figure 12-9 The contents of the `web.xml` Web Application Deployment Descriptor for the EPS application.

This completes the deployment of the EPS application onto Tomcat. In the next section, we run the application and monitor the SOAP messages that are transmitted between the EPS application and each of the Web services it consumes.

Running the Application

In this section, we run the EPS application and also analyze the SOAP messages that are exchanged between the application and each Web service. By analyzing these SOAP messages, we can get a deeper understanding of the entire EPS application, as well as of the client-side binding stubs.

We can run the EPS Web application by simply typing in the appropriate URL into any browser. As we saw in the previous section, the URL for the EPS application is:

```
http://localhost:8080/epsdemo
```

Once we type in this URL, the `EPS.html (index.html)` page should be displayed within the browser. This page presents an HTML form prompting the user to enter the desired part number, required quantity, and optimization criteria. Enter the following information:

```
Part Number: 15151
Required Quantity: 4
Optimize For: Lead-time
```

Based on this information, the application will contact each of the vendor Web services and return the name of the vendor with the lowest lead-time for the component with part number 15151. Assuming that Vendor A has the lowest lead-time with 2 days, the EPS application will return the message: `The component has been successfully located. The shortest leadtime is offered by Vendor A, and the lead time is 2 days.`

To monitor the messages that are exchanged between the EPS application and each Web service, we use the TCP/IP Monitor utility, `tcpmon`, which is bundled with the Axis distribution. The `tcpmon` utility works by listening on a particular port for incoming messages. When an incoming message arrives, `tcpmon` displays the message and then forwards it to another port for handling.

The default listening port for Tomcat is `8080`, and all of our SOAP messages are sent to that port. We can have `tcpmon` listen on another port, say port `1234`, and then forward the message to port `8080`.

To make this change, we must modify the port numbers within each of the ServiceLocator files (`VendorAProcurementServiceLocator.java`, `VendorBProcurement-ServiceLocator.java`, `AltPartServiceServiceLocator.java`) of the client-side binding stubs. For instance, within the VendorBProcurementServiceLocator.java file, we change port `8080` in this line:

```
private final java.lang.String VendorBProcurement_address =
"http://localhost:8080/axis/services/VendorBProcurement";
```

to

```
private final java.lang.String VendorBProcurement_address =
"http://localhost:1234/axis/services/VendorBProcurement";
```

This changes the port number to which each SOAP message is sent from port `8080` to port `1234`.

Now, we can compile these simple changes into the `epsdemo` Web application. Next, we run the `tcpmon` utility by typing:

```
java org.apache.axis.utils.tcpmon 1234 localhost 8080
```

This instructs the `tcpmon` utility to run and listen for incoming messages on port `1234` and then to forward those messages to port `8080` on the host `localhost`. Now, run the EPS application (by typing `http://localhost:8080/epsdemo` into a browser) and then enter Part Number: 15151, Required Quantity: 4, and Optimize For: Lead-time. The ServiceServlet will send SOAP messages to each of the two vendor Web services, and each of these messages will be displayed by the `tcpmon`.

Figure 12-10 lists the SOAP request message that is sent from the `ServiceServlet` to the `VendorAProcurement` Web service, as well as the response message.

```
POST /axis/services/VendorAProcurement HTTP/1.0
Content-Type: text/xml; charset=utf-8
Accept: application/soap+xml, application/dime, multipart/
related, text/*
User-Agent: Axis/1.1
Host: 127.0.0.1
Cache-Control: no-cache
Pragma: no-cache
SOAPAction: ""
Content-Length: 484
<?xml version="1.0" encoding="UTF-8"?>
<soapenv:Envelope xmlns:soapenv="http://schemas.xmlsoap.org/
soap/envelope/" xmlns:xsd="http://www.w3.org/2001/XMLSchema"
xmlns:xsi="http://www.w3.org/2001/XMLSchema-instance">
 <soapenv:Body>
  <ns1:getLeadTime soapenv:encodingStyle="http://
schemas.xmlsoap.org/soap/encoding/" xmlns:ns1="http://
DefaultNamespace">
   <in0 xsi:type="xsd:int">15151</in0>
   <in1 xsi:type="xsd:int">4</in1>
  </ns1:getLeadTime>
 </soapenv:Body>
</soapenv:Envelope>
```

(a) The SOAP request message from the `ServiceServlet` to the Web service `VendorAProcurement`

```
HTTP/1.1 200 OK
Content-Type: text/xml; charset=utf-8
Date: Sat, 16 Aug 2003 16:17:08 GMT
Server: Apache Coyote/1.0
Connection: close
<?xml version="1.0" encoding="UTF-8"?>
<soapenv:Envelope xmlns:soapenv="http://schemas.xmlsoap.org/
soap/envelope/" xmlns:xsd="http://www.w3.org/2001/XMLSchema"
xmlns:xsi="http://www.w3.org/2001/XMLSchema-instance">
 <soapenv:Body>
  <ns1:getLeadTimeResponse soapenv:encodingStyle="http://
schemas.xmlsoap.org/soap/encoding/" xmlns:ns1="http://
DefaultNamespace">
   <ns1:getLeadTimeReturn xsi:type="xsd:int">2</
ns1:getLeadTimeReturn>
  </ns1:getLeadTimeResponse>
 </soapenv:Body>
</soapenv:Envelope>
```

(b) The SOAP response message from the Web service `VendorAProcurement`.

Figure 12-10 The (a) request and (b) response messages between the EPS application's ServiceServlet and the Web service VendorAProcurement.

By analyzing Figure 12-10, we see that the SOAP message is requesting an invocation of the getLeadTime operation of the VendorAProcurement Web service with the arguments 15151 and 4. The response message listed in Figure 12-10 shows the leadtime is 2 days.

Figure 12-11 lists the SOAP request message that is sent from the ServiceServlet to the VendorBProcurement Web service, as well as the response message.

```
POST /axis/services/VendorBProcurement HTTP/1.0
Content-Type: text/xml; charset=utf-8
Accept: application/soap+xml, application/dime, multipart/
related, text/*
User-Agent: Axis/1.1
Host: 127.0.0.1
Cache-Control: no-cache
Pragma: no-cache
SOAPAction: ""
Content-Length: 496
<?xml version="1.0" encoding="UTF-8"?>
<soapenv:Envelope xmlns:soapenv="http://schemas.xmlsoap.org/
soap/envelope/" xmlns:xsd="http://www.w3.org/2001/XMLSchema"
xmlns:xsi="http://www.w3.org/2001/XMLSchema-instance">
 <soapenv:Body>
  <ns1:componentLeadtime soapenv:encodingStyle="http://
schemas.xmlsoap.org/soap/encoding/" xmlns:ns1="http://
DefaultNamespace">
   <in0 xsi:type="xsd:int">4</in0>
   <in1 xsi:type="xsd:int">15151</in1>
  </ns1:componentLeadtime>
 </soapenv:Body>
</soapenv:Envelope>
```

(a) The SOAP request message from the ServiceServlet to the Web service VendorBProcurement

```
HTTP/1.1 200 OK
Content-Type: text/xml; charset=utf-8
Date: Sat, 16 Aug 2003 16:17:08 GMT
Server: Apache Coyote/1.0
Connection: close
<?xml version="1.0" encoding="UTF-8"?>
<soapenv:Envelope xmlns:soapenv="http://schemas.xmlsoap.org/
soap/envelope/" xmlns:xsd="http://www.w3.org/2001/XMLSchema"
xmlns:xsi="http://www.w3.org/2001/XMLSchema-instance">
 <soapenv:Body>
  <ns1:componentLeadtimeResponse
soapenv:encodingStyle="http://schemas.xmlsoap.org/soap/
encoding/" xmlns:ns1="http://DefaultNamespace">
   <ns1:componentLeadtimeReturn xsi:type="xsd:int">4</
ns1:componentLeadtimeReturn>
  </ns1:componentLeadtimeResponse>
 </soapenv:Body>
</soapenv:Envelope>
```

(b) The SOAP response message from the Web service VendorBProcurement.

Figure 12-11 The (a) request and (b) response messages between the EPS application's ServiceServlet and the Web service VendorBProcurement.

By analyzing request (a), we see that the SOAP message is requesting invocation of the `componentLeadtime` operation of the `VendorBProcurement` Web service with the arguments 4 and 15151. The response message (b) lists the lead-time as 4 days.

Based on these two response messages, the business logic of the `ServiceServlet` is able to select Vendor A as the vendor with the shortest lead-time for procuring 4 units of part 15151. Now we have successfully developed and run our EPS application based on Web services for component ordering and fulfillment.

Direct Web Service Invocations (without Binding Stubs)

In our development of the EPS application, we used client-side binding stubs to facilitate communication between the client-application and the consumed Web services. Although binding stubs are automatically generated from a Web service's WSDL description and support a simple programming model, they do incur some overhead. Each time a Web service is used, all of the binding stub files must be generated, instantiated within the client program, and compiled. Each of the binding stub files must also be co-located with the client application. For applications that consume a large number of Web services, the binding stub files represent a significant footprint. This is especially so for mobile applications.

Client applications can also invoke Web service operations without using binding stubs. In order to invoke Web service operations without binding stubs, the application must simply configure metadata for each Web service operation and then make the actual invocation. The simplest way to do this is to use standard JAX-RPC (Java API for XML-based Remote Procedure Call) objects.

Within the `ServiceServlet` servlet of the EPS application we used client-side binding stubs to invoke Web service operations as follows:

```
try
{
  // Instantiate the VendorAProcurement Service Locator
  VendorAProcurementService vapService =
    new VendorAProcurementServiceLocator ();

  // Now use the locator to get a stub which
  //  implements the SDI.
  VendorAProcurement vapPort =
    vapService.getVendorAProcurement ();

  // Call the getLeadTime operation of the Web service
  //  through the client proxy method
  int vendorAResult = vapPort.getLeadTime ( 15151, 4);

  // Now use the result
}
```

```
catch ( Exception e )
{
   System.out.println ( "Error in client proxy." );
}
```

The same invocation can be accomplished without using any binding stubs as follows:

```
try
{
  // Specify the Web service endpoint
  String endpoint =
   "http://localhost:8080/axis/services/VendorAProcurement";

  Service service = new Service ();
  Call call = ( Call ) service.createCall ();

  call.setTargetEndpointAddress (
    new java.net.URL ( endpoint ) );

  // Specify the Web service operation to
  //  invoke - getLeadTime
  call.setOperationName ( new QName (
    "http://soapinterop.org/" , "getLeadTime" ) );

  // Optionally, specify the operation and return type
  //  parameter names, types, and modes
  call.addParameter ( "partNumber" ,
                      org.apache.axis.Constants.XSD_INT ,
                      javax.xml.rpc.ParameterMode.IN );
  call.addParameter ( "quantity" ,
                      org.apache.axis.Constants.XSD_INT ,
                      javax.xml.rpc.ParameterMode.IN );
  call.setReturnType ( org.apache.axis.Constants.XSD_INT );

  // Invoke the Web service operation by providing the
  //  actual parameter data of 15151 and 4
  Object retObj = call.invoke ( new Object[]{
                                new Integer ( 15151 ),
                                new Integer ( 4 )} );

  // Now we can cast the return value into an integer
  //  and use it.
    .
    .
    .

}
catch ( Exception e )
{
  System.err.println ( e.toString () );
}
```

The imports required for this code segment are:

```
import org.apache.axis.client.Call;
import org.apache.axis.client.Service;
import javax.xml.namespace.QName;
```

By simply specifying the metadata for each Web service to invoke, we are able to consume any Web service without generating any client-side binding stubs. Although binding stubs support a simple programming model, direct calls to Web services from the client application support dynamic invocations and are easier to maintain over time.

Where Are the Holes?

In this chapter we implemented the EPS application using only the core Web services technologies discussed in the first part of the book. Based on this core platform, we have been able to write a distributed application using industry standard messaging based on XML and HTTP.

The current EPS application certainly works, but there are numerous limitations to this application—both in terms of functionality as well as manageability. For example, the current implementation provides a simple means to compare the prices or lead times from the two vendors, but the application does not actually procure the components, that is, it does not support transactions. The application also does not support access from mobile devices.

The application is also difficult to manage and maintain as more and more vendor Web services are added. As it stands now, each time a new Web service is added (or removed), significant development time is needed to re-architect the system, write additional program code, and subject the entire system to rigorous testing processes.

Applications that provide full functionality are no doubt quite useful. Enterprise applications must not only implement the required functionality, but they must also be architected to operate within enterprise environments and meet enterprise needs for manageability. In the next chapter, we expand on this application to support these additional needs for enterprises.

Summary

In this chapter we have gone step-by-step and developed a Web services-based enterprise procurement application. We discussed both sides of the application—the client application that consumes Web services to present a coherent value-added functionality as well as the individual Web services.

We also implemented the entire system by using only the technologies of the core Web services platform—SOAP and WSDL. In the next chapter, we build on and extend this application, using the technologies and standards discussed in the second section of this book, and develop an enterprise-class system that supports transactions, workflow, mobility, and security.

Architect's Notes

- Client-side binding stubs support a simple programming model for Web services. The binding stubs are automatically generated by tools from each Web service's WSDL description, and provide a local interface for each remote Web service.
- Direct calls (without the use of binding stubs) to Web services are slightly more complicated, but incur significantly less overhead. There is no need to generate or maintain binding stubs for each Web service, and direct calls support dynamic invocations.
- The basic Web services infrastructure, comprising SOAP, WSDL, and UDDI, provide a good platform for industry-standards-based XML messaging between applications. However, this basic platform does not support additional enterprise-class requirements such as support for mobility, transactions, workflow, and security. (See the next chapter for how to implement an enterprise application that supports these requirements.)

CHAPTER 13

Real World Web Service Application Development—Advanced Technologies

In the previous chapter, we developed a Web services-based application from the ground up using fundamental Web services technologies like SOAP and WSDL. However, the exchange of messages between businesses is only the tip of the iceberg as far as enterprise computing is concerned. To enable true enterprise-level computing with Web services, we must address the non-functional requirements, which enable dependable applications to be built. In this chapter we address those requirements by adding security, transactionality, configurability, and mobility into our basic architecture to develop a full enterprise class application out of the basic enterprise procurement system.

Introduction

While the enterprise procurement application in its present form addresses the basic functional requirements of ordering parts, traditionally enterprise computing has had much stronger non-functional requirements which the current architecture does not address. The challenge is, therefore, to meet the following non-functional requirements to make the application truly dependable:

- **Configurability**—Enterprises live and die on the ability to react quickly to market conditions. Those enterprises whose computing systems and processes can be reconfigured quickly gain advantage in the market place.
- **Transactionality**—High quality data is central to the successful enterprise and the ability to maintain the consistency of that data is paramount, especially where business processes are automated. Failure to guard against inconsistent data is a real Achilles' heel for any wired enterprise.

- **Security**—Trading partners must be able to identify those parties they are interacting with, and be assured that the messages exchanged are not tampered with.[1]
- **Mobility**—Like the ability to reconfigure processes quickly, mobility is a key factor in business agility. A modern enterprise needs to empower its people wherever they may be and so the IT infrastructure must be equally mobile.

Given the modular and extensible nature of Web services, we can add each of these features into our architecture in a piecemeal fashion, building up the overall functionality of the system one step at a time until we can support all of our non-functional requirements, as shown in Figure 13-1.

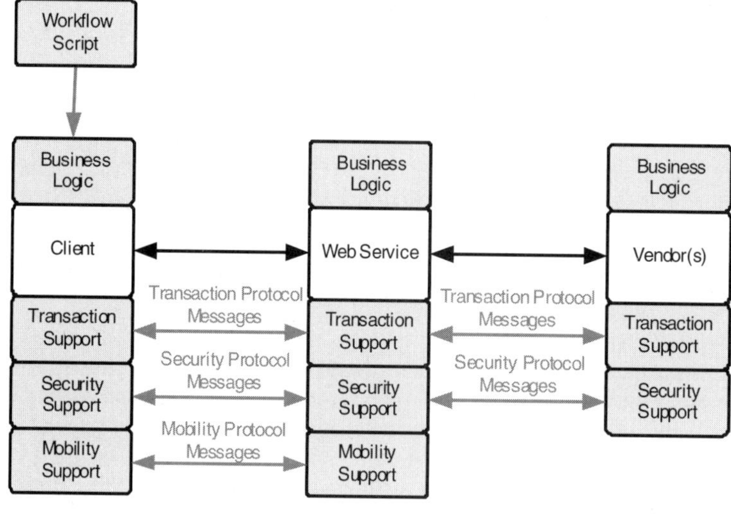

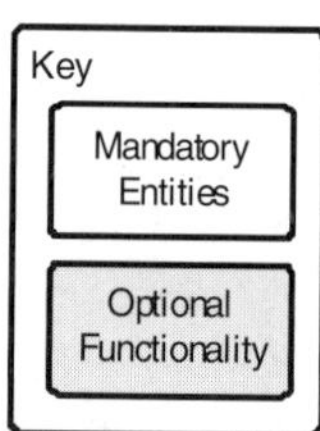

Figure 13-1 A Secure, Mobile, Configurable, Transaction-Aware Web Services-based Application

1. At time of writing, there are no freely available WS-Security implementations to use to secure the application. Instead, we assume that transport-level security mechanisms like HTTPS can be used to implement privacy and message integrity concerns, as well as (via certificates) to address authenticity concerns.

It should be kept in mind that while the overall architecture of a complete system may resemble that shown in Figure 13-1, Web services—uniquely among current distributed systems technology—allow a great deal of flexibility in the composition of underlying infrastructure. While as developers we may be expected to build secure, mobile, transaction-aware, reconfigurable services, we may equally be expected to produce simply a secure Web service. As we progress through this chapter, remember that each highlighted technology can be taken as a discrete component in its own right, and does not depend on any of the other technologies. That is, we are free to mix-and-match technologies in keeping with the general Web services philosophy, and so each example can be seen as a specific application in its own right and the examples can be taken as a whole composite application.

Building Evolvable and Composable Workflows

The previous revision of the enterprise procurement application relied on a static HTML page and a human to drive the application. While this may be a suitable approach for a small business, it does not scale well. In a large enterprise it may be preferable to capture the knowledge of the human operator and automate the process, freeing the human operator to work on more interesting work and allowing the process to execute more quickly.

A simple automation solution would involve screen-scraping techniques to allow a computer program that has been written to mimic the behavior of a human operator to drive the Web page itself via standard HTTP commands. However, this is a rather poor and brittle approach for three reasons:

- If the Web page's HTML changes, the program's screen scraping routines will fail and have to be updated.
- If the rules change, the program will have to be edited and rebuilt—which is not an approach that supports rapid reconfiguration.
- Composing such a standalone screen-scraping program into a larger system then gives rise to Enterprise Application Integration (EAI) headaches further down the track.

The advantages of using Web services-based workflow technology to orchestrate service interactions compared to the previous human-driven Web-based approach are twofold. First, human knowledge is encoded into XML, which can be easily re-encoded and evolved as and when the problem domain changes. Had this knowledge been encoded into compiled program code, its maintenance and rapid evolution would involve software engineers, system administrators and so forth that necessarily reduces the pace at which updates can be made. In this XML form (and indeed even more so if graphical tools that target the BPEL language are used), the job of evolving the workflow can be delegated to business analysts without necessarily having to resort to heavyweight software maintenance practices.

Second, as a Web service itself, the workflow script can easily form a component to be re-used by other Web services-based applications. Compared to the either the human-driven or programmatic screen-scraping approach, this method permits much more robust re-use of components. However, to reap these benefits, we must first automate the process into a workflow.

Of course, we could resort to traditional (proprietary) middleware to integrate the Web-based application. However, this is short sighted since it then produces another proprietary system that we may need to integrate at a later date. Better just to switch all integration work over to the canonical form that Web services provides now, unless there are extremely compelling reasons not to.

Not using Web services for integration work just stores headaches for later!

Automating the Procurement Process

A better solution is to cut out the middleman (the Web page and human operator) altogether and instead capture the process as a workflow script that encodes the kinds of decisions that humans would make. That workflow script can then be executed and interact directly with the back-end Web services, and can itself be exposed as a Web service allowing aggregation into larger applications, as shown in Figure 13-2.

From the perspective of a consumer, the workflow-based Web service that drives the procurement is no different from any other Web service insofar as it is an endpoint through which messages are exchanged. In this case, the message exchanges need to be able to describe procurement of items based on cost, part number, and lead time.

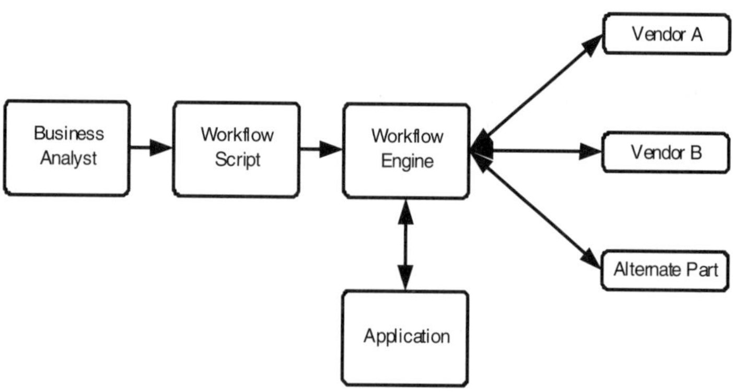

Figure 13-2 Encoding Business Rules into a Workflow.

It also needs to determine whether it is cost of lead time that is the most important factor for this order—that is, whether the parts have to be procured quickly or cheaply. Given these criteria, as a first step toward designing the workflow, we can design a WSDL interface that describes this interface, which is shown in Figure 13-3.

```
<?xml version="1.0"?>
<definitions targetNamespace="http://procurement.example.org"
xmlns:tns="http://procurement.example.org" xmlns:wsdl="http://
schemas.xmlsoap.org/wsdl/" xmlns:xsd="http://www.w3.org/2001/
XMLSchema" xmlns:slnk="http://schemas.xmlsoap.org/ws/2002/07/
service-link" xmlns:soap="http://schemas.xmlsoap.org/wsdl/
soap/" xmlns="http://schemas.xmlsoap.org/wsdl/"
xmlns:ele="http://procurement.example.org/elements">
  <types>
    <schema targetNamespace=
      "http://procurement.example.org/elements"
      xmlns="http://www.w3.org/2001/XMLSchema">
      <xsd:element name="partNumber" type="xsd:int"/>
      <xsd:element name="quantity" type="xsd:int"/>
      <xsd:element name="costOverLeadtime"
        type="xsd:boolean"/>
      <xsd:element name="orderNumber" type="xsd:int"/>
    </schema>
  </types>
  <message name="OrderPartsRequest">
    <part name="partNumber" element="ele:partNumber"/>
    <part name="quantity" element="ele:quantity"/>
    <part name="costOverLeadtime"
      element="ele:costOverLeadtime"/>
  </message>
  <message name="OrderPartsResponse">
    <part name="orderNumber" element="ele:orderNumber"/>
  </message>
  <portType name="PartsServicePortType">
    <operation name="orderParts">
      <input message="tns:OrderPartsRequest"/>
      <output message="tns:OrderPartsResponse"/>
    </operation>
  </portType>
  <slnk:serviceLinkType name="OrderPartsLT">
    <slnk:role name="PartServer">
      <slnk:portType name="tns:PartsServicePortType"/>
    </slnk:role>
  </slnk:serviceLinkType>
</definitions>
```

Figure 13-3 Procurement Service WSDL (Abstract) Interface.

The WSDL shown in Figure 13-3 is the basis for all interaction with the procurement Web service. Through this interface, external applications can invoke the logic captured as a BPEL script, which will interact with the vendor services on the users' behalf. The service description is straightforward, and simply consists of a set of types which are composed into two messages (`OrderPartsRequest` for inbound requests and `OrderPartsResponse` for outgoing responses), and a single `portType` declaration, which supports the `orderParts` operation. Thus the orderParts operation has a signature that we can approximate to the semantically equivalent Java, `int orderParts(int partNumber, int quantity, boolean costOrLeadtime)`. The return value for this method is the order number for the specified quantity of parts and the arguments represent a part number that has relevance for a particular part with a particular vendor—the number of those parts required and whether cost or leadtime is the overriding priority.

The only element that is different from a vanilla WSDL document is the `serviceLinkType` element, which is a BPEL construct that specifies which services can link to (are allowed to invoke) the part ordering service. In this case, the `serviceLinkType` specifies only a single role, which is the `PartsServicePortType`. This means that the service places no constraints on the interfaces of other services that may wish to invoke the part ordering service. Had another role been specified, it would have meant that any service invoking the part ordering service would have had to fulfill the indicated role—that is, a `portType` for the part ordering service to call back to must be supported by the invoker of the part ordering service.

The choice of using a synchronous message exchange pattern as opposed to a one-way pattern has been made under the assumption that the procurement process will be short-lived. This approach has the benefit that it is simple to understand and matches the message exchange pattern exhibited by the underlying vendor services.

However, the one-way approach would have the benefit that network resources would not be consumed while waiting for the procurement process to finish, and also decouples the procurement service from the procurer so they may fail and recover independently of one-another without upsetting the behavior of the system.

Augmenting Remote WSDL Interfaces

Having understood the interface and message exchanges between the client and the workflow-based service, we now need to analyze the interfaces and message exchanges that occur at the back end so we can utilize the functionality exposed by those services within the workflow script. To utilize the functionality of a Web service from within a BPEL workflow, the service's interface needs to be augmented with appropriate `serviceLinkType` declarations, just like the WSDL for the workflow itself. This is achieved most easily via the WSDL import directive.

We can use the WSDL `import` directive to extend the existing WSDL documents without having to re-write them. In this case we write a new WSDL document for each service, but include only the `serviceLinkType` declarations that BPEL workflows require. The WSDL descriptions of each of the vendor services, and the alternate part service as shown in Figure 13-4, Figure 13-5 and Figure 13-6, respectively. In each case, the original WSDL interface is imported and augmented by an appropriate `serviceLinkType` declaration.

```
<?xml version="1.0" encoding="UTF-8"?>
<definitions
targetNamespace="http://procurement.example.org/va"
xmlns:vas="http://localhost:8080/axis/services/VendorAService"
xmlns="http://schemas.xmlsoap.org/wsdl/" xmlns:slnk="http://
schemas.xmlsoap.org/ws/2002/07/service-link">
  <import
namespace="http://localhost:8080/axis/services/VendorAService"
location=
  "http://localhost:8080/axis/services/VendorAService?wsdl"/>
  <slnk:serviceLinkType name="VendorAServiceLT">
    <slnk:role name="VendorAServiceRole">
      <slnk:portType name="vas:VendorAService"/>
    </slnk:role>
  </slnk:serviceLinkType>
</definitions>
```

Figure 13-4 The vendor a service WSDL interface.

Figure 13-4 shows the `serviceLinkType` that defines the role of the Vendor A service in the workflow. Since Vendor A is a synchronous service, it specifies only a single role for itself and does not place any restrictions on a particular `portType` that must be supported by the caller. This is also true of the Vendor B service shown in Figure 13-5.

Like the Vendor A and Vendor B augmentations, the AlternatePartService also declares a unary `serviceLinkType`, as shown in Figure 13-6.

Now that we have our BPEL augmented interfaces in place, the next step is to build the workflow that will drive the services behind the interfaces.

Implementing the BPEL Workflow Script

The final goal of our automation project is to capture the rules that a human operator would use when procuring parts in BPEL format. When building the workflow script, the problem can be broken down into these sections:

```
<?xml version="1.0" encoding="UTF-8"?>
<definitions
targetNamespace="http://procurement.example.org/vb"
xmlns:vbs="http://localhost:8080/axis/services/VendorBService"
xmlns="http://schemas.xmlsoap.org/wsdl/" xmlns:slnk="http://
schemas.xmlsoap.org/ws/2002/07/service-link">
  <import
namespace="http://localhost:8080/axis/services/VendorBService"
location=
"http://localhost:8080/axis/services/VendorBService?wsdl"/>
  <slnk:serviceLinkType name="VendorBServiceLT">
    <slnk:role name="VendorBServiceRole">
      <slnk:portType name="vbs:VendorBService"/>
    </slnk:role>
  </slnk:serviceLinkType>
</definitions>
```

Figure 13-5 The Vendor B service WSDL interface.

```
<?xml version="1.0" encoding="UTF-8"?>
<definitions
targetNamespace="http://procurement.example.org/ap" xmlns:aps=
 "http://localhost:8080/axis/services/AlternatePartService"
xmlns="http://schemas.xmlsoap.org/wsdl/" xmlns:slnk=
 "http://schemas.xmlsoap.org/ws/2002/07/service-link">
  <import namespace=
  "http://localhost:8080/axis/services/AlternatePartService"
location=
"http://localhost:8080/axis/services/AlternatePartService?wsdl"/>
  <slnk:serviceLinkType name="AlternatePartServiceLT">
    <slnk:role name="AlternatePartServiceRole">
      <slnk:portType name="aps:AlternatePartService"/>
    </slnk:role>
  </slnk:serviceLinkType>
</definitions>
```

Figure 13-6 The alternate part service WSDL interface.

1. Declaring the services that the script will interact with, the role that each plays respective to the workflow and the `serviceLinkType` which references them in the `<partners>` section of the BPEL script.
2. Declaration of `<containers>` to hold messages that are sent and received from the vendor and alternate part services and between the workflow instance and the client application that instantiated it.
3. Creation of the algorithmic aspect of the workflow script that drives the constituent Web services through the procurement process.

The algorithm that we will implement, which captures the human operator behavior, is straightforward to understand. In the first phase of the algorithm the vendor services are asked for the price and leadtimes for a specific quantity of a particular part, using the alternate part service to lookup the equivalent part number for Vendor B. This is done in parallel, using `<sequence>` activities nested inside `<flow>` activities, for performance reasons, and is safe to execute in this manner because only read-only operations are invoked on the vendor services.

Once the cost and leadtime have been discovered, the algorithm then checks to see which is the most important factor, based on the contents of the message sent by the invoking application. Based on that decision, the cheapest or fastest offer is taken up by placing the order with the appropriate vendor service and returning the order number to the invoking application. This is depicted in Figure 13-7.

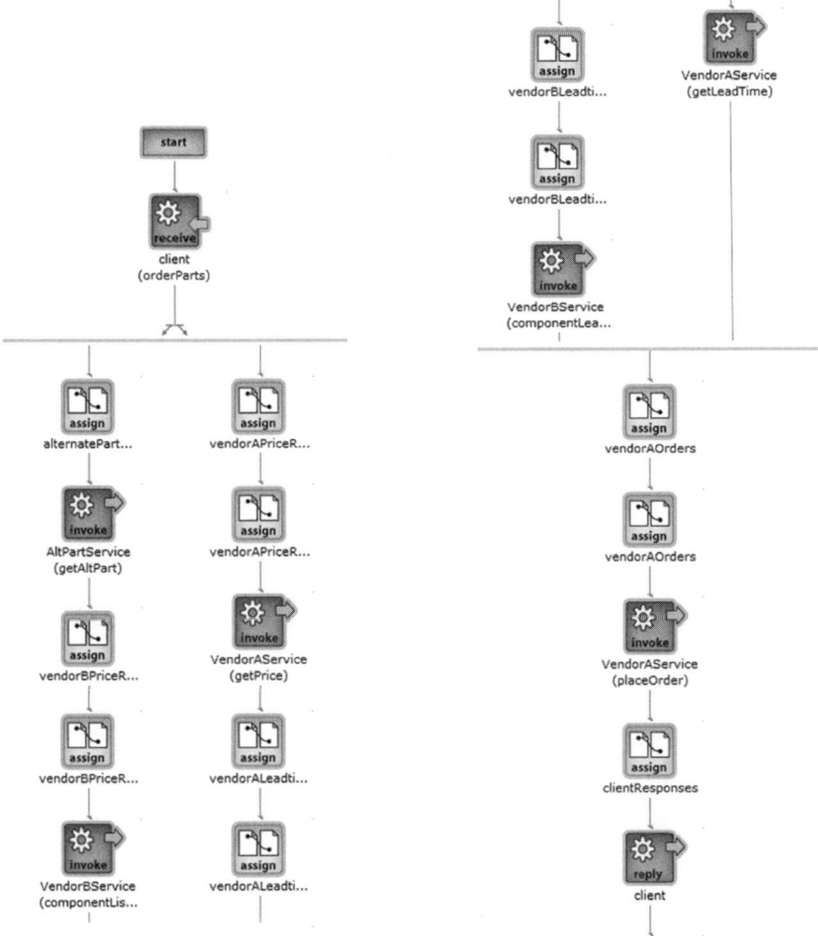

Figure 13-7 BPEL procurement workflow diagram.

The workflow is shown graphically in Figure 13-7 (which is, in fact, an audit trail from the engine used to execute the workflow). The workflow instance is created on receipt of a message from an invoking application. From there a parallel activity follows where Vendor A service is asked for price and leadtime information (in the right-hand side of the parallel activity) while Vendor B is asked for the same *after* the alternate part service has retrieved the alternate appropriate part number.

Once both threads of parallel activity have completed, there is a synchronization at which point the decision for cheapest versus fastest is taken and an order placed with one or other of the vendor services in the subsequent (serial) activity. This strategy is captured in the BPEL workflow script shown in Figure 13-8 and Figure 13-9.

```
<process name="Procurement"
targetNamespace="http://procurement.example.org"
suppressJoinFailure="yes" xmlns:tns="http://
procurement.example.org" xmlns:wsdl="http://schemas.xmlsoap.org/
wsdl/" xmlns:sref="http://schemas.xmlsoap.org/ws/2002/07/service-
reference/" xmlns="http://schemas.xmlsoap.org/ws/2002/07/business-
process/" xmlns:vas="http://localhost:8080/axis/services/
VendorAService" xmlns:vbs="http://localhost:8080/axis/services/
VendorBService" xmlns:aps="http://localhost:8080/axis/services/
AlternatePartService"
xmlns:vasn="http://procurement.example.org/va" xmlns:vbsn="http://
procurement.example.org/vb" xmlns:apsn="http://
procurement.example.org/ap">
```

Figure 13-8 BPEL procurement workflow script.

The XML in Figure 13-8 shows the opening tag of a BPEL process. It declares a process element (the root for all BPEL processes) and the namespaces of the procurement workflow service, its partners and `serviceLinkType` declarations, and the BPEL namespaces.

Once we have these namespaces, we can start to use their contents to author the workflow script itself, starting with the partner declarations as shown in Figure 13-9.

```
<partners>
  <partner name="VendorAService"
    serviceLinkType="vasn:VendorAServiceLT"
    partnerRole="VendorAServiceRole"/>
  <partner name="VendorBService"
    serviceLinkType="vbsn:VendorBServiceLT"
    partnerRole="VendorBServiceRole"/>
  <partner name="AltPartService"
    serviceLinkType="apsn:AlternatePartServiceLT"
    partnerRole="VendorBServiceRole"/>
  <partner name="client" serviceLinkType="tns:OrderPartsLT"
    myRole="PartServer"/>
</partners>
```

Figure 13-9 Partner declarations.

Figure 13-9 declares each `partner` that is involved in the process, and their roles in terms of the `serviceLinkTypes` that we defined earlier in Figure 13-4, Figure 13-5, and Figure 13-6. Once each partner has been declared, it becomes a reference to a Web service we can interact with as part of our workflow.

To interact with partners (and to do local processing where necessary), we need to be able to send them messages. The `container` declarations for this workflow are shown in Figure 13-10.

```
<containers>
  <container name="clientRequests"
    messageType="tns:OrderPartsRequest"/>
  <container name="clientResponses"
    messageType="tns:OrderPartsResponse"/>
  <container name="vendorAOrders"
    messageType="vas:placeOrderRequest"/>
  <container name="vendorAOrderNumbers"
    messageType="vas:placeOrderResponse"/>
  <container name="vendorAPriceRequests"
    messageType="vas:getPriceRequest"/>
  <container name="vendorAPriceResponses"
    messageType="vas:getPriceResponse"/>
  <container name="vendorALeadtimeRequests"
    messageType="vas:getLeadTimeRequest"/>
  <container name="vendorALeadtimeResponses"
    messageType="vas:getLeadTimeResponse"/>
  <container name="vendorBOrders"
    messageType="vbs:orderComponentRequest"/>
  <container name="vendorBOrderNumbers"
    messageType="vbs:orderComponentResponse"/>
  <container name="vendorBPriceRequests"
    messageType="vbs:componentListPriceRequest"/>
  <container name="vendorBPriceResponses"
    messageType="vbs:componentListPriceResponse"/>
  <container name="vendorBLeadtimeRequests"
    messageType="vbs:componentLeadtimeRequest"/>
  <container name="vendorBLeadtimeResponses"
    messageType="vbs:componentLeadtimeResponse"/>
  <container name="alternatePartRequests"
    messageType="aps:getAltPartRequest"/>
  <container name="alternatePartResponses"
    messageType="aps:getAltPartResponse"/>
</containers>
```

Figure 13-10 Container declarations.

Each of the variables used in the process is typed according to the WSDL messages found in the interfaces of the partners and in the procurement service itself. The containers element is placed at process scope in Figure 13-10 because all variables have process scope in BPEL 1.0— in BPEL 1.1 this has (fortunately) been changed to allow the equivalent of `containers` (called `variables`) to be declared within arbitrary scopes.

Having containers and partners gives us the ability to exchange the messages held in containers with the Web services represented by partners. The first of these message exchanges in this process is presented in Figure 13-11, and iscaptured in graphical form (from the audit trail of the workflow instance) in Figure 13-12.

```
<sequence>
  <!-- receive input from requestor -->
  <receive partner="client"
    portType="tns:PartsServicePortType"
    operation="orderParts" container="clientRequests"
    createInstance="yes"/>
```

Figure 13-11 Initiating a workflow instance.

Figure 13-12 Graphical representation of initiating a Workflow instance.

The workflow logic begins in the `receive` activity in Figure 13-11. This activity receives an `OrderPartsRequest` message through the orderParts operation in the `PartsServicePortType` portType, which it deposits into the `clientRequests` container. Since the receipt of this message is the logical beginning of the workflow logic, a new instance of the workflow is created by setting the `createInstance="yes"` attribute.

Once we have the client request, we can begin to compute how best to meet the procurement needs of the client, as per Figure 13-13.

The flow from Figure 13-12 is codified in Figure 13-14 where we invoke operations on Vendor A's service to determine the price of the requested part. In Figure 13-14 we declare a `flow` activity that we use to support the parallel execution of activities in Figure 13-14 (where the workflow interacts with Vendor A's Web service) and in Figure 13-16 (where the workflow interacts with the alternate part service and Vendor B).

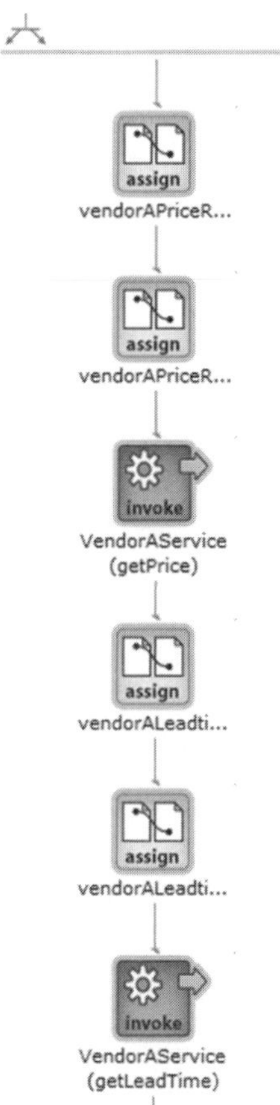

Figure 13-13 Graphical representation of invoking operations on VendorA.

The activities in Figure 13-14 are scoped within a sequence to serialize their execution. The strategy is to build a request message to invoke the price operation of VendorA and then the same for the leadtime operation. These results are then stored in the `vendorAPriceResponses` and `vendorALeadtimeResponses` containers for later processing. Hence, in Figure 13-14 we see a set of assignment activities to build the outgoing message, an invocation on VendorA's Web service using that message, and then more assignment logic to store the response from the invocation in the appropriate containers.

```
<!-- Ask vendor A service for a price and leadtime -->
<flow>
  <sequence>
    <assign>
      <copy>
        <from container="clientRequests"
          part="partNumber"/>
        <to container="vendorAPriceRequests"
          part="partNumber"/>
      </copy>
    </assign>
    <assign>
      <copy>
        <from container="clientRequests"
          part="quantity"/>
        <to container="vendorAPriceRequests"
          part="quantity"/>
      </copy>
    </assign>
    <invoke partner="VendorAService"
      portType="vas:VendorAService" operation="getPrice"
      inputContainer="vendorAPriceRequests"
      outputContainer="vendorAPriceResponses"/>
    <assign>
      <copy>
        <from container="clientRequests"
          part="partNumber"/>
        <to container="vendorALeadtimeRequests"
          part="partNumber"/>
      </copy>
    </assign>
    <assign>
      <copy>
        <from container="clientRequests"
          part="quantity"/>
        <to container="vendorALeadtimeRequests"
          part="quantity"/>
      </copy>
    </assign>
    <invoke partner="VendorAService"
      portType="vas:VendorAService"
      operation="getLeadTime"
      inputContainer="vendorALeadtimeRequests"
      outputContainer="vendorALeadtimeResponses"/>
  </sequence>
```

Figure 13-14 Invoking operations on VendorA in parallel with other operations.

This same strategy is used to invoke operations on Vendor B's Web service and the alternate part service (in parallel with the invocations on Vendor A because they are within the scope of the same `flow` activity), as shown in Figure 13-15 and expressed in BPEL in Figure 13-16.

Figure 13-15 Graphical representation of invoking operations on Vendor B and the alternate part service.

```
<!--First find out the alternative part name -->
<sequence>
  <assign>
    <copy>
      <from container="clientRequests"
        part="partNumber"/>
      <to container="alternatePartRequests"
        part="partNo"/>
    </copy>
  </assign>
  <invoke partner="AltPartService"
    portType="aps:AlternatePartService"
    operation="getAltPart"
    inputContainer="alternatePartRequests"
    outputContainer="alternatePartResponses"/>
  <!-- And ask the VendorB service for the price and
    leadtime -->
  <assign>
    <copy>
      <from container="alternatePartResponses"
        part="getAltPartReturn"/>
      <to container="vendorBPriceRequests"
        part="partNumber"/>
    </copy>
  </assign>
  <assign>
    <copy>
      <from container="clientRequests"
        part="quantity"/>
      <to container="vendorBPriceRequests"
        part="quantity"/>
    </copy>
  </assign>
  <invoke partner="VendorBService"
    portType="vbs:VendorBService"
    operation="componentListPrice"
    inputContainer="vendorBPriceRequests"
    outputContainer="vendorBPriceResponses"/>
  <assign>
    <copy>
      <from container="alternatePartResponses"
        part="getAltPartReturn"/>
      <to container="vendorBLeadtimeRequests"
        part="partNumber"/>
    </copy>
  </assign>
  <assign>
    <copy>
```

Figure 13-16 Invoking operations on Vendor B and the alternate part service in parallel with operations on Vendor A.

```
          <from container="clientRequests"
            part="quantity"/>
          <to container="vendorBLeadtimeRequests"
            part="quantity"/>
        </copy>
      </assign>
      <invoke partner="VendorBService"
        portType="vbs:VendorBService"
        operation="componentLeadtime"
        inputContainer="vendorBLeadtimeRequests"
        outputContainer="vendorBLeadtimeResponses"/>
    </sequence>
  </flow>
```

Figure 13-16 Invoking operations on Vendor B and the alternate part service in parallel with operations on Vendor A (continued).

In Figure 13-16, the workflow script first builds a message in the alternatePartRequests container through a set of assign activities to send to the alternate part service. Once that message has been constructed, it is sent to the alternate part service via an invoke activity, which synchronously receives a response from the alternate part service and stores the message in the alternatePartResponses container.

The getAltPartReturn part of the alternatePartResponses container is then used with the quantity part of the clientRequests container (which contains the original order details) to create messages in the vendorBPriceRequests and vendorBLeadtimeRequests containers. These messages are then used to invoke the componentListPrice and componentLeadtime operations on Vendor B's Web service, and the synchronous responses from those invocations are stored in the vendorBPriceResponses and vendorBLeadtimeResponses containers, respectively, ready for further processing.

Once the price and leadtime requests from Vendor A and Vendor B have been received, the parallel activity in this workflow (the sequence activities enclosed in the flow activity) comes to an end, the processing of the information received from partner Web services can begin, as shown in Figure 13-17.

The BPEL fragment shown in Figure 13-17 deals with procuring parts where cost is the most important metric, that is where the costOverLeadtime part of the clientRequests container contains the value "true" as computed by the outermost switch activity (if this value was set to "false" then the code in Figure 13-20 would instead be executed since it constitutes the otherwise branch of the outermost switch).

Inside the outermost switch, there is a nested switch activity which, depending on whether Vendor A or Vendor B delivered the cheapest quote, executes either the case branch (Vendor B's quote is greater than Vendor A's) or the otherwise branch (where by implication Vendor A's price is the largest).

```
<switch>
  <case condition=
    "bpws:getContainerData('clientRequests',
      'costOverLeadtime')">
    <!-- cost is most important -->
    <switch>
      <case condition=
        "bpws:getContainerData('vendorBPriceResponses',
          'componentListPriceReturn') >
         bpws:getContainerData('vendorAPriceResponses',
          'getPriceReturn') ">
        <sequence>
          <!-- Vendor A is cheapest -->
          <assign>
            <copy>
              <from container="clientRequests"
                part="partNumber"/>
              <to container="vendorAOrders"
                part="partNumber"/>
            </copy>
          </assign>
          <assign>
            <copy>
              <from container="clientRequests"
                part="quantity"/>
              <to container="vendorAOrders"
                part="quantity"/>
            </copy>
          </assign>
          <invoke partner="VendorAService"
            portType="vas:VendorAService"
            operation="placeOrder"
            inputContainer="vendorAOrders"
            outputContainer="vendorAOrderNumbers"/>
          <assign>
            <copy>
              <from container="vendorAOrderNumbers"
                part="placeOrderReturn"/>
              <to container="clientResponses"
                part="orderNumber"/>
            </copy>
          </assign>
        </sequence>
      </case>
      <otherwise>
        <!-- VendorB is cheapest -->
        <sequence>
          <assign>
            <copy>
```

Figure 13-17 Ordering from either vendor based on cost.

```
                <from container="alternatePartResponses"
                  part="getAltPartReturn"/>
                <to container="vendorBOrders"
                  part="partNumber"/>
              </copy>
            </assign>
            <assign>
              <copy>
                <from container="clientRequests"
                  part="quantity"/>
                <to container="vendorBOrders"
                  part="quantity"/>
              </copy>
            </assign>
            <invoke partner="VendorBService"
              portType="vbs:VendorBService"
              operation="orderComponent"
              inputContainer="vendorBOrders"
              outputContainer="vendorBOrderNumbers"/>
            <assign>
              <copy>
                <from container="vendorBOrderNumbers"
                  part="orderComponentReturn"/>
                <to container="clientResponses"
                  part="orderNumber"/>
              </copy>
            </assign>
          </sequence>
        </otherwise>
      </switch>
    </case>
```

Figure 13-17 Ordering from either vendor based on cost (continued).

The logic is straightforward in either case in that whichever service offered the cheapest price has a message created and the appropriate "purchase" operation is invoked. This is highlighted in Figure 13-18 where in the audit trail for a particular instance, we see that Vendor A offered the least expensive option and that accordingly messages are exchanged with Vendor A to procure parts.

The results from this invocation are then stored in the `clientResponses` container ready to return the results of the procurement to the original client, highlighted in Figure 13-19.

Our workflow logic also has the ability to procure items based on timeliness criteria. Figure 13-20 shows the continuation of the switch activity that began in Figure 13-17 and is executed where timeliness, rather than cost, is the overriding priority. This part of the workflow is executed when the condition `<case condition= "bpws:getContainerData('clientRequests', 'costOverLeadtime')">` evaluates to false—i.e., when the message that the client used to initiate the workflow contained the value `false` in the `costOverLeadtime` part.

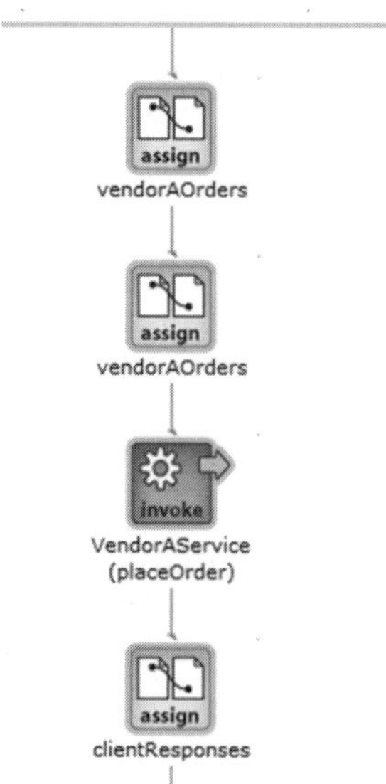

Figure 13-18 Graphical representation of ordering from VendorA based on cost.

Figure 13-19 Graphical representation of replying with the cheapest procurement offer to the client.

```
<otherwise>
 <!-- speed is most important -->
 <switch>
   <case condition=
    "bpws:getContainerData('vendorBLeadtimeResponses',
     'componentLeadtimeReturn') >
    bpws:getContainerData('vendorALeadtimeResponses',
     'getLeadTimeReturn') ">
     <!-- Vendor A is fastest -->
     <sequence>
       <assign>
         <copy>
```

Figure 13-20 Ordering from either vendor based on leadtime.

```
            <from container="clientRequests"
              part="partNumber"/>
            <to container="vendorAOrders"
              part="partNumber"/>
          </copy>
        </assign>
        <assign>
          <copy>
            <from container="clientRequests"
              part="quantity"/>
            <to container="vendorAOrders"
              part="quantity"/>
          </copy>
        </assign>
        <invoke partner="VendorAService"
          portType="vas:VendorAService"
          operation="placeOrder"
          inputContainer="vendorAOrders"
          outputContainer="vendorAOrderNumbers"/>
        <assign>
          <copy>
            <from container="vendorAOrderNumbers"
              part="placeOrderReturn"/>
            <to container="clientResponses"
              part="orderNumber"/>
          </copy>
        </assign>
      </sequence>
    </case>
    <otherwise>
      <!-- VendorB is fastest -->
      <sequence>
        <assign>
          <copy>
            <from container="alternatePartResponses"
              part="getAltPartReturn"/>
            <to container="vendorBOrders"
              part="partNumber"/>
          </copy>
        </assign>
        <assign>
          <copy>
            <from container="clientRequests"
              part="quantity"/>
            <to container="vendorBOrders"
              part="quantity"/>
          </copy>
        </assign>
        <invoke partner="VendorBService"
          portType="vbs:VendorBService"
```

Figure 13-20 Ordering from either vendor based on leadtime (continued).

```
                    operation="orderComponent"
                    inputContainer="vendorBOrders"
                    outputContainer="vendorBOrderNumbers"/>
                  <assign>
                    <copy>
                      <from container="vendorBOrderNumbers"
                        part="orderComponentReturn"/>
                      <to container="clientResponses"
                        part="orderNumber"/>
                    </copy>
                  </assign>
                </sequence>
              </otherwise>
            </switch>
          </otherwise>
        </switch>
```

Figure 13-20 Ordering from either vendor based on leadtime (continued).

Figure 13-20 is almost identical to Figure 13-17, with the caveat that orders are placed based on lead time, not price. Again, the logic is straightforward in that whichever service offered the fastest turnaround has a message created and the appropriate "purchase" operation is invoked. The results from this invocation once again stored in the `clientResponses` container ready to return the results of the procurement to the original client.

The final part of the workflow script is to respond to the original client the invoked the workflow. This is shown in Figure 13-21.

```
    <!-- respond output to requestor -->
    <reply partner="client"
      portType="tns:PartsServicePortType"
      operation="orderParts"
      container="clientResponses"/>
  </sequence>
</process>
```

Figure 13-21 Replying with the cheapest or fastest procurement offer to the client.

The `reply` activity shown in Figure 13-21 simply takes the message that has been built by the script in the `clientResponses` container and uses it to respond to the invocation it received through the `PartsServicePortType` `portType` from the client, before terminating and closing both the sequence that the reply activity was part of and the process as a whole.

Deploying and Executing BPEL Workflows

Having developed the workflow script that captures the knowledge of the human worker, we must deploy it onto a workflow server to expose its functionality to the network.

> For this example, we chose the Collaxa 2.0 (beta 8) to host our scripts. This software provides the ability to develop and execute BPEL workflow scripts, and to expose those workflows as Web services. It is available with a free 30-day license from http://www.collaxa.com/product.welcome.html. There are other toolkits available from other vendors (including IBM's BPWS4J and Microsoft's BizTalk), but it should be noted that while the actual workflow scripts we developed are, by definition, portable between different engines, the configuration and method of deployment will differ.

The deployment configuration that we ultimately want to arrive at is shown in Figure 13-22. In this case, both the workflow script and the WSDL augmentation are hosted by the BPEL engine. The engine takes the workflow script WSDL and creates the additional binding and service entries in that WSDL so it can expose the workflow script as a Web service. It also takes the additional WSDL augmentations supplied at deploy time and imports the WSDL served by the vendor and alternate part services, so the underlying engine can process all the necessary binding information for the remote services.

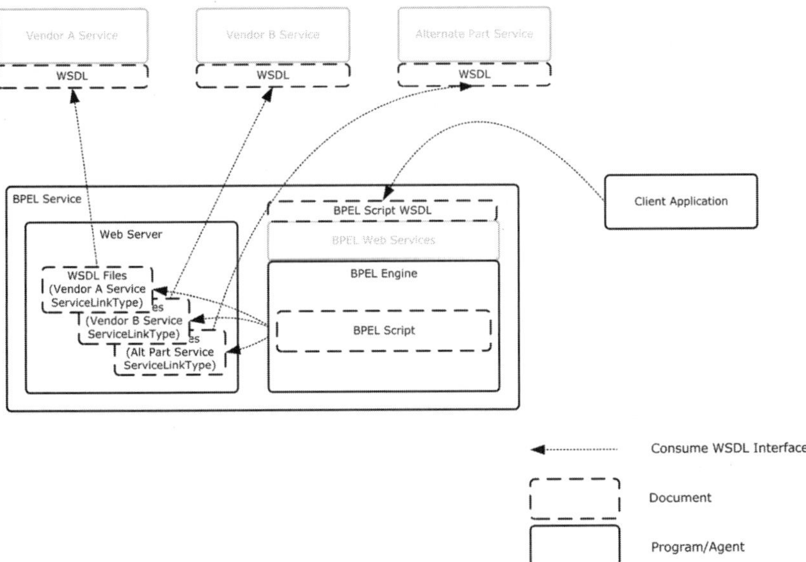

Figure 13-22 The procurement workflow collaxa deployment.

The key to deploying this configuration is the project file that ties together the workflow script, its (abstract) WSDL definition and the WSDL of the remote services. This is shown in Figure 13-23.

```
<?xml version="1.0" encoding="UTF-8"?>
<bpel-scenario src="Procurement.bpel Procurement.wsdl">
  <properties id="VendorAService">
    <property name="wsdl-location">
      http://localhost:9700/xmllib/VendorAService.wsdl
    </property>
  </properties>
  <properties id="VendorBService">
    <property name="wsdl-location">
      http://localhost:9700/xmllib/VendorBService.wsdl
    </property>
  </properties>
  <properties id="AltPartService">
    <property name="wsdl-location">
      http://localhost:9700/xmllib/AlternatePartService.wsdl
    </property>
  </properties>
</bpel-scenario>
```

Figure 13-23 A collaxa project configuration file.

The key point about Figure 13-23 is that each service name matches exactly the name of a partner in the BPEL workflow script that we presented in Figure 13-22. Additionally, each `wsdl-location` property references the locally hosted WSDL file which in turn imports the remotely hosted WSDL at each Web service invoked by the workflow.

```
<?xml version="1.0"?>
<project name="Procurement" default="main" basedir=".">
  <property name="deploy" value="true"/>
  <property name="rev" value="1.0"/>
  <property name="out"
    value="${CXHome}/server-default/classes"/>
  <target name="main">
    <copy file="${basedir}/AlternatePartService.wsdl"
      todir="${CXHome}/server-default/xmllib/"/>
    <copy file="${basedir}/VendorAService.wsdl"
      todir="${CXHome}/server-default/xmllib/"/>
    <copy file="${basedir}/VendorBService.wsdl"
      todir="${CXHome}/server-default/xmllib/"/>
    <bpelc input="${basedir}/Procurement.xml" rev="${rev}"
      sourcepath="${basedir}" deploy="${deploy}"/>
  </target>
</project>
```

Figure 13-24 A Collaxa `ant` script.

The final stage in deploying this workflow is to execute the compiler/deployment tool on the project file, and to deploy the additional WSDL onto the workflow engine server where it can be accessed by workflow instances. To simplify matters, the Collaxa 2.0 engine comes with a variant of the popular Apache Ant build scripting language and, thus, the entire deployment can be achieved by issuing the command `cxant` in the same directory as the Ant script shown in Figure 13-24. This is, in fact, a standard Ant script for which the cxant program automatically sets the Collaxa-specific variables (like `CXHome` which is the location of the Collaxa installation). Other than that, the script uses the standard Ant `copy` task to move the WSDL files into the server's WSDL directory and the Collaxa `bpelc` task that invokes the toolkit's BPEL compilation and deployment utility.

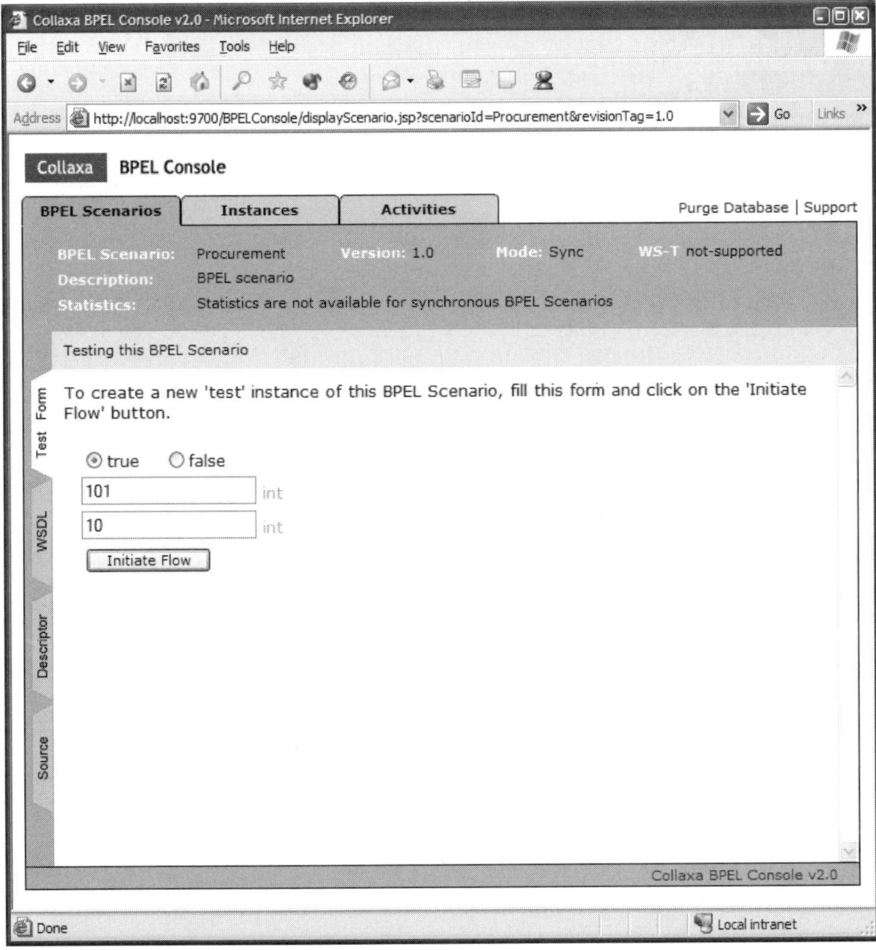

Figure 13-25 Executing a workflow instance.

Having successfully deployed the workflow script, we are now able to execute it. The easiest way to do this is to simply use the Collaxa 2.0 console to execute an instance of the workflow, as shown in Figure 13-25. The form presented to the user allows the construction of the initial message to the workflow instance and is, therefore, composed from a part number (integer), a quantity (integer), and a preference for leadtime or cost (Boolean value). Once the "initiate flow" button is clicked, the code behind the Web page sends these values as an `OrderPartsRequest` to the Web service endpoint exposed by the engine and execution proceeds as shown in Figure 13-26.

However, it is generally not the case that we would want this workflow to be executed from the server console. So instead of using the console to invoke the service on our behalf, it is possible to access the workflow Web service programmatically through its WSDL interface. To do this, we obtain the address of the (full) WSDL for the service from the console, and use the client-side tools from a Web services toolkit to consume that WSDL and create appropriate proxies for use within other applications and services.

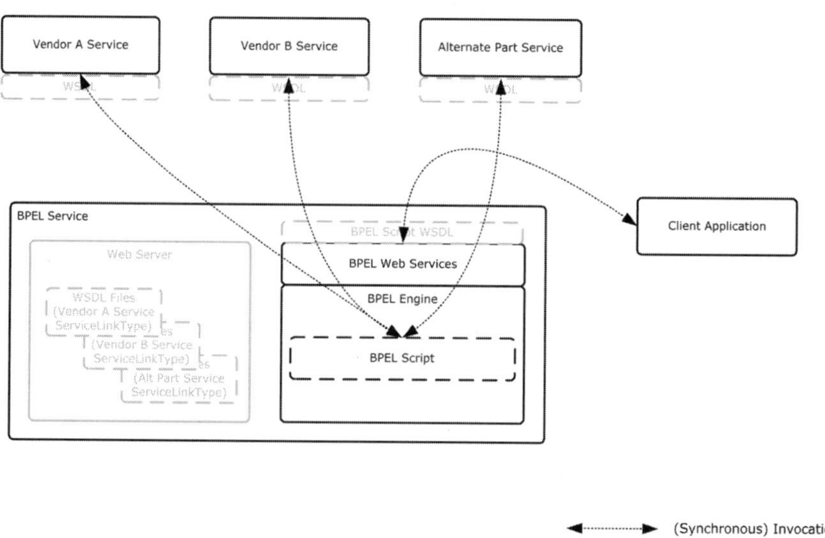

Figure 13-26 Executing the procurement workflow in the Collaxa 2.0 environment.

Adding Transaction Support

Of course in enterprise procurement, sometimes creativity is required to obtain the right materials at the right time. While this creativity often rests in the heads of the staff involved in the procurement process, the computing systems that support those roles must also be able to deal with the logistics of the kinds of situations where staff order numerous partial shipments of parts from a number of suppliers to fulfill a single order. In this situation, we need a mechanism that permits orders to execute seamlessly across a number of Web services as though it was a single order sent to a single provider. In short, we need transactional support.

> In this section we use Java code to illustrate how to transaction-enable Web services and applications which consume those services. Although BPEL supports transactional semantics with its compensate activity, and furthermore supports distributed transactions via the WS-Transaction Business Activity protocol, at time of writing no BPEL toolkits are available that support this. However, bear in mind that mapping BPEL activity scopes onto transactions is relatively straightforward, and once BPEL tool support improves, transactional underpinnings for BPEL workflows will become commonplace.

Adding transaction support into a Web services-based application is a multistage process that must be implemented by the software agents of all parties intending to participate in transactions. Though each party's responsibilities are generally different, they can be categorized into one of two roles:

- Client application—is usually the software entity that drives the business logic of the application, now additionally demarks the transaction boundaries within that application which in effect groups calls on disparate Web services into a single logical, reversible piece of work.
- Web service provider—the Web services consumed by the client application must be augmented to understand the transaction protocol SOAP headers and, additionally, provide a *participant* that will handle transaction protocol messages on behalf of its associated service. The Web service provider generally also requires some work at the back end to integrate the business Web service and the associated participant.

In addition, the transacting Web services also need to agree on a mutually trusted transaction coordinator to control the execution of the transaction. While the nature of this trust varies (it can be based on physical location, or implemented using a WS-Security-based approach), Web services administrators may refuse to allow transactions involving their services to be driven by an unknown or untrusted coordinator. Such a refusal is usually on the basis that a rogue coordinator may attempt to interrupt the enterprise by holding up any resources involved with the transaction in a denial of service attack.

For each of the vendor's Web services involved in our EPS application, we need to perform the following tasks:

1. Register header processors in the SOAP stacks of both vendors' Web services. The header processors are software entities that map transactional contexts onto local threads of activity within the Web service.
2. Create a participant Web service for each vendor that deals with Web services transaction protocols (in this case, the OASIS BTP protocol) at the front end and maps that onto back-end resources in an appropriate manner.

The alternate part Web service is slightly different. Since it is effectively stateless and so does not require transactional support per se (transactions are for supporting consistent state changes across services), we don't need to register a header processor in the SOAP stack for the alternate part service, nor do we require that the service enrolls a participant since it has no interest in the outcome of the transaction and it knows that none of its state will be changed either way by its outcome.

Once the additional infrastructure to support transactionality has been added into the application, the architecture looks a little different. The architecture of the transaction-aware application is shown in Figure 13-27, where we see transaction-aware Vendor A and Vendor B services with their transaction protocol handlers that deal with SOAP header blocks containing transaction contexts, collocated with participants which deal with the transaction protocol messages. The business-level services and the participants are both able to invoke operations on the back end, which provides the implementation for the service. In a typical enterprise application, the transaction protocol messages will be mapped onto back-end database systems to determine whether the business-level changes made to the data will be made persistent when the transaction has finished.

Now that we have considered the additional non-functional requirements that adding transactions places on the application as a whole and designed an architecture that can accommodate those requirements, the next step in the engineering process is to implement and integrate the new system components.

For this example, the ArjunaWST 1.1 toolkit was used. ArjunaWST 1.1 provides a transaction manager, client libraries, participant-side infrastructure, and service protocol handlers for building BTP-based applications. It is available with a free 30-day license from http://www.arjuna.com/products/arjunawst/. It should be noted that other toolkits that implement BTP are available from a number of other vendors. Also bear in mind that while this example utilizes a BTP toolkit, the overall strategy and architecture are equally applicable to other Web services transactions protocols.

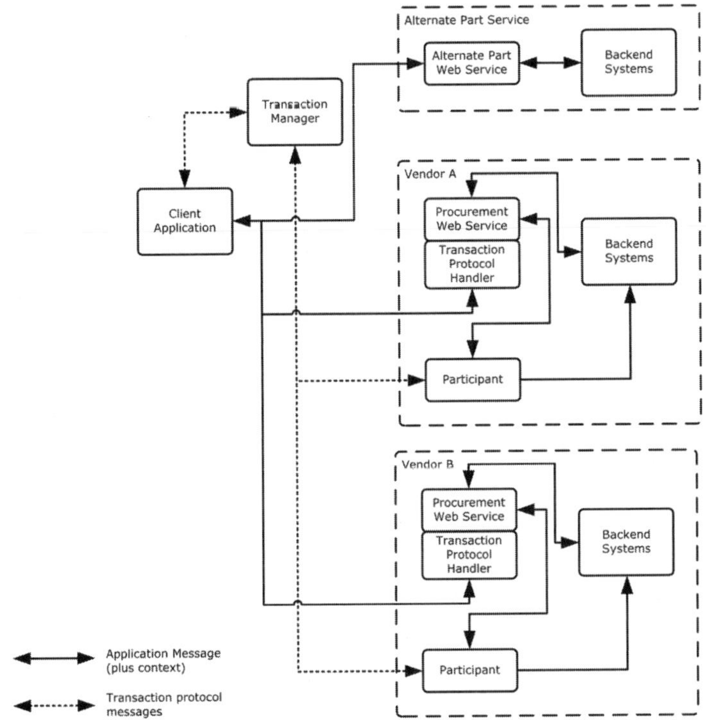

Figure 13-27 The transaction-aware procurement application architecture.

Changes to the Back End Systems

Transactions are a mechanism that helps to safeguard the consistency of state across Web services. However, in our previous back end implementation there was no mechanism available to allow changes to the back end state to be reversed. While we could order parts from the vendor services, there was no way of canceling that order once it had been made.

Clearly for a transactional system, we need to be dealing with data structures with which we can back out changes if needed—i.e., if a transaction fails. Therefore in this example, we chose to extend the original back end implementation so it supported a rudimentary `cancel` operation which, given an order number, will cancel the order and return parts to stock.

> The ability to undo work is the kind of behavior we would have available had we used a message queue or database at the back end. We use a simple data structure in preference to databases or queues because we want to concentrate specifically on Web services aspects of the application and not get into the detail of writing back-end enterprise systems.

The implementation of the enhanced back end system is shown in Figure 13-28.

```
package com.backend;

import java.util.Hashtable;

/**
 * A more complex model of an enterprise back-end, designed
 * to simulate some scenarios where databases, queues and
 * so forth are used to implement a Web service. It's not a
 * "true" enterprise back-end because it is necessarily
 * simplified, but the overall concepts are very similar.
 */
public class ComplexBackend extends SimpleBackend
{

  public ComplexBackend(){}


   /**
    * The orderParts method picks items from stock and
    * readies them for shipping.
    * It gives the caller a unique order number which
    * references the shipping items.
    *
    * @param   int  partNo The part  number of the part being
    *          ordered.
    * @param   int  quantity The number  of those parts that
    *          are  required.
    * @return   The  order number for the ordered parts.  Will
    *           return  -1 if the order could not be honored
    *           (e.g. not enough in stock).
    */
  public int orderParts(int partNo, int quantity)
  {
    if(_inventory.getQuantityInStock(partNo) >=  quantity)
    {
      _orderNumber++;

      // Place parts onto  shipping queue
      InventoryEntry shippingParts =
        new InventoryEntry
         (_inventory.getPartFromPartNumber(partNo),
          quantity);
      _shippingOrders.put(new  Integer(_orderNumber),
        shippingParts );

      // Remove parts from stock.
      _inventory.removeItem
        (_inventory.getPartFromPartNumber(partNo),
         quantity);
```

Figure 13-28 Back end system implementation.

```
      // Give  a visual indicator that  parts are shipping
      System.out.println("Shipping: \n" +  shippingParts);
      System.out.println
       (shippingParts.getPart().getPartNumber() +
        " left  in stock: "  +
        _inventory.getQuantityInStock
       (shippingParts.getPart().getPartNumber()));

      return _orderNumber;
    }
    return -1; // Could  not  honor order
  }

  /**
   * The cancel order method can be used to send an order
   * from shipping back into inventory. While this method
   * could be consumed directly by,  Web services  clients,
   * in  this example we  use  it as an example of
   * application level compensation which  is invoked by the
   * underlying transaction system.
   *
   * @param  int  orderNo  The  order of the number  that is
   *         to be cancelled. This will be  the  same int
   *         value that  was  returned when the order was
   *         placed.
   */
  public void  cancelOrder(int  orderNo)
  {
    if(_shippingOrders.containsKey(new Integer(orderNo)))
    {
      // If there  is an order  in shipping, stop and return
      // the parts to the inventory
      InventoryEntry entry = (InventoryEntry)
               _shippingOrders.remove(new Integer(orderNo));
      _inventory.addItem(entry.getPart(),
                  entry.getQuantity(), entry.getLeadtime());

      // Alert user
      System.out.println("Returned to inventory: ");
      System.out.println(entry);
    }
  }

  private  Hashtable _shippingOrders =  new  Hashtable();
}
```

Figure 13-28 Back end system implementation (continued).

The back end now consists of a more fully featured `orderParts` method that not only removes items from stock, but also immediately places them into a second structure that holds shipping orders. The back end is said to behave *optimistically* because it commits resources for shipping immediately. The `cancelOrder` method provides an application-level logical reverse of the `orderParts` method that removes the order from the set of shipping orders, and increments the inventory with the number of parts that have been removed from shipping.

> Ordinarily, mechanisms like the `cancelOrder` method are not required since the underlying (transactional) database or queue is available to both the transaction infrastructure and the business logic. However, in this case the back end system effectively plays the role of the database and so it must be equipped with rollback-like features.

At this point, we now have the back end system in place for each vendor service, and we know that the back ends are now suitable for running transactions across. The next step is to expose our new "transactional" resource to the network through its associated business Web service.

Transaction-Aware Service Implementation

Now that we understand the architectural changes that have taken place and seen how the back end has been remodeled to support transactional behavior, we can develop our strategy for supporting transactions at the Web services level. There are two distinct aspects to this support, the first being the construction of a service that is transaction-context aware and the second being the integration of this context-aware service with the underlying transaction toolkit.

To make the business-level Web service transaction-context aware, we need to integrate it with the underlying transaction toolkit and SOAP server. In the transaction toolkit we use in this example, this is a matter of registering a *handler* for transaction contexts at the same time that the service itself is deployed onto the SOAP server. Since we use the standard Apache Axis toolkit to deploy our sample application, we enhance our deployment configuration file (deploy.wsdd) and specify the name of the handler class that we want to support our service. This is shown in Figure 13-29.

The Axis deployment description shown in Figure 13-29 registers both the transactional services and handlers for transaction contexts for those services that require transactional support (i.e., those services that rely on transactions to guarantee consistent state). In fact, for each transactional service, we need to register three items with the underlying SOAP engine. These are:

- The name of the class that provides the service implementation.
- The name of the handler that provides the transaction-context processing capabilities for incoming contexts in SOAP header blocks (i.e., the SOAP actor that handles thread-transaction mapping).

```
<deployment name="TransactionalServiceDeployment"
 xmlns="http://xml.apache.org/axis/wsdd/"
 xmlns:java="http://xml.apache.org/axis/wsdd/providers/java">
  <handler name="BTPContextProcessor"
    type=

"java:com.hp.mw.xts.platforms.java.axis.service.BTPContextProc
essor"/>
  <service name="TransactionalVendorAService"
    provider="java:RPC">
    <requestFlow>
     <handler type="BTPContextProcessor" />
    </requestFlow>
    <responseFlow>
      <handler type="BTPContextProcessor" />
    </responseFlow>
    <parameter name="className"
      value="com.vendora.TransactionalVendorAService"/>
  </service>
  <service name="TransactionalVendorBService"
    provider="java:RPC">
    <requestFlow>
     <handler type="BTPContextProcessor"/>
    </requestFlow>
    <responseFlow>
      <handler type="BTPContextProcessor" />
    </responseFlow>
    <parameter name="className"
     value="com.vendorb.TransactionalVendorBService"/>
  </service>
  <service name="AlternatePartService" provider="java:RPC">
    <parameter name="className"
      value="com.altpart.AlternatePartService"/>
  </service>
</deployment>
```

Figure 13-29 Deploying a transactional service with an Axis deployment file.

- The name of the handler that provides the transaction context processing capabilities for outgoing contexts.

With the transaction toolkit that we use in this example, incoming and outgoing context management are both handled by the same implementing class, `com.hp.mw.xts.platforms.java.axis.service.BTPContextProcessor`, and so the element `<handler type="BTPContextProcessor"/>` appears in both the `<requestFlow>` and `<responseFlow>` elements. Since we intend for our service to be invoked via SOAP-RPC, we register it with the RPC provider using `provider="java:RPC"` in the `<service>` element. Finally, the implementing class for the service is specified as a parameter `<parameter name="className" value="com.altpart.AlternatePartService"/>`.

Once we have our deployment file written, we use the Axis administrative features to register the service with a running SOAP server. This is easily achieved on the command line with the command:

```
java org.apache.axis.client.AdminClient
 -lhttp://localhost:8080/axis/services/AdminService
```

where the URL specified as the –l switch is the location where your Axis installation is hosted. Once this command is executed, the Axis SOAP server will alter its configuration in accordance with the configuration file, as shown in Figure 13-30, and we are ready to invoke it and include it in business transactions.

In addition to the changes at the back end and the introduction of transaction-processing infrastructure, we have also enhanced the Web service itself such that it exposes information about the business level operations. This enhancement consists of an additional static method and hash table, which maintains a mapping between transaction contexts (provided by the underlying transaction toolkit) and order numbers (generated by the back end). Thus, given a transaction context, it is possible to discover the order numbers associated with that context, so that should the associated transaction fail, the orders (via their order numbers) can be readily cancelled.

> Note that context to order number mapping method is not itself exposed as a Web service since it is intended to be consumed by a collocated participant. If, however, the participant needed to be remotely located from the service (for logistical or performance reasons), it is simple enough to provide a Web service to support remote invocations—and indeed this is well within the capabilities of most SOAP toolkits to automate.

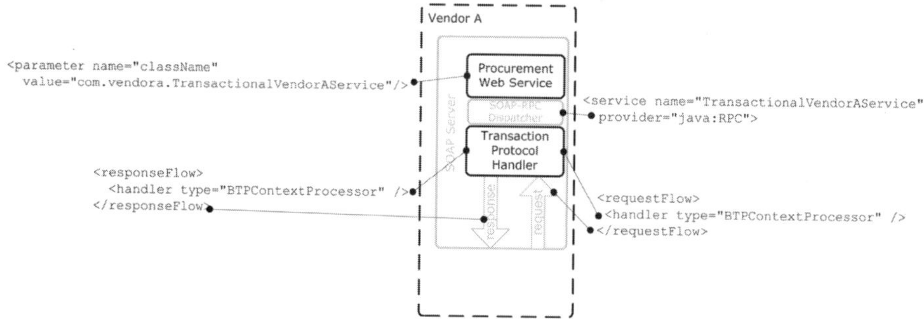

Figure 13-30 The Web service-side infrastructure after deployment.

The service implementation for the vendor services is shown in Figure 13-31. Although we show only the Vendor A service here, the Vendor B service is similar enough (though with Vendor B-specific method names) that it has been omitted for the sake of brevity.

```
package  com.vendora;

import java.util.Hashtable;

/**
 * The TransactionalVendorAService provides additional
 * infrastructure to support transactionality for the
 * VendorAService.
 */
public class TransactionalVendorAService
                extends VendorAService
{
  /**
   * The placeOrder method has the same functionality  as the
   * method from  the  parent class, aside  from it  stores
   * an in-memory  mapping between the order number  and  the
   * transaction  context  that it  was created within.
   *
   * Note: in a true enterprise system, this in-memory
   * mapping would have to be persistent (e.g. serialized to
   * disk or database) in case the service crashed. It is
   * not made  persistent here  for the sake  of clarity.
   *
   * @param int partNumber The part number of the
   *        requested parts.
   * @param int quantity The quantity of the parts
   *        requested.
   */
  public int placeOrder(int partNumber, int quantity)
  {
    int  orderNo  = super.placeOrder(partNumber, quantity);

    try
    {
      // Do the mapping thing with the TX context
      // and  order ID
      com.hp.mw.ts.arjuna.common.Uid currentTxUid  =
    com.hp.mw.xts.management.ServiceManagement.getUidFromContext();

      if(currentTxUid  != null)
      {
        if(_txContextOrderMappings.containsKey(currentTxUid))
```

Figure 13-31 The transaction-aware Vendor A service implementation.

```
        {
          Integer[] existingOrders = (Integer[])
                  _txContextOrderMappings.get(currentTxUid);
          Integer[] newOrders =
                     new Integer[existingOrders.length + 1];

          for(int i = 0; i < existingOrders.length; i++)
          {
            newOrders[i] = existingOrders[i];
          }
          newOrders[newOrders.length-1] =
                                       new Integer(orderNo);

          for(int i = 0; i < newOrders.length; i++)
          {
            System.out.println(newOrders[i]);
          }
        }
      }
    }
    catch(Exception e)
    {
      // If we get here, there's no transaction to
      // worry about.
    }

    return orderNo;
  }

  /**
   * The getOrderID method returns the orderID(s) associated
   * with the current transaction context.
   *
   * @return int[] The order ID's associated with the
   * current transaction context.
   */
  static int[] getOrderID()
  {
    try
    {
      // Retrieve the array of orders that are associated
      // with this context
      com.hp.mw.ts.arjuna.common.Uid currentTxUid =
     com.hp.mw.xts.management.ServiceManagement.getUidFromContext();

      Integer[] orderNumbers =
        (Integer[])_txContextOrderMappings.get(currentTxUid);
```

Figure 13-31 The transaction-aware Vendor A service implementation (continued).

```
        if(orderNumbers  == null)
        {
          return null;
        }
        else
        {
          int[] result = new int[orderNumbers.length];
          for(int  i =  0; i < result.length; i++)
          {
            result[i] =  orderNumbers[i].intValue();
          }

          return result;
        }
      }
      catch(Exception  e)
      {
        return null;
      }
    }

    /**
     * This hashtable is keyed on transaction context, and
     * stores arrays of integers which  are  themselves order
     * numbers.
     */
    private  static Hashtable _txContextOrderMappings =
                                            new Hashtable();
}
```

Figure 13-31 The transaction-aware Vendor A service implementation (continued).

The final piece of work to complete this service is the configuration of the transaction infrastructure from the chosen transaction toolkit, so that when the service is invoked within the scope of a transaction (that is, it receives a message with a transaction context in the SOAP header) an appropriate participant is enrolled into the transaction. If we recall the explanation offered in Chapter 6, the participant is the entity that deals with the transaction protocol on behalf of the associated business-level Web service. However, the enrollment of participants by a service is more of an administrative task than an architectural or development task, and as such the underlying transaction toolkit allows us to administratively specify the location of a participant to enroll whenever a transactional invocation occurs. This is achieved through a configuration file, which is shown in Figure 13-32.

The `default-service-rule-engine-config.xml` configuration file is used to declare a set of simple rules that the underlying transaction toolkit can use to make choices about which participants to enroll in response to certain invocations, based on what is being invoked and within the scope of what kind of transaction the invocation occurred.

```
<sre:default-service-rule-engine xmlns:sre=
  "http://www.arjuna.com/schemas/xts/service-rule-engine/2002/
10/">
  <sre:rule>
    <sre:transaction-type>any</sre:transaction-type>
    <sre:service-endpoint>
     http://localhost:8080/axis/services/
TransactionalVendorAService
    </sre:service-endpoint>
    <sre:participant>
      http://localhost:8080/axis/services/VendorAParticipant
    </sre:participant>
  </sre:rule>
  <sre:rule>
    <sre:transaction-type>any</sre:transaction-type>
    <sre:service-endpoint>
     http://localhost:8080/axis/services/
TransactionalVendorBService
    </sre:service-endpoint>
    <sre:participant>
      http://localhost:8080/axis/services/VendorBParticipant
    </sre:participant>
  </sre:rule>
</sre:default-service-rule-engine>
```

Figure 13-32 `default-service-rule-engine-config.xml` configuration file.

A `rule` consists of a triplet of values for `transaction-type`, `service-endpoint`, and `participant`. That is, a rule allows the administrative specification of which participant to enroll when a particular service is invoked within the scope of a particular type of transaction. For instance, one of the rules in Figure 13-32 states that whenever any kind of transaction context arrives with an invocation on the `TransactionalVendorAService`, that `VendorAParticipant` will be enrolled. This can be refined as necessary such that different participant implementations can be enrolled based on specific transaction types, or even a combination of transaction type and service invoked without having to resort to code.

> The use of a `default-service-rule-engine-config.xml` configuration file is particular to the transaction toolkit that we used in this example (Arjuna's WST 1.1), and will differ from vendor to vendor. For instance the HP toolkit that we used in Chapter 6 relied on the service developer to implement enrollments through a programmatic API.

From this point the business-level service is complete, and we have constructed a service-side architecture that looks like the diagram shown in Figure 13-33.

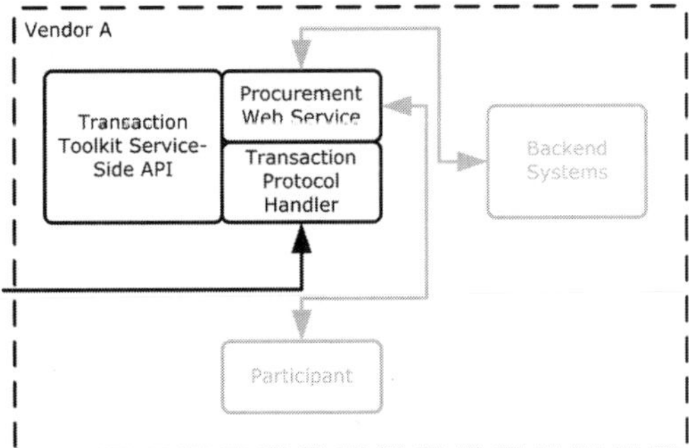

Figure 13-33 The service-side infrastructure up close.

As Figure 13-33 shows, although we had to upgrade our service to expose order numbers associated with particular transactions, most of this work is handled by the underlying transaction toolkit. The Web services aspects of the application have not forced changes onto the actual business logic back end, if we ignore that we had to emulate transactionality with additional cancellation methods in the back end (since that functionality is usually provide by default by a database or other transactional resource). At this point we are ready to join together the transaction-aware service with the underlying transaction protocol, which is done through the development and deployment of a participant.

Implementing Participants

The participant implementation is the piece of logic that determines what back end transactional behavior occurs in response to transaction protocol messages out on the Web services network. Using our toolkit, integrating participants into an application is a two-stage process which involves developing the participant logic, and specifying rules for its enrollment (which are complimentary to the rules that the service uses to enroll participants) into a transaction.

However, let's begin our discussion of the participant looking at the implementation for the Vendor A participant, as shown in Figure 13-34. Note that the implementation for Vendor B's participant is once again similar enough to Vendor A's that we can safely omit a full discussion of its implementation here.

The methods that the `VendorAParticipant` supports in Figure 13-34 directly correspond to the messages exchanges that a participant is involved in within the scope of a BTP transaction. The most important of these methods are the three that are involved in the two-phase confirm aspects of BTP: prepare, confirm, and cancel.

The `prepare` method returns a Vote that indicates to the calling transaction coordinator whether it will proceed to make the work done in the scope of the transaction durable—to indicate whether state changes in the service will remain or be deleted when the transaction finishes. In this case, the method is hardwired to always return a `VoteConfirm` object, which indicates

```
package com.vendora;

import com.hp.mw.xts.participant.*;
import com.hp.mw.ts.arjuna.common.Uid;

import com.hp.mw.xts.core.exceptions.*;

import com.hp.mw.xts.core.common.Vote;
import com.hp.mw.xts.core.common.VoteConfirm;
import com.hp.mw.xts.core.common.VoteCancel;
import com.hp.mw.xts.qualifiers.Qualifier;
import com.hp.mw.xts.management.ParticipantManagement;

import com.hp.mw.ts.arjuna.state.InputObjectState;
import com.hp.mw.ts.arjuna.state.OutputObjectState;

/**
 * The VendorAParticipant provides the transaction
 * participant (the actor that understands the transaction
 * protocol) for the TransactionalVendorAService.
 */
public class VendorAParticipant implements Participant
{
    /**
     * Implements the Participant.prepare operation.
     *
     * @param id The identifier of the entity that is to be
     *       prepared
     * @param qualifiers ignored in this implementation
     * @return Vote to CONFIRM or CANCEL the transaction
     */
    public Vote prepare(Uid id, Qualifier[] qualifiers)
        throws GeneralException, InvalidInferiorException,
        WrongStateException, HeuristicHazardException,
        HeuristicMixedException
    {
        // VendorA takes an optimistic strategy and always
        // internally commits resources and votes to confirm.
        return new VoteConfirm();
    }

    /**
     * Implements the Participant.confirm operation.
     *
     * @param id The inferior which is to have <i>confirm</i>
     *       invoked on it
     * @param qualifiers ignored in this implementation
     */
```

Figure 13-34 The VendorAParticipant implementation.

```
    public void confirm(Uid id, Qualifier[] qualifiers)
        throws GeneralException, InvalidInferiorException,
        WrongStateException, HeuristicHazardException,
        HeuristicMixedException
    {
        // Do nothing on confirm because VendorA's strategy
        // is to confirm immediately.
    }

    /**
     * Implements the Participant.cancel operation.
     *
     * @param id The inferior which is to have <i>cancel</i>
     *       invoked on it
     * @param qualifiers ignored in this implementation
     */
    public void cancel(Uid id, Qualifier[] qualifiers)
        throws GeneralException, InvalidInferiorException,
        WrongStateException, HeuristicHazardException,
        HeuristicMixedException
    {
        // The resources have already been committed. Must
        // now perform compensating action.

        // Get the orderNos from the
        // TrasactionalVendorAService
        int[] ordersToCancel =
                    TransactionalVendorAService.getOrderID();
        if(ordersToCancel != null)
        {
            for(int i = 0; i < ordersToCancel.length; i++)
            {
                // Invoke compensating action at the back end
                TransactionalVendorAService.
                     _backend.cancelOrder(ordersToCancel[i]);
            }
        }
    }

    /**
     * Implements the Participant.contradiction operation.
     *
     * @param id The inferior to inform
     * @param qualifiers ignored in this implementation
     */
    public void contradiction(Uid id, Qualifier[] qualifiers)
        throws GeneralException, InvalidInferiorException,
        WrongStateException
    {
```

Figure 13-34 The `VendorAParticipant` implementation (continued).

```
        // There has been a contradiction, shout for help!
        System.err.println(
                    "\t\tVendorAParticipant.contradiction(" +
                    id.stringForm() + ")");
    }
    /**
     * Implements the Participant.superiorState operation.
     *
     * Not required for this example
     *
     * @param id
     * @param qualifiers
     * @return null in all cases
     */
    public String superiorState(Uid id,
                                Qualifier[] qualifiers)
        throws GeneralException, InvalidInferiorException
    {
        return null;
    }

    /**
     * Implements the Participant.defaultIsCancel operation.
     *
     * The underlying business logic does not support
     * timeouts.
     *
     * @param id The inferior to query
     * @return false in all cases because default action is
     *         to confirm.
     */
    public boolean defaultIsCancel(Uid id)
    {
        return false;
    }

    /**
     * Implements the Participant.confirmedReceived
     * operation.
     *
     * This implementation does not acknowledge receipt of
     * confirm messages.
     *
     * @param id The inferior to query
     * @return false in all cases
     */
    public boolean confirmedReceived(Uid id)
    {
        return false;
    }
```

Figure 13-34 The `VendorAParticipant` implementation (continued).

```
    public int status(Uid id, Qualifier[] qualifiers) throws
                    GeneralException, InvalidInferiorException
    {
        System.err.println(
                    "\t\tVendorAParticipant.superiorState(" +
                    id.stringForm() + ")");

        return
          com.hp.mw.xts.core.common.TwoPhaseStatus.UNKNOWN;
    }

    public String name()
    {
        return "VendorAParticipant implementation";
    }

    // These are left empty because the VendorAParticipant
    // does not need to be recoverable.
    public boolean packState (OutputObjectState os)
    {
        return true;
    }

    public boolean unpackState (InputObjectState os)
    {
        return true;
    }
}
```

Figure 13-34 The `VendorAParticipant` implementation (continued).

to the invoking transaction manager that state changes associated with this participant will be persisted after the transaction is finished. Since we have chosen this optimistic approach, only in those (presumably minor number of) cases where something goes wrong will the participant have to take restorative action.

Since we have chosen to commit state changes in the first phases of the two-phase confirm process (during the prepare phase), there is nothing to do if the transaction gets to the confirm phase and so the `confirm` method is left empty. Conversely, should the transaction coordinator decide to cancel the transaction, the `cancel` method will be invoked, which will perform a compensating action to reverse the work done by the service. In this case that compensation will be to invoke the `cancelOrder` method on the back end system for each part that was ordered within the scope of the transaction.

Like the business-level Web services, the participant is also deployed into the SOAP server. The only difference here is that the consumer of the participant service is always another Web service (the transaction manager service) and not client applications. Deploying the service is straightforward and relies on a simple deployment descriptor file as shown in Figure 13-35.

```
<deployment name="ParticipantDeployment" xmlns="http://
xml.apache.org/axis/wsdd/" xmlns:java="http://xml.apache.org/
axis/wsdd/providers/java">
  <service name="VendorAParticipant" style="message">
    <parameter name="className" value=
"com.hp.mw.xts.platforms.java.axis.documentHandlers.Participan
tDocumentHandler"/>
    <parameter name="allowedMethods" value="invoke"/>
  </service>
  <service name="VendorBParticipant" style="message">
    <parameter name="className" value=
"com.hp.mw.xts.platforms.java.axis.documentHandlers.Participan
tDocumentHandler"/>
    <parameter name="allowedMethods" value="invoke"/>
  </service>
</deployment>
```

Figure 13-35 Deploying a participant with an Axis deployment file.

Like business Web services, participants must also be deployed into a SOAP server to be accessible. However, the participant services don't require any additional SOAP actors to be registered as handlers in their service stacks, since they only deal with transaction protocol messages and not application-plus-context messages. Thus, the deployment configuration files are correspondingly simpler, as we see in Figure 13-35.

There are, however, a few remarkable differences between the participant deployment configuration file and the transactional service deployment configuration file that we saw in Figure 13-29. First, the participant service uses document-style SOAP to exchange messages (it exchanges arbitrary XML documents in its SOAP payload, not SOAP-schema encoded payloads) and so the style attribute in the `service` element is set to `style="message"`.

Furthermore, because the service now needs to understand arbitrary SOAP message encodings, it needs to be configured with an implementation class that can decode those messages and dispatch them appropriately. This is handled by the `className` parameter, which specifies a particular document handler to which incoming messages will be routed. The `ParticipantDocumentHandler` class is a component from the underlying transaction toolkit that understands the transaction protocol messages and is able to dispatch them appropriately at the back end.

The final parameter, `allowedMethods`, specifies a list of the methods from the `ParticipantDocumentHandler` class that will be exposed as a Web service. In this case, we only require that the invoke method is exposed since this is the only necessary conduit to enable BTP messages to be routed through to the back end.

The last piece in the puzzle for service-side transactionality is the administration of the participant. For this we complete the participant-side rule engine configuration, from the underlying transaction engine toolkit, where we specify a mapping from endpoints to particular implementations. This is in effect the reciprocal feature of the service side rule engine configuration, and allows a particular participant implementation to be used based on the endpoint of the `ultimateReceiver` so that many different participant implementations can be hosted and routed by a single SOAP server instance.

```
<?xml version="1.0" encoding="UTF-8"?>
<pre:default-participant-rule-engine xmlns:pre="http://
www.arjuna.com/schemas/xts/participant-rule-engine/2002/10/">
  <pre:rule>
    <pre:participant-endpoint>
      http://localhost:8080/axis/services/VendorAParticipant
    </pre:participant-endpoint>
    <pre:participant-implementation>
      com.vendora.VendorAParticipant
    </pre:participant-implementation>
  </pre:rule>
  <pre:rule>
    <pre:participant-endpoint>
      http://localhost:8080/axis/services/VendorBParticipant
    </pre:participant-endpoint>
    <pre:participant-implementation>
      com.vendorb.VendorBParticipant
    </pre:participant-implementation>
  </pre:rule>
</pre:default-participant-rule-engine>
```

Figure 13-36 `default-participant-rule-engine-config.xml` configuration file.

In Figure 13-36, we map the participant endpoint onto the implementing Java class. Now when a BTP message arrives and is processed by the `ParticipantDocumentHandler`, it will automatically be dispatched to the correct participant implementation. Like the equivalent service-side rules, this means that a system can be evolved over time without having to resort to coding.

As we see in Figure 13-37, at this point the transactional service is ready for consumption. The participant implementation can cooperate with the service to provide the additional transactional quality of service that enterprises require. All that is left now is to consume the functionality offered by the service, and see how we can drive its transactional aspects.

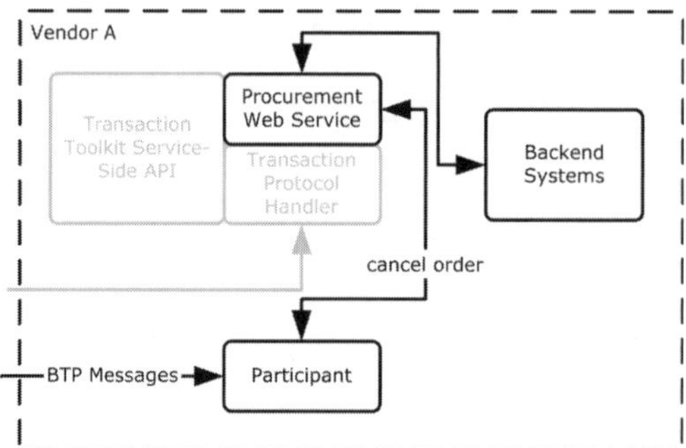

Figure 13-37 Participant and service-side infrastructure.

Consuming Transactional Web Services

Writing transactional applications involves not only developing business logic, but also controlling the underlying transactional behavior of the system. The key to developing such applications is to partition the work into suitable transactions so that work can be reversed, replayed and so forth as necessary.

In this example, we try to purchase components from both suppliers where we will only proceed with the order if both suppliers commit to providing the necessary parts. Where either one of the suppliers is unable to meet its commitment, or where there is a failure that prevents the order from making progress, we will cancel the transaction. Canceling the transaction causes the transaction manager to instruct all enrolled participants to perform the appropriate restorative action at the back end of their associated service. As we saw in Figure 13-34, this ultimately has the effect of reversing any work done so that the transaction appears to have never run. A sample client application is shown in Figure 13-38.

```
package  client;

import com.hp.mw.xts.*;
import com.hp.mw.xts.core.common.StatusItem;
import com.hp.mw.xts.core.common.Vote;
import com.hp.mw.xts.core.common.VoteConfirm;

import com.hp.mwlabs.xts.portability.xml.XMLProvider;

import com.vendora.VendorAStub;
import com.vendorb.VendorBStub;
import com.altpart.AlternatePartStub;
```

Figure 13-38 Client application implementation.

```
/**
 * Runs a simple transactional invocation on each service.
 */
public class TransactionalClient
{
  public static void main(String[] args)
  {
    try
    {
      TransactionManager tm =
        TransactionFactory.getTransaction(
                        XMLProvider.getDOMDocument(CONFIG));
      UserTransaction  ut = (UserTransaction)tm;

      // We're going to repeat this order  until someone is
      // out of stock to show transactions cancelling...
      // We happen to  know that there  are  only 250 spark
      // plugs available in VendorB,  so 7 times round will
      // do it
      for(int  i =  0; i < 6; i++)
      {
        // Start the transaction - in this case an atom
        ut.begin(TxTypes.ATOM);

        // Business  logic
        VendorAStub  vas  = new VendorAStub(new java.net.URL(
"http://localhost:8080/axis/services/TransactionalVendorAService"));
        VendorBStub  vbs  = new VendorBStub(new java.net.URL(
"http://localhost:8080/axis/services/TransactionalVendorBService"));

        // Going to order 2 Head Gaskets from VendorA and
        // 45 spark  plugs from B, or nothing at  all.
        int  orderA = vas.placeOrder(101, 2);
        int  orderB = vbs.orderComponent(45,  888);

        // Terminate the transaction

        Vote prepareResult = ut.prepare();

        if(prepareResult instanceof  VoteConfirm  &&
            orderA >= 0 && orderB >=  0)
        {
          System.out.println("Orders:  " +  orderA + " and "
             + orderB +  " have successfully  been placed.");
          ut.confirm();
        }
        else
```

Figure 13-38 Client application implementation (continued).

```
            {
              System.out.println("Orders:  " +  orderA + " and "
                              + orderB +  " have been  cancelled.");
              ut.cancel(null);
            }
          }

          System.exit(0);
        }
        catch(Exception  e)
        {
          e.printStackTrace(System.err);
          System.exit(1);
        }

    }

    private static final String CONFIG = "<proxy-config
    xmlns=\"http://www.arjuna.com/schemas/xts/proxy/2002/10/\">"
       +"\n<properties>"
       +"\n<property name=\"usertransaction_implementation\" "
       +"value=com.hp.mwlabs.xts.api.proxy.UserTransactionProxy\"/>"
       +"\n<property name=\"transactionmanager_implementation\" "
       +"value=\"com.hp.mwlabs.xts.api.proxy.TransactionManagerProxy\" />"
       +"\n</properties>"
       +"\n<transaction-manager-url>"
       +"http://localhost:8080/axis/services/WebTransactionManager"
       +"</transaction-manager-url>"
       +"\n</proxy-config>";

}
```

Figure 13-38 Client application implementation (continued).

This application can be broken down into four broad phases. The first of these phases is where the client binds to the transaction manager that will support the subsequent transactional behavior. This is realized by the opening lines of the `main` method that create and initialize a `TransactionManager` and `UserTransaction` instance (which is achieved through an XML configuration file which the application encodes as a static string).

It is the `UserTransaction` instance that is then subsequently used to delimit the transactional behavior of the application. The begin method of the `UserTransaction` instance is called to instruct the remote transaction manager to create a new BTP atom. Once this call completes any further work, including Web services invocations (where the Web services support transactions), is implicitly within the scope of this transaction. At the client application side, the current thread is associated with the context. Whenever a Web services invocation is made, the XML form of the context travels in a SOAP header block to the invoked service where, as we have seen, the service-side infrastructure handles thread-context association and enrollment of participants.

The real work of this application is contained within its business logic. In this case the application simply orders parts from the two vendor services. Supported by the transaction, the orders continue until such point that either there is an underlying fault or until the order process fails which causes the transaction to cancel, and any orders and parts currently unsettled to be cancelled are returned to stock.

It is important to understand that this is possible because of the *open-top* nature of the underlying transaction protocol. Since both the prepare and confirm/cancel phases of the two-phase confirm are driven by the client application, it is possible for the application to affect the transaction directly and assert that the transaction confirm or cancel, just like the transaction manager. Application-level rules can be used to complete or abort transactions in addition to the standard semantic where faults are the cause of transactional aborts.

Once the client application is developed and built, the final stage is to deploy and execute. Since we have chosen the Apache Axis platform for building this demo application, we need to configure our application to use the Axis client-side infrastructure to propagate transaction contexts on our behalf. The configuration for this is shown in Figure 13-39. Like the service-side configuration, the client configuration registers handlers that deal with thread-context association at the client side. Once this configuration is in place, the application is ready to execute.

```
<?xml version="1.0" encoding="UTF-8"?>
<deployment xmlns="http://xml.apache.org/axis/wsdd/"
xmlns:java="http://xml.apache.org/axis/wsdd/providers/java">
  <globalConfiguration>
   <parameter name="sendXsiTypes" value="true"/>
   <parameter name="sendMultiRefs" value="true"/>
   <parameter name="sendXMLDeclaration" value="true"/>
   <requestFlow>
    <handler
   type=
   "java:com.hp.mw.xts.platforms.java.axis.client.OutgoingContextHandler"/>
   </requestFlow>
   <responseFlow>
    <handler
   type=
   "java:com.hp.mw.xts.platforms.java.axis.client.IncomingContextHandler"/>
   </responseFlow>
  </globalConfiguration>
  <transport name="http"
   pivot="java:org.apache.axis.transport.http.HTTPSender"/>
</deployment>
```

Figure 13-39 An Axis `client-config.wsdd` configuration file.

Programming for Mobility

In this section, we extend the application to support mobile access. As we saw in Chapter 10, supporting mobile access to an application can be accomplished by using either a proxy-based architecture or communicating with the individual Web services directly from the mobile application.

For existing enterprise applications, a proxy-based mobile solution is usually easier to develop. Minimally, the application view or presentation layer is simply mobilized and migrated to the mobile device. The remainder of the application, including the business logic and Web service invocations, remains on the server. This server then acts as a proxy between the mobile application and the remote Web services.

Figure 13-40 depicts the architecture that will mobilize the application.

The MobileServlet proxy interprets the data from the mobile application, MobileClient-Application, and in turn invokes the appropriate Web services that implement the required business logic to handle the requests. The proxy combines information from the Web services, as well as other business logic implemented by the proxy itself, and responds to the mobile request in a format acceptable to the mobile device and application. It is important to note that this is not a browser-based solution, but instead uses a mobile application that communicates with the Servlet using HTTP.

Figure 13-41 shows a screenshot of the mobile user interface of the `MobileClientApplication`. The user interface is simple and allows the user to enter the desired part number and quantities from both Vendors A and B. When the user depresses the `FINDIT` button, it submits the data to the `MobileServlet` as HTTP POST form data. The message returned by the MobileServlet is displayed within the rectangular textarea widget.

The source code of the `MobileClientApplication` is listed in Figure 13-42. The application basically consists of two major sections. The first section builds the entire graphical user interface by appropriately placing textboxes and labels throughout the frame widget. The widget is sized to fit within a personal digital assistant (PDA) device. The second section is comprised of the `goButtonActionPerformed` method, and implements the business logic that exchanges messages to the `MobileServlet` based on the data input by the user into the form fields.

Figure 13-40 Mobilizing the application by using a proxy-based architecture.

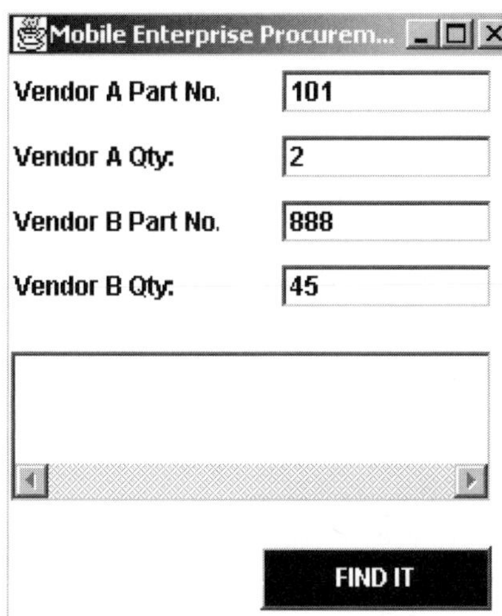

Figure 13-41 Mobile user interface of the MobileClientApplication.

```
import java.awt.*;
import java.awt.event.ActionEvent;
import java.io.IOException;
import java.io.InputStream;
import java.io.OutputStreamWriter;
import java.io.PrintWriter;
import java.net.HttpURLConnection;
import java.net.MalformedURLException;
import java.net.URL;
import java.net.URLEncoder;

public class MobileClientApplication extends Frame
{
   // The graphical user interface widget variable
   //  definitions
   TextField vendorAPartNumberTextField;
   Label vendorAPartNumberLabel;
   TextField vendorAQuantityTextField;
   Label vendorAQuantityLabel;

   // The vendorBPartNumberTextField,
   //  vendorBPartNumberLabel, vendorBQuantityTextField,
   //  vendorBQuantityLabel have been removed for brevity

   // The button that the user presses after entering
   //  all of the requested information
```

Figure 13-42 MobileClientApplication source code.

```
Button goButton;

// The textfield where the results from the Web
//  service invocation are displayed
TextArea resultsTextField;


public MobileClientApplication ()
{
}

// Build the graphical user interface
public void createTextEntry ()
{
   vendorAPartNumberLabel = new Label ();
   vendorAPartNumberLabel.setForeground ( Color.black );
   vendorAPartNumberLabel.setBackground ( Color.white );
   vendorAPartNumberLabel.setText("Vendor A Part No.: " );
   vendorAPartNumberLabel.setLocation ( 5 , 30 );
   vendorAPartNumberLabel.setBounds ( 5 , 30 , 100 , 20 );
   vendorAPartNumberLabel.setFont ( new java.awt.Font
                                ( "Dialog" , 1 , 12 ) );

   vendorAPartNumberTextField = new TextField ();
   vendorAPartNumberTextField.setColumns ( 4 );
   vendorAPartNumberTextField.setForeground(Color.black );
   vendorAPartNumberTextField.setBackground(Color.white );
   vendorAPartNumberTextField.setText ( "111" );
   vendorAPartNumberTextField.setColumns ( 15 );
   vendorAPartNumberTextField.setLocation ( 135 , 30 );
   vendorAPartNumberTextField.setBounds ( 135 , 30 , 100 ,
                                          20 );
   vendorAPartNumberTextField.setFont ( new java.awt.Font
                                ( "Dialog" , 1 , 12 ) );

   vendorAQuantityLabel = new Label ();
   vendorAQuantityLabel.setForeground ( Color.black );
   vendorAQuantityLabel.setBackground ( Color.white );
   vendorAQuantityLabel.setText ( "Vendor A Qty: " );
   vendorAQuantityLabel.setLocation ( 5 , 60 );
   vendorAQuantityLabel.setBounds ( 5 , 60 , 100 , 20 );
   vendorAQuantityLabel.setFont ( new java.awt.Font
                               ( "Dialog" , 1 , 12 ) );

   vendorAQuantityTextField = new TextField ();
   vendorAQuantityTextField.setColumns ( 2 );
   vendorAQuantityTextField.setForeground ( Color.black );
   vendorAQuantityTextField.setBackground ( Color.white );
   vendorAQuantityTextField.setText ( "33" );
   vendorAQuantityTextField.setLocation ( 135 , 60 );
```

Figure 13-42 MobileClientApplication source code (continued).

```
        vendorAQuantityTextField.setBounds ( 135 , 60 , 100 ,
                                                20 );
        vendorAQuantityTextField.setFont ( new java.awt.Font
                                       ( "Dialog" , 1 , 12 ) );


        // The vendorBPartNumberTextField,
        //  vendorBPartNumberLabel, vendorBQuantityTextField,
        //  vendorBQuantityLabel have been removed for brevity

        resultsTextField = new TextArea ( "" , 20 , 5 ,
                           TextArea.SCROLLBARS_HORIZONTAL_ONLY );
        resultsTextField.setEditable ( false );
        resultsTextField.setForeground ( Color.red );
        resultsTextField.setBackground ( Color.white );
        resultsTextField.setLocation ( 05 , 160 );
        resultsTextField.setBounds ( 05 , 160 , 230 , 70 );
        resultsTextField.setFont ( new java.awt.Font
                                     ( "Dialog" , 1 , 12 ) );

        goButton = new Button ();
        goButton.setBackground ( Color.black );
        goButton.setForeground ( Color.black );
        goButton.setFont ( new java.awt.Font ( "Dialog" , 1 ,
                                                12 ) );
        goButton.setForeground ( SystemColor.activeCaptionText );
        goButton.setLabel ( "FIND IT" );
        goButton.setLocation ( 125 , 250 );
        goButton.setBounds ( 125 , 250 , 110 , 30 );
        goButton.addActionListener ( new
          java.awt.event.ActionListener ()
        {
           public void actionPerformed ( ActionEvent e )
           {
              goButtonActionPerformed ( e );
           }
        } );

        this.add ( vendorAPartNumberLabel , "North" );
        this.add ( vendorAPartNumberTextField , "North" );
        this.add ( vendorAQuantityLabel , "North" );
        this.add ( vendorAQuantityTextField , "North" );
        // The vendorBPartNumberTextField,
        //  vendorBPartNumberLabel, vendorBQuantityTextField,
        //  vendorBQuantityLabel have been removed for brevity
        this.add ( resultsTextField , "North" );
        this.add ( goButton , "North" );
    }
```

Figure 13-42 MobileClientApplication source code (continued).

```
// Close the user interface window and exit if the
//  user so chooses
public boolean handleEvent ( Event evt )
{
   if ( evt.id == Event.WINDOW_DESTROY )
   {
      System.exit ( 0 );
   }
   return super.handleEvent ( evt );
}

// This method is called when the user presses the
//  goButton (pressed after the user enters all of
//  the requested information.
void goButtonActionPerformed ( ActionEvent e )
{
   byte buf[] = new byte[ 4012 ];
   int n;
   String confirmStr = "";

   StringBuffer sb = new StringBuffer ();
   sb.append ( URLEncoder.encode ( "vapn" ) + "=" );
   sb.append ( URLEncoder.encode (
               vendorAPartNumberTextField.getText () ) );
   sb.append ( "&" + URLEncoder.encode ( "vaq" ) + "=" );
   sb.append ( URLEncoder.encode (
               vendorAQuantityTextField.getText () ) );

   // The information for vbpn and vbq (read from
   //  vendorBPartNumberTextField and
   //  vendorBQuantityTextField)
   //  have been removed for brevity

   String formData = sb.toString ();

   try
   {
      URL url = new URL (
             "http://localhost:8080/meps/MobileServlet");
      HttpURLConnection urlcon = ( HttpURLConnection )
                                   url.openConnection();
      urlcon.setRequestMethod ( "POST" );
      urlcon.setRequestProperty ( "Content-type" ,
                "application/x-www-form-urlencoded" );
      urlcon.setDoOutput ( true );
      urlcon.setDoInput ( true );
      PrintWriter pout =
               new PrintWriter ( new OutputStreamWriter (
                                 urlcon.getOutputStream (),
                                 "8859_1" ) , true );
```

Figure 13-42 MobileClientApplication source code (continued).

```
         pout.print ( formData );
         pout.flush ();

         InputStream in = urlcon.getInputStream ();
         while((n = in.read(buf , 0 , buf.length)) != -1 )
         {
            confirmStr =
                  confirmStr.concat (new String(buf ,0 , n));
         }

         if ( confirmStr != null )
         {
            resultsTextField.setText ( confirmStr );
         }
      }
      catch ( MalformedURLException err )
      {
         System.out.println ( err );
      }
      catch ( IOException err2 )
      {
         System.out.println ( err2 );
      }
   }

   public static void main ( String args[] ) throws Exception
   {
      MobileClientApplication window =
                           new MobileClientApplication ();
      window.setTitle ( "Mobile Enterprise Procurement" );
      window.setLayout ( null );
      window.setBackground ( Color.white );
      window.createTextEntry ();
      window.pack ();
      window.resize ( 250 , 320 );
      window.show ();
   }
}
```

Figure 13-42 MobileClientApplication source code (continued).

The source code for the `MobileServlet` is listed in Figure 13-43. The `MobileServlet` serves as a proxy between the `MobileApplicationClient` and the back-end server-side business logic, as was implemented by the `TransactionalClient` class.

```
import javax.servlet.ServletConfig;
import javax.servlet.ServletException;
import javax.servlet.http.HttpServlet;
import javax.servlet.http.HttpServletRequest;
import javax.servlet.http.HttpServletResponse;
import java.io.IOException;
import java.io.PrintWriter;

public class MobileServlet extends HttpServlet
{
   private static final String CONTENT_TYPE = "text/html";

   static String paramVendorAPartNumber;
   static String paramVendorAQuantity;
   static String paramVendorBPartNumber;
   static String paramVendorBQuantity;
   String resultString = "empty";

   public void init ( ServletConfig config )
                                  throws ServletException
   {
      super.init ( config );
   }

   // Forward the doGet to the doPost
   public void doGet ( HttpServletRequest request ,
                       HttpServletResponse response )
                       throws ServletException , IOException
   {
      doPost ( request , response );
   }

   // Service the HTTP POST request
   public void doPost ( HttpServletRequest request ,
                        HttpServletResponse response )
                        throws ServletException , IOException
   {
      boolean serviceConfirm;
      boolean formReady = true;

      paramVendorAPartNumber = request.getParameter("vapn");
      paramVendorAQuantity = request.getParameter ("vaq");
      paramVendorBPartNumber = request.getParameter ("vbpn");
      paramVendorBQuantity = request.getParameter ("vbq");

      response.setContentType ( CONTENT_TYPE );
      PrintWriter out = response.getWriter ();

      // All of the fields must be filled in,
```

Figure 13-43 MobileServlet source code.

```
    // otherwise, print a message to fill everything in.
    // This is done by setting formReady to false
    if ( ( paramVendorAPartNumber == null ) ||
       ( paramVendorAQuantity == null ) ||
       ( paramVendorBPartNumber == null ) ||
       ( paramVendorBQuantity == null ) )
    {
       formReady = false;
    }
    else
    {
       if ((paramVendorAPartNumber.trim ().length () == 0 )
       || ( paramVendorAQuantity.trim ().length () == 0 )
       || ( paramVendorBPartNumber.trim ().length () == 0 )
       || ( paramVendorBQuantity.trim ().length () == 0 ) )
       {
          formReady = false;
       }
    }

    if ( !formReady )
    {
       // If the form is not ready, then return a message
       //  to completely fill-in the required fields.
       resultString = "Please complete the above form!";
    }
    else
    {
       // If the form is ready, then we simply have to
       //  invoke the transactionalClient which implements
       //  the business logic for completing the
       //  transaction. The message returned by the
       //  TransactionalClient is returned to the mobile
       //  application.
       resultString = invokeTransactionalClient
                         (paramVendorAPartNumber,
                          paramVendorBPartNumber,
                          paramVendorAQuantity,
                          paramVendorBQuantity);
    }
    out.println (resultString);
 }

 public void destroy ()
 {
 }

 private static String invokeTransactionalClient (vapn,
                                        vbpn, vaq, vbq)
```

Figure 13-43 MobileServlet source code (continued).

```
    {
        String returnString = "return sting from ITC";

        // The body of the TransactionalClient class
        //  goes here. The only changes are (1) instead
        //  of outputting messages to the console, the
        //  the messages should be returned as part of
        //  the method's return value, and (2) the hard-
        //  coded Vendor A and B part number and quantities
        //  must be set based on the vapn, vbpn, vaq, and
        //  vbq variables.

        return ( returnString );
    }
}
```

Figure 13-43 MobileServlet source code (continued).

The `MobileServlet` is a standard J2EE Servlet that accepts messages from the `MobileClientApplication` as HTTP POST form parameters. These parameters are read and parsed by the `MobileServlet` to ascertain that all of the required fields have been filled in by the user. If some of the form fields are empty, a message to completely fill in all of the form fields is returned to the `MobileClientApplication` which, in turn, displays it for the user.

If all of the form fields are properly filled in, then the `MobileServlet` invokes the `invokeTransactionalClient` method. This method is basically a replica of the `TransactionalClient` class from Figure 13-38, and has not been shown for the sake of brevity. The only changes between the implementation of the `TransactionalClient` and the `invokeTransactionalClient` are as follows:

1. Messages must be output not to the system console, but instead must be returned as part of the method's return value. For example, the `System.out.println`'s within the `TransactionalClient` class that output user messages must simply be returned as the return value of the `invokeTransactionalClient` method.
2. The Vendor A and B part numbers and quantities that are hardcoded in the `TransactionalClient` class must be set based on the `vapn`, `vbpn`, `vaq`, and `vbq` variables. That is, the following two lines must be replaced as shown:

```
int  orderA = vas.placeOrder(101, 2);
       int  orderB = vbs.orderComponent(45,  888);
```

with

```
int  orderA = vas.placeOrder(vapn, vaq);
       int  orderB = vbs.orderComponent(vbq,  vbpn);
```

With these simple changes, our mobilization of the `TransactionalClient` is complete.

Securing the Application

Security and how to properly secure a Web service application is one of the most important issues facing developers charged with building Web service systems. Unfortunately, this is also an area of tremendous flux. The security standards specifications are yet to be fully fleshed out and, not surprisingly, commercial infrastructure does not yet provide good implementations of these security specifications.

WS-Security together with the other WS-* specifications are becoming the de facto standard for establishing secure, trust relationships within Web service environments. In the long-term, all Web service applications will use WS-Security to implement transport-independent, secure communications between client applications and Web services.

Until the WS-* specifications are fully completed and good commercial implementations are available, alternative security solutions are necessary. Waiting to add security until these specifications are complete and building Web services that do not use encryption or any sort of authorization is probably not a good idea. Luckily, for the majority of Web service applications today, the use of standard HTTP security mechanisms will suffice. Over the next few years, as Web services are used in larger and broader environments, the HTTP security mechanisms will need to be replaced by implementations of WS-Security.

In the remainder of this section, we look at how to secure our procurement application by using HTTP security mechanisms, including SSL and basic authorization. See Chapter 8 for a detailed coverage of WS-Security as well as the underlying XML security specifications, including XML Encryption and XML Digital Signatures.

HTTP Security

HTTP security mechanisms are well-understood and proven technologies that have been used for years to secure Web sites. As we discussed in Chapter 8, although they work well for securing Web sites, HTTP security mechanisms have several shortcomings when used within a Web services environment. Nonetheless, until the WS-Security specifications are completed and fully implemented, for most Web services today, HTTP security presents a viable solution for data protection and authorization.

Web service transactions can be secured by using the following HTTP security techniques:

- HTTP with Secure Sockets Layer (SSL), commonly referred to as HTTPS, for data protection.
- HTTP basic authorization using usernames and passwords for access control and overall authorization.

Together, these two techniques provide a near-complete, point-to-point HTTP transport-level security solution for Web services. The aspect of security that is not covered by these two techniques is non-repudiation. Luckily, for the vast majority of Web service applications today, this is not critical.

We start by describing the steps necessary to configure support for HTTP basic authorization using username and password for access to the Web services of the EPS application. The configuration steps are as follows:

1. Define user credentials.

   Credentials, in this case, are username and password pairs that are associated with different "roles" that are granted access to various protected resources. For our purposes, these protected resources are Web services, and potential users must present the appropriate username-password pair before they are given access to consume the Web service.

   To define new user credentials, we must edit the `%TOMCAT_HOME%\conf\tomcat-users.xml` file. Add a new role named `webserviceauthorized`, and specify its username as `wsuser` and its associated password as `wsuserpw`. The default `tomcat-users.xml` file with the required additions is shown below:

```
<?xml version='1.0' encoding='utf-8'?>
<tomcat-users>
  <role rolename="tomcat"/>
  <role rolename="role1"/>
  <role rolename="manager"/>
  <role rolename="admin"/>
  <user username="tomcat" password="tomcat" roles="tomcat"/>
  <user username="both" password="tomcat"
        roles="tomcat,role1"/>
  <user username="role1" password="tomcat" roles="role1"/>
  <user username="admin" password="admin"
        roles="admin,manager"/>

<!-- Add new usernames and passwords for new roles here -->
<user username="wsuser" password="wsuserpw"
      roles="webserviceauthorized"/>

</tomcat-users>
```

2. Provide a security constraint for each set of Web service URLs.

   In this step, we associate a security constraint for the role we defined in the previous step for all Web services that are available from this Tomcat server. In particular, we specify that all Web services that are available on this Tomcat server whose endpoint URL includes the pattern `/services/*` will only be accessible to those users that belong to the `webserviceauthorized` role (created in the previous step).

To do this, we must edit the %TOMCAT_HOME%\webapps\axis\WEB-INF\web.xml file. Add the following lines to immediately before the closing </web-app> element:

```
<security-constraint>
  <web-resource-collection>
    <web-resource-name>
      Protected Web Services
    </web-resource-name>

    <!-- Specify the URL pattern for the protected
         Web Services -->
    <url-pattern>/services/*</url-pattern>
  </web-resource-collection>
  <auth-constraint>

  <!-- Specify the role name to be associated with
       this security constraint -->
    <role-name>webserviceauthorized</role-name>
  </auth-constraint>
</security-constraint>

<!-- Specify the login configuration -->
<login-config>
<auth-method>BASIC</auth-method>
<realm-name>Protected Web Services</realm-name>
</login-config>
```

3. Specify the username and password within the client application.

Now that we have configured Tomcat and Axis to verify the username and password before allowing access to any of the Web services, we must make sure that each time our client application invokes a Web service it provides the appropriate username-password pair as part of the SOAP request.

We do this by setting the username and password within the call object of the invocation. If you are invoking Web services directly from the client application (without using client-side binding stubs), then add the following lines to the call object of the invocation. If you are using client-side binding stubs (as we are in the EPS application), then add the following two lines to the binding stubs of each of the Web services used by the application.

```
call.setUsername("wsuser");
call.setPassword("wsuserpw");
```

Now we have fully configured the Web services as well as the client application to use HTTP basic authentication based on the username-password pair: `wsuser-wsuserpw`. Only those SOAP messages that use HTTP as their transport and incorporate this username-password pair as part of the HTTP header will be allowed access to any of the Web services.

Next, we look at the steps necessary to configure support for HTTPS for exchange of SOAP messages. The configuration steps are as follows:

1. Download and install the Java Secure Socket Extension (JSSE) package. If your Java JDK is 1.4.0 or above, the JSSE is already bundled with the distribution and there is no need to download any additional package.
2. Create or obtain a SSL certificate that will be used to authenticate and encrypt data within the exchanged SOAP messages. Refer to Chapter 8 for an overview of the concepts underlying SSL, certificates, authentication, and encryption.

   If you do not have or cannot obtain a certificate from a Certificate Authority, java provides a tool to generate and sign your own digital certificate. To run this tool, type in the following command:

```
JAVA_HOME%\bin\keytool -genkey -alias tomcat -keyalg RSA
```

   The tool will prompt you to enter a variety of information about yourself and your organization that will be the basis for the generated certificate. The tool will also ask for a password. Although any password can be used, the default password used by Tomcat is `changeit`. The result of running this tool will be a file named `.keystore` locate on the user's home directory.

   A certificate will need to be created for both the server (where the Web services are) and for the client. If both reside on a single machine (a rare case in most enterprise deployments), a single certificate can be used.
3. Enable SSL support on Tomcat.

   To enable support for SSL on Tomcat, simply delete the comment tags around the following connector element within the `%TOMCAT_HOME%\conf\ server.xml` file:

```
<!-- Define a SSL Coyote HTTP/1.1 Connector on port 8443 -->
<!-- Delete this line to enable SSL support
<Connector className=
           "org.apache.coyote.tomcat4.CoyoteConnector"
           port="8443" minProcessors="5" maxProcessors="75"
           enableLookups="true" acceptCount="100" debug="0"
           scheme="https" secure="true"
           useURIValidationHack="false"
           disableUploadTimeout="true">
  <Factory className=
    "org.apache.coyote.tomcat4.CoyoteServerSocketFactory"
    clientAuth="false" protocol="TLS" />
</Connector>
Delete this line to enable SSL support -->
```

4. **Modify the client application to access each Web service using HTTPS.**
   To instruct the client application to use HTTPS to communicate with each Web service, the endpoint of each Web service must be updated to include the HTTPS protocol and the port number 8443, which is the default configured port on which Tomcat listens for secure connections. To do this, change each Web service endpoint from `http://<hostname>:8080/<Web service path>` to `https://<hostname>:8443/<Web service path>`.
   For instance, in the EPS application, the endpoint:

```
http://localhost:8080/axis/services/TransactionalVendorAService
```

would be changed to:

```
https://localhost:8443/axis/services/TransactionalVendorAService
```

Then finally, specify the location of the client SSL certificate for use during message authentication and encryption. If you are invoking Web services directly from the client application (without using client-side binding stubs), add the following line prior to instantiating the `service` object and creating the `call` object. If you are using client-side binding stubs (as we are in the EPS application), add the following line to the binding stubs of each of the Web services used by the application:

```
System.setProperty("javax.net.ssl.trustStore", "C:\\Documents
and Settings\\Administrator\\.keystore");
```

Together, the specification of the HTTPS within the Web service endpoint and the specification of the location of the client certificate should be done as follows:

```
// Add these two lines
String endpoint =
  "https://localhost:8443/axis/services/VendorAProcurement";

System.setProperty("javax.net.ssl.trustStore",
  "C:\\Documents and Settings\\sandeep\\.keystore");

// The above lines should be generally placed before
//  the new service is instantiated (below), either
//  within the client application (if client-side
//  binding stubs are not used), or within the
//  binding stubs (if they are used).
Service service = new Service ();
Call call = ( Call ) service.createCall ();
call.setTargetEndpointAddress (
  new java.net.URL ( endpoint ) );

// Invocation code...
```

On completing these steps, the application is configured for secure communications over a point-to-point HTTPS channel. HTTP basic authentication over SSL-based HTTPS provides a security solution that is sufficient for most Web service environments today. Together, these two HTTP security mechanisms provide the following capabilities within a Web service environment: message authentication, authorization, confidentiality, and integrity.

Summary

Perhaps the single most important factor that sets Web services apart from previous distributed systems frameworks is not interoperability as we might at first think (since if vendors were enthusiastic enough they could have made prior systems interoperate), but extensibility. In contrast to previous systems like CORBA, where the message format and content were closely tied together—each bit in a message field was fixed and had significance for some a priori determined protocol—SOAP is modular and arbitrarily extensible for new protocols. This extensibility has been exemplified in this chapter. We have seen disparate enterprise requirements like transactions and security implemented in such a way that they are both independent of one-another and yet can operate seamlessly side-by-side in the same application, even without having to alter any application code.

As more and more enterprise processes are automated and made electronic, the need for 24 hours by 7 days-a-week access to these automated environments becomes increasingly important. Mobile devices such as personal digital assistants and Internet-capable cellular phones present a good platform for providing such pervasive access. We have shown how mobilizing an existing enterprise Web services-based application can be simplified by using a proxy-based architecture. A few simple changes to the existing application together with a mobile client application and a mobile proxy that intermediates between the mobile client and the back-end application is all that is needed. Development and testing times are minimized, thus reducing time-to-market and costs.

Of course, while Web services solve a number of problems for architects and developers, they do not necessarily solve any problems for the business user directly, since they are a system development aid and not a business tool. However, we are already seeing Web services becoming encapsulated behind "business analyst-friendly" APIs with efforts like BPEL (and its tool support) abstracting away much of the detail of the underlying Web services-based infrastructure and presenting the user with a business-focused view of the problem domain.

It is finally becoming clear that enterprise-level quality of service can be implemented in a Web services environment, though the implementations are necessarily less advanced than the equivalent software designed for proprietary systems. This will improve as the whole industry moves its focus to Web services.

Architect's Notes

- Expect security (at all levels, not just transport), transactions, and workflow to become widespread technologies in Web services applications. Plan to use these wherever appropriate without resorting to proprietary mechanisms which jeopardize interoperability between systems that you have not yet even dreamt of connecting.
- Adding support for a protocol to a Web service—even retrospectively—does not affect any other supported protocols since the SOAP header processing mechanisms are extensible and modular. With Web services, adding the right mix of support for your application should be easier than ever before.
- Plan to base integration projects on Web services technology unless they involve homogeneous systems. To do otherwise is a false economy since the common denominator platform that Web services provides will be supported by toolkits on most, if not all, systems that are likely to require integration effort.

CHAPTER 14

Epilogue

Web services are at the very beginning of their reign as the infrastructure of choice for distributed computing systems and electronic commerce. We have seen in previous chapters how we can use current Web services technologies to create truly robust enterprise applications. In this chapter, we recap the set of current standards and take a look at both the future of Web services standards and platforms for building Web services, as well as the organizations that are driving the evolution technology into the future.

Current Standards and Future Trends

In this book we have surveyed many Web services standards and seen how they can be deployed to support enterprise-class Web services applications. As we draw our discussion to a close, it is useful both to reflect over how far the individual technologies have come, and look into the near future to see how they may evolve for use in our next software projects.

XML

Given the investment that organizations have now made in this technology, there is significant inertia against changing the core XML technologies (XML, XML Infoset, and XML Schema). This core XML work is now solid (XML is an ISO standard, and each of these technologies is a W3C recommendation) and has provided the basis of the entire Web services stack. It is not expected that much will happen over time to change XML and XML Schema, and though XML 1.1 is being worked on, changes are likely to be minor and incremental.

For the peripheral XML technologies like XSL, XPath and so forth some less minor revisions are occurring. While it is anticipated that revisions to these technologies will be backwardly compatible—that XML inertia helping out again—the newer versions of these technologies are adding additional levels of functionality and richness that has been found lacking by current XML and Web services work. A classic example of this is the greater breadth of types available in XPath 2.0 compared to its predecessor.

The popular XML processing technologies SAX and DOM are also undergoing revision. While SAX has stabilized at version 2.0 and is being worked on at implementation level by the community, DOM has now evolved from level 2 to level 3 where its interfaces have been refined in the light of experience from the DOM level 2 compliant implementations. Though DOM level 3 is indeed a major revision, anyone comfortable with level 2 will have little difficulty migrating once level 3 becomes widespread.

SOAP and WSDL

SOAP 1.1 and WSDL 1.1 are already the single most ubiquitous de facto standards for Web services. Going forward, SOAP 1.1 will be replaced by SOAP 1.2 whose features have matured in the light of amassed experience with both SOAP 1.0 and 1.1.

> SOAP 1.1 and 1.2 are sufficiently different to cause interoperability problems at the wire level. However, semantically they remain similar, so that we expect SOAP servers and toolkits to be able to support both versions and encapsulate the protocol detail away from applications behind APIs.

While the move to SOAP 1.2 will ultimately be thought of as more of an incremental upgrade than a major revolution, something more fundamental is happening to WSDL. In the future, we expect to see more high-level protocols exploiting WSDL extensibility elements and thus extending WSDL to build new Web services technology. WSDL will, in addition to its role as the Web services IDL, become the protocol toolkit for the description and development of new Web services protocol.

To summarize the evolution of these two technologies is simple: SOAP bootstrapped the whole Web service architecture and was the single most important standard—until now. The SOAP community will continue to innovate and simplify, but their efforts will begin to go more unnoticed as the Web services community takes SOAP for granted. WSDL will be where future business-focused innovation in the Web services space will occur, and it is WSDL which will drive the second phase of Web services development and deployment.

UDDI

In the heyday of Web services hyperbole, UDDI was touted as the central hub of the Web services universe. These early days of UDDI focused almost exclusively on the Universal Business Registry as the technology that would allow services to automatically locate, bind, and interact with one another seamlessly across the Internet.

While the great promise of an Internet-scale network of Web services supported by UDDI has yet come to fruition—and it may never do so—UDDI has continued to grow in popularity in private networks. From being the glue that binds the universal Web services network together, UDDI has started to become an invaluable service for providing in-house Web services directories for individual enterprises, and for bringing together networks of partner Web services.

As we look forward to the future of UDDI, it is almost certain that the current sparsely populated Universal Business Directory will not dominate the Web services network globally. Instead, it is more likely that federations of smaller, more private UDDI registries will begin to build upward toward that ultimate goal. Though it is not necessarily the case that a truly global federated network of UDDI registries will ever reach the same scale as that originally envisioned UDDI is certain to remain a feature of the Web services landscape.

Transactions

With the advent of WS-Transaction, the incumbent OASIS BTP standard for Web services transactions has a new rival. This rivalry goes beyond technical differences between the specifications, of which there are many, and is really a symptom of the larger battle for the Web services environment.

Given that the WS-Transaction specification has the support of arguably the two biggest players in the Web services arena (IBM and Microsoft), it has been suggested that WS-Transaction will naturally be the transaction protocol of choice for the industry. However, to ensure success, WS-Transaction must counter the fact that the OASIS BTP standard is more mature and has the support of several shipping implementations, as well as the backing of a number of relatively influential players in the Web services field (such as Sun, HP, and Oracle).

What is clear at time of writing is that the arrival of WS-Transaction has put the brakes on much of the potential BTP deployments as the industry waits to see which of the two protocols will become dominant, or indeed whether there is any scope for convergence. Technically, both models have strengths and weaknesses, but ultimately which protocol dominates might come down to pure muscle on behalf of their backers.

Security

The lack of understanding of security issues for Web services together with the immaturity of technologies and standards to address these issues are one of the most important reasons of limiting the deployment of enterprise Web services. Much of the experience companies have with security is with Web sites and Web applications. Both of these applications involve sending HTML between the server and the client (e.g., Internet browser). Web services involve applications exchanging data and information through defined application programming interfaces (APIs). These APIs can contain literally dozens of methods and operations, each of which presents hackers with potential entry points to compromise the security and integrity of a system. Moreover, information that is exchanged between client applications and Web services must be secured and kept confidential, while not overburdening applications and servers with the large overheads associated with encrypting and decrypting all packets and all parts of each packet.

The XML security specifications, XML Encryption and XML Digital Signatures, make great strides in specifying security constructs that are sufficiently robust and flexible to meet the demands and trade-offs inherent to securing enterprise systems. The WS-Security specification builds on the XML security specifications and encapsulates them within SOAP envelopes. This brings to bear all of the benefits of the XML security specifications while removing any dependence on the specific transport layer, and also furthers interoperability. The WS-Security specifications are quickly emerging as the de facto standard for Web service security, and address many of the critical security needs of Web service environments. The remainder of the WS specifications roadmap (as laid out by IBM and Microsoft), once fully completed, will result in a comprehensive framework that supports and enables securing of many scenarios that are not possible today.

Conversations

Although WSCL received the accolade of being the conversation language of choice for UDDI.org, there has been no widespread acceptance of temporal interfaces for Web services as many architects and developers have only recently become familiar with static WSDL interfaces. While the technology undoubtedly has promise, the value of advertising temporal interfaces can only be realized when they are widely deployed, perhaps at the same order of magnitude as WSDL itself.

However, WSCL is not about to disappear completely. While it now seems likely that take-up of single-party conversation technology may be low in the near future, WSCL has become one of the technologies (along with WSCI) for the W3C's choreography working group that aims to tackle the general concepts of business process management over Web services. If this is ultimately the line taken, we may see elements of WSCL taken forward as single endpoint conversations become a subset of more general process choreography involving multiple parties.

Workflow

In the Web services workflow arena, BPEL4WS enjoys a dominant position in the field by dint that it is second-generation technology supported by arguably the most important commercial Web services players. While the royalty-free status of BPEL4WS is yet to be ascertained, implementations are already available from the BPEL4WS creators and third-party implementers, all of which add to its momentum. BPEL4WS itself is going through another revision, as alluded to in the "future directions" part of the specification. However, most of the work on the spec will be in integrating the BPEL4WS technology with other supporting Web services technologies, like reliable messaging and context management, and it is not thought that that BPEL4WS will undergo any radical changes in semantics.

All other competing standards in the Web services orchestration and choreography area have been subsumed by the W3C Choreography working group that has a two year charter to produce a choreography standard that meshes with the W3C's overall Web services architecture. This effort has the backing of some major players in the Web services arena and has taken onboard the WSCL and WSCI specifications as well as other non-Web services specifications to try to take a broad view of the problem.

However, given the broad view and lengthy charter of this group, it is entirely possible that BPEL4WS, with a smaller and nimbler set of participants backed up by huge engineering organizations, will steal a march on the W3C's efforts in the mean time.

Quality of Service

As more and more Web services become available, quality of service (QoS) becomes an important differentiating feature that will directly drive the popularity and the overall usefulness of a service. Exposing a piece of business logic as a Web service is not difficult; architecting the system so that it meets the needs of potential users with respect to performance, latency, reliability, and so on is the difficult part.

To support QoS, Web services themselves must be carefully architected and implemented, but standards and technologies must also emerge to monitor the QoS of individual Web services and then publish that information to potential client applications and Web service brokers. Although no dominant standard exists for monitoring and publishing QoS information, there are some likely candidates including extending WSDL to support QoS.

Mobile and Wireless

Mobile and wireless devices are no longer just novelty items within corporations. In fact, mobile devices are critical tools within the arsenal of 24x7 enterprise operations. Many challenges exist in the development of mobile systems that are usually not an issue in the development of non-mobile systems. Issues such as application energy consumption, network bandwidth utilization, limited computational resources, and small form factor user interfaces all come together to make the design of mobile applications difficult.

J2EE servlets are a well-understood and standard technology for bridging between existing systems (or new ones) and mobile environments. The servlet acts either as a proxy for mobile applications or generates the actual content that is displayed through a mobile browser.

Since servlets can accommodate data in any format, the mobile system does not need to parse or generate XML data (e.g., SOAP envelopes), thus obviating the need for large footprint XML parsers.

Mobile devices can also directly access Web services without any proxy. In these situations, resource-limited SOAP and XML platforms, such as kSOAP and kXML, can be used. The Java 2 Micro Edition (J2ME) Web Service specification (JSR-172) is also emerging as a de facto standard for a larger framework for Web services operating within mobile environments. Once fully defined, the specification will articulate mechanisms by which to efficiently access Web services from mobile devices as well as to deploy Web services onto mobile devices.

Standards Organizations

Given that Web services are extensible by nature and adaptable to a range of business computing scenarios, it should come as no surprise to learn that there are a number of standards organizations vying to push forward future Web services specifications. It is almost certain that distributing the standards management of a technology would ultimately be the death-knell for other architectures. However, since Web services protocols are largely mutually unaware, aside from the basic SOAP and WSDL infrastructure, and designed to be extended by third parties, it is quite possible for distinct groups with diverse interests in applying Webs services to each progress the state of the art of the overall technology largely independently. This has led to the situation that we have today where a number of bodies each produce new protocol standards for the emergent Web services architecture, with the World Wide Web Consortium (W3C), Organization for the Advancement of Structured Information Systems (OASIS), and Web Services Interoperability Organization (WS-I)—each providing a focus for their own particular areas of interest within the Web services arena.

W3C

> The World Wide Web Consortium (W3C) develops interoperable technologies (specifications, guidelines, software, and tools) to lead the Web to its full potential. W3C is a forum for information, commerce, communication, and collective understanding.
>
> *http://www.w3c.org*

The W3C has a prestigious history as far as Web services are concerned, being the driving force behind the development of the XML specifications and the home of the two most fundamental Web services standards: SOAP and WSDL. As part of an increasingly large industry-wide effort, the various committees within the W3C are engaged not only in future revisions of DOM, XML, XML Schema, XML Encryption and Signature, SOAP, and WSDL, but are also actively involved in forging an overall architecture for Web services and trying to reconcile the various Web services choreography efforts into a single endorsed standard.

However, some in the Web services community have begun to express concerns that W3C is losing ground to other bodies and may become marginalized since it also maintains its traditional role in overseeing World Wide Web standards, and provides relatively long-lived charters for its working groups (the choreography working group, for instance, has a two-year charter). Furthermore, given its strong stance on royalty-free standards and the increasing propensity for vendors to look to produce revenue from intellectual effort expended in producing Web services protocols, it is clear that the W3C is approaching an interesting epoch in its history.

OASIS

> OASIS is a not-for-profit, global consortium that drives the development, convergence and adoption of e-business standards.
>
> *http://www.oasis-open.org*

OASIS was originally formed as a forum for those interested in SGML in 1993. In 1998, its name was changed to OASIS along with a change in emphasis to XML (OASIS also runs the XML.org web site) and related technologies. OASIS is currently renowned for being the home of ebXML. However, OASIS has grown with the advent of Web services and is now active in such diverse areas as UDDI, security, and management in addition to its work on transactions with BTP.

Unlike the W3C, OASIS does not strive to develop overarching architectures for Web services or drive particular areas toward standards unilaterally. Instead, OASIS acts as a mediator for third parties to collaborate on standards and as such is very industry driven. Because of this pragmatic piecemeal approach, OASIS has become almost the antithesis of the W3C and is beginning to look like the main body to oversee the individual technologies that will ultimately form the Web services stack.

WS-I

> WS-I is an open industry organization chartered to promote Web services interoperability across platforms, operating systems, and programming languages. The organization works across the industry and standards organizations to respond to customer needs by providing guidance, best practices, and resources for developing Web services solutions.
>
> *http://www.ws-i.org*

The Web Services Interoperability Organization, or WS-I, has been created to foster interoperability between different vendors' implementations of the Web services standards being developed through W3C, OASIS, OMG, and so forth. The group is not chartered with the creation of standards per se, but with creating common "profiles" of the output from other standards bodies and supporting vendors in creating versions of their software that adhere to these profiles and thus interoperate.

At present, the WS-I is immersed in the creation of its basic profile for Web services, which includes specific conventions on the use of SOAP 1.1 and WSDL 1.1 to foster interoperability between services. It also provides some conventions on the use of UDDI (version 2.04) so that lookups may be made in a consistent manner across UDDI implementations and organizations. The WS-I basic profile also includes a number of security mechanisms for securing communication channels (e.g., HTTPS) and establishing authenticity (X.509 certificates).

On top of the basic profile, the WS-I working groups will continue up the Web services stack to provide conformance profiles for the other higher-level requirements by layering existing and forthcoming standards. Going forward, WS-I will become the prevalent organization for Web services middleware developers. It will also provide Web services application developers with a standard and well-known means of both assuring interoperability and choosing Web services infrastructure based on standard capabilities.

Vendor Specifications

In addition to the work of standards bodies, it has become almost commonplace for individual vendors or groups of vendors with shared interests (both in the technical and commercial sense) to release their own specifications to the world independent of any formal standards body. While the backers of such specifications generally maintain that they intend to present the specifications to appropriate standards bodies eventually, this approach causes some muddying of waters in the Web services community.

While there is undoubtedly value in many of these proto-specifications, developers and architects should have their wits about them when implementing or buying technology based on them. For example, some vendor-backed specifications like WS-Reliability and WS-ReliableMessaging directly and openly compete with one another. Furthermore, once a specification goes to standardization, it does not necessarily mean that the outcome from that process will resemble the input (as testified to by BEA's and HP's initial submissions to the OASIS BTP effort which bear little resemblance to the final protocol).

However, sound judgment on which specifications are likely to make it to broad acceptance largely unchanged, does mean that a savvy architect or developer can march on the market (albeit with a certain amount of risk). When appraising proto-specifications for bleeding-edge technologies, it makes sense not only to investigate whether the technology itself is sound, but also the relative business cases put forward by its backers and the position (and indeed likely position) of those backers within the Web services community and wider industry.

Platforms

The two major platforms for developing Web services are Sun's J2EE and Microsoft's .Net. On paper, there isn't much to separate the two technologies insofar as they both offer similar features in terms of a component model, data access, rich runtime environment, broad library support, and of course the all-important Web services aspects.

Microsoft .Net

Perhaps the biggest single differentiator of the .Net approach is that everything is supplied by a single vendor and has thus been honed to work together harmoniously, and that same vendor has provided some of the most sophisticated tool support on the market to make working with the .Net framework a pleasant and productive experience.

This ease-of-use is carried forward to the Web services features, ASP.Net, where to expose a piece of functionality to the network (including the automatic production of WSDL and handling of SOAP messages) is simplicity itself, requiring only a single line of code per operation. This ease-of-use does not, however, mean that the platform handles only simple cases; in fact the truth is far from it. The ASP.Net features allow advanced developers to handcraft the way in which SOAP messages are handled, and there is rich support for other useful technologies like XSLT and DOM.

J2EE

In stark contrast to the single-vendor approach of the .Net framework, the J2EE standard is maintained by a single body (Sun) supported by a plethora of vendors such as IBM, BEA, and Oracle. In theory, this means that developing Web services on J2EE-based application servers opens up a wealth of choice and allows true mix-and-match component based solutions to be built. In practice, however, things are not always quite so straightforward since each vendor supports its own set of conventions for aspects like component deployment and configuration, while they can still remain faithful to the J2EE standard. Furthermore, not all platforms ship with useful features like XSLT processing components, DOM, or in some cases even a SOAP stack.

However, if we consider Web services level in isolation from the rest of the J2EE stack, things are significantly better. In particular, the open-source AXIS toolkit from the Apache group is a firm favorite for building Java-based Web services since it has kept apace with the feature list of the best of breed Web service platforms, including ASP.Net and WASP server (Systinet). Furthermore, since AXIS has partial support for JAXM and JAXRPC interfaces, code written to use AXIS can be ported to other Java Web services platform with a minimum of effort.

A Single Web Services Platform?

There is one certainty in the battle between the platforms: There is no certain winner. Regardless of what statistics the Java and Microsoft camps can roll out and, irrespective of the views of platform zealots, both platforms will exist in the future Web services landscape (in addition to a plethora of other "niche" platforms).

For your own part, remember that Web services are simply user interfaces for computers. Just as we wouldn't necessarily decide on a particular platform just because it makes writing GUIs easier, the same is true in the Web services arena. Your choice of platform will be made based on the constraints of existing infrastructure and the needs of the project as a whole, not just the Web services aspects.

The only way to be sure that you will have full coverage is to learn the key APIs on both platforms. While this might sound like a lot of additional work, experience shows that it is not—the hard work is in understanding the underlying protocols and not in the APIs—while the number of API calls needed to get up and running on both platforms is relatively small.

Summary

While we cannot with any certainty predict what the future holds for Web services, there do seem to be some commonsense observations that we can offer. The first of these is that the Web services community by and large consists of a plethora of small vendors offering technologies and services at the bottom end, and a handful of large vendors (dominated by IBM and Microsoft) at the top end of the scale. Given the sheer number of smaller vendors (and the prevailing economic conditions), we expect there will be a degree of consolidation with the larger vendors using their financial muscle to add smaller vendors' niche technologies into their portfolios.

On a technical level, we expect that a number of technologies, which largely follow the technologies we have seen in this book, will rise to prominence:

- XML and XML Schema will become the fundamental building blocks of all enterprise technology and will remain the basis of Web services throughout their lifetime.
- SOAP 1.2 and WSDL 1.2 will prevail as the messaging and protocol-description languages of Web services, respectively, though at the time of this writing, SOAP 1.2 is a new recommendation and WSDL 1.2 remains a work in progress which means that toolkit support for both is currently limited.
- UDDI will increase in its use for inter-enterprise Web service discovery and integration purposes. The use of UDDI at runtime for system reliability and failover will also increase.
- An eventual standard for transactions will likely be influenced to a great extent by the WS-Transaction standard. While we think it unlikely that WS-Transaction will remain

in its current form, any future transaction standard will share a number of its characteristics. It is unlikely that BTP will become a widespread transaction protocol simply because its list of backers is somewhat less prestigious and powerful in the Web services arena than those of WS-Transaction.

- WS-Security, as well as its associated WS specifications, will emerge as the dominant standard for securing Web service environments. As IT organizations become more familiar and more experienced with securing Web services, the adoption of Web services by enterprises as well as the release of Web services from within the firewall to the outside world will increase.
- Conversations, choreography, and orchestration are becoming increasingly intertwined. It is anticipated that a single standard (either based on BPEL4WS or perhaps as the output from the W3C's choreography working group) will subsume all of these and so conversations and workflow will become one.
- Web services that are accessible by mobile devices will steadily increase. In the near term, most mobile systems will be based on proxy architectures (e.g., using J2EE servlets as the proxy) instead of direct Web service invocations.

Generally, we expect the near-term future to be punctuated by both continued work in the specification space and for software engineers to begin projects that utilize basic aspects of this technology (like SOAP and WSDL). If all goes well, then by the time that we as engineers are ready to tackle more advanced features, the standards groups will have completed their own work and we should find ourselves in a position where the technology is mature and engineers will have already scaled the learning curve to be able to use it. All of this means that Web services have a bright future ahead of them.

INDEX

N

O

P

Q

R

S

Prentice Hall Professional Technical Reference
http://www.phptr.com/
Prentice Hall PTR InformIT InformIT Online Books Financial Times Prentice Hall ft.com PTG Interactive Reuters
PRENTICE HALL PTR
TOMORROW'S SOLUTIONS FOR TODAY'S PROFESSIONALS
Prentice Hall Professional Technical Reference
Browse
Book Series
What's New
User Groups
Alliances
Special Sales
Contact Us
Search | Help | Home
Quick Search
PTR Favorites
Find a Bookstore
Book Series
Special Interests
Newsletters
Press Room
International
Best Sellers
Solutions Beyond the Book
Shopping Bag
Keep Up to Date with
PH PTR Online
We strive to stay on the cutting edge of what's happening in professional computer science and engineering. Here's a bit of what you'll find when you stop by www.phptr.com:
What's new at PHPTR? We don't just publish books for the professional community, we're a part of it. Check out our convention schedule, keep up with your favorite authors, and get the latest reviews and press releases on topics of interest to you.
Special interest areas offering our latest books, book series, features of the month, related links, and other useful information to help you get the job done.
User Groups Prentice Hall Professional Technical Reference's User Group Program helps volunteer, not-for-profit user groups provide their members with training and information about cutting-edge technology.
Companion Websites Our Companion Websites provide valuable solutions beyond the book. Here you can download the source code, get updates and corrections, chat with other users and the author about the book, or discover links to other websites on this topic.
Need to find a bookstore? Chances are, there's a bookseller near you that carries a broad selection of PTR titles. Locate a Magnet bookstore near you at www.phptr.com.
Subscribe today! Join PHPTR's monthly email newsletter!
Want to be kept up-to-date on your area of interest? Choose a targeted category on our website, and we'll keep you informed of the latest PHPTR products, author events, reviews and conferences in your interest area.
Visit our mailroom to subscribe today! http://www.phptr.com/mail_lists